## Useful Windows Command Prompt Commar



| Command | Description |
|---|---|
| *ipconfig* | Displays information about the TCP/IP |
| *ftp* | Enables file transfers |
| *net continue* | Resumes a service that has been paused |
| *net file* | Shows the currently open shared files and file locks and is used to close designated files or to remove file locks |
| *net helpmsg* | Determines the meaning of a numeric network error message |
| *net pause* | Pauses a service |
| *net print* | Used to view and manage queued print jobs by computer, share name, and job number |
| *net send* | Sends a message to designated users or to all users currently connected to the server |
| *net session* | Shows the users currently connected to a server and is used to disconnect designated user sessions or all user sessions |
| *net share* | Creates, deletes, or shows information about a shared resource |
| *net start* | Shows the started services or is used to start a designated service |
| *net stop* | Stops a network service on a computer |
| *net use* | Shows information about shared resources or is used to configure, connect, and disconnect shared resources |
| *net user* | Used to view, add, or modify a user account set up on a server or in a domain |
| *net view* | Presents a list of domains, the computers and servers in a domain, and all resources shared by a computer in a domain |
| *nbstat* | Shows the server and domain names registered to the network (only on server versions) |
| *netstat* | Displays information about the Transmission Control Protocol/Internet Protocol (TCP/IP) session at the computer |
| *ping* | Polls another TCP/IP node to verify you can communicate with it |
| *tracert* | Displays the number of hops and other routing information on the path to the specified computer or network device |

## Useful Linux Command-Line Commands for Configuring and Troubleshooting Networks

| Command | Description |
|---|---|
| *finger* | Provides information about a user |
| *ftp* | Enables file transfers |
| *ifconfig* | Sets up a network interface and displays network interface configuration information |
| *netstat* | Shows network connection information |
| *nfsstat* | Shows statistics for Network File System (NFS) file upload and download activity |
| *nslookup* | Queries information on Internet Domain Name System (DNS) servers |
| *ping* | Polls another TCP/IP node to verify you can communicate with it |
| *route* | Displays routing table information and can be used to configure routing |
| *showmount* | Shows clients that have mounted volumes on an NFS server |
| *traceroute* | Displays the number of hops and other routing information on the path to the specified computer or network device |
| *who* | Shows who is logged on |

# Guide to Operating Systems

# Guide to Operating Systems

Fifth Edition

**Greg Tomsho**

CENGAGE

Andover • Melbourne • Mexico City • Stamford, CT • Toronto • Hong Kong • New Delhi • Seoul • Singapore • Tokyo

**Guide to Operating Systems, 5th edition**
Greg Tomsho



ISBN-13: 978-93-866-5090-0
ISBN-10: 93-866-5090-8

Cengage Learning India Private Limited
418, F.I.E., Patparganj
Delhi 110092
India

Tel: 91-11-43641111
Fax: 91-11-43641100
Email: asia.infoindia@cengage.com

Cengage Learning is a leading provider of customized learning solutions with office locations around the globe, including Andover, Melbourne, Mexico City, Stamford (CT), Toronto, Hong Kong, New Delhi, Seoul, Singapore, and Tokyo. Locate your local office at: www.cengage.com/global

Cengage Learning Products are represented in Canada by Nelson Education, Ltd.

For product information, visit our website at **www.cengage.co.in**

Printed in India
First Indian Reprint 2017

**Disclaimer:**
This book contains link to resources which are a part of the US edition. The same may not be available with the Indian edition. The buyer needs to purchase a copy of the US edition to have full access to those resources. In no event the publisher shall be liable for any limitation or performance due to unavailability of these resources.

# Brief Contents

# Table of Contents

# Introduction

**If you use a computer, you also use a computer operating system to tap into the** computer's power. The more you know about a computer's operating system, the more you are able to enjoy the full versatility of your computer. This book opens the door to understanding your computer's operating system. Also, the book enables you to understand many types of operating systems so you can compare the advantages of each for your personal and professional use.

In this book, you learn about the most popular operating systems in use today:

- Windows, with emphasis on Windows 10 and Windows Server 2012, and coverage of Windows Server 2016
- UNIX/Linux, with emphasis on Fedora 23
- Mac OS X, with emphasis on El Capitan

The book starts at a basic level and builds with each chapter to put you on track to become an accomplished user of each operating system.

You learn the operating systems in clear language through a hands-on, practical approach. An advantage of studying several operating systems is that you can compare the functions of each side-by-side as you learn. If you are taking an introductory operating systems course or an operating systems survey course, this book offers a strong foundation for mastering operating systems. Also, if you are preparing for one or more computer certifications, such as for hardware systems, networking, programming, or security, you'll find this book provides a vital background for your preparations. The book is particularly useful as background for the CompTIA A+ certification. If you are relatively new to computers, the book starts with the basics to build your confidence. If you are more experienced in computers, you'll find lots of useful information to further build your repertoire of knowledge and experience.

## The Intended Audience

*Guide to Operating Systems, Fifth Edition* is written in straightforward language for anyone who uses a computer and wants to learn more. No prior computer experience is required, although some previous basic experience with a computer is helpful. The hands-on projects in this book use a variety of operating systems. You can learn the concepts if you have access to one or a combination of the operating systems presented. The more operating systems that are available to you, the better the opportunity to compare their features. For the most part, the projects can be performed in a classroom, computer lab, or at home.

## What's New to this Edition

*Guide to Operating Systems, Fifth Edition* is extensively updated to include the most current operating systems and operating system features. This includes all-new coverage of Windows 10, Windows Server 2012, Windows Server 2016, Fedora Linux with the GNOME desktop, and Mac OS X El Capitan. Coverage of legacy operating systems is greatly reduced to provide mainly an historical perspective.

The book also includes extensive updates for new hardware and new operating system installation and management activities. New hardware coverage includes the latest CPUs and peripheral devices. The interaction of operating systems and new storage devices is also significantly updated, as well as new networking capabilities, including wireless networking advances and cloud computing. An entire chapter has been added for operating system virtualization, including VMware, Microsoft Hyper-V, and VirtualBox.

Screen captures, figures, and tables are virtually all new. The hands-on projects are fully updated or are all new for the new operating systems. A new end-of-chapter section called Challenge Labs gives readers one or more hands-on activities that require research and synthesis of information already learned.

## Chapter Descriptions

The chapter coverage is balanced to give you a full range of information about each topic. The following is a summary of what you will learn in each chapter. Besides the instruction provided throughout the chapter text, you can build on your knowledge and review your progress using the extensive hands-on projects, challenge labs, case projects, key terms, and review questions at the end of each chapter.

- *Chapter 1: Operating Systems Fundamentals* gives you a basic introduction to operating systems, including the types of operating systems and how they work. You also learn about the history of operating systems.

- *Chapter 2: Popular Operating Systems* presents in-depth descriptions of modern Windows OSs, Linux and UNIX, and Mac OS X. You also briefly learn about earlier Microsoft operating systems. This chapter gives you a starting point from which to compare features of operating systems and to understand advancements in the latest versions.
- *Chapter 3: The Central Processing Unit (CPU)* enables you to understand how processors work and the essential characteristics of modern processors. The chapter concludes with an overview of popular modern processors.
- *Chapter 4: File Systems* explains the functions common to all file systems and then describes the specific file systems used by different operating systems, from a brief introduction to FAT to more in-depth coverage of NTFS, ufs/ext, HFS, and HFS+.
- *Chapter 5: Installing and Upgrading Operating Systems* shows you how to prepare for installing operating systems and then shows you how to install each operating system discussed in this book. You learn about installing operating systems from scratch and how to upgrade operating systems.
- *Chapter 6: Configuring Input and Output Devices* explains how devices such as monitors, keyboards, mice, disk drives, network cards, and other devices interface with operating systems. You learn about the latest input and output technologies for modern operating systems and computers.
- *Chapter 7: Using and Configuring Storage Devices* describes popular storage devices, including hard drives, removable drives, RAID, CD and DVD technologies, flash and solid-state drive storage, network storage, USB devices, and the latest emerging technologies. Storage device configuration is covered for the operating systems and you learn how to perform backups for Windows, UNIX/Linux, and Mac OS X operating systems.
- *Chapter 8: Virtualization and Cloud Computing Fundamentals* introduces you to virtualization, its terminology, and some of the popular virtualization products that can be used on the OSs this book discusses.
- *Chapter 9: Configuring a Network Connection* provides an introduction to how networks function, including network technologies and protocols. You learn how to configure protocols in each operating system and you learn about the basic structure of local and wide area networks. You also learn how operating systems interface with networks.
- *Chapter 10: Sharing Resources and Working with Accounts* shows you many ways to share resources through a network, including sharing disks, folders, and printers. Besides covering how to share resources, the chapter also discusses how to secure them through accounts, groups, and access privileges.
- *Chapter 11: Operating Systems Management and Maintenance* presents many techniques for maintaining systems, such as cleaning up unused files, defragmenting disks, making file system repairs, tuning virtual memory, and addressing problems. The chapter also addresses planning for backups and how to tune systems for top performance.
- *Appendix A: Operating System Command-Line Commands* shows you how to access the command line in each operating system and presents tables that summarize general and network commands. This appendix provides a place to quickly find or review the operating system commands.

## Features

To aid you in fully understanding operating system concepts, there are many features in this book designed to improve its pedagogical value.

- **Chapter Objectives.** Each chapter in this book begins with a detailed list of the concepts to be mastered within that chapter. This list provides you with a quick reference to the contents of each chapter as well as a useful study aid.
- **Illustrations and Tables.** Numerous illustrations of operating system screens and concepts aid you in the visualization of common setup steps, theories, and concepts. In addition, many tables provide details and comparisons of both practical and theoretical information.
- ***From the Trenches* Stories and Examples.** Each chapter contains boxed text with examples from the author's extensive experience to add color through real-life situations.
- **Chapter Summaries.** Each chapter's text is followed by a summary of the concepts it has introduced. These summaries provide a helpful way to recap and revisit the ideas covered in each chapter.
- **Key Terms.** A listing of the terms that were introduced throughout the chapter, along with definitions, is presented at the end of each chapter.
- **Review Questions.** The end-of-chapter assessment begins with a set of review questions that reinforce the ideas introduced in each chapter.
- **Hands-On Projects.** The goal of this book is to provide you with the practical knowledge and skills to install and administer desktop and server operating systems as they are employed for personal and business use. To this end, along with theoretical explanations, each chapter provides numerous hands-on projects aimed at providing you with real-world implementation experience.
- **Critical Thinking Sections.** The end-of-chapter Critical Thinking section gives you more opportunities for hands-on practice with **Challenge Labs**, which enable you to use the knowledge you've gained from reading the chapter and performing hands-on projects to solve more complex problems without step-by-step instructions. This section also includes **Case Projects** that ask you to evaluate a scenario and decide on a course of action to propose a solution. These valuable tools help you sharpen decision-making, critical thinking, and troubleshooting skills.

## Text and Graphic Conventions

Whenever appropriate, additional information and activities have been added to this book to help you better understand what is being discussed in the chapters. Icons throughout the text alert you to additional materials. The icons used in this textbook are as follows:

The Note icon is used to present additional helpful material related to the subject being described.

Tips are included from the author's experience to provide extra information about how to configure an operating system, apply a concept, or solve a problem.

Cautions are provided to help you anticipate potential problems or mistakes so you can prevent them from happening.

Each hands-on project in this book is preceded by the Hands-On Projects icon and a description of the practical exercise that follows.

Case Project icons mark each case project. Case projects are more involved, scenario-based assignments. In each extensive case example, you are asked to implement what you have learned.

# MindTap

MindTap for *Guide to Operating Systems* is an online learning solution designed to help students master the skills they need in today's workforce. Research shows that employers need critical thinkers, troubleshooters, and creative problem-solvers to stay relevant in our fast-paced, technology-driven world. MindTap helps users achieve this with assignments and activities that provide hands-on practice, real-life relevance, and mastery of difficult concepts. Students are guided through assignments that progress from basic knowledge and understanding to more challenging problems.

All MindTap activities and assignments are tied to learning objectives. The hands-on exercises provide real-life application and practice. Readings and "Whiteboard Shorts" support the lecture, while "In the News" assignments encourage students to stay current. Pre- and post-course assessments allow you to measure how much students have learned using analytics and reporting that makes it easy to see where the class stands in terms of progress, engagement, and completion rates. You can use the existing content and learning path or pick and choose how the material will wrap around your own content. You control what the students see and when they see it. Learn more at *www.cengage.com/mindtap/*.

# Instructor Resources

Everything you need for your course in one place! This collection of book-specific lecture and class tools is available online via *www.cengage.com/login*. Access and download PowerPoint presentations, images, the Instructor's Manual, and more.

- *Electronic Instructor's Manual*—The Instructor's Manual that accompanies this book includes additional instructional material to assist in class preparation, including suggestions for classroom activities, discussion topics, and additional quiz questions.

- *Solutions*—The instructor's resources include solutions to all end-of-chapter material, including review questions and case projects.
- *PowerPoint presentations*—This book comes with Microsoft PowerPoint slides for each chapter. They're included as a teaching aid for classroom presentations, to make available to students on the network for chapter review, or to be printed for classroom distribution. Instructors, please feel free to add your own slides for additional topics you introduce to the class.
- *Figure files*—All the figures and tables in the book are reproduced in bitmap format. Similar to the PowerPoint presentations, they're included as a teaching aid for classroom presentations, to make available to students for review, or to be printed for classroom distribution.

## About the Author

Greg Tomsho is director of the Computer Networking Technology Department and Cisco Academy at Yavapai College in Prescott, Arizona. He has earned the CCNA, MCTS, MCSA, A+, Network+, Security+, Server+, and Linux+ certifications. A former software engineer, technical support manager, and IT director, he has more than 30 years of computer and networking experience. His other books include *MCSA Guide to Installing and Configuring Microsoft Windows Server 2012/R2; MCSA Guide to Administering Microsoft Windows Server 2012/R2; MCSA Guide to Configuring Advanced Microsoft Windows Server 2012/R2 Services; MCTS Guide to Windows Server 2008 Active Directory Configuration; MCTS Guide to Microsoft Windows Server 2008 Applications Infrastructure Configuration; Guide to Networking Essentials; Guide to Network Support and Troubleshooting*; and *A+ CoursePrep ExamGuide.*

## Acknowledgments

I would like to thank the team at Cengage Learning for this opportunity to improve and expand on the fifth edition of this book. This team includes Kristin McNary, Product Team Manager; Natalie Pashoukos, Senior Content Developer; Brooke Greenhouse, Senior Content Project Manager; and Serge Palladino, Nicole Spoto, and Danielle Shaw of Manuscript Quality Assurance, who tested projects for accuracy. Thanks also go to my development editor, Dan Seiter, for his guidance in creating a polished product. Additional praise and special thanks go to my beautiful wife, Julie; our daughters, Camille and Sophia; and our son, Michael. As always, they have been patient and supportive throughout the process and I truly appreciate their support.

### Reviewers

**Guy Garrett, M.S., M.B.A.**
Associate Professor, Cybersecurity & Information Technology
Manager, Network Systems Technology/Cybersecurity Program
Gulf Coast State College
Panama City, FL

**Emily Harrington**
CIT Coordinator/Faculty
Pitt Community College
Winterville, NC

**Todd Koonts, MSIT, CCE**
Program Chair
CTI/Information Assurance and Digital Forensics
Central Piedmont Community College
Charlotte, NC

# Before You Begin

The importance of a solid lab environment can't be overstated. This book contains hands-on projects that require a variety of operating systems, including Windows 10, Linux Fedora 23, and Mac OS X El Capitan. Using virtualization can simplify the lab environment. For example, you can use VMware Player, VMware Workstation, VirtualBox, and other products to install Windows and Linux in a virtual machine, regardless of the OS running on your physical computer. Installing Mac OS X in a virtual machine running on Windows requires some creativity, but it can be done. If you want to run El Capitan as a VMware virtual machine running on Windows, do a little Internet research on the topic. The following section lists the requirements for completing hands-on activities and challenge labs.

## Lab Setup Guide

Most of the hands-on projects and challenge labs require a Windows 10, Linux Fedora 23, or Mac OS X El Capitan computer. The computers should have a connection to the Internet, but only a few of the activities actually require Internet access. The use of virtual machines is highly recommended.

### Windows 10 Computers

- Windows 10 Enterprise or Education Edition is recommended, but other versions are acceptable
- An account that is a member of the local Administrators group
- Workgroup name: Using the default workgroup name ("Workgroup") is acceptable, but the name is not important
- Memory: 1 GB required, 2 GB or more recommended
- Hard disk 1: 60 GB or more (Windows installed on this drive)
- Hard disk 2: Unallocated 60 GB or more
- IP address via DHCP server or static if required on your network
- Internet access

### Fedora 23 Computers

- Fedora 23 Linux locally installed (a live CD boot will work for some activities, but not all)
- An administrator account and access to the root password
- Memory: 1 GB
- Hard disk 1: 60 GB or more (Fedora 23 installed on this drive)
- Hard disk 2: 20 GB or more
- IP address via DHCP server or static if required on your network
- Internet access

### Mac OS X Computers

- Mac OS X El Capitan
- An administrator account and access to the root password
- Memory: 1 GB
- Hard disk 1: 60 GB or more (Mac OS X El Capitan installed on this drive)
- IP address via DHCP server or static if required on your network
- Internet access

### Additional Items

- Windows 10 installation media (DVD or .iso file)—Using an evaluation copy is acceptable. You can download evaluation copies of Windows from *www.microsoft.com/en-us/evalcenter/*
- Windows Server 2012 R2 installation media (DVD or .iso file)—Using an evaluation copy is acceptable
- Linux Fedora 23 installation media (DVD or .iso file)

chapter 1

# Operating Systems Fundamentals

**After reading this chapter and completing the exercises, you will be able to:**

- Explain basic operating system concepts
- Understand the history of operating system development
- Discuss how operating systems work
- Describe the types of operating systems
- Discuss single tasking versus multitasking
- Differentiate between single-user and multiuser operating systems
- List and briefly describe current operating systems

**Computers come in many and varied physical forms. There are supercomputers that** perform complex computing tasks at incredible speeds, business servers that provide enterprise-level networked applications, desktop and laptop PCs, tablets, smartphones, and wearable computers. Plus, there are many devices you may not even think of as having a computer, such as those embedded in everyday devices like cars, televisions, and even dishwashers. Without an operating system, however, these devices are only a collection of electronic parts. It takes an operating system to turn a computer into a functioning device for work or play. The operating system is the software that starts the basic functions of a computer, displays documents on the computer's monitor, accesses the Internet, and runs applications—it transforms the computer into a powerful tool. There are many kinds of operating systems, but only a few have captured a wide audience. Server operating systems like Windows Server 2016 and UNIX run on network servers, and client operating systems like Windows 10, Mac OS X, and Ubuntu Linux run on desktop computers. Some operating systems are very specialized and rarely seen, such as those that run the electronics in a car. Others are ubiquitous, such as Android and iOS, which run mobile devices.

This book is your guide to the most popular operating systems. In the beginning chapters, you take an in-depth look at popular desktop or client operating systems: Windows 10, Windows 8.1, Windows 7, UNIX/Linux (particularly Linux), and Mac OS X El Capitan. Later in the book, you examine popular server operating systems: Windows Server 2016, Windows Server 2012, and UNIX/Linux. (Note that several distributions of Linux/UNIX can be either client or server operating systems.) This chapter sets the foundation for understanding desktop and server operating systems by introducing you to concepts that apply to most operating systems. With this knowledge under your belt, you will have a solid frame of reference to understand operating system specifics as they are discussed in later chapters.

## About the Hands-On Projects

Be sure to read and complete the activities in the "Before You Begin" section of the Introduction. The Hands-On Projects in this book require that you first set up your lab environment so it is ready to go. The "Before You Begin" section gives you step-by-step instructions for the suggested lab configuration to use with all activities in this book.

Completing the Hands-On Projects is important because they contain information about operating systems that is best understood through hands-on experience. If for some reason you can't do some of the projects, you should at least read through each one to make sure you don't miss important information.

# An Introduction to Operating Systems

Before we discuss how an operating system works, let's review the basic functions of any computer. A computer's functions and features can be broken down into the three basic tasks all computers perform: input, processing, and output. Information is input to a computer from a device such as a keyboard or from a storage device such as a hard drive; the central processing unit (CPU) processes the information, and then output is usually created. The following example illustrates the process:

- *Input*—A user running a word-processing program types the letter *A* on the keyboard, which results in sending a code to the computer representing the letter *A*.
- *Processing*—The computer's CPU determines what letter was typed by looking up the keyboard code in a table.
- *Output*—The CPU sends instructions to the graphics cards to display the letter *A*, which is then sent to the computer monitor.

The three functions described above involve some type of computer **hardware**, but the hardware is controlled and coordinated by the operating system. Without an operating system, every application you use would have to know the details of how to work with each of the hardware devices. Without the operating system to coordinate things, only one application could run at a time. So, you couldn't open a Web browser while working on a Word document, for example. The operating system can be seen as the go-between for the applications you run and the computer hardware.

In a nutshell, an **operating system (OS)** is a specialized computer program that provides the following features:

- *User interface*—The **user interface** provides a method for users to interact with the computer, usually with a keyboard and mouse or touch screen. A user clicks, touches, or types; the computer processes the input and provides some type of output.
- *File system*—The **file system** is the method by which an OS stores and organizes files and manages access to files on a storage device, such as a hard drive.
- *Processes and services*—A **process** is a program that's loaded into memory and run by the CPU. It can be an application a user interacts with, such as a word-processing program or a Web browser, or a program with no user interface that communicates with and provides services to other processes. This type of process is usually called a **service** in Windows and a *daemon* in Linux, and is said to run in the background because there's no user interface.
- *Kernel*—The **kernel** is the heart of the OS and runs with the highest priority. It schedules processes to run, making sure high-priority processes are taken care of first; manages memory to ensure that two applications don't attempt to use the same memory space; and makes sure I/O devices are accessed by only one process at a time, in addition to other tasks.

Each of the above OS components are discussed in more detail throughout this book. For now, let's look more closely at various types of OSs.

## Desktop Versus Server Operating System

A **computer program** is a series of instructions executed by the computer's CPU. A computer program can be large and complex, like an operating system, or it can be small and fairly simple, such as a basic app running on a mobile device. What's special about an operating system program compared to an app is that the operating system is loaded when the computer is turned on and remains running until you turn the computer off. Its job is to make the computer useful so you can run apps, access the Internet, and communicate with other computers.

While there are many types of OSs, and they are designed for different purposes, this book focuses on desktop or client OSs, and server OSs. A **desktop operating system**, or *client operating system*, is typically installed on a personal computer (PC) that is used by one person at a time, and is almost always connected to a network, either wired or wirelessly. The hardware used with a client OS can be in several forms, such as:

- A full desktop computer consisting of separate components for the monitor, CPU box, keyboard, and mouse
- A portable or laptop unit that combines the monitor, CPU box, keyboard, and pointing device in an all-in-one device that is easy to carry
- A combination such as the iMac computer in which the monitor and CPU are in one unit with a separate keyboard and mouse
- A fourth category, often referred to as a 2-in-1, consists of a large tablet computer such as the iPad Pro or Microsoft Surface, along with a detachable keyboard

A **server operating system** is usually installed on a more powerful computer that typically has a wired connection to a network, and can act in many roles to enable multiple users to access information, such as e-mail, files, and software. The server hardware can also take different forms, including traditional server hardware, rack-mounted server hardware, and blade servers.

The traditional server, often used by small or medium-sized businesses, consists of a monitor, CPU box, keyboard, and mouse. **Rack-mounted servers** are CPU boxes mounted in racks that can hold multiple servers. Each rack-mounted server typically has its own power cord and network connection—but these servers often share one monitor and pointing device. Depending on the height of the rack and the height of the servers, one rack can hold a few servers or several dozen. **Blade servers** conserve even more space than rack-mounted servers; each blade server typically looks like a card that fits into a blade enclosure. The **blade enclosure** is a large box with a backplane that contains slots for blade servers; the box provides cooling fans, electrical power, connection to a shared monitor and pointing device, and even network connectivity, depending on the blade enclosure. A single blade enclosure can house over 100 blade servers. Medium-sized and large organizations use rack-mounted and blade servers to help conserve space and to consolidate server management.

TIP

Visit *www.hpe.com*, *www.dell.com*, or *www.supermicro.com* to view examples of traditional, rack-mounted, and blade servers. Also, note that the actual hardware design of rack-mounted and blade servers varies by manufacturer.

Modern desktop and server operating systems are designed to enable network communications so that the operating systems can communicate with one another over a network cable, through wireless communications, and through the Internet. Network communications enable sharing files, sharing printers, and sending e-mail.

## Input and Output

One of the most basic tasks of an operating system is to take care of **input/output** (I/O) functions, which let other programs communicate with the computer hardware. The I/O functions take requests from the software the user runs (the application software) and translate them into low-level requests that the hardware can understand and carry out. In general, an operating system serves as an interface between application software and hardware, as shown in Figure 1-1. Operating systems perform the following I/O tasks:

- Handle input from the keyboard, mouse, and other input devices
- Handle output to the monitor and printer
- Manage network communications, such as for a local network and the Internet
- Control input/output for devices such as network interface cards
- Control information storage and retrieval using various types of storage media such as hard drives, flash drives, and DVDs
- Enable multimedia use for voice and video composition or reproduction, such as recording video from a camera or playing music through speakers

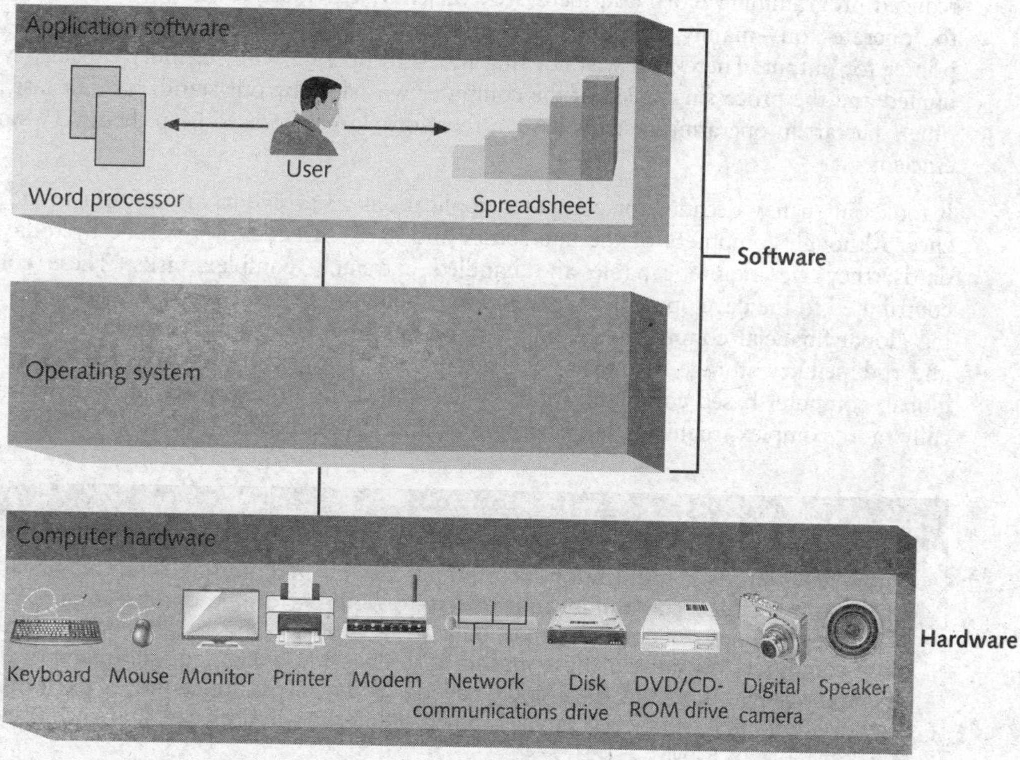


**Figure 1-1** General tasks for all operating systems

# A Short History of Operating Systems

The history of operating systems is a very elaborate subject. As a matter of fact, there are many books on this subject. This short history is not meant to be comprehensive; it merely presents enough background information to show how some of the features in modern PCs and PC operating systems developed.

Initially, computers were used as large automated calculators to solve all sorts of mathematical and statistical problems. Computers were extremely large, often taking up entire rooms. Although you can legitimately trace the history of today's digital computers back 100 years or more, no practical designs were used by significant numbers of people until the late 1950s. Scientists programmed these computers to perform precise tasks. The operating systems were rudimentary, often not able to do more than read punch cards or tape and write output to Teletype machines (machines resembling typewriters). A tape or deck of cards was loaded, a button was pushed on the machine to indicate the input was ready, and the machine started to read the tape and perform the operations requested. If all went well, the work was done and the output was generated. This output would be sent to the Teletype, and that was that.

Yes, there was computer history before this point, but it did not involve any sort of operating system. Any program that the computer ran had to include all logic to control the computer. Because this logic was rather complex, and not all scientists were computer scientists, the operating system was a tool that allowed non-computer scientists to use computers. The OS reduced programming work and increased efficiency. Obviously, there was not all that much to "operate" on—mainly the punch card and punch tape readers for input and the Teletype printer for output. There also was not that much to operate with; memory capacity was very limited and the processing speed of the computer was slow by our standards (but fast for that time). The art in operating systems design, therefore, largely was to keep them very small and efficient.

It took only a few decades for computer applications to evolve to appeal to a broader audience. Although computers of the late sixties and early seventies were crude by today's standards, they were quite capable and handled extremely complex tasks. These computers contributed to the development of space travel, submarine-based ballistic missiles, and a growing global financial community. Computers of this time used only a few kilobytes of RAM and rudimentary storage of only a few megabytes. This period also saw the beginning of a global, computer-based communications system called the *Internet*. Applications became logically more complex, requiring larger programs and large amounts of data.

**From the Trenches ...**

In the 1990s, student registration, accounting, student aid, and all other administrative functions in a state's community college system were performed on one large computer at each community college—that had only 4 MB of RAM. The system administrators of those computers considered these machines to have more than enough memory to run all administrative functions for a single college. Today, those functions are performed at each location on servers; each server is much smaller in physical size, and each uses tens of GB or more of RAM.

As always, necessity was the mother of invention. Input and output devices were created, and computer memory capacity and speed increased. With more devices to manage, operating systems became more complex and extensive, but the rule of thumb—small and fast—was still extremely important. This round of evolution, which really began to take off in the mid-seventies, included the display terminal, a Teletype machine with a keyboard that did not print on paper, but projected letters on a screen (commonly referred to as a *cathode ray tube* or *CRT*). The initial CRT was later followed by a terminal that could also show simple graphics; the terminal looked like an early computer, but it was only a monitor and a keyboard without a CPU or processing capability. The magnetic tape drive, used to store and retrieve data and programs on tape, could store more and was less operator intensive than paper tape. It was quickly followed by numerous manifestations of magnetic disks.

The next evolution was the ability to share computer resources among various programs. If a computer was very fast and could quickly switch among various programs, you could do several tasks seemingly at once and serve many people simultaneously. Some of the operating systems that evolved in this era are long lost to all but those who worked directly with them. However, there are some notable players that were responsible for setting the stage for the full-featured functionality we take for granted today. Digital Equipment Corporation's (DEC's) PDP series computers, for example, ran the DEC operating system, simply known as OS, in one version or another. A popular one was OS/8, which came in various versions, such as Release 3Q; OS/8 was released in 1968. PDP-8 computers were general-purpose machines that at one time were the top-selling computers across the world. The PDP series could also run Multics, which was the basis for the development of the first version of UNIX, a multiuser, multitasking operating system. (Multics is widely considered to be the first multiuser, multitasking operating system. You'll learn about multitasking later in the chapter.)

TIP

To find out more about the once popular PDP-8 computers, visit *www.cs.uiowa.edu/~jones/pdp8*.

The original UNIX was developed at AT&T Bell Labs in 1969 by Kenneth Thompson and Dennis Ritchie as an improvement on Multics. Later, DEC VAX computers used Virtual Memory System (VMS), a powerful, multitasking, multiuser operating system that was strong on networking. IBM mainframes made a series of operating systems popular, starting with GM-NAA I/O in the early sixties and later with System/360. Many others would follow, including CICS, which is still in use today.

Programming computers at this time was still a very complicated process best left to scientists. In the mid-1960s, right after the first interactive computer game was invented at the Massachusetts Institute of Technology (MIT), a simple programming language was developed at Dartmouth College, aimed at the nonprogrammer. It was dubbed **BASIC**, or **Beginner's All-purpose Symbolic Instruction Code**, and became a widely used programming language for many years to follow. A few years later, in 1975, Bill Gates discovered BASIC, and became interested enough to write a compiler for it. (A compiler is software that turns computer code written by people into code that is understood by computers.) Gates then sold the compiler to a company called Micro Instrumentation Telemetry Systems (MITS). MITS was the first company to produce a desktop computer that was widely accepted and could conduct useful work at the hands of any knowledgeable programmer. That same year, Gates dropped out of Harvard to dedicate his time to writing software. Other programming languages introduced around this time included Pascal, C, and other versions of BASIC supplied by various computer manufacturers. Only a couple of years later, Gates' new company (Microsoft) and others adapted popular mainframe and minicomputer programming languages, such as FORTRAN and COBOL, so they could be used on desktop computers. There were also proprietary languages that gained some popularity—languages primarily designed for database programming, for example—but they didn't last and aren't significant to this book.

The introduction of the microcomputer in the mid-1970s was probably the most exciting thing to happen to operating systems. These machines typically had many of the old restrictions, including slow speed and little memory. Many microcomputers came with a small operating system and Read-Only Memory (ROM) that did no more than provide an elementary screen, keyboard, printer, and disk input and output. Gates saw an opportunity and put together a team at Microsoft to adapt a fledging version of a new microcomputer operating system called *86-DOS*, which ran on a prototype of a new microcomputer being developed by IBM called the *personal computer*. 86-DOS was originally written by Tim Paterson (from Seattle Computer Products) as the Quick and Dirty Operating System (QDOS) for the new 8086 microprocessor. 86-DOS (or QDOS) evolved in 1980 through a cooperative effort between Paterson and Microsoft into the **Microsoft Disk Operating System**, or **MS-DOS**. MS-DOS was designed as a **command-line interface**, which means that users typed in commands instead of using the **graphical user interface (GUI)** point-and-click method that is common today.

The original MS-DOS did not offer a GUI desktop from which to click menus and icons. The command-line interface is available in modern Windows operating systems, as well as in Linux and Mac OS X. Some server administrators prefer to use a command-line interface because it offers more individualized and specialized control over the operating system. You'll have an opportunity to use command-line interfaces in Windows, Linux, and Mac OS X throughout the projects in this book.

MS-DOS became a runaway success for Microsoft, and it was the first widely distributed operating system for microcomputers that had to be loaded from disk or tape. There were earlier systems, including Control Program/Monitor (CP/M), that used some features and concepts of the existing UNIX operating system designs, but when IBM adopted MS-DOS for its PC (calling it PC DOS), the die was cast.

What did MS-DOS do? It provided the basic operating system functions described earlier in this chapter, and it was amazingly similar to what was used before on larger computers. It supported basic functions, such as keyboard, disk, and printer I/O—and communications. As time went on, more and more support functions were added, including support for such things as hard disks. Then along came the Apple Macintosh in 1984, with its GUI and mouse pointing device, which allowed users to interact with the operating system on a graphical screen. The mouse allowed users to point at or click icons or to select items from menus to accomplish tasks. Initially, Microsoft chose to wait on development of a GUI, but after Microsoft saw the successful reception of the interface on Apple computers, it developed one of its own.

When the Macintosh was introduced, it seemed light years ahead of the IBM PC. Its operating system came with a standard GUI at a time when MS-DOS was still based on entering text commands. Also, the Macintosh OS managed computer memory closely for the software, something MS-DOS did not do. And, because Mac OS managed all computer memory for the application programs, you could start several programs and switch among them. Mac OS was also years ahead in I/O functions such as printer management. In MS-DOS, a program had to provide its own drivers for I/O devices; MS-DOS provided only the most rudimentary interface. On Mac OS, many I/O functions were part of the operating system.

Microsoft, however, did not stay behind for long. In 1985, Microsoft shipped an extension to its DOS operating system, called Microsoft Windows, which provided a GUI and many of the same functions as Mac OS. The first Windows was really an operating "environment" running on top of MS-DOS, made to look like a single operating system. Today's Windows is no longer based on DOS and is a full-fledged operating system.

Although Apple was six years ahead of Microsoft in offering a friendly GUI-based OS, Apple ultimately fell well behind Microsoft in sales because it chose not to license the Mac OS to outside hardware vendors.

Numerous incarnations of operating systems have come and gone since those days. Today, both Windows and Mac OS X are very similar in what they can do and how they do it; they have a wealth of features and drivers that make the original DOS look elementary. Their principal functions are unchanged, however: to provide an interface between the application programs and hardware, and to provide a user interface for basic functions, such as file and disk management.

Let's review the important pieces of operating system development history. Although pre-1980s computing history is interesting, it doesn't hold much relevance to what we do with computers today. Tables 1-1 and 1-2 show the major milestones in operating system development. The tables summarize 8-, 16-, 32-, and 64-bit operating systems. In general, a 64-bit operating system is more powerful and faster than a 32-bit system, which is more powerful and faster than a 16-bit system, and so on. You will learn more about these differences in Chapter 2, "Popular Operating Systems," and Chapter 3, "Operating System Hardware Components."

**Table 1-1 Operating system releases from 1968 to 1999**

| Operating system | Approximate date | Bits | Comments |
|---|---|---|---|
| UNIX (Bell/AT&T) | 1968 | 8 | First widely used multiuser, multitasking operating system for minicomputers. |
| CP/M | 1975 | 8 | First operating system that allowed serious business work on small personal computers. VisiCalc, a spreadsheet application released in 1978, was the first business calculation program for CP/M, and to a large extent made CP/M a success. |
| MS-DOS | 1980 | 16 | First operating system for the very successful IBM PC family of computers. Lotus 1-2-3 was to MS-DOS in 1981 what VisiCalc was to CP/M. Also in 1981, Microsoft introduced the first version of Word for the PC. |

(continues)

**Table 1-1 Operating system releases from 1968 to 1999 (*continued*)**

| Operating system | Approximate date | Bits | Comments |
|---|---|---|---|
| PC DOS | 1981 | 16 | IBM version of Microsoft MS-DOS. |
| Mac OS | 1984 | 16 | The first widely distributed operating system that was totally graphical in its user interface. Also, Mac OS introduced the use of a mouse to PC-based systems. |
| Mac System Software 5 | 1987 | 16 | Mac OS implemented cooperative multitasking so that more than one application could be run at one time. |
| Mac System Software 6 | 1988 | 16 | Mac OS was significantly stabilized and was also adapted to run on portable computers. |
| Windows 3.0 | 1990 | 16 | First usable version of a graphical operating system for the PC. |
| Linux 0.01 | 1991 | 16 | Linus Torvalds made the first version of Linux available through an FTP download site. |
| Mac System Software 7 | 1991 | 32 | Mac OS was redesigned to have a new interface, more applications, and to use 32-bit addressing. |
| MCC Interim Linux | 1992 | 16 | The first actual distribution of Linux was offered through the University of Manchester in England. |
| Windows for Workgroups (Windows 3.11) | 1993 | 16 | First version of Microsoft Windows with peer-to-peer networking support for the PC. |
| Windows NT (New Technology) | 1993 | 32 | Microsoft's first attempt to bring a true 32-bit, preemptive, multitasking operating system with integrated network functionality to the world of personal computing. Windows NT was later offered in a Workstation version and a Server version. |
| Red Hat Linux, SUSE, and the Linux kernel 1.0 | 1994 | 16/32 | Linux kernel version 1.0 was released, as were the first distributions of Red Hat Linux and SUSE Linux. |
| Windows 95 | 1995 | 16/32 | An upgrade to Windows 3.x, mostly 32-bit code, with a much improved user interface and increased support for hardware. It offered native support to run 32-bit applications and many networking features. Windows 95 represented a different direction than Windows NT because it was intended to provide backward compatibility for 16-bit applications, and it continued to allow applications to directly access hardware functions. |
| Windows 98 | 1998 | 32 | Implemented many bug fixes to Windows 95, more extended hardware support, and was fully 32-bit. |
| GNOME 1.0 desktop | 1999 | 16/32 | The GNOME 1.0 desktop (similar in function to Windows) became available as free software and grew to become one of the most popular UNIX/Linux desktops. |

**Table 1-2 Operating system releases from 2000 to the present**

| Operating system | Approximate date | Bits | Comments |
|---|---|---|---|
| Windows 2000 | 2000 | 32 | A major revision of the Windows NT operating system; Windows 2000 was much faster and more reliable than Windows NT. The Windows 2000 kernel contained over twice the lines of code used in Windows NT. Windows 2000 came in several versions, including Professional, Server, Advanced Server, and Datacenter. |
| Windows Millennium Edition (Me) | 2000 | 32 | Microsoft's operating system upgrade of Windows 98, designed specifically for the home user, with improved multimedia capabilities. |
| Mac OS X | 2001 | 32 | Introduced as a significant departure from the earlier Mac OS versions because it was rewritten to have UNIX-based Darwin as the foundation for the operating system code. Updated versions of Mac OS X continue to be issued with the Snow Leopard version (Mac OS X 10.6) at this writing. |
| Linux kernel 2.4 | 2001 | 32/64 | Enabled compatibility with Plug and Play devices, including USB devices. |
| Windows XP | 2001 | 32/64 | The successor to Windows Me and Windows 2000 Professional, available in four editions: Home, Professional, Tablet PC, and Media Center. The Home Edition was a 32-bit system that focused on home use for photos, music, and other multimedia files. The Professional Edition, available in 32-bit and 64-bit versions, was intended for office and professional users who needed more computing power and extensive networking capabilities. The Tablet PC Edition was tailored for tablet PCs that use speech and pen capabilities and offered great mobility, such as native wireless communications. Finally, the Media Center Edition was for enhanced digital media use involving television, audio, video, and graphics. |
| Windows Server 2003 | 2003 | 32/64 | Available in Standard Edition, Web Edition, Enterprise Edition, and Datacenter Edition, this operating system was designed as a server platform for Microsoft's .NET initiative, which integrated all types of devices—PCs, handheld computers, cell phones, and home appliances—for communications over the Internet. |
| Linux kernel 2.6 | 2003 | 32/64 | Provided support for larger file system storage, new CPUs, more stable 64-bit CPU support, and support for many more simultaneous users. |
| Windows Vista | 2006 | 32/64 | Introduced a newer security philosophy that employed a restricted user account control mode. Came in five editions: Home Basic, Home Premium, Business, Enterprise, and Ultimate. |
| Windows Server 2003 | R2 2006 | 32/64 | An interim release, called *Release 2* (R2), of Windows Server 2003 for compatibility with Windows Vista and to add new features, particularly for medium-sized and large organizations. Offered the same editions as Windows Server 2003. |
| Windows Server 2008 | 2008 | 32/64 | Employed the new security philosophy begun with Windows Vista and extended security for servers in part by offering greater modularity to achieve a smaller attack profile. The main editions included Standard, Enterprise, Datacenter, Web, and HPC (High Performance Computing). |

(*continues*)

**Table 1-2 Operating system releases from 2000 to the present (*continued*)**

| Operating system | Approximate date | Bits | Comments |
|---|---|---|---|
| Mac OS X Snow Leopard | 2009 | 32/64 | Dropped support for PowerPC processors and switched to using only Intel processors. |
| Windows 7 | 2009 | 32/64 | Employed enhanced security features, with fewer headaches and stumbling blocks for the user, compared to Windows Vista. Offered many new desktop features. The editions included Home Basic, Home Premium, Professional, Enterprise, and Ultimate. |
| Windows Server 2008 R2 | 2009 | 64 only | An interim release (Release 2 or R2) for Windows Server 2008 that included built-in compatibility with Windows 7. It had desktop changes similar to Windows 7. Offered the same versions as Windows Server 2008. Microsoft's current plans are only to develop new operating systems for 64-bit computers. |
| Chrome OS | 2009 | 32/64 | An OS based on the Linux kernel and developed by Google. Chrome OS is intended to be an online OS, meaning that you must be connected to the Internet to get the best use of it. Chrome OS runs primarily Web applications and is only available pre-installed on a device from a manufacturer, such as a Chromebook. |
| Linux Kernel 3.0 | 2011 | 32/64 | New features include automatic defragmentation, a feature to wake up a computer from a wireless interface (Wake on WLAN), support for containers (a type of virtualization), and support for new devices. |
| Windows 8/8.1 | 2012/2013 | 32/64 | Windows 8 was Microsoft's first attempt to unify the mobile and desktop computing space. The touch-centric interface was not well accepted; to mollify users, Microsoft quickly released Windows 8.1, which walked back some of the disliked user interface changes from previous Windows versions. |
| Windows Server 2012/R2 | 2012/2013 | 64 only | Windows Server 2012 was released along with Windows 8 and had the same user-interface problems. Windows Server 2012 R2 was released along with Windows 8.1. Windows Server 2012/R2 made substantial enhancements to its virtualization engine, Hyper-V, and added cloud-centric features. Windows Server 2012/R2 had Standard and Datacenter editions along with Foundation and Essentials. Enterprise edition was later dropped. |
| Linux Kernel 4.0 | 2015 | 32/64 | This release includes live updating of the kernel without requiring a system shutdown, a feature called *lazytime* that supports better file time stamping, and a number of driver and performance enhancements. |
| Windows 10 | 2015 | 32/64 | Windows 10 finished walking back the user interface problems of Windows 8 while providing a single OS that worked well on the desktop as well as on touch-centric mobile devices like the Microsoft Surface. Speculation is that Windows 10 may be the last named version of Windows. |
| Mac OS X El Capitan | 2015 | 32/64 | This release includes the Split View feature, an updated Spotlight search app, and new swipe gestures. |
| Windows Server 2016 | 2016 | 64 only | Windows Server 2016 is slated for release about the time this book goes to press (fall 2016). This version emphasizes virtualization, flexible storage solutions, and cloud computing, and includes a version called *Nano Server* that has a very small footprint for embedded and virtual deployments. |

TIP

Check out Paul Thurrott's SuperSite for Windows at: *http://winsupersite.com/server/windows-server-0* to read about the latest in Windows 10 and Windows Server.

All of these PC operating systems changed the roles of the big machines' dynasty. Many big machines are now obsolete; others are used for calculation and data storage as back-end functions for the PC. Even in this arena, they are threatened today as PC operating systems and hardware extend further and further.

Many older operating systems are no longer around because of hardware changes. In Chapter 3, you look more closely at hardware architecture and what it means for the operating system. A good example of hardware that is no longer feasible to run an OS is the Z80 CPU produced by Zilog. Zilog manufactures semiconductors and created the first microprocessor.

When the cheaper and more flexible Intel 8088 and 8086 microprocessors were introduced in the IBM PC, the MS-DOS platform was a more attractive choice for most users. The Z80 and its CP/M operating system slowly died out. The same happened to some operating systems that used IBM PC hardware for other reasons. A prime example is IBM's own OS/2 operating system, first released in 1987 and developed jointly with Microsoft. The OS/2 system required extensive hardware, and it could not run older MS-DOS applications. Many people wanted to continue to run MS-DOS applications, so OS/2 was not a big hit. Because new software for OS/2 was slow to come and offered no substantial new features, people were hesitant to use it. Today, you will find OS/2 mainly in environments where it is used to interface to large IBM mainframes with custom-developed applications. For an operating system to be successful, many things must work together: availability of hardware and application programs, the right mix of features, and good timing. Try Hands-On Project 1-1 at the end of this chapter to learn more about the history of operating systems.

# Understanding How Operating Systems Work

Many elements go into enabling an operating system to work with the computer on which it is loaded. These include:

- The kernel
- Resource managers
- Device drivers
- Application software
- BIOS

In the next sections you learn about each of these elements. The sections are followed by a summary to help you put the information together.

## The Kernel

The kernel consists of the essential program code of the operating system. To help illustrate this concept, you might draw a parallel to a general contractor on a job site. The general contractor is there to schedule all the specific tasks that must be completed to finish the job and to ensure that all the subcontractors have the necessary resources and tools to do their jobs in a timely manner. Tasks are scheduled, resources are allocated, and then tasks are terminated and resources released so they can be used for other tasks. Scheduling computer processes and managing resources, such as memory and processing time, are key tasks of the OS kernel.

The term *kernel* has evolved from the UNIX operating system, but is also used to apply to the core code in the Windows and Mac OS X operating systems. In UNIX and Linux systems, the basic interface with the kernel is called the **shell**, which is a program that enables users to execute commands. You learn how to identify the UNIX/Linux shell in the Hands-On Projects in Chapter 2.

The jobs performed by the kernel can include:

- Managing interactions with the CPU
- Starting, managing, and scheduling programs that handle I/O activities, including device and networking activities
- Handling basic computer security
- Managing use of the computer's memory (RAM)
- Managing priority levels assigned to programs and computer processes

In Windows systems, the name of the kernel file is ntoskrnl.exe. In Mac OS X, the kernel is called *XNU*. The actual kernel name in Linux depends on the distribution and release of Linux. You can determine information about the kernel by using the *uname -sr* command in Linux (see Hands-On Project 1-5 to learn how to execute the *uname* command).

UNIX and Linux are available in distributions. A **distribution** is an issuance of UNIX or Linux that is based on a standard kernel, but that also has customizations added by a particular private or commercial development group. For example, Red Hat Enterprise Linux has customizations that are useful for organizations and businesses; this distribution is sold through the Red Hat company. GNU Linux is a distribution built on a Linux kernel, but with added tools from the GNU Project and the Free Software Foundation. GNU Linux is free. Fedora Linux is sponsored by Red Hat to serve as a development vehicle for testing customizations that may or may not be incorporated into Red Hat Enterprise Linux. Fedora Linux is offered free as a way to encourage the public to test new features prior to incorporating them into Red Hat Enterprise Linux.

## Resource Managers

One of the functions of the operating system is to manage RAM and central processor use. For example, programs and devices require access to memory. If two devices or programs use the same memory space at the same time, they will not function properly, and they might cause the computer and operating system to hang. Even the computer's CPU contains memory that must be properly managed to avoid problems. The operating system uses specialized programs called **resource managers** to help ensure that memory is used properly and there are no memory conflicts.

The operating system also manages how programs access the processing capabilities of the CPU. Even if a computer has two or more CPUs, it is still important that one program not dominate the processing time on any one CPU. If one program were able to take over all of the time on a CPU, the computer might appear to hang and the work by other programs would come to a halt, possibly crashing the computer. When multiple programs and processes are running, the operating system manages the amount of time each is given by the CPU. For example, if there is one CPU and 10 programs that want to access it, the operating system will give each program a time slice on the CPU—as determined by the priority the CPU gives a particular program or process. Each program or process does a little work during its time slice, and then the kernel gives the next program or process CPU access for its time slice. Often programs associated with operating system tasks have a higher priority than user programs, because operating system programs are necessary for the smooth functioning of the computer.

## Device Drivers and the Operating System

The operating system communicates and works directly with many devices, including the monitor, keyboard, disk drives, mouse, network adaptor, sound card, and so on. Some operating system programs exchange information with specific hardware (chips) inside the computer that control these devices. The code (instructions) for this information exchange is typically referred to as a device driver. A **device driver** translates computer code to display text on a screen, or translates movements of a mouse into action, for example. A separate device driver is usually present for each I/O device, as shown in Figure 1-2. In general, operating systems have a standardized way of communicating with a certain type of device driver. The device driver contains the actual code (instructions) to communicate with the chips on the device. This way, if another piece of hardware is introduced into the computer, the operating system code does not have to change. To enable the computer to communicate with the new device, you simply need to load a new device driver onto the operating system.

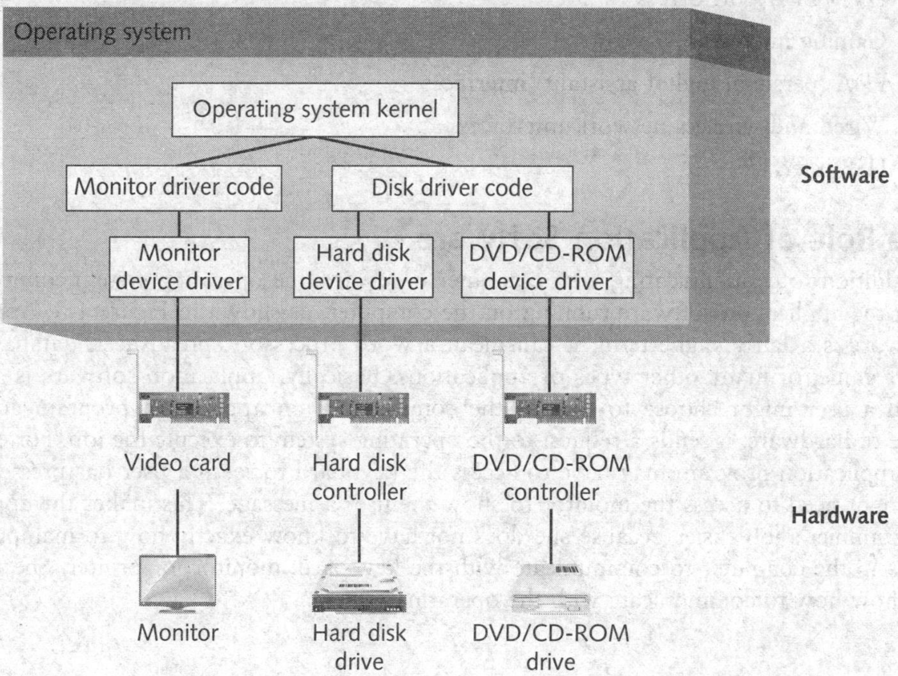


**Figure 1-2** Device drivers provide communication between the OS and hardware devices

TIP

If a particular device is not working, one way to troubleshoot the problem is to obtain and install the latest driver for that device, which can usually be downloaded from the manufacturer's Web site.

For example, high-capacity removable hard drives that connect through a Universal Serial Bus (USB) were introduced after some earlier operating systems were written. Thus, earlier versions of operating systems did not natively support USB-based removable hard drives. However, because removable hard drives are similar to other types of disk drives, early versions of operating systems could be adapted to use removable hard drives by loading a few simple drivers for the operating system. You may encounter device drivers that interface with your operating system for other devices, including:

- Fixed internal hard disk drives (HDDs) and solid state drives (SSDs)
- Computer monitors
- Keyboards
- Mouse and trackball devices
- Remote communications modems
- Printers and scanners
- Tape drives, flash drives, hard drives, and other removable media
- Digital cameras and video hardware
- MP3 players or other audio hardware
- DVD/CD-ROM drives
- Gaming interfaces
- PDA (personal digital assistant) interfaces
- Wired and wireless network interfaces
- USB interfaces

## The Role of Application Software

In addition to communicating with computer hardware, the operating system communicates with the application software running on the computer, as shown in Figure 1-3. **Application software** is a fairly vague term; it can mean a word processor, spreadsheet, database, computer game, or many other types of applications. Basically, application software is any program a user might choose to run on the computer. If an application program accesses a piece of hardware, it sends a request to the operating system to execute the job. For example, the application program may have to access the keyboard to see if a user has pressed a key, or might need to access the monitor to show the user a message. This makes the application programmer's job easier because she does not have to know exactly how to manipulate the chips in the computer to communicate with the keyboard, monitor, or printer. She only has to know how to communicate with the operating system.

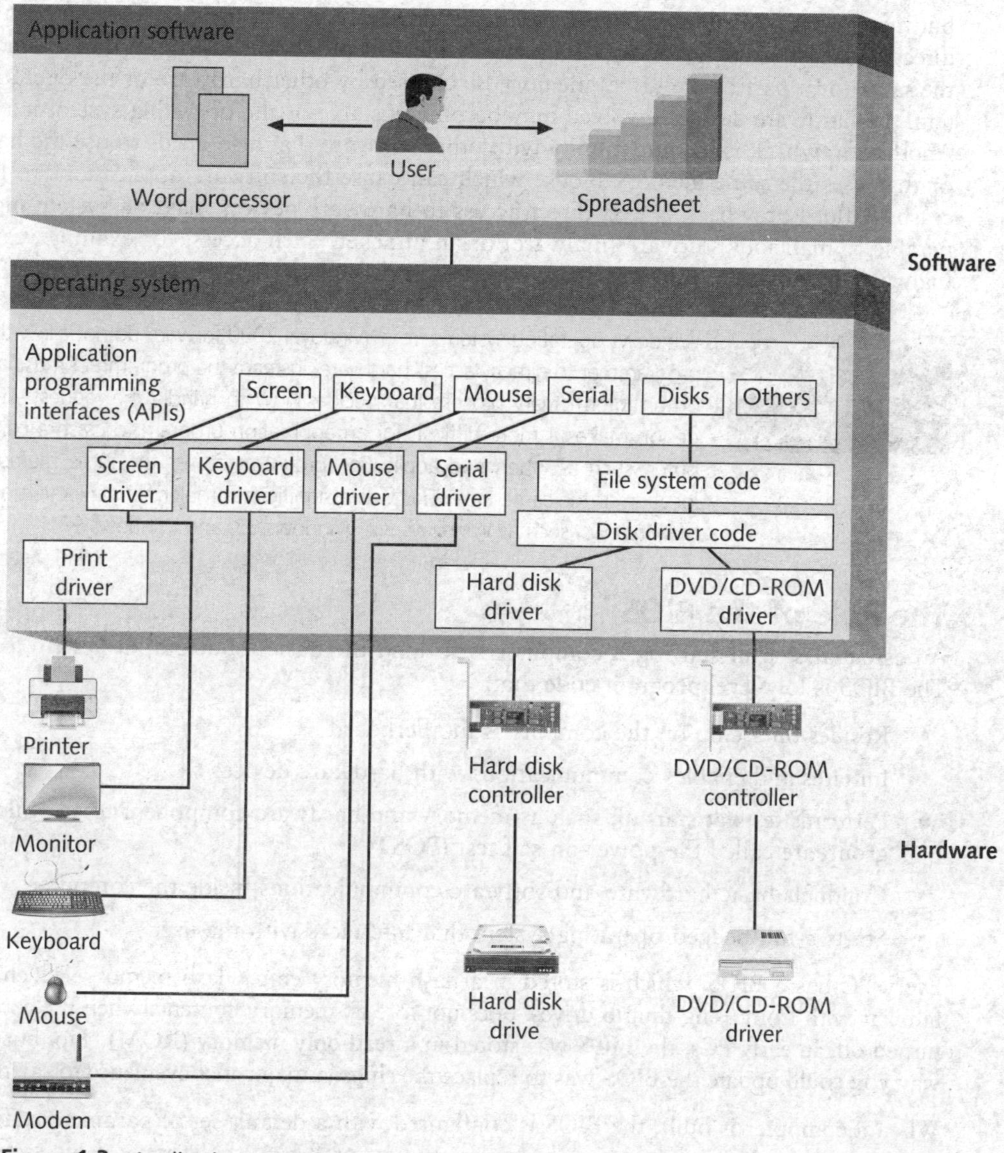


**Figure 1-3** Application programs communicate with hardware through the operating system

In its most basic form, an operating system manages the communication among the application programs, the user, and the computer. This level of management allows application programmers to concentrate on applications that will run on any hardware, as long as the operating system can control them. In other words, an application program can submit a general request to the operating system, such as "write this information to disk," and the operating system handles the details. The application programmer doesn't have to worry about how to queue data, update the disk directory, or physically copy data from memory to the disk drive.

In early operating systems, programmers designed code to directly access hardware and improve overall application performance. This practice can make hardware response fast, but there are serious drawbacks. A significant drawback is that memory is often required for directly managing the hardware. If a memory block is programmed for use that conflicts with the same (or a part of the same) memory block used by other hardware or the operating system, the hardware devices involved may become unstable or the operating system may crash. Another drawback is incompatibility with other software that also needs to use the hardware or that uses the same memory block, which can cause the software applications to hang or crash. A third drawback is that direct access to hardware devices makes a system more vulnerable to malicious software (malware) or an attacker. Such access, for example, can allow malware to damage a disk or extensively damage disk files.

Windows operating systems from Windows 2000 forward do not allow the programmer to directly access hardware. Instead, the programmer must call on an intermediary process that decides how to handle the request. This design makes it more difficult for an application program to crash a computer, such as when two application programs access the same memory location at the same time. This was a significant problem in earlier versions of Windows, such as Windows 3.x, Windows 95, and Windows 98.

## The Role of the BIOS

An essential step in starting a computer is to load the **basic input/output system,** or **BIOS.** The BIOS is low-level program code that:

- Resides on a chip on the computer's motherboard
- Initiates and enables communications with hardware devices
- Performs tests at startup, such as memory and hardware component tests, which as a group are called the **power-on self test (POST)**
- Conducts basic hardware and software communications inside the computer
- Starts a full-fledged operating system that interfaces with the user

Every PC has a BIOS, which is stored in a flash memory chip. Flash memory, which you are familiar with from using thumb drives, does not lose its memory contents when the computer is turned off. In early PCs, the BIOS was stored in a **read-only memory (ROM)** chip, but the only way you could update the BIOS was to replace the chips, a major inconvenience to say the least.

When a computer is built, the BIOS is configured with a default set of parameters. The BIOS configuration stores information about the amount of RAM, the storage devices, and other I/O devices on the computer. The BIOS configuration is stored in a memory chip called **complementary metal oxide semiconductor** (**CMOS**). A CMOS chip uses a low-power memory technology that is powered by a small battery. Users can make changes to the BIOS configuration by accessing the BIOS setup screen before the computer boots. Figure 1-4 shows a sample BIOS setup screen on a computer. Whenever you turn on your PC, the machine wakes up and begins executing the startup program inside the BIOS. This program initializes the screen and keyboard, tests computer hardware, such as the CPU and memory, initializes the hard disk and other devices, and then loads the main operating system—Windows 10 or Linux, for example—that provides more advanced functionality for application programs. Figure 1-5 illustrates the main operating system components, including the relationship of an operating system to the BIOS.

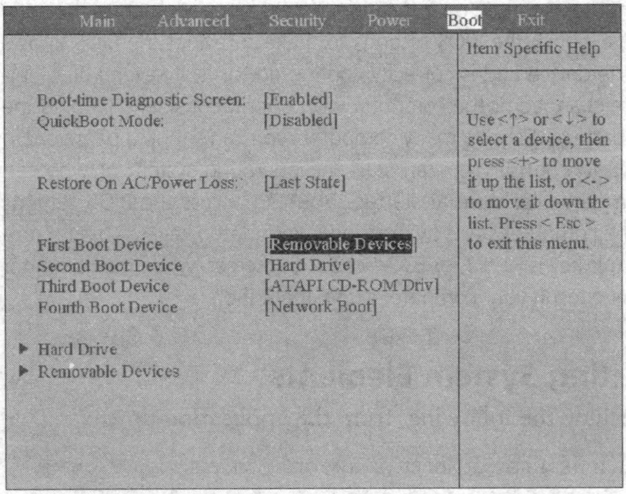


**Figure 1-4** Sample BIOS setup screen

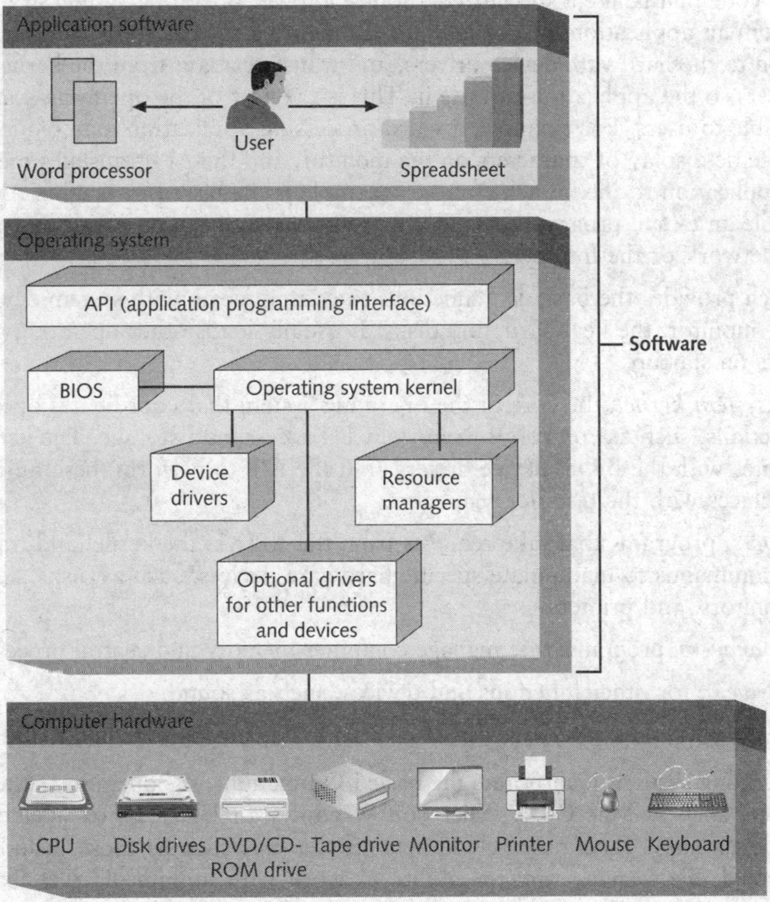


**Figure 1-5** General operating system design

TIP

If a computer is turned on but cannot access a device, such as the main disk drive, check the BIOS settings to make sure that the BIOS knows about the device and is correctly configured for it. If several BIOS settings are changed or the computer won't boot, consider changing the CMOS battery. Also, on many computers you can set up a password in the BIOS to control who can start the operating system or who can access a particular drive at startup. You can access the BIOS settings when the computer starts by pressing a designated key. On many computers, this key is F1, F2, or ESC—check the screen when the computer boots, or consult your computer's documentation.

## A Summary of Operating System Elements

The elements in Figure 1-5 include the following, from the application down:

- *Application software*, such as a spreadsheet or a word processor.
- *Application programming interface*. An **application programming interface (API)** is software designed to communicate with the application software and the user. The API is program code that is like a specialized "hook" into the operating system. It translates requests from an application into code that the operating system kernel can understand and pass on to the hardware device drivers, and translates data from the kernel and device drivers so the application can use it. This is the part of the operating system that is most visible to users. For example, a word-processing application may request to create a specific display of characters on the monitor, and the API translates the request from the application to the kernel. Another example is the use of messaging APIs, which enable an e-mail program to send a message through the operating system to a computer network or the Internet.
- *BIOS*, which provides the basic I/O functions to communicate with system devices, such as the monitor, the keyboard, and disks. It usually loads other operating system components on startup.
- *Operating system kernel*, the core of the operating system that coordinates operating system functions, such as control of memory, CPU access, and storage. The kernel communicates with the BIOS, device drivers, and the API to perform these functions. It also interfaces with the resource managers.
- *Device drivers*, programs that take requests from the API via the kernel and translate them into commands to manipulate specific hardware devices, such as disks, keyboards, monitors, and printers.
- *Resource managers*, programs that manage computer memory and central processor use.
- *Optional drivers*, for other functions and devices, such as sound.
- *Computer hardware*, such as storage devices, CPU, mouse, keyboard, monitor, and printer.

Although all operating systems incorporate the basic I/O functions, the operating systems you are accustomed to, such as Mac OS X, Microsoft Windows, or UNIX/Linux, include many additional functions. These functions include network services such as those included with the TCP/IP protocol, file systems, and the ability to work with multimedia files like audio and video files.

The Hands-On Projects at the end of this chapter enable you to view the interfaces (desktops) of Windows 10, Linux, and Mac OS X—all of which enable users to interact with the operating system.

## Types of Operating Systems

There are many types of computer operating systems, which work in very different ways and are intended for very different purposes. To a large extent, the functions required by a computer dictate what the operating system will do and how. As an example, the computer in a microwave oven needs device drivers for the light-emitting diode (LED) display, numeric keypad, and door-closing switches, whereas the computer in a television needs drivers to monitor the remote control and tell the tuner to change the channel. The same goes for various types of small and large computers; a computer designed to handle a high volume of numerical operations for many users needs different functions than the PC used to run a word processor.

In general, operating systems are organized by the size, type, and purpose of the computer on which they run. For example, PC-class computers are designed for individual users to perform tasks, such as word processing, database and spreadsheet management, and networking with other computers. Over the years, PCs have become faster, more complex, and more powerful, offering the user more features. As a result, many PCs can now handle complex operations that go beyond simply running a user's application software. This ability has resulted in advanced operating systems that are designed to provide complex graphical user interfaces and advanced services and applications. The lines of division by size, type, and purpose are therefore getting more vague every day. Hardware is becoming more compact, but capable of doing more, and operating systems are getting larger and more complex.

One example of how PC operating systems have become more complex is the comparison of lines of code. Windows 3.1, released in 1992, had about 3 million lines of code, whereas modern OSs like Mac OS X and recent Windows versions have more than 50 million lines of code.

For instance, in the seventies, corporate computing was confined to mainframe- and minicomputer-class devices. These were refrigerator-sized or larger computers that required a full staff to manage them, and large, expensive air-conditioned rooms to hold them. The operating systems for these machines were quite complex and often included such intrinsic functions as text editing (not quite "word processing" by today's standards), database management, networking, and communications. There were few PC-class devices at the time. Those that were available were capable of minimal functionality, and used what could only be described as rudimentary operating systems. Many of those early devices didn't support any storage hardware (disk drives), or if they did, it was frequently serial, low-density tape. In this comparison, it should be easy to see that "in the old days," operating systems for large machines were very different from operating systems used for smaller machines.

**From the Trenches ...**

In the early 1990s, one of the authors managed the installation of a new IBM 9000-class mainframe. Installing the hardware and operating system, plus porting (relocating) programs and data from the previous mainframe, was such a complex process that it took several months to plan and many more months to test and execute. The computer equipment was so large that it was delivered by a moving van. Compare that task to setting up a new PC server and operating system, which requires very little space and can take as little as a few hours to a few days to complete.

At the same time, applications for these early large machines were written with efficient code so they could maximize all of the resources on the computer. As a result, appearance, programming, and management were very terse and basic.

To a lesser extent, this is still true today. There are still "big" machines and "small" machines, except that much of today's computer equipment is no longer physically large. The days of room-sized or even refrigerator-sized computers are nearly gone. A "big" machine today simply has more processing power, more memory, more storage (disk drive capacity), and better network connectivity. Very high-capacity computing is often accomplished by linking together several servers to appear as one.

Some of today's supercomputers are still physically large, such as those made by the Cray supercomputer company (visit *www.cray.com*). A **supercomputer** is one that has extreme processing power and speed to handle complex computations that are beyond the reach of other computers. A supercomputer might be used to simulate constantly changing and complex molecular structures, for example.

To operate today's more powerful computers, more powerful and more capable operating systems are employed. For example, a company that sells Internet access and Web hosting to thousands of other users—an Internet service provider (ISP), for instance—requires computers capable of performing multiple tasks for many users at the same time.

Although the computers used for such large installations typically don't look much different from the PC or Macintosh designed for a single user, they are quite different inside. They have powerful multitasking, multiuser capabilities with high-speed network connections. Also, they may include multiple CPUs and have more powerful I/O capabilities. The differences are significant, but also subtle. For example, Linux is a popular desktop operating system (used by a single person) based on UNIX, and it is also used to host Web servers, mail servers, and other Internet-related multiuser applications. Again, the hardware for a single-user Linux computer is likely much different from that of a Linux computer used to host Internet services, even though the operating system is the same. On the other hand, even with the enhanced hardware, an ISP wouldn't likely replace Linux or any other server operating system, such as Windows Server 2016, with a system intended for the desktop, such as Windows 10.

So-called high-end workstations are used by engineers for graphical design, or by editors for film design and animation. Again, these machines may look much like a school or home PC, but inside they include extremely fast hard disk controllers, 3D graphics interfaces, lots of memory, and often support for multiple CPUs. The needs of these workstations are very different from the multitasking, multiuser needs of an Internet server, but they too have special requirements that can't be met by some operating systems. Although some graphics applications use Linux or UNIX, the Windows and Mac OS X operating systems are more popular foundations for these applications, and can be used for powerful business applications as well.

So, there must be other factors that differentiate high-end and low-end computers. The main factor is the application software used with the computers. Again, the differentiation among computers is getting less defined. You have seen some of these factors, but the confusing concept is that even high-end applications can often run on what are considered low-end machines on the same operating system. When this is the case, the main differentiating factor is the hardware: the speed of the disk controller, size and speed of the storage media, amount and speed of memory, size of the data pathways in the computer (such as 32-bit, 64-bit, or larger), or speed and number of CPUs.

One way to look at computer and operating systems is to consider them in terms of one or more of the following characteristics:

- Time sharing
- Real-time
- Multiuser

## Time Sharing

A **time-sharing system** is a central computer system that is used by multiple users and applications simultaneously. Mainframe computers typically fall into this category. These computers are used to conduct massive calculations or manipulate huge amounts of data. Mainframe computers, such as IBM System z mainframes, are used at scientific institutions, banks, and insurance companies. They are built to quickly perform tasks, such as keeping track of thousands of checking account balances. Most of their work is done in batches, using **batch processing**—such as clearing two million checks and updating their associated bank accounts—instead of single, sequential repetitive tasks. When the batch process is finished—all checks have been posted, for example—the statements can be printed. Contrast this approach to that of smaller computers, such as PCs, that are interactive and use **sequential processing**, where each process request is completed and the data returned before the next process is started.

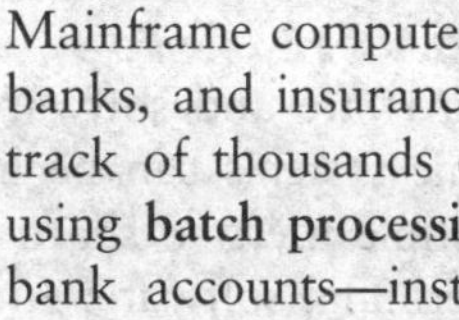


Big batch processing jobs, or multiple batch jobs that must occur in a specific order on large computers, are often scheduled to run after work hours because they require so many machine resources. This makes batch processing less convenient than the instant response you get with a sequential process.

Besides batch processing, many clerks, customer representatives, and ATM machines often use a mainframe to do daily transactions. They all share the resources, or processor time, of the large machine, which is why such machines are called *time-sharing systems*.

**From the Trenches ...**

A downside of batch processing is that if the order of processing is inadvertently changed, the result may be a disaster to the data. A bank experienced this problem when performing its fiscal year-end closing. Some preliminary financial calculations and database updates were scheduled after all files were formally closed for the fiscal year. To restore the files to their year-end condition, it was necessary to restrict access to the mainframe the next day, and the batch processes were rescheduled. No new business could be done on the mainframe for a day until the data was restored and corrected.

## Real-Time Systems

A **real-time operating system (RTOS)** receives and processes inputs and produces the required outputs in a specified amount of time. It is more important for the response time of an RTOS to be consistent than fast, although RTOSs are also built for speed. For example, an RTOS might be used in an industrial plant to control machinery. Inputs to the computer controlling the machinery dictate how the machines respond; the responses must be consistent and predictable, or the entire process may be thrown off.

Examples of RTOSs include VxWorks from Wind River Systems, QNX, and Windows CE. These OSs are typically used in **embedded systems**, which means the computer has a dedicated function within a larger system such as a piece of machinery. Examples of embedded systems include the computer that runs all the systems of a modern automobile or the computers that run the robots on an automated assembly line.

## Multiuser Systems

A **multiuser system** supports multiple users who access the hardware and software of the computer and operating system. Both time-sharing and real-time systems can be multiuser systems. To review, time sharing is a method for enabling multiple users to share in using CPU resources, such as through terminals or computers with terminal software. A terminal consists of a keyboard and monitor without a CPU. For example, a time-sharing mainframe was originally accessed by running cables from terminals to a specialized communications box connected to the mainframe, creating a multiuser system, as shown in Figure 1-6. In time sharing, users may experience delays as the processor and operating system handle all of the processing requests and processing time becomes available. Today, multiple users typically access mainframes through a computer network.

Servers, such as a Linux server or Windows Server 2016, can provide computer access to multiple users over a network, as shown in Figure 1-7. In this environment, multiple users can do many different things on the multiuser computer at the same time. Access to resources is designed to be instantaneous by all users. Most modern OSs run both on personal computers and servers and are considered multiuser operating systems. Even though Windows 10, for example, doesn't typically have multiple monitors and keyboards attached to it with several users running applications, these OSs can support multiple user connections through a network.

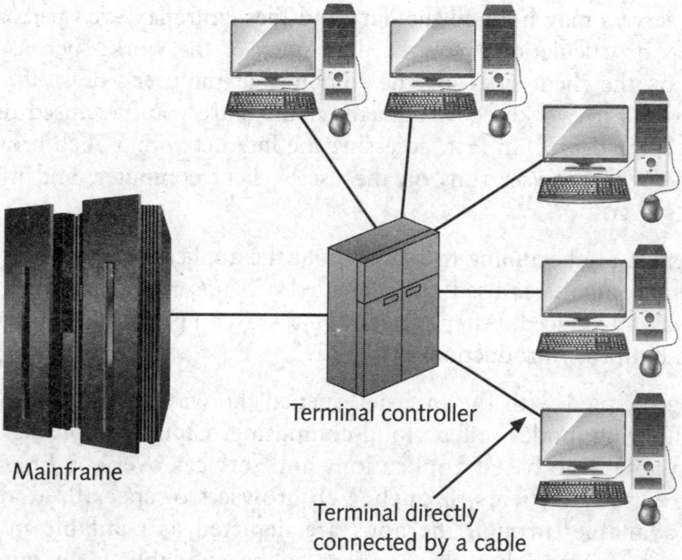


**Figure 1-6** Time-sharing mainframe with terminals

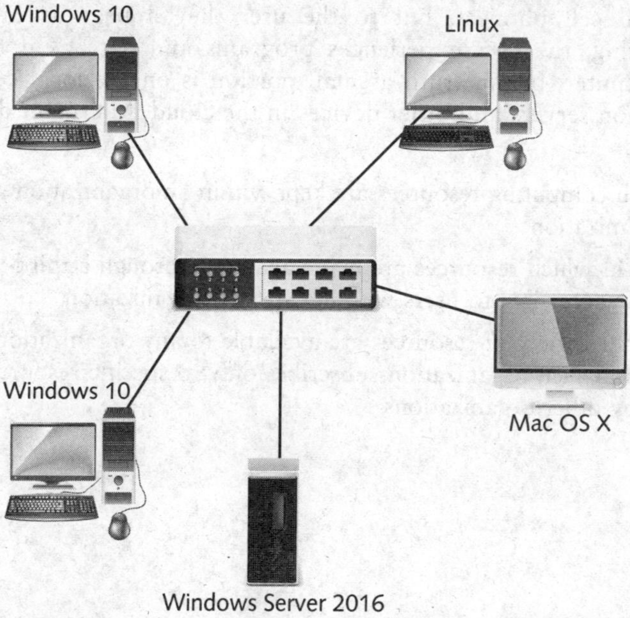


**Figure 1-7** Using a network to access a Windows server

In a departure from mainframes and time sharing, one of the newer approaches to multiuser operations is the use of **client/server systems**. On a multiuser mainframe, all of the work is typically done on the big machine, including running programs, storing data, and accessing data. In the client/server model, only some of the work is done on the central servers. In a client/server system, the servers may hold all the data and files, and may even perform some of the database functions or calculations required, but much of the work, such as running programs, is performed on the client side—on the computer at the user's desk. If you have used PC-class computers in a networked environment, chances are you have used the client/server model, at least to some degree. In fact, accessing the Internet with a Web browser is a client/server activity. The Web browser runs on the user's client computer, and it requests Web pages from a Web server.

Operating system differences are beginning to narrow, but the applications that run on them help differentiate how the computer is used and classified. Client/server computing was not possible until the PC was introduced. After all, it requires a computer at the user's desk, which was not available until the introduction of the PC.

Client/server computing coupled with the Internet opened the way to an even more efficient and powerful computing model called cloud computing. **Cloud computing** involves providing a host of scalable Web-based applications and services over the Internet or a private network that are used by clients through Web browsers or specialized apps. The servers and resources available through the apps are depicted as available in a cloud because there are many resources, but they appear to be available from one unified resource (see Figure 1-8). You might compare this technology to using telephone services. There are many telephone companies and telephone technologies (such as land lines, satellite phones, and cell phones), but to the user they appear as one giant resource. In cloud computing, the user experiences programs and data as if they are installed on the user's computer, but in truth a small portion is on the local computer and all other resources are on servers and other devices in the cloud. Microsoft describes three types of cloud models:

- *Private cloud*—In which computing resources are kept within an organization and used exclusively by that organization
- *Hosted private cloud*—In which resources are made available through a third-party outsourcer, but are only accessible to users within a specific organization
- *Public cloud*—In which a variety of resources are available to any organization through a third party and each organization subscribes only to specific resources, which may be shared by other organizations

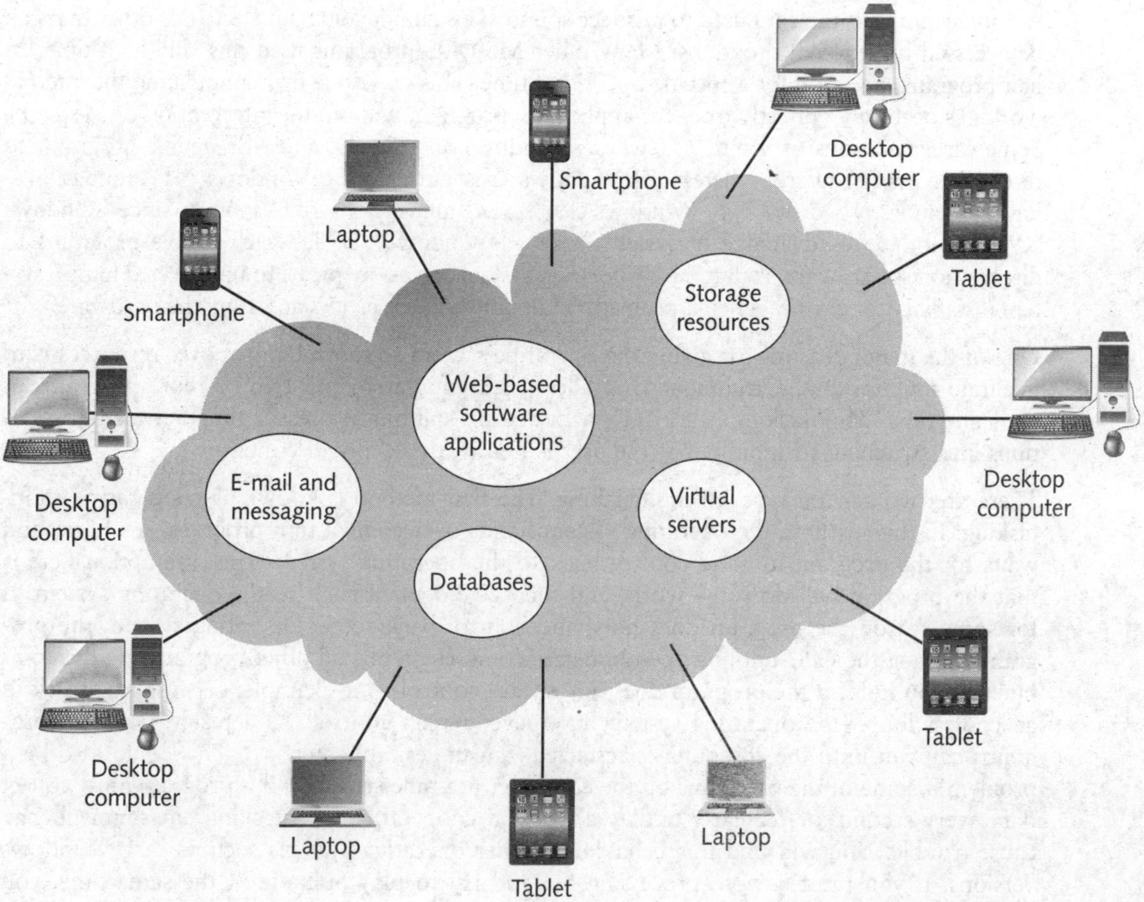


**Figure 1-8** Cloud computing

Common cloud service providers include Amazon Web Services (AWS), Microsoft Azure, and Dropbox. AWS and Microsoft Azure are full-service cloud computing companies that can offer customers anything from cloud storage to an entire network of servers and services. Dropbox, as you may know, is a cloud storage company that provides seamless access to files through the Internet.

## Single Tasking Versus Multitasking

A few aspects of operating systems deserve a closer look. As pointed out earlier, today's PC operating systems go way beyond basic I/O. In practice, almost every resource in the computer, such as the memory and the microprocessor (CPU), is managed by the operating system. This is both good and bad; it results in a lot more consistency and a lot of added functionality. However, application programs can no longer directly access hardware in creative ways as they could before, particularly under MS-DOS and in early Windows systems.

A good example is the chip used to produce sound. This chip includes an electronic timer that can be accessed by external programs. Many older MS-DOS programs used this chip as a timer to halt program execution for a specified period of time. This was done by manipulating the internal workings of the chip directly from the application program, without the intervention of MS-DOS. Some earlier versions of Windows, such as Windows 3.x, 95, 98, and ME, enable programs to directly access hardware, whereas all Windows OSs built on the Windows NT foundation—which includes Windows NT, Windows 2000, and all versions of Windows since Windows XP—do not. A disadvantage of systems such as Windows 95/98, which enable programs to directly access hardware, is that these operating systems are more prone to unexpected hangs, system instability, or crashes when a problem occurs in software as it is accessing the hardware.

One of the major reasons for giving the operating system so much control over resources is to facilitate **multitasking**, a technique that allows a computer to run two or more programs at the same time. Multitasking is typically achieved by splitting processor time between applications and switching so rapidly that the user is not aware of any discontinuity.

There are two general types of multitasking. The first method is known as **cooperative multitasking**. In this method, the operating system hands over control to a program, sits back, and waits for the program to hand control back to the operating system. The assumption here is that the program will do some work, and then give control back to the operating system. If for some reason the program does not hand control back to the operating system, the program will hog the CPU until its operations are complete, while all other programs on the computer are on hold. If the program does not release control—for example, because it is stuck in an endless loop—the operating system may never regain control. As a result, no other programs can run until the computer is restarted—an undesirable scenario. This could also be a problem if some of the programs on the computer are time sensitive. If a program must collect data every second, or regularly update a clock, a cooperative multitasking environment may cause trouble. You will find this behavior in older operating systems such as early Windows versions. If you print a word-processing file and try to play Solitaire at the same time, you will find that you cannot play a card until the print job is finished. Figure 1-9 shows the basic concept of cooperative multitasking.

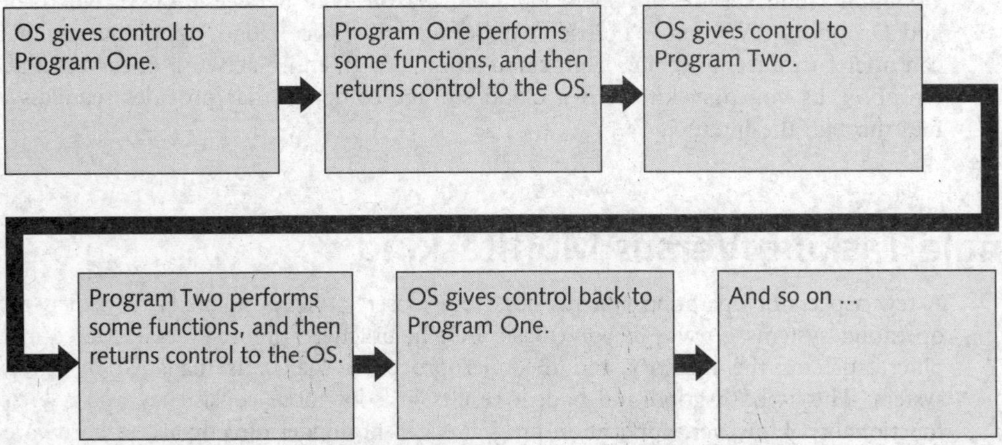


**Figure 1-9** Cooperative multitasking basics

A better method is the second alternative, **preemptive multitasking**, illustrated in Figure 1-10. Modern operating systems developed since the early 2000s use preemptive multitasking. These systems include all Windows OSs since Windows XP, along with Mac OS X and all Linux/UNIX variations. In preemptive multitasking, the operating system is in control of the computer at all times. It lets programs execute a little bit of code at a time, but immediately after the code executes, it forces the program to relinquish control of the CPU back to the operating system. It then takes the next program and repeats the same process. Because the operating system is in charge, it has a lot of control over how much of the computer's resources are allocated to each program. As a result, the computer must use more of its processor power and memory to support the operating system, but the behavior of programs and the computer as a whole are a little more predictable. Playing Solitaire while printing a word-processing file within a preemptive multitasking system is not a problem—both processes get enough CPU time to do their jobs—and the user is often unaware that the system has been rapidly switching between tasks.

Linux/UNIX OSs have always included preemptive multitasking since the original UNIX developed by Bell Labs in the 1970s.

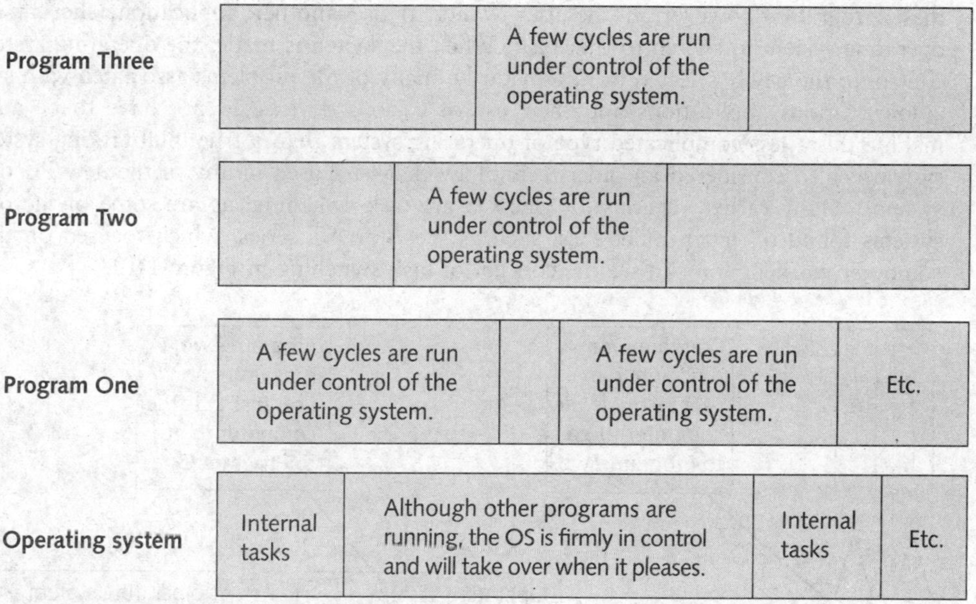


**Figure 1-10** Preemptive multitasking basics

Some older operating systems, such as MS-DOS, were single-tasking operating systems. A **single-tasking** operating system executes one program at a time (see Figure 1-11). To do something else, one program must be stopped and a new program must be loaded and executed. Because multiple programs are not trying to use the same resources, single-tasking operating systems are a lot simpler. These systems, however, are considered older technology, and as new operating systems are released, they are seldom single-tasking. New single-tasking operating systems are found only in computers with very limited processor capacity, such as older personal digital assistants (PDAs), which have long since been replaced by smartphones and tablets that sport their own multitasking OSs.

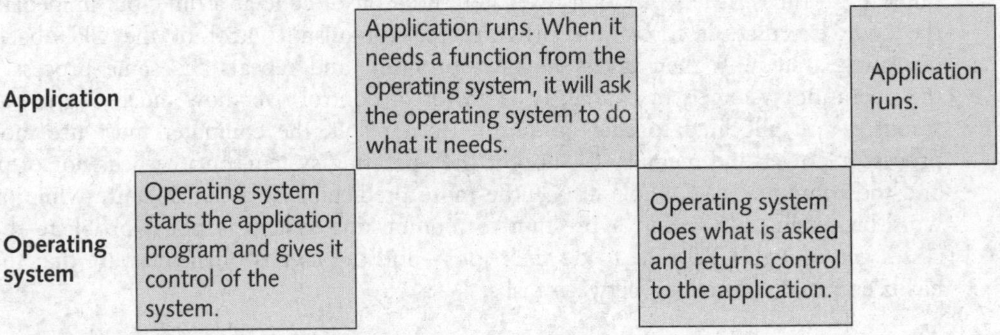


**Figure 1-11** Single-tasking operating system

A special note must be made of a hybrid system called a **task-switching** operating system. This system offers many of the device management functions of the multitasking operating system, and it can load multiple application programs at once. It will actively execute only one of these programs, however. If the user wants to use another application, she can ask the operating system to switch to that task. When the switch is made, the operating system gives control to the newly selected task. Obviously, many of the problems associated with switching among various applications and their use of various devices do not have to be addressed, making this a less complicated type of operating system than a true multitasking system. This system is also considered an older technology that isn't used in any of the new PC operating systems. Many earlier versions of Mac OS are task switching, as are some of the operating systems found on much older PCs, such as the Atari ST series, which focused on the home computer market. You can see the concept of task switching in Figure 1-12.

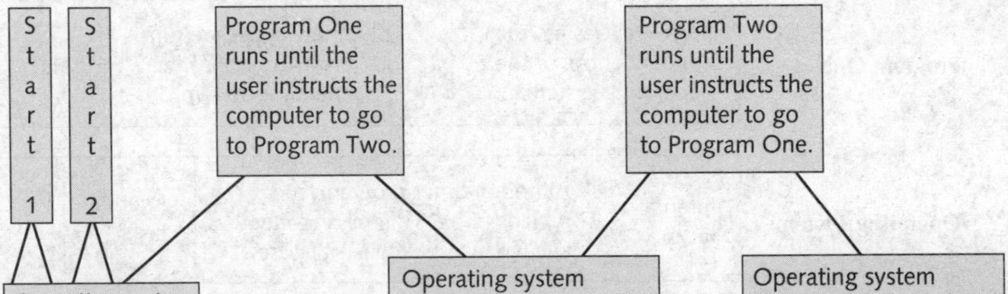


**Figure 1-12** Task switching

Multitasking should not be confused with **multithreading**. Multithreading is the ability of programs to be written so that they run several program code blocks, called *threads*, independently. For example, a database program might run a thread to pull data from the database and another thread to simultaneously sum figures to create a subtotal. You learn more about multithreading in Chapter 3.

## Single-User Versus Multiuser Operating Systems

Some operating systems, in addition to being able to run multiple programs at the same time with multitasking technology, allow multiple users to use an application simultaneously. These systems are known as *multiuser operating systems*. By definition, a multiuser system is almost a multitasking system. Most multiuser systems use preemptive, multitasking technology. The desktop operating systems covered in this book initially were designed as **single-user systems** (only one user at a time), with the exception of UNIX and Linux, which have always been multiuser operating systems by design. From the start, all Windows server systems, from Windows NT onward, were designed as full-featured multiuser systems. Mac OS X Server is also a full-featured multiuser system. The desktop versions of operating systems, such as Windows 10 and Mac OS X, are also multiuser systems, but they do not have the full multiuser capacity of the server systems. All of these desktop systems are intended to handle only 10 to 20 simultaneous users before they bog down under the load. A server system is designed to handle hundreds of users at once.

While modern OSs are multitasking as well as multiuser, Windows 98 was a good example of an operating system that was multitasking but not multiuser. Windows 98 could handily run a word-processing program while running a Web browser and an e-mail client for a single user, but it wasn't designed to run applications for multiple users simultaneously. Table 1-3 compares single-user and multiuser operating systems.

**Table 1-3 Comparing single-user and multiuser operating systems**

| Single-user operating system | Multiuser operating system |
|---|---|
| Handles only one user at a time | Handles multiple users at a time |
| Some older desktop operating systems are only single-user | All server operating systems are multiuser, and some desktop operating systems have limited multiuser capability |
| Some single-user operating systems do not use multitasking and some do | Always employs multitasking |
| Single-user systems that can use multitasking may use either cooperative or preemptive multitasking | Uses preemptive multitasking |

# Current Operating Systems

The operating systems surveyed in this book are the most common in today's computing environments, and they fall into several families:

- Windows 7, 8.1, and 10
- Windows Server 2008, 2012, and 2016
- The different distributions of UNIX/Linux operating systems, focusing particularly on Fedora, which is used as a leading-edge development environment for the popular Red Hat Enterprise Linux (new features in Red Hat Enterprise Linux come from Fedora)
- Apple Macintosh Mac OS X (version 10.11 El Capitan)

Windows 8 was not well-received and almost all systems that were initially configured with Windows 8 were upgraded to Windows 8.1 when it became available, so this book does not cover features particular to Windows 8.

In Chapter 2, you learn about these families in more detail. This section provides a brief summary.

At the time of this writing, three popular desktop operating systems were used most frequently in corporate America—Windows 7, 8.1, and 10. These three operating systems offer a stable work environment that is appealing for office use. Further, Microsoft continually issues updates for Windows systems that increase their security and performance. It is also possible to find some corporate users hanging on to older versions of Windows and even MS-DOS, but they have become rare. The most popular Microsoft server operating systems are Windows Server 2008/R2 and Windows Server 2012/R2. Support for Windows Server 2003 has ended and most companies have upgraded or are upgrading to a newer version of Windows Server. Windows Server 2016 will be released about the time this book publishes, and features and screenshots will be based on preview release 4.

The multiuser UNIX operating system has been popular among industrial-strength users for many years. It is especially appealing to members of the scientific and research communities for its power to perform complex tasks and maintain large databases. There are many flavors of UNIX, but the two main design standards are the Berkeley Software Distribution (BSD) standard and the System V Release 4 (SVR4) standard. This book focuses on SVR4 UNIX. Linux is a UNIX look-alike system that is popular as a server operating system in business, education, and government and is rapidly replacing UNIX. Linux operating system distributions are particularly popular for servers and are gaining ground on the desktop, in part because they take advantage of a huge open source software community. Open source software is typically developed by hundreds or thousands of volunteers, relies on peer review, contains code in the public domain, and is typically distributed for free.

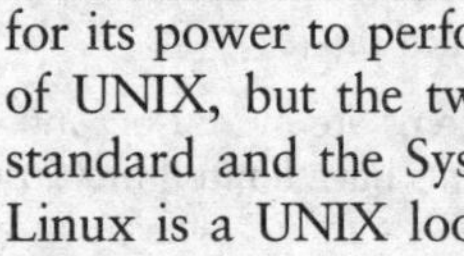


You can learn more about open source software at *www.opensource.org* and *sourceforge.net*.

The Mac OS X operating system for Apple Macintosh computers is popular in the educational and graphics sectors, particularly for video editing and desktop publishing. Its use in the corporate world is often for these applications, and it is also very popular among home users. Corporate users sometimes regard Mac OS X as difficult to set up for networking in a medium-sized to large organization with complex networks, although Apple has addressed many of these concerns. Mac OS X is popular with home users because the desktop is intuitive and home network setup is user friendly. Also, some home users are already familiar with Mac OS X from using it at school.

In Chapter 2, you will take a much closer look at the individual operating systems mentioned here. You will find out more about the hardware required to run each operating system, and which versions you will see in which environments. Try the Hands-On Projects at the end of Chapter 1 to learn more about the Windows-based, Linux, and Mac OS X operating systems, including how to use tools for obtaining system information, how to view device drivers, how to see multitasking in operation, and how to use desktop applications.

## Chapter Summary

- All computers perform three basic tasks: input, processing, and output. An operating system is a specialized computer program that provides a user interface, file system, processes and services, and a kernel.
- An operating system provides the foundation upon which to run the components of a computer and execute applications.
- A basic task of an operating system is to enable a computer to perform I/O functions so that it can use software applications and communicate with computer hardware.
- Two common types of operating systems are desktop (or client) and server operating systems.
- The history of operating systems and computers represents a progression from physically huge computers to large computers to desktop-sized computers that have powerful processing capabilities and operating systems.
- Device drivers can extend the native functions of an operating system to provide access and control over different types of devices, such as printers and DVD drives.
- The BIOS is low-level program code that operates between the computer hardware and a higher-level operating system to initiate communications with hardware devices, perform hardware tests at startup, and enable the startup of the higher-level operating system.
- An operating system may be geared to run a large mainframe computer or a small PC. However, small PC systems can now be very powerful; when combined, they can be used in many places instead of mainframe systems.
- Operating systems can be understood in terms of characteristics such as time sharing, real-time operation, and multiuser capabilities.

- From a user standpoint, one of the most significant advances in operating systems was the refinement of the GUI, as seen in the development of Windows-based and Mac OS systems.
- Early operating systems tended to be single tasking, but modern systems are largely multitasking.
- A true multiuser system is one in which multiple users access and run a single application on a single computer at the same time.
- Current popular operating systems include Windows 7, 8.1, and 10, Server 2008/R2, Server 2012/R2, Server 2016, UNIX/Linux, and Mac OS X El Capitan. Of the systems listed, the server operating systems are primarily discussed in the last three chapters of the book, along with some networking basics.

# Key Terms

**application programming interface (API)** Functions or programming features in an operating system that programmers can use for network links, links to messaging services, or interfaces to other systems.

**application software** A word processor, spreadsheet, database, computer game, or other type of application that a user runs on a computer. Application software consists of computer code that is formatted so the computer or its operating system can translate the code into a specific task, such as writing a document.

**basic input/output system (BIOS)** Low-level program code that conducts basic hardware and software communications inside the computer. A computer's BIOS basically resides between computer hardware and the higher-level operating system, such as UNIX or Windows.

**batch processing** A computing style frequently employed by large systems. A request for a series of processes is submitted to the computer; information is displayed or printed when the batch is complete. Batches might include the processing for all of the checks submitted to a bank for a day, or for all of the purchases in a wholesale inventory system, for example. Compare to *sequential processing*.

**Beginner's All-purpose Symbolic Instruction Code (BASIC)** An English-like computer programming language originally designed as a teaching tool, but which evolved into a useful and relatively powerful development language.

**blade enclosure** A large box with slots for blade servers; the box also provides cooling fans, electrical power, connection to a shared monitor and pointing device, and even network connectivity. The actual design depends on the manufacturer.

**blade server** A server unit that looks like a card that fits into a blade enclosure. Blade servers are intended to save space. See *blade enclosure*.

**client/server systems** A computer hardware and software design in which different portions of an application execute on different computers, or on different components of a single computer. Typically, client software supports user I/O and server software conducts database searches, manages printer output, and the like.

**cloud computing** A computing technology that provides a host of scalable Web-based applications and services over the Internet or a private network used by clients through Web browsers.

**command-line interface** An interface that enables the user to display a command line from which to enter commands. These interfaces include the Command Prompt window in Windows operating systems and the terminal window in Linux and Mac OS X.

**complementary metal oxide semiconductor (CMOS)** A type of memory that stores a computer's BIOS configuration. A CMOS chip uses a low-power memory technology that is powered by a small battery.

**computer program** A series of instructions executed by the computer's CPU.

**cooperative multitasking** A computer hardware and software design in which the operating system temporarily hands off control to an application and waits for the application to return control to the operating system. Compare to *preemptive multitasking*.

**desktop operating system** A computer operating system that is typically installed on a PC, usually used by one person at a time, and may or may not be connected to a network. Also called a *client operating system*.

**device driver** Computer software designed to provide the operating system and application software access to specific computer hardware.

**distribution** An issuance of UNIX or Linux that is based on a standard kernel, but that also has customizations added by a particular private or commercial development group.

**embedded system** A computer that has a dedicated function within a larger system, such as a piece of machinery.

**file system** The method by which an OS stores and organizes files and manages access to files on a storage device.

**graphical user interface (GUI)** An interface between the user and an operating system that presents information in an intuitive graphical format, including multiple colors, figures, icons, windows, toolbars, and other features. A GUI is usually deployed with a pointing device, such as a mouse, to make the user more productive.

**hardware** The physical devices in a computer, including the CPU, circuit boards (cards), disk drives, monitor, and modem.

**input/output (I/O)** Input is information taken in by a computer device to handle or process; an example is characters typed at a keyboard. Output is information sent out by a computer device after the information is handled or processed; an example is the display of typed characters on the monitor.

**kernel** An essential set of programs and computer code built into a computer operating system to control processor, disk, memory, and other functions central to a computer's basic operation. The kernel communicates with the BIOS, device drivers, and the API to perform these functions. It also interfaces with the resource managers.

**Microsoft Disk Operating System (MS-DOS)** The first widely distributed operating system for microcomputers, created by Tim Paterson and a team at Microsoft that included Bill Gates. This generic computer code was used to control many basic computer hardware and software functions. MS-DOS is sometimes referred to as DOS.

**multitasking** A technique that allows a computer to run two or more programs at the same time.

**multithreading** Running several program processes or parts (threads) at the same time.

**multiuser system** A computer hardware and software system designed to service multiple users who access the computer's hardware and software applications simultaneously.

**operating system (OS)** A specialized computer program that provides a user interface, file system, services, and a kernel to a computer. An OS runs on computer hardware and facilitates application execution.

**power-on self test (POST)** Tests, such as memory and hardware component tests, that are run by the BIOS when a computer starts and that must complete before the operating system is loaded. See *basic input/output system (BIOS)*.

**preemptive multitasking** A computer hardware and software design for multitasking of applications in which the operating system retains control of the computer at all times. See *cooperative multitasking* for comparison.

**process** A program that is loaded into memory and run by the CPU. It can be an application a user interacts with, such as a word-processing program or a Web browser, or a program with no user interface that communicates with other processes and provides services to them.

**rack-mounted server** CPU boxes mounted in racks that can hold multiple servers, each with its own power cord and network connection—and that often share one monitor and pointing device.

**read-only memory (ROM)** Memory that contains information that is not erased when the power is removed from the memory hardware.

**real-time operating system (RTOS)** An operating system that receives and processes inputs and produces the required outputs in a specified amount of time.

**resource managers** Programs that manage computer memory and CPU use.

**sequential processing** A computer processing style in which each operation is submitted, acted upon, and the results displayed before the next process is started. Compare to *batch processing*.

**server operating system** A computer operating system usually found on more powerful PC-based computers than those used for desktop operating systems. A server OS is connected to a network and can act in many roles to enable multiple users to access information via e-mail, files, software, and other means.

**service** A process that runs in the background because there is no user interface. See *process*.

**shell** An interface that enables users to interact with an operating system kernel. The shell enables the user to execute commands. See *kernel*.

**single-tasking** A computer hardware and software design that can manage only a single task at a time.

**single-user system** A computer hardware and software system that enables only one user to access its resources at a particular time.

**supercomputer** A computer that has extreme processing power and speed to handle complex computations that are beyond the reach of other computers.

**task switching** A hybrid between single-tasking and multitasking that permits the user or application software to switch among multiple single-tasking operations.

**time-sharing system** A central computer system, such as a mainframe, that is used by multiple users and applications simultaneously.

**user interface** A component of an operating system that provides a method for users to interact with the computer, usually with a keyboard and mouse or touch screen.

## Review Questions

1. Which of the following is a basic function all computers perform? (Choose all that apply.)
   a. processing
   b. Internet access
   c. graphics
   d. input
   e. e-mail
   f. output
2. Which of the following executes instructions provided by computer programs?
   a. NIC
   b. USB
   c. CPU
   d. drive
3. The large bank where you work uses an older mainframe to make a customer service database available for complex reports and queries about customer profiles. Which of the following occurs when 12 users run large reports on the mainframe at the same time?
   a. batching
   b. interfacing
   c. overload
   d. time sharing
4. Which of the following is a feature typically provided by an operating system? (Choose all that apply.)
   a. file system
   b. spreadsheet
   c. database app
   d. kernel

5. What is another name for a client operating system?
   a. real-time operating system
   b. multiuser operating system
   c. server operating system
   d. desktop operating system
6. While on a coffee break, your colleague asserts that cooperative multitasking is the best operating system design. What is your response? (Choose all that apply.)
   a. A disadvantage of cooperative multitasking is that it relies on each program to decide when to give control back to the operating system.
   b. Cooperative multitasking can be faster than other forms of multitasking because it increases the clock speed of the processor.
   c. Cooperative multitasking OSs can get stuck in an endless loop.
   d. Modern operating systems use preemptive multitasking so that the operating system is fully in control.
7. You are called into a small business in which 25 people are using one Windows 10 computer to share files. The business wants you to diagnose why file sharing is often slow or seems to grind to a halt. What is your assessment?
   a. Windows 10 is only meant for 20 or fewer simultaneous users. The company should upgrade to a server system.
   b. Windows 10 is working in batch mode and should be reset for multitasking mode.
   c. The company should switch to Windows 7.
   d. Windows 10 is experiencing task locks and task locking should be turned off.
8. Which type of server plugs into slots in an enclosure that contains a backplane?
   a. rack-mounted
   b. blade
   c. tower
   d. mainframe
9. What is the core code of an operating system called?
   a. kernel
   b. blade
   c. driver
   d. bus

10. You are using e-mail to send a message over the Internet. Which of the following types of software acts like a hook in the operating system to enable e-mail transmissions over the Internet?
    a. software compiler
    b. hook driver
    c. Internet translator
    d. application programming interface
11. Which of the following operating systems only comes in a 64-bit version and not a 32-bit version?
    a. Mac OS X Leopard
    b. Linux
    c. Windows Server 2016
    d. Windows 10
    e. No current operating system operates only on a 64-bit computer.
12. Which processor was used in the original IBM PC?
    a. Zilog Z80
    b. Motorola 68000
    c. AMD Opteron
    d. Intel 8088
13. Which of the following operating systems are multitasking systems? (Choose all that apply.)
    a. MS-DOS
    b. Windows 10
    c. Mac OS X
    d. Linux
14. To help manage access to the CPU, programs and processes are assigned which of the following by the operating system?
    a. a time-stamp
    b. 100 KB of RAM
    c. a program unit interval
    d. a priority

15. Today's class discussion is a comparison of high-end computers and lower-end computers. Which of the following factors help to differentiate these types of computers? (Choose all that apply.)
    a. number of CPUs
    b. size of the monitor
    c. size of the data pathways in the computer
    d. number of USB ports
16. Where is a computer's BIOS typically stored in modern computers?
    a. RAM
    b. flash memory
    c. ROM
    d. hard disk
17. Which of the following is performed by the BIOS? (Choose all that apply.)
    a. runs the power-on self test
    b. starts the operating system
    c. manages the file system
    d. allocates memory to applications
18. Operating systems that give programs direct access to manipulating hardware are more susceptible to which of the following problems? (Choose all that apply.)
    a. malicious software vulnerabilities
    b. runaway BIOS
    c. memory block conflicts that make hardware devices unstable
    d. CPU clocking problems
19. Which type of operating system is most likely to be part of an embedded system?
    a. task-switching
    b. cooperative multitasking
    c. real-time
    d. time sharing
20. What are two types of cloud computing models? (Choose two.)
    a. private cloud
    b. public cloud
    c. preemptive cloud
    d. cooperative cloud

# Hands-On Projects

Please read the "Before You Begin" section of this book's Introduction for details on the suggested lab configuration for all the projects.

At the end of each chapter in this book, Hands-On Projects give you direct experience in applying what you have learned about operating systems. As you are completing the Hands-On Projects, keep a lab book, notebook, or word processor handy so you can record your findings for later reference.

These projects use a variety of OSs, including a Windows client and a Windows server. For people who use a Windows client, note that the instructions apply to Windows 10. For projects that use a Windows server, instructions will apply to Windows Server 2012 R2. Projects that use Linux will use Fedora 23 with the default GNOME desktop, and those that use Mac OS X will use El Capitan. Other OS versions and releases can be used with small changes to the instructions. The Linux projects are tailored for the Fedora 23 distribution. If you choose to use a different Linux distribution, plan to use one with the GNOME desktop; the steps in the Hands-On Projects will still apply in most cases. All of the Linux commands you learn to use in the terminal window will work on any Linux distribution and desktop, and in many UNIX distributions as well. The Mac OS X projects primarily use the default Mac OS X desktop. Because Mac OS X is built on BSD UNIX (the Darwin distribution), some projects also use the terminal window in Mac OS X for practicing UNIX commands.

In some Windows projects, you may see the User Account Control (UAC) box, which is used for security to help thwart intruders. If you see this box, click Continue. Because computer setups may be different, the box is not mentioned in the actual project steps.

**Table 1-4 Which operating system is used in each project?**

| Operating system | Projects |
|---|---|
| Any | 1-1 |
| Windows 10 | 1-2 through 1-4 |
| Fedora Linux | 1-5 and 1-6 |
| Mac OS X El Capitan | 1-7 and 1-8 |

## Project 1-1: Explore the History of the Computer

The Internet can be a rich source of information about the history of computers. In this project, you use the Internet to review the history of computers, software, and the Internet. You will need a computer with any OS installed that has access to the Internet.

1. Start and log on to any computer with Internet access and a Web browser. Open a Web browser and go to *www.computerhistory.org/timeline*.
2. Determine the answers to the following:
   a. Which three PCs were released in 1977?
   b. What was the first non-kit PC developed in 1973?
   c. What important data storage medium was released in 1983?
   d. What does ASCII stand for, and in what year did it come out?
   e. What was the name of the first fully transistorized computer, which was developed in 1955?
   f. What input and output devices were used by the Manchester Mark I computer?
   g. In what year was the World Wide Web born via the development of Hypertext Markup Language (HTML), and who developed HTML?
3. Visit the Hobbes' Internet Timeline 10 (Hobbes' Internet Timeline Copyright © 1993–2016 by Robert H. Zakon) by accessing *www.zakon.org/robert/internet/timeline*. Determine the answers to the following:
   a. BITNET, one of the predecessors of the Internet, was launched in 1981. What does BITNET stand for?
   b. What worm struck the Internet in 2001?
   c. What food could you order through the Internet in 1994?
   d. What famous person sent an e-mail in 1976?
   e. What country offered Internet voting for local elections in 2005?
   f. In 2008, what kind of network did NASA test?
4. Close your browser.

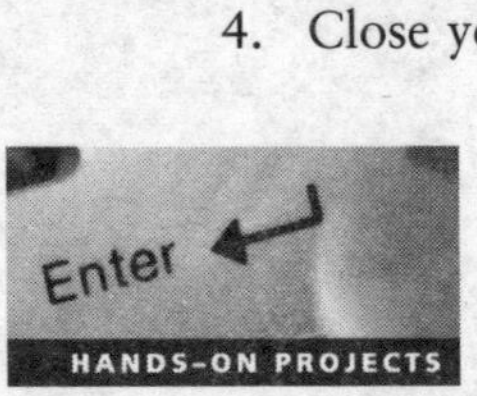


## Project 1-2: Explore the Windows 10 Interface

A good place to start learning about an operating system is to perform a preliminary exploration of its user interface and the tools available to work with and manage the system. In this project, you explore the Windows 10 interface and some of its tools.

1. Start your Windows 10 computer. If necessary, log on by pressing **Ctrl+Alt+Del.**
2. Enter your user name, password, and domain name (if required), and then press **Enter** or click the **Submit** button.
3. Notice the taskbar, which is at the bottom of the desktop on most systems.
4. Click **Start** to view the available applications you can run and tasks you can complete. Record some of the options.

5. On Windows 8.1 and Windows 10, you can right-click the **Start** button to see a list of administrative tasks that are particularly important to an IT administrator or computer technician (see Figure 1-13). Right-click **Start** and browse through the available tools. (Note: The same menu is also available in Windows Server 2012 R2 and later.)

**Figure 1-13** Right-clicking the Start menu in Windows 8.1 and Windows 10

6. Right-click the **Start** button, and then click **Command Prompt**. Notice the option for Command Prompt (Admin), which runs the command prompt with the administrative privileges required for some commands.

7. Type **help** and press **Enter** to see a list of commands you can run from the command prompt. Type **exit** and press **Enter** to close the command prompt.

8. Right-click **Start**, and click **System** (see Figure 1-14). This window displays information about the installed OS and the computer. From here you can change the computer name and join a workgroup or domain. This window also tells you whether Windows is activated. Close the System window by clicking the **X** in the upper-right corner.

**Figure 1-14** The Windows System window

9. Right-click **Start** and click **Computer Management**. In the tree (see the left pane) under Computer Management and System Tools, click **Device Manager**.

10. What types of devices that you can use with the computer are displayed in the right pane? Record some of your observations.

11. Double-click **Processors**. What type of processor or processors are installed in the computer? Double-click **Network adapters**. How many network adapters are installed? What kind are they?

12. Close the Computer Management window.

13. Stay logged on if you're going on to the next project.

## Project 1-3: View Devices and Device Drivers in Windows 10

Devices connected to a computer, such as the keyboard, are linked into the operating system through device drivers. In this project, you view the keyboard device drivers installed in Windows 10.

1. Start your Windows 10 computer and log on, if necessary.

2. Right-click **Start**, and then click **Device Manager**.

3. Double-click **Keyboards**.

4. Double-click the keyboard description under Keyboards to open the keyboard Properties dialog box.

5. Click the **Driver** tab. Who is the provider of the keyboard device driver, and is the device driver digitally signed (for security)? Record your observations.
6. Click the **Driver Details** button to see the names of the driver files (see Figure 1-15).

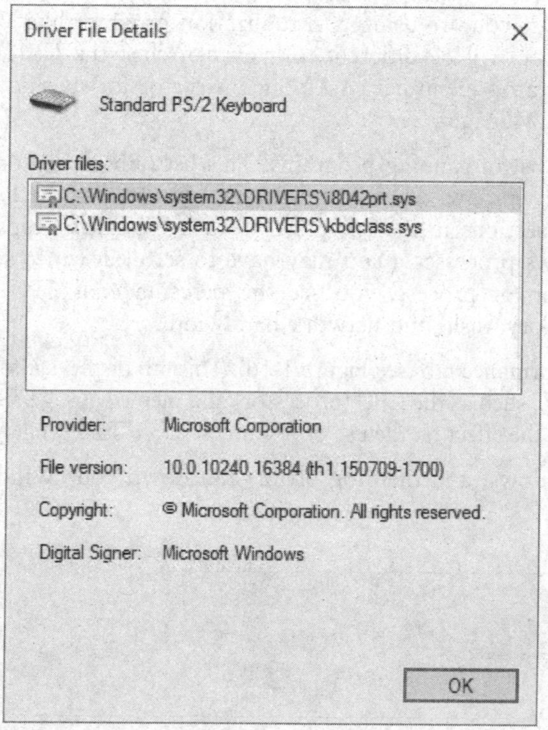


**Figure 1-15** Driver details in Windows 10

7. Click **OK**, click **Cancel**, and then close the Device Manager window.
8. Stay logged on if you're going on to the next project.

## Project 1-4: Examine Multitasking in Windows 10

Multitasking enables the user of a desktop operating system to perform many activities at once, such as running a word processor, using a spreadsheet, and running a Web browser. In this project, you take advantage of multitasking using Windows 10.

1. Start your Windows 10 computer and log on, if necessary.
2. Click in the **Search the web and Windows** text box next to the **Start** button, type **notepad,** and press **Enter** to start the Notepad program. (If Cortana is enabled, you will see "Ask me anything" in the text box instead of "Search the web and Windows.")
3. Click in the **Search the web and Windows** text box, type **calculator,** and press **Enter** to start the Calculator program.

4. Click in the **Search the web and Windows** text box, type **paint,** and press **Enter** to start the Paint program. You now have three programs running.
5. Notice that an icon appears for each application in the taskbar. Windows is now multitasking. Click the **Calculator** icon in the taskbar to bring its window to the front of the others.
6. Press **Ctrl+Alt+Del.** (Note that if you are using a virtualization program like VMware for these projects, this keystroke will be different, or you can click the Ctrl+Alt+Del icon on the virtualization program's menu bar. Ask your instructor for specific instructions, if necessary.) Click **Task Manager.**
7. In Task Manager, you see the list of running programs. This list only shows programs you started that have an open window. Click **More details.** Ensure that the **Processes** tab is selected. You see three sections in the left pane of Task Manager: Apps, Background processes, and Windows processes. (You may have to scroll down to see Windows processes.) For each app or process, you see the percentage of CPU each is using, and the amount of memory, disk, and network bandwidth.
8. In Task Manager, click the **Performance** tab (see Figure 1-16). This tab displays information about the system resources in use, such as the CPU (processor) and memory usage. Close one or two applications and observe the effect on the use of resources. Close Task Manager.
9. Close the remaining open windows, and then log off or shut down your Windows 10 computer.

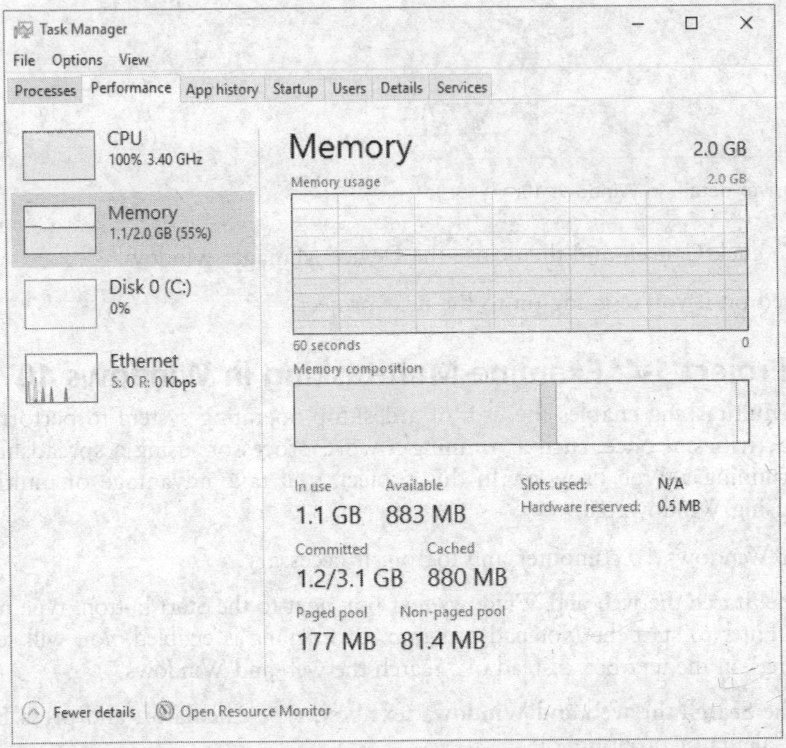


**Figure 1-16** Windows Task Manager: Performance tab

## Project 1-5: Explore the Fedora Linux Interface

In this project, you briefly explore the Fedora 23 desktop and view some of the common tools available in Fedora 23. While you can use other versions of Linux, Fedora 23 is suggested for these projects because they are written with that distribution in mind. Note that Fedora 23 comes with the GNOME desktop by default.

1. Start your Linux computer and log on.
2. Notice the bar at the top of the desktop. This is the top panel, which contains the Activities menu, a digital clock, and a place to access settings for the network, control the sound volume, and log on and off from the system. Click **Activities** to access common tasks.
3. In the Activities Overview window (see Figure 1-17), you have access to common applications such as a Web browser, e-mail client, image browser, and file browser. Click the **Show Applications** icon (it looks like a square grid of white dots) at the bottom of the screen to see more tasks and apps.

**Figure 1-17** Fedora 23 with the GNOME desktop and Activities Overview window

*Source: Fedora 23 (Linux)*

4. Click **Settings** to see a list of settings tools. Click **Details** near the bottom of the All Settings window (see Figure 1-18). The Overview window displays basic information about the system hardware as well as the GNOME version. Close the Details window.

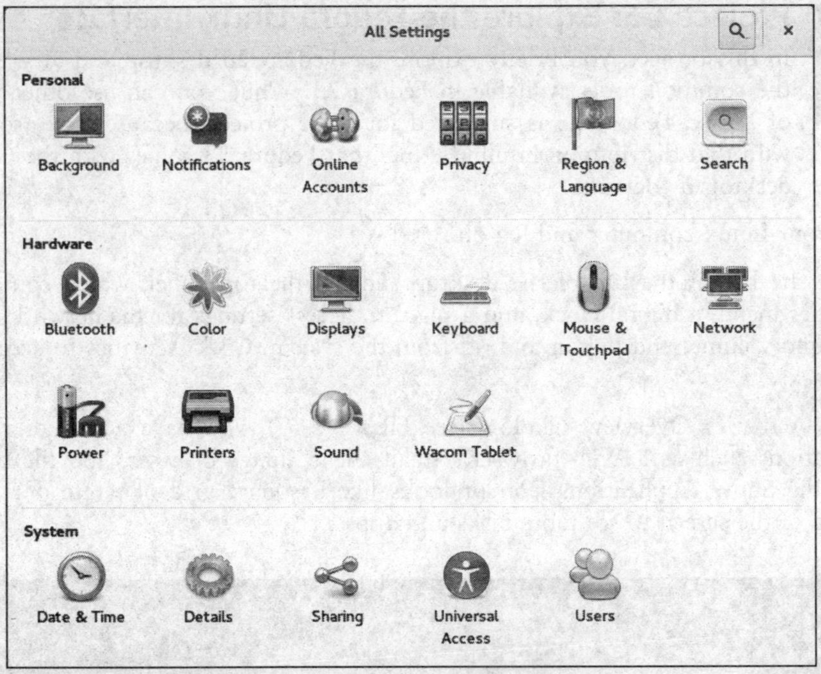


**Figure 1-18** The All Settings window in Linux

*Source: Fedora 23 (Linux)*

5. Click **Activities** and click the **Show Applications** icon. Click **Utilities** to see a list of utilities that come with Fedora, including a calculator, disk management utilities, and system monitoring.

6. Click **Terminal** to open the terminal application, which provides a command-line interface to Linux, much like the command prompt in Windows. In the terminal window, type **uname –a** to see detailed version information for the Linux OS and the kernel.

7. Type **man ls** and press **Enter**. The resulting display provides documentation about the *ls* command that is used to list files. (The *man* command is used to access the Linux online help.)

8. Press the **Spacebar** to page through the manual information for the *ls* command. Keep pressing the Spacebar until you reach the end of the documentation. Press **q** to exit the manual documentation.

9. Type **ls -la** and press **Enter** to view information about files.

10. Click the **X** in the upper-right corner of the terminal window to close it and return to the desktop.

11. On the far right side of the top panel, click the **power** icon. A small panel opens. Here you can adjust the sound volume, manage network connections, view information about the current user, log off the system, and shut down or lock the system, among other things. On the lower-right side of the open panel, click the **power** icon. You are informed that the system will power off in 60 seconds. Click **Cancel** if you are continuing to the next project.

## Project 1-6: View Device Drivers in Linux

In this project, you list the contents of a particular driver file in Fedora Linux, but the same procedures apply to many versions of UNIX/Linux. In this example, the *sda* file contains driver information pertaining to hard drives.

1. Start your Fedora Linux system and log on, if necessary. In the panel at the top of the desktop, click **Activities**, click **Show Applications**, click **Utilities**, and then click **Terminal**. (Remember these steps to open a Linux terminal window, as you will be doing so frequently throughout the book. Later instructions simply tell you to open a terminal window.)
2. Type **ls -l /dev** and press **Enter** to display the contents of the /dev directory, which contains the Linux device drivers.
3. To see information about the hard disk driver, type **ls –l /dev/sda** and press **Enter**. Notice in the output the word *disk*, which indicates the driver is for a disk device. Device drivers will be discussed in more detail in Chapter 6, "Configuring Input and Output Devices."
4. Type **exit** and press **Enter** to close the terminal window, or close the window by clicking the **X** in the upper-right corner.

## Project 1-7: Explore the Mac OS Interface

This project enables you to briefly explore the Mac OS X El Capitan desktop. Depending on the setup of your Mac OS X system, you may or may not need an account and password to access the operating system.

1. Boot the Mac OS X system. If you need to provide logon information, enter your name and password and press **Enter** or **Return**. (If you are using a Mac keyboard, the key is labeled *Return*. On PCs, the key is labeled *Enter*. Throughout this book, the term *Enter* will be used, but just substitute *Return* if you are using a Mac keyboard.)
2. Notice the menu options in the menu bar at the top of the screen and record them (see Figure 1-19).
3. Next, observe the bar that appears at the bottom of the screen (by default on most systems). This is called the *Dock*.
4. Point to each icon in the Dock to see what it does and record some of the icon names. (Note that the contents of the Dock can be customized, so different systems may have different icons.)
5. Click the **Go** menu at the top of the desktop. From here, you can explore files, view the network, access the iCloud drive, and open applications and utilities.
6. Click an open area of the desktop to close the Go menu.
7. Click the **Apple** icon at the far left side of the menu bar. Click **About This Mac** to see information about the system. Explore each of the six tabs in the About This Mac

window (see Figure 1-19). Close the About This Mac window by clicking the red **X** at the top of the window.

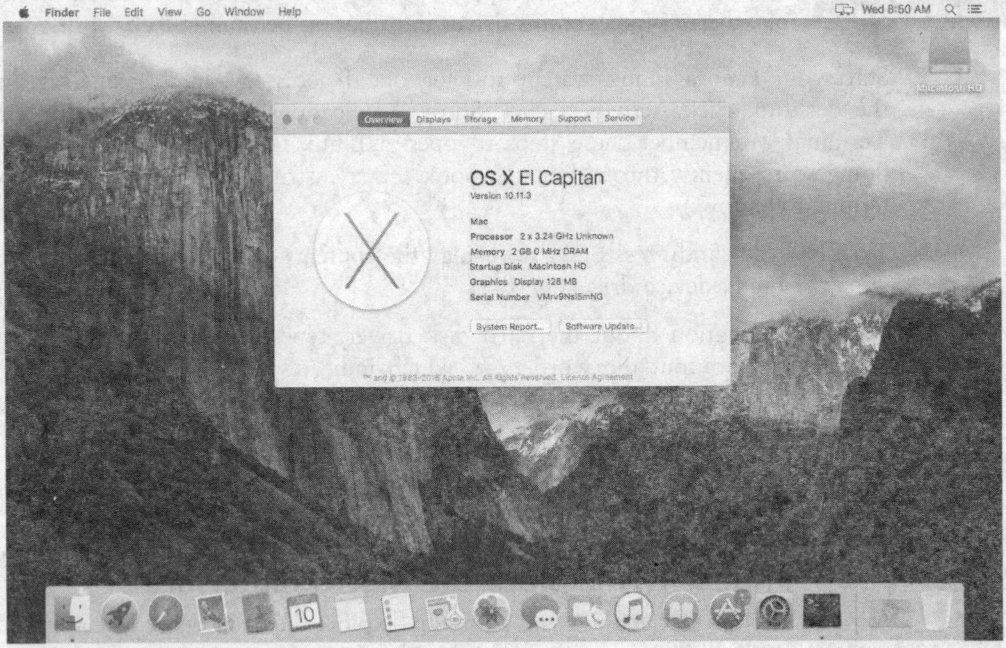


**Figure 1-19** Mac OS X El Capitan desktop and About This Mac window

*Source: Mac OS X El Capitan*

8. Click **Help** on the menu bar at the top of the desktop. Click **Mac Help.**
9. Type **Using USB devices** in the Spotlight search box, which includes a magnifying glass icon. Press **Enter** and notice the range of topics from which to choose.
10. Close the Mac Help window by clicking the **red button** on the upper-left side of the window. An X appears in the button when you point to it.
11. Click **Go** in the menu bar at the top of the screen. Click **Utilities.**
12. Double-click **Terminal.** Use the scroll bar, if necessary, to find the Terminal icon.
13. Type **man ls** and press **Enter** to view documentation about the *ls* command.
14. Press the **Spacebar** to page through the documentation.
15. Press **q** to exit the documentation and return to the command prompt in the terminal window.
16. Type **ls -la** and press **Enter** to see a listing of files similar to those you saw with Fedora.
17. Click the **Terminal** menu at the top of the desktop and click **Quit Terminal.**
18. Close the Utilities window. Stay logged on to your Mac OS X computer if you are continuing to the next project.

## Project 1-8: Examine Multitasking in Mac OS X

Mac OS X is another example of a multitasking operating system in which you can run several applications at the same time. This project enables you to start three applications in Mac OS X to demonstrate multitasking.

1. Start your Mac OS X computer and log on, if necessary. Double-click **Macintosh HD** on the desktop.
2. Double-click the **Applications** folder.
3. Double-click **TextEdit**. Notice that TextEdit is added to the Dock when you start the program.
4. Click the **Applications** window to bring it to the front, and then double-click **Calculator**. Calculator is added to the Dock.
5. Click the **Applications** window and double-click **Safari**. Note that you can also start Safari from its icon in the Dock.
6. Click the **Applications** window to activate it. Note that Go is displayed as an option in the menu bar at the top of the screen. Next, click **Go** in the menu bar and click **Utilities**.
7. Double-click **Activity Monitor** in the Utilities window.
8. Make sure that **CPU** is selected at the top of the Activity Monitor window. Click the **% CPU** column heading to sort programs by activity. Notice the changes (or lack of them) in CPU activity as you close windows in the following steps. (If necessary, move or maximize the Activity Monitor window so it is not obscured by other windows as they are clicked.)
9. Click the **Utilities** window and close it.
10. Click the **Calculator** on the desktop or its icon in the Dock to bring it to the front. Click **Calculator** in the menu bar at the top of the desktop and click **Quit Calculator**. You can also click the red **X** on the upper-left side of the application's window.
11. Close TextEdit and Safari. Note any changes in Activity Monitor.
12. Close Activity Monitor.
13. Notice that the icons from the applications you just closed are removed from the Dock (except Safari, which is always on the Dock).
14. Shut down or log off your Mac OS X computer.

# Critical Thinking

The following activities give you critical thinking challenges. Challenge Labs give you an opportunity to use the skills you have learned to perform a task without step-by-step instructions. Case Projects present a practical problem for which you supply a written solution. Not all chapters contain Challenge Labs. There is not always a specific right or wrong answer to these critical thinking exercises. They are intended to encourage you to review the chapter material and delve deeper into the topics you have learned.

## Case Projects

### Case Project 1-1: Basic Operating System Functions

The Lawson City and County Planning Department has recently received a new budget allocation to purchase new desktop and server systems. Because the budget has been strapped for many years, the department hasn't been able to upgrade its systems. Most of the desktop computers are running Windows XP or Windows 7. The server systems are Windows Server 2003 and Windows Server 2008. The department has network and Internet connectivity through a combination of older wired and wireless technologies.

Before they begin making decisions, the planning office managers ask you to make a presentation to cover the basics of operating systems. They ask you to begin the presentation by explaining basic functions that operating systems perform. Create a presentation and give it to the class or your instructor. Consider using diagrams or slides.

### Case Project 1-2: Device Drivers

This is a follow-on case project to Case Project 1-1.

One of the managers has heard that current device drivers are important to consider when choosing an operating system. Improve your presentation by including an explanation of device drivers and why they are important.

### Case Project 1-3: Choose a New Server

This is a follow-on case project to Case Project 1-1.

High on the list of needs is implementing a new server. A small committee of planning department employees has been formed to look at options for a server operating system. What options should they consider, which do you recommend, and why do you recommend them? Write a short memo for your instructor.

### Case Project 1-4: Choose New Desktop Systems

This is a follow-on case project to Case Project 1-1.

What desktop operating systems might be used to replace the Windows XP and Windows 7 computers? What operating system capabilities should the planning department look for when replacing these computers? Also, how might system costs affect the decision? Write a short memo for your instructor.

## Case Project 1-5: A Problem with a Newly Released Operating System

While the planning department is researching computer options, a computer support person comes across an article in a computer magazine about a newly released operating system that is experiencing frequent memory and CPU problems, such as slow or no response when accessing disk drives or displaying characters on the monitor. What might be the cause of these problems? Write a short memo for your instructor.

chapter 2

# Popular Operating Systems

**After reading this chapter and completing the exercises, you will be able to:**

- Describe early Microsoft operating systems and their characteristics
- Identify the features of modern Microsoft operating systems
- Identify the features and characteristics of UNIX and UNIX-like operating systems
- Identify the features and characteristics of Mac OS and Mac OS X

**This chapter examines the features of the most popular operating systems as well** as their general characteristics, strengths, and weaknesses. Chapter 1 provided a brief historical survey of operating systems. This chapter takes a closer look at early Microsoft operating systems that laid the groundwork for current desktop and server operating systems. You will then focus on these more recent operating systems, which include Windows 7 and later versions, Windows Server 2012 and later versions, as well as UNIX/Linux and Mac OS X El Capitan. This overview will provide the background you need to choose the operating system that is best suited for a particular work or home environment, and to determine which operating system to use when new computers are installed or existing computers are upgraded. Likewise, you will be able to identify situations in which the wrong operating system is used.

System hardware requirements for the current operating systems discussed in this book are listed in Chapter 5.

# Early Microsoft Operating Systems

Earlier operating systems were very primitive compared to those available today. They laid the groundwork for the look and feel, features, and characteristics of current operating systems. This section describes some early Microsoft operating systems and shows the progression from these systems to more modern ones.

## MS-DOS and PC DOS

Microsoft's original operating system for the IBM PC hardware platform was called MS-DOS, or more simply, DOS. The version of MS-DOS that ran on early IBM computers was called PC DOS because it was customized and marketed by IBM. Most programs operating under DOS used a simple text-based, command-line user interface similar to what you see when you open a command prompt on a modern Windows computer. Both versions could only access up to 640 KB of memory.

## Windows 3.x

Microsoft released the first version of Windows in 1984, implementing a graphical user interface (GUI) to compete with the Apple Macintosh. This early version of Windows was quite slow and not well accepted. Windows 3.1 in the early 1990s was the first popular, usable Microsoft GUI, and it paved the way for Windows to become the dominant PC operating system (see Figure 2-1).

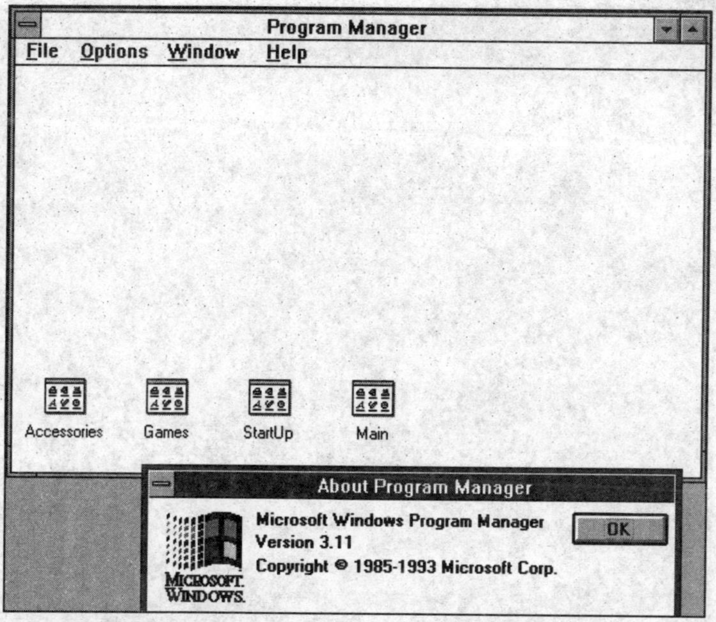


**Figure 2-1** The Windows 3.x GUI

## Windows 95

As the PC platform became more powerful and the Pentium architecture became more common, Microsoft created a true 32-bit operating system that could use the functionality of the new 32-bit computer architecture. Windows 95 eliminated the 640 KB memory limit and the 16-bit code. By being able to use more computer resources, Windows 95 could introduce several advanced functions that have now become standard Windows features:

- The Windows desktop
- Plug and Play
- ActiveX and the Component Object Model (COM)
- The registry
- Multitasking
- Enhanced network and Internet capabilities

**The Windows Desktop** Windows 95 introduced a new GUI, now called the *desktop* (see Figure 2-2), which became the foundation for the GUI used in all later versions of Windows. The Windows 95 GUI introduced the Start button that provides direct access to system utilities and application programs. Other desktop features included the taskbar at the bottom of the screen, which contains icons that represent currently running programs and other information about the system's operation, and shortcut and program icons to seamlessly run programs, manipulate files, and access network connections from one place.

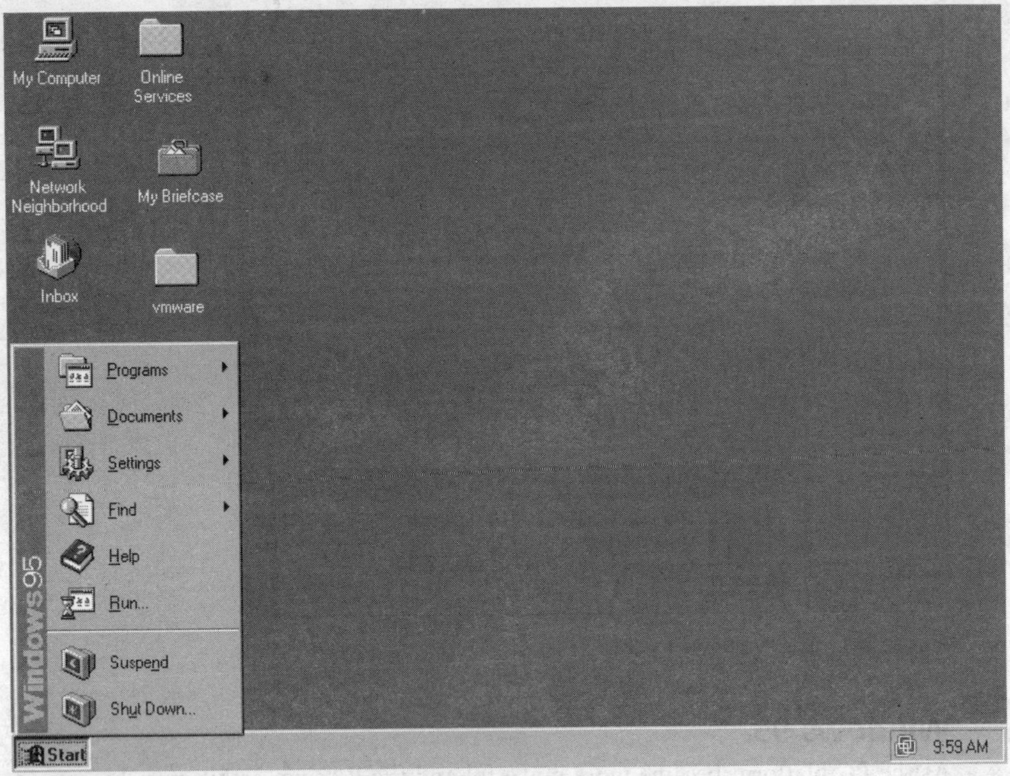


**Figure 2-2** The Windows 95 desktop shortcuts, Start button, and taskbar

**Plug and Play** Plug and Play (PnP) was possibly the most exciting hardware feature introduced in Windows 95 and continued in later versions of Windows (except Windows NT). PnP enables the operating system to automatically detect newly installed hardware. Before PnP, devices had to be configured using hardware in the form of little switches or jumpers on the expansion card or motherboard. This manual configuration was fraught with difficulties due to resource conflicts and the risk of incorrect switch or jumper settings. PnP put the configuration of devices in the hands of software, which is not a perfect solution, but it is considerably better than manual configuration.

**ActiveX and the Component Object Model (COM)** Much of the easy manipulation of the user interface in Windows 95 was made possible by a Microsoft technology called ActiveX. **ActiveX**, along with its parent, the **Component Object Model** (COM), is a standardized way for objects to communicate with each other. These objects include programs, files, computers, printers, control panels, windows, and icons.

**The Registry** Windows 95 also introduced a new way of storing and managing operating system information. Up to this point, such information was kept in files in various locations on the hard disk. The new concept was called the **registry**, a database that stores operating system information, information about hardware and software configuration, and general information that is shared by parts of the operating system or application programs to make COM and ActiveX work. You explore the registry in Hands-On Project 2-2.

The registry is a hierarchical database that provides the following information:

- Operating system configuration
- Service and device driver information and configuration
- Software and application parameters
- Hardware configuration
- Performance information
- Desktop configuration

**Multitasking** Multitasking in Windows 95 was cooperative for 16-bit applications, but preemptive for 32-bit applications. Windows 95 introduced a **task supervisor**, which detects tasks that appear stuck, and presents the option to close hung tasks without having to restart the operating system. A hung task occurs when an application no longer responds to keyboard or mouse input. In earlier versions of Windows, and sometimes even with Windows 95 and later, a hung task could hang the entire OS, requiring a restart and reboot of the computer. Starting with Windows 95 and preemptive multitasking, a hung task did not hang the entire system and only the problematic task had to be restarted.

**Enhanced Network and Internet Capabilities** The networking functionality in Windows 95 was substantially extended from earlier versions of Windows. Unlike earlier versions of Windows, in Windows 95 the network drivers were part of the Windows operating system. In all but the early versions of Windows 95, all the networking code was written as a 32-bit application. This resulted in a significant boost in network performance. When Windows 95 was released, Microsoft did not support Internet connectivity, but by 1997, Microsoft integrated Internet access through its Web browser, Internet Explorer, and the ability to share computer resources over the Internet into its operating systems.

## Windows 98/Me

Windows 98 and its slightly newer sibling, Windows Millennium Edition (Me), were similar to Windows 95 in many ways. They ran on similar computers and provided roughly the same capabilities. Windows Me included all Windows 98 features but expanded multimedia and networking capabilities.

**Windows 98** The Windows 98 user interface differed slightly from Windows 95, with little changing of the desktop's appearance except for the ability of Windows 98 to view items on the desktop as a Web page, a feature called Active Desktop.

Some of the additional changes from Windows 95 to Windows 98 included:

- Expanded PnP support
- Automatic registry checks and repairs
- Advanced power management features

- Support for new hardware standards such as Universal Serial Bus (USB)
- Improved cooperative multitasking for 16-bit applications
- Greater integration of Internet and networking features
- Extended multimedia support
- Expanded support for high-speed networking
- Ability to perform upgrades over the Internet

Windows 98 also supported newer hardware standards, such as **Universal Serial Bus (USB)** 1.0, a relatively high-speed (at the time) input/output (I/O) port, and updated standards for multimedia, data storage, and networking.

USB is a bus standard that enables you to attach all types of devices—keyboards, cameras, pointing devices, telephones, tape drives, and flash memory, for example—to one bus port on a computer. Up to 127 devices can be attached to one port, and it is not necessary to power off the computer when you attach a device. USB was developed to replace the traditional serial and parallel bus technologies on computers.

**Windows Millennium Edition (Me)** Windows Millennium Edition (Me) was developed for home computer users, not office or professional users, and it implemented applications that appealed to home users more than Windows 95 or 98. These applications included playing music, storing family photos, playing games, and accessing the Internet. Windows Me offered better support for infrared devices, such as **Infrared Data Association (IrDA)** support, and implemented the enhanced PnP standard, called **Universal Plug and Play (UPnP)**. UPnP is a set of protocols that allows network devices to be automatically discovered and configured by network client computers. While Windows Me brought a number of enhancements to the Windows OS, its hardware support and reliability problems hampered its success in the marketplace. Customers opted to stay with Windows 98 until Windows XP came out in late 2001.

## Windows NT

While Microsoft was developing the Windows line of operating systems to run on the lower end of IBM PC hardware, it also developed a high-end operating system intended for powerful workstations and servers. This OS was called Windows New Technology, or Windows NT. Over the course of its development, Windows NT supported the IBM PC architecture, the Alpha architecture, and for a while, the PowerPC architecture, as each of these hardware platforms gained its time in the industry spotlight. The idea was to make an operating system that could be used on some very powerful computers. One very significant difference between Windows 95/98 (often referred to as Windows 9x) and Windows NT was that the operating system kernel in Windows NT ran in **privileged mode,** which protected it from problems created by a malfunctioning program or process. Privileged mode gives the operating system an extra level of security from intruders, and prevents system crashes due to out-of-control applications.

Windows NT 4.0 was the first widely successful version of Windows NT. It was released at about the same time as Windows 95 and sported the new Windows 95 look.

Windows NT was offered in two versions: Windows NT Workstation and Windows NT Server. Windows NT Workstation was the operating system for users who needed a high-end, stable, and secure graphical operating system. Windows NT Server was designed as a multiuser server operating system for access over a network. For all the changes inside the operating system, however, Windows NT looked remarkably like Windows 9x on the outside. Users could easily move from the Windows desktop OS (Windows 9x) to Windows NT because of the familiar user interface.

**Networking Support** Windows NT supported network connectivity protocols that were compatible with IBM mainframes, UNIX computers, Macintosh computers, Novell NetWare servers, all Windows-based computers, and others. It also supported high-speed networking connectivity and remote access over telephone lines or the Internet.

**Security** Security was a significant feature of Windows NT. The operating system required the user to log on and be authenticated by submitting a username and password to gain access to the computer. Windows NT 4.0 Server had a C2 top-secret security rating from the United States government. The C2 rating means that the Windows NT Server network operating system provided security at many levels, including the following:

- File and folder protection
- User accounts and passwords
- File, folder, and account auditing
- File server access protection on a network
- File server management controls

The **domain** was an integral part of the Windows NT security model. In every Windows NT domain, there was one Primary Domain Controller (PDC). The PDC computer was responsible for keeping all usernames and passwords for all users who wanted to contact the domain. Any other server that was part of the domain could request password and permission information from the PDC. This allowed a user to sign on to the domain once and gain access to any server that was a member of the domain, a feature called *single sign-on*. In addition to user and password information, the PDC could also contain system policies, which provided general information on what users were allowed to do on certain computers on the network, down to what function and features of the user interface should be enabled.

## Windows 2000

Built on the Windows NT technology, Microsoft Windows 2000 was a more robust operating system. The operating system represented a significant rewrite of the Windows NT kernel, and ran about 30 percent faster than Windows NT. Also, like its Windows NT predecessor, Windows 2000 used preemptive multitasking and multithreading, and the kernel ran in privileged mode.

Windows 2000 had more advanced networking support than Windows NT and supported new networking technologies, such as **virtual private networks (VPNs)**. A VPN is a private network that is like an encrypted tunnel through a larger network—such as the Internet, an enterprise network, or both—and is restricted only to designated member **clients**. With a VPN, you can securely access network resources on a private home or company network from anywhere you have Internet access.

People who have experience troubleshooting problems with mismatched drivers, or who have overwritten portions of the operating system in previous versions of Windows, appreciated the built-in protection of the core operating system files and driver-signing features of Windows 2000. Windows 2000 kept a copy of operating system files in a safe place, so if a critical file was overwritten or deleted, the operating system automatically replaced it. **Driver signing** means that you can set up all drivers so they cannot be inadvertently overwritten by earlier driver versions, and only certified versions of drivers can be installed.

New features in Windows 2000 included:

- *Active Directory*—**Active Directory** is a database used to store information about resources such as user accounts, computers, and printers; it groups resources at different levels (hierarchies) for local and universal management. These groupings are called *containers* because they are like storage bins that can hold network resources and other bins at lower levels. Active Directory also provides a centralized means to quickly find a specific resource through indexing. Active Directory was only available on the server version of Windows 2000.
- *Distributed network architecture*—Windows 2000 offered new ways to distribute network and management resources to match the needs of most types of networks. In Windows 2000 Server, multiple servers could be designated as domain controllers, each containing a copy of Active Directory and able to verify a user who wanted to log on to the network. This was an important change from Windows NT Server 4.0, in which one server, the PDC, maintained the master copy of account and security information; and one or more servers, called *backup domain controllers (BDC)*, kept copies of this information as a backup. On Windows 2000 Server, each computer that had Active Directory installed was referred to as a Domain Controller (DC).
- *Kerberos security*—**Kerberos** is a security system and authentication protocol that authenticates users and grants or denies access to network resources based on a user's log-on name and password. The primary goal of Kerberos is to prevent unauthorized users from accessing computer and network resources. Kerberos works through a special communications protocol that enables a client to initiate contact with a server and request secure communication. The server responds by providing an encryption key that is unique to that communication session, and it does so by using a protected communication called a *ticket*. Windows 2000 Server and Professional and all successive versions of Windows support Kerberos.
- *IntelliMirror*—IntelliMirror was a concept built into Windows 2000. It was intended to enable Windows 2000 clients to access the same desktop settings, applications, and data from wherever they accessed the network, even if they were not on the network. IntelliMirror also used information in Active Directory to ensure that consistent

security and group policies applied to the client, and that the client's software was upgraded or removed on the basis of a central management scheme.

- *International language compatibility*—Windows 2000 supported more languages and language capabilities than previous versions of Windows, and included Hindi, Chinese, and multiple versions of English. This feature was important because servers are used all over the world.

## Windows 2000 Server and Windows 2000 Professional

Microsoft offered versions of Windows 2000 designed for server and workstation implementations. The basic server version was called Windows 2000 Server, and Windows 2000 Professional was designed for workstations. When it introduced Windows 2000, Microsoft's overall goal was to combine Windows 2000 Server and Windows 2000 Professional on a server-based network to achieve a lower **total cost of ownership** (TCO). The TCO is the total cost of owning a network, including hardware, software, training, maintenance, and user support costs. Windows 2000 Professional was intended as a reliable, easy-to-configure, workstation operating system to be used in a business or professional environment. Recognizing that professionals are highly mobile, Windows 2000 Professional was designed to work equally well on a desktop computer or a notebook computer. Windows 2000 Server was intended to play a key management role on the network by administering Active Directory and a multitude of network services. By combining Windows 2000 Professional workstations and Windows 2000 Server on the same network, along with Active Directory, it was possible to centralize software updates and workstation configuration via a server.

Windows 2000 Server supported up to four processors, while Windows 2000 Professional supported up to two. Windows 2000 Server also offered more services and user connectivity options that are appropriate for a server instead of a workstation. These services included the following:

- The capability to handle virtually unlimited numbers of users simultaneously (depending on the hardware platform; Windows 2000 Professional is designed for up to 10 simultaneous users only)
- Active Directory management
- Network management
- Web-based management services
- Network-wide security management
- Network storage management
- Remote network access, network-wide communications services, and high speed network connectivity
- Application services management
- Network printer management through Active Directory

## Windows 2000 Server, Advanced Server, and Datacenter Server

Windows 2000 Server was divided into three different products to match the network application: Windows 2000 Server, Windows 2000 Advanced Server, and Windows 2000

Datacenter Server. Windows 2000 Server provided a comprehensive set of server and Web services for up to four processor systems, and supported up to 4 GB of RAM. Windows 2000 Advanced Server was intended for high-end enterprise networks that require up to eight processor servers, clustered servers, or both. **Clustering** is a technique in which two or more servers are linked to equally share the server processor load, server storage, and other server resources (see Figure 2-3). Windows 2000 Advanced Server also had the ability to handle up to 8 GB of RAM. Windows 2000 Datacenter Server was targeted for large database and data manipulation services. The Datacenter version supported 64 GB of RAM, clustering, and individual servers with up to 32 processors.

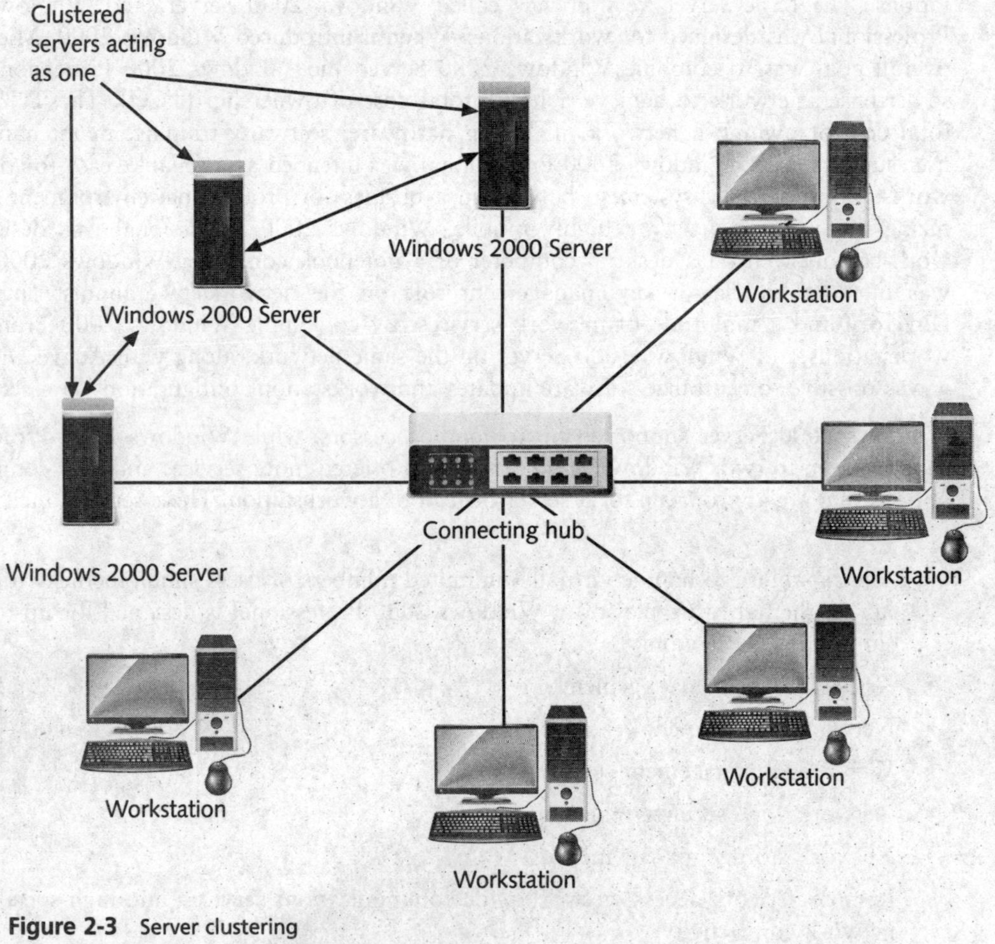


**Figure 2-3** Server clustering

Microsoft discontinued support for all versions of Windows 2000 Server in 2010.

## Windows XP and Windows Server 2003

Windows 2000 evolved into two products, both containing the core elements of the Windows 2000 kernel: Windows XP and Windows Server 2003. Windows XP was the desktop version of the operating system, while Windows Server 2003 was the server version. Both of these operating systems offered a refreshed desktop GUI, with changes apparent in the two-column Start menu, as shown in Figure 2-4.

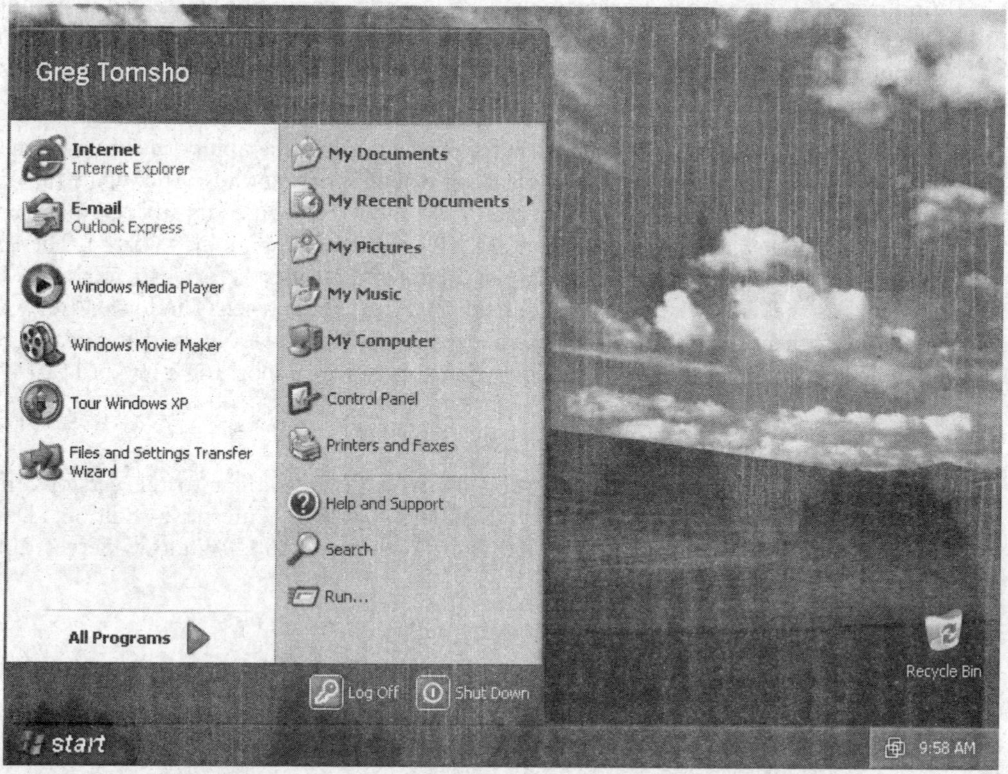


**Figure 2-4** The Windows XP desktop and Start menu

In addition to the new GUI, Windows XP and Windows Server 2003 offered more capabilities for keeping photo albums, playing music, running video and audio files, playing games, and using other multimedia applications. Windows XP and Windows Server 2003 also offered better Internet security through a built-in firewall and the ability to remotely control the computer over an Internet connection via a tool called Remote Desktop. Remote Desktop is designed to be secure; the computer being controlled must first grant access. Another feature introduced with Windows XP was that you had to **activate** it after installation. The OS could be activated automatically online or by calling Microsoft with the activation key that came with the system. The activation code is linked to a particular computer on which the operating system resides. System activation is a mechanism to help ensure that software is not pirated.

Windows XP came in several versions, including Windows XP Home, Windows XP Professional, Windows XP Tablet PC, Windows XP Media Center, and Windows XP 64-Bit.

**Windows XP Home and Professional Editions** Windows XP, which stands for "Windows Experience," originally came in two versions: Windows XP Professional and Windows XP Home Edition. Windows XP Professional was intended for office and professional use. This version of Windows XP had the ability to create accounts for different users who might use the operating system. Windows XP Professional, like Windows 2000 Professional, could be used as a small server for up to 10 users. Windows XP Home Edition was meant to be the next upgrade from Windows 9x/Me, and was a scaled-down version of Windows XP Professional. For example, user accounts could not be created in Windows XP Home Edition. Another difference was that Windows XP Professional could run on computers using up to two processors and on 64-bit Itanium computers, whereas Windows XP Home Edition ran only on 32-bit single-processor computers.

Windows XP contained many other new features, including the ability to configure themes for the desktop, a better help system, and plenty of troubleshooting tools. And, while the kernel for Windows XP was vastly different from that of Windows 9x, you could still run many programs written for Windows 9x using the Windows XP Program Compatibility Wizard. These features and more made Windows XP a mainstay in homes and businesses for years to come. Windows XP lasted as the Windows flagship OS from 2001 to 2007, when Windows Vista was introduced. Even then, people were not eager to give up Windows XP, and it remains today in many homes and businesses even though Microsoft ended support for it in April 2014.

## Windows Server 2003/R2

Windows Server 2003 came in four versions, which were similar to the versions that were available for Windows 2000 Server: Standard Edition, Enterprise Edition, Datacenter Edition, and Web Edition. An upgrade from Windows 2000, Windows Server 2003 contained new features, including:

- The GUI interface used with Windows XP
- Improvements for faster network logon authentication through Active Directory
- Several hundred new group policies that can be set to manage user workstations via Active Directory
- New tools for managing server resources
- Ability to run on 64-bit Itanium processors
- Remote server management through the Remote Desktop tool
- Enhanced ability for users to run programs on the server, through Microsoft Terminal Services
- Runtime code for the Windows .NET development environment to run applications through the Internet on all types of devices

Microsoft listened to the demands for tighter security in their operating systems. With Windows Server 2003, they took a step in that direction. After the initial installation, most Windows server features had to be set up manually, which was a change from previous versions of the operating system, where many functions were set up by default. In Windows Server 2003, you set up only the functions you wanted to use. (Operating system installation is covered in Chapter 5.)

Windows Server 2003 Release 2 (R2) was an interim version of Windows Server. It upgraded Windows Server 2003 with many new features that were then incorporated into Windows Server 2008 and beyond. Some of the Windows Server 2003 R2 enhancements included a new version of the **Microsoft Management Console (MMC)**, faster code execution (depending on the server hardware), a new **Print Management Console**, strong integration with **.NET Framework**, and improved security. Organizations that used Active Directory, **Distributed File System (DFS)**, clustered servers, and group policies found valuable new features for managing their enterprise networks. Microsoft continued to emphasize improvements in security for all of its operating systems, and Windows Server 2003 R2 was no exception. From the security standpoint, the R2 version came with a new Windows Firewall, first introduced in Windows XP Service Pack 2. The R2 version also integrated new security patches into the operating system code, and added a new feature, called Post-Setup Security Updates, to guide server managers through new configuration activities related to patches and updates.

Windows Server 2003 R2 offered many new features that organizations wanted for even more reliable, heavy-duty, and uninterrupted computing. Some of these features are summarized here:

- Better performance
- Improved group policy management
- MMC 3.0 and the Print Management Console
- New server clustering capabilities
- Virtual server options
- Dynamic Systems Initiative
- Better identity and access management
- Better options for branch office servers
- DFS enhancements
- Subsystem for UNIX-based applications
- Improved storage management

**From the Trenches ...**

A college had limited IT server staff who were familiar with the Windows Server 2003 operating system. With the release of Windows Server 2003 R2, they used the Print Management Console to give access to the help desk personnel. The help desk was able to set up, reset, check status, and customize printers on the network. All of this took place remotely at the help desk. Customers were happy that they got immediate assistance and did not have to wait for a technician to come to their office. The server staff were also pleased that they did not have to make as many trips out of the office to fix problems.

Microsoft ended support of Windows Server 2003 in July 2015, and has urged companies to move to Windows Server 2008 or Windows Server 2012.

# Modern Windows Operating Systems

While many Windows XP and Windows Server 2003 computers are still operating, both OSs are now considered legacy systems. Microsoft no longer supports them or earlier Windows versions, and users should update their computers to more recent versions to ensure better reliability and security. Even Windows 7 and Windows Vista, which are described next, no longer receive mainstream support from Microsoft. Extended support ends for Vista in April 2017 and in January 2020 for Windows 7.

## Windows Vista/Windows 7

Microsoft Windows Vista, released in January 2007, is a workstation operating system that followed Windows XP. Features in Windows Vista grew out of Windows XP and the development process for Microsoft Windows Server 2008. Not long afterward, in July 2009, Windows 7 was introduced. Like Windows Me, Windows Vista was not well received, which is why Windows 7 was introduced fairly quickly after it was apparent that Windows Vista was struggling in the marketplace (people still loved Windows XP). This section focuses on Windows 7, which is far more prevalent in homes and businesses even in 2016, even though most of what is discussed applies equally to Windows Vista as well. In addition, most features were carried forward from Windows 7 to Windows 8/8.1 and Windows 10.

Windows 7 was geared to make desktop computing more intuitive and more reliable for users than previous versions of Windows. For example, every computer user has had trouble finding a specific document or file they know is buried in a folder somewhere. Windows 7 is designed to enable users to quickly find documents, files, and resources—even if they don't remember the exact location. This is accomplished through enhanced search facilities and new ways to organize information.

In terms of security and reliability, Windows 7 has more built-in security features than previous versions and requires less rebooting. For instance, the Windows 7 firewall is enhanced to monitor both incoming and outgoing communications. When used with Windows 7, Internet Explorer has stronger security to avoid spyware and malicious software attacks. Further, when you install a software patch to enhance security or for other reasons, there are fewer instances that require you to reboot the computer right away, which makes your system more reliable.

Code enhancements "under the hood" in Windows 7 make this operating system about a third faster than Windows XP and Windows 2000. In terms of what you see on the desktop, Windows 7 provides what Microsoft calls a "unified presentation subsystem for Windows," which means that the windows you see are consistently designed and offer many new features for quickly accessing information. The new desktop presentation, called Aero (Authentic, Energetic, Reflective, and Open), also enables organizations to more effectively manage user desktops for uniformity and to reduce common problems in computer use. To the developer, the unified subsystem means there is a more consistent set of application programming interfaces (APIs) for linking programs with the operating system. Visually, Aero can use 3D graphics accelerators to render transparent and other visual effects called "Glass" display effects.

For most users, the reasons to upgrade to Windows 7 include greater speed, more productivity through the use of intuitive features, uniformity of the desktop, and greater security and reliability. These factors are particularly important to users who rely on a computer for school, work, entertainment, and important functions in a home.

While many home users upgrade their OS for new features, corporate IT departments often upgrade only when there is a business reason for doing so. Business reasons may include new features that increase employee productivity, but many businesses only upgrade because the OS is no longer supported with security and reliability enhancements.

Windows 7 implements many new features that represent changes from earlier Windows operating systems. A sampling of new features includes:

- Desktop and windows interface
- Libraries
- Folder resource sharing options
- Reliability features
- Security features
- User Account Protection
- Management options

Each of these is explained in the following sections.

**Desktop and Windows Interface** When you use Windows 7, you'll notice that, as in Windows XP, there is a Start button on the taskbar. The taskbar can contain icons for currently running programs or ones you can choose to run. A notification area on the right side contains the time and other elements, such as the speaker volume. Windows 7 also has a feature called desktop **gadgets** (first introduced with Vista), or small applications for readily accessing information and tools, such as a clock, calendar, or weather updates.

Desktop gadgets posed a security risk, and support for them ceased starting with Windows 8.

The Windows 7 Search box at the bottom of the Start menu is an important feature that enables fast searching for a specific document or file. The Search feature provides very fast searches for resources. Figure 2-5 shows the Windows 7 Start menu with the Search box at the bottom and the desktop with a clock gadget and a CPU meter gadget running on the right side.

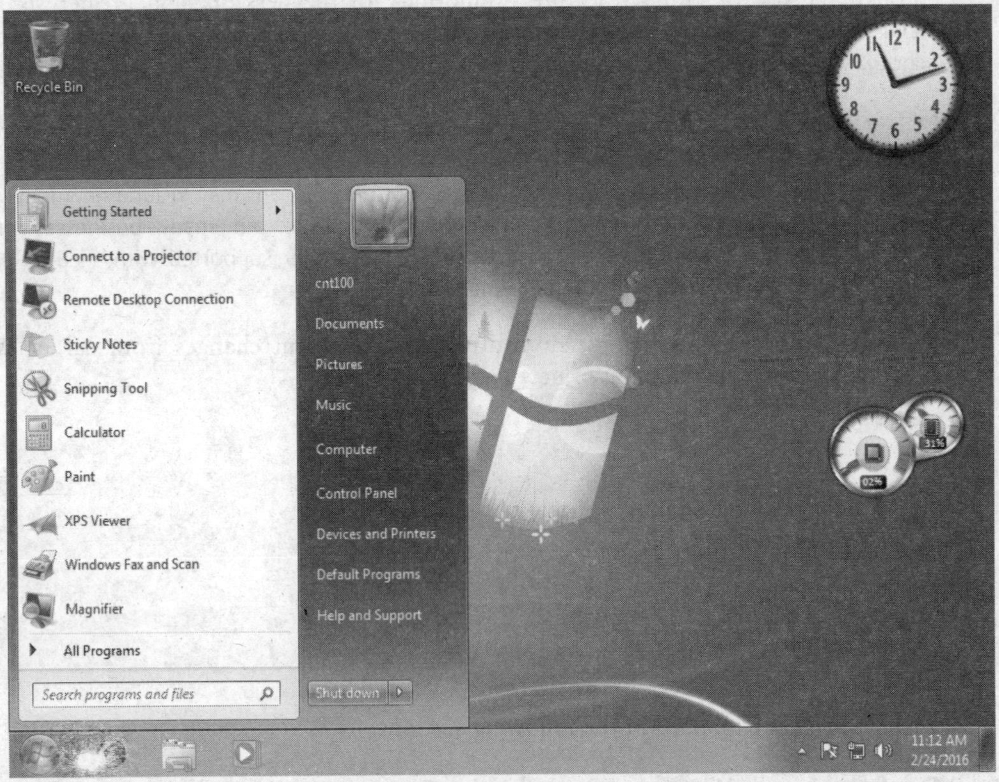


**Figure 2-5** The Windows 7 desktop and Start menu

As in previous Windows versions, the Windows 7 Control Panel is the place to configure your computer. Control Panel still offers the Classic view, which is comparable to pre-Windows XP versions. You can also see Control Panel contents in the Category view introduced in Windows XP. When you use the Category view, the presentation of information is designed to more quickly address a specific task, such as configuring a network connection. Figure 2-6 shows a list of the Control Panel categories in Windows 7.

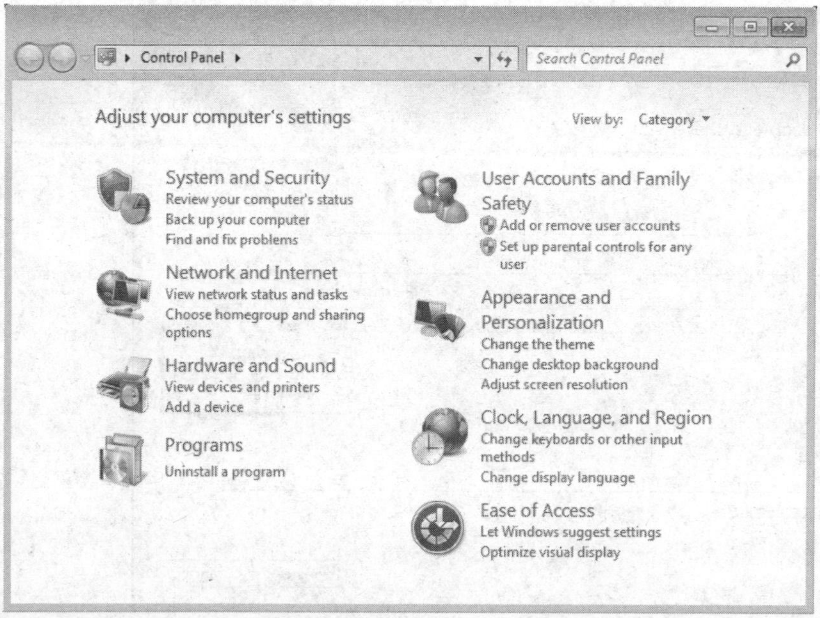


**Figure 2-6** Windows 7 Control Panel categories

**Libraries** A library is an innovation for organizing files from multiple locations on your computer and the network. Libraries can be optimized based on the content of the files, such as documents, music, pictures, and videos. A library is not really a folder in the traditional sense, such as Documents. It is a dynamic folder that houses files from one or more different locations.

**Folder Resource Sharing Options** Sharing folders over a network is a powerful tool for making information resources available to multiple network users (see Chapter 10). In Windows 7, you have the option to configure folder sharing in one of two ways: (1) by selecting the folder and clicking the Share with button in the Explorer window or (2) by right-clicking the folder and clicking Share with. After you elect to share a folder, you see the Sharing Wizard that enables you to specify which users can access the folder (see Figure 2-7). You can choose from a list of users who have accounts on the computer or you can use the Find button to locate other users on a network, such as those in Active Directory. There are three permission levels:

- *Read*—Permissions to open and view the file
- *Read/write*—Permissions to view, use, and change the file contents, and to remove the file
- *Owner*—Permissions to view, use, and change the file contents as well as change permissions on the file

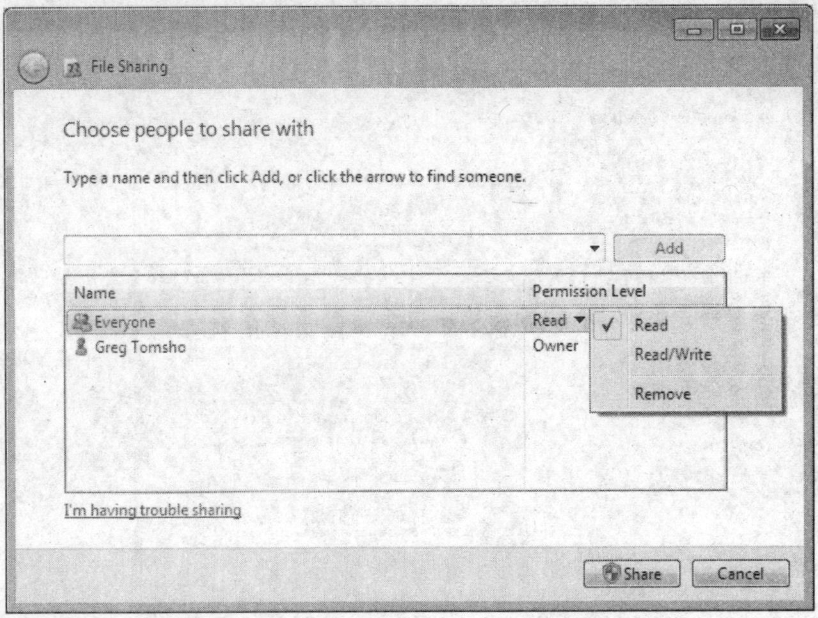


**Figure 2-7** Sharing a folder in Windows 7

As in Windows XP, a Windows 7 folder or file also has file permissions that control who accesses the folder or file. If the file permissions deny access to a user or group, that person or group will not have share access. File permissions are configured by right-clicking the folder or file, clicking Properties, and clicking the Security tab.

In addition to the Sharing Wizard, users can specify the use of a file on the basis of a personal or public profile established on their computers. Files not to be shared can be saved into a personal profile and files to be shared can be saved into a public profile.

**Reliability Features** Windows 7 has features for increased reliability so users experience fewer interruptions and information is kept intact. These features include the following:

- *Startup Repair Tool*—Automatically launched when a boot problem is detected. It can detect and solve driver problems, incorrect startup settings, and corrupted startup information on the disk.
- *New code to prevent interruptions*—Additional safeguards to prevent system crashes and hangs.
- *Self-diagnosis for problems*—Built-in diagnostics for common hardware problems, such as disk or memory failures.
- *Restart Manager*—Reduces the number of times you have to reboot your computer due to installed updates or patches. Instead of rebooting the entire computer, certain processes that are updated can simply be restarted.
- *Service-failure recovery*—The operating system can automatically detect when a service has failed and attempt to restart it.

**Security Features** Building a secure operating system means building in security from the ground up. If you are a user of earlier Windows operating systems, you are probably aware of the continual need to install security updates and patches. Because computer attackers use a multitude of ways to invade operating systems, manufacturers have had to plug all kinds of unanticipated holes. Today we know more about how systems are attacked and there are more available defenses. In Windows 7 and beyond, Microsoft is working to change coding structures at the foundation of the operating system to reduce the opportunities for attackers. Besides locking down the code, Microsoft has implemented additional security features, including:

- A more comprehensive firewall
- User Account Protection
- Built-in security software to find and eliminate malicious software
- Status information

The Windows firewall monitors traffic going into and coming out of the computer. This capability was initially implemented in Windows XP with Service Pack 2. Another firewall element used in Windows 7 is the ability to link it to the use of group policy settings. This means that a server manager can set up a group policy to have consistent desktop and system settings on that server's clients. In an office or organization, the group policy configuration can be used to ensure that all users have enabled the firewall and are using exactly the same security settings within the firewall. Even if a user changes his or her firewall settings, the group policy ensures the settings are back the next time that user logs on (or the group policy can be set to prevent users from changing firewall settings). Having consistent firewall settings is vital for an organization, because its network is no more secure than the least secure client.

Another feature of the Windows firewall is that it is compatible with **IP Security (IPsec)**. IPsec is a set of secure communications standards and standards for encryption to protect network communications between computers. IPsec is supported by Microsoft and other server systems, such as all Windows systems since Windows 2000 Server and Linux.

**User Account Protection (UAP)** was introduced in Windows Vista and is intended to make user accounts more secure. UAP enables the user account administrator to better protect accounts by controlling permissions and by limiting the software applications that can be run from an account. UAP protects the registry and specified folders so their contents are only available to a specific user. If you regularly use virus checking or other system protection software, you have probably noticed that the software often corrects changes to a computer's registry that have been introduced by malicious software. UAP is designed to address this important security problem.

Some users log on to their computers using an account that has Administrator permissions. Because this type of account can make significant changes to the operating system, there is a risk in running all applications with Administrator permissions in effect. UAP limits the permissions given to applications so that system-wide changes are not made inadvertently or through malicious software. One downside to UAP is that some applications you could formerly run in Windows XP may not run in new versions of Windows.

In Windows 7, Microsoft has integrated programs to search for and eliminate malicious software, including viruses, worms, and Trojan horses. If the integrated programs cannot successfully delete specific malicious software, they may instead be able to block the effect of the malicious software on the local computer.

Windows 7 also includes what Microsoft calls Windows Service Hardening. One common avenue for attackers is through an open service, such as through FTP. Windows Service Hardening limits the effect a service can have in Windows, so attacks are limited or thwarted.

It can be difficult for a user to determine if new security patches and other updates are implemented on a computer. Windows 7 provides status information to show whether recent patches and updates have been installed. This is part of Microsoft's Network Access Protection initiative for networks using Windows client OSs (Windows Vista and later) and Windows Server OSs (Windows Server 2008 and later). These servers have the ability to set up network access protection that is enforced on all clients, such as maintaining security patches and updates.

**Windows 7 Management Options** Windows 7 and later extend the TCO initiatives of Microsoft to save on support costs incurred by users and organizations. Windows 7 comes with more group policy settings than earlier Windows versions, which means that computers in an office, department, or organization can be standardized for easier use. For example, if all users in the customer service department in a business use the same order entry program, that program can be set up to start the same way on all department computers via group policy. A customer service representative can go to any computer in the department and access the program in a familiar way. By creating consistency in the way computer systems are used, group policy saves on support costs.

Sometimes one computer is used by many people, such as a public computer in a coffee shop or library. In this situation, one computer might have different group policies, depending on who logs on. Windows 7 includes the Group Policy Management Console (GPMC). The GPMC enables the computer's administrator to configure different group policies for different kinds of users.

In Windows 7 it is more difficult to change system settings and files, such as the registry, because the system can be configured so that only an authorized installer makes these changes—instead of users or software that do not have authorization. This system protection is accomplished through the Windows Resource Protection (WRP) feature.

For more versatile management, Windows 7 brings back the Administrative Tools menu first introduced in Windows NT. To access the Administrative Tools menu, click Start, click Control Panel, click System and Security, and click Administrative Tools. Some of the Administrative Tools that are available include:

- *Computer Management*—Opens the Computer Management tool that provides access to many general management functions, such as Event Viewer, Shared Folders, Task Scheduler, Reliability and Performance, Device Manager, Disk Management, and Services and Applications.
- *Performance Monitor*—Shows monitors for utilization of the CPU, disk, network, and memory.
- *Task Scheduler*—Permits you to set up tasks or applications to run at a certain time, such as starting a backup at 6:00 p.m.
- *Event Viewer*—Enables you to access the computer system's logs to track activities and errors.

## Windows Server 2008/R2

Windows Server 2008 was released by Microsoft in February 2008 and Windows Server 2008 R2 was released in October 2009. It is available in versions similar to Windows Server 2003. Windows Server 2008 and Windows Vista share the same code base and thus the same new features, as do Windows Server 2008 R2 and Windows 7.

Windows Server 2008 R2 is the first Windows OS not to be available in a 32-bit version; it is only available in a 64-bit version.

Compared with its predecessors, Windows Server 2008 and Windows Server 2008 R2 include some new and enhanced features:

- Active Directory
- Failover clustering
- Hyper-V
- Self-healing NTFS
- Server Core
- Server Manager

**Active Directory** With Windows Server 2008, a read-only domain controller (RODC) was implemented. This is great for servers in locations that do not have the desired security for a domain controller. Hackers cannot make changes at remote locations that would then be replicated to the main domain controller at the corporate headquarters. In addition, RODCs limit the amount of sensitive information stored on the server, such as user passwords.

**Failover Clustering** **Failover clustering** is a server OS feature in which two or more servers are tightly linked; one server is the active server and the others are considered standby servers. The active server provides services to network clients while the standby servers monitor the availability of the active server. If the active server fails, one of the standby servers (as determined by an algorithm) begins providing its network services. Failover clustering is enhanced significantly in Windows Server 2008 Enterprise and Datacenter editions with the addition of a cluster validation wizard. This wizard runs validation tests on the servers you are going to cluster. It tests the software and hardware on each server and provides a report on how well failover clustering will run.

**Hyper-V** Microsoft rolled out **Hyper-V** in Windows Server 2008; a stand-alone release of Hyper-V Server is available. It allows the server to run multiple independent operating systems at the same time on the same hardware. Hyper-V allows server administrators to combine multiple virtual servers on one physical server.

**Self-Healing NTFS** In the past, if you experienced problems with NTFS volumes on a disk, you used Chkdsk.exe to fix the problem. This meant taking down the volume to run the utility. With self-healing NTFS, the utility runs in the background to correct hard disk problems. The availability of the file system is far greater than the previous way of using the Chkdsk.exe utility, data is preserved as much as possible, and better reports are provided to describe modifications made to the volume.

**Server Core** Microsoft describes **Server Core** as being "designed for use in organizations that either have many servers, some of which need only to perform dedicated tasks but with outstanding stability, or in environments where high security requirements require a minimal attack surface on the server." Server Core is a bare-bones installation with a limited GUI that is meant to reduce hacker attacks to the operating system. It is ideal for branch offices, remote locations, and office servers.

**Server Manager** Server Manager combines and replaces the Manage Your Server, Configure Your Server, and Security Configuration Wizards found in Windows Server 2003. It centralizes these features and provides one location to set up, deploy, and manage servers, add server roles, and check the status of servers. Figure 2-8 shows the Server Manager.

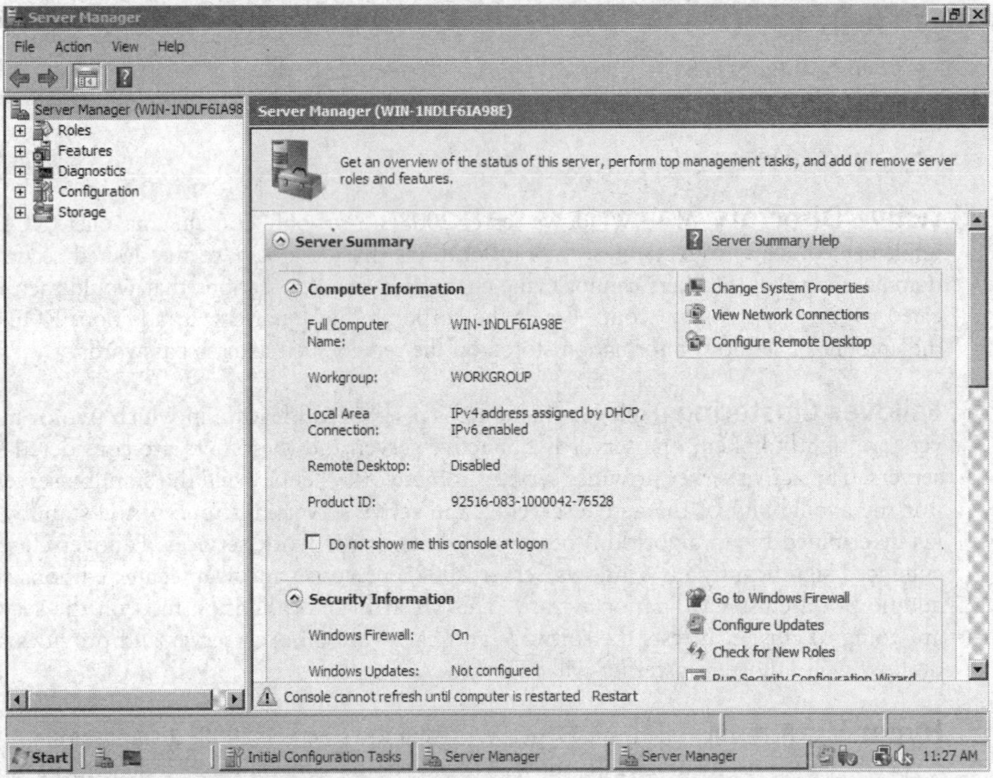


**Figure 2-8** Windows Server 2008 Server Manager

Windows Server 2008/R2 supports up to 64 physical processors in a system and up to 64 TB of RAM. Windows Server 2008/R2 is available in Datacenter Edition, Enterprise Edition, Standard Edition, and Web Server Edition. The Web Server edition does not support Windows Hyper-V and cannot be configured as a domain controller.

Some of the new, updated, and enhanced features found in Windows Server 2008 R2 include:

- Integration with Windows 7
- File services management
- Scalability
- Reliability
- Virtualization
- Web platform updates

**Integration with Windows 7** The features described here are only available to Windows 7 client computers attached to Windows Server 2008 R2 systems. Mobile connectivity is becoming more important as organizations are finding ways to do more with fewer resources. As discussed under Windows 2000, a popular way to remotely connect to the corporate servers is via a VPN. Users will most likely need to install a VPN client on their mobile device and then establish a connection. This can be time-consuming and difficult. Many times, it requires the assistance of the company help desk or even the server administrator.

Microsoft introduced DirectAccess to provide the functionality of a VPN without the hassles of setting one up and then initiating it each time you want access to the remote network. The remote computer is automatically authenticated before the user logs on. Thus, when the user logs on, the process is very fast and requires very little effort. This allows Windows Server 2008 R2 to manage the Windows 7 client without waiting for the client to log on. DirectAccess uses IPsec encryption over the Internet to protect the organization's data.

Organizations are turning more to centralized applications on the corporate server. This reduces the costs of remote and branch IT groups. It also puts a greater burden on the connections between the branch group and organization headquarters. On one hand, centralized applications save money, but on the other, there is the additional cost of increased bandwidth. The BranchCache feature allows the remote network to cache frequently accessed applications and information at the branch office, greatly reducing the traffic over the network link.

**File Services Management** With the price of server storage declining and the centralization of data in **storage area networks** (SANs), the management and security of this data is becoming increasingly important. A SAN is a fast network that contains components that can be shared for storage and access to the storage. Windows **File Classification Infrastructure** (FCI) provides the information you need to manage the data. It automates the classification of data based on predefined categories, including what is contained in the data. If the data contains sensitive information, FCI may move this information to a more secure server and even encrypt it.

**Scalability** Windows Server 2008 R2 includes components to help reduce the number of physical servers. This reduces the organization's costs for servers, administrators, physical space, and power consumption. Windows Server 2008 R2 supports up to 256 logical processors along with Hyper-V, which supports up to 64 logical processors.

**Reliability** Windows Hardware Error Architecture (WHEA) now supports memory and cache error recovery. This is done without the application or the operating system being aware of the process. Windows Server 2008 R2 also supports "hot add" capabilities for memory, processors, and I/O resources. A server administrator can add memory, processors, and I/O resources to a server when the need arises without taking the server down, reconfiguring it, and then rebooting it. In today's 24/7 world of operations, reliability and uptime are critical to the success of the organization. This is accomplished through Dynamic Hardware Partitioning.

**Virtualization** Modern data centers rely heavily on virtualization to keep operational costs as low as possible both for power consumption and the purchase of new physical servers. Windows Server 2008 R2 provides Hyper-V for server virtualization, which includes Live Migration. This allows the server administrator to move a virtual machine from one physical server to another. The users of the server will see no service interruption.

Virtual machines are growing in popularity because it is easy to set them up quickly on servers already in the data center. Management of virtual machines becomes a growing task as the number of these machines increases. Windows Server 2008 R2 provides enhancements that assist the server administrator, such as Hyper-V Management Console and System Center Virtual Machine Manager 2008.

**Web Platform Updates** Internet Information Services (IIS) 7.5 and enhanced support for .NET on Server Core are two of the Web platform updates in Windows Server 2008 R2. IIS 7.5 provides centralized Web management, more reliability, and improved security.

There is also a new administration console called IIS 7.5 Manager. This console allows for both local and remote administration. Configuration management allows Web site administrators to delegate control over content to the owners of the information. IIS 7.5 comes with enhanced troubleshooting tools such as the failed request tracing tool, which keeps a record of failed requests based on a set of rules the server administrator creates. Finally, IIS 7.5 provides a better server footprint. It has a modular architecture so that the server administrator can load just the modules needed for the specific type of Web services being offered. This, along with the Windows Server 2008 R2 Server Core option, reduces the amount of code and thus the vulnerability to attack.

## Windows 8/8.1

Windows 8 was released in October 2012 and was intended to unify the operating system user interface and code base to work on mobile touch-centric devices as well as traditional desktops. Just a year later, in October 2013, Microsoft released Windows 8.1 to correct for some egregious miscalculations, not the least of which was the abandonment of the beloved Start button. The touch-centric interface of Windows 8 was not well received, particularly because so few Windows mobile devices were in use and very few people had a touch screen as their desktop or laptop monitor. The mouse and keyboard were still the input devices of choice on the vast majority of Windows systems.

In Windows 8, the Windows Start button is replaced by the Start screen (see Figure 2-9), which contains live tiles you can press or click to start applications or access the desktop.

When Windows 8 boots, users are placed directly into the Start screen rather than the desktop. To get to the desktop, users must click a live tile on the Start screen. With no Start button on the desktop, users must find a spot in a corner of the screen and touch or click it to bring up the Start screen.

**Figure 2-9** Windows 8 Start screen

Despite the shortcomings of the user interface, Windows 8 and its immediate successor, Windows 8.1, have a number of improvements over Windows 7 under the hood, most of which would carry forward to the better-received Windows 10. Some of the new and improved features include the following:

- User interface changes
- Storage enhancements
- Security enhancements
- Client Hyper-V
- Integration with online services

**User Interface** While the user interface is the primary knock on Windows 8, there are some notable and well-received changes. Windows Explorer is renamed File Explorer and gets a ribbon-style interface to replace the traditional command bar. Task Manager got a facelift, making it easier to see what processes are running and what resources are being used. Also, a new touch-optimized Settings app provides access to common PC settings without making users wade through all of the options in Control Panel (although the full Control Panel remains). While the Start button was missing from Windows 8, Microsoft brought it back in a reduced form in Windows 8.1. In Windows 8.1, clicking the Start button opens the Start screen, but right-clicking it gives administrators and power users quick access to frequently used administrative tools such as Programs and Features, Power Options, Event Viewer, System, Device Manager, Network Connections, Disk Management, Computer Management, and several more (see Figure 2-10).

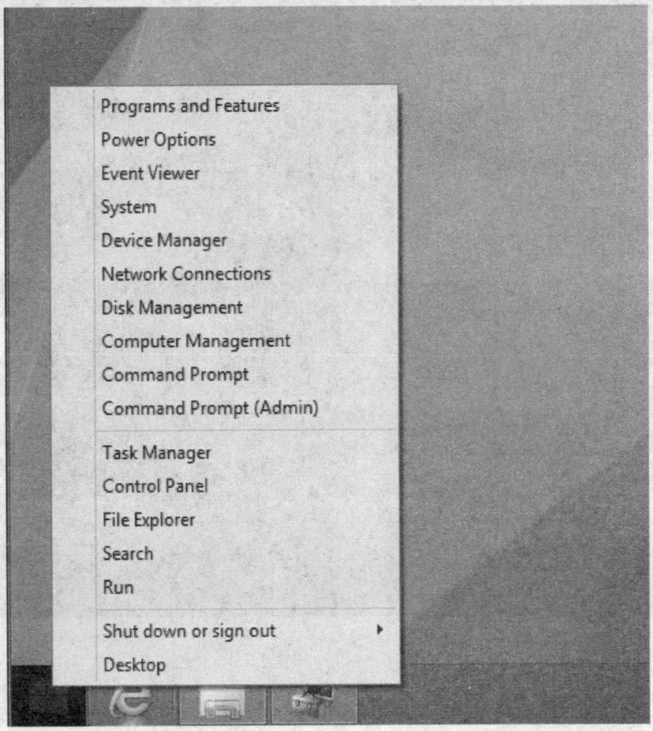


**Figure 2-10** The Windows 8.1 Start button and right-click menu

**Storage Enhancements** Windows 8 introduces Storage Spaces, a storage management and configuration tool that allows users (and server administrators on Windows Server 2012) to manage disks of different sizes and interfaces (including external disks) as a single pool of storage, creating virtual disks and virtual volumes from the storage pool as necessary. Another nice feature in Windows 8 is the ability to mount CD and DVD images with a simple double-click on an ISO file. After double-clicking (or right-clicking and clicking Mount), a new drive letter is created and the ISO file is opened in a File Explorer window. This feature allows you to explore the contents of a DVD image without burning it to a disk. In a similar fashion, you can mount virtual disks if they are in the Microsoft VHD or VHDX format used by Hyper-V and Storage Spaces. Mounted virtual disks can then be used as if they were a physical disk attached to the system with a drive letter assigned. Storage and storage devices are discussed in more detail in Chapter 7.

**Security Enhancements** Windows 8 adds the option to sign in with a Microsoft online account rather than using a local user account and password. In addition, you can sign in using a PIN or a picture password instead of a traditional password. To use a picture password, you choose a picture and then use a touch screen to create a combination of lines, circles, and taps. To use the picture password when you sign in, you repeat the pattern you created on the displayed picture. Windows 8 also offers a variety of controls to allow parents to monitor their children's activities. And, if your system starts acting up, new recovery options allow you to refresh your PC without losing any files or reset the machine to factory settings and completely start over.

**Client Hyper-V** Microsoft brings the success of Hyper-V on Windows Server OSs to its client line of OSs starting in Windows 8. Client Hyper-V uses the same virtualization technology that is found on Windows Server, allowing you to run multiple OSs on a single physical computer. This feature allows you to upgrade to the latest Windows version and still be able to run older versions of Windows in a virtual machine. For example, if you have an application designed for Windows XP, Windows Vista, or even earlier versions that will not run in Windows 8 and later versions, you can run the application in a virtual machine with the required guest OS installed.

**Online Services** Users who choose to sign in using a Microsoft online account gain the benefits of synchronized applications and settings between devices. In addition, the client necessary to access Microsoft's OneDrive cloud storage service is built into Windows 8. As part of the Windows 8 user interface makeover, Microsoft introduced Windows Store apps that run on desktop and mobile computers alike. These touch-centric apps run full-screen in Windows 8, but Microsoft changed course in Windows 10, allowing Windows Store apps to be run in a window like most other programs.

## Windows Server 2012/R2

Windows Server 2012/R2 is Microsoft's deep dive into the private cloud. This new version is chock-full of new tools and features designed to help server administrators increase the availability of network services and limit security risks. Microsoft has also emphasized features that help datacenter operators deploy and manage a private cloud. Windows Server 2012/R2 comes in two primary editions and two special editions. Standard and Datacenter editions return from Windows Server 2008, but there is no longer an Enterprise edition. Standard Edition is suitable for most mid-sized to large companies, while Datacenter Edition is designed for organizations that rely heavily on Hyper-V virtualization. The two special editions are Essentials and Foundation. Essentials is aimed at small businesses with 25 or fewer users. It supports most of the roles and features in Standard and Datacenter editions, but some roles have restrictions or limited functions. Essentials Edition is automatically configured as a root domain controller, which is the first domain controller installed in an Active Directory forest. Foundation Edition, the entry-level Windows Server 2012/R2 edition, is suitable for small businesses that need to purchase a complete server solution for file and printer sharing, centralized control over user accounts and network resources, and common services used in most networks, such as Web services, DNS, and DHCP. Foundation Edition is available as an OEM version only, installed on a server by the manufacturer, and supports only 15 users. The features already discussed in the Windows 8/8.1 section are present in Windows Server 2012/R2, with the exception of some of the user-specific features. Also, Windows Server 2012/R2 boots directly to the desktop instead of the Start screen.

Windows Server 2012/R2 maintains all the core technologies used in Windows Server 2008, including Server Manager, NTFS, Active Directory, and Windows file and printer sharing and networking features, although many of these technologies later received enhancements, as discussed in the following sections.

**Server Manager** Server Manager has been updated to allow administrators to manage all the servers in the network from a single management console. The left pane of Server Manager displays the major views: Dashboard, Local Server, and All Servers. You use the Local Server view to manage just the server where you're running Server Manager, and the All Servers view to manage aspects of all servers. To add servers you want to manage, right-click All Servers and click Add Servers or use the Manage menu. When you click All Servers in the left pane, you see a list of servers you can manage in the right pane (see Figure 2-11).

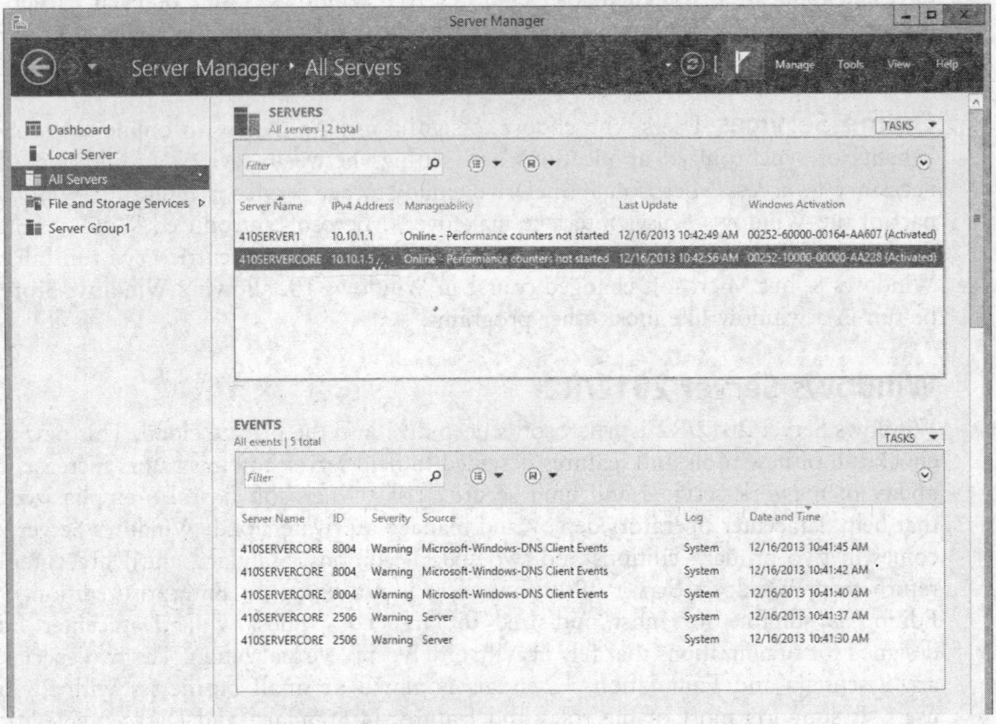


**Figure 2-11** Windows Server Manager in Windows Server 2012/R2

**NTFS File System** NTFS was introduced in Windows NT in the early 1990s. Although it has been updated throughout the years, NTFS has remained a reliable, flexible, and scalable file system. One of the most noticeable improvements of NTFS versus its predecessor,

FAT32, is file and folder permissions. Since its debut in Windows NT, NTFS has added many new features, including disk quotas, built-in file compression and encryption, BitLocker drive encryption, and a host of performance and reliability improvements.

**Active Directory** Active Directory is the foundation of a Windows network environment. This directory service enables administrators to create and manage users and groups, set network-wide user and computer policies, manage security, and organize network resources. With Active Directory, you transform a limited, nonscalable workgroup network into a Windows domain with nearly unlimited scalability. Windows Server 2012/R2 continues to add features to Active Directory, including an easy-to-use Recycle Bin to restore deleted objects, and a user interface to create password policies that can be applied to individual users and groups.

**New Features in Windows Server 2012/R2** Microsoft has added several new features and improved a host of existing features to make Windows Server 2012/R2 a secure, highly available, enterprise-class server OS. Microsoft's emphasis on the private cloud is clear, with several features focused on this burgeoning sector of IT. Some of the new and improved features are discussed briefly in the following list and covered in more detail in later chapters.

- *Server Core*—Server Core has no taskbar or Start screen, just a command prompt window on a black background. Its use might not be obvious, but Server Core has quite a bit going on under the hood. Server Core's lightweight interface hides powerful server capabilities that aren't encumbered by a resource-intensive GUI. A fresh installation of Server Core uses a little more than 5 GB of disk space compared with more than 9 GB for a fresh installation of Windows Server 2012/R2 with a GUI. A major enhancement made to Server Core in Windows Server 2012/R2 is the ability to switch between Server Core mode and GUI mode. In the Windows Server 2008 version, after you installed it in Server Core mode or GUI mode, you couldn't switch to the other mode.
- *Minimal Server Interface*—The benefits of Server Core mode are substantial, but some people just can't live without being able to point and click. Microsoft recognized this fact and found a happy medium between Server Core mode and the full GUI: Minimal Server Interface (also called MinShell). Minimal Server Interface allows users to perform most local management tasks with a GUI tool but lacks many aspects of the full user interface.
- *Hyper-V 3.0*—Hyper-V is the Windows Server virtualization environment introduced in Windows Server 2008. Although it's not new, the enhancements in Hyper-V version 3.0 make Windows Server a leader in virtualization software. Hyper-V 3.0 is a major component of Microsoft's private cloud initiative and includes these new features: multiple concurrent live migrations, Hyper-V Replica, support for up to 32 virtual processors, virtual machines with up to 32 GB of RAM, and several additional performance and reliability enhancements.
- *PowerShell 4.0*—PowerShell is a command-line interactive scripting environment that provides the commands for almost any management task in a Windows Server 2012/R2 environment. It can be used much like a command prompt, where you enter one command at a time and view the results, or as a powerful scripting engine that enables

you to create and save a series of commands for performing complex tasks. Although PowerShell 1.0 was introduced in 2006, it has been substantially enhanced in Windows Server 2012/R2 with more than 50 new cmdlets, job scheduling, enhanced auto-completion, and improved performance.

- *Storage Spaces*—As discussed in the sections on Windows 8, Storage Spaces provides administrators with the ability to manage storage of different sizes and interfaces, creating virtual disks that can be anything from a simple volume to a fault-tolerant RAID 5.
- *Resilient File System*—Resilient File System (ReFS) is a new file system in Windows Server 2012/R2 that's intended for large data storage applications that require a high degree of reliability. It's largely backward-compatible with NTFS but doesn't support some features, such as file-based compression, disk quotas, and Encrypting File System (EFS).
- *Dynamic Access Control*—Dynamic Access Control (DAC) gives you fine-tuned control over shared resources without some of the limitations of traditional file permissions. DAC works alongside traditional permissions, giving administrators more flexibility in assigning access to resources. Traditional permissions are based on user and group accounts, and in a large network with hundreds or thousands of users and resources, group-based permissions can be limiting and complex. DAC allows classifying data and assigning permissions by user attributes rather than group memberships. As a simple example, a folder can be classified as belonging to the Accounting Department, making access available only to users whose Department attribute equals Accounting, or the folder can be classified as highly sensitive so that its contents are encrypted automatically, relieving an administrator from having to encrypt it manually.

**From the Trenches ...**

The Computer Networking Technology department at a college runs its own network, including routers, switches, and Windows servers. The servers used hardware RAID controllers for fault-tolerant disk storage. However, every time the OS was updated or a disk needed to be replaced, the RAID controllers seemed to have problems. For example, when the servers were upgraded from Windows Server 2008 R2 to Windows Server 2012, the drivers for the RAID controllers weren't available. The department turned to Storage Spaces, the new feature in Windows Server 2012, so that standard disk controllers could be used while maintaining fault tolerance with virtual RAID disks. Now, disk space can be expanded simply by adding a new disk without the need to worry about compatibility with the existing disks. In addition, there is no further need to be concerned about updated drivers for finicky RAID controllers.

## Windows 10

Windows 10 is the current release of the client version of Windows, and some say it may be the last numbered release of Windows, with enhancements coming as regular feature updates automatically when they are released. Windows 10 was released in July 2015. What, no Windows 9, you might ask? Microsoft decided to forego Windows 9 and leap directly from

Windows 8.1 to Windows 10. The official explanation is that the new Windows was too big a leap forward to advance just one version number, but some suspect it was a way for Microsoft to distance itself from what is considered a poor showing with Windows 8. In fact, Microsoft offered a free upgrade to Windows 10 during its first year of availability to anyone who possessed a valid license for Windows 7 or Windows 8/8.1.

Windows 10 builds on the successful features of Windows 8/8.1, discards some of the less successful, and brings back some popular Windows 7 features that had been left out of Windows 8. Some of the key features of Windows 10 include:

- *Virtual desktops*—A feature long available on Linux desktop managers, virtual desktops let users create multiple desktops and switch between them to access open application windows that were started in each desktop. To create a new desktop, click the new Task View icon on the taskbar, and click the plus sign that appears in the bottom right of the screen. Alternatively, press Windows+Ctrl+D to create a new desktop and switch to it. To move an open application window to a different desktop, press the Task View icon, right-click the window you want to move, click Move to, and select the desktop you want (see Figure 2-12). In the figure, you see the Task View icon to the right of the Search bar on the taskbar, and you can see two desktops. The window with Microsoft Edge, the new Windows Web browser, is about to be moved to Desktop 2. Virtual desktops help you organize your workspace and easily switch between sets of applications you are working on, making multitasking more efficient.

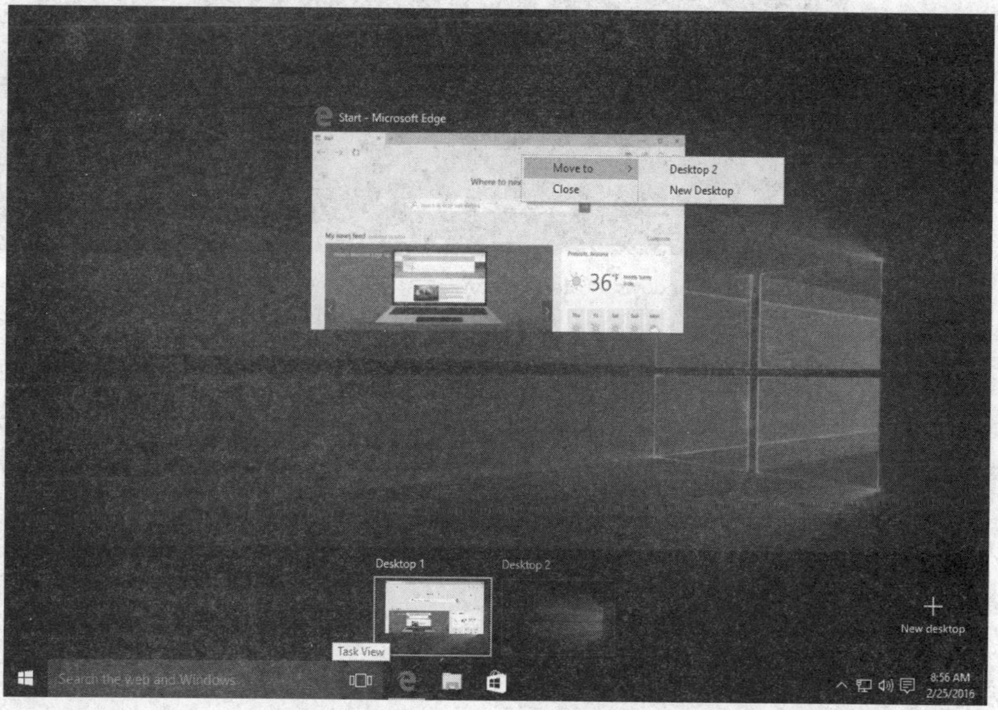


**Figure 2-12** Windows 10 virtual desktops

- *Return of the Start button*—The Start button is back and is a hybrid between the Windows 7 Start button and the Windows 8 Start screen. There are essentially two columns; the left column looks somewhat like the old Windows 7 Start button, with frequently used applications and shortcuts to settings and a power button for log-off/shutdown options. The right pane looks like a scaled-down version of the Start screen from Windows 8, with live tiles pointing to apps you can run (see Figure 2-13). For IT pros and power users, the right-click functionality of the Start button added with Windows 8.1 remains.

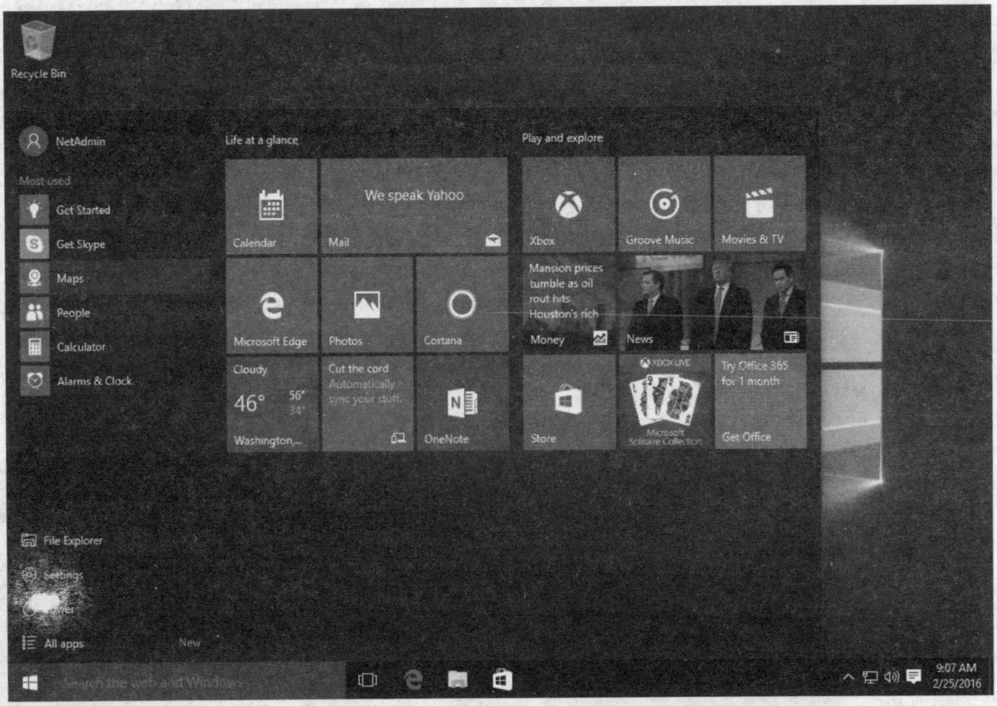


**Figure 2-13** Windows 10 Start button

- *Microsoft Edge Web browser*—Microsoft started from scratch to come up with Microsoft Edge, an eventual replacement for Internet Explorer. Edge is a slimmed-down Web browser built around standards such as HTML5, but it doesn't support ActiveX controls, so you can't get rid of Internet Explorer right away if you need those capabilities. However, it does have a built-in PDF reader and Adobe Flash Player. It integrates nicely with Microsoft's new digital assistant, Cortana (discussed next), has a reading mode, and supports annotations directly on Web pages that can be stored and shared in the cloud (see Figure 2-14).

**Figure 2-14** Microsoft Edge Web browser

- *Cortana digital assistant*—If you have ever used an iPhone or iPad to talk to Siri, or said "Okay Google" into your Android phone, you have some ideas what Cortana is all about. In order to use Cortana on your computer, you must be signed in with a Microsoft online account. With Cortana, you can use voice commands to ask questions (Cortana uses Bing as its search engine), open applications, set reminders and appointments, and so forth.
- *Quick access*—File Explorer adds a feature called Quick access that lets you pin any folder or search result to the Quick access section in the left pane of File Explorer.
- *Universal application architecture*—The Metro-style apps that Microsoft first released with Windows 8 are designed to run across Windows 10 desktops, tablets, smartphones, and other portable devices—even Xbox One. Windows 10 automatically recognizes whether you are on a device with a touch screen and selects between a mouse-oriented interface and a touch screen interface.
- *Sign-in options*—A new feature called Windows Hello allows you to expand your sign-in options. Aside from using a password or PIN, you can now sign into your device using your facial features or fingerprint if your hardware supports it. To use the face recognition option, you'll need an Intel RealSense 3D camera; a regular Web cam won't work. For fingerprint sign-in, you'll need a compatible fingerprint scanner, which you can buy as a USB device for as little as $15.

There are many more features in Windows 10, and Microsoft will be releasing new features as updates as they are completed.

### Windows Server 2016

Still under development at this writing, Windows Server 2016 comes with the Windows 10 user interface and builds upon features found in Windows Server 2012/R2. Here are a few of the highlights you can expect to find in Windows Server 2016, which was due to be released in the fall of 2016:

- *Hyper-V*—A host of improvements to Hyper-V are included in the new Windows Server 2016, including nested virtualization (the ability to run a virtual machine in a virtual machine), Linux Secure Boot, production checkpoints, hot add and remove for memory and network adapters, and many more.
- *Nano Server*—Nano Server is a new install option for Windows Server 2016. It goes beyond Server Core, with an even smaller footprint, and doesn't support a local logon—all management tasks are done remotely. Nano Server is designed for single-task virtual machines, a DNS server, a storage host, or a Web server.
- *Failover clusters*—Failover clusters can now be upgraded from Windows Server 2012 R2 to Windows Server 2016 without Hyper-V or file server cluster downtime.
- *Windows Containers*—Windows Server 2016 expands its virtualization options with Windows Server Containers and Hyper-V Containers. Containers allow you to run applications that are isolated from one another, improving reliability. Windows Server Containers provide a moderate level of isolation while sharing various system libraries and Hyper-V Containers give you virtual-machine levels of isolation without the resource overhead of an actual virtual machine.

## UNIX and UNIX-like Operating Systems

The UNIX operating system comes in many different formats. Of all the operating systems covered in this book, it is the oldest, most diverse, and most complicated. The reason for this is that one manufacturer does not have the exclusive license for UNIX. After UNIX was developed at AT&T, the company never formally licensed the kernel to prevent others from using it and implementing their own specialized utilities. AT&T used the operating system within the company and made the source code available outside the company. The end result is that there are many UNIX versions with many diverse utilities.

Versions of UNIX today adhere to one of the two main design standards: the **Berkeley Software Distribution (BSD)** standard or the **System V Release 4 (SVR4)** standard. Examples of BSD-style UNIX include the freely available NetBSD and FreeBSD operating systems, as well as the commercially available BSDi UNIX. SVR4 versions include freely available versions of Linux and commercial versions such as Oracle (formerly Sun Microsystems) Solaris and SCO UNIX. All UNIX systems include security features. Table 2-1 lists several versions of UNIX or UNIX-like OSs, along with the manufacturer and origin. It also includes Web addresses to check for additional information.

**Table 2-1 UNIX or UNIX-like OSs**

| Version | Manufacturer/source | Origin | Web address |
|---|---|---|---|
| AIX | IBM | A combination of SVR4 and BSD | *www-03.ibm.com/systems/power/software/aix/* |
| Debian | Debian | BSD | *www.debian.org* |
| Fedora | Fedora (supported by Red Hat) | SVR4 | *https://getfedora.org* |
| FreeBSD | The FreeBSD Project | BSD | *www.freebsd.org* |
| HURD | GNU | BSD | *www.gnu.org/software/hurd/hurd.html* |
| Mac OS X | Apple Computer | BSD (Darwin UNIX) | *www.apple.com* |
| NetBSD | The NetBSD Project | BSD | *www.netbsd.org* |
| OpenBSD | The OpenBSD Project | BSD | *www.openbsd.org* |
| Red Hat Linux | Red Hat | SVR4 | *www.redhat.com* |
| Solaris | Oracle | BSD | *www.oracle.com* |
| openSUSE | MicroFocus | SVR4 | *www.suse.com* |
| Turbolinux | Turbolinux, Inc. | SVR4 | *www.turbolinux.com* |
| Ubuntu | Canonical | BSD | *www.ubuntu.com* |

This book uses Linux for its UNIX examples; Linux is modeled after UNIX and shares many of the same features and commands. Most Linux versions are available free of charge, but some enhanced versions of Linux must be purchased. Linux is considered "UNIX-like" based on standards that were developed after UNIX originally came out. Linux runs on Intel-based and AMD-based processors.

There are a number of Linux versions available worldwide. Red Hat Linux, Ubuntu, and Debian are well known in the United States, but are also popular worldwide. OpenSUSE Linux is another popular product, especially in Europe. The product comes in both a professional and personal version. Turbolinux is the leading Linux distributor in the Asian-Pacific region. It provides workstation, desktop, and server versions of its product.

Because UNIX comes in such a wide variety of implementations, it runs on almost any hardware. There are UNIX versions available for all hardware mentioned up to this point. For this reason, it is hard to define exactly what specifications a platform should meet to run UNIX.

UNIX is a true multitasking, multiuser operating system. This means, as explained before, that it can fully serve all the computing needs of multiple users running multiple applications at the same time. Depending on the hardware, a single UNIX computer can support from one to several thousand users.

After startup, UNIX typically presents you with a request for a login, or username, followed by a request for a password. The username and password you provide determine what privileges you will be granted on the system. When your identity has been verified, you are presented with a shell—that is, the user interface. This is another point where UNIX is substantially different from most other operating systems: by default, most UNIX versions come with several different shells, and it is up to users to pick the shell they want to use. Different shells provide different levels of functionality, but all of the shells function much like the shell in a Windows command prompt, with a series of built-in commands and the ability to call **external commands** (operating system commands that are stored in a separate program file on disk) and application programs simply by typing commands at the command line.

The most popular UNIX shells are the Bourne shell (sh), its cousin the Bourne Again shell (bash), and a version of the Bourne shell called the *C shell* (csh), in which some of the commands are formatted to be similar to the C programming language. Overall, these shells function in the same way: you get a prompt, you type a command, and they do what you ask. When you are done with the shell, you can exit using the *exit* command. Typically, this returns you to the login prompt. Try Hands-On Project 2-5 to determine which UNIX shell you are using.

Many versions of UNIX can also provide you with a GUI. The most popular interface is the X11 Window System, known commonly as X Window. **X Window** is similar to other windowed interfaces. A unique feature of X Window is that it is network enabled. Using an X terminal, it is possible to run X Window and all the application programs on a remote UNIX computer, and to remotely interact with your applications. One UNIX system can support many X terminals and users. X Window, however, is an optional part of many UNIX versions. Just as there are many different UNIX versions, there are also many different versions of X Window. Linux generally uses a version called Xfree that can be obtained for free. X Window, by default, does not include programs analogous to Windows Explorer for managing files, or the Windows-based Start menu for starting programs, but many utilities are available to provide file and application management.

Fedora Linux, for example, offers an X Window-like GUI interface called GNOME (see Figure 2-15), which can be installed or omitted. Even when GNOME is installed, you can still execute regular Linux commands by starting the terminal emulation program window shown in Figure 2-16. To start the terminal emulation program in Fedora, for instance, click Activities, Show Applications, Utilities, and then click Terminal. Hands-On Project 2-6 enables you to learn more about the Fedora GNOME interface, while Hands-On Project 2-7 helps you to learn about the *find* command in a terminal window.

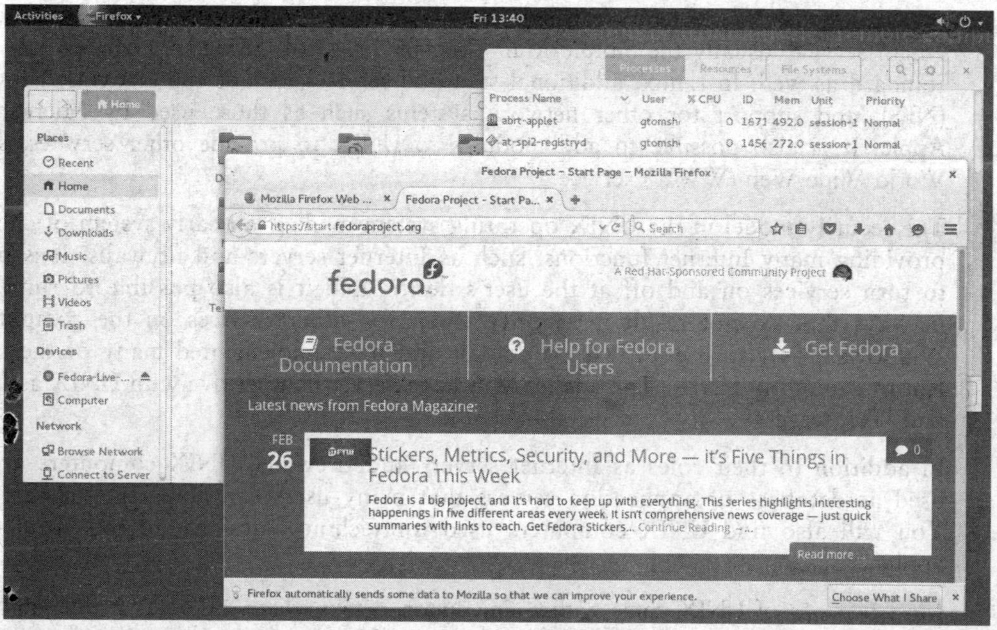


**Figure 2-15** The GNOME desktop in Fedora

*Source: Fedora Linux*

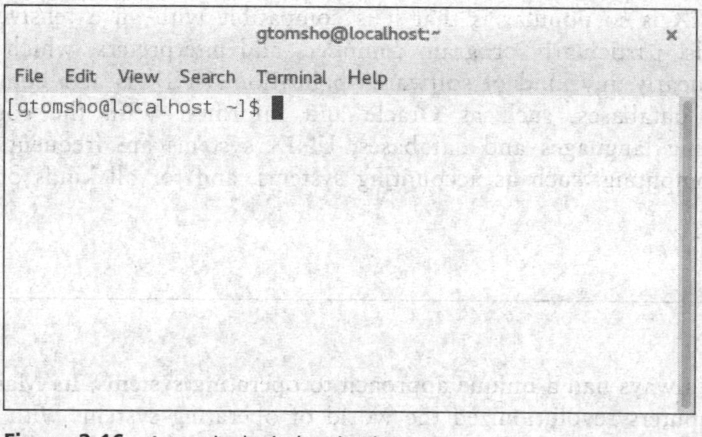


**Figure 2-16** A terminal window in Linux

*Source: Fedora Linux*

All networking functions in UNIX are based on the BSD networking model, which provides support for the Transmission Control Protocol/Internet Protocol (TCP/IP). This is the standard protocol in use on the Internet, and as such, UNIX computers are qualified to provide numerous Internet services. (Network protocols are discussed later in this book.) The standard UNIX operating system does not provide many network functions. Most of these functions are provided by add-ons. The standard functions include login services, which allow a user to connect to the UNIX computer from another remote computer on the network; file transfers through the File Transfer Protocol (FTP); and some form of e-mail service, usually the Simple Mail Transfer Protocol (SMTP). Other services can be standard as well. In Linux, additional standard services include the Network File System (NFS), and support for other network systems such as those used by Microsoft and Apple. It is also possible to add modules to UNIX to provide other services, such as World Wide Web (WWW) service.

The security model in the UNIX operating system made it an early system of choice for providing many Internet functions, such as Internet servers and firewalls. It is possible to turn services on and off at the user's desire, and it is also possible to run services in ways that do not result in security issues for other services on the computer. All Windows OSs also use TCP/IP by default and have implemented many of the security features found in UNIX. This makes Windows Server competitive with UNIX as Internet and Web servers.

In addition to their roles as Internet servers and firewalls, UNIX computers are often used as database or application servers that many users can access at the same time. You will also find UNIX computers used for technical design and industrial control applications.

Most versions of UNIX come with a line editor, a text editor, or both. A **line editor** is an editor used to create text one line at a time. Line editors are often used to create scripts, programs in which each line executes a specific command. A text editor enables you to edit text in a full-screen mode.

One reason that UNIX is so popular is that it is compatible with an extensive range of programming tools, particularly program compilers and interpreters, which means that you can create nearly any kind of software application. UNIX is also compatible with many popular databases, such as Oracle and Informix. With the combined power of programming languages and databases, UNIX systems are frequently used for administrative computing, such as accounting systems, and for all kinds of scientific applications.

# Mac OS

Apple Computer has always had a unique approach to operating systems. Its Macintosh line of personal computers revolutionized the world of operating systems with its all-graphical user interface and an all-graphical shell. Although there are subtle differences between Microsoft Windows and Mac OS in the way they function, you will see many similarities as well, which many would say is because Windows was designed to mimic the look and feel of Mac OS. Mac OS X is built on Darwin UNIX, which is a distribution of the BSD UNIX version. The Mac OS X El Capitan desktop is shown in Figure 2-17.

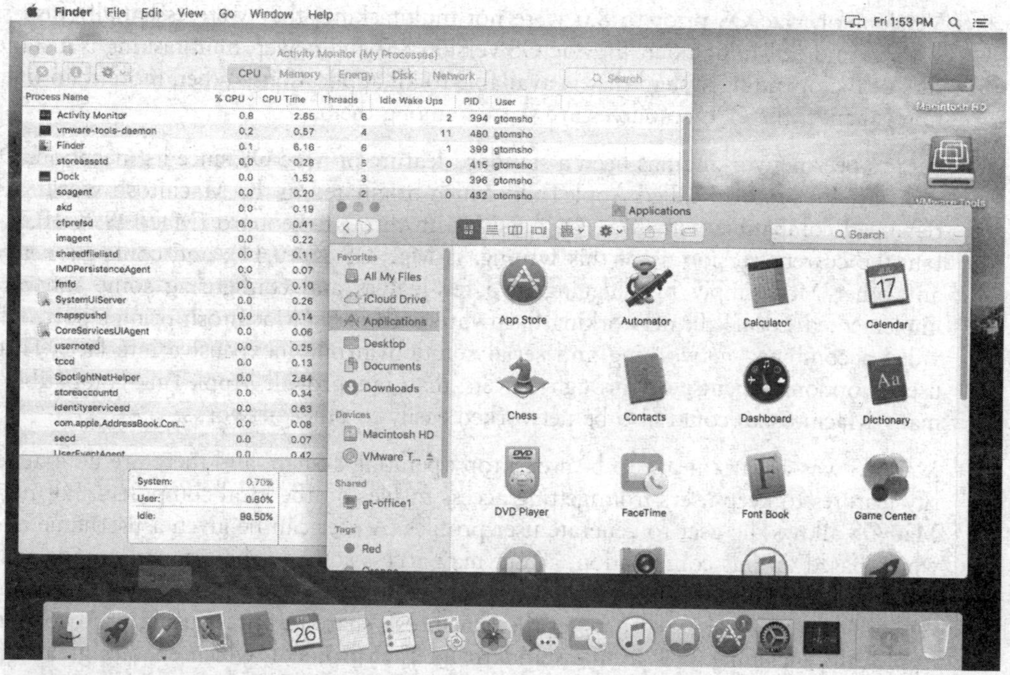


**Figure 2-17** The Mac OS X El Capitan desktop

*Source: Mac OS X El Capitan*

The hardware architecture of Mac OS is substantially different from the architecture used on most other platforms, especially because many of the graphical functions are included in the basic input/output system (BIOS) functions, which are located in the read-only memory (ROM) of the hardware. (Apple calls this "firmware.") Beginning with System 7.1, Apple began using system enabler files that allowed the previous version of the operating system to support new hardware. When the next version of the operating system was released, support for the most recent Macs was included so the enabler file was no longer needed for that model. The hardware architecture needed to run Mac OS is very dependent on the version of the operating system. If you run version 7.0, you could be using any Macintosh hardware architecture, except for the PowerPC platform, which is supported as of version 7.5. If you are running the newest generation of hardware (Intel-based), you are required to run Mac OS X. Apple has always made the hardware and software closely interconnected, which results in strict requirements when it comes to operating system/hardware coordination.

One significant difference between Mac OS and other operating systems covered in this chapter is that only one company (Apple) makes hardware capable of running Mac OS. Mac OS runs on Intel processors, but the hardware is still Apple hardware. Several years back, Apple licensed Power Computing, Motorola, and other companies to make Mac OS-compatible hardware, but that is no longer the case. In short, using Apple software means using Apple hardware.

Versions of Mac OS prior to 8.0 were not multitasking; they were essentially task switching with the aid of MultiFinder. In Mac OS version 8.0 and newer, multitasking is a standard feature of the operating system that is available to all applications. When more than one application is active, the CPU resources are shared among them.

**Peer-to-peer networking** has been a standard feature of Mac OS since its inception. Older versions used a protocol called AppleTalk, which originated in the Macintosh world. AppleTalk remained compatible with Mac OS versions up through Leopard (Mac OS X 10.5; El Capitan, the current version as of this writing, is Mac OS X 10.11), and could be networked to any other Mac simply by plugging in a few cables and configuring some software. Apple implemented LocalTalk networking hardware with every Macintosh printer port, which provided a combined networking and serial solution in one inexpensive interface. Through the use of optional clients, or through servers that can provide AppleTalk-compatible services, many Macintoshes could also be networked easily to other networks.

Mac OS was always meant to be a desktop operating system, and there are no extended security features to keep users from getting access to files on the local computers. For networking, Mac OS allows the user to generate user profiles. A user can be given a username and a password. Based on this combination, a user may access some of the resources made available on the network. Mac OS can use its networking features to share printer and disk resources. In version 8.x and later, extensions let the Macintosh share resources using protocols other than AppleTalk, including TCP/IP, the standard Internet protocol, which enables greater flexibility in how Macs can be networked. Beginning with Mac OS X version 10.6 (Snow Leopard), AppleTalk is no longer supported. Snow Leopard supports TCP/IP networking.

Throughout its history, Mac OS has been known for its support of graphics, video, and sound capabilities. In this respect, Mac OS has been ahead of the industry. Because Apple has had tight control over both the Macintosh hardware architecture and operating system, and because it chose to actively enhance the audiovisual functions of both hardware and software, the Mac and the Mac OS are favored by people in the graphics, sound, and video fields. Macintosh computers are used in many different environments, especially those that deal with the creative process. The Mac font management and ColorSync color matching technologies have endeared it to graphic arts and prepress professionals, while QuickTime has made the Mac popular for multimedia sound and video production. You will also find many Macs in educational environments. The home computer market has a small but substantial share of computers running Mac OS. MacBook Air notebook computers continue to be popular, even in organizations that have settled primarily on the Windows-Intel platform.

Mac OS 9.x introduced features for better hardware and Internet access. For example, version 9.1 introduced a Printer Sharing panel to manage and share a USB printer on a network. There is a capability to connect to another computer over the Internet by using the Point-to-Point Protocol (PPP), a network communications protocol designed for remote communications. (You will learn more about protocols later in this book.) Mac OS 9.x added Personal Web Sharing for creating a Web page that others can access over the Internet or through a private network. Also, Mac OS 9.x included a runtime execution tool for running Java applets from the Finder tool. The Network Assist Client tool can be used by network administrators to control the computer.

## Mac OS X

Mac OS X, where X means version 10, is a significant update because it sports the "Aqua" interface. One of the main changes for users of Mac OS 9.x and earlier is that some programs and utilities were replaced. The Apple menu can no longer be customized as in the past. New menu features include System Preferences, which is similar to the Control Panel on Windows systems. System Preferences enables you to set functions such as the time and date, display settings, startup functions, energy saving functions, and network functions. The Dock function can be customized through the System Preferences tool for the applications you want to include. Through Dock, you can start multiple applications and switch between them in a multitasking environment.

Out of the box, Mac OS X is configured so that different users can access the operating system in their own workspaces, without affecting other users. If one user wants to log out so that another user can access Mac OS X, the first user can now select the new Log Out option from the Apple menu, instead of turning off the computer and then rebooting.

Many windows in Mac OS X now can be customized so that their contents appear in columns, similar to Windows-based systems. Also, the title bar in a window displays buttons to close, minimize, or maximize (zone) that window. Throughout each window, the icons have a modern look. Also, some windows have "drawers" that slide out like file cabinet drawers to offer information.

Internet connectivity is enhanced in Mac OS X through the Internet Connect tool, which performs functions that users of previous Mac OS versions associated with the Remote Access tool. Internet Connect enables you to set up an Internet connection, configure a modem, and monitor the status of a connection. Internet applications include the Mail application from Apple, which is used for e-mail; and Internet Explorer, a Web browser from Microsoft. Some notable changes and enhancements of Mac OS X that have occurred through the years include:

- *Mac OS X 10.6 Snow Leopard*—This was the first version of Mac OS X that would support only Intel-based processors. A download called Rosetta could be installed to retain support for PowerPC applications.
- *Mac OS X 10.7 Lion*—With the success of the iPad and iOS, it was only natural for Apple to incorporate some of the popular features found in iOS into Mac OS X. Mac OS X Lion included Launchpad to easily browse installed applications, and the use of multi-touch gestures was expanded for hardware that supported it. Mission Control unified a number of utilities into a single interface.
- *Mac OS X 10.8 Mountain Lion*—The success of iOS on mobile devices continued to color Mac OS X with support for iMessage, iWork, and iCloud, along with Notification Center. In addition, all software updates were available only through the App Store.
- *Mac OS X 10.9 Mavericks*—Running on Intel 64-bit processors, Mavericks was a modest release with mostly minor feature and performance improvements. This was also the first departure from using big cat names for each Mac OS X release. From here on, at least for a while, well-known California locations would be used to name the OS.
- *Mac OS X 10.10 Yosemite*—Yosemite gave Mac OS X a face lift, with a user interface that was based on iOS 7, giving window edges a more flat appearance. Probably the biggest new feature is called Handoff, which allows users of iOS 8.1 and later mobile

devices to "hand off" work in progress (such as SMS messages, e-mails, and phone calls) from their mobile device to their Mac.

## Mac OS X 10.11 El Capitan

Mac OS X 10.11 El Capitan is the current release of Mac OS X that started shipping in September 2015. Most would not call this a major release, but there are some improvements to features and performance. A feature called Split View lets you work in two applications at the same time, with each application snapped to opposite sides of the screen (see Figure 2-18). The Spotlight search app was updated, Pinned Sites lets you easily recall your favorite Web sites, and some new swipe gestures were added to apps. Finally, El Capitan introduces Metal for Mac, a set of 3D development tools for designing games and other 3D apps.

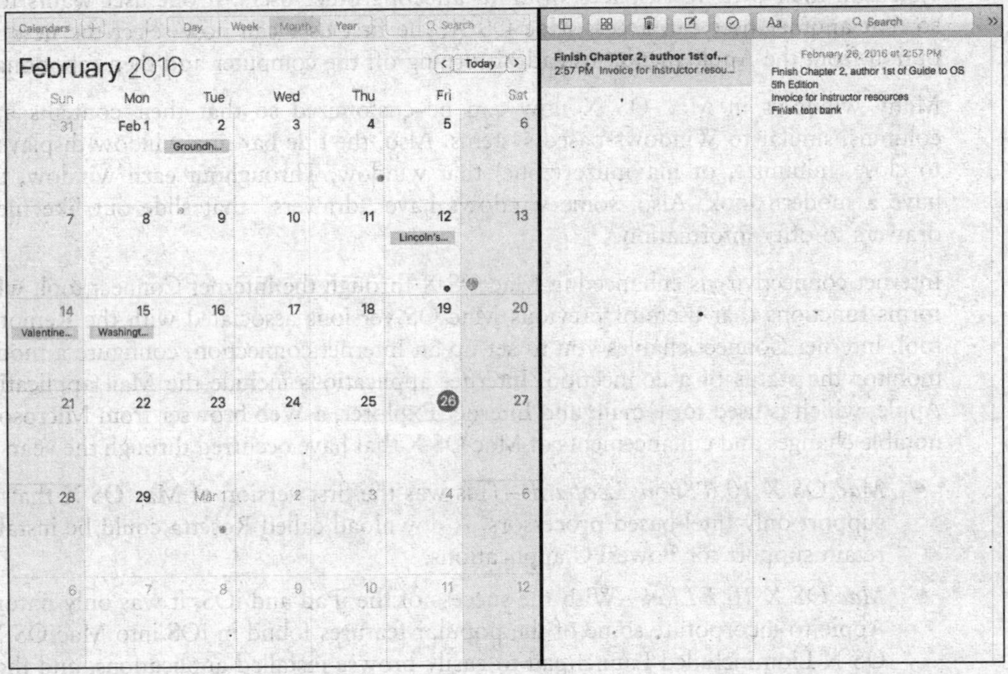


**Figure 2-18** Split View on Mac OS X El Capitan

*Source: Mac OS X El Capitan*

# Chapter Summary

- Early computer operating systems were primitive compared to current operating systems, but they were significant during their time and moved us toward a desktop computing environment. Server operating systems followed to allow for file sharing and printing.
- Windows, Macintosh, and Linux/UNIX are popular current operating systems, with new releases announced on a regular basis. Each release has new features and enhancements.

- Server operating systems have evolved to allow clustering, virtual servers, self-healing NTFS, a storage manager for SANS, single sign-on, network management, and security features.
- Mac OS X is built on Darwin UNIX, which is a distribution of the BSD UNIX version. Mac OS X 10.11 El Capitan is the latest Mac OS X release.

# Key Terms

**activate** To register your copy of a Windows operating system, starting with the Windows XP version. Without this activation, you can only run your operating system for a very brief time.

**Active Directory** A Windows Server installable service that consists of a database of computers, users, shared printers, shared folders, and other network resources and resource groupings used to manage a network and enable users to quickly find a particular resource.

**ActiveX** An internal programming standard that allows various software running under the Windows operating system to communicate with Windows and other programs.

**Berkeley Software Distribution (BSD)** A variant of the UNIX operating system upon which a large proportion of today's UNIX software is based.

**client** In a networking environment, a computer that handles certain user-side software operations. For example, a network client may run software that captures user data input and presents output to the user from a network server.

**clustering** The ability to share computing load and resources by linking two or more discrete computer systems (servers) to function as though they are one.

**Component Object Model (COM)** Standards that enable a software object, such as a graphic, to be linked from one software component to another one.

**Distributed File System (DFS)** A set of client and server services to organize distributed shared files into a logical file system.

**domain** A logical grouping of Windows computers and computer resources that helps manage these resources and user access to them.

**driver signing** Setting up all drivers so that they cannot be inadvertently overwritten by earlier driver versions and only certified versions of drivers can be installed.

**external commands** Operating system commands that are stored in separate program files on disk. When these commands are required, they must be loaded from disk storage into memory before they are executed.

**failover clustering** A group of two or more servers configured so that if one server fails, another server can resume the services the first one was providing.

**File Classification Infrastructure (FCI)** A system that allows files to be located on servers in an organization based on predetermined naming conventions.

**gadgets** Small applications for readily accessing information and tools.

**Hyper-V** A Windows feature that allows a server to run multiple independent operating systems at the same time and to run multiple virtual servers on one physical server.

**Infrared Data Association (IrDA)** A group of peripheral manufacturers that developed a set of standards for transmitting data using infrared light. Printers were some of the first devices to support the IrDA specifications.

**IP Security (IPsec)** A way to secure Internet Protocol (IP) traffic by encrypting and authenticating each packet.

**Kerberos** A security system and authentication protocol that authenticates users and grants or denies access to network resources based on a user's log-on name and password. Kerberos creates a unique encryption key for each communication session.

**library** A combination of folders that can be in any location on the local computer or the network.

**line editor** An editor that is used to create text one line at a time.

**Microsoft Management Console (MMC)** A flexible system that allows server administrators to configure the servers and monitor their function in one place.

**.NET Framework** A large library, available to all programming languages supported by .NET, that allows multiple programming languages to use code from other languages.

**peer-to-peer networking** A network setup in which any computer can communicate with other networked computers on an equal or peer-like basis without going through an intermediary, such as a server or network host computer. Mac OS is a peer-to-peer operating system.

**Plug and Play (PnP)** Software utilities that operate with compatible hardware to facilitate automatic hardware configuration. Windows versions starting with 95 recognize PnP hardware when it is installed, and in many cases can configure the hardware and install required software without significant user intervention.

**Print Management Console** A console that allows a system administrator to manage printers and printing throughout the network.

**privileged mode** A feature of the operating system kernel introduced in Windows NT that protected it from problems created by a malfunctioning program or process.

**registry** A Windows database that stores information about a computer's hardware and software configuration.

**Server Core** A scaled-back version of Windows Server 2008 in which all configurations and maintenance are done via the command-line interface.

**storage area network (SAN)** A set of storage devices that appear to the server to be locally attached, but in fact are on their own network with access granted to the server.

**System V Release 4 (SVR4)** A variation of the UNIX operating system. It is very popular today along with the Berkeley Software Distribution (BSD).

**task supervisor** A process in the operating system that keeps track of applications running on the computer and the resources they use.

**total cost of ownership (TCO)** The cost of installing and maintaining computers and equipment on a network. TCO includes hardware, software, maintenance, and support costs.

**Universal Plug and Play (UPnP)** An initiative of more than 80 companies to develop products that can be quickly added to a computer or network. These products include intelligent appliances for the home. For more information, go to *http://openconnectivity.org/upnp*.

**Universal Serial Bus (USB)** A serial bus designed to support up to 127 discrete devices with data transfer speeds up to 5 Gbits/s (gigabits per second).

**User Account Protection (UAP)** A feature of some Microsoft operating systems that allows for better protection of user accounts by controlling permissions and limiting the software applications that can be run from an account.

**virtual private network (VPN)** A private network that is like an encrypted tunnel through a larger network—such as the Internet, an enterprise network, or both—and is restricted to designated member clients.

**Windows Hardware Error Architecture (WHEA)** An architecture that supports memory and cache error recovery without the operating system being aware of the process.

**X Window** A windowed user interface for UNIX and other operating systems.

## Review Questions

1. What was the original Microsoft operating system for the IBM PC?
   a. Windows 3.1
   b. Windows 1.0
   c. MS-DOS
   d. Windows 95
2. Windows 2000 Server was the first Windows server to contain Active Directory. True or False?
3. What does it mean if a driver is signed?
   a. The driver file contains a digital certificate.
   b. Only certified versions of drivers can be installed.
   c. The driver can only work in Windows 10 and later versions.
   d. The driver must be installed on a server.
4. What is the default authentication protocol used by Windows 2000 Server and later versions?
   a. Kerberos
   b. MS-CHAP
   c. PAP
   d. IntelliMirror
5. In Windows Server 2003, most features and services are installed and enabled by default. True or False?
6. With which client OS does Windows Server 2008 share the same code base?
   a. Windows Server 2003
   b. Windows XP
   c. Windows Vista
   d. Windows Server 2003 R2

7. Self-Healing NTFS is a process to repair disk drives on an off-line server. True or False?
8. What feature introduced with Windows Server 2008 provides only a limited GUI?
   a. Active Directory
   b. Server Core
   c. Plug and Play
   d. RODC
9. Which of the following best describes a virtual private network (VPN)?
   a. a stand-alone virtual network
   b. a virtual network residing within one computer
   c. a private network that is like an encrypted tunnel through a larger network
   d. a network that can only be observed from the outside on rare occasions
10. Windows Server 2008 R2 supports up to 64 physical processors. True or False?
11. What features available starting with Windows Server 2008 R2 provide the functionality of a VPN without requiring users to initiate a connection each time they want one?
    a. remote desktop protocol
    b. IntelliMirror
    c. Hyper-V
    d. DirectAccess
12. FCI automates data classification based on predefined categories. True or False?
13. Windows 8 has a Start button that supports only right-click functionality. True or False?
14. The X Window-like GUI interface in Red Hat Linux is called which of the following?
    a. KDE
    b. RDP
    c. BSD
    d. GNOME
15. Which of the following best describes Hyper-V?
    a. the fifth version of the overdrive section on the Intel chip
    b. a method to increase the speed of memory access on a personal computer
    c. the server virtualization code used to create multiple logical servers on one physical server
    d. extremely fast communication over the USB port
16. Looking at Windows Server 2008 R2, which of the following statements is true?
    a. It was released in both a 32-bit and 64-bit version.
    b. It shares a core operating system with Windows Vista.
    c. It supports Live Migration.
    d. It has integration features with Windows XP and Windows Vista.

17. What was the first version of Windows Server to come in Essentials and Foundation editions?
    a. Windows Server 2016
    b. Windows Server 2012
    c. Windows Server 2008
    d. Windows Server 2003
18. What are the two main design standards to which most versions of UNIX adhere? (Choose two.)
    a. BSD
    b. USB
    c. SVR4
    d. SCO
19. What company supports Fedora Linux?
    a. Oracle (formerly Sun Microsystems)
    b. Red Hat
    c. IBM
    d. Hewlett-Packard (HP)
20. Virtualization allows you to do which of the following?
    a. Combine multiple physical servers into one logical server.
    b. Run a live and test environment on separate physical servers.
    c. Set up multiple operating systems on one physical server.
    d. Access multiple physical servers through one virtual console.

## Hands-On Projects

In some Windows projects you may see the User Account Control (UAC) box, which is used for security to help thwart intruders. If you see this box, click Yes to continue. Because computer setups may be different, the box is not mentioned in the actual project steps.

### Project 2-1: Use the Windows Search Function

Windows 10 offers a convenient search program to quickly find files and start applications. In this project you learn how to use the "Search the web and Windows" search box in Windows 10.

1. Start and log on to your Windows 10 computer. Click the **Search the web and Windows** text box next to the Start button. (Note that if Cortana is enabled, the search box will display the prompt "Ask me anything.")

2. Type **file**. Notice that the operating system interactively searches as you are typing (see Figure 2-19).

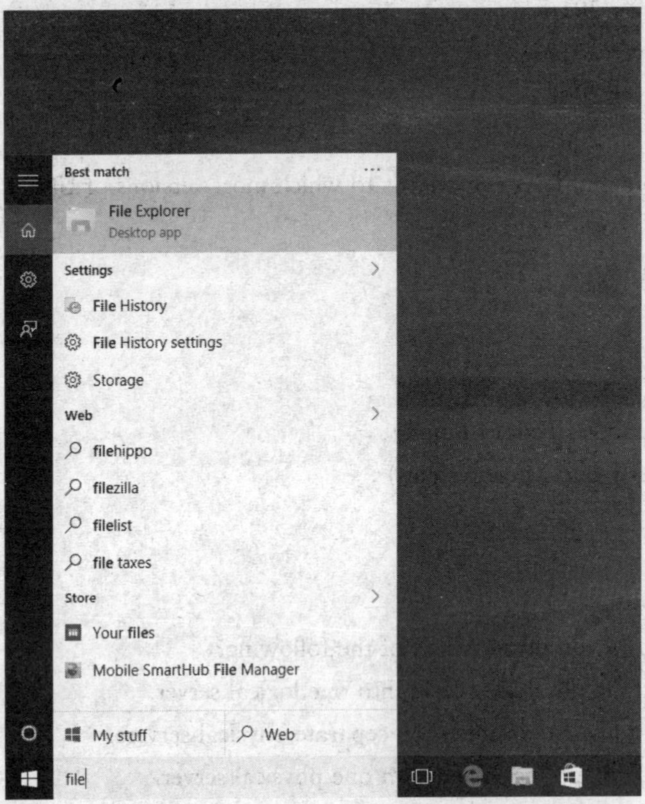


**Figure 2-19** Windows 10 "Search the web and Windows" search box

3. Click **File Explorer** in the search results menu to start File Explorer.
4. Close the File Explorer window.
5. As an alternative, you can start a program by entering its file name in the search box. Click the **Search the web and Windows** text box. Type **explorer.exe.** Press **Enter** or click **explorer.exe** in the search results to start File Explorer.
6. Close File Explorer.
7. Click the **Search the web and Windows** text box.
8. Type **cmd** and press **Enter**. You'll see the Command Prompt window.
9. In the Command Prompt window, type **dir** at the command prompt and press **Enter** to list the directories and files in your current directory. Type **dir /a** and press **Enter**. You will see a long list of files and directories, including system and hidden files. The */a* option in the *dir* command specifies that all files should be listed.

10. Close the Command Prompt window.
11. Stay logged on if you are continuing to the next project.

## Project 2-2: Browse the Windows 10 Registry

In this project, you browse the registry of Windows 10. Be careful not to make any changes to the registry. The Registry Editor does not have a Save or OK function, so any changes you make take effect immediately. Also, there is no Undo key.

1. Log on to Windows 10, if necessary.
2. Click the **Search the web and Windows** text box, type **regedit**, press **Enter**, and click **Yes**.
3. You see an interface like File Explorer that shows five folders, called *keys*. Each key contains information about different aspects of the system, such as hardware settings, user environment settings, application settings, and Windows system settings.
4. In the left pane, click to expand **HKEY_LOCAL_MACHINE\SOFTWARE\Microsoft\Windows\CurrentVersion\Authentication** and then click **LogonUI**. The right pane displays a number of values related to the current user (see Figure 2-20).

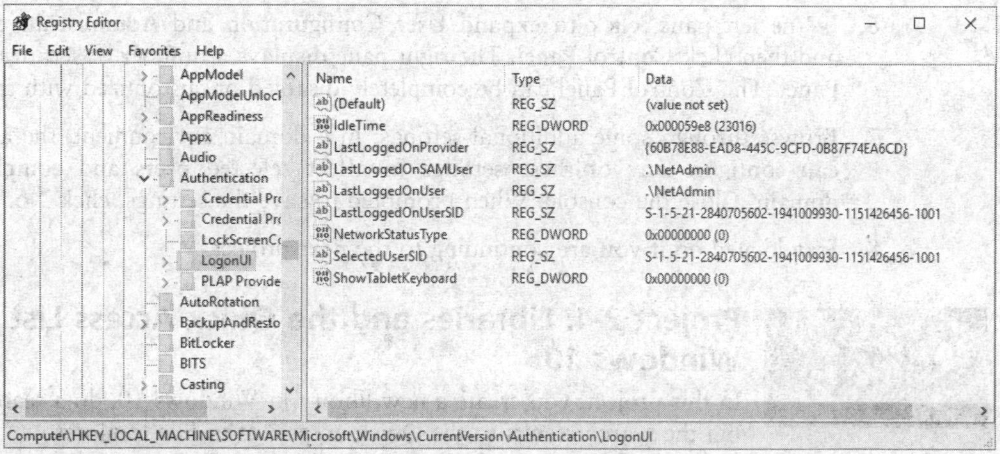


**Figure 2-20** Windows 10 registry

5. In the left pane of the registry editor, navigate to **HKEY_CURRENT_USER\Control Panel.** Right-click **Control Panel** and click **Find.** In the Find dialog box, click to uncheck **Keys** and **Data**, leaving only Values checked. In the Find what box, type **Wallpaper** and click **Find Next.** The value shows the path to the wallpaper used by the current user.
6. Close the Registry Editor.
7. Stay logged on if you are continuing to the next project.

## Project 2-3: Work with MMC and Group Policy Editor

In this project, you use the Microsoft Management Console (MMC) and load a snap-in called Local Group Policy Editor. Group Policy is used to configure aspects of your system, including the working environment. In a Windows domain, the IT administrator can configure Group Policy on Windows servers that are pushed down to domain members to maintain a consistent security and working environment for all client computers.

1. Log on to Windows 10, if necessary.
2. Click the **Search the web and Windows** text box, type **mmc**, press **Enter**, and click **Yes**.
3. In the console that opens, click **File** and click **Add/Remove Snap-in**. In the Add or Remove Snap-ins dialog box, browse through the available snap-ins. Scroll down and click **Group Policy Object Editor** (part of the name may be cut off), and then click **Add**.
4. In the Select Group Policy Object window, click **Finish**. Click **OK**.
5. In the left pane of the console, click to expand **Local Computer Policy**, **Computer Configuration**, and **Windows Settings**. Then click **Security Settings**. In the right pane, double-click **Account Policies** and then **Password Policy**. This is where policies are configured that control password and account lockout settings.
6. In the left pane, click to expand **User Configuration** and **Administrative Templates**, and then click **Control Panel**. The right pane displays a number of settings for Control Panel. The Control Panel can be completely disabled or customized with these settings.
7. Browse through some additional settings. In a domain environment, the administrator can configure any of these settings to affect selected users and computers in the domain. Close the console. When prompted to save the settings, click **No**.
8. Stay logged on if you are continuing to the next project.

## Project 2-4: Libraries and the Quick Access List in Windows 10

In this project, you create a new library in Windows 10, do a search, and then pin the search results to the Quick access list in File Explorer.

1. Log on to Windows 10, if necessary.
2. Open File Explorer by right-clicking **Start** and clicking **File Explorer**.
3. To work with libraries, you must enable them in the Navigation pane. To do so, click **View** in the File Explorer menu bar, and then click **Navigation pane**. Click to select **Show libraries**. (If Show libraries is already checked, skip this step.)
4. In the left pane of File Explorer, right-click **Libraries**, point to **New**, and click **Library**. Type **Programs** and press **Enter** to give the new library a name.
5. Right-click **Programs**, and click **Properties**. Click **Add** to add a new folder. Navigate to the C: drive and click **Program Files (x86)**. Click **Include folder**.

6. Click **Add** to add a new folder. Navigate to the C: drive and click **Program Files.** Click **Include folder.**
7. Click **Change library icon.** Choose an icon from the list and click **OK.** Click **OK** to finish creating your library. Click to expand **Programs.** In the right pane, you see a list of files and folders contained in the two folders.
8. Click the **Search Programs** text box at the top right of the File Explorer window, and type **Internet.** This search will show all files and folders whose name or contents contain the word "Internet."
9. Click the **Home** menu in File Explorer and then click **Pin to Quick access.** A new item is added under the Quick access list in the left pane of File Explorer. You see a search icon named Internet. Click **Internet** to see the search results in the right pane. From now on, you can click the Internet search icon in the Quick access list to repeat the search results. Close File Explorer.
10. Log off or shut down your Windows 10 computer.

## Project 2-5: Determine the Shell in Linux

In this project, you learn how to determine what shell you are using while in the Linux operating system. The shell serves as an interface between the user and the operating system—for example, when the user instructs the operating system to execute a program or command.

1. Start your Linux computer and log on.
2. Access the shell prompt by opening a terminal window in the Linux GNOME interface. To open a terminal window, click **Activities,** click the **Show Applications** icon, click **Utilities,** and click **Terminal.**
3. Look at the shell prompt. The $ prompt means that you are in either the Bourne, Bourne Again, or Korn shell.
4. At the shell prompt, type **echo $SHELL,** making sure that the word "SHELL" is in all capital letters. Press **Enter.** A response of /bin/bash means you are using the Bourne Again shell. If /bin/sh appears, you are in the Bourne shell. A response of /bin/ksh signifies the Korn shell.
5. If you got an error message in Step 4, enter **echo $shell,** making sure that the word "shell" is in all lowercase letters. You should see the response /bin/csh, which means that you are in the C shell.
6. At the shell prompt, type **man bash** and press **Enter** to read the online manual information about the Bourne Again shell, which is the default shell used in Fedora and Red Hat Linux distributions.
7. Press the **Spacebar** one or two times to continue reading the introductory information about the Bourne Again shell. When you are finished reading the first few pages, press **q** to exit the documentation.
8. Close the terminal window, but stay logged on to Linux for the next project.

## Project 2-6: Create a Shortcut on the Linux Activities Dash

In this project, you start a program from the Activities dash and then create a shortcut on the Activities dash.

1. From your Linux desktop, click **Activities**. You see a list of icons in a panel called the dash on the left side of the screen.
2. Click **Files** (the icon that looks like a filing cabinet) to open Files, the Linux GNOME file manager.
3. Notice that a new item is placed next to the Activities menu. The active application is shown here. Click **Files** next to Activities to see a list of options. You can open a new window, perform tasks specific to the application, view the application's preferences, get help, and quit.
4. Click the Files window again. Click **Computer** in the left pane to open the root of the file system. Double-click **Home** to open the home folder for the current user. Close **Files.**
5. Click **Activities,** click **Show Applications,** and then click **Utilities.** Right-click **Terminal** and click **Add to Favorites.** From now on, you can open a terminal window directly from the Activities dash. Click the **Activities** menu to show the desktop again.
6. Click **Activities** and then click the **Terminal** icon to start a shell prompt in a terminal window. Type **gedit** and press **Enter** to start the GNOME text editor. This editor is like Windows Notepad but has more features. Type your name and the name of the class you are taking, and then click **Save.**
7. When prompted, type **myfile** as the name of the file, click **Documents** in the left pane, and click **Save.**
8. Open Files by clicking **Activities** and clicking **Files.** Double-click **Documents** in the right pane to see the file you just created. Also notice that Files appears in the Applications menu next to Activities. Close Files. Notice that gedit now appears in the Applications menu. Close **gedit.** Close the terminal window.
9. Stay logged on if you are continuing to the next activity.

## Project 2-7: Find Files in Linux

In Linux, you can search for a file using the *find* command from the Terminal window. Alternatively, you can use the search tool in the GNOME Activities menu.

1. Open a terminal window. (Hint: You just created a shortcut to it in the previous project.)
2. At the shell prompt, type **find /home -name Desktop** and press **Enter** to search for the desktop directory within your account's home directory (see Figure 2-21). In this

context, *find* is the command to search for one or more files, */home* tells the *find* command to search for files in the /home directory, which is the parent directory for all user account directories, and *-name Desktop* is an instruction to look for all files that contain *Desktop* as part of the name.

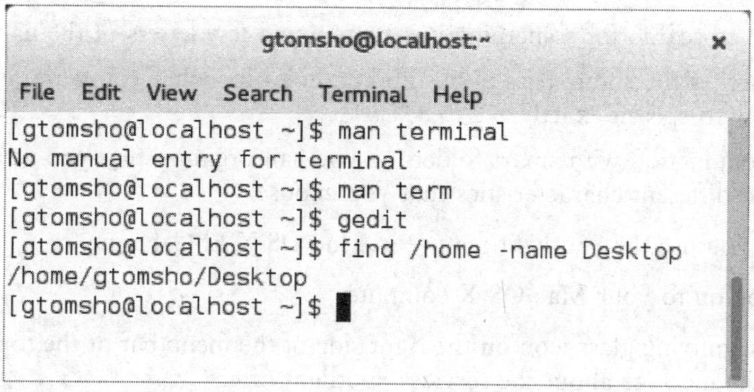


**Figure 2-21** Using the *find* command in the Linux shell

*Source: Linux*

3. Type **man find** and press **Enter** to see the manual pages for the *find* command. Scroll through the man pages to see the options available with the *find* command. Press **q** when you are finished.

4. Type **locate Desktop | more** and press **Enter**. This *locate* command uses an index to find all files and folders on the disk that include the word *Desktop*. The *| more* part of the command pipes output to the *more* command, which paginates the output. Press the **Spacebar** if necessary to scroll through the files.

5. Type **touch myDesktopfile** and press **Enter** to create a new file named myDesktopfile. Type **locate Desktop** and press **Enter**. The command does not find the file because the index has not been updated.

6. Type **sudo updatedb** and press **Enter** to update the index. Type your password when prompted, if necessary. The *updatedb* command must be run as the superuser and therefore requires you to enter your password in most cases.

7. Type **locate Desktop | more** and press **Enter**. You should see the myDesktopfile in the listing. Close the Terminal window.

8. Click **Activities**, click the **Type to search** text box, and type **Desktop.** Don't press Enter. Linux finds all items related to the desktop and all files that have the word *Desktop* as part of the name. If you press Enter, you will run any applications found that are related to Desktop.

9. In the search results, click the folder named **Desktop** to open the folder in Files.

10. Close **Files**.

11. Log off or shut down your Linux computer.

## Project 2-8: Use Spotlight in Mac OS X

Mac OS X was among the first operating systems to offer faster searches by providing Spotlight. Spotlight offers the following:

- Indexes files so you can find them faster
- Enables you to search for something just by typing a few letters of the name
- Quickly searches the computer's nooks and crannies for what you want, even if you're not sure how to spell it exactly
- Works in conjunction with smart folders so you can organize files you've found according to different characteristics that you choose

In this project, you use the Spotlight feature in Mac OS X El Capitan.

1. Start and log on to your Mac OS X computer.
2. Click the magnifying glass icon on the right side of the menu bar at the top of the desktop. Read the message about the services Spotlight offers.
3. Type **d**. Notice that Spotlight starts an instant search (see Figure 2-22).

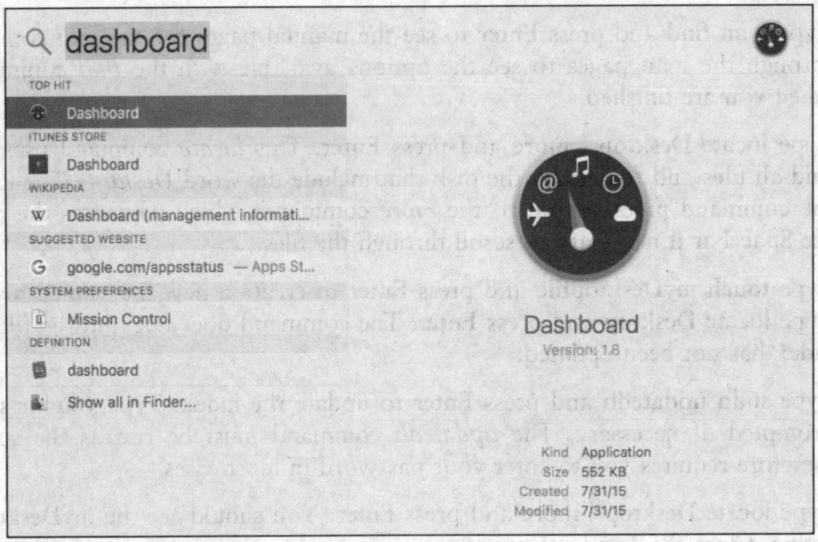


**Figure 2-22** Performing a Spotlight search in Mac OS X
*Source: Mac OS X El Capitan*

4. Slowly type the remaining letters, **ashboard**, to see how Spotlight changes its display.
5. In the right pane, double-click **Dashboard** to open it. Dashboard is a collection of widgets. Close Dashboard by clicking the circle icon with the arrow in the lower-right corner.
6. Open Spotlight again by clicking the magnifying glass icon.
7. Delete **dashboard** in the search box.

8. Type **itunes**. The item under Top Hits is Spotlight's best guess about which item is most likely the one you want.
9. Delete **itunes** and type **jpg**.
10. Click one of the images listed (with a .jpg extension). Notice that the picture is previewed in the right pane.
11. Click somewhere on the desktop to close Spotlight.
12. Stay logged on if you are continuing to the next project.

## Project 2-9: Examine the Menus in Mac OS X

In this project, you examine the Mac OS X menu bar options on the desktop.

To view the Mac OS X desktop and menu bar options:

1. Log on to your Mac OS X computer, if necessary.
2. Click **Finder** in the menu bar to display the Finder menu selections. Finder enables you to manage features on the desktop as well as empty the trash (deleted files and folders) or secure emptied trash. Click **Preferences** in the Finder menu. The Finder Preferences window enables you to set up preferences for desktop features, such as specifying items to display on the desktop, including disk drives (see Figure 2-23).

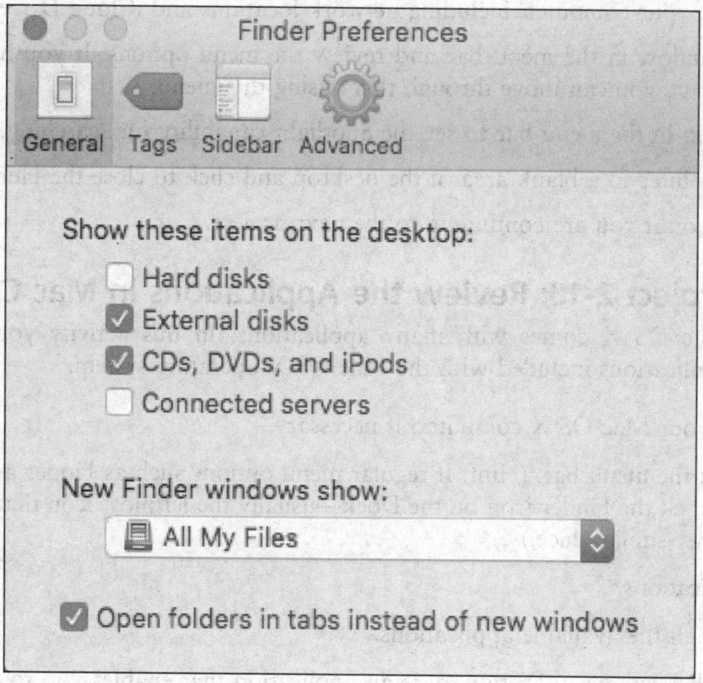


**Figure 2-23** Finder preferences

*Source: Mac OS X El Capitan*

3. Click each of the buttons in the Finder Preferences window as listed below:
    - **General**—Specify items to display on the desktop, such as hard drives, and determine where to open windows and set folder properties.
    - **Tags**—Color-code labels used in windows so that windows can be sorted by color.
    - **Sidebar**—Designate what appears in the Sidebar shown in open windows. For example, you can display links for quick access to devices, documents, and shared resources.
    - **Advanced**—Configure options for file extensions, emptying the trash (deleted files), and where to perform searches.
4. Close the Finder Preferences window.
5. Click **File** in the menu bar and review the options in the File menu. From here you can open a new Finder window, open and create files, and save items to a portable drive.
6. Point to **Edit** in the menu bar and notice the options that can be used while editing, such as cut and copy. (These options are only available if you are editing a file.)
7. Point to **View** in the menu bar. Notice the options that can be used to manage the presentation of items in a window, such as displaying items as icons or a list.
8. Point to **Go** in the menu bar and notice its options. From here, you can open various locations on your computer, including network locations and iCloud Drive.
9. Point to **Window** in the menu bar and review the menu options. If you have multiple windows open, you can move through them using this menu.
10. Point to **Help** in the menu bar to see the Spotlight capability for searching.
11. Move the pointer to a blank area of the desktop and click to close the Help menu.
12. Stay logged on if you are continuing to the next project.

Enter
HANDS-ON PROJECTS

## Project 2-10: Review the Applications in Mac OS X

Mac OS X comes with many applications. In this activity you review the applications included with the Mac OS X operating system.

1. Log on to your Mac OS X computer, if necessary.
2. Click **Go** in the menu bar. (Hint: If regular menu options such as Finder and Go aren't displayed, click the Finder icon on the Dock—usually the leftmost icon that looks like a blue and gray smiling face.)
3. Click **Applications.**
4. Scroll through the available applications.
5. Double-click **Dictionary**. Dictionary is an application that enables you to quickly look up the meaning of a word or determine its spelling.
6. Type **folder** in the Spotlight box.

7. Read the definition for *folder*. Close the Dictionary window.
8. Double-click **TextEdit** in the Applications window. Like most OSs, Mac OS X has a basic text editor. Close TextEdit.
9. Double-click **Safari** in the Applications window. Safari is the native Mac OS X Web browser. Close Safari.
10. Double-click **LaunchPad** in the Applications window. LaunchPad provides another method for starting applications in Mac OS X. Click **Notes.** Notice that you only need to single-click the application icon to start it. Leave Notes open.
11. Click the **Safari** icon in the Dock. Press and hold the green maximize button in Safari, and then slide the Safari window to the left side of the screen until it snaps into place. Double-click the Notes window; it snaps into place on the right side of the screen. This is called Split View.
12. Close the Safari window and the Notes window. Close the Applications window.
13. Log off or shut down your Mac OS X computer.

## Critical Thinking

The following activities give you critical thinking challenges. Challenge Labs give you an opportunity to use the skills you have learned to perform a task without step-by-step instructions. Case Projects present a practical problem for which you supply a written solution. Not all chapters contain Challenge Labs. There is not always a specific right or wrong answer to these critical thinking exercises. They are intended to encourage you to review the chapter material and delve deeper into the topics you have learned.

## Case Projects

The following scenario is used for Case Projects 2-1 through 2-6:

Darts is a sporting goods company with outlets in most of the western states. This company has a network of 10 servers and 273 client computers that have the following operating systems:

- Eight Windows Server 2008 servers
- Two Linux servers running Red Hat Linux Enterprise
- 20 computers running Mac OS X version 10.7 Lion
- 32 computers running Windows 10
- 80 computers running Windows 8.1
- 46 computers running Windows Vista
- 95 computers running Windows XP

Darts realizes that with the projected growth of the company, they need to upgrade the computers and servers on their network.

## Case Project 2-1: Accounting Department Upgrade

The Accounting Department has all of the Windows XP computers. The accounting director wants to upgrade to Windows 10. What are the advantages of upgrading for this department in terms of the enhanced operating system functions that are available in Windows 10? What are some possible disadvantages?

## Case Project 2-2: Legacy Billing System

If the Accounting Department does upgrade to Windows 10, will the department be able to run a legacy 16-bit billing program that was designed for Windows XP?

## Case Project 2-3: New Computer for the Marketing Department

The Marketing Department uses the Mac OS X version 10.7 Lion computers. Because they plan to purchase new computers, what is the newest Mac operating system to which they can upgrade? What would be the advantage of this upgrade for their department?

## Case Project 2-4: President's Problem

The president of Darts is convinced that the processor on his Windows Vista system is overloaded. How can you help him determine if there is a problem with the processor?

## Case Project 2-5: Chief Financial Officer's Concerns

The new chief financial officer believes that all of the Windows XP computers should be upgraded to Windows 10 because Windows 8.1 was not well received in the marketplace. What are the advantages and disadvantages of upgrading to Windows 10 compared to Windows 8.1? Include a discussion of the total cost of the upgrade (TCO).

## Case Project 2-6: Server Upgrades

What would be the advantage of upgrading the Windows Server 2008 servers, and if you recommend upgrading them, what operating system do you recommend? Why?

chapter 3

# The Central Processing Unit (CPU)

**After reading this chapter and completing the exercises, you will be able to:**

- Describe the function and features of CPUs
- Identify features of popular CPUs from various manufacturers

**Operating systems and hardware work together to make computers useful for** business, educational, personal, network, and cloud computing applications. The features of an operating system used for a particular application depend on the capabilities of the hardware. In many cases, modern operating systems do not support older hardware. When you upgrade an operating system, you may need to upgrade the hardware to match the new operating system's capabilities.

This chapter focuses on the CPU and its surrounding electronics, including CPU architecture, clock speeds, and buses. In addition, you learn how CPUs are used by particular operating systems.

# Understanding CPUs

As you learned in Chapter 1, "Operating Systems Fundamentals," one of the main functions of the operating system is to provide the interface between the various application programs running on a computer and the hardware inside. Central to understanding the hardware is the system architecture of the computer, which is built around the CPU, or processor. The **system architecture** includes the number and type of CPUs in the hardware, and the communication routes, called buses, between the CPUs and other hardware components, such as memory and disk storage. A **bus** is a path or channel between a computer's CPU and the devices it manages, such as memory and I/O devices.

The CPU is the chip that performs the actual computational and logic work. Most modern PCs have one such chip, and are referred to as **single-processor computers**. In reality, to ensure complete functionality, the CPU requires several support chips, such as chips that help manage communications with devices and device drivers.

Chip technology continues to develop with the addition of multicore processors. A processor **core** is the part of a CPU that reads and executes very basic instructions, such as reading and writing data from and to memory or executing an arithmetic operation. CPUs were originally created to have only one core and thus perform only one instruction at a time. A multicore processor has two or more cores—for example, a dual-core processor contains two cores and a quad-core processor has four. The most processor cores used in traditional PC desktops and servers is 16 as of this writing, but high-end CPUs, such as Intel's Knights Landing, have up to 72 cores. Development continues in this area, and scientists so far have put as many as 1000 cores on a single CPU chip.

Some computers have multiple physical CPUs; many have two, and some have as many as 128 or more. This type of computer is generally referred to as a **multiprocessor computer**. You will take a closer look at single-processor, multiprocessor, and multicore computers later in this chapter.

# Basic CPU Architecture

We will discuss different design types of CPUs and various components of a CPU, but before we do, let's take a look at its basic architecture. Most CPUs are composed of the following elements (see Figure 3-1):

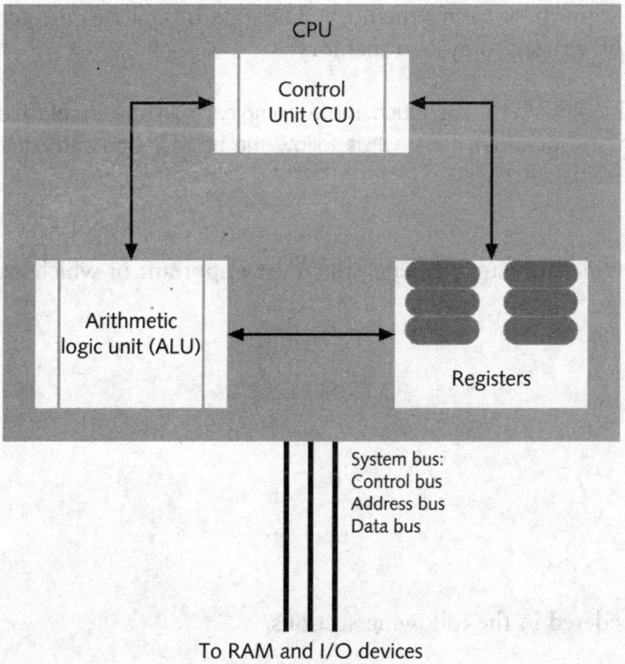


**Figure 3-1** Basic architecture of a CPU

- *Control unit*—The **control unit** (CU) is the director of operations in the CPU. The control unit provides timing and coordination between the other parts of the CPU, such as the arithmetic logic unit, registers, and system bus. For example, when a new instruction should be executed, the control unit receives and decodes the instruction and tells the arithmetic logic unit to execute it.
- *Arithmetic logic unit*—The **arithmetic logic unit** (**ALU**) performs the primary task of any CPU, which is to execute instructions. These might be arithmetic instructions, such as addition or multiplication of integers, or logic instructions, such as binary AND or binary OR instructions. Most CPUs also contain a **floating point unit** (**FPU**) that performs floating point operations.
- *Registers*—A **register** is a temporary holding location on a CPU where data must be placed before the CPU can use it. There are instruction registers that hold the instruction the CPU executes, such as add, multiply, or store. Also, the CPU uses address registers to access data stored in RAM, and data registers that hold the data the CPU is currently working with, such as two numbers used in an add or multiply instruction.
- *System bus*—The system bus is a series of lanes that are used to communicate between the CPU and other major parts of the computer, such as RAM and input/output (I/O) devices. There are actually three types of buses: the control bus, address bus, and data bus. The **control bus** carries status signals between the CPU and other devices. Status signals inform the CPU that a device needs attention; for example, when an input device has data ready, the CPU must execute the device driver code to read the data from the device. The **address bus** carries address signals to indicate where data should

be read from or written to in the system's memory. The **data bus** carries the actual data that is being read from or written to system memory.

While modern CPUs are much more complex than the simple block diagram in Figure 3-1, most CPUs follow the basic design and contain the elements described.

CPUs can be classified by several hardware elements, the most important of which are:

- Design type
- Speed
- Cache
- Address bus
- Data bus
- Control bus
- CPU scheduling

Each of these elements is considered in the following sections.

## Design Type

Two general CPU designs are used in today's computers: **Complex Instruction Set Computing (CISC)** and **Reduced Instruction Set Computing (RISC)**. The main difference between the two is the number of different instructions the chip can process and the complexity of the instructions. When a program executes on a computer, the CPU reads instruction after instruction from the program to perform the tasks specified in the program. When the CPU has read such an instruction, it carries out the associated operations. The CPU can process as many as 20 million complex operations per second on the low end, and several billion on the high end. Clock speed and CPU design are the factors that determine how fast operations are executed. It is convenient for the programmer to have many instructions available to perform many different operations.

Let's say, for example, that the programmer wants to multiply two numbers. It would be convenient to give the CPU the two numbers, then tell it to multiply them and display the result. Because different kinds of numbers (such as integers and real numbers) must be treated differently, it would be nice if there were functions to perform this multiplication on all number types. You can see that as we require the CPU to perform more and more functions, the number of instructions can rapidly increase. The **instruction set**, or the list of commands the CPU can understand and carry out, can become quite complex as programs perform more functions. A processor that works like this is called a CISC CPU.

CISC and RISC CPUs differ in the following ways:

- *Complex versus simple instructions*—CISC CPUs are generally more complex, meaning each instruction does more work than a single RISC instruction. Some instructions carried out by CISC CPUs may require several RISC instructions to perform the same task. For example, say you want to add two numbers that are stored in memory locations X and Y and store the result back in memory location X. The CISC CPU code might look like the following:

```
add X, Y
```

Behind the scenes, the CPU must load the data from location X into one of its registers, load the data from location Y into another one of its registers, perform the calculation, the result of which is stored in another register, and then move the result back into memory location X. To perform the same task with a RISC processor, you might have several instructions:

```
load R1, X
load R2, Y
add R1, R2
stor R1, X
```

In the above example, the RISC CPU requires four instructions: two to load the numbers to be added from memory (X and Y) into registers (R1 and R2), one to perform the addition, and one to store the result from its register (R1) back to memory (X). As you can see, CISC instructions are much more complex because they do a lot of work that doesn't require specific instructions, whereas RISC CPUs require the programmer (or compiler) to explicitly write those instructions. Based on the above example, what advantage is there in using a RISC CPU? It has to do with clock cycles.

- *Clock cycles*—The single add instruction on a CISC CPU might take four CPU clock cycles, whereas each of the four instructions carried out by the RISC CPU will take one clock cycle each. In this example, it takes both CPU types the same number of clock cycles to perform the same task. Some instructions on CISC CPUs might require one clock cycle; others might need two, four, or more clock cycles. Conversely, most instructions on RISC CPUs take only one clock cycle. Because the instructions on RISC CPUs take a uniform number of clock cycles, designers can use this fact to their advantage with pipelining.
- *Pipelining*—**Pipelining** is the ability of the CPU to perform more than one task on a single clock cycle. For example, if you have a series of additions to perform, a RISC processor doesn't have to wait for all four instructions to complete before it moves on to the next addition. While the second load instruction of the first addition is being performed, the RISC processor can be loading the first value for the next addition. While pipelining does occur in CISC CPUs, the varying number of cycles it takes to complete each instruction makes pipelining more difficult and not as effective, compared to RISC CPUs. Figure 3-2 shows how pipelining and the number of cycles required per instruction can affect execution time. In the figure, a CISC CPU and RISC CPU are each performing a series of three additions. With the CISC CPU, only three instructions are required, but each instruction takes four clock cycles and the first instruction is completed before the second instruction is started. With the RISC CPU, each addition takes four instructions of one clock cycle each, but using pipelining, the second addition is started while the first addition is still under way, allowing the RISC CPU to complete all three additions in only six cycles, as opposed to 12 cycles for the CISC CPU.

CISC CPU

Three additions in 12 clock cycles

| Clock cycles | | | | | | | | | | | |
|---|---|---|---|---|---|---|---|---|---|---|---|
| 1 | 2 | 3 | 4 | 5 | 6 | 7 | 8 | 9 | 10 | 11 | 12 |
| add (1st addition) | | | | add (2nd addition) | | | | add (3rd addition) | | | |

RISC CPU

Three additions in 6 clock cycles

| Clock cycles | | | | | | |
|---|---|---|---|---|---|---|
| 1 | 2 | 3 | 4 | 5 | 6 | |
| load | load | add | stor | | | 1st addition |
| | load | load | add | stor | | 2nd addition |
| | | load | load | add | stor | 3rd addition |

**Figure 3-2** CISC processing versus RISC processing using pipelining

- *Hardware versus microcode*—Because CISC instructions are so complex, there is actually a small program inside the chip that must interpret and execute each instruction. This small program is called **microcode**. RISC instructions are all executed directly by the CPU hardware, with no microcode middleman. This approach makes for faster execution of individual instructions.
- *Compiler*—A **compiler** is a computer program that takes a high-level language like C# or Java and turns it into assembly code that is executed by the CPU. Due to the complexity of CISC-based instructions, the compiler has less work to do because the high-level language code need not be broken down into as many assembly language steps. Taking the example of an addition instruction from before, the C# or Java code might look like the following:

```
X = X + Y;
```

The compiler then translates that statement into assembly code for a CISC CPU. The assembly code might also be a single line of code:

```
add X, Y
```

By comparison, several lines of code might be needed when the compiler translates the statement into assembly code for a RISC CPU:

```
load R1, X

load R2, Y

add R1, R2

stor R1, X
```

After a high-level language program is compiled to assembly language, another step called *assembly* is needed before it can be executed by the CPU. Assembly translates assembly code into machine code. With machine code, each assembly language statement is translated into a series of numbers—for example, the statement *load R1, X* might be translated to something like 09 101 2215. Remember, computers can only interpret numeric values; the software they run translates numbers into human-readable form, and vice versa.

- *Number and usage of registers*—As mentioned, a register is a temporary holding location on a CPU where data must be placed before the CPU can use it. Because so much room is used for microcode on CISC CPUs, there are far fewer registers than on a RISC chip, which doesn't use microcode. The more registers there are, the more simultaneous operations the CPU can perform, as you saw with pipelining. One of the reasons pipelining is easier with RISC CPUs is because there are more registers to store data for pipelined instructions. In addition, CISC CPUs erase their registers after each instruction and require them to be reloaded with each successive instruction, whereas RISC CPUs can leave data in registers until the register is needed for another operation.

CISC and RISC CPUs continue to be produced. The debate between which is better is muddied by the inclusion of CISC features in RISC CPUs and RISC features in CISC CPUs. Intel processors are still considered to be CISC.

## Speed

The speed of a CPU defines how fast it can perform operations. There are many ways to indicate speed, but the most frequently used indicator is the **internal clock speed** of the CPU. As you may know, a CPU runs on a very rigid schedule along with the rest of the computer. The clock provides this schedule to make sure that all the chips know what to expect at a given time. The internal clock speed tells you how many clock pulses, or ticks, are available per second. Typically, the CPU performs some action on every tick. The more ticks per second there are, the faster the CPU executes commands, and the harder the electronics on the CPU must work. The clock speed for a CPU can be lower than 1 million ticks per second (1 megahertz or MHz) or higher than 4 billion ticks per second (4 gigahertz or GHz). The faster the clock is, the faster the CPU, and the more expensive the hardware. Also, as more components are needed to make a CPU, the chip uses more energy to do its work. Part of this energy is converted to heat, causing faster CPUs to run warmer, which requires more fans in the chassis. Overheating of computer components in general and CPUs in particular is a constant battle faced by IT departments; it requires considerable investment in the cooling systems of data centers.

**From the Trenches ...**

A college upgraded from 1.8 GHz computers to a model running at 3.06 GHz. The computers were plugged in and ran for about five minutes before the video became scrambled and stopped working. Several calls were made to customer service; after four days of work, technicians determined that the computers had a heating problem. The computers were built at sea level, where they worked just fine, but the college was in a city at an elevation of over 5000 feet. Air contains fewer molecules as the altitude increases. Molecules hitting the surface of the CPU carry away the heat, and at higher elevations, there aren't as many molecules, so there is less air movement to cool the warmer CPUs. These warmer CPUs were overheating the video circuitry and causing the problems. The manufacturer's addition of dual-chassis fans to each computer corrected the problem.

In addition to performing fast operations inside the CPU, the chips must be able to communicate with the other chips in the computer. This is where the **external clock speed** of the CPU comes in. While a CPU may run internally at a speed of 3 GHz, it typically uses a lower clock speed to communicate with the rest of the computer. The reason for the lower speed is again cost, to a large extent. It would be extremely expensive to make every component in the computer run as fast as the CPU. Therefore, the other components in the computer typically run at a reduced clock rate. Usually, the external clock speed is one-half, one-third, one-fourth, or one-eighth the speed of the internal CPU clock.

## Cache

If a CPU wants to get a few numbers out of memory, and its internal clock speed is four times faster than its external clock speed, it obviously must wait on the external clock, which could be very inefficient. To avoid this problem, modern CPUs have **cache memory** built into the chip. Cache memory works by providing extremely fast access to data so the CPU doesn't have to wait for main RAM. While the CPU is executing program code, instructions or data that are most likely to be used next are fetched from main memory and placed in cache memory. When the CPU needs the next bytes of data or the next instruction, it looks in cache first. If the information cannot be found, the CPU then fetches it from main memory. The more often the CPU can find the data in cache, the faster the program will execute. There are different levels of cache, with each successive level becoming larger, but slower:

- *Level 1 cache*—**Level 1 (L1) cache** is the fastest of the cache types; usually it runs at the same speed as the CPU, so the CPU won't have to wait for data if it can be found in L1 cache. However, L1 cache is the least plentiful—typically 8 to 32 KB per processor core—so it can't hold much data. L1 cache is usually divided into two parts: instruction cache and data cache. L1 cache is always an integral part of the CPU chip on modern CPUs.
- *Level 2 cache*—**Level 2 (L2) cache** is somewhat slower than L1 cache, but much larger. Many CPUs today have 256 KB of L2 cache per processor core. The combination of L1 cache and L2 cache greatly increases the chances that the data the CPU needs will

be located in cache, so the CPU will not have to access much slower main memory. L2 cache is also an integral part of the CPU chip on modern CPUs.

- *Level 3 cache*—**Level 3 (L3) cache**, until the last several years, was not part of the CPU chip, but was instead a part of the motherboard. This meant that L3 cache could be fairly large, but considerably slower than L1 and L2 cache. On the more advanced CPUs, L3 cache is part of the CPU and is shared among the CPU cores. L3 cache can often be found in sizes of 8 MB, 16 MB, and greater.
- *Level 4 cache*—**Level 4 (L4) cache**, if it exists, will usually be found on the motherboard. If a CPU has L1, L2, and L3 cache and is installed on a motherboard that has built-in cache, the cache on the motherboard will become L4 cache. If a CPU only has L1 and L2 cache, the motherboard cache will become L3 cache. The exception is the high-end version of some CPUs that are starting to come with on-board L4 cache. Some of these high-end CPUs have as much as 128 MB of L4 cache that is shared among the CPU cores.

The amount of cache, especially for larger CPUs, determines the speed of the CPU. In many cases, up to 95 percent of the data a CPU needs to transfer to and from memory is present in one of the caches when the CPU needs it. A specialized piece of hardware called the **cache controller** predicts what data will be needed, and makes that data available in cache before it is needed. Most modern CPUs can also use the cache to write data to memory and ensure that the CPU will not have to wait when it wants to write results to memory. You can see that intelligent, fast cache controllers and large amounts of cache are important components for increasing the speed of a CPU.

## Address Bus

The address bus is an internal communications pathway that specifies the source and target addresses for memory reads and writes. It is instrumental in the transfer of data to and from computer memory. The address bus typically runs at the external clock speed of the CPU. The address, like all data in the computer, is in digital form and is conveyed as a series of bits. The width of the address bus is the number of bits that can be used to address memory. A wider bus means the computer can address more memory, and therefore store more data or larger, more complex programs. For example, a 16-bit address bus can address 64 kilobytes, or KB (65,536 bytes) of memory, and a 32-bit address bus can address roughly 4 billion bytes, or 4 gigabytes (GB) of memory. Modern processors have a 64-bit address bus, allowing them to address 16 terabytes (TB) of memory.

## Data Bus

The data bus allows computer components, such as the CPU, display adapter, and main memory, to share information. The number of bits in the data bus indicates how many bits of data can be transferred from memory to the CPU, or vice versa, in a single operation. A CPU with an external clock speed of 1 GHz will have 1 billion ticks per second to the external bus. If this CPU has a 16-bit data bus, it could theoretically transfer 2 GB (2,000,000,000 bytes) of data to and from memory every second. (One byte consists of 8 bits, so 1 billion × 16 bits/8 bits per second = 2 GB per second.) A CPU with an external clock speed of 1 GHz and a 64-bit data bus could transfer as much as 8 GB per second (1 billion × 64 bits/8 bits per byte). That is four times as much data in the same time period, so in theory, the CPU will work four times as fast.

There are a couple of catches here. First, the software must be able to instruct the CPU to use all of the data bus, and the rest of the computer must be fast enough to keep up with the CPU. Most CPUs work internally with the same number of bits as on the data bus. In other words, a CPU with a 64-bit data bus can typically perform operations on 64 bits of data at a time. Almost all CPUs can also be instructed to work with chunks of data narrower than the data bus width, but in this case the CPU is not as efficient because the same number of clock cycles is required to perform an operation, whether or not all bits are used. All Windows versions from Windows XP forward include a 64-bit version, and starting with Windows Server 2008 R2, all server versions are 64-bit only.

## Control Bus

The CPU is kept informed of the status of the computer's resources and devices, such as the memory and disk drives, by information transported on the control bus. The most basic information transported across the control bus indicates whether a particular resource is active and can be accessed. If a disk drive becomes active, for example, the disk controller provides this information to the CPU over the control bus. Other information that may be transported over the control bus includes whether a particular function is for input or output. Memory read and write status is transported on this bus, as well as **interrupt requests (IRQs)**. An interrupt request is a request to the processor to "interrupt" whatever it is doing to take care of a process, such as a read from a disk drive, which in turn might be interrupted by another process, such as a write into memory.

## CPU Scheduling

CPU scheduling determines which process to execute when multiple processes are waiting to run. For example, if you have three applications open on your computer, each application must be scheduled to get CPU time. The CPU switches between the applications very quickly based on factors like priority, so users don't typically notice that this switching, or *time-slicing*, is occurring. CPU scheduling is not a function built into the CPU; rather, it is a function of the operating system. However, the architecture of the CPU can greatly facilitate a system's ability to efficiently schedule multiple processes. Recall from Chapter 1 that a process is a program that's loaded into memory and run by the CPU. Most PC operating systems of the 1970s and 1980s were basically single threaded, meaning they could only schedule the process to run as a whole. Beginning with the Windows NT operating system, the use of CPU scheduling algorithms began to evolve to allow **multithreading**, which is the ability to run two or more parts of a process, known as threads, at the same time. A **thread** is the smallest piece of computer code that can be independently scheduled for execution. For example, if a user is running a word processor, one thread might accept input from the keyboard and format it on the screen while another thread does a spell check as the user types. Switching between threads takes a considerable number of CPU instructions to accomplish, so it was only practical to begin including this feature in OSs when CPUs became powerful enough to support it. Modern CPUs with multiple cores are designed specifically for multithreading, so switching between threads is extremely efficient when compared to the operation in older CPUs. Some Intel CPUs contain a feature called Hyper-Threading.

**Hyper-Threading** (HT) allows two threads to run on each CPU core simultaneously. In some ways, this feature doubles the amount of work a CPU can do. When monitoring a CPU with a program such as Task Manager, each CPU core is actually seen as two logical processors, so a 4-core CPU will be reported as having 8 logical processors.

# Popular PC Processors

The following sections provide an overview of the CPUs found in PCs and of more powerful 64-bit processors that are available for PCs and servers.

## Intel

The most popular CPUs used in PCs today are designed by Intel. The first player in this line of processors was the 8088, the CPU found in the original IBM PC. Early Intel CPUs were identified by model numbers: 8088, 8086, 80286, 80386, and 80486. The model numbers are sometimes shown without the 80 prefix, or are preceded by an "i," as in 80486, 486, or i486. The Pentium family of chips followed the 486 (*penta* means five in Greek). Pentium chips are sometimes identified with just a P and a number—for example, P4 for Pentium 4. Table 3-1 lists single-processor Intel CPUs, including the Celeron, Pentium III, and Pentium 4. The Intel Itanium and Itanium 2 are 64-bit processors designed for higher-end PCs and servers. Notice the trends in Table 3-1 toward ever-faster internal and external clock speeds, more and larger cache, and increasing capability to handle multimedia and large amounts of data.

**Table 3-1 Single-core Intel CPUs**

| CPU | Year introduced | Data bus/ address bus bits | Internal clock speed | External clock speed | Cache | Comments |
|---|---|---|---|---|---|---|
| 8088 | 1978 | 8/20 | 4–8 MHz | 4–8 MHz | No | CPU of the first IBM PC. |
| 8086 | 1978 | 16/20 | 4–16 MHz | 4–16 MHz | No | First Intel CPU to have a 16-bit data path. |
| 80286 | 1982 | 16/24 | 8–40 MHz | 8–40 MHz | No | Beginning of the 80x86 line. |
| 80386SX | 1985 | 16/24 | 16–40 MHz | 16–40 MHz | No | Less expensive version of 386 chip; supported only 16-bit data bus. |
| 80386DX | 1985 | 32/24 | 16–40 MHz | 16–40 MHz | No | Introduced 32-bit data bus. |
| 80486SX | 1989 | 16/24 | 16–80 MHz | 16–40 MHz | Yes | Less expensive version of 486 chip; supported only 16-bit data bus. |
| 80486DX | 1989 | 32/24 | 16–120 MHz | 16–40 MHz | Yes | First Intel chip to use different internal and external clocks, include a math coprocessor, and include L1 cache on the chip as well as features for external L2 cache. |
| Pentium | 1993 | 32/28 | 16–266 MHz | 16–66 MHz | Yes | More instructions added and L1 cache was made more efficient. |

(*continues*)

**Table 3-1 Single-core Intel CPUs (*continued*)**

| CPU | Year introduced | Data bus/ address bus bits | Internal clock speed | External clock speed | Cache | Comments |
|---|---|---|---|---|---|---|
| Pentium Pro | 1995 | 64/28 | 33–200 MHz | 33–50 MHz | Yes | Optimized for running 32-bit instructions. Intel also released the Multimedia Extension (MMX), with new instructions to deal with multimedia and handling large amounts of data. |
| Pentium II | 1997 | 64/36 | 66–550 MHz | 66–100 MHz | Yes | Inclusion of L1 cache running at internal clock speed as well as L2 cache running at external or twice the external clock speed; both were built right onto the CPU module. |
| Xeon | 1998 | 64/36 | 500 MHz–3.66 GHz | 400–800 MHz | Yes | Offered as a version of the Pentium II and Pentium III processors. Used a new L2 caching technique that was twice as fast as non-Xeon processors. The newer Xeon MP chips also had a new instruction set that improved video, encryption, and authentication performance—features important for busy Web servers. It also used Hyper-Threading technology, and L3 cache of 512 KB, 1 MB, or 2 MB was available. |
| Celeron | 1998 | 64/36 | 850 MHz–3.06 GHz | 66–800 MHz | Yes | Low-end processor for PC multimedia and home markets. |
| Pentium III | 1999 | 64/36 | 600 MHz–1.2 GHz | 100–133 MHz | Yes | Introduced Streaming SIMD Extensions. SIMD, which stands for *single-instruction, multiple-data* stream processing, is an instruction set designed to provide better multimedia processing. |
| Pentium 4 | 2001 | 64/36 | 1.3–3.88 GHz | 400–1066 MHz | Yes | Included two math coprocessors; also used execution-based cache. Extreme Edition supported Hyper-Threading, a technology that enables a single processor to appear to the operating system as two separate processors. The Pentium 4 had a similar architecture to the Xeon MP but added an execution-based cache, which was even faster than the original Xeon cache. |

**Table 3-1** Single-core Intel CPUs (*continued*)

| CPU | Year introduced | Data bus/ address bus bits | Internal clock speed | External clock speed | Cache | Comments |
|---|---|---|---|---|---|---|
| Itanium | 2001 | 64/128 | 733–800 MHz | 266 MHz | Yes | First RISC-based Intel chip, 64-bit with EPIC architecture; designed for high-end PC workstations and servers. |
| Itanium 2 | 2002 | 64/128 | 1.3–1.5 GHz | 400 MHz | Yes | Extended the Itanium family of CPU chips; optimized for dual-processor servers and workstations. |
| Pentium M | 2003 | 64/36 | 900 MHz–2.26 GHz | 400–533 MHz | Yes | Pentium M referred to a group of mobile single-core processors. |
| Multicore processors | Table 3-2 lists Intel multicore processors starting with the Pentium D. | | | | | |

A very important feature of Intel CPUs is **backward compatibility**, which means that a significant number of features from an older chip can function on a newer chip. For example, code written to run on an 8088 processor runs on a newer CPU without change. Because the 8088 code is 16-bit code, it does not use many of the advanced features of the newer CPUs, and it runs more slowly than code written especially for the CPU. Backward compatibility is one of the major reasons for the success of the Intel line of CPUs. The Itanium line of Intel CPU chips is not backward-compatible.

The Intel Itanium and Itanium 2 processors are a significant departure from previous Intel processors in two respects: they are built on the RISC-based EPIC architecture and they are 64-bit chips. The Itanium features the complete EPIC design allotment of 256 64-bit registers that can operate as rotating registers. In order to use the capabilities of the Itanium 64-bit processor, the operating system and applications must be recompiled or rewritten to use 64-bit processing.

The Intel Itanium processor is intended for very large-scale operations that match powerful mainframes. For this reason, the chip architecture and bus design include the capability to run more than 1000 processors as a group.

Initially, processors were developed with one core, which executed the program instructions. Today, these cores are independent of each other and are packaged on a single chip. Some processors today contain 6, 8, 12, 16, and even more cores. Multicore processors are the norm today, and even smartphones and tablets frequently contain two or four cores.

Table 3-2 lists multicore Intel CPUs along with the number of cores and the cache size. Notice that the Intel Core i3, i5, and i7 processors have bus speeds referred to in terms of GT/s, or gigatransfers per second.

These tables are not intended to be comprehensive; rather, they are intended to show the progression of CPUs and CPU architecture through the years.

**Table 3-2 Multicore Intel CPUs**

| CPU | Year introduced | Cores | Speed | Bus speed | Cache |
|---|---|---|---|---|---|
| Pentium D | 2005 | 2 | 2.64–3.60 GHz | 533–1055 MHz | 1–2 MB |
| Xeon | 2005 | 2–8 | 1.68–3.73 GHz | 667–1600 MHz | 2–24 MB |
| Itanium | 2006 | 2–4 | 1.40–1.73 GHz | 400–667 MHz | 8–24 MB |
| Intel Core Solo | 2006 | 1 | 1.06–1.86 GHz | 533–667 MHz | 2 MB |
| Intel Core Duo | 2006 | 2 | 1.06–2.33 GHz | 533–667 MHz | 2 MB |
| Pentium Dual-Core | 2007 | 2 | 1.60–3.33 GHz | 800–1066 MHz | 1–2 MB |
| Intel Core 2 Duo | 2007 | 2 | 1.86–3.33 GHz | 800–1333 MHz | 3–6 MB |
| Intel Core 2 Quad | 2007 | 4 | 2.33–3.00 GHz | 1066–1333 MHz | 4–12 MB |
| Intel Core 2 Extreme | 2008 | 2 | 2.00–3.20 GHz | 1066–1600 MHz | 6–12 MB |
| Atom | 2008 | 1 | 800 MHz–2.13 GHz | 400–533 MHz | 512 KB–1 MB |
| Intel Core i7 | 2009 | 4–6 | 1.06–3.33 GHz | 2.5 GT/s–4.8 GT/s | 4–12 MB |
| Intel Core i5 | 2009 | 2–4 | 1.06–3.76 GHz | 2.5 GT/s | 3–8 MB |
| Intel Core i3 | 2010 | 2 | 1.20–3.06 GHz | 2.5 GT/s | 4 MB |

Table 3-2 stops with processors released in 2010, but that doesn't mean Intel stopped developing new CPUs. For the most part, Intel has maintained the same naming structure for its products, with new processors named Pentium, Core i3, Core i5, and Core i7. Intel differentiates its models by adding a number and microarchitecture code name after the name of the CPU. **Microarchitecture** is the description of a CPU's internal circuitry, defining characteristics such as the technology used to create the chip, the supported instruction set, the bit size, and so forth. For example, the Intel Core i7-5820 Haswell-E is a 6-core process running at 3.3 GHz based on the Haswell microarchitecture, which was released in 2013. The most current microarchitecture, released in 2015, is called Skylark. It has bus transfer speeds up to 8 GT/s, up to 128 MB L4 cache, and four cores; it runs at speeds up to 4 GHz.

Try Hands-On Projects 3-1 through 3-6 to practice monitoring processor usage and obtain information on the CPU in Windows-based, Linux-based, and Mac-based operating systems.

## AMD

Advanced Micro Devices, Inc. (AMD) manufactures CPU chips that compete with Intel PC chips. Table 3-3 lists single-core AMD chips, some of which are still being manufactured. More recent versions of these chips use multicore technology, and are listed in Table 3-4.

**Table 3-3 Single-core AMD processors**

| Processor | Latest clock speeds (MHz or GHz) | Compares to Intel chip | System bus speed (MHz) |
|---|---|---|---|
| AMD-K6-2 | 166–475 MHz | Pentium II, Celeron | 66, 95, 100 |
| AMD-K6-III | 350–450 MHz | Pentium II | 100 |
| Duron | 1–1.3 GHz | Celeron | 200 |
| Athlon | Up to 1.9 GHz | Pentium III | 200 |
| Athlon Model 4 | Up to 1.4 GHz | Pentium III | 266 |
| Athlon MP | 1.4–2.1 GHz | Pentium III | 200 to 400+ |
| Athlon XP | Up to 2.2 GHz | Pentium 4 | 266, 333, 400 |
| Opteron (64-bit) | 1.4–2.0 GHz | Itanium | 244 |

**Table 3-4 Multicore AMD processors**

| Processor | Clock speeds (MHz or GHz) | Cores | Compares to Intel chip |
|---|---|---|---|
| Athlon II | 1.8–3.3 GHz | 2–4 | Intel Core 2 Duo |
| Phenom II | 2.5–3.5 GHz | 2–6 | Intel Core 2 Quad |
| Phenom | 1.8–2.6 GHz | 3–4 | Intel Core 2 Quad |
| Athlon X2 | 2.3–2.8 GHz | 2 | Intel Core 2 Duo |
| Opteron 4000 Series | 1.7–2.8 GHz | 8–12 | Itanium/Xeon |
| Opteron 6000 Series | 1.7–2.4 GHz | 6 | Itanium/Xeon |

Like Intel, AMD continues to develop CPUs with names based on the series, such as Athlon and FX, and the core architecture, such as Zambezi and Vishera. As of 2016, one of AMD's most current processors for desktop computers is the FX-8320 Vishera, which sports 8 cores running at up to 4.7 GHz, with 8 MB L2 and 8 MB L3 cache.

## Other Processors

In addition to Intel and its direct competitors, several other manufacturers produced processors for various types of computers, including Motorola, PowerPC, SPARC, and Alpha chips.

**Motorola** Motorola chips were typically found in Macintosh computers. Its line of CISC CPUs is used in many older Macintosh computers, as well as in many older UNIX computers. The popular models were the 68000, 68020, 68030, and 68040. The development of the chips' features was roughly similar to the development in the Intel line; the 68020 showed many similarities to the 80286, the 68030 was similar to the 80386, and the 68040 was similar to the 80486. Motorola has discontinued these chips.

**PowerPC** This line of chips used different instruction sets and a different general architecture than the Motorola 68xxx line, and was developed jointly by Apple Computer, IBM, and Motorola, an alliance referred to as AIM. These RISC chips were known as the PowerPC line. In 2005, Apple moved to using Intel chips and Motorola left the CPU manufacturing business.

**SPARC** SPARC, which stands for Scalable Processor Architecture, is a RISC processor designed by Sun Microsystems and continued with Oracle Corporation's acquisition of Sun Microsystems. SPARC CPUs have gone through many incarnations, and the RISC processor is the most popular on the market today. The SPARC M7 from Oracle is the current version of the SPARC processor. It is a 64-bit chip with 64-bit address and data buses. The SPARC M7 contains 32 cores, runs at speeds up to 4.1 GHz, and has an L3 cache of 64 MB.

Primarily, you will see various implementations of the UNIX operating system running on these CPUs, performing high-end engineering and networking duties. The most popular operating system that uses the chip is Oracle Corporation's Solaris. (Solaris is SunOS with a desktop window system.) Dell and HP have announced they will resell Oracle Solaris for their platforms.

**Alpha** Another CPU of interest is the Alpha CPU, originally designed by Digital Equipment Corporation (DEC). DEC was purchased by Compaq, which in turn was purchased by HP. The Alpha CPU was found in older high-end HP Compaq servers; it had a 64-bit data bus and a 64-bit address bus. The internal clock speed could be as high as 1.3 GHz. It was the first chip to reach a speed of 1 GHz. The Alpha used a traditional 64 KB L1 cache and an external L2 cache that could go up to 8 MB. Similar to the SPARC, Alpha chips were widely used in the UNIX environment. Also like the SPARC, Alpha chips were found in computers that had heavy networking, engineering, and graphics duties. Many proprietary devices, such as file servers, firewall products, and routers, ran custom operating systems based on an Alpha architecture.

HP has moved away from Alpha chips in its high-end server computers, replacing the Alpha with the Intel chipset. HP continued development of the Alpha into 2004, production through 2006, and support through 2011.

There are many other CPUs, but many of the details about these chips are beyond the focus of this book. The CPUs discussed here are the most popular in PCs today and the most often used by the operating systems covered in this book.

# Chapter Summary

- One of the main functions of the operating system is to provide the interface between the various application programs running on a computer and the hardware inside. Processor hardware improvements have marched steadily from the early 8088 chip to the modern 64-bit multicore processors. Operating systems paralleled these changes to take advantage of the capabilities of new processors at each stage of development. Processors continue to become faster and more efficient.
- Most CPUs are composed of a control unit, arithmetic logic unit, registers, and a system bus, which is composed of a control bus, address bus, and data bus.
- CPUs can be classified by several elements, including design type, speed, cache, address bus, data bus, control bus, and CPU scheduling. Design types include CISC and RISC. CISC makes programming less complex but RISC can be faster in many instances.
- The amount of cache is critical to a CPU's overall speed because it is much faster than RAM. Modern CPUs have L1, L2, L3, and sometimes L4 cache built into the processor chip.
- CPU scheduling allows an operating system to schedule multiple processes or threads. Multicore processors facilitate efficient CPU scheduling.
- Intel processors are the most popular CPUs in PCs today, but AMD processors are also frequently used. Some processors come with 16 or more cores. The most current Intel microarchitecture is called Skylake, which has bus transfers up to 8 GT/s. Among the most current AMD processors is the FX Vishera line of processors, which have up to 8 cores.
- Other processors include the Motorola, PowerPC, the SPARC, and the Alpha.

# Key Terms

**address bus** An internal communications pathway inside a computer that specifies the source and target address for memory reads and writes.

**arithmetic logic unit (ALU)** A component of a CPU that executes instructions.

**backward compatibility** The ability of features from an older chip to function on a newer chip.

**bus** A path or channel between a computer's CPU and the devices it manages, such as memory and I/O devices.

**cache controller** Internal computer hardware that manages the data going into and loaded from the computer's cache memory.

**cache memory** Special computer memory that temporarily stores data used by the CPU. Cache memory is physically close to the CPU and is faster than standard system memory, enabling faster retrieval and processing time.

**compiler** A computer program that takes a high-level language like C# or Java and turns it into assembly code that is executed by the CPU.

**Complex Instruction Set Computing (CISC)** A computer CPU architecture in which processor components are reconfigured to conduct different operations as required. Such computer designs require many instructions and more complex instructions than other designs. Compare to *Reduced Instruction Set Computing (RISC)*.

**control bus** An internal communications pathway that keeps the CPU informed of the status of particular computer resources and devices, such as memory and disk drives.

**control unit (CU)** A component of a CPU that provides timing and coordination between the other parts of the CPU, such as the arithmetic logic unit, registers, and system bus.

**core** The part of a processor used to read and execute instructions.

**data bus** An internal communications pathway that carries data between the CPU and memory locations.

**external clock speed** The speed at which the processor communicates with the memory and other devices in the computer; usually one-fourth to one-half the internal clock speed.

**floating point unit (FPU)** A component of a CPU that executes floating point mathematical operations.

**Hyper-Threading (HT)** A feature of some Intel CPUs that allows two threads to run on each CPU core simultaneously.

**instruction set** In a computer CPU, the group of commands (instructions) the processor recognizes. These instructions are used to conduct the operations required of the CPU by the operating system and application software.

**internal clock speed** The speed at which the CPU executes internal commands, measured in megahertz (millions of clock ticks per second) or gigahertz (billions of clock ticks per second). Internal clock speeds can be as low as 1 MHz or more than 4 GHz.

**interrupt request (IRQ)** A request to the processor so that a currently operating process, such as a read from a disk drive, can be interrupted by another process, such as a write into memory.

**level 1 (L1) cache** Cache memory that is part of the CPU hardware. See *cache memory*.

**level 2 (L2) cache** Cache memory that is somewhat slower than L1 cache but is much larger. See *cache memory*.

**level 3 (L3) cache** Cache memory that is slower than L1 or L2 cache but is much larger. L3 cache is located on the CPU chip on most modern CPUs, and is shared among multiple cores. See *cache memory*.

**level 4 (L4) cache** Cache memory that is found on some advanced modern CPUs. See *cache memory*.

**microarchitecture** The description of the internal circuitry of a CPU that defines characteristics such as the technology used to create the chip, the supported instruction set, and the bit size.

**microcode** A small program inside a CISC CPU that must interpret and execute each instruction.

**multiprocessor computer** A computer that uses more than one CPU.

**multithreading** Running several processes or parts (threads) of processes at the same time.

**pipelining** A CPU design that permits the processor to operate on one instruction at the same time it is fetching one or more subsequent instructions from the operating system or application.

**Reduced Instruction Set Computing (RISC)** A computer CPU design that dedicates processor hardware components to certain functions. This design reduces the number and complexity of required instructions and often results in faster performance than CISC CPUs. Compare to *Complex Instruction Set Computing (CISC)*.

**register** A temporary holding location in a CPU where data must be placed before the CPU can use it.

**single-processor computer** A computer capable of supporting only a single CPU.

**system architecture** The computer hardware design that includes the processor (CPU) and communication routes between the CPU and the hardware it manages, such as memory and disk storage.

**thread** The smallest piece of computer code that can be independently scheduled for execution.

## Review Questions

1. Which component of the CPU is responsible for executing arithmetic and logic instructions?
   a. CU
   b. ALU
   c. data bus
   d. control bus
2. Instruction pipelining is a processing technique that allows the processor to operate on one instruction at a time with the pipeline keeping the instructions in order. True or False?
3. Which part of a CPU carries signals to indicate where data should be read from or written to in the system's memory?
   a. register
   b. data bus
   c. control unit
   d. address bus
4. Which of the following is true about CISC CPUs?
   a. They have a simple instruction set.
   b. They require a more complex compiler.
   c. They use microcode.
   d. Pipelining is easy.

5. Which of the following is used to keep the CPU informed of the status of resources and devices connected to the computer?
   a. control bus
   b. ALU
   c. microcode
   d. pipeline
6. What type of computer program takes a high-level language and turns it into assembly code?
   a. interpreter
   b. compiler
   c. assembler
   d. translator
7. What was the first widely used personal computer CPU manufactured by Intel?
   a. RISC
   b. 80286
   c. Alpha
   d. 8088
8. Where must data be placed on a CPU before it can use the data for arithmetic instructions?
   a. FPU
   b. register
   c. data bus
   d. CU
9. Manufacturers rate their CPU speeds based on which characteristic?
   a. external clock speed
   b. pipelining speed
   c. internal clock speed
   d. core speed times the number of cores
10. Which of the following is true about RISC CPUs versus CISC CPUs? (Choose all that apply.)
    a. They use microcode.
    b. They use a complex compiler.
    c. They use more registers.
    d. They have complex instructions.

11. Which cache level provides the fastest access to its data?
    a. L1
    b. L2
    c. L3
    d. L4
12. A CPU with an external clock speed of 2 GHz and a 64-bit data bus can transfer how much data per second?
    a. 8 GB/s
    b. 16 GB/s
    c. 32 GB/s
    d. 128 GB/s
13. The list of commands a CPU can execute is referred to as which of the following?
    a. instruction set
    b. instruction cache
    c. data set
    d. data cache
14. AMD manufactures which of the following chips? (Choose all that apply.)
    a. Atom
    b. Duron
    c. Xeon
    d. Phenom
15. Which manufacturer developed the Celeron line of CPUs?
    a. Intel
    b. Apple
    c. Motorola
    d. AMD
16. Which line of CPUs is a RISC processor?
    a. 68000
    b. Atom
    c. SPARC
    d. Pentium D

# Hands-On Projects

## Project 3-1: Monitor Processor Usage with Task Manager

Use Windows Task Manager to monitor processor usage.

1. Start your Windows 10 computer and log on.
2. Right-click the **taskbar** and click **Task Manager** on the shortcut menu. Click the **More details** button, if necessary.
3. Click the **Performance** tab and click **CPU** in the left pane, if necessary (see Figure 3-3).

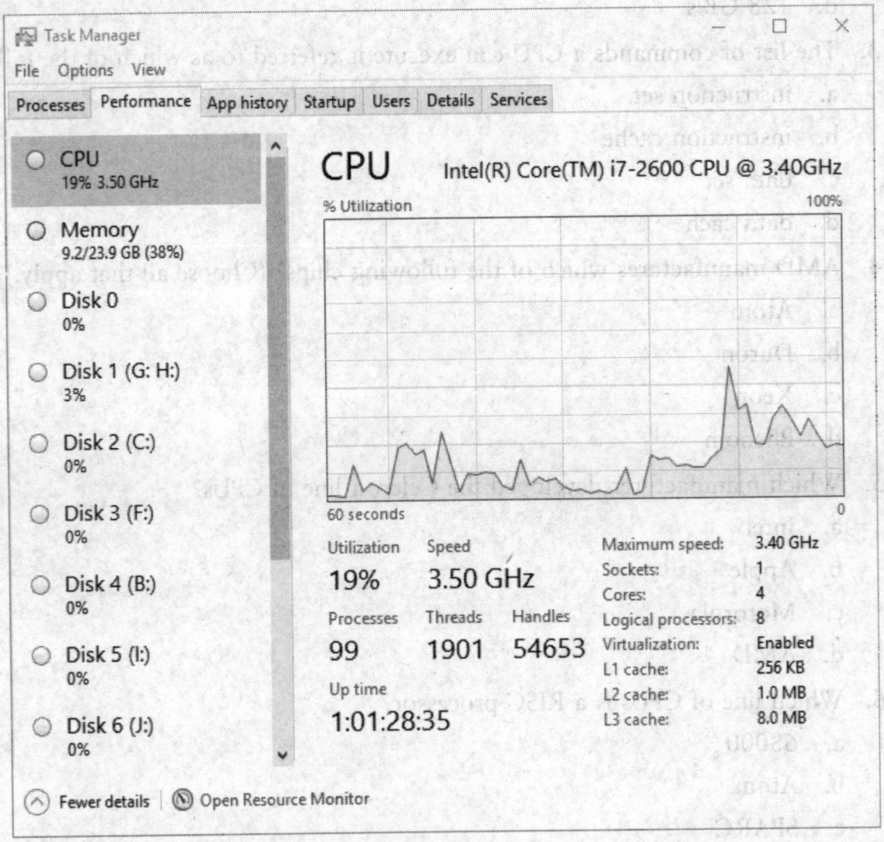


**Figure 3-3** The Performance tab in Task Manager

4. Watch the CPU history graph and note how it changes over time. Open and close a Web browser three or four times. Look at the CPU history graph now. You should see a distinct increase in CPU utilization.

5. Review the other information you can learn about the CPU. In Figure 3-3, you see the CPU model at the top of the graph. Below the graph, you see the maximum speed of the CPU, the number of cores, the number of logical processors, and the amount of L1, L2, and L3 cache, as well as other information. Your display will likely look different depending on the type of CPU running on your system. Can you tell by looking at Figure 3-3 if the CPU that is being monitored supports Hyper-Threading? How can you tell?

6. Close Task Manager. Stay logged on if you are continuing to the next project.

Do not leave Task Manager running in the background when you are not using it. Task Manager uses CPU and memory resources and could slow down the computer.

## Project 3-2: Check Processor Status in Device Manager

Most Windows-based systems can report on whether the processor (or any other hardware device) is working properly. This project shows you how to check the status of the processor.

1. Log on to your Windows computer, if necessary.

2. Right-click **Start**, and click **Device Manager**.

3. Double-click **Processors** (see Figure 3-4). How many processors are displayed? Double-click a processor in the list.

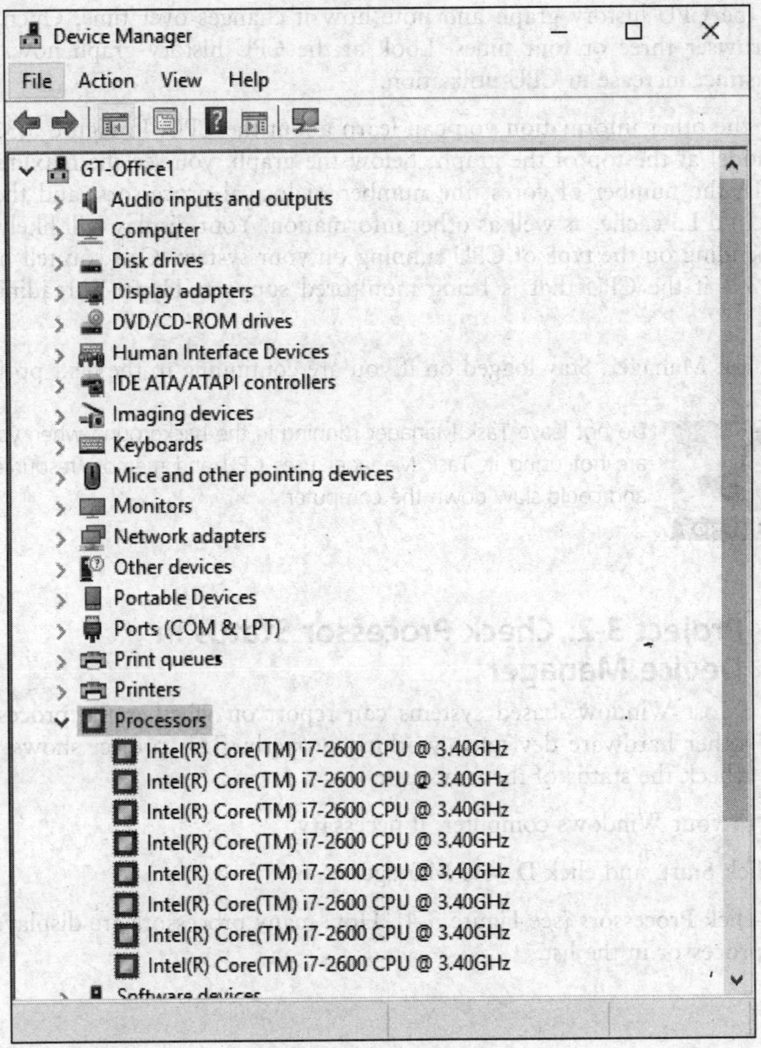


**Figure 3-4** Viewing processors in Device Manager

4. Click the **General** tab, if necessary. The General tab shows the manufacturer and model of the CPU, and the Device status box shows the status.

5. Click the **Details** tab. Here, you can see a variety of information about the device and the device driver. Click the selection arrow under Property and browse through the properties. Click **Power data** to see the various power states supported by the CPU.

6. Click **Cancel** to close the Processor Properties dialog box, and then close Device Manager.

7. Log off or shut down your Windows computer.

## Project 3-3: Use System Monitor in Linux

The GNOME desktop in Linux offers the System Monitor tool for tracking processor activity. In this project, you learn how to use the System Monitor tool.

1. Start your Linux computer and log on.
2. Click **Activities** and click **Show Applications.** Click **Utilities** and then click **System Monitor.**
3. Click the **Resources** tab, if necessary (see Figure 3-5).

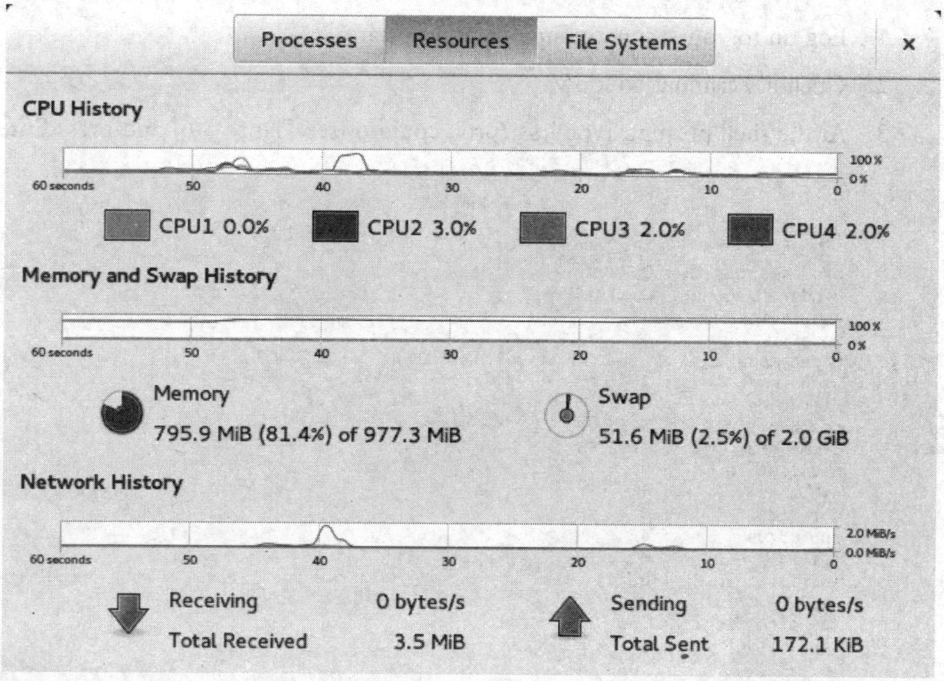


**Figure 3-5** System Monitor in Linux

*Source: Linux*

4. If your computer has more than one processor, you'll see a color-coded line for each processor in the CPU History section of System Monitor. (Figure 3-5 shows there are four processors.)
5. Notice the Memory and Swap History section of System Monitor. The Memory information shows the amount of memory that is currently in use, as a percentage of the total amount of memory. In Figure 3-5, 795.9 MiB (or MB), or 81.4 % of the total memory is in use in a computer that has 977.3 MiB (or MB) of RAM. Review the memory statistics for your computer.
6. Open and close several applications, such as a Web browser, terminal window, and file editor. Return to System Monitor to see the changes in the graphs. Close System Monitor and any open windows.

7. Click **Activities,** click **Show Applications,** and then click **Settings.** Click **Details** in the System section. The Overview window shows basic system information, such as the amount of memory installed, the CPU, the bit size of the OS (32-bit or 64-bit), and the GNOME version. Close the Details window.

8. Stay logged on if you are continuing to the next project.

## Project 3-4: View the cpuinfo File in Linux

In addition to using the GNOME System Monitor, you can determine information about the CPU in a Linux computer by displaying the contents of the /proc/cpuinfo file via the *less* command. You learn how to do so in this project.

1. Log on to your Linux computer, if necessary.
2. Open a **Terminal** window.
3. At the shell prompt, type **less /proc/cpuinfo** (see Figure 3-6) and press **Enter.**

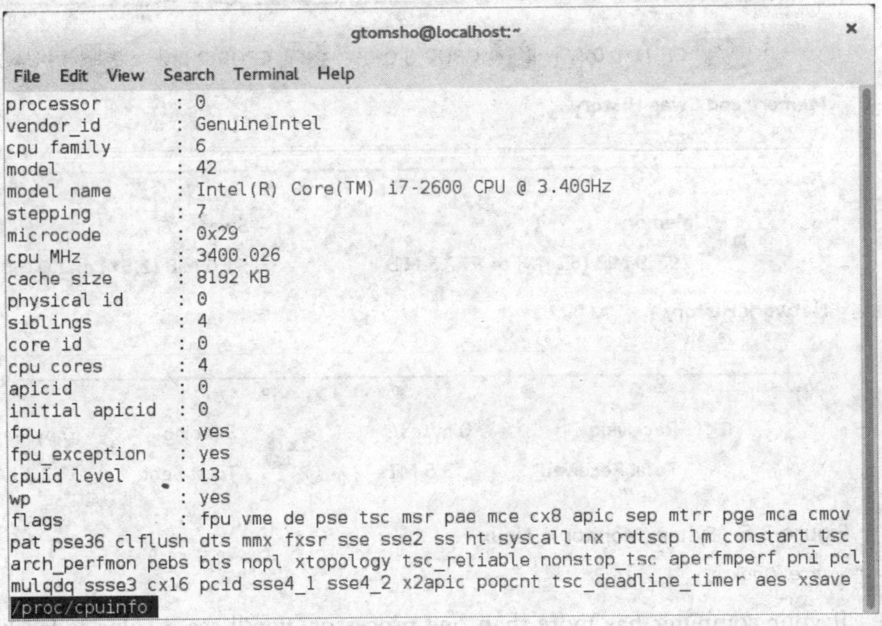


```
processor       : 0
vendor_id       : GenuineIntel
cpu family      : 6
model           : 42
model name      : Intel(R) Core(TM) i7-2600 CPU @ 3.40GHz
stepping        : 7
microcode       : 0x29
cpu MHz         : 3400.026
cache size      : 8192 KB
physical id     : 0
siblings        : 4
core id         : 0
cpu cores       : 4
apicid          : 0
initial apicid  : 0
fpu             : yes
fpu_exception   : yes
cpuid level     : 13
wp              : yes
flags           : fpu vme de pse tsc msr pae mce cx8 apic sep mtrr pge mca cmov
pat pse36 clflush dts mmx fxsr sse sse2 ss ht syscall nx rdtscp lm constant_tsc
arch_perfmon pebs bts nopl xtopology tsc_reliable nonstop_tsc aperfmperf pni pcl
mulqdq ssse3 cx16 pcid sse4_1 sse4_2 x2apic popcnt tsc_deadline_timer aes xsave
/proc/cpuinfo
```

**Figure 3-6** Viewing /proc/cpuinfo in Linux

*Source: Linux*

4. Press the **Page Down** key or press the **Spacebar** to view more of the file's contents one page at a time. The **Page Up** key takes you back through the previous pages of the file. You can also use the up or down arrows to navigate through the file one line at a time.
5. This file shows you how many processors are in the computer, indexed by 0. If you see only one section of information under processor 0, then you have one processor. A second section, showing processor 1, would mean you have two processors, and so on. Look for the model name, speed, cache size, and number of cores.
6. Press **q** to exit the display of the /proc/cpuinfo file's contents.

7. Type **top** and press **Enter**. Top is an interactive task manager that runs in a terminal window. Look for the Tasks field. It should be displayed in the second row on the left side of the window.
8. To toggle from task mode to thread mode, press **H**. (A capital H is required, so you probably need to press **Shift-H**.) The Tasks field is changed to Threads and the number increases because many tasks contain two or more threads.
9. Press **q** to quit the top task manager.
10. Close the Terminal window and log off or shut down your Linux computer.

Enter
HANDS-ON PROJECTS

## Project 3-5: View Hardware Information in Mac OS X

In Chapter 1, "Operating Systems Fundamentals," you briefly used the About This Mac feature in Mac OS X. This feature is worth reviewing because it provides a fast way to determine what processor is in a Macintosh computer and the amount of memory. This information can save you time, for example, if you are planning to upgrade multiple computers to the latest version of Mac OS X and you want to determine which ones have Intel processors and whether they have enough RAM for the upgrade. In this project, you review how to open the About This Mac window for information about the processor(s) and RAM.

1. Start your Mac OS X computer and log on.
2. Click the **Apple** icon in the top left corner of the menu bar.
3. Click **About This Mac** on the menu.
4. The About This Mac window not only shows the operating system version, as you learned in Chapter 1, it also shows the number of processors, the model name and speed of the processors, plus the amount and type of memory installed (see Figure 3-7).

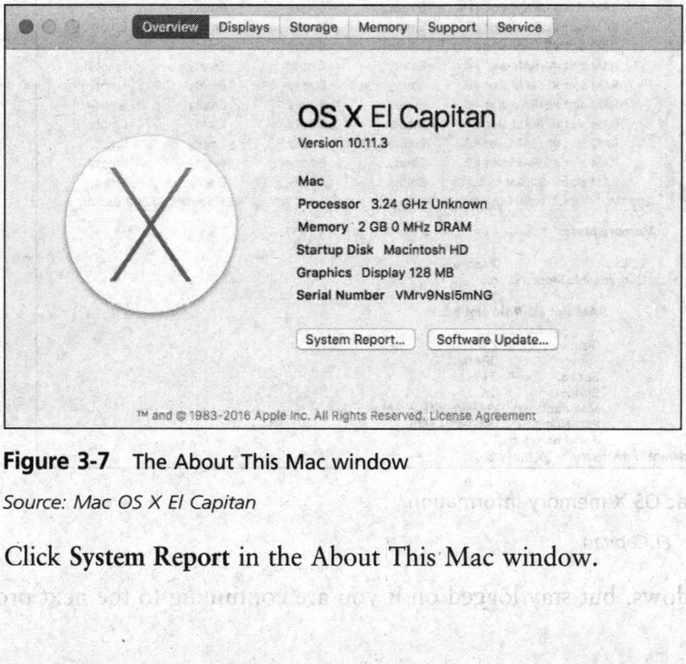


**Figure 3-7** The About This Mac window

*Source: Mac OS X El Capitan*

5. Click **System Report** in the About This Mac window.

6. Make sure that **Hardware** is highlighted in the left pane. Here you learn more about the processor, including the speed, the number of cores, and the amount of L2 and L3 cache, if present (see Figure 3-8).

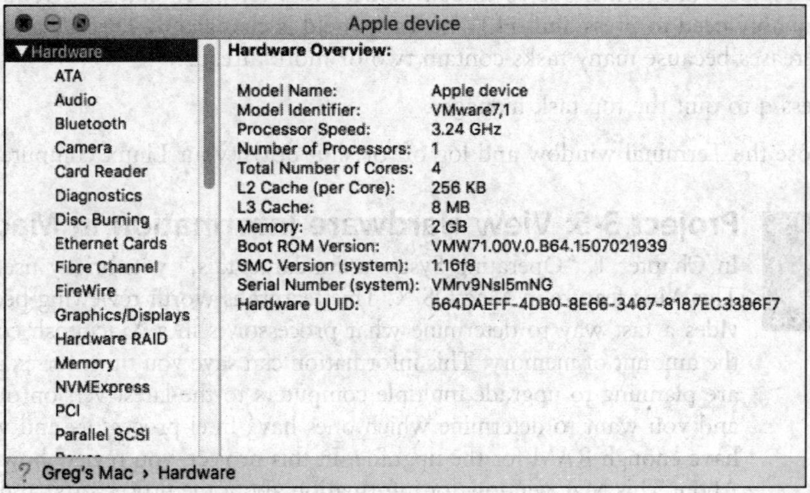


**Figure 3-8** Mac OS X hardware overview

*Source: Mac OS X El Capitan*

7. In the left pane, click **Memory** under Hardware. The right pane shows information about the number of memory slots and the RAM (if any) plugged into each slot (see Figure 3-9).

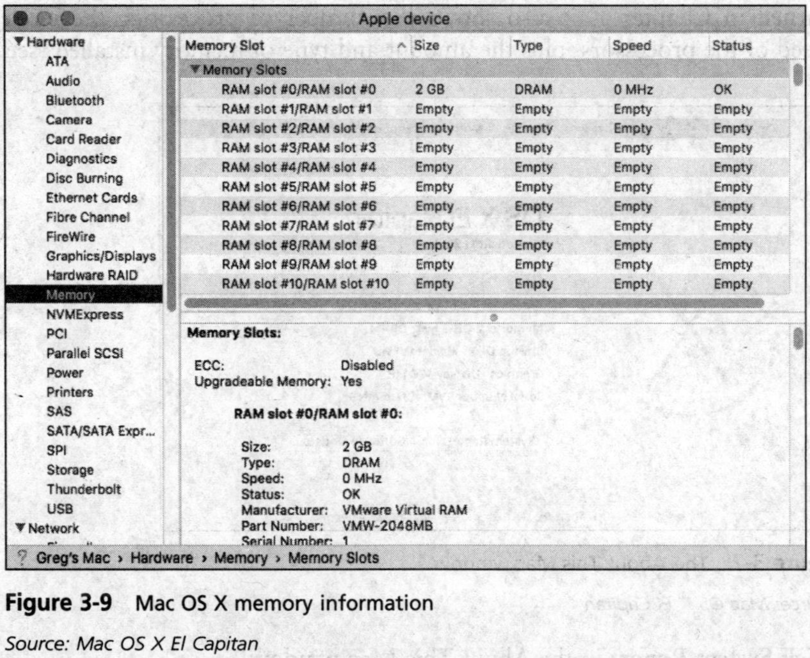


**Figure 3-9** Mac OS X memory information

*Source: Mac OS X El Capitan*

8. Close all windows, but stay logged on if you are continuing to the next project.

## Project 3-6: Use Activity Monitor in Mac OS X

You can also use a feature called Activity Monitor to find information about the processor and memory in a Mac OS X computer.

1. Log on to your Mac OS X computer, if necessary.
2. Ensure that Finder is active by clicking **Finder** in the Dock, if necessary.
3. Click **Go** in the menu bar and click **Utilities**.
4. Double-click **Activity Monitor** in the Utilities window.
5. Make sure the **CPU** button is selected to display CPU activity. A small CPU meter is displayed at the bottom of the Activity Monitor window so that you can follow the current CPU usage. Also, as you learned in Chapter 1, the upper portion of the window shows the amount of CPU used (under the % CPU column) by each active program or process.
6. Click the **Memory** button in the Activity Monitor window (see Figure 3-10). The Memory column gives you information about the amount of RAM used by each program or process, and the bottom portion of the window provides statistics about memory use.

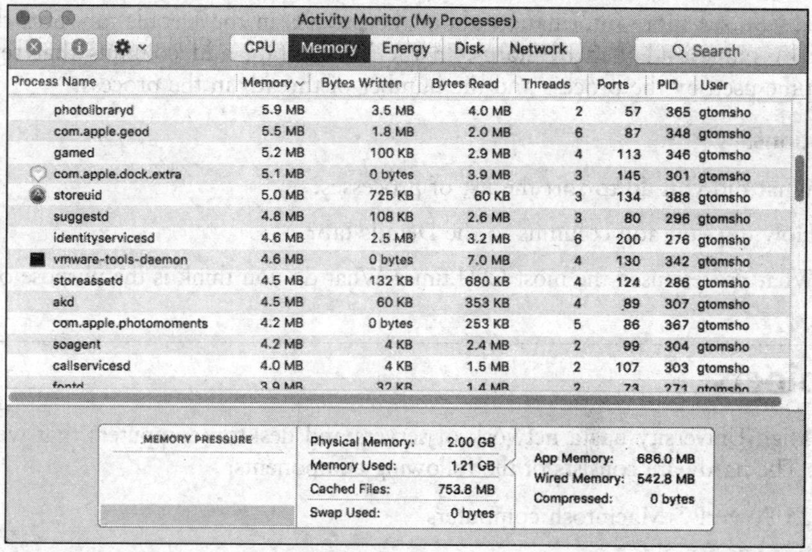


**Figure 3-10** Activity Monitor in Mac OS X

*Source: Mac OS X El Capitan*

7. Right-click any of the column headers, such as **User**. You can choose which columns should be displayed. Click **Bytes Written**, right-click a column again, and click **Bytes Read**. These columns show you the amount of data read from and written to disk; you'll also find these columns if you click the Disk button at the top of the window. You can click and drag the columns to put them in any order you want.
8. Close Activity Monitor and any open windows.
9. Log off or shut down your Mac OS X computer.

## Critical Thinking

The following activities give you critical thinking challenges. Challenge Labs give you an opportunity to use the skills you have learned to perform a task without step-by-step instructions. Case projects offer a practical problem for which you supply a written solution. Not all chapters contain Challenge Labs. There is not always a specific right or wrong answer to these critical thinking exercises. They are intended to encourage you to review the chapter material and delve deeper into the topics you have learned.

## Challenge Labs

### Challenge Lab 3-1: Work with Task Manager in Windows

In this challenge lab, you explore Task Manager in more depth. You may have to research how to perform some of the tasks. Once you are finished, you will answer some questions.

On your Windows computer, start Task Manager and be sure you see the Processes, Performance, and other tabs. From the Processes tab, right-click any process and click **Go to details**. You see more information about the process in the Details tab. Sort the list of processes by name and then by status. In the Details tab, add columns that report the total CPU time used by the process and the number of threads in the process.

**Questions:**

1. What did you do to sort the list of processes?
2. How did you add columns to the Details tab?
3. What process used the most CPU time? What do you think is the purpose of this process?

## Case Projects

Mile High University has a network of servers and desktop computers that were installed in 2000. The hardware consists of the following components:

- 25 PowerPC Macintosh computers
- Four Dell Pentium 4 servers
- Two HP servers running on the Alpha CPU
- 160 desktop computers running on the AMD Duron CPU
- 25 desktop computers running on the Intel Core Duo CPU
- 45 desktop computers running on the Pentium 4 CPU

Using the information you learned in this chapter and previous chapters, you will be able to make informed recommendations in the following case projects.

## Case Project 3-1: Server Upgrades

The new Director of Information Technology has asked you to recommend a strategy to upgrade the servers on their network. Recommendations on server hardware, CPU chip set, speed, and caching are needed. You should also recommend which servers to upgrade first and determine whether any servers are still appropriate to keep.

## Case Project 3-2: Desktop Computing

The director has evaluated your server recommendations and asks you to design a strategy for upgrading the desktop hardware. He feels that most of the university's desktop computers need to be replaced. You should explain your strategy.

## Case Project 3-3: Hardware Overheating

The university is having some problems with the desktop computer that runs the Intel Core Duo CPU. The computers will suddenly scramble the display screens and freeze. Because of this, the university wants to stay away from having desktops running any of the Intel CPUs. What would you recommend to address the problem? Research some of the causes of overheating hardware and suggest possible remedies. In addition, what desktop CPUs would you recommend for replacing their older hardware? Provide an explanation for your recommendation and what the university should do in the future.

chapter 4

# File Systems

**After reading this chapter and completing the exercises, you will be able to:**

- List the basic functions common to all file systems
- Use and describe the file systems used by Windows OSs
- Use and describe the file systems used by UNIX and Linux systems, including ufs and ext
- Use and describe the Mac OS X Extended (HFS+) file system

**In this chapter, you learn the general characteristics and functions of file systems,** including their organization and specific features. You then explore the file systems used by Windows, UNIX/Linux, and Macintosh operating systems. You also learn about the tools available for file systems, such as tools for locating files and fixing damaged files.

# Understanding File System Functions

One of the basic functions of an operating system is to enable you to store and access information on a computer or other digital device. This information might be letters, a report, spreadsheet files, your favorite music, or pictures of your family. All of this vital information is managed, stored, and retrieved through a **file system**. In one sense, a file system is like your personal assistant, properly saving and keeping track of the location of your important data. The file system allocates locations on a disk for storage and keeps a record of where specific information is kept. When you need the information, the file system consults its records to determine the location and then retrieves the information. Some file systems also implement recovery procedures when a disk area is damaged or when the operating system unexpectedly goes down, such as during a power failure.

To fulfill all these functions, the file systems used by computer operating systems perform the following general tasks:

- Provide a convenient interface for users and applications to open and save files
- Provide a hierarchical structure to organize files
- Store file metadata to provide detailed information about files
- Organize space on a storage device

## User Interface

When a user double-clicks a file to open it, the user interface calls the file system with a request to open the file. The file type determines exactly how the file is opened. If the file is an application, the application is loaded into memory and run by the CPU. If the file is a document, the application associated with the document type is loaded into memory and opens the file. For example, on Windows computers, if you double-click the Budget.xls file, the Excel application is loaded into memory and then opens the file. If a user creates a file or changes an existing file and wants to save it, the application calls the file system to store the new or changed file on the disk. Most users of an OS interact with the file system by using a file manager program, such as File Explorer in Windows or Files in the GNOME desktop in Linux. As a future computer or network professional, you need to have a deeper understanding of how a file system works so that you can make informed choices when you need to install a file system or troubleshoot file system-related problems.

## Hierarchical Structure

The overall purpose of a file system is to create a structure for filing data. The analogy that is typically used for a file system is that of file cabinets, file drawers, and file folders. For example, the computer could be considered the file cabinet and the disk drives the drawers. Within each drawer (drive), information is organized into hanging folders, manila folders, and individual documents (files), as shown in Figure 4-1.

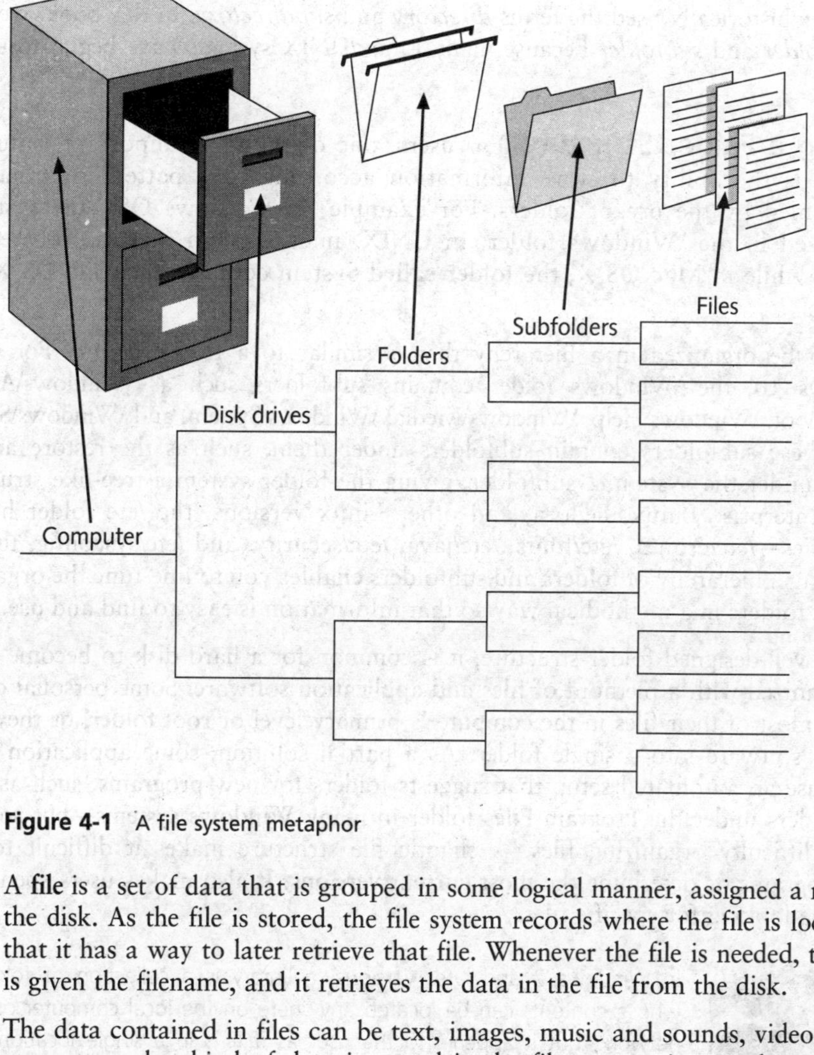


**Figure 4-1** A file system metaphor

A **file** is a set of data that is grouped in some logical manner, assigned a name, and stored on the disk. As the file is stored, the file system records where the file is located on the disk so that it has a way to later retrieve that file. Whenever the file is needed, the operating system is given the filename, and it retrieves the data in the file from the disk.

The data contained in files can be text, images, music and sounds, video, or Web pages. But no matter what kind of data is stored in the file system, it must be converted into digital format—a series of 1s and 0s—that the computer understands. The operating system, along with the applications you use for word processing, graphics, and so on, performs this function of converting data into digital format for the computer, and back into the end-user format as text or pictures, for example.

Moreover, there must be a way to write digital information to disk, track it, update it when necessary, and call it back when the user or a user-controlled program wants it. To achieve all this, the operating system typically groups file data in some logical way, creates a record of this structure, and builds a folder or directory to track the type of data stored in each file. A **folder** or **directory** is an organizational structure that contains files and may additionally contain subfolders (or subdirectories) under it. The folder connects names to the files that are stored on the disk, which makes it easy for users and programs to obtain the right data at the right time. Windows systems use the terms *folder* and *subfolder* and Linux/UNIX systems have historically used the terms *directory* and *subdirectory*. In this book, we will use the terms *folder* and *subfolder* because many Linux/UNIX systems have begun to use those terms.

**Designing a Folder Structure** For users, one of the most important features of a file system is the ability to store information according to a pattern of organization that is enabled by the use of folders. For example, in Windows OSs, the system files are organized in the \Windows folder. In UNIX, many system files are located in the /etc folder, while in Mac OS X, the folder called System contains the Mac OS X critical system files.

Folders can be organized in a hierarchy that is similar to a tree structure. For example, in Windows 10, the \Windows folder contains subfolders such as \Windows\AppPatch, \Windows\Boot, \Windows\Help, \Windows\Media, \Windows\System, and \Windows\System32. Many of these subfolders contain subfolders under them, such as the restore and spool subfolders under the System32 subfolder, giving the folder system a tree-like structure. In Red Hat Enterprise Linux, Fedora, and other Linux versions, the /etc folder has many subdirectories—/etc/cron.d, /etc/fonts, /etc/java, /etc/security, and /etc/sysconfig, to name a few. Building a hierarchy of folders and subfolders enables you to fine-tune the organization of files and folders in a methodical way so that information is easy to find and use.

Without a well-designed folder structure, it is common for a hard disk to become cluttered and disorganized with a plethora of files and application software. Some personal computer users keep most of their files in the computer's primary level or **root folder**, or they load all application software into a single folder. As a partial solution, some application software programs use an automated setup that suggests folders for new programs, such as creating new subfolders under the Program Files folder in many Windows systems—but some users still have difficulty organizing files. A chaotic file structure makes it difficult to run or remove programs or determine the most current versions. It also makes users spend unproductive time looking for specific files.

In Windows 7 and later versions, a library is a collection of folders whose contents can be located anywhere on the local computer or its network, but it appears to the user as if it is in a single location. A library is a convenient way to access folders in different locations from one central location.

To avoid confusion, carefully design the file and folder structure from the start, particularly on servers that are accessed by many users. Plan to design a folder structure that complements the one already set up by the operating system, and then implement access controls that prevent unauthorized users from bypassing the structure. The default operating system structure, along with the structure that you add, might consist of folders for the following:

- Operating system files (typically set up by the operating system)
- Software applications (often set up both by the operating system, the software applications that you install, and decisions you make about how to install those applications)
- Work files, such as word-processing, graphics, spreadsheet, and database files (set up by you and by applications such as Microsoft Word)
- Public files that you share over the network (set up by you)
- Utilities files (set up by the operating system, the utilities applications, and your decisions about how to install specific utilities)
- Temporary files (set up by the operating system, applications that use temporary files, and your decisions about where to store temporary files)

Keeping temporary files for an extended period is a security risk. Temporary files should be purged as soon as they are no longer needed.

In deciding how to allocate folders for specific types of files, consider following some general practices. For instance, the root folder should not be cluttered with files or too many directories or folders. Each software application should have its own folder or subfolder so updates and software removal are easy to administer. For easy access control, similar information should be grouped, such as accounting systems or office productivity software. Operating system files should be kept separate and protected so important files are not accidentally deleted by a user. On Windows systems, some critical files are hidden from casual users and marked as system files so they cannot be easily deleted. In addition, most OS files are protected by access controls. Directories and folders should have names that clearly reflect their purposes. For example, consider a law office administrator who uses legal time-accounting software, legal forms software, Microsoft Office, confidential and shared spreadsheets, and Word documents—all on a computer running Windows 10. The same office administrator also maintains specialized Web pages for the law firm's Web site. The folder structure from the root might be as follows:

- *Windows* for the system files (the default folder set up by the operating system)
- *Program Files* for general software and utilities (the default folder set up by the operating system)
- *Documents and Settings* for work files such as Word documents and confidential spreadsheets (the default folder set up by the operating system)
- *Shared* for spreadsheets that are shared over the network (a sample folder the user could set up, or the user could employ the default Public Documents folder set up by the operating system, as noted below)

- *Forms* for specific types of forms used by the legal forms software (a sample folder the user might set up)
- *Inetpub* for Web pages (a sample folder the user might set up in conjunction with the installation of Web design software)

By default, Windows Vista and later versions create a \Users\Public\Public Documents folder for sharing. Some users choose to use this folder for sharing files over a network. However, make sure that you know what security is set on shared folders so you do not host unwelcome guests. In server environments, the IT administrator typically disables the use of Public folders. You will learn about file system security later in this chapter.

Each major folder has subfolders to keep grouped files or application software separate. For example, the Program Files folder contains subfolders for each different software package, such as \Program Files\Microsoft Office for the Microsoft Office software, and \Program Files\Time Accounting for the legal time-accounting software folder. The Users *username* folder would have a Documents subfolder to contain confidential spreadsheets and Word documents, while shared spreadsheets would be in the Public Documents folder. Figure 4-2 illustrates this folder structure.

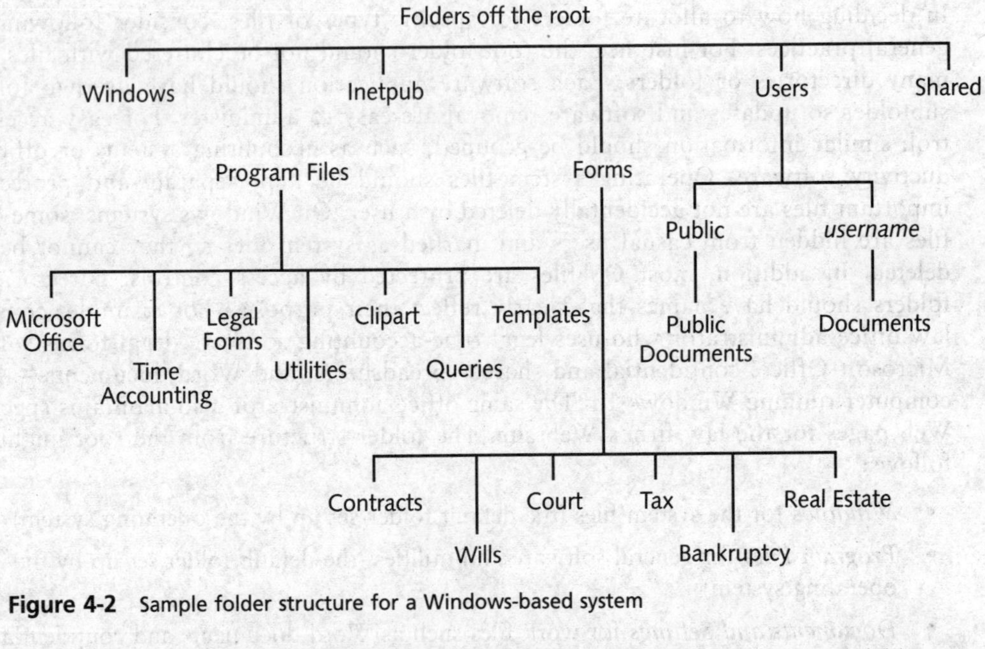


**Figure 4-2** Sample folder structure for a Windows-based system

For Linux systems, such as Red Hat Enterprise Linux or Fedora, a typical folder structure already provided by the operating system is as follows:

- *bin* for user programs and utilities (binary files)
- *sbin* for system administration utilities (system binary files)

- *lib* for runtime library files needed by programs stored in the /bin and /sbin directories
- *usr* for user files and programs
- *var* for files in which content often varies or for files that are used only temporarily
- *tmp* for files used only temporarily
- *dev* for devices
- *mnt* for DVD/CD-ROM drives, flash drives, and other removable media
- *etc* for system and configuration files
- *root* for files used by the root account
- *home* for users' home directories (or folders) and typically stored in subfolders named for each user
- *proc* for system resource tracking

Figure 4-3 shows Fedora root folders in the GNOME Files tool. In Linux, the term *root folder* is used in two ways. One way is to refer to the root or main level from which all folders are created. All of the folders in the previous list are in the root, which is designated as /. The other *root folder* is the folder named /root, which is used as the home folder by the root account. Recall that the root account has complete permission to all files and applications on a Linux system.

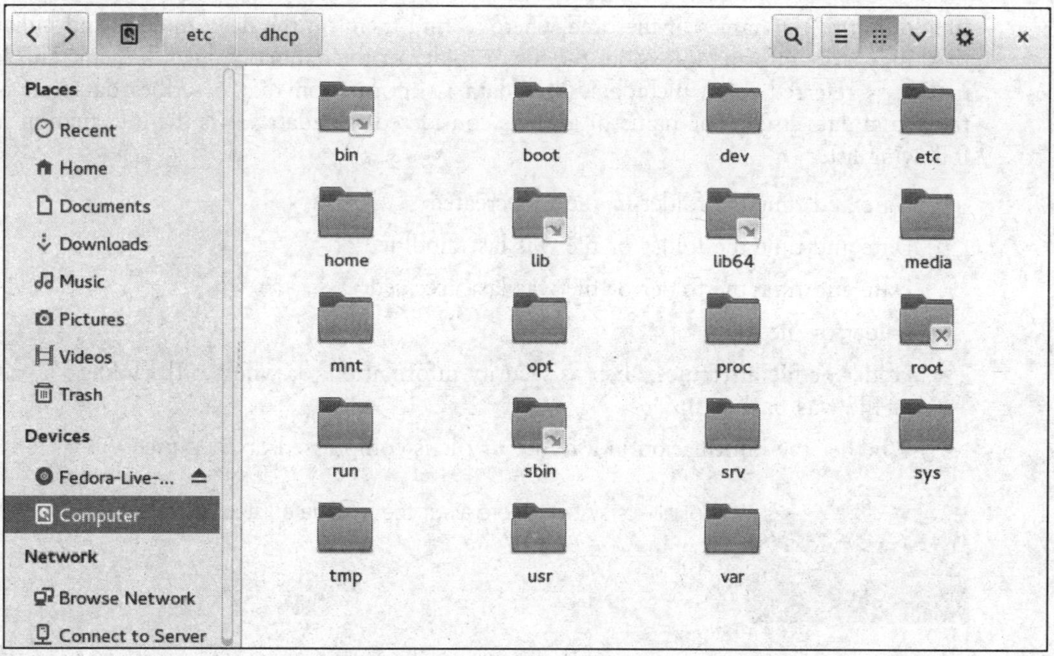


**Figure 4-3** Fedora root folders in the GNOME Files tool

*Source: Fedora Linux*

> **NOTE**
> Windows operating systems use backslashes to designate a folder, but UNIX and Linux use a forward slash. For example, the main level root is / and the bin folder is denoted as /bin.

You can view folders in Linux from the command line—for example, by using a terminal window—and from the Files tool, as demonstrated in Hands-On Project 4-7.

In Mac OS X, the default folder structure created by the operating system from the root level includes:

- *Applications* for Mac OS X software applications
- *System* for Mac OS X system files
- *Library* for library files (such as fonts)
- *Users* for user accounts, with subfolders for each user account to store files
- *Documents* for documents

Do Hands-On Projects 4-2, 4-4, and 4-6 to practice making folders in different operating systems.

## File Metadata

In addition to the names of files and where to find them on the disk, folders (and individual files) may store information about the file or folder or the data contained in them. This information is referred to as metadata. **Metadata** is information that describes data but is not the actual data itself. The name of a file is considered metadata, as is the information in the following list:

- Date and time the folder or file was created
- Date and time the folder or file was last modified
- Date and time the folder or file was last accessed
- Folder or file size
- Folder or **file attributes**, such as security information, or whether the folder or file was backed up
- Whether the information in a folder or file is compressed or encrypted

> **NOTE**
> Not all file systems store all of the metadata listed above.

Figure 4-4 illustrates some of the metadata that is stored for a file in Windows 10; this metadata can be displayed using File Explorer. As you learn later in this chapter, the way in which this information is stored depends on the design of the file system.

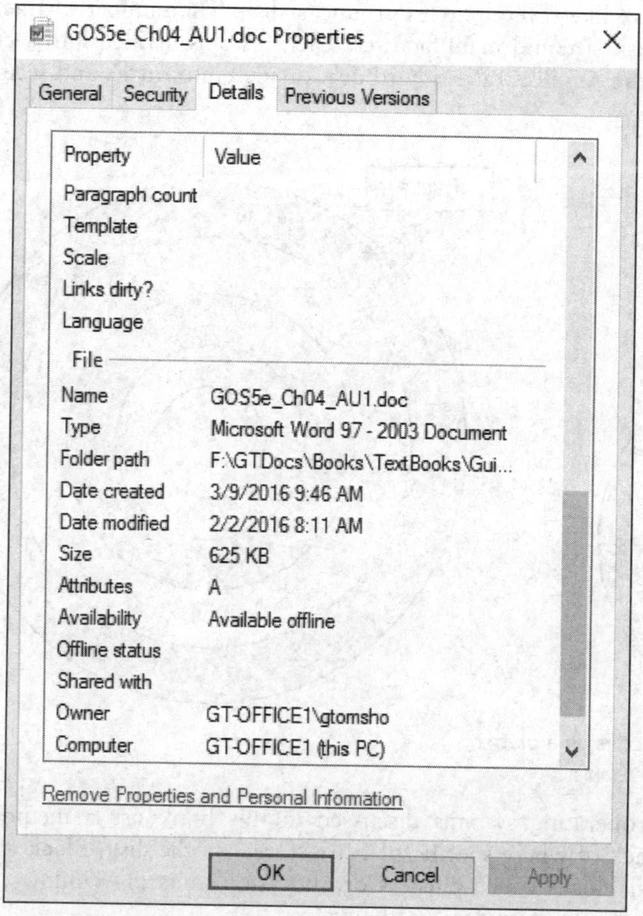


**Figure 4-4** Windows file metadata

In Hands-On Project 4-2, you view folder and file information in File Explorer. Also, Hands-On Projects 4-7 and 4-8 give you experience viewing folders and files using the Files tool in Linux and the Macintosh HD desktop icon in Mac OS X.

## Storage Device Space Organization

This section discusses storage in the context of mechanical hard disk drives (HDDs); however, the concepts and procedures are the same for solid-state drives (SSDs). The differences are primarily in their physical characteristics. For example, HDDs have platters and read/write heads, but SSDs do not.

When a hard disk is delivered from the manufacturer, it is low-level formatted. A **low-level format** is a software process that marks the location of disk tracks and sectors. Every disk is divided into **tracks**, which are like several circles around a disk. The number of tracks on a hard disk depends on the disk size and manufacturer. Each track is divided into sections of equal size called **sectors**. Figure 4-5 illustrates a hard disk divided into tracks and sectors on a platter.

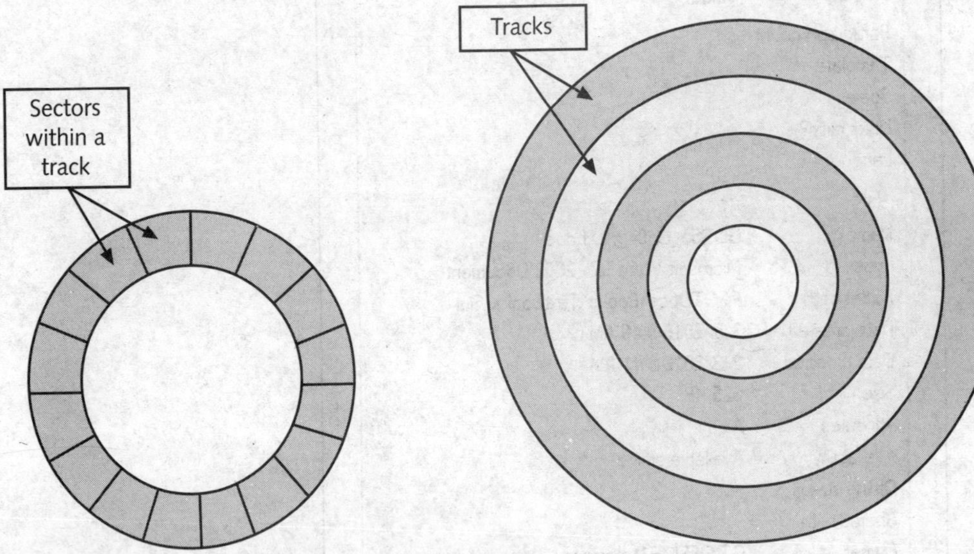


**Figure 4-5** Disk tracks and sectors on a platter

**Block Allocation** The operating systems discussed in this book use a method called **block allocation** to keep track of where specific files are stored on the disk. Block allocation divides the disk into logical blocks called **clusters** or allocation units in Windows systems, which in turn correlate to a group of sectors on the disk.

Block allocation data is stored on the disk itself using one of two techniques. One technique uses a fixed portion of the disk to store this data—for example, the **file allocation table (FAT)** file system initially implemented in MS-DOS and supported by all versions of Windows and most other OSs. The other technique uses various locations on the disk to store a special type of file that is used for folder and file allocation information; examples include the **New Technology File System** (**NTFS**) and the UNIX/Linux file systems. On NTFS-formatted disks, the allocation table is called the Master File Table (MFT), which is discussed later in the chapter. As you can imagine, the areas of the disk in which allocation information and folder information are stored are very important; without this data, it would be impossible to access any of the files on the system without using specialized disk repair tools.

If a system uses a specific area or set of areas on the disk to store this file allocation data, obviously that disk area is accessed frequently. This is why many problems in accessing disk files arise as problems in file allocation tables and folder information. Because this data is also stored in a location separate from the actual file, you can see that when there is a problem with the disk, some of the folder or allocation data may not match the data actually stored on the disk. These occurrences are less common today, but it is very important to exercise proper care of disks to minimize such problems.

Proper disk care includes regularly maintaining a Windows disk through defragmenting (discussed later in this chapter), periodically deleting unused files (see Chapter 11), maintaining good security (see Chapter 10), implementing protection from viruses and malicious software, and providing stable power (such as through an uninterruptible power supply or UPS).

All operating systems have special tools that let you check, and sometimes repair, common file system and disk problems. Some operating systems can perform checks on the file system on an ongoing basis. These tools are discussed in more detail later in this chapter.

**Partitions** Before a file system can be placed on a hard disk, the disk must be partitioned and formatted. **Partitioning** is the process of blocking a group of tracks and sectors to be used by a particular file system, such as FAT or NTFS. After a disk is partitioned, it must be **high-level formatted** (or simply formatted) so that the partition contains the disk divisions and patterns needed by a particular operating system to store files. With today's technology creating disks of greater capacity, and as disks are used in more diverse applications, sometimes it is desirable to have more than one file system on a single disk, which is accomplished by having a partition for each file system. You might need multiple file systems to allow the installation of Windows 10 alongside Windows 7, or to install Red Hat Enterprise Linux and Windows 10 on the same computer, for example. Multiple operating systems may be required on a single system to accommodate certain applications designed for Linux and other applications designed for Windows 10.

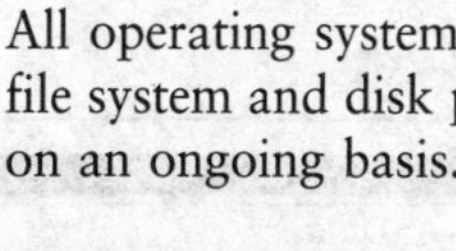


The use of virtualization can provide some of the same benefits, and more, of installing multiple OSs on a computer system. Its use is generally preferred over installing multiple OSs on separate disk partitions. Virtualization is discussed in Chapter 8.

When you want to have multiple file systems on one disk, you can partition the disk so that different file systems can be installed on different disk partitions. You can also create partitions in one operating system to segment a single **physical drive**, the hard disk in a computer, into multiple logical volumes to which you can assign distinct drive letters. This technique of dividing a hard disk into multiple **logical drives** is very useful for organizing file storage, and was necessary with older operating systems, such as MS-DOS and Windows 3.1, which did not recognize very large hard drives.

Figure 4-6 illustrates a Windows 10 system that has multiple partitions (FAT32, NTFS, and **Universal Disk Format or UDF**, a format used for DVDs and other optical media) used for segmenting data on a hard disk.

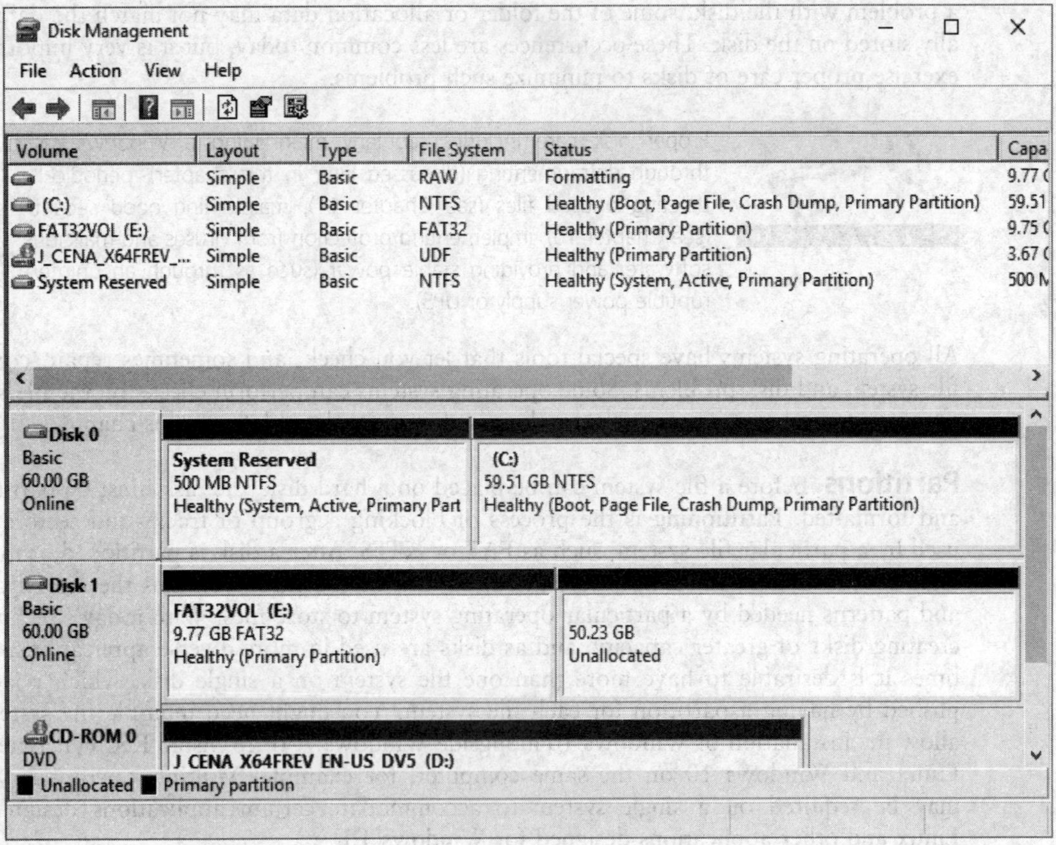


**Figure 4-6** Multiple partitions used in one Windows 10 system

Partitioning can typically be done only on hard disks, SSDs, or large removable disks. Low-capacity media do not support partitioning because there simply is not enough room on these low-capacity disks to make partitioning practical. Also, some larger-capacity media, such as DVDs, CDs, and tapes, are not partitioned by the user.

The logical programming that creates disk partitions resides at an even lower level than the actual file system, and it lets you divide the disk into "slices." The slices are done at the low-level format portion of the disk, and are stored in special sections of the hard drive itself, separate from the operating system. Obviously, the partitioning scheme must be communicated to the operating system and file system. On most disks, there is a separate area that stores the partition information. This area has room to hold information about a set number of partitions. Whenever you create a partition, information about it is stored in this special area of the disk. On systems in the IBM/Intel PC hardware architecture, for example, there is typically room to store information for up to four partitions on each disk. This area is known as the **partition table** in MS-DOS, Mac OS, and Windows, and the **disk label** in UNIX/Linux. In addition to the disk label and partition table, another piece of disk is reserved, known as the **boot block** in UNIX/Linux and Mac OS X, or the **Master Boot Record** (MBR) in MS-DOS and Windows. In Windows systems, the MBR can be up to 512 bytes long and consists of four elements:

- The *boot program*, which examines the partition table to determine the partition from which to boot (the **active partition**) and enables the program code in the active partition's start area to execute and then point to the code that starts the operating system
- The *disk signature*, which stores information about the disk and is used by management software such as the Windows registry
- The *partition table* for the active partition
- The *end-of-MBR marker*, which signifies where the MBR contents end on the disk

Hands-On Project 4-3 shows you how to repair an MBR or a damaged boot sector in Windows 10.

Not all operating systems support partitions in the same way, which you will discover in the following sections on file systems for individual operating systems. Each operating system also uses specific utilities to create partitions. When a disk partition is created, the file system is stored inside the partition. The folder structures are then built inside the file system. When files are stored on the disks, they are given some space inside the partition, and data about the files is written in the folder area.

Windows supports two types of drive partitioning: basic and dynamic. Basic disks are the default type and have been around since the early 1980s, starting with the original IBM PC. Basic disks support up to four partitions per hard drive: four primary partitions or three primary partitions and one extended partition. The extended partition may then be divided further into logical drives (see Figure 4-7). Each of these logical drives can hold an individual FAT16, FAT32, or NTFS file system. Under control of the operating system, up to 26 logical drives (pointers to separate file systems), each with its own file system, can be active at one time. In Figure 4-7, the disk is divided into three primary partitions, one with FAT32 and two with NTFS, and the extended partition is divided into two logical drives, one with FAT (FAT16) and one with NTFS. Free space is also still available on the extended partition to create additional logical drives.

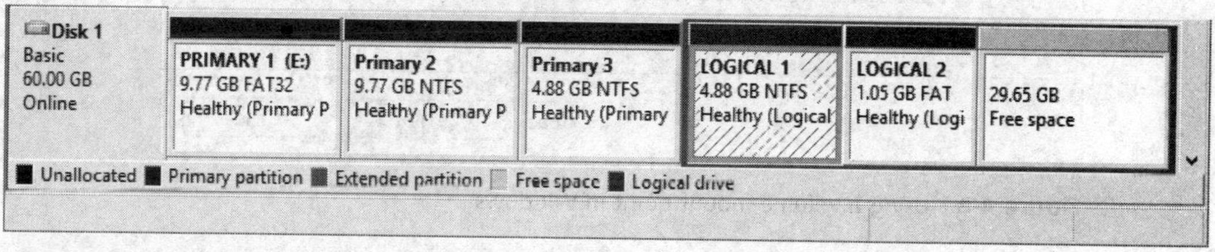


**Figure 4-7** A disk with primary and extended partitions

Microsoft generally refers to a partition that has a file system installed as a **volume**. In most cases, this book will do the same.

Each volume is usually assigned a letter followed by a colon: A:, B:, C:, and so on through Z:. This design lets you easily address the individual file systems by specifying a drive letter. Letters A: and B: were traditionally reserved for two removable file systems on floppy disk drives. Because floppy drives are no longer found on modern systems, the A: and B: drive letters can be used for any storage medium. Typically, C: is reserved for the first volume, and is normally the system that contains the Windows OS. All other file systems located on fixed disks and controlled by the hard disk drivers in the operating system follow in sequential order. So, a machine with two hard disks of two partitions each will have the drive letters C: for the first volume on the first disk, D: for the second volume on the first disk, E: for the first volume on the second disk, and F: for the second volume on the second disk. Disks that require special drivers, such as DVD/CD-ROM drives or removable disks, can be assigned any unused drive letter. By default, they will be assigned the next letter after the drive letter used by the last hard disk. In the previous example, a DVD/CD-ROM drive would be drive G:.

Since Windows XP, you can access a volume as a folder on another NTFS volume. This means that instead of assigning a drive letter to a volume, you mount the volume in an empty folder on an NTFS volume that is assigned a drive letter. When you format a disk using the Windows Disk Management utility, you have the option to **mount** the disk instead of assigning a drive letter (see Figure 4-8). The empty folder into which a volume is mounted is called a **volume mount point.**

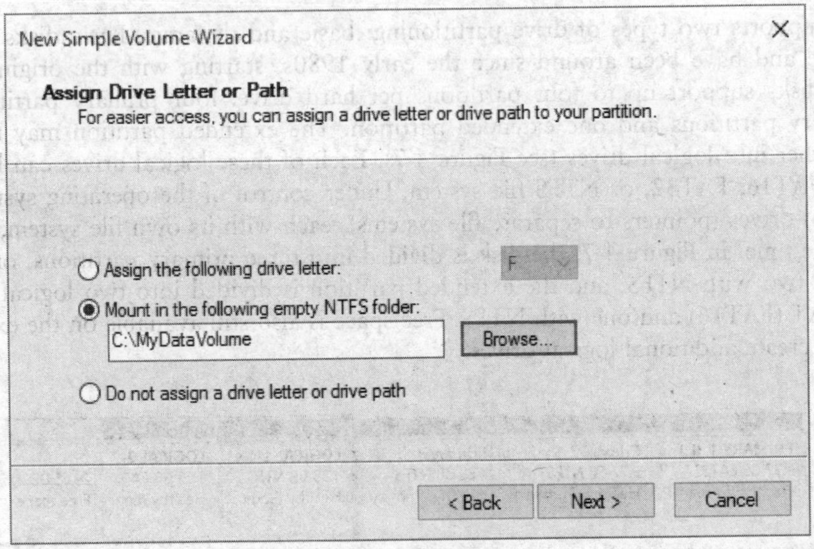


**Figure 4-8** Using a volume mount point in Windows

In earlier versions of Windows, it was common to use the *fdisk* utility to partition hard disks. However, in versions of Windows starting with Windows 2000, you typically partition disks during the installation of the operating system and can add or reconfigure partitions after the operating system is installed. During the installation, it is necessary to partition at least the area on which the operating system is loaded. If your disks are currently unpartitioned, Windows will provide the option to automatically create the necessary volumes: one called System Reserved that is active and holds the boot configuration data and another that will be assigned the C: drive and hold the Windows OS. The System Reserved volume is about 500 MB and is not assigned a drive letter.

After the operating system is loaded, you can use the Disk Management tool to partition additional free space and disks. Refer to Figure 4-6 for an example of the Disk Management tool in Windows 10. The fastest way to access the Disk Management tool in Windows 8.1 and later versions is to right-click Start and then click Disk Management in the menu. The tool can also be accessed from the Control Panel and the Computer Management console. You learn more about managing disks with this tool in Chapter 7.

**Formatting** After you partition a disk, it is time to place the file system on the partition using the process called **formatting**. When you first install a Windows operating system, Windows will automatically create and format the necessary partitions, as mentioned, or you can create and format the partitions manually. The installation process then creates the folder structure and writes the OS files to the disk. After the operating system is installed, you can use the Disk Management tool to create additional volumes. Another option for formatting a hard disk is to use the *format* command from the Command Prompt window. This command writes all of the file system structure to the disk. As with many system-level commands, *format* includes several additional switches that modify precise program operation. You can view a list of these switches by typing *format /?* in the Command Prompt window. See Table 4-1 for a list of *format* switches.

Commands frequently use switches. A **switch** in a command changes the way a particular command operates. In many operating systems, these extra commands follow a forward slash and take the form of a letter or combination of letters, such as the *dir* command in Windows systems, which shows the contents of one or more directories and can take several switches or arguments, including */p* (pause when the screen is full) and */s* (include subdirectories). In UNIX/Linux systems, the command switches frequently begin with one (-) or two (--) dashes.

Formatting a disk removes all data that was on the disk. On disks that have never been formatted, the *format* command writes new sector and track markers on the disk. On disks used previously, you can use the */q* (quick format) option. This tells *format* to dispense with the disk check and simply write a new root folder and FAT or MFT. Using the */q* switch makes the format operation a lot faster, but it also skips the detailed checking of the disk, which can cause trouble later if an application tries to write information to a bad disk location.

**Table 4-1** ***Format*** **command switches**

| Switch | Function |
|---|---|
| */v:label* | Specifies the volume label |
| */q* | Uses a quick format technique that does not check the disk for damaged clusters or bad spots |
| */f:size* | Specifies the size of the floppy disk to format (such as 160, 180, 320, 360, 720, 1.2, 1.44, or 2.88, where the file sizes are in KB or MB) |
| */fs:filesystem* | Specifies whether to format for FAT16, FAT32, or NTFS |

*(continues)*

**Table 4-1** ***Format*** **command switches (*continued*)**

| Switch | Function |
|---|---|
| */t:tracks* | Designates the number of tracks on a side (disks can be formatted on both sides) |
| */n:sectors* | Designates how many sectors are in a track |
| */c* | NTFS only: this causes files created on the volume to be compressed |
| */p:count* | Write zeros in all sectors for the number of times specified in the count parameter. This option causes all data on the disk to be overwritten with 0 bits for security reasons to ensure that no data is recoverable. This is not valid with the */q* switch. |
| */X* | Forces the volume to dismount first, if necessary |
| */R:revision* | UDF only: forces a specific UDF format revision |
| */L* | NTFS only: use large file records |
| */A:size* | Overrides the default allocation unit (cluster) size |
| */N:sectors* | Specifies the number of sectors per track. |
| */S:state* | Specifies support for short filenames. The state is either "enable" or "disable." Short names are disabled by default. |
| */I:state* | ReFS only: Specifies whether integrity should be enabled on the new volume. The state is either "enable" or "disable." Integrity is enabled on storage that supports data redundancy by default. |

TIP

It is possible to run Windows operating systems and UNIX/Linux systems on one machine. For example, if you only format a portion of a partitioned hard disk for Windows, you can format another portion for UNIX/Linux if you save the room required by the operating system—but it is advised that you use the appropriate disk formatting utility for your UNIX/Linux operating system or let the UNIX/ Linux installation program do the formatting.

The boot block is placed in the first sector on the disk, which also contains the root folder (the highest-level folder). The root folder is also where the system stores file information, such as name, start cluster, file size, file modification date and time, and file attributes (file characteristics such as Hidden, Read-only, Archive, and so on). The root folder on every partition has a fixed size that can contain a maximum of 512 entries in FAT16 and unlimited entries in FAT32 and NTFS. Each entry corresponds with a cluster address or sector on the disk. When the file system performs its format operation, it divides the disk into clusters that are sequentially numbered. Each of the two copies of the FAT has exactly one entry for each cluster.

When a file is stored to disk, its data is written in the clusters on the disk. The filename is stored in the folder, along with the number of the first cluster in which the data is stored. When the operating system fills the first cluster, data is written to the next free cluster on the disk. The FAT entry corresponding with the first cluster is filled with the number of the second cluster in the file. When the second cluster is full, the operating system continues to write in the next free cluster. The FAT entry for the second cluster is set to point to the cluster number for the third cluster, and so on. When a file is completely written to the disk, the FAT entry for the final cluster is filled with all 1s, which means the end of the file. At this time, the folder entry for the file is updated with the total file size. This is commonly referred to as the **linked-list** method.

Clusters are of a fixed length, and if a file does not exactly match the space available in the clusters it uses, you can end up with some unused space at the end of a cluster. This is a little wasteful, and it also explains why a file's folder entry must include the exact file size. The operating system sets all FAT entries to 0s when it formats the disk, indicating that none of the clusters is being used. When you write a file to disk, the operating system finds free space on the disk simply by looking for the next FAT entry that contains all 0s. In most cases, the *format* command reads every address on the disk to make sure they are usable. Unusable spots are marked in the FAT as **bad clusters**, and these areas are never used for file storage. The *format* command then writes a new root folder and file allocation table, and the disk is ready for use.

When formatting a hard disk, the size of each entry in the FAT16 table is 16 bits long on any disk larger than 16 MB. On a hard disk, several sectors are combined into a cluster; exactly how many sectors per cluster depends on the size of the hard disk.

Recall that the largest possible partition in a FAT16 file system is 4 GB. Keep in mind that the smallest allocation unit is one cluster. If you store a file that is 300 bytes long on a file system that has clusters of 64 KB, you will waste a lot of space. For this reason, smaller cluster sizes are generally considered desirable. As a result, Windows systems using FAT with large hard disks frequently have many hard disk partitions.

Each partition stores an extra copy of the FAT in case the first copy gets damaged. However, there is only one copy of the root folder on each partition. This concept is shown in Figure 4-9.

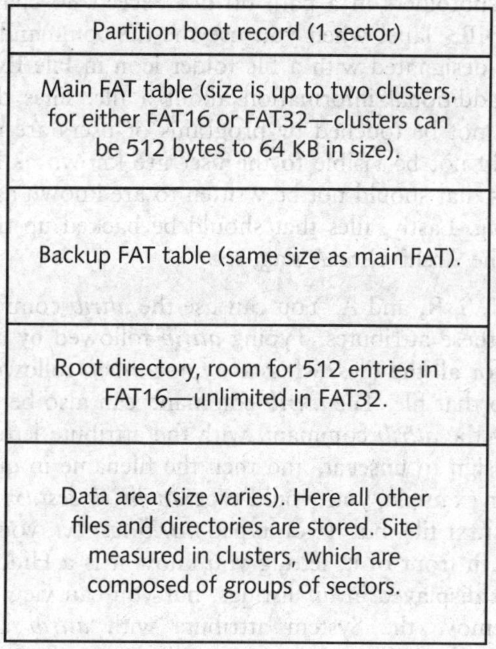


**Figure 4-9** Typical FAT directory structure

The FATs and root folder are found at the beginning of each partition, and they are always at the same location. This makes it possible for the boot program to easily find the files needed to start the operating system. Other directories in the file system are specialized files. They are identical to any other file in the operating system, with the exception of having the folder attribute set in their own folder entry. There can be a virtually unlimited number of directories, with a virtually unlimited number of files in each (limited only by the amount of storage space on the disk).

The FAT folder structure is simple. In each folder entry, information about the file is stored, including the filename, the file revision date and time, the file size, and the file attributes. The filename consists of two parts: the name and the extension, which contains up to three characters. Extensions can have a special meaning. For example, files with a .sys extension are generally device drivers; files with .com or .exe extensions are program files the operating system can execute; and files with the .bat extension are batch files of commands that can be executed as if they were typed in a command prompt window. The filename and extension are separated by a period.

Apart from the filename, each folder entry also contains some **status bits** that identify the type of filename contained in each entry. The status bits in use are Volume, Folder, System, Hidden, Read-only, and Archive. The Volume bit indicates a file system **volume label**, or a nickname for the file system. The volume name can be set with the */v* option of the *format* command, or by using the *volume* command. The volume name appears at the top of folder listings (using the *dir* command). The Folder bit is used to signify that a file contains folder data and should be treated as a folder by the file system. Folders may in turn contain subfolders, as long as the names of all subfolders in a path do not exceed 80 characters. You will see a folder marked with a <DIR> label when you use the *dir* command in the Command Prompt window, or it will be designated with a file folder icon in File Explorer. The four remaining attributes indicate additional information about a file. Files that are part of the operating system and should not be touched by programs or users are marked with a System or S flag. Files that should not be visible to the user are known as Hidden files and are marked with the H bit. Files that should not be written to are known as Read-only files and are marked with the R flag. Lastly, files that should be backed up the next time a backup is made are said to have the Archive, or A flag, set.

Overall, there are four optional flags—H, S, R, and A. You can use the *attrib* command at the Command Prompt to look at or set these attributes. Typing *attrib* followed by a folder name shows all of the attribute settings for all the files, whereas typing *attrib* followed by a filename shows only attributes specific to that file. The *attrib* command can also be used to set file attributes. To do this, you follow the *attrib* command with the attribute letter, then the + sign to set the attribute or the – sign to unset it, and then the filename in question. To make a file named test.txt hidden, for example, you would type *attrib +h test.txt*. If you then typed *dir*, you would not see the test.txt file, but if you typed *attrib test.txt*, you would once again see test.txt, with the letter *H* in front of it, letting you know it is a Hidden file. A file with the S attribute set is also not displayed in *dir* listings, but you can view it with the *attrib* command, and you can remove the System attribute with *attrib* as well. Table 4-2 shows the various arguments and switches you can use with the *attrib* command.

**Table 4-2 Attribute command (*attrib*) arguments and switches**

| Argument/switch | Description |
|---|---|
| *r* | Read-only file attribute |
| *a* | Archive file attribute |
| *s* | System file attribute |
| *h* | Hidden file attribute |
| *i* | Not a content-indexed file attribute; the contents of the file will not be included in the search index |
| *x* | No scrub file attribute; only supported on ReFS file systems |
| *v* | Integrity attribute; only supported on ReFS file systems |
| */s* | Processes files in all folders in the specified path |
| */d* | Processes folders as well as files |

# Windows File Systems

Windows XP through Windows Server 2008 R2 support three file systems: extended FAT16, FAT32, and NTFS. Windows 8, Windows Server 2012, and later versions also support ReFS. All of these operating systems also support file systems for DVD/CD-ROM drives and USB devices like flash drives.

## FAT16 and Extended FAT16

The extended FAT16 file system under Windows evolved from the FAT16 system used in early versions of MS-DOS and Windows (3.x/95/98/Me). An extended file system can be divided into multiple logical file systems. FAT uses a file allocation table to store folder information about files, such as filenames, file attributes, and file location. The "16" in FAT16 means that this file system uses 16-bit entries in the file allocation table and uses $2^{16}$ clusters. Remember that clusters are blocks of space containing one or more sectors into which the disk is divided.

In extended FAT16, the maximum size of a volume is 4 GB, and the maximum size of a file is 2 GB. One advantage to using the extended FAT16 file system is that it has been around for a long time, and even non-Windows operating systems, such as UNIX/Linux, can read disks written in FAT16 format. Further, because the file system is simple, relatively little can go wrong, which makes it a stable file system.

Originally, FAT16 used "8.3" **filenames**, which can be up to eight characters long followed by a period and an **extension** of three characters, such as Filename.ext. Examples of extensions are .txt for text files, .doc or .docx for word-processing files, .xls or .xlsx for Excel spreadsheets, and so on. The limitations of this naming convention contributed to the development and use of **long filenames (LFNs)** in extended FAT16. An LFN:

- Can contain as many as 255 characters
- Is not case sensitive
- Cannot include characters such as " / \ [ ] : ; =, (this applies both to 8.3 filenames and LFNs)

Because LFN characters are stored in **Unicode**, a coding system that allows for representation of any character in any language, it is possible to use most legitimate characters in Windows in a filename (see the previous bulleted list for some exceptions). The advantage of LFNs and Unicode is that LFNs can be read by other operating systems, including Mac OS and UNIX/Linux systems (such as on a Windows 2008 server that has file services installed for Mac OS and UNIX/Linux clients).

Until fairly recently, letters and digits were represented by ASCII (American Standard Code for Information Interchange, pronounced *as-key*) values. The problem with this standard is that it uses an entire byte to represent each character, which limits the number of characters that can be represented to 255. This is not enough to handle all the characters needed to represent world languages, which use several different alphabets (Greek, Russian, Japanese, and Hindi, for example). ASCII deals with this problem by employing many different character sets, depending on the characters you're trying to represent. The Unicode Consortium, a not-for-profit organization, represents an alternative in which there is a single, unique code for each possible character in any language. The first 128 characters in Unicode are the 128 ASCII characters. Unicode allows over a million characters to be defined. It includes distinct character codes for all modern languages and many historic scripts like Egyptian hieroglyphs. To the user who communicates primarily in English, Unicode will not make a big difference, but in this age of worldwide communication, it is a necessity.

## FAT32

Starting with Windows 95 Release 2, all Windows versions support FAT32. FAT32 is designed to accommodate larger-capacity disks than FAT16 and avoid the problem of cluster size limitations. A file allocation table entry in FAT32 is 32 bits in length and FAT32 supports up to $2^{28}$ clusters (this figure is not to the 32nd power because some extra space is reserved for the operating system). In FAT32, the root folder does not have to be at the beginning of a volume; it can be located anywhere. Also, FAT32 can use disk space more efficiently than FAT16 because it can use smaller cluster sizes. FAT32 partitions have a theoretical size of 2 terabytes (TB); however, the largest volume that can be formatted is 32 GB (still much larger than FAT16). The maximum file size in FAT32 is raised to 4 GB.

FAT32 shares characteristics of extended FAT16, such as the double FAT structure at the beginning of a partition for fault tolerance and the use of LFNs and Unicode.

Sometimes users choose to employ extended FAT16 or FAT32 because they are familiar with these file systems or they have dual-boot systems, such as a system with Windows XP and the older Windows 98. Another reason for using extended FAT16 or FAT32 is that these file systems offer fast response on small, 1 or 2 GB partitions.

Windows file systems can be converted from FAT16 or FAT32 to NTFS, either during installation or at a later date. If you convert at a later date, use the *convert* command in the Command Prompt window. However, you cannot convert from NTFS to FAT16 or FAT32, except by reformatting to use FAT16 or FAT32 and then performing a full restore. You can use the Windows Backup tool to perform a backup or a restore from a previous backup.

If a partition is set up for FAT and is 2 GB or smaller, Windows will format it as FAT16 during installation (if the option to use FAT is selected). Partitions that are over 2 GB are formatted as FAT32.

## FAT64

FAT64, also known as exFAT, is a proprietary file system. Microsoft introduced it for mobile personal storage needs to handle large files. As the size of pictures, videos, and other media files grows, the file size limits of FAT16 and FAT32 are an important consideration. The size limit for FAT16 is 2 GB minus one byte, and for FAT32 it is 4 GB minus one byte. FAT64 with a limit of 16 EB is a good choice for USB flash devices when you will be storing very large files.

FAT64 is available starting in Service Pack 1 for Windows Vista. It is also available for Linux from a third party. Apple added support in Mac OS X Snow Leopard in late 2010.

## NTFS

NTFS is the primary Windows file system for all Windows operating systems starting with Windows NT 3.1. It is a modern system designed for the needs of a networked environment.

The way NTFS keeps track of files and clusters is a little different from that of FAT file systems. Rather than using a structure of FATs and directories, NTFS uses a **Master File Table (MFT)**. Like the FATs and directories, this table is located at the beginning of the partition. The boot sector is located ahead of the MFT. Following the MFT, there are several system files that the file system uses to make all the features of NTFS work. Note that the MFT in itself is nothing more than a file on the file system, as are all other system files. The second file on the disk is a copy of the first three records of the MFT. This ensures that if the MFT is damaged, it can be re-created. File number five, known as $, contains the entries in the root folder, whereas file number six, known as $Bitmap, contains data about which clusters on the disk are in use. Normally, the MFT and related files take up about 1 MB of disk space when the disk is initially formatted.

When a file is created in NTFS, a record for that file is added to the MFT. This record contains all standard information, such as filename, size, dates, and times. It also contains additional attributes, such as security settings, ownership, and permissions. If there is not enough room in an MFT record to store security settings, the settings that don't fit are put on another cluster somewhere on the disk, and the MFT record points to this information. If a file is very small, there is sometimes enough room in the MFT record to store the file data. If there is not enough room, the system allocates clusters elsewhere on the disk. The

MFT record reflects the sequence of clusters that a file uses. The attributes can generally be repeated; it is possible to have a whole series of different security attributes for different users. It is also possible to have multiple filenames that refer to the same file, a technique known as **hard linking**. This is a feature, also available in UNIX/Linux file systems, that is sometimes used to make the same file appear in multiple directories without having to allocate disk space for the file more than once.

NTFS is referred to in two ways. The first is by the actual release numbering and the second is the more accepted way, which very roughly refers to a Windows operating system. Table 4-3 shows the five versions of NTFS, the operating system they correspond to, and the generally accepted version number for NTFS.

**Table 4-3 NTFS versions**

| Official version number | Generally accepted version number | Windows operating system |
|---|---|---|
| 1.0 | NTFS | |
| 1.1 | NTFS | |
| 1.2 | NTFS 4 | Windows NT 3.51 and NT 4.0 |
| 3.0 | NTFS 5.0 | Windows 2000 |
| 3.1 | NTFS 5.1/5.2 | Windows XP/Windows Server 2003/Windows Server 2008/Vista |
| 3.1 | NTFS 6.0 | Windows Server 2008 R2/Windows 7 and later |

Some of the basic features incorporated into NTFS include:

- Long filenames
- Built-in security features
- Better file compression than FAT
- Ability to use larger disks and files than FAT
- File activity tracking for better recovery and stability than FAT
- **Portable Operating System Interface for UNIX (POSIX)** support
- Volume striping and volume extensions
- Less disk fragmentation than FAT

As a full-featured network file system, NTFS is equipped with security features that meet the U.S. government's C2 security specifications. C2 security refers to high-level, "top-secret" standards for data protection, system auditing, and system access, which are required by some government agencies. One security feature is the ability to establish the type of access allowed for users of folders and files within folders. The file and folder access can be tailored to the particular requirements of an organization. For example, the system files on a server can be protected so only the server administrator has access. A folder of databases can be protected with read access, but no access to change data; also, a public folder can give users in a designated group access to read and update files, but not to delete files.

File compression is a process that significantly reduces the size of a file by removing unused space within it or using compression algorithms. Some files can be compressed by more than 40 percent, saving important disk space for other storage needs. This is particularly useful for files that are accessed infrequently. NTFS provides the ability to compress files as needed. Try Hands-On Project 4-4 to compress files in Windows.

NTFS can be scaled to accommodate very large files, particularly for database applications. A Microsoft SQL Server database file might be 20 GB or larger, for example. This means an organization can store pictures, scanned images, and sound clips in a single database. The NTFS system can support files up to $2^{64}$ bytes (in theory).

Another NTFS feature is **journaling**, the ability to keep a log or journal of file system activity. This is a critical process if there is a power outage or hard disk failure. Important information can be retrieved and restored in these situations. FAT does not offer this capability.

NTFS supports POSIX standards to enable portability of applications from one computer system to another. POSIX was initially developed as a UNIX standard designed to ensure portability of applications among various versions of UNIX, but now POSIX is used by other file systems and operating systems as well. NTFS follows the POSIX 1 standard, which includes case-sensitive filenames and use of multiple filenames (called *hard links*, a concept discussed later in this chapter). For example, the files Myfile.doc and MYFile.doc are considered different files (except when using File Explorer or the Command Prompt window).

An important volume-handling feature of NTFS is the ability to create extensions on an existing volume, such as when new disk storage is added. Another feature is volume striping, which is a process that equally divides the contents of each file across two or more volumes to extend disk life, enable fault tolerance features, and balance the disk load for better performance.

Last, NTFS is less prone to file corruption than FAT in part because it has a **hot fix** capability, which means that if a bad disk area is detected, NTFS automatically copies the information from the bad area to another disk area that is not damaged.

In addition to the NTFS 4 features already described, NTFS 5 adds several new features:

- Ability to encrypt files
- No system reboot required after creating an extended volume
- Ability to reduce drive designations
- Indexing for fast access

- Ability to retain shortcuts and other file information when files and folders are placed on other volumes (In Windows systems, a shortcut is a link or icon that can start software in the same location or in a different location through a simple mouse click or double-click.)
- Ability to establish disk quotas

With NTFS 5, files can be encrypted so that their contents are available only to those granted access. Also, volume extensions can be set up without the need to reboot the system. (In NTFS 4, you must reboot after adding an extension to an existing volume.) Volume mount points, as previously discussed, can be created as a way to reduce the number of drive designations for multiple volumes, instead of designating a new drive for each new volume. In Windows, a mount point appears to the user as a folder, but it is really a link to a hard drive, DVD/CD-ROM drive, or other storage medium. NTFS 5 incorporates fast indexing in conjunction with Active Folder to make file searching and retrieval faster than in NTFS 4. A new technique called **Distributed Link Tracking** is available in NTFS 5 so that shortcuts you have created are not lost when you move files to another volume. Finally, NTFS 5 enables you to set up **disk quotas** to control how much disk space users can occupy. Disk quotas are a vital tool for disk capacity planning to ensure that there is enough disk space for all server operations and critical files.

The latest version of NTFS, referred to as NTFS 6, adds several new features:

- Transactional NTFS
- Partition resizing
- Self-healing

Transactional NTFS is used to perform operations on an NTFS volume in transaction mode; that is, all specified file system transactions take place or none of them takes place. You can package registry and file system operations in a transaction so that all of the operations take place or none of them succeed. If one of the file system operations does not work, then everything is aborted and nothing takes place. Transactional NTFS is used heavily in Windows Server 2008.

Beginning with Windows Vista, Microsoft allowed for the expanding and shrinking of partitions, so you could adjust the amount of space used by a volume without having to delete the partition and reformat the disk. The capability is still very limited and there are third-party products that are more capable and robust.

In the past, if you had problems with NTFS volumes on your disk, you used *chkdsk.exe* to fix the problem. This meant taking down the volume to run the utility. With self-healing NTFS, the utility runs in the background to correct hard disk problems. The availability of the file system is far greater than the previous way using the *chkdsk.exe* utility, data is preserved as much as possible, and better reports are provided to describe modifications made to the volume. Table 4-4 compares FAT16, FAT32, FAT64, and NTFS.

**Table 4-4 FAT16, FAT32, FAT64, and NTFS compared**

| Feature | FAT16 | FAT32 | FAT64 (exFAT) | NTFS |
|---|---|---|---|---|
| Total volume size | 2–4 GB | 2 TB to 16 TB | 512 TB | 2 TB |
| Maximum file size | 4 GB | 4 GB | 16 EB (exabytes); 1 EB equals a billion gigabytes | Theoretical limit of 264 bytes |
| Compatible with floppy disks | Yes | No | No | No |
| Security | Limited security based on attributes and shares | Limited security based on attributes and shares | Limited security based on attributes and shares | Extensive security and auditing options |
| File compression | Supported with extra utilities | Supported with extra utilities | Supported with extra utilities | Supported as part of NTFS |
| File activity tracking | None | None | None | Tracking via a log |
| POSIX support | None | Limited | Limited | POSIX 1 support |
| Hot fix | Limited | Limited | Yes | Yes |
| Large database support | Limited | Yes | Yes | Yes |
| Multiple disk drives in one volume | No | No | No | Yes |

When you copy a file from an NTFS system to a FAT16 or FAT32 system, the security permissions of the file are lost because permissions are not supported in FAT16 or FAT32.

**Basic and Dynamic Disks** Basic disks use traditional disk partitioning techniques, meaning they are limited to four primary partitions or three primary partitions and one extended partition. Windows 2000 Server introduced dynamic disks, which do not use traditional partitioning techniques. Dynamic disks make it possible to set up a large number of volumes on one disk and provide the ability to extend volumes onto additional physical disks. You can convert basic disks to dynamic disks using the Disk Management tool.

**NTFS File System and Disk Utilities** Sometimes disk performance is affected by corrupted files, or when the file allocation table loses pointers to certain files. You can correct these problems and maintain the integrity of the data by periodically running the "Check disk" utility, called *chkdsk*. All versions of Windows starting with Windows 2000 come with *chkdsk*, which is run from the Command Prompt window or by clicking Start, clicking Run, entering *chkdsk*, and pressing OK. The *chkdsk* utility can detect and fix an extensive set of file system problems in FAT and NTFS systems. Table 4-5 presents a list of the switches that are available for this utility and Figure 4-10 illustrates *chkdsk* results for a computer running Windows 10.

**Table 4-5** ***Chkdsk* switch options**

| Switch/parameter | Purpose |
|---|---|
| *[volume]* (such as C:) | Specifies that *chkdsk* check only the designated volume |
| *[filename]* (such as *.dll) | Enables a check of the specified file or files only |
| /c | For NTFS only, *chkdsk* uses an abbreviated check of the folder structure |
| /f | Instructs *chkdsk* to fix errors that it finds and locks the disk while checking |
| /i | For NTFS only, *chkdsk* uses an abbreviated check of indexes |
| /L:size | For NTFS only, enables you to specify the size of the log file created by the disk check |
| /r | Searches for bad sectors, fixes problems, and recovers information (if possible, or use the *recover* command afterward) |
| /v | On FAT, shows the entire path name of files; on NTFS, shows clean-up messages associated with errors |
| /b | In NTFS only, clears the list of bad clusters stored on the volume and rescans everything. This feature was added in Vista. |
| /x | Dismounts or locks a volume before starting (/f also dismounts or locks a volume) |

In Hands-On Project 4-5, you run *chkdsk* in Windows.

In Windows versions starting with Windows 2000, *chkdsk* runs automatically at bootup if it detects that the operating system was previously shut down with a file system problem, or shut down before the operating system had the opportunity to clean up temporary files on the disk.

```
Administrator: C:\WINDOWS\system32\cmd.exe

C:\Windows\System32>chkdsk
The type of the file system is NTFS.
Volume label is Win10OS.

WARNING!  /F parameter not specified.
Running CHKDSK in read-only mode.

Stage 1: Examining basic file system structure ...
  335104 file records processed.
File verification completed.
  5788 large file records processed.
  0 bad file records processed.

Stage 2: Examining file name linkage ...
  405214 index entries processed.
Index verification completed.
  0 unindexed files scanned.
  0 unindexed files recovered to lost and found.

Stage 3: Examining security descriptors ...
Security descriptor verification completed.
  35056 data files processed.
CHKDSK is verifying Usn Journal...
  41092544 USN bytes processed.
Usn Journal verification completed.

Windows has scanned the file system and found no problems.
No further action is required.

 499644415 KB total disk space.
 107024852 KB in 192502 files.
    129164 KB in 35057 indexes.
         0 KB in bad sectors.
    459915 KB in use by the system.
     65536 KB occupied by the log file.
 392030484 KB available on disk.

      4096 bytes in each allocation unit.
 124911103 total allocation units on disk.
  98007621 allocation units available on disk.

C:\Windows\System32>
```

**Figure 4-10** Results of the *chkdsk* command

If *chkdsk* finds any problems, it either fixes them (depending on the error) or displays an error message. Or, you have the option of letting it fix all problems automatically by using the */f* or Fix option. The most common problems are files with sizes of 0, which is caused when a file is not properly closed, or chains of clusters (file allocation units) that have no folder entries attached. When *chkdsk* finds lost allocation units or chains, it prompts you with a yes-or-no question: "Convert lost chains to files? Answer 'yes' to the question so that you can save the lost information to files." The files that *chkdsk* creates for each lost chain are labeled Filexxx.chk and can be edited with a text editor such as Notepad to determine their contents. The presence of some bad sectors is normal; many disks have a few bad sectors that are marked by the manufacturer during the low-level format on which data cannot be written. If there are hundreds of bad sectors, however, this indicates a problem with the disk.

If you frequently see errors when you run *chkdsk*, you should look for a bigger problem. Sometimes the operator is to blame. Systems that are not used properly—for example, because software is not closed correctly—can cause problems in the file system. Often, disks that are about to fail will show small glitches (*chkdsk* errors) a long time before they finally fail, so be alert for possible future system failure if you see frequent errors.

### From the Trenches ...

A customer who purchased a newly manufactured computer ran *chkdsk* on the hard drive to verify its condition. *Chkdsk* showed that nearly half of the disk had bad clusters that were quarantined via the low-level format so they could not be used. Because the customer ran *chkdsk* right after receiving the computer, he was able to discover the problem right away and returned the computer for a more functional hard drive.

NTFS 6 introduced the concept of self-healing, which was mentioned earlier in this chapter. Because it runs in the background and attempts to correct problems automatically, the need to run *chkdsk.exe* has been greatly reduced.

All versions of Windows since Windows 2000 have a built-in disk defragmenting tool. Over time, disk space becomes fragmented with pockets of open space. For example, when an operating system writes a file to disk, it looks for the first place in the first empty disk location and uses the cluster (allocation unit) indicated there. It continues to use the next empty cluster until there are no more clusters free immediately following the last cluster. At that point, it skips ahead to find the next open cluster. As a result, files written to disk may be scattered all over the disk. Imagine a scenario in which four small files are written—we'll call them A, B, C, and D. On an empty disk, these files will occupy sequential clusters on the disk. If files A and C are removed, there will be some open clusters on the disk. If file E, which is larger than A and C combined, is written to the disk, it will start using the clusters formerly occupied by A, then use those formerly used by C, and then continue beyond the clusters occupied by D. When a disk is highly fragmented, the read heads have to work harder to obtain data, wasting time and creating more wear. For this reason, it is wise to periodically defragment your disks. A **defragmenter** is a tool that rearranges data on the disk in a continuous fashion, ridding the disk of scattered open clusters.

Windows versions since Windows 2000 all have Disk Defragmenter (see Figure 4-11). Disk Defragmenter can be used on volumes formatted for FAT16, FAT32, FAT64, and NTFS.

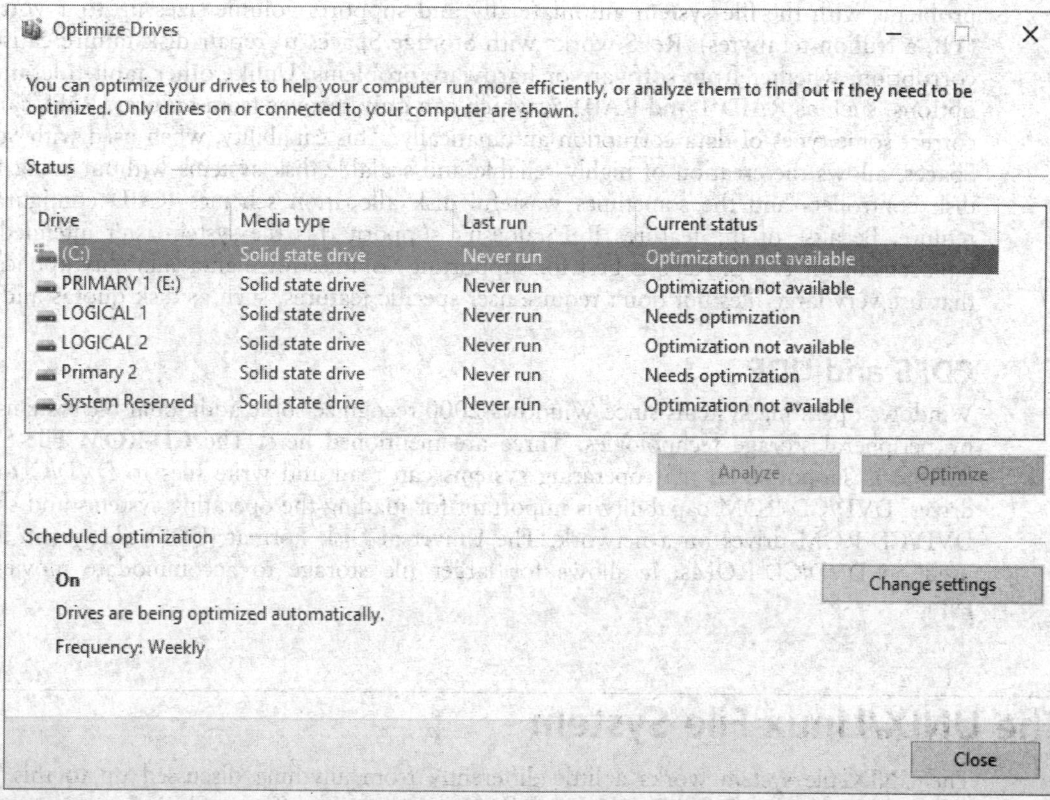


**Figure 4-11** Disk Defragmenter in Windows 10

Windows versions after XP come with a Disk Cleanup utility that deletes temporary Internet files, temporary program files, program files that are not used, and files in the Recycle Bin. To start this utility from File Explorer, right-click the disk and click Properties. From the General tab, click Disk Cleanup.

Care should be taken to use only utilities designed to work with NTFS; serious damage can occur if other utilities are used. If utilities designed for MS-DOS or Windows 95/98/Me are used on NTFS file systems, they may reach incorrect conclusions regarding file system layout. This can result in loss of data, damaged files, or even destruction of the complete file system and all of its contents.

## Resilient File System (ReFS)

ReFS became available starting with Windows Server 2012. The main use of **Resilient File System (ReFS)** is in large file-sharing applications where volumes are managed by Storage Spaces (which was introduced in Chapter 2). Although ReFS is mostly backward-compatible with NTFS, it doesn't support file compression, disk quotas, and EFS (Encrypting File System). Also, Windows can't be booted from an ReFS volume. ReFS can repair minor problems with the file system automatically and supports volume sizes up to 1 yottabyte (YB, a trillion terabytes). ReFS works with Storage Spaces to repair disk failure caused by corruption, whether from software or hardware problems. Unlike other fault-tolerant disk options, such as RAID 1 and RAID 5, which can only recover from failures, ReFS can also correct some types of data corruption automatically. This capability, when used with Storage Spaces, allows the creation of highly reliable and scalable disk systems without using RAID disk controllers and the sometimes wasteful disk allocation schemes RAID configurations require. Because of the features ReFS doesn't support, this file system isn't intended as a replacement for NTFS. ReFS is best for supporting volumes for high-availability applications that use very large files but don't require user-specific features, such as disk quotas and EFS.

### CDFS and UDF

Windows operating systems since Windows 2000 recognize some additional file systems used by peripheral storage technologies. Three are mentioned here. The **CD-ROM File System (CDFS)** is supported so that operating systems can read and write files to DVD/CD-ROM drives. DVD/CD-ROM capability is important for loading the operating systems and sharing DVD/CD-ROM drives on a network. The Universal Disk Format (UDF) file system is also used on DVD/CD-ROMs; it allows for larger file storage to accommodate movies and games.

## The UNIX/Linux File System

The UNIX file system works a little differently from anything discussed up to this point. "UNIX file system" is really a misnomer. In reality, many different file systems can be used, but some are more "native" to specific UNIX operating systems than others. Most versions of UNIX and Linux support the **UNIX file system (ufs)**, which is the original native UNIX file system. Ufs is a hierarchical (tree structure) file system that is expandable, supports large storage, provides file and folder security, and is reliable. In fact, many qualities of NTFS are modeled after ufs. Ufs supports journaling so that if a system crashes unexpectedly, it is possible to reconstruct files or to roll back recent changes, resulting in minimal or no damage to the integrity of the files or data. Ufs also supports hot fixes to automatically move data on damaged portions of disks to areas that are not damaged.

In Linux, the native file system is called the **extended file system (ext or ext fs)**, which is installed by default. Ext is modeled after ufs, but the first version contained some bugs, supported files to only 2 GB, and did not offer journaling. However, in Linux, ext provides an advantage over all other file systems because it enables the full range of built-in Linux commands, file manipulation, and security. Newer versions of Linux use either the second (ext2), third (ext3), or fourth (ext4) versions of the extended file system. Ext2 is a reliable file system that handles large disk storage. Ext3 has enhancements of ext2 with the addition of journaling. Ext4 supports file sizes up to 16 TB.

TIP

If you are not sure what file systems are incorporated in UNIX/Linux, you can determine them by viewing the contents of the /proc/filesystems file, or by using the *mount* command to display the mounted file systems. Table 4-6 lists a sampling of file systems that are compatible with UNIX/Linux systems.

**Table 4-6 Typical file systems supported by UNIX/Linux**

| File system | Description |
|---|---|
| Extended file system (ext or ext fs) and the newer versions, second extended file system (ext2 or ext2 fs), third extended file system (ext3 or ext3 fs), and fourth extended file system (ext4 or ext4 fs) | File system that comes with Linux by default (compatible with Linux and FreeBSD) |
| High-performance file system (hpfs) | File system developed for use with the OS/2 operating system |
| msdos | File system that offers compatibility with FAT12 and FAT16 (does not support long filenames); typically installed to enable UNIX to read floppy disks made in MS-DOS or Windows |
| International Standard Operating system (iso9660 in Linux, hsfs in Solaris, cd9660 in FreeBSD) | File system developed for DVD/CD-ROM use; does not support long filenames |
| Proc file system | File system that presents information about the kernel status and the use of memory (not truly a physical file system, but a logical file system) |
| Network file system (nfs) | File system developed by Sun Microsystems for UNIX systems to support network access and sharing of files (such as uploading and downloading files) and supported on virtually all UNIX/Linux versions as well as by many other operating systems |
| Swap file system | File system for the swap space; swap space is disk space used exclusively to store spillover information from memory, when memory is full (called *virtual memory*), and is used by virtually all UNIX/Linux systems |
| UNIX file system (ufs; also called the Berkeley Fast File System) | Original file system for UNIX that is compatible with virtually all UNIX systems and most Linux systems |
| umsdos | File system that is compatible with extended FAT16 as used by Windows NT, 2000, XP, Server 2003, Vista, 7, and Server 2008, but it also supports security permissions, file ownership, and long filenames |
| vfat | File system that is compatible with FAT32 and supports long filenames |
| ntfs | File system used by Windows starting with Windows NT 3.1 |
| Global File System (GFS and GFS2) | File system used by Linux computer clusters |
| XFS | 64-bit high-performance journaling file system that is excellent at handling large files |

The main difference between native UNIX file systems, such as ufs and ext, and those covered earlier in the chapter lies in the way information is physically stored on the disk. Because ufs and ext are the most popular file systems across UNIX platforms, we detail them here and lump them under the heading of "The UNIX/Linux file system." Both file systems use the same structure, which is built on the concept of information nodes, or **inodes**. Each file has an inode and is identified by an inode number. Inode 0 contains the root of the folder structure (/) and is the jumping-off point for all other inodes. This concept is shown in Figure 4-12.

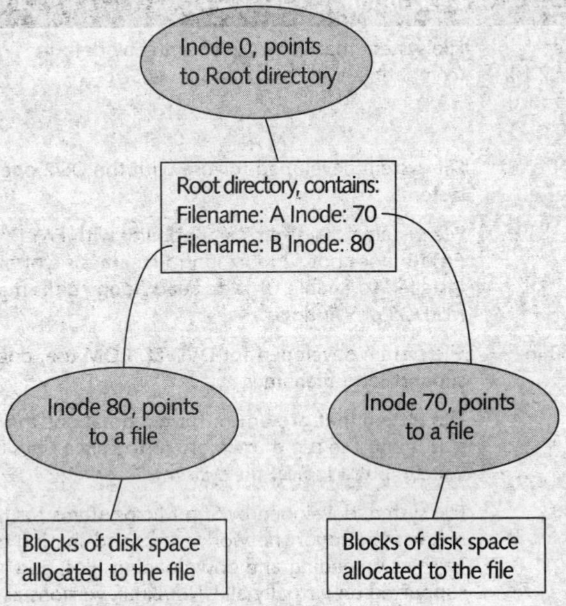


**Figure 4-12** UNIX/Linux information nodes (inodes) design

TIP

You can display inode information for directories and files by using the *ls -i* command. Also, note that in most UNIX/Linux systems (commonly referred to as *nix*), a folder is technically just a file that can hold other files.

An inode contains the name of a file and general information about that file. In terms of general information, each inode indicates user and group ownership, access mode (read, write, and execute security permissions), the size and type of the file, the date the file was created, and the date the file was last modified and read.

The pointer information is based on logical blocks. Each disk is divided into logical blocks ranging in size from 512 to 8192 bytes or more, depending on the version of UNIX/Linux, but blocks can also be divided into multiple sub-blocks or fractions as needed by the file system. The inode for a file contains a pointer (number) that tells the operating system how to locate the first in a set of one or more logical blocks that contain the specific file contents. The inode can also specify the number of blocks or links to the first block used by the folder or file. In short, the inode tells the operating system where to find a file on the hard disk.

The file system itself is identified by the superblock. The **superblock** contains information about the layout of blocks, sectors, and cylinder groups on the file system. This information is the key to finding anything on the file system, and it should never change. Without the superblock, the file system cannot be accessed. For this reason, many copies of the superblock are written into the file system at the time of file system creation. If the superblock is damaged, you can copy one of the superblock copies over the damaged superblock to restore access to the file system.

Note that the inode does not contain a filename; the filename is stored in a folder, which in itself is no more than a file. In it is stored the names of the files and the inode to which they are connected.

Several folder entries can point to the same inode; this is called a hard link. Hard links make it possible to have one file appear in several folders, or in the same folder under several names, without using extra disk space. In Figure 4-13, there are two folders: Marketing and Sales. In the Marketing folder is a file named ClientsFile that points to inode 20301, and in the Sales folder a file named CustomerFile points to the same inode. ClientsFile and CustomerFile are the exact same file.

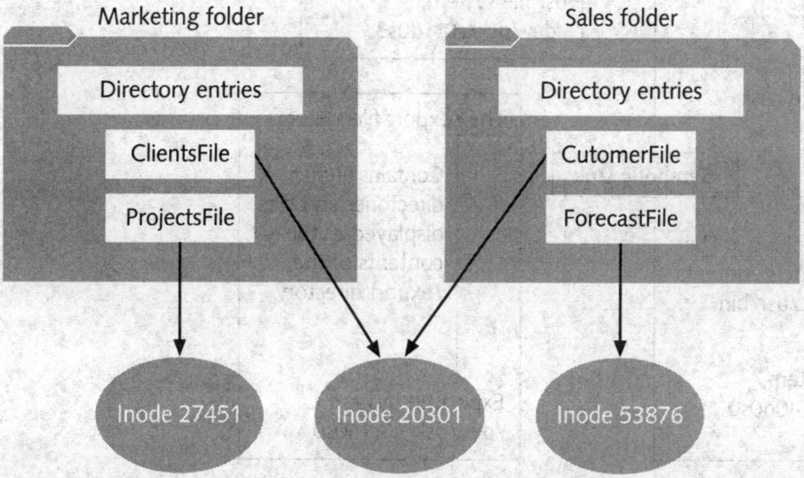


**Figure 4-13** Hard links—multiple folder entries point to the same inode

The inode keeps a counter that tells how many folder entries point to a file. Deleting a file is achieved by deleting the last folder entry, which brings the inode link count down to 0, meaning the file has effectively been removed.

A UNIX/Linux system can have many file systems. Unlike the Windows environment, where drive letters are often used to access each file system, UNIX/Linux uses only mount points, in which each file system is a subfolder of the root of the file system, which is always designated as /.

In UNIX/Linux, all file systems are referred to by a path (see Figure 4-14). The path starts with root (/). If other file systems are to be used, a folder is created on the root file system—for example, a folder named "usr." Then, using the *mount* command, the UNIX/Linux operating system is told to associate the root inode of another file system to the empty folder. This process can be repeated many times, and there is no hard limit to the number of file systems that can be mounted this way, short of the number of inodes in the root file system. Every file in every file system on a computer is thus referred to by a long folder path, and jumping from one file system to another is seamless.

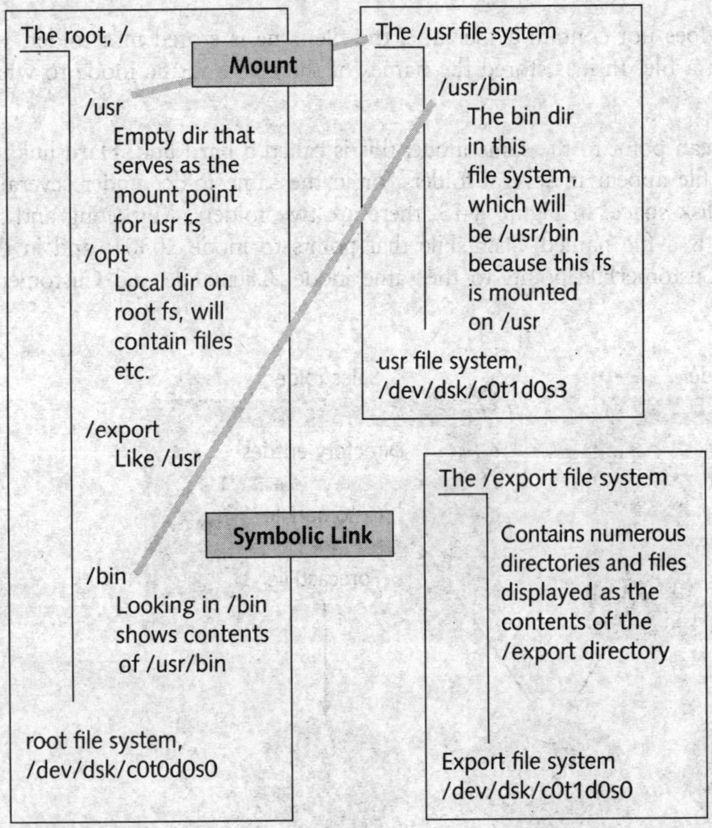


**Figure 4-14** UNIX/Linux file system paths

The *mount* command has several options; typing it without parameters results in a display of the disks (and file systems) that are currently mounted. For each disk, you will see the name of the partition and the path on which it was mounted.

The UNIX/Linux operating system and file system treat uppercase and lowercase characters as different characters; a file named HELLO is different from a file named hello, which is in turn different from one named Hello. Therefore, it is extremely important to type UNIX/Linux filenames exactly as they appear.

As mentioned, a folder is nothing more than a special file. There are several other special files in the UNIX/Linux file system. For example, disks themselves are referenced by a special inode called a device. There are two types of devices: raw devices and block devices. A **raw device** has no logical division in blocks, whereas a **block device** does. Every device the UNIX/Linux computer uses must be represented by a device inode, whether it is a disk, a serial port, or an Ethernet (network) card. These devices have special parameters in the inode that enable the OS to figure out how to get to them. All partitions of all disks appear as devices. For example, an ext3 partition on a hard disk may be represented as /dev/hda1. Devices are normally kept in the /dev or /devices folder. When you look at the output of the *mount* command, you will see your disks referenced this way.

The **symbolic link** is another special feature of the UNIX/Linux file system we should mention here. As previously indicated, it is possible to link multiple folder entries to one inode. For this to work, the inode and the folder entry must be on the same disk partition. If you want to link a folder entry to a file that is on a different partition, you must use a symbolic link. This is a special file that has a flag set in the inode to identify it as a symbolic link. The content of the file is a path that, when followed, leads to another file. Note that a hard link, when created, must point to a valid inode and will therefore always be valid. A symbolic link is merely a pointer to a file. It is possible to create symbolic links that point to files that do not exist, or to remove the file to which a symbolic link points without removing the link. In such cases, you might end up with a symbolic link that appears to be a valid file when viewed in a folder, but when opened returns a "no such file" error. Another interesting effect of using symbolic links is that it is possible to create loops. You can make a Folder A, which contains a Folder B, which contains a link back to Folder A. However, this can become extremely confusing. Hard links and symbolic links are made with the *ln* command. The *ln* command used with no options makes a hard link, and with the *-s* option makes a symbolic link. The first option is the name of the existing file, followed by the name of the link you want to create.

**TIP**

One way to save time in typing is to create a link to a folder that has a long path. For example, assume that you store many files in the /user/bus/inventory folder. Each time you want to see a listing of that folder, you must type *ls /user/bus/inventory*. If you enter *ln / user/bus/inventory* to create a link to that folder, in the future you only have to type *ls inventory* to see its contents. To learn more about the *ln* command, type *man ln* in a terminal or command prompt window, and then press Enter. *Man* is the command for displaying the contents of the online manual pages for a specific command, such as *ls*.

As with all other operating systems discussed so far, you first have to partition a disk to use the UNIX/Linux file system. The command used to partition the disk differs slightly from one version of UNIX to another. In most UNIX systems, either *fdisk* or *format* does the job. Typing *man fdisk* or *man format* and pressing Enter at the command prompt gives you an overview of available command options. Figure 4-15 shows the man page for the *fdisk* command in Fedora Linux.

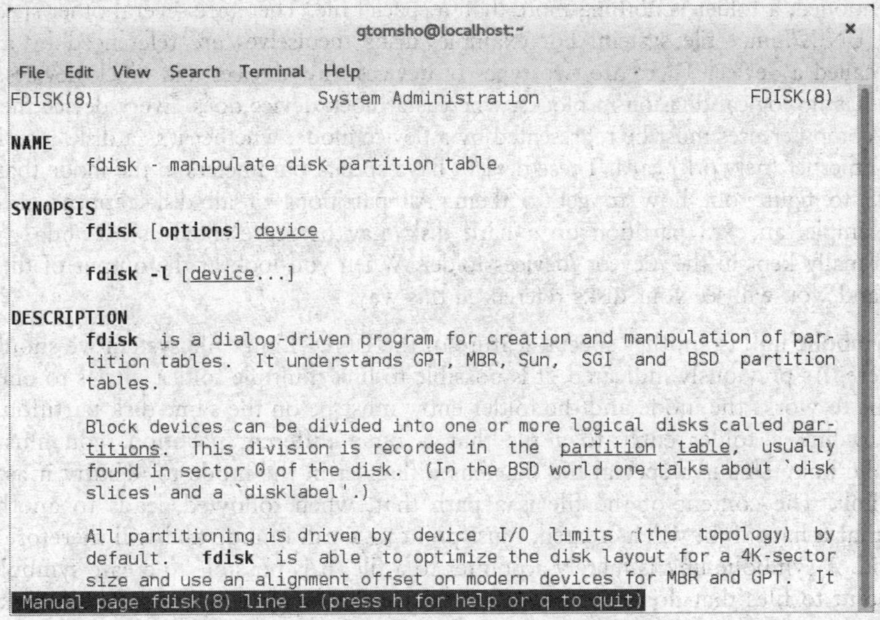

```
gtomsho@localhost:~
File Edit View Search Terminal Help
FDISK(8)                    System Administration                    FDISK(8)

NAME
       fdisk - manipulate disk partition table

SYNOPSIS
       fdisk [options] device

       fdisk -l [device...]

DESCRIPTION
       fdisk  is a dialog-driven program for creation and manipulation of par-
       tition tables.  It understands GPT, MBR, Sun,  SGI  and  BSD  partition
       tables.

       Block devices can be divided into one or more logical disks called par-
       titions.  This division is recorded in  the  partition  table,  usually
       found in sector 0 of the disk.  (In the BSD world one talks about `disk
       slices' and a `disklabel'.)

       All partitioning is driven by  device  I/O  limits  (the  topology)  by
       default.   fdisk  is  able  to optimize the disk layout for a 4K-sector
       size and use an alignment offset on modern devices for MBR and GPT.  It
 Manual page fdisk(8) line 1 (press h for help or q to quit)
```

**Figure 4-15** The man page for the *fdisk* command

*Source: Fedora Linux*

Once a partition is made, it is time to create the file system. To do this, you must know the device name of the partition on which you want to create the file system. This name can be obtained from the *print partition table* command in *fdisk* or *format*. The most convenient way to create a new file system is with the *newfs* command. Simply type *newfs*, followed by the name of the device. After you confirm that you want to create a new file system, you will see a progress report that shows you where copies of the superblocks are written, as well as some information about the cylinder group and the number of inodes. When *newfs* is completed, you can make a mount point for the new file system using the *mkdir* command. (Note that a mount point in UNIX/Linux is nothing more than an empty folder—the disk location in which the file system contents will appear.) If, for example, you created a file system on */dev/sdb1* and you want to mount it in the /test mount point, you type *mkdir /test*. Next, you mount the file system by typing *mount /dev/sdb1 /test*, and now you are ready to use the new file system. *Newfs* is available in many versions of UNIX, such as in Solaris UNIX, but it is not available in all versions of Linux, including Red Hat Enterprise Linux and Fedora. In UNIX/Linux varieties where *newfs* is not available, *mkfs* should be used instead. (*Mkfs* is available in Red Hat Enterprise Linux and Fedora.) The use of *mkfs* is less desirable because it requires the user to specify many parameters, such as the size of the file system, the block size, number of inodes, number of superblock copies and their locations, and a few others, depending on the version of UNIX/Linux. The *newfs* utility takes care of all these details automatically.

UNIX/Linux is very picky when it comes to file system consistency. If it finds problems on the file system in the inodes, superblock, or folder structures, it will shut down. When you save a file to disk, the system first stores part of the data in memory, until it has time to write the file to disk. If for some reason your computer stops working before the data is written to disk, you can end up with a damaged file system. This is why UNIX/Linux machines should always be shut down using the proper commands, which ensure that all data is stored on disk before the machine is brought down. In normal operation, all data waiting to be saved to disk in memory is written to disk every 30 seconds. You can manually force a write of all data in memory by using the *sync* command. When the system is properly shut down, the file systems are unmounted. Whenever the machine starts up, UNIX/Linux checks the file systems to make sure they are all working properly. To do this, the operating system verifies the integrity of the superblock, the inodes, all cluster groups, and all folder entries. The program that performs this operation is the file system checker, also known as *fsck*.

You can manually run *fsck* at any time to perform file system checks after the system is up, but take great care when doing this. If data on the disk is changed while an *fsck* is in progress, the results may be disastrous. The most common problems found when *fsck* is run are unlinked inodes, folder entries with no associated inodes, and wrong free block counts. All of these can be a result of a system that was not properly shut down. If these errors occur frequently, hardware failure may be imminent.

Table 4-7 presents a summary of useful commands for managing UNIX/Linux file systems.

**Table 4-7 UNIX/Linux file system commands**

| Command | Description |
|---|---|
| *cat* | Displays the contents of a file to the screen |
| *cd* | Changes to another folder |
| *cp* | Copies a file to another folder (and you can rename the file at the same time) |
| *fdisk* | Formats and partitions a disk in some UNIX systems, such as Linux |
| *format* | Formats and partitions a disk in some UNIX systems, such as Solaris |
| *ls* | Lists contents of a folder |
| *mkdir* | Creates a folder |
| *mkfs* | Creates a file system (but requires more parameters than *newfs*) |
| *mount* | Lists the disk currently mounted; also mounts file systems and devices (such as a DVD/CD-ROM) |
| *mv* | Moves a file to a different folder |
| *newfs* | Creates a new file system in some versions of UNIX/Linux |
| *rm* | Removes a file or folder |
| *sync* | Forces information in memory to be written to disk |
| *touch* | Creates an empty file |
| *umount* | Unmounts a file system |

# The Macintosh File System

The original **Macintosh Filing System** (MFS) of 1984 was limited to keeping track of 128 documents, applications, or folders. This was a reasonable limit when the only storage device was a 400 KB floppy disk drive. As larger disks became available, however, the need for folders and subfolders became obvious, and Apple responded with the **Hierarchical Filing System** (HFS) in 1986.

Like FAT16, HFS divides a volume into, at most, $2^{16}$ (65,536) units. (*Volume* is the Mac term for a disk or disk partition.) On PC systems, these units are called *clusters* or *allocation units*. On the Mac, they are called **allocation blocks**, but the principle is the same. Interestingly, while UNIX/Linux and Windows operating systems report file sizes in terms of their actual size, the Macintosh operating system sometimes reports file sizes in terms of logical size, based on the number of allocation blocks occupied by the file. The best way to view the actual size of a file is to use the Mac's Get Info option, which shows many other types of information about a file.

In 1998, Apple released Mac OS 8.1, which introduced a new disk format, Hierarchical Filing System Extended Format. This format was variously referred to as Mac OS HFS+, Mac OS Extended, or Mac OS **Extended (HFS+)**, which is used today in Mac OS X. The newer HFS+ format increases the number of allocation blocks per volume to $2^{32}$. This format creates smaller allocation blocks (clusters) and more efficient disk utilization. Systems that use Mac OS 8.1 or later can format disks in either the Mac OS Standard (HFS) or Mac OS Extended (HFS+) format. However, Macintoshes with pre-8.1 versions of the OS can't read disks in Extended format. Volumes that are smaller than 32 MB must also continue to use Standard format.

In Mac OS X version 3.0, Mac OS Extended (HFS+) includes several new features:

- An optional case-sensitive format to make the file system more compatible with other UNIX/Linux systems
- Journaling, which is turned on by default (see Figure 4-16) so that data can be recovered from a journal file if a disk or system problem occurs while data is being updated or modified
- The ability to store up to 16 TB of data, which is particularly important for the Mac OS X Server version

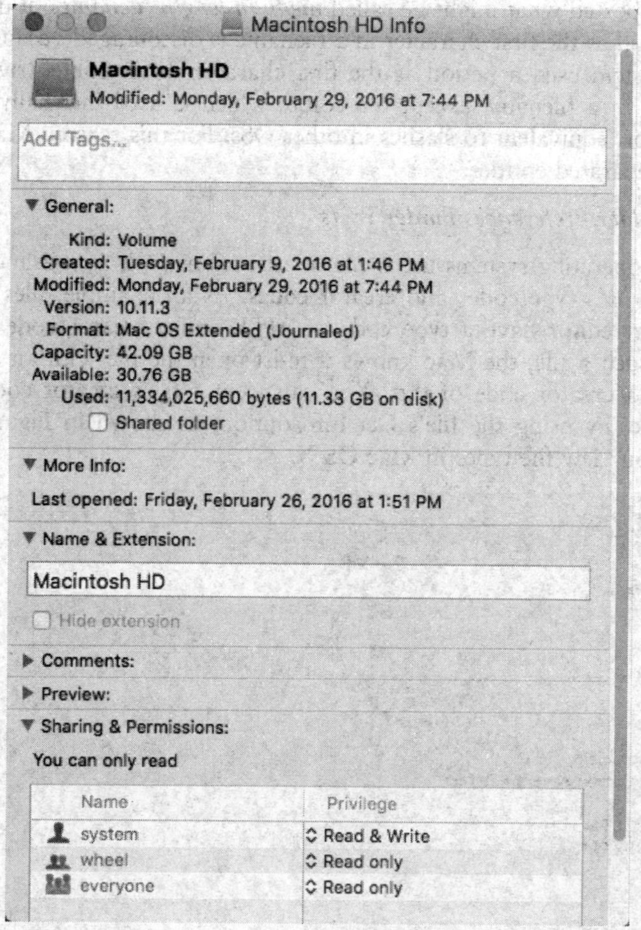


**Figure 4-16** Mac OS X using the Mac OS Extended (HFS+) file system

*Source: Mac OS X*

The first two sectors of a Mac-formatted disk are the boot sectors, or boot blocks in Macintosh terminology. The boot blocks identify the filing system, the names of important system files, and other important information. The boot blocks are followed by the **volume information block**, which points to other important areas of information, such as the location of the system files and the catalog and extents b-trees.

The **catalog b-tree** is the list of all files on the volume. It keeps track of a file's name, its logical location in the folder structure, its physical location on the disk surface, and the locations and sizes of the file's data fork and resource forks (as discussed later in the chapter). The **extents b-tree** keeps track of the location of file fragments, or extents.

Macintoshes can read and write to disks from other operating systems. For instance, Macs can read iso9660 DVD/CD-ROMs using a dedicated driver. Macs can also read all manner of MS-DOS- and Windows-formatted disks, thanks to pre-Mac OS X tools such as the PC Exchange control panel, and thanks to various Mac OS X tools, such as those offered through System Preferences and as disk utilities.

The Mac OS has always supported what might be called *medium-length filenames* of up to 31 characters. The use of a period as the first character in a filename is discouraged because older versions of the operating system used a period as the first character of invisible driver files. Any character may be used in a filename except the colon, which is used internally by the Mac OS as a folder separator, equivalent to slashes in other OSs. For this reason, Macintosh paths are written as colon-separated entities:

*Hard Drive:System Folder:Preferences:Finder Prefs*

UNIX/Linux and Windows operating systems use filename extensions such as .txt and .gif to identify file types. The Mac uses **type codes** and **creator codes**. As an example, files created with Apple's SimpleText text editor have a type code of APPL and a creator code of ttxt. When a user double-clicks such a file, the Mac knows it must open the file with an application (type code APPL) and a creator code of ttxt. You can view a file's creator code, such as a JPEG file for a graphic, by using the file's Get Info option, as shown in Figure 4-17. In Hands-On Project 4-9, you view file types in Mac OS X.

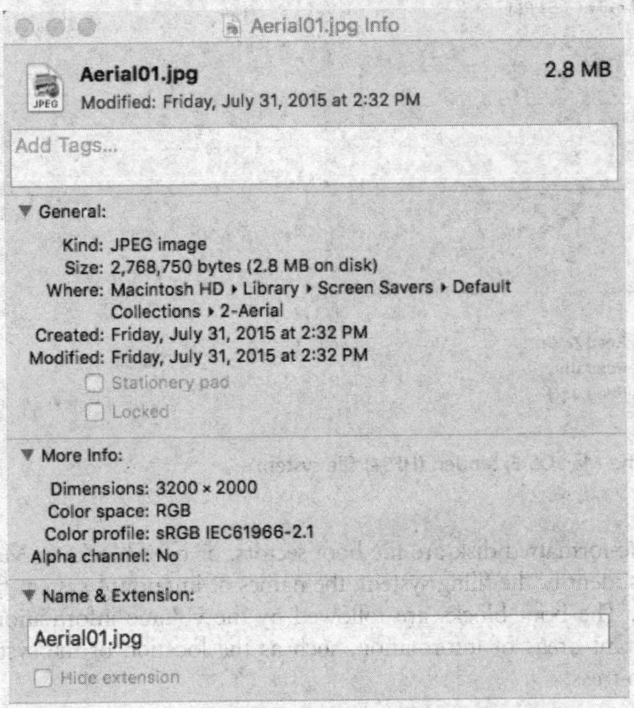


**Figure 4-17** Using the Get Info option for a JPEG file

*Source: Mac OS X*

The type and creator codes facilitate the Mac's use of icons. Documents do not store their own icons; instead, the Mac gets the icon from the creating application. Instead of accessing the application each time the icon must be displayed, the Mac stores the icons and file associations in invisible files called the *desktop databases*. Each disk or volume has its own desktop databases. "Rebuilding the desktop" on a Macintosh means rebuilding these database files, and is a common troubleshooting step when icons appear incorrectly. You can rebuild the desktop on a disk at startup by holding down the command and option keys. For removable media, hold down the command and option keys before inserting the disk.

One way in which Macintosh files are unique is that they can contain two parts, or forks: the data fork and the resource fork. The **data fork** contains frequently changing information, such as word-processing data, while the **resource fork** contains fixed information, including a program's icons, menu resources, and splash screens. One advantage of resource forks for programmers is that they modularize the program. For instance, it becomes very easy to change the text of a warning dialog or the name of a menu item without having to change the underlying code, so customization and internationalization are easier.

Folders can be created using the New Folder option in the Finder's File menu and in the Save and Save As dialog boxes in most applications. All volumes have two special, invisible folders: Trash and Desktop. If you move a file's icon from a USB drive to the desktop, the file still resides in the USB drive's Desktop folder. Likewise, you can move the file's icon to the Trash can without deleting it, and it will still reside in the USB drive's Trash folder. You can prove this to yourself by ejecting the USB drive and inserting it in another Macintosh. The files will appear on the desktop, and the Trash can will bulge.

Apple's equivalent of the UNIX/Linux symbolic link and Windows shortcut is the **alias**, which was introduced in System 7.0 in 1991. Files, folders, applications, and disks can be aliased. The system-level Alias Manager keeps track of the original item, even if it is moved or renamed. The word *alias* is added to the filename when the alias is created, and the filename is presented in italicized text. Beginning in OS 8.5, aliases also have small arrows on their icons, similar to shortcuts in Windows-based operating systems. In Hands-On Project 4-9, you create an alias.

Mac OS X comes with two important disk utilities: Disk Utility for managing disk drives and Disk First Aid for repairing disk problems. Figure 4-18 shows Disk Utility after running First Aid on Macintosh HD.

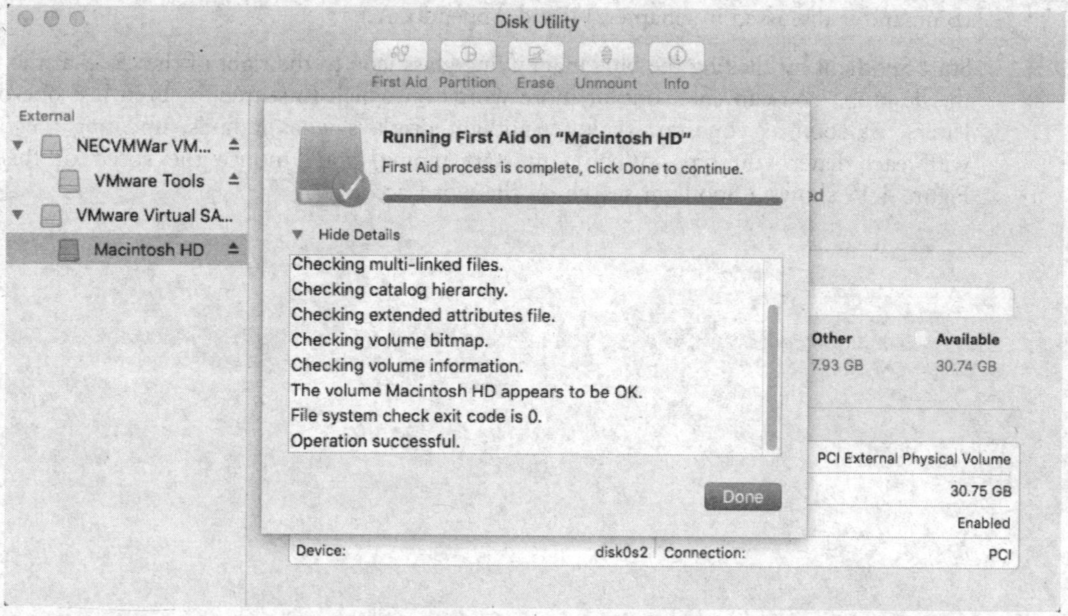


**Figure 4-18** Mac OS X Disk Utility running First Aid

*Source: Mac OS X*

Older versions of Mac OS X came with the Sherlock program, which can search disks for filenames and text within files. These operations are extremely fast because Sherlock pre-indexes local disks, just as search engines index Web pages. Because indexing takes significant processor time, it can be scheduled for times when the computer is not heavily used. Sherlock also functions as a program for querying multiple Internet search engines or the site search engines available on many Web sites.

**Spotlight** replaced Sherlock in Mac OS X 10.4 Tiger, although Sherlock continued to ship with Mac OS until it was officially retired with the release of Mac OS X 10.5 Leopard. Mac OS X users have always faced the same problems as Windows users when it comes to organizing and finding files. Nothing is more frustrating than knowing you have created and saved a document, spreadsheet, song, or photo and being unable to find it. Spotlight does the following for you:

- Indexes files so you can find them faster
- Enables you to search for something just by typing a few letters of the name
- Quickly searches the computer's nooks and crannies for what you want, even if you're not sure how to spell it exactly
- Works in conjunction with the smart folders capability so you can organize files you've found according to different characteristics you choose

One reason for Spotlight's speed is that it indexes not only by filenames, but by metadata associated with documents, such as the author, creation, date, and lots of other information. It also indexes based on individual words inside regular text files, word-processing files, and even PDF files used by Adobe. Spotlight does not work on files in the UNIX system and kernel. For these files you have to use UNIX commands, such as *find* or *locate*. (The *find* command is discussed in Chapter 11 and Appendix A.)

Start Spotlight by clicking the blue magnifying-glass icon to the right of the clock at the top of the desktop. You can enter one or more words on which to search, or even just one or two letters. As soon as you start typing, Spotlight displays what it finds, updating the display with each letter you type. When you start typing, you'll notice the speed of this tool. Figure 4-19 shows a Spotlight search on the word *account*.

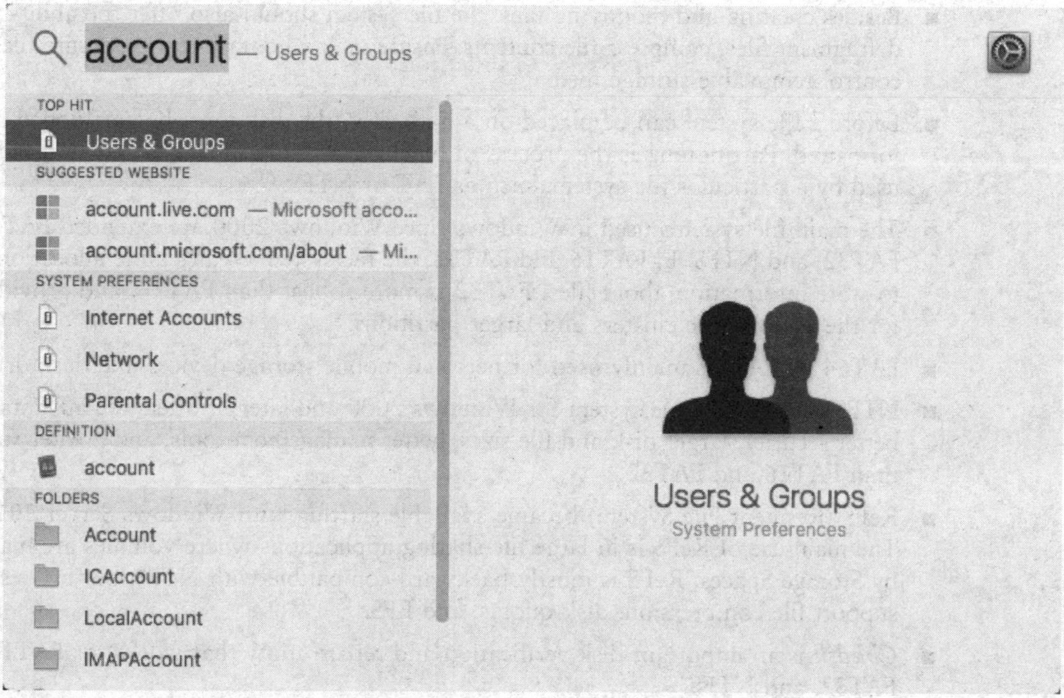


**Figure 4-19** A Spotlight search in Mac OS X

*Source: Mac OS X*

When the Mac is shut down normally using the Apple menu's Shut Down option, a flag is set on the hard drive. In the event of a crash or forced reboot, this flag is not set. If the flag is not set, the Mac will see during the next startup that the computer was not shut down properly and run a disk integrity check.

The Mac is extremely versatile at booting from different devices. Like other operating systems, the Mac will boot from a DVD/CD-ROM inserted during the boot sequence. If the disk does not contain a valid System Folder, the Mac will eject the disk and continue searching for a bootable device, such as a SCSI device. Since the early 1990s, Macs have been able to boot from a DVD/CD-ROM drive—simply press the C key while booting up. Pressing the Shift-Option-Delete-Apple (SODA) keys during the boot sequence will bypass the internal hard drive and boot from the next drive in the SCSI chain.

# Chapter Summary

- One of the basic functions of an operating system is to enable you to store and access information on a computer or other digital device. This information is managed, stored, and retrieved through a file system.
- Some of the tasks performed by a file system include providing a convenient interface, providing a hierarchical structure, storing file metadata, organizing space on a storage device, and providing utilities to maintain and manage the file system.

- Besides creating and modifying files, the file system should also offer the ability to defragment files, compress file contents, ensure file and data integrity, secure files, and control removable storage media.
- Before a file system can be placed on a hard disk, the disk must be partitioned and formatted. Partitioning is the process of blocking a group of tracks and sectors to be used by a particular file system, such as FAT or NTFS.
- The main file systems used in Windows since Windows 2000 are extended FAT16, FAT32, and NTFS. In FAT16 and FAT32, the file system creates a file allocation table to store information about files. FAT32 is more robust than FAT16, and provides for the use of more clusters and larger partitions.
- FAT64 (exFAT) is mainly used for personal mobile storage devices like flash drives.
- NTFS is the native file system for Windows 2000 and later; it offers the advantages of better security, larger disk and file sizes, better management tools, and greater stability than FAT16 and FAT32.
- ReFS (Resilient File System) became available starting with Windows Server 2012. The main use of ReFS is in large file-sharing applications where volumes are managed by Storage Spaces. ReFS is mostly backward-compatible with NTFS, but it doesn't support file compression, disk quotas, and EFS.
- *Chkdsk* is an important disk verification and repair utility that works for FAT16, FAT32, and NTFS.
- UNIX and Linux support many different file systems, but typically they employ ufs or ext.
- Ufs and ext use information nodes (inodes) to organize information about files. Also, a UNIX/Linux system can have many file systems mounted as subfolders of the root.
- Different varieties of UNIX/Linux use different file system utilities, such as *fdisk* and *format*, to partition and format disks. The *fsck* (file system checker) utility is used to verify the integrity of UNIX/Linux file systems.
- Mac OS X uses the Mac OS Extended (HFS+) file system, which is an enhancement of HFS and was introduced in 1998 with Mac OS 8.1. Like NTFS, the Mac OS Extended file system makes more efficient utilization of disk space and supports larger disk sizes, and in Mac OS X version 10.3 and higher, it offers a case-sensitive capability, journaling, and support for 8 EB disk storage.
- Two important Mac OS X disk tools include the Disk Utility and Disk First Aid.

## Key Terms

**8.3 filenames** An older filename format in which the name of the file can be up to eight characters long, followed by a period and an extension of three characters. See also *extension*.

**active partition** The logical portion of a hard disk drive that is currently being used to store data. In a PC system, the partition that contains the bootable operating system.

**alias** In the Macintosh file system, a feature that presents an icon representing an executable file. Equivalent to the UNIX/Linux link and the Windows shortcut.

**allocation block** In the Macintosh file system, a division of hard disk data, equivalent to the Windows disk cluster. Each Macintosh volume is divided into $2^{16}$ (65,535) individual units.

**bad clusters** On a hard disk drive, areas of the surface that cannot be used to safely store data. Bad clusters are usually identified by the *format* command or one of the hard drive utilities, such as *chkdsk* or *fsck*.

**block allocation** A hard disk configuration scheme in which the disk is divided into logical blocks, which in turn are mapped to sectors, heads, and tracks.

**block device** In the UNIX/Linux file system, a device that is divided or configured into logical blocks. See also *raw device*.

**boot block** The UNIX/Linux and Mac OS X equivalent of the Windows Master Boot Record (MBR), the area of the hard disk that stores partition information for the disk. For example, on a Mac-formatted disk, the first two sectors are boot blocks that identify the filing system, the names of important system files, and other important information. See also *volume information block*.

**catalog b-tree** In the Macintosh file system, a list of all files on a given volume. Similar to a folder in the Windows file system.

**CD-ROM File System (CDFS)** A 32-bit file system used on CD-ROMs and DVDs.

**cluster** In Windows-based file systems, a logical block of information on a disk containing one or more sectors. Also called an *allocation unit*.

**creator codes** Hidden file characteristics in the Macintosh file system that indicate the program (software application) that created the file. See *type code*.

**data fork** The portion of a file in the Macintosh file system that stores the variable data associated with the file. Data fork information might include word-processing data, spreadsheet information, and so on.

**defragmenter** A tool that rearranges data on a disk in a continuous fashion, ridding the disk of scattered open clusters.

**directory** An organizational structure that contains files and may additionally contain subdirectories under it. A directory contains information about files, such as filenames, file sizes, date of creation, and file type. More commonly referred to as a *folder* in modern OSs.

**disk label** The UNIX/Linux equivalent of a partition table in MS-DOS or Windows systems. The disk label is a table containing information about each partition on a disk, such as the type of partition, size, and location.

**disk quota** Allocation of a specific amount of disk space to a user or application with the ability to ensure that the user or application cannot use more disk space than is specified in the allocation.

**Distributed Link Tracking** A technique introduced in NTFS 5 so that shortcuts, such as those on the desktop, are not lost when files are moved to another volume.

**extended file system (ext or ext fs)** The file system designed for Linux that is installed by default in Linux operating systems.

**Extended (HFS+)** A file system released in 1998 with Mac OS 8.1 and the file system used in Mac OS X.

**extension** In MS-DOS and Windows-based systems, the part of a filename that typically identifies the type of file associated with the name. File extensions are typically three characters long and include standard notations such as .sys, .exe, .bat, and so on.

**extents b-tree** A file system component that keeps track of the location of file fragments, or extents, in the Mac OS HFS file system.

**file** A set of data that is grouped in some logical manner, assigned a name, and stored on the disk.

**file allocation table (FAT)** A file management system that defines the way data is stored on a disk drive. The FAT stores information about a file's size and physical location on the disk.

**file attributes** File characteristics stored with the filename in the disk folder; attributes specify certain storage and operational parameters associated with the file, such as hidden, read-only, archive, and so on.

**file system** A design for storing and managing files on a disk drive.

**folder** See *directory*.

**formatting** The process of installing a file system on a disk partition.

**hard link** In Windows versions starting with Windows 2000 and UNIX/Linux, a file management technique that permits multiple folder entries to point to the same file.

**Hierarchical Filing System (HFS)** An early Apple Macintosh file system storage method that uses a hierarchical folder structure.

**high-level formatting** A process that prepares a disk partition (or removable media) for a specific file system.

**hot fix** A procedure used by a file system that can detect a damaged disk area and then automatically copy information from that area to another disk area that is not damaged.

**inode** Short for "information node." In UNIX/Linux, a system for storing key information about files.

**journaling** The ability of a file system or software (such as database software) to track file changes so that if a system crashes unexpectedly, it is possible to reconstruct files or to roll back changes with minimal or no damage.

**linked list** Used in FAT file systems so that when a file is written to disk, each cluster containing that file's data has a pointer to the location of the next cluster of data.

**logical drive** A software definition that divides a physical hard drive into multiple drives for file storage.

**long filename (LFN)** A name for a file, folder, or folder in a file system in which the name can be up to 255 characters in length. Long filenames in Windows, UNIX/Linux, and Mac OS systems are also POSIX compliant in that they honor uppercase and lowercase characters.

**low-level format** A software process that marks tracks and sectors on a disk. A low-level format is necessary before a disk can be partitioned and formatted.

**Macintosh Filing System (MFS)** The original Macintosh filing system, introduced in 1984. MFS was limited to keeping track of 128 documents, applications, or folders.

**Master Boot Record (MBR)** An area of a hard disk in MS-DOS and Windows that stores partition information about the disk. MBRs are not found on disks that do not support multiple partitions.

**Master File Table (MFT)** A storage organization system used with the NTFS file system. The MFT is located at the beginning of the partition.

**metadata** Information that describes data but is not the actual data.

**mount** A process that makes a disk partition or volume available for use by the operating system.

**New Technology File System (NTFS)** The file storage system that is the native system in Windows versions starting with Windows NT.

**partitioning** Blocking a group of tracks and sectors to be used by a particular file system, such as FAT or NTFS. Partitioning is a hard disk management technique that permits the installation of multiple file systems on a single disk or the configuration of multiple logical hard drives that use the same file system on a single physical hard drive.

**partition table** A table containing information about each partition on a disk, such as the type of partition, size, and location. Also, the partition table provides information to the computer about how to access the disk.

**physical drive** A hard drive in a computer that you can physically touch and that can be divided into one or more logical drives.

**Portable Operating System Interface for UNIX (POSIX)** A UNIX standard designed to ensure portability of applications among various versions of UNIX.

**raw device** In the UNIX/Linux file system, a device that has not been divided into logical blocks. See also *block device*.

**Resilient File System (ReFS)** A file system in Windows Server 2012 and later that is used in large file-sharing applications and that can correct some types of data corruption automatically.

**resource fork** In the Macintosh file system, the portion of a file that contains fixed information, such as a program's icons, menu resources, and splash screens.

**root folder** The highest-level folder in the structure of files and folders in a file system.

**sectors** Equally sized portions of a disk track. See *tracks*.

**Spotlight** The new way to search in Mac OS X, starting with version 10.4 Tiger. Spotlight stores a virtual index of everything on the system.

**status bits** Bits used as part of a folder entry to identify the type of file contained in each entry. The status bits in use are Volume, Folder, System, Hidden, Read-only, and Archive.

**superblock** In the UNIX/Linux file system, a special data block that contains information about the layout of blocks, sectors, and cylinder groups on the file system. This information is the key to finding anything on the file system, and it should never change.

**switch** An operating system command option that changes the way certain commands function. Command options, or switches, are usually entered as one or more letters, separated from the main command by a forward slash (/) in Windows and by a dash (-) in UNIX/Linux.

**symbolic link** A special file in the UNIX/Linux file system that permits a folder link to a file that is on a different partition.

**tracks** Concentric rings that cover an entire disk like grooves on a phonograph record. Each ring is divided into sectors in which to store data.

**type code** In the Macintosh file system, embedded file information that denotes which applications were used to create the files. Mac OS type codes are used in much the same way as Windows file extensions that identify file types with .txt, .doc, and other extensions. See *creator codes*.

**Unicode** A 16-bit character code that allows for the definition of up to 65,536 characters.

**Universal Disk Format (UDF)** A removable disk formatting standard used for large-capacity CD-ROMs and DVD-ROMs.

**UNIX file system (ufs)** A file system supported in most versions of UNIX/Linux; ufs is a hierarchical (tree structure) file system that is expandable, supports large storage, provides excellent security, and is reliable. Ufs employs information nodes (inodes).

**volume** A portion of a disk that has a file system installed and is ready to be accessed for data storage and retrieval.

**volume information block** On a Mac-formatted disk, the sector after the boot blocks. See also *boot block*. The volume information block points to other important areas of information, such as the location of the system files and the catalog and extents trees.

**volume label** A series of characters, commonly used as a nickname, that identify a volume.

**volume mount point** An empty folder into which a volume is mounted. See *mount*.

## Review Questions

1. As you are using some files on a workstation running Linux, you determine that a few of the files seem to be corrupted. What should you do?
   a. Close all files and applications and run *fsck*.
   b. Start DiskScan to check for file links.
   c. Reformat your disk using the *format* command.
   d. Use the Disk Check utility, which can be run at any time.
2. You are installing Windows 10 on a new disk that has only been low-level formatted. What is the first thing you need to do to prepare the disk?
   a. Use Disk Scrub to ensure there are no bad spots on the disk.
   b. Format the disk for NTFS.
   c. Partition the disk.
   d. Initialize the disk with the root folder.

3. You need to create a new folder in a Linux system and you choose to do so from a terminal window. Which of the following commands enables you to create a folder?
   a. *fdisk*
   b. *mkdir*
   c. *mkfs*
   d. *mkfsdir*
4. What file system is used on a hard disk in a computer running Mac OS X?
   a. Macintosh Filing System (MFS)
   b. Macintosh Network File System (MNFS)
   c. Extended file system (ext)
   d. Mac OS Extended (HFS+) file system
5. Your assistant has documentation that shows how to modify a device file in Linux, but the documentation does not mention which folder to find the file in. Which folder should you suggest?
   a. /mnt
   b. /var
   c. /dev
   d. /proc
6. On a Windows-based system, which of the following are contained in the Master Boot Record? (Choose all that apply.)
   a. disk signature
   b. boot program
   c. boot block
   d. partition table for the active partition
7. You developed a proposal for the president of your company several months ago. You know you saved it, but you are not sure where. You created the proposal on your Mac OS X El Capitan computer. Which of the following is the easiest option for finding the document? (Choose all that apply.)
   a. Use Get Info on each of the folders that you think the document might be in. Check the creation date. When you find dates that look promising, open the folder and check the documents.
   b. Use the search tool Sherlock to search for text within files.
   c. Use the UNIX command-line prompt to search your Mac for the proposal using *find* or *locate*.
   d. Use Spotlight to search for the document on your Mac.

8. You need to find the date and time a file was created and the file's size. Where should you look?
   a. in the volume label
   b. in the Master File Table
   c. in the file metadata
   d. in the file allocation table
9. You need to find out more about the *fdisk* utility and the commands associated with it before you set up a new Linux system in addition to the one you are already using. What command can you use on your present system to find out more about *fdisk*?
   a. *man fdisk*
   b. *fdisk /?*
   c. *fdisk /help*
   d. *find fdisk*
10. Mac OS X files can contain which of the following? (Choose all that apply.)
    a. application generator
    b. data fork
    c. extension marker
    d. resource fork
11. Users on your organization's Windows Server 2012 R2 server are beginning to take up excessive disk space on the NTFS volumes. You have plenty of disk space now, but you're concerned about this situation in the future. What can you do?
    a. Enforce stronger security so it is harder for users to write files to their home directories.
    b. Establish disk quotas.
    c. Encrypt portions of the users' home directories so they can only be used by the Administrator account.
    d. Use bigger blocks for the partition.
12. In which file system would you find the Master File Table?
    a. FAT12
    b. NFS
    c. NTFS
    d. ufs
13. What command in Windows Server 2012 can you use to format a disk for FAT32?
    a. *fdisk:FAT32*
    b. *format /fs:FAT32*
    c. *part /FAT32*
    d. *mkdisk FAT32*

14. You are installing a file-sharing application on a Windows Server 2012 R2 server in which the volumes are managed by Storage Spaces and fault tolerance is a major consideration. Which file system should you use?
    a. FAT64
    b. ReFS
    c. NTFS
    d. ext4
15. In what file system(s) would you find inodes? (Choose all that apply.)
    a. FAT16
    b. ufs
    c. ext3
    d. NTFS
16. The president of your company uses Mac OS X and wants to find out more about a file, such as whether the file is a TIFF document. What tool should she use?
    a. the Get Info option for the file
    b. Explorer
    c. Files
    d. the Window options for the file
17. Which of the following is a process that marks the location of tracks and sectors on a disk?
    a. disk tracking
    b. a low-level format
    c. a high-level format
    d. etching
18. In FAT32, file characteristics such as Hidden and Read-only are examples of ______________.
    a. cluster designations
    b. formatting properties
    c. file attributes
    d. properties applied only to files and folders in the root
19. You run a computer support business and one of your customers calls to say he formatted his hard drive because it seemed to contain lots of bad clusters. The problem is that now the operating system won't start. What might be the problem?
    a. He performed a quick format that does not fix bad clusters.
    b. A hard disk can only be formatted once.
    c. He formatted using the wrong driver.
    d. Formatting the disk destroyed all the files on it, including the operating system files.

20. Which of the following holds information about the layout of blocks and sectors in the UNIX file system?
    a. root
    b. file allocation table
    c. superblock
    d. folder flag

# Hands-On Projects

## Project 4-1: Explore the File System in Windows

File systems store and manage files, like a personal assistant to the file system user. In this project, you employ File Explorer to view folders and files in Windows. Also, you view the information that is stored for files.

1. Start your Windows 10 computer and log on. Right-click **Start** and click **File Explorer**.
2. In the left pane, click to expand **This PC**, if necessary. Double-click **Local Disk (C:)** to view folders and files on the hard drive.
3. In the right pane, double-click **Windows** to view more folders and files.
4. Click the **View** menu and then click **Content** in the Layout section of the Ribbon to change the view of the folders and files.
5. Click to select the **File name extensions** and **Hidden items** check boxes, if they are not already checked. You'll see additional folders and file extensions.
6. Close File Explorer.
7. Stay logged on if you are continuing to the next project.

## Project 4-2: Create Folders in Windows

When you use an operating system, you will often need to create a new folder. In this project, you learn how to create a new folder in Windows.

1. Start your Windows 10 computer and log on, if necessary. Right-click **Start** and click **File Explorer**.
2. In the left pane, click to expand **This PC**, if necessary. Double-click **Local Disk (C:)** to view folders and files on the hard drive.
3. In the right pane, double-click the **Users** folder and then double-click the folder that has the same name as the account you used to log on.
4. Click the **Home** tab on the Ribbon and click **New folder**.

5. Type your initials and then the word **folder**. For example, the user entered "GTfolder" as the folder name in Figure 4-20. Press **Enter**. (Don't delete this folder because you will use it again in Hands-On Project 4-3.)

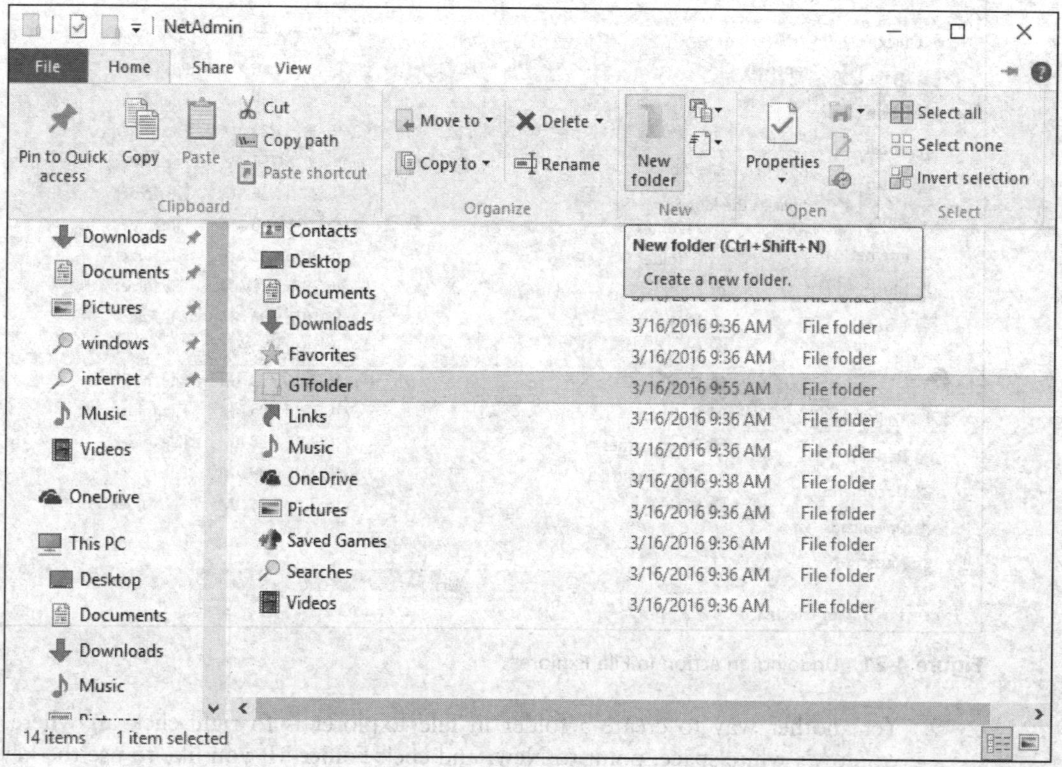


**Figure 4-20** Creating a folder in Windows 10

6. Right-click the folder you just created and click **Properties** to view its associated properties. Click each tab to quickly get an overview of the kinds of properties you can configure for the folder.
7. Click **Cancel**.
8. Another method for creating a folder is available in File Explorer. Open File Explorer, and then click the **Folder** icon in the Quick access menu, next to the name of the folder you are viewing. (In Figure 4-20, it is the Folder icon next to NetAdmin on the upper-left side of the window.) You see a new folder, ready to be named. Click the down arrow next to the folder icon you just clicked, and click **Undo** to remove the folder you just created (see Figure 4-21). Close **File Explorer**.

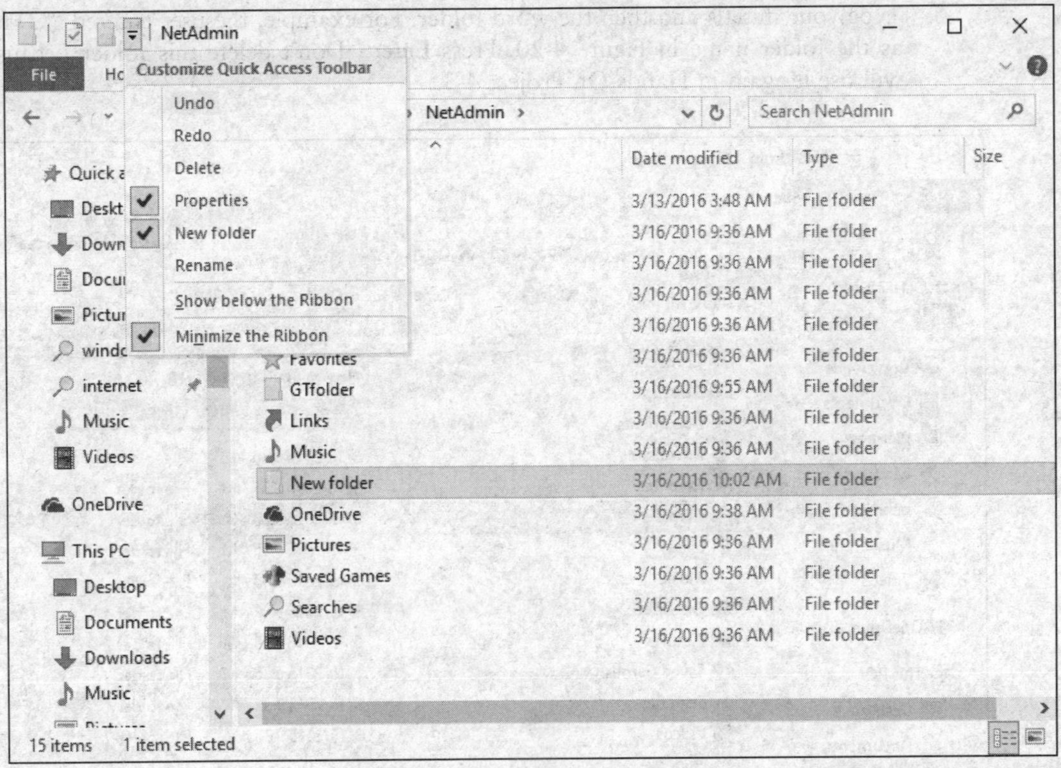


**Figure 4-21** Undoing an action in File Explorer

9. Yet another way to create a folder in File Explorer is to right-click anywhere in the window's white space, point to **New**, and click **Folder**. (If you like to use the keyboard rather than the mouse, click Ctrl+Shift+N to create a new folder.) Undo the creation of this new folder.

10. To create a folder at the Windows Command Prompt, right-click **Start** and click **Command Prompt**. The prompt shows the path in the file hierarchy where any file system command you enter will be applied by default. The Command Prompt opens in C:\Users*CurrentUser*, where CurrentUser is the currently logged-on user.

11. Type **dir** and press **Enter**. Notice the folder you created earlier. To create a new folder named MyDocs, type **mkdir MyDocs** and press **Enter**. To verify that the folder was created, type **dir** and press **Enter**.

12. Type **cd mydocs** and press **Enter**. (Remember that Windows folder names and filenames are not case sensitive, so you don't have to capitalize these names in commands.) Notice that the prompt changes by adding MyDocs to the path. Type **dir** and press **Enter**.

13. The *dir* command shows two folders named "." and "..". These are more like placeholders than actual folders. The "." folder simply refers to the current folder and the ".." folder refers to the parent folder. Type **cd .** and press **Enter**; you'll see that your

prompt doesn't change because the command basically tells the operating system to "go to the current folder." Type **cd ..** and press **Enter** to return to the C:\Users*Current User* folder.

14. Navigate to the root of the drive by typing **cd ** and pressing **Enter**. The prompt changes to C:\> to indicate that you are in the C:\ folder, which is the root of C:. Close the command prompt. Figure 4-22 shows the commands you entered and their output, although some of the *dir* output has been omitted to save space.
15. Shut down your Windows computer in preparation for the next project.

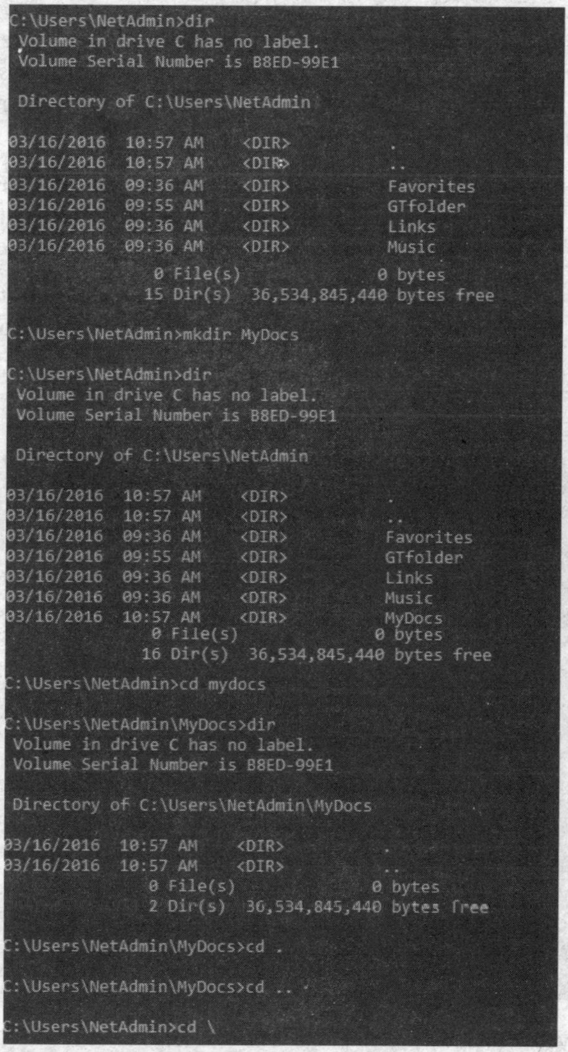


**Figure 4-22** A series of file system commands at a Windows command prompt

## Project 4-3: Fix a Corrupted MBR in Windows

A sudden power failure or a bad spot on a disk can corrupt the Master Boot Record and prevent a computer from booting. In Windows, you can fix the Master Boot Record using the Recovery Console. This project shows you how to start the Recovery Console and fix the Master Boot Record in Windows. For this project, you'll need the installation DVD/CD-ROM for the operating system. Also, you need to make sure all files are saved and that all users are logged off the server. Insert the DVD/CD-ROM for your operating system, but take no action if you see an installation start-up window. Shut down the operating system and computer.

1. Place the Windows installation DVD in the DVD player. You want to boot to the DVD, so you will need to enter the appropriate keystroke while the system is booting to access the boot menu. Ask your instructor to identify this keystroke; some systems use Esc, and others use F2 or another function key. Turn on your Windows computer to the boot menu and select the DVD as the boot device.

2. After the Windows Setup program starts, click **Next** until you see the screen that displays the Install now prompt and the Repair your computer option in the lower-left corner (see Figure 4-23). Press **R** (for repair) to open the Windows Recovery Menu.

3. On the Choose an option screen, click **Troubleshoot**. On the Troubleshoot screen, click **Advanced options**. On the Advanced options screen, click **Command prompt** to enter the Recovery Console.

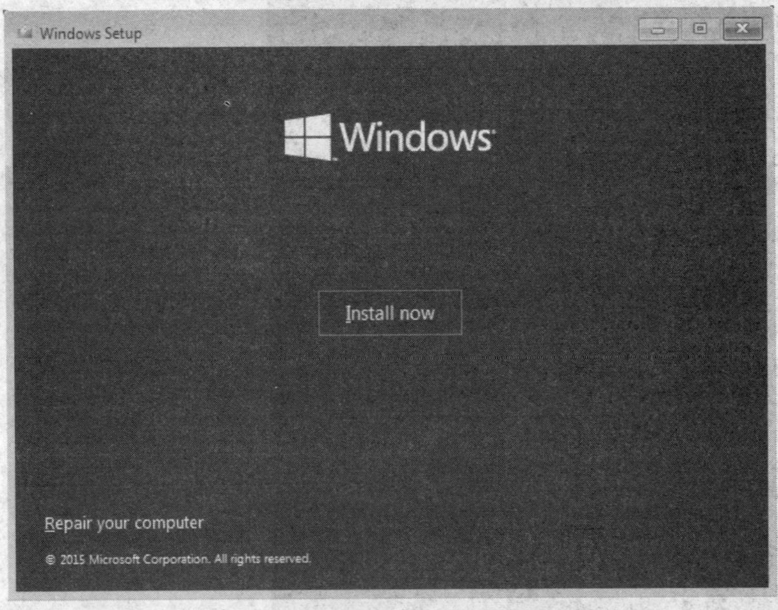


**Figure 4-23** The Repair your computer option in the Windows setup screen

4. The *bootrec /fixmbr* command is used to fix the Master Boot Record from the command line. Type **bootrec /?** and press **Enter** to view the help information for this command.

Read the description for each option. As you can see, *bootrec* can solve more problems than just a bad MBR.

5. If you have permission from your instructor, type **bootrec /fixmbr** and press **Enter**. Because nothing is wrong with the MBR, this command should not cause any problems, but be sure you have permission if you are not using your own computer. The command should output a message that "The operation completed successfully."
6. Type **exit** and press **Enter** to close the Recovery Console. Click **Continue** to boot to Windows.

## Project 4-4: Compress Files in Windows

In this project, you learn how to compress files in Windows. You need a computer with a drive formatted for NTFS.

1. Start your Windows computer and log on, if necessary. Open **File Explorer**.
2. Navigate to the folder you created in Project 4-2 (C:\Users*CurrentUser**YY* folder), where *CurrentUser* is the logged-on user account and *YY* represents your initials. Double-click the folder to open it. The right pane should be empty.
3. Create a new folder named **SubFolder** using one of the methods described in Project 4-2.
4. Right-click **SubFolder** and click **Properties**.
5. Click the **Advanced** button to view a dialog box similar to Figure 4-24. Notice the advanced attributes you can configure.

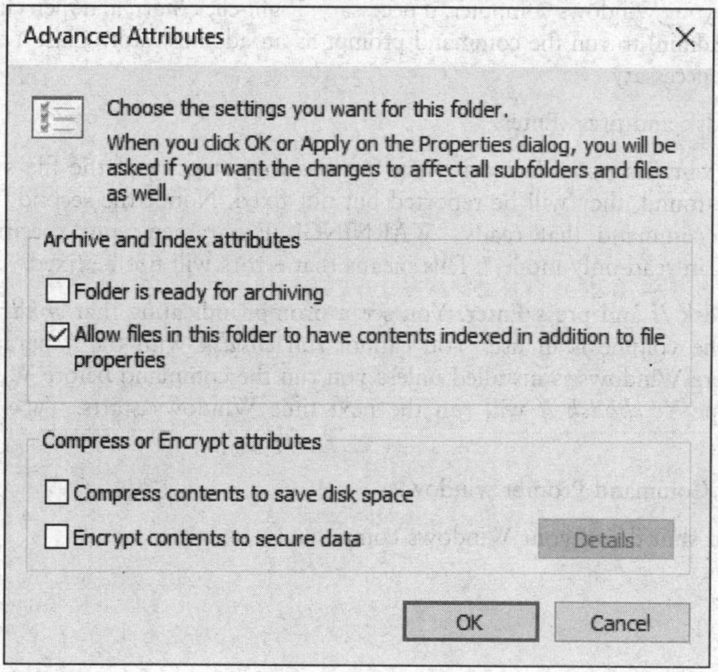


**Figure 4-24** The Advanced Attributes dialog box

6. Click **Compress contents to save disk space** and click **OK.**
7. Click **OK** to exit the folder's Properties dialog box.
8. Notice the change to the SubFolder icon. It now displays two blue arrows pointing toward each other in the upper-right corner, indicating that the folder and its contents are compressed.
9. Double-click **SubFolder** to open it. Right-click in the right pane, point to **New**, click **Text Document**, and press **Enter** to keep the default name. Notice that the file displays the two blue arrows to indicate it is compressed. All files that are placed in a compressed folder are automatically compressed.
10. Close File Explorer.
11. Stay logged on if you are continuing to the next project.

You cannot compress a folder that is encrypted.

## Project 4-5: Run *chkdsk* in Windows

*Chkdsk* is an important utility included in Windows that verifies the integrity of a disk and its file system. It also can fix problems that it encounters. In this project, you run *chkdsk* to see how it works.

1. Log on to your Windows computer, if necessary. Right-click **Start**, and then click **Command Prompt (Admin)** to run the command prompt as an administrator. Click **Yes** at the UAC prompt, if necessary.
2. Type **chkdsk** and press **Enter**.
3. *Chkdsk* examines your disk drive and verifies the integrity of the file system. If any errors are found, they will be reported but not fixed. Notice the second line of output from the command that reads "WARNING! /F parameter not specified. Running CHKDSK in read-only mode." This means that errors will not be fixed.
4. Type **chkdsk /f** and press **Enter**. You see a prompt indicating that *chkdsk* cannot run because the volume is in use. You cannot run *chkdsk* with the */f* parameter on the drive where Windows is installed unless you run the command before Windows starts. If you type Y, *chkdsk /f* will run the next time Windows starts. Type **N** and press **Enter**.
5. Close the Command Prompt window.
6. Log off or shut down your Windows computer.

Another way to have *chkdsk* start is to save all your work and simply turn off the computer without properly shutting it down. When you reboot, the system will run *chkdsk* if it detects a problem with the way the computer was shut down. In most cases, this is a safe test because you will most likely not cause damage to files or the file system if your work is saved and all programs are closed.

## Project 4-6: Navigate the Linux Folder Structure from the Shell Prompt

There are two common ways to view and manage folders and files in Linux: from the shell prompt and from the GNOME Files tool. In this project, you use the shell prompt in Fedora, although the steps are similar in many UNIX/Linux systems.

1. Start and log on to your Linux computer. Open a terminal window.
2. Type **ls -a** and press **Enter** to view the folders and files in your home folder, including those that are hidden. (Hidden files are represented by a period in front of the filename.)
3. Type **ls -l /** and press **Enter** to view the main folder structure in the system (see Figure 4-25).

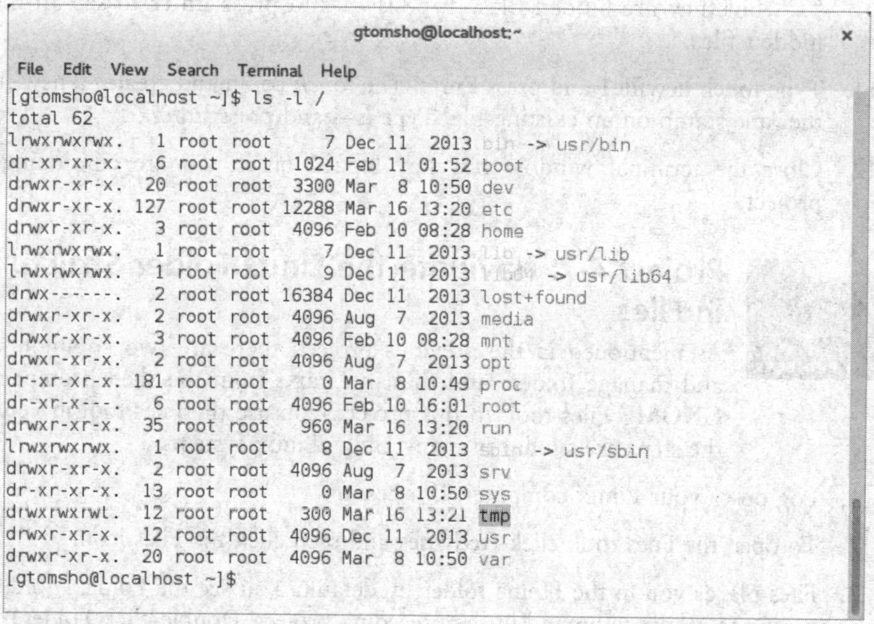


**Figure 4-25** The Linux folder structure

*Source: Fedora Linux*

4. At the Linux shell prompt, you see a "~" character, which indicates you are in your home folder. Type **cd /** and press **Enter** to move to the root; notice how the prompt changes.
5. Type **cd** and press **Enter** to go back to your home folder. Notice the prompt again. Type **cd /** and press **Enter**. You can also go to your home folder by typing **cd ~** and pressing **Enter**.
6. Type **cd /home** and press **Enter**. Type **ls** and press **Enter**. You see a list of all the home folders. You might see folders other than your own, depending on how many users are on your Linux computer.
7. Type **cd *username***, where ***username*** is the account you used to log on. If you are in the correct folder, the prompt again changes to ~.
8. Type **mkdir Folder1** and press **Enter** to create a new folder in your home folder. Type **cd folder1** and press **Enter**. If you used the folder capitalization specified in both commands, you will receive an error because Linux considers Folder1 and folder1 to be different names.
9. Type **cd Folder1** and press **Enter**. Your prompt changes to indicate you are in the Folder1 folder.
10. Type **ls** and press **Enter**. There is no output because the folder is empty, or at least it seems that way. Like Windows, Linux has two folders named "." and "..", but they are hidden files. Type **ls –a** and press **Enter** to see all files, including hidden files.
11. Type **touch newfile1** and press **Enter**. The *touch* command creates a new file or updates the time stamp on an existing file. Type **ls -l** and press **Enter**.
12. Close the terminal window but stay logged on if you are continuing to the next project.

## Project 4-7: Navigate the Linux Folder Structure in Files

As mentioned in the previous project, there are two common ways to view and manage folders and files in Linux: from the shell prompt and from the GNOME Files tool. In this project, you use the Files tool in Fedora, although the steps are similar in many UNIX/Linux systems.

1. Log on to your Linux computer, if necessary.
2. To open the Files tool, click **Activities** and then click the **Files** icon.
3. Files places you in the Home folder by default. You see the Folder1 folder you created using the *mkdir* command in the preceding project. Double-click **Folder1**.
4. You see the file you created using the *touch* command in the preceding project.

5. In the left pane, double-click **Computer** to go to the root of the file system. (The Computer entry should be listed under the Devices category in the left pane of Files—you may need to scroll the left pane to see it.) Double-click the **home** folder.

6. Double-click the folder that represents your home folder. Right-click **Folder1**, view the options, and then click **Compress.**

7. The compression function is different in Linux than in Windows. In Linux a new file is created from the folder and its contents are called a compressed tar file by default. See Figure 4-26. Notice also that the system creates the compressed tar file in your home directory. Click **Create**, and then click **Close.** You see a new file named Folder1.tar.gz in your home directory.

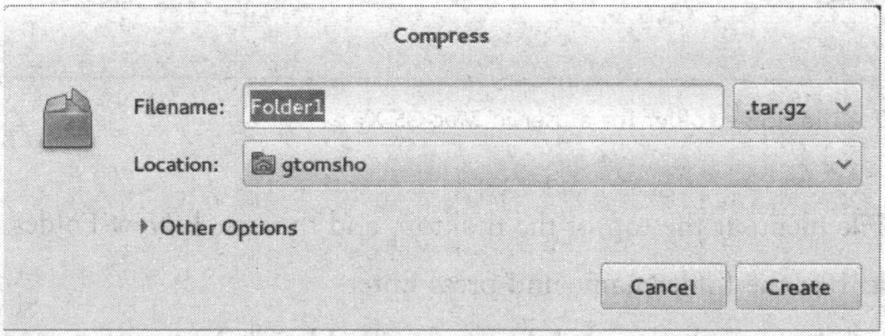


**Figure 4-26** Creating a compressed file in Linux

*Source: Fedora Linux*

8. Close Files and log off or shut down your Linux computer.

## Project 4-8: Navigate the Mac OS X Folder Structure

In this project, you learn to use the Macintosh HD desktop icon in Mac OS X to access files and folders.

1. Start and log on to your Mac OS X computer. Double-click the **Macintosh HD** icon on the desktop.

2. Double-click the **Users** folder. You should see a folder for each user account on the system, and a Shared folder.

3. Double-click your account's home folder, which looks like a house.

4. Your home folder contains a combination of folders and files. Typically, documents that you create using this account are placed in the Documents folder. There are also folders in which to store Downloads, Movies, Music, Pictures, and so on, as shown in Figure 4-27.

**Figure 4-27** The home folder for a user in Mac OS X

*Source: Mac OS X*

5. Click the **File** menu at the top of the desktop, and then click **New Folder.**
6. Type **Folder1** as the folder name and press **Enter.**
7. Right-click **Folder1** and then click **Compress "Folder1".** Notice that a new file named Folder1.zip is created in your home folder.
8. Click the **Go** menu at the top of the desktop, and then click **Utilities.**
9. Double-click **Terminal** in the Utilities window.
10. Type **ls** and press **Enter** to view the contents of your home folder. You see the folder you created in Step 6.
11. Type **mkdir Folder2** and press **Enter.**
12. Type **ls** and press **Enter** to verify that your folder was created. Note that you also used the *ls* and *mkdir* commands in Linux to work with files.
13. Click the **Terminal** menu at the top of the desktop, and then click **Quit Terminal.**
14. Close the Utilities window, but stay logged on if you are continuing to the next project.

## Project 4-9: Create Aliases with Mac OS X

Mac OS X includes the Get Info option to allow you to view file types. Also, aliases are a useful feature in Macintosh file systems. Like shortcuts in Windows, aliases let you create custom icons and names to place on your desktop, menus, or elsewhere to point to other applications. Aliases give you multiple ways to access the same application and let you easily place these access points in various convenient locations. In this project, you view the file type of an application and create an alias.

1. From your Mac OS X desktop, click **Go** in the menu bar at the top of the desktop and then click **Applications.**
2. Click **Contacts.** (Don't double-click, because you do not want to open the application.)

3. Click the **File** menu and then click **Get Info.** Review the information you see. Close the Contacts Info window.
4. Make sure **Contacts** is still selected, and then click the **File** menu and click **Make Alias.**
5. If necessary, click to move the cursor to the box under the Contacts icon and change the text to insert your initials before Contacts. For example, the user entered GT Contacts as the alias in Figure 4-28.

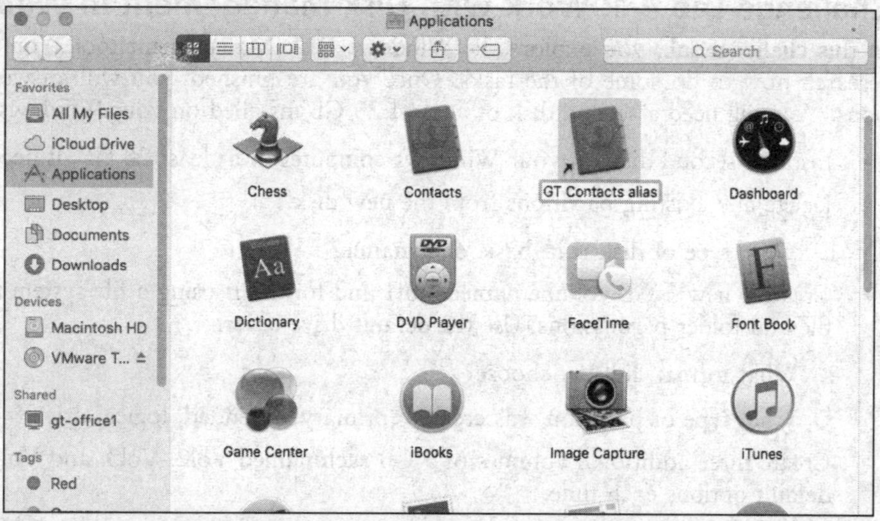


**Figure 4-28** Creating a new alias in Mac OS X

*Source: Mac OS X*

6. Right-click the new alias and click **Copy.** Right-click the desktop and click **Paste Item.** The new alias is copied to the right side of the desktop.
7. Double-click the alias on the desktop to see that it opens the Contacts application.
8. Log off or shut down your Mac OS X computer.

Although an alias only points to the actual application, you can treat an alias like an application. For example, you can drag a file onto an alias icon to open the file with the application to which the alias points. You can also create an alias for a folder instead of an application, which lets you save files into a folder by choosing its alias. Further, you can create an alias from a network connection so you can open the server it represents simply by double-clicking the alias icon.

## Critical Thinking

The following activities give you critical thinking challenges. Challenge Labs give you an opportunity to use the skills you have learned to perform a task without step-by-step instructions. Case projects offer a practical problem for which you supply a written solution. Not all chapters contain Challenge Labs. There is not always a specific right or wrong answer to these critical thinking exercises. They are intended to encourage you to review the chapter material and delve deeper into the topics you have learned.

# Challenge Labs

## Challenge Lab 4-1: Work with Disk Management in Windows

In this challenge lab, you explore the Windows Disk Management tool. You may have to research how to do some of the tasks. Once you are finished, you will answer some questions. You will need a second disk of at least 20 GB installed on your Windows computer.

- Install a second disk on your Windows computer of at least 20 GB, if necessary.
- Delete any existing partitions from the new disk.

  1. What type of disk is it: basic or dynamic?

- Create a new 3 GB volume named Vol1 and format it using a file system that supports file and folder permissions. Use the default drive letter.

  2. What format did you choose?
  3. What type of partition was created (primary, extended, logical drive)?

- Create three additional volumes of 3 GB each named Vol2, Vol3, and Vol4. Accept the default options each time.

  4. For each partition, what was the partition type you created?
  5. Explain what happened when you created the fourth volume.

- Convert the disk to a dynamic disk. (Convert only the new disk you installed; do not convert Disk 0, which is the Windows boot disk.)

  6. How did this change the way the volumes and partitions are labeled?

- Close Disk Management.

# Case Projects

GT Yummy Ice Cream is a company that produces ice cream and sells it to distributors in North America. The company's headquarters are in a large building in downtown Chicago. All of the senior management—the president and all vice presidents—use Macintosh computers with the Mac OS X operating system. The Marketing Department uses Windows 10, as does the Accounting Department. The Manufacturing and Operations Department uses workstations running Linux, which have specialized software for their area, including a complex inventory and distribution client/server system. The servers used by the company include a combination of Windows Server 2008 R2 and Windows Server 2012 R2. There has been some turnover in the company's Computer Support area, so you have been hired as a consultant to provide help.

## Case Project 4-1: Train a New Vice President in Using Mac OS X Folders

A new vice president has just been hired, and she is not familiar with Macintosh computers. You have been asked to provide her with a set of simple written instructions for how to access the documents in the home folder, which were left by her predecessor. Also, provide instructions for how to create a new folder in Mac OS X. Note that both the predecessor and the new vice president have the same user account name, which is VP Financials. Finally, the vice president needs your advice for creating a folder structure under her home folder. She wants a separate location for each of the following:

- Rulings by the board of directors
- Financial spreadsheets
- Word-processed documents that pertain to her division
- Word-processed documents that relate to senior management activities
- Marketing reports

Explain how you would set up the folder structure and what you would name the folders.

## Case Project 4-2: Determine Whether a File System is Mounted for a DVD/CD-ROM Drive

An inventory specialist in the Manufacturing and Operations Department needs to determine what file systems are mounted on his Linux computer because he is not sure that the DVD/CD-ROM drive is properly mounted. Explain the steps he should use to determine the mounted file systems, and note which file system should be mounted for the DVD/CD-ROM drive.

## Case Project 4-3: Choose a File System for Windows 10

A new computer has just been purchased for the accounting manager. The company purchased the computer without an operating system because they already have extra licensed copies of Windows 10. You need to set up the computer. What Windows 10 file system do you implement, recognizing that the accounting manager needs a secure system? Explain your decision and briefly discuss the advantages of this file system. Also, the accounting manager asks you to set up a preliminary folder structure to contain:

- Accounting reports
- Word-processed documents
- Department memos
- Personnel evaluations

Explain where you would set up this folder structure and show how you would name the new folders.

## Case Project 4-4: The Advantages of the Windows Server 2012 File System

GT Yummy Ice Cream has just hired a new person who is training to be a Windows Server administrator. She has worked with computers in many capacities, but has never managed a Windows Server 2012 server. You are asked to train her, and as part of the orientation to Windows Server 2012, you decide to explain the advantages of its file system. Create a short report that summarizes the advantages you will discuss in your training.

## Case Project 4-5: Repair a File Problem

The copywriter in the Marketing Department uses a Windows 10 computer that has some problems. Each time the copywriter accesses certain files, he sees an error message. He is concerned because the files will be used for an upcoming catalog that will go into print soon. Explain the steps needed to fix these files. The files are on the D: drive and the Windows OS is installed on the C: drive.

chapter 5

# Installing and Upgrading Operating Systems

## After reading this chapter and completing the exercises, you will be able to:

- Explain the overall process of installing and upgrading operating systems
- Prepare to install an operating system and understand the factors involved in an upgrade
- Install and upgrade the following operating systems and understand the various options:
  - Windows 7 and Windows 10
  - Windows Server 2008 and Windows Server 2012
  - Linux using the Fedora 23 distribution
  - Mac OS X El Capitan
- Obtain operating system patches and minor upgrades via the Internet

**For many, the installation or upgrade of an operating system (OS) sounds like a** daunting task. This chapter takes the mystery out of the process by showing you, step by step, how to install or upgrade modern OSs. First you learn some of the basic tasks and planning you must do before installing or upgrading an OS, and then you step through actual installations and upgrades in the Hands-On Projects at the end of the chapter. When you are finished, you will know how to prepare for an OS installation or upgrade; what to expect, what to watch for, and what to avoid during the process; and how to update your OS once it is installed. It is beyond the scope of this book to cover all possible options and settings, so only typical installations and upgrades are presented. For easier reading, the chapter is divided into two parts:

- Part 1: Introduction and Initial Preparations
- Part 2: OS Installations and Upgrades

# Part 1: Introduction and Initial Preparations

In Part 1, you learn general concepts about OS installations and upgrades. You also learn how to make advance preparations to help maximize the success of an installation, such as by verifying hardware and hardware drivers, backing up OSs before starting, and conducting a test upgrade.

## Introduction to Installing an OS

There are two basic types of OS installations: clean installations and upgrade installations. A **clean installation** is performed in one of the following scenarios:

- The installation is performed on a computer that has no OS installed (a new hard drive or one that has been formatted)
- The computer has an OS already installed; it is deleted and replaced by the new OS
- The computer has an OS installed and the new OS is installed on another volume, making it possible to boot either to the old OS or the new one

An **upgrade installation** occurs on a computer that already contains an earlier version of the OS. The upgrade replaces the earlier version with a new version, and usually retains some or all of the original settings, user accounts, applications, data files, and other existing user files.

The process of installing an OS varies from one OS to another, but certain features are common to all installations. OS installation can be divided into three general stages: preparation, the installation itself, and the configuration tasks performed following the installation.

Preparing for installation involves the following:

- Choosing a computer configuration that meets or exceeds the minimum requirements for the OS you are installing
- Ensuring that all computer hardware is operating correctly
- Having the OS installation media available (DVDs, ISO files, setup programs) and any license or activation codes

- Understanding the general features of the OS you are installing so you can decide which modules to install and which to omit
- Having device drivers that might not be included with the OS installation files. This preparation is particularly important for disk controllers. (During the Windows installation process, you will be prompted to add drivers for any disks that are not recognized by the setup program.)
- Having accurate information available about your computer and peripheral devices
- Being aware of the network environment in which you are installing the OS; this preparation may involve having information about how and where the computer should be connected to the network or having Wi-Fi access information, knowing how IP addressing is done on the network, and knowing what to name the computer

During the installation, you may need to provide some or all of the following information:

- Where (in which drive, folder, or path) to install the OS and what to name the folder that contains the OS
- Whether you want to perform a clean installation or an upgrade and the name(s) the OS uses for these different installation types (for example, Windows uses the term *Custom install* for a clean installation)
- Information about you, your company, and your computer; this information might include your name, company name, computer name, or workgroup name
- A license or activation code that verifies your right to install the OS
- Which components of the OS you want to install

After you complete an installation, keep the product key, ID number, or activation code in a safe place so you can reinstall the OS in the event that your computer or hard drive fails. Also, always keep the installation DVDs and other media in a safe place after completing the installation.

Modern OSs can automatically detect and configure devices such as monitors, keyboards, printers, mice, network cards, video cards, and sound cards, as long as the OS has the appropriate device driver as part of the installation media. However, automatic detection may also misidentify a device, and you might need to reinstall the correct driver.

Some installation programs are primarily GUI-based or use a combination of GUI- and text-based screens. Modern versions of Windows, Linux, and Mac OS X primarily use GUI screens during an installation, and they use automated "wizards" to step you through the process. OSs can usually be installed from DVDs, and in many cases over a network. (Network installations are not covered in this book.)

The installation itself consists of some or all of the following general functions:

- Running the installation program
- Gathering system information
- Determining which elements of the OS will be installed
- Copying OS files to your computer

- Configuring devices and drivers
- Restarting the system and finalizing configuration of devices

For most OSs, device and driver configuration is part of the installation process. The Plug and Play (PnP) feature automatically configures internal and external devices as part of the installation and at startup whenever a new device is added.

Windows 95 was the first OS to be compatible with PnP. Besides Windows, UNIX/Linux distributions and Mac OS X are also PnP compatible.

Even with a PnP-capable OS, you may have to configure devices to work optimally with the OS. For example, your computer may detect a video card in the system and a monitor, but it may not have the correct or newest driver for the card. Also, the monitor settings may need to be configured for optimal performance. In some cases, the OS may search for and download the correct driver automatically, or you might have to supply a disc or flash drive that contains the driver or download it manually.

## Preparing for Installation

Before you can install any OS, you must make a few advance preparations. Naturally, you must select a computer on which you will install the OS. You might have an existing computer or a new computer that was purchased specifically for the OS. The "computer" may also be a virtual machine in which the "hardware" is virtual hardware emulated by virtual machine software, such as VMware or Microsoft Hyper-V. (Virtualization is discussed in more detail in Chapter 8.) In any case, the computer must meet the minimum specifications for the OS you are installing. Most commonly, the minimum specifications cover the speed and type of CPU, the amount of memory, and the amount of free disk space.

## Checking the Hardware

First, and most important, the machine must be working correctly. If you have defective hardware, such as a bad disk drive, a bad DVD/CD-ROM drive, or a bad memory chip, the OS installation can be extremely difficult or impossible. Most OSs interface with the hardware on many levels.

Before you begin an installation, you should be sure that all hardware needed for the installation is turned on and ready for use, including the computer, monitor, and any external peripheral devices, such as USB devices and external disk drives.

You should remove or disconnect any removable media that contain important data or that are not necessary for the installation. In general, an OS installation will not destroy data on removable media, unless it is specifically instructed to do so. However, if important data is backed up and removable media are taken out of their drives or disconnected, there is no chance of losing anything.

You should also have available information about your hardware, including how many hard disks you have, their size, and their type, such as SAS or SATA disks. (You learn about these disks in Chapter 7, "Using and Configuring Storage Devices.") You should also know how much memory you have in your machine. For any expansion cards, such as your video card, network card, sound card, and disk controllers, you should know the make and model. If you have a printer, modem, scanner, or other device, you should keep the device driver disks handy and know their types. Table 5-1 is an example of how you might organize this information for installation.

**Table 5-1 Hardware component information**

| Component | Description/setting |
|---|---|
| CPU (type and bit size) | The computer's basic input/output system (BIOS) knows the CPU information, and the OS should automatically make all required adjustments. One caveat, however, is that the bit size (32-bit or 64-bit) of the CPU must match the bit size of the OS you are installing. |
| Amount of RAM | Your OS should automatically detect the amount of random access memory (RAM) in your computer. However, guidelines supplied with your OS tell you how much RAM is recommended. You should know how much you have to ensure that minimum requirements are met. |
| Type of buses | Before you install the OS, you might want to install any expansion cards you want to use. You'll need to know what expansion buses your computer supports and how many slots are available before you purchase the expansion cards. Examples of expansion bus slot types include PCI Express, PCI-X, and PCI. |
| Hard disk(s) | You need to know the type and size of your hard disks and whether they are empty or have a file system installed. If you are doing an upgrade or installing alongside an existing OS, you need to know how much free space is available. Most new hardware includes BIOS routines to automatically detect the type of hard drive installed, as well as critical drive settings. |
| Keyboard | Unless your keyboard has special features that require custom drivers, the type of keyboard you have should not be a factor during OS installation. |
| Mouse | The type of mouse or pointing device can be important; there can be differences between a wired mouse and a wireless mouse. In some cases, a custom driver may be needed for a mouse that has extra features. |
| Video card | Most modern OSs will detect your video card and automatically include required drivers. However, special features of your video card may become available only with the use of a special driver provided by the manufacturer. This is particularly true of video cards that support multiple monitors. |
| DVD/CD-ROM type | Your OS automatically detects this information. |
| Sound card | Some OSs include drivers for common sound card hardware. If your card isn't one of the popular models, make sure you have the required drivers supplied by the card's manufacturer. |
| Network interface card (NIC) | Most OSs will automatically detect your NIC. However, it may still be a good idea to use the manufacturer's custom drivers for best performance. |
| Printer | You should have custom drivers from your printer manufacturer. |
| Other input/output (I/O) devices | If your OS doesn't detect other hardware during the installation, you must understand hardware basics and have access to any custom drivers required to make it function properly with your OS. Most motherboards come with a DVD that contains drivers for all the on-board devices, but it's a good idea to check the motherboard manufacturer's Web site and see if there are updated drivers for the OS you are installing. |

NOTE

Chapter 6, "Configuring Input and Output Devices," and Chapter 7, "Using and Configuring Storage Devices," provide more detailed information on devices and device drivers.

Some cards installed in the computer include their own settings. In the Intel PC architecture, these cards must often be configured to interface with the computer in a certain way. Modern OSs use the PnP capability to do this. If you install an OS that supports PnP, card configuration is usually automatic. If you do not use an OS that supports PnP, or if you install a component that does not support PnP, you may be in for a few surprises. Many PnP cards come with a utility that lets you configure them to work in non-PnP mode; this utility is usually included on the manufacturer's disk with the drivers.

All modern Windows OSs support PnP. Most Linux distributions also support PnP, but the use of drivers in Linux can be more complex than in Windows systems, so there can be occasional problems in detecting PnP cards and devices in Linux. If a detection problem occurs, contact the card or device manufacturer. Interface cards in the Apple Mac architecture don't usually need any special configuration for the hardware to work properly because Mac OS X is specifically designed for Mac hardware.

NOTE

Newer hardware may have BIOS settings that can turn PnP compatibility on or off. PnP should be enabled by default. If it isn't, check your computer's BIOS documentation to find out how to turn it on before installing a new OS. USB devices, such as flash or removable hard drives, can be hot-plugged into a computer and recognized because they are equipped with PnP capability. A hot-plug device can be installed and removed from the computer while the computer is on and the OS is running.

## Checking Drivers

Many devices, such as DVD drives, SCSI drives, network interface cards, printers, and scanners, require special drivers to work correctly. In general, drivers are included on the disks that come with the devices, but often these disks do not include drivers for all possible OSs or the most up-to-date drivers. Also, your device may not be on the list of drivers that come with the OS, which can result in some installation problems.

If you install drivers that came with your hardware, the hardware should operate properly. However, in some cases, you may get significantly better performance by installing later drivers that you secure from the manufacturer. The easiest way to access the latest drivers is to go to the hardware manufacturer's Web site for drivers and support information, or contact the manufacturer and ask for the latest driver disks for your device.

Even though you may have driver disks on hand, it is best to obtain recent drivers because driver updates often fix bugs or performance problems in older versions. In some cases, your strategy may involve reading forums about manufacturers' devices so you are aware of any problems with the newest drivers. For example, a new driver that is relatively untested in the market may have some problems, in which case you want to use the driver issued just prior to the newest driver.

You should also check the documentation that came with any hardware you want to use with your new OS. In many cases, the manufacturer includes a disclaimer indicating which OSs are certified for use with particular hardware.

## Ensuring Hardware Compatibility

Because of the wide range of hardware available today, you will find that many OSs have certain hardware requirements. These are usually listed on the vendor's Web site or in the OS's documentation. Some OSs enable you to look up compatible hardware online. For example, you can find compatibility information for Windows servers on Microsoft's Windows Server Catalog Web site, at *www.windowsservercatalog.com/*. For client OSs such as Windows 10, go to the Windows Compatibility Products List Web site: *https://sysdev.microsoft.com/en-us/hardware/lpl/*. Red Hat has a certified products catalog that combines Red Hat hardware, software, and plug-in compatibility information into a single publication (*https://access.redhat.com/ecosystem/*). For Mac OS X, use Apple Macintosh hardware such as the iMac to ensure compatibility.

If you are installing the OS on a virtual machine, the virtual machine software allows you to select the OS you are installing and the virtual machine is configured appropriately to ensure the virtual hardware is compatible.

## Migrating to a New OS

No matter how comfortable you are with an OS, there comes a time when you must upgrade or migrate to the next version. In this context, an upgrade refers to an installation in which the original settings and user files are retained; we use **migration** to more broadly refer to moving from one OS to another, which may or may not involve implementing a new computer.

For instance, a migration may be necessary when you find that your current OS version does not support new software or certain devices you want to use. Also, older versions of OSs don't have the new security features required for safer network and Internet access, or to protect e-mail systems. Whether it is a small upgrade to fix bugs or a larger upgrade or migration, many of the procedures are similar to those required for an initial installation. In this section, you'll learn about general upgrade and migration considerations, backup and safety recommendations, and the specific steps and possible pitfalls involved in upgrading or migrating computer OSs.

## Deciding Whether to Perform an Upgrade or Clean Installation

When you consider migrating to a newer OS version, decide whether you can perform an upgrade installation or whether you need to do a clean installation. An upgrade installation can be an advantage in that it typically costs less to purchase an upgrade license than a new license for an OS. In many cases, you can also elect to retain your existing settings, data files, and applications, which can save time and money.

Alternatively, the advantage of a clean installation is that you can start fresh by reformatting the hard disk used by the OS, which enables disk problems to be identified and remedied before they become a headache later. In some cases, reformatting may also help your system to run faster. The downside of a clean installation is that it takes extra time to configure the OS, restore data files, and reinstall applications.

Although it takes time to reinstall applications, the reinstallation may solve problems with applications that don't work properly or that have become sluggish. When you reinstall applications, also plan to apply application updates that manufacturers often distribute through the Internet.

In some cases, you need to perform a clean installation because the new OS version does not support your old hardware. For example, organizations that were using Windows XP may need to upgrade to Windows 10 because Windows XP is no longer supported; the computers running Windows XP will probably not meet the minimum requirements of Windows 10, so clean installations on new hardware are required.

## Preparing for an Upgrade or Migration

Before you upgrade or migrate, the first thing to consider is whether this step is truly necessary. For example, will it enable you or your organization to perform tasks or use software you can't use now? Will it save money in the long run by increasing productivity or enabling new services? Is your current OS no longer supported, or does it have security vulnerabilities that a new OS resolves?

If you are certain that an upgrade or migration is necessary and desirable, then you must make sure you have the necessary hardware and software (including device drivers) for the new OS version, as well as information about your computer that may be needed. You should also make a complete backup of your current system and data before starting. If you are upgrading or migrating more than two or three computers at once, consider performing a test upgrade or migration on one or two computers to identify and solve possible problems. These types of considerations are discussed in the following sections.

If you are upgrading or migrating a large number of desktop or server OSs, investigate automated installation methods, such as Microsoft's unattended installation option, or large-scale installation options such as Windows Deployment Services (available in Windows Server). There is not room in this chapter to discuss these automated techniques, but it is important to be aware they are available.

**Deciding to Upgrade or Migrate** When new versions of OSs are released that promise new features, bug fixes, enhanced capabilities, and more speed, it is tempting to jump immediately on the upgrade bandwagon. However, before taking such a step, especially in a large production environment, you should carefully consider whether you need to upgrade or migrate and whether the time is right. Although newer versions of OSs promise great new features, you should ask yourself whether you actually need the new functionality. Objective analysis of the situation may show that an upgrade or migration may not be cost effective. In other cases, the result might significantly lower the total cost of ownership (TCO) if the OS you are upgrading to can be more easily managed. For example, Group Policy is a feature that works in Windows domains to manage security, configuration, settings, and other configurable features on Windows client computers. Generally speaking, Microsoft enhances the capabilities of Group Policy with each release of its server and client OS versions, making newer OSs easier to manage while improving security in an enterprise network.

In some cases, moving to a new OS has little immediate effect on the functions performed by the computers and users for which you are responsible. However, you may want to upgrade to newer hardware for warranty, performance, and reliability reasons. In this case, your old OS may not support the new hardware features, making your decision to upgrade to a newer version an easy and necessary one.

Sometimes OS vendors publish a list of the applications tested on the new OS. These tests may not be comprehensive enough to ensure that all features of the applications work properly, or that they work on all types of computers. Install the new OS and the applications your organization uses on a test computer so that you can verify them before implementing them on a large scale.

Experience has also shown that it is best not to upgrade or migrate shortly after a new OS is released. If you can put off moving to a new OS for several months, or maybe even a year, you benefit from the experiences of many other users solving problems that might have been yours. If you wait, you will have access to many patches and bug fixes that are not available for early releases. If you feel you must upgrade or migrate soon after a new version is released, consider using the test strategy covered later in this chapter.

**The OS Version Development Cycle** Some OS vendors offer prerelease or beta software for you to try. Microsoft, for example, typically offers prereleases in the form of alpha software, beta versions, and release candidate (RC) versions. **Alpha software** is an early development version of software in which there are likely to be bugs, and not all of the anticipated software functionality is present. **Beta software** has successfully passed the alpha test stage. Beta testing may involve dozens, hundreds, or even thousands of people, and may be conducted in multiple stages, such as beta 1, beta 2, and so on. Beta software likely still has bugs, but is at a more tested stage. A **release candidate** (RC) is software at the final stage of testing by vendors and users before the official release that is sold commercially. A release candidate is usually tested by a very large audience of customers.

When an OS has been well tested and contains all of the new features, it is ready to go to market. At this stage Microsoft calls the software a **release to manufacturing (RTM)** version. Never install anything other than an official release or RTM version of an OS on **production computers** because preliminary versions can have bugs, security vulnerabilities, and reliability problems. In addition, some OS vendors put a time limit on preliminary releases so that they stop working or receiving updates after a specified date.

NOTE

A production computer is any computer used to perform real work. If it were to become unusable for any reason, it would cause an inconvenience, hinder workflow, or cause data to be lost.

TIP

If you plan to implement a new OS for an organization, consider obtaining an alpha or beta version, and put it on a machine used specifically for testing. Use this computer for training and investigation to learn about the new features of the OS and how they will affect your work environment, particularly your existing software. Virtual machines are excellent choices for testing preliminary software releases because they can be quickly built and just as quickly removed when you are finished with them.

**Checking Hardware and Software** Before you decide to upgrade or migrate, you should carefully check the affected computers against the requirements of the new OS. As already noted, newer OSs often require more advanced hardware, including increased memory, disk space, CPU speed, and sometimes even improved display properties. Take special note of the hardware installed in the computer, such as network cards, scanners, sound cards, and other devices that require special drivers. If your organization supports many computers, consider obtaining network software that can automatically inventory the hardware components of the computers on your network. Or, you can inventory the hardware yourself, as illustrated in the example hardware inventory list in Table 5-2.

**Table 5-2 Sample hardware inventory for multiple computers**

| Computer ID | CPU/clock speed | RAM | Disk capacity | DVD/CD-ROM | Video | Special devices |
|---|---|---|---|---|---|---|
| CFNP9012 | 2.8 GHz | 4 GB | 750 GB | DVD/CD-ROM | On board | None |
| D3FX1931 | 3.2 GHz | 8 GB | 1 TB | Blu-ray disc and DVD/CD-ROM | VisionTEK PCIe | Tablet |
| ... | ... | ... | ... | ... | ... | ... |

Also, before you migrate to a new OS, make sure that the current drivers for I/O devices and storage media work with the new version, or that drivers are available for these devices on the new OS. It is a good idea to contact hardware vendors and get some assurance that their devices will continue to work properly after the upgrade. Do not leave this to chance; older or discontinued hardware may not be supported in newer OS versions.

TIP

The issue of drivers is another reason to delay your migration until an OS has been on the market for several months. Sometimes OS vendors release a system before hardware manufacturers have had time to develop and test new drivers. Waiting to migrate usually means there will be more drivers—and hardware—available to use with an OS.

Make sure that you have all the device drivers needed for the hardware available on a DVD, flash drive, or removable hard drive. If there are drivers that exist only on the hard disk of the computer, copy them to a flash drive, removable hard drive, or some other safe place. Otherwise, if the installation fails, you will not have the drivers you need to get the computer back to work. If there are new drivers for the new version of the OS, keep them handy, as well as copies of your current drivers. You will then be able to reinstall the old OS if you cannot complete the upgrade for some reason.

It is also a good idea to keep detailed records of custom software settings—changes in the default settings for the OS and other software—so that these custom settings can be restored if necessary after any OS or other software upgrade. For example, it is not uncommon for users to modify display or other settings after they run an OS for a while; they may use an automated backup program, run special disk tools on a regular basis, or have customized network settings. Upgrade installations may reset some settings to their defaults, which may not be what you want.

Determine what software is used on systems prior to an upgrade or migration so that you can check to see if there are any compatibility problems. Windows 10 has a Program Compatibility Troubleshooter that can help you configure an application that will run on an older Windows version but won't run on Windows 10.

Another way to run older applications on new operating systems is to use virtualization. Using a virtualization program such as VMware Player, Hyper-V, or VirtualBox, you can run the old OS as a virtual machine in the new OS. In addition, some virtualization programs let you create a virtual machine from your physical computer, a process called *physical to virtual (P2V)*. Using this procedure, the OS and applications on your old computer are put into virtual disks that are attached to a virtual machine you can run in your new OS.

## Making Backups Before Migrating to a New OS

A **backup** involves copying files from a computer system to another medium, such as tape, a DVD, another hard drive, or a removable drive. It is essential to have a complete backup of your old OS, software, and data before beginning a migration. Making backups of software and data is also a very important part of day-to-day computer operation because unexpected things happen, such as hard disk crashes or unintentional file deletions. As OSs and computers get more complicated, failures can even happen for unexplainable reasons during normal computer operation. If you use computers long enough, eventually you will lose critical information. Backups are essential to recovering from such a loss.

Most OSs have a backup utility, and software vendors offer many other choices that provide plenty of additional backup options.

If a program is lost, you may be able to simply reinstall it, but when data files are lost, the damage may take hours or days to repair. For this reason, regular backup of your system during normal operations and full backup prior to an upgrade are necessities.

Consider the following points when backing up your information:

- Close all open windows and save all files before starting a backup because many backup tools do not back up open files.
- Make sure that you have the software needed to restore the backups under both the old and new OSs. There is nothing more frustrating than having a backup but not being able to restore it. Even though you probably tested the backup and restore software with the old OS, there is no guarantee it will work properly with the new one. Before you perform an upgrade, you should test the restore software, preferably by making a backup and restoring it to the computer you set up to test the new OS.
- Make sure that you make a full backup of the system. You should make a backup of the entire contents of all disks connected to the computer, not just the disk the OS is installed on.

NOTE

When you perform a backup, make sure that you back up critical system files, such as the system state data in Windows desktop and server OSs, which includes the registry. In the backup utility that comes with these OSs, and for some third-party utilities, you can manually select a system state backup. Another way to make sure that you have a backup of all files, including system files, is to perform an image (binary) backup by using tools in the OS's backup software or third-party software. Disk imaging software vendors include Paragon, Acronis, and Symantec.

Some computers you upgrade will not have a built-in drive, such as a tape drive or dedicated backup drive, that is suitable to make a full backup. In this situation, consider using a removable external hard drive or a network drive. Another option is to back up to another computer on the network that is equipped with an appropriate backup device. Keep in mind that almost all OSs support easily removable external drives that connect to the USB, FireWire, or eSATA port on a computer. It is worth the money to have one of these devices handy to make full backups before an upgrade installation. Chapter 7 and Chapter 11 provide more information about backups.

NOTE

Upgrading an OS can be very simple; it may take only 20 minutes, and you may never need the backup media you created or the test system you used to verify the restore would work properly. However, if the upgrade does not go as planned, you will be very happy to have the backup. The time spent backing up, including testing the backup, can prevent many headaches and problems with your system upgrade.

**From the Trenches ...**

A small credit union was migrating from an older UNIX server to a new Linux server. They used third-party backup software that was advertised as supporting both OSs, so they did not run a test to ensure the software worked with both OSs. After upgrading to the Linux server, the information on the tapes made from the old UNIX system could not be read by the new Linux server. In fact, the backup could not be read even by the old UNIX system. Fortunately, the credit union staff had not dismantled the old UNIX system before discovering this problem.

## Conducting a Test Migration

You should plan to test an upgrade or migration before you apply it to a production computer. If you have only one or two computers to upgrade or migrate, this may not be an option, but when you have five or more computers to upgrade or migrate, it can be beneficial to perform a test on one or more.

The purpose of a test is to simulate what would happen in a real upgrade or migration and discover any problems that might occur. To run the test, you need a working computer that closely resembles the computers you will be upgrading or migrating. Choose a computer that resembles the "lowest common denominator" of the computers you are upgrading or migrating, in terms of their amount of memory, CPU speed, size of the hard disk, and any connected devices. You should also install all software that is typically found on a production computer in your situation. If you are in a network environment, connect the computer to the network and make sure everything is fully functional. You should be able to use this machine as if it were a production computer. At the beginning of the test, this computer will run the old version of the OS, the version you currently run on your production computers. Part of the test is to practice upgrading or migrating this OS.

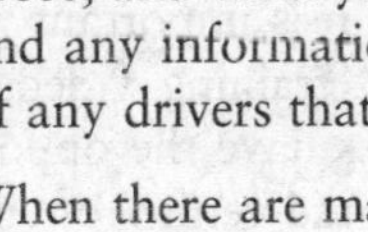
TIP

Consider using virtual machines as part of your upgrade test. Virtual machines don't test hardware compatibility, but you can at least install the applications in the new OS on a virtual machine to verify that the applications will work correctly.

When the test computer is fully functional, you can perform the upgrade or migration. It is helpful to take specific notes describing the steps of the installation, any problems that arose, and what you did about them. Also note any questions you had about the installation, and any information you had to look up to complete the installation. Write down the names of any drivers that you needed. These notes will serve as a guide in later installations.

When there are many computers to upgrade or migrate, it is common to do so over a period of several weeks or months, so having notes on the exact steps of the process will help you remember the information you need and the problems you found. Another approach is to create a written checklist that documents the upgrade or migration process step by step, including how to handle problems as well as special driver and software installations and configurations.

Once you complete the upgrade or migration on the test computer and immediately deal with any software issues that arise, test the computer for a couple of days. Perform tasks that you would normally perform, and take note of any changes in the computer and the user interface.

If you find no apparent problems, you may want to ask an experienced user whose computer is on the list to be upgraded or migrated to use the test computer for work for a few days. Keep in close communication with this person, taking note of any problems and anything that does not work properly. After moving to a new OS, one of the first things to check is whether all application software functions normally. Sometimes after upgrades or migrations, particular functions in software packages do not work, or work differently. If there are problems, chances are they will not surface until a user tries to access a certain function you never thought to test.

During the testing phase for an upgrade installation, ensure that the upgrade did not change any settings or move or remove files or programs. If you encounter significant problems with hardware or software, delay the upgrade or migration until they are resolved. Just as a prerelease test will uncover major and minor problems with a new OS design, an upgrade or migration test can uncover conflicts between the new OS and your particular system configuration.

After resolving any problems, repeat the test installation process. Install the old OS, then all software, then upgrade or migrate the OS, and make the changes you think will resolve the issues you encountered earlier. Test the computer yourself for a couple of days, and then let a user test the computer. In this way, you have another chance to test the upgrade or migration and your installation notes.

These tests can be time consuming; you may need a week or longer to get through them. In some cases, you may perform many test installations before you get every detail worked out. Or, you may decide after repeated tries that the upgrade or migration will not work and cancel the plan. Either way, the test results, when carefully documented, will tell you what to expect. Obviously it is better to find out in a test situation that an OS upgrade or migration won't work for you. Your test results can also be used to explain to employees and management why an upgrade or migration should or should not be carried out. If you decide that the plan should proceed, you will know the steps, you will know what to expect, and you will be efficient in performing the upgrade or migration.

## Training

In small to large organizations that migrate to a new desktop OS, it is important to arrange for user training. This training might be in the form of classes, training videos, training DVDs, or other means. The important thing is to ensure that users have the opportunity to learn the new OS. There is an initial expense for training, but the return on investment (ROI) can be worth it in terms of user productivity as well as user morale.

Also, training for server administrators on new server systems is important. Training the server administrators will help them understand the new features of the server and how to best use those features to improve reliability, security, and productivity.

# Part 2: OS Installations and Upgrades

The second half of this chapter focuses on the practical steps to install and upgrade the OSs discussed in this book. For each OS you learn:

- Information about OS versions
- Minimum and recommended hardware configurations
- Installation steps
- Upgrade steps
- How to install minor upgrades or patches (minor enhancements or fixes are often made available through the Internet on a weekly, monthly, or as-needed basis)

## Installing and Upgrading Windows 7

Mainstream support for Windows 7 ended in January 2015, but it's still widely used in business and at home. Extended support for Windows 7 is scheduled to end in January 2020. The editions available in Windows 7 include:

- *Starter edition*—A stripped-down version of Windows 7 that offers limited functions, including fewer desktop display options. It is often preinstalled on **netbook computers,** which are small portable or laptop computers that have limited computing capabilities and are designed for lightweight portability. Netbook computers are generally used for Web access, e-mail, and basic document creation. Starter edition could originally handle only three simultaneously open applications, but this restriction no longer applies.
- *Home basic edition*—Just a step above Starter edition, the Home Basic edition is intended for Web surfing, e-mail, photos, music, and basic document handling. It has only limited support for the Aero desktop feature.
- *Home premium edition*—Offers more digital capabilities than Home Basic edition for expanding home entertainment, use of photos, and more capable document handling. Home Premium is particularly well suited to entertainment activities involving games, TV, music, and multimedia. Home Premium edition provides full support for the Aero desktop.
- *Professional edition*—A platform for accomplishing professional activities on the computer in a home, small office, or larger office work environment. Windows Professional is well suited to setting up projectors, networks, printers, and other shared resources. It enables the user to set up automatic backups in a home or work context.
- *Business edition*—Intended for business users to enable the use of business applications, network mobility throughout an office, and for remote access, document collaboration, versatile backup and shadow copy capabilities, and strong security. Business edition is also well adapted for membership in a Windows Server domain.
- *Ultimate edition*—A union of the home entertainment and business productivity capabilities of the Home Premium and Business editions. Ultimate edition also offers advanced battery management for portable computers and the most advanced security protection, including BitLocker Drive Encryption. BitLocker is a whole-disk encryption system that can prevent the system from booting without the necessary key.

- *Enterprise edition*—Contains the same features as Ultimate edition except that it is sold to large companies using volume licensing instead of to individual users.

All Windows 7 editions, except Starter edition (32-bit only), come in 32- and 64-bit versions. The user's direct experience of security in Windows 7 is toned down from Windows Vista, in that it requires less user intervention. However, the actual security is strengthened to meet new security threats.

**Hardware Requirements** For satisfactory performance, users should consider purchasing a computer that has a 1.2 GHz dual-core or better CPU, 2 GB or more of RAM, and 100 GB or more of storage. These aren't the minimum requirements (see Table 5-3), but they are recommended for satisfactory performance.

Windows 7 offers visual features that can take full advantage of the high resolution and display capabilities of systems with advanced graphics features. When you use a computer with an advanced graphics processor, Windows 7 can display high-quality results for multimedia and gaming applications.

The hardware requirements for Windows 7 are summarized in Table 5-3.

**Table 5-3 Windows 7 hardware requirements**

| Hardware | Minimum | Recommended |
|---|---|---|
| CPU | 1 GHz 32- or 64-bit processor | Multicore processor or multiple processors for better performance; also, an Intel-VT or AMD-V capable processor for handling virtual desktop software to run multiple OSs |
| RAM | 1 GB (32-bit)<br>2 GB (64-bit) | 2 GB or more for 32-bit systems (2 GB is required to run Windows Virtual PC)<br>3 GB or more for 64-bit systems |
| Storage | 16 GB (32-bit)<br>20 GB (64-bit) | 50 GB or much more depending on the applications to be used |
| Video card | DirectX 9 graphics device with WDDM 1.0 or higher | Video capabilities appropriate for the applications to be used; gaming and multimedia applications may require specialized video capabilities |

**Installing Windows 7** The Windows installation process is simple and straightforward. With the installation DVD inserted in the drive, start the computer. The system boots from the DVD and the setup program begins. You are prompted for the language and locale settings, as shown in Figure 5-1.

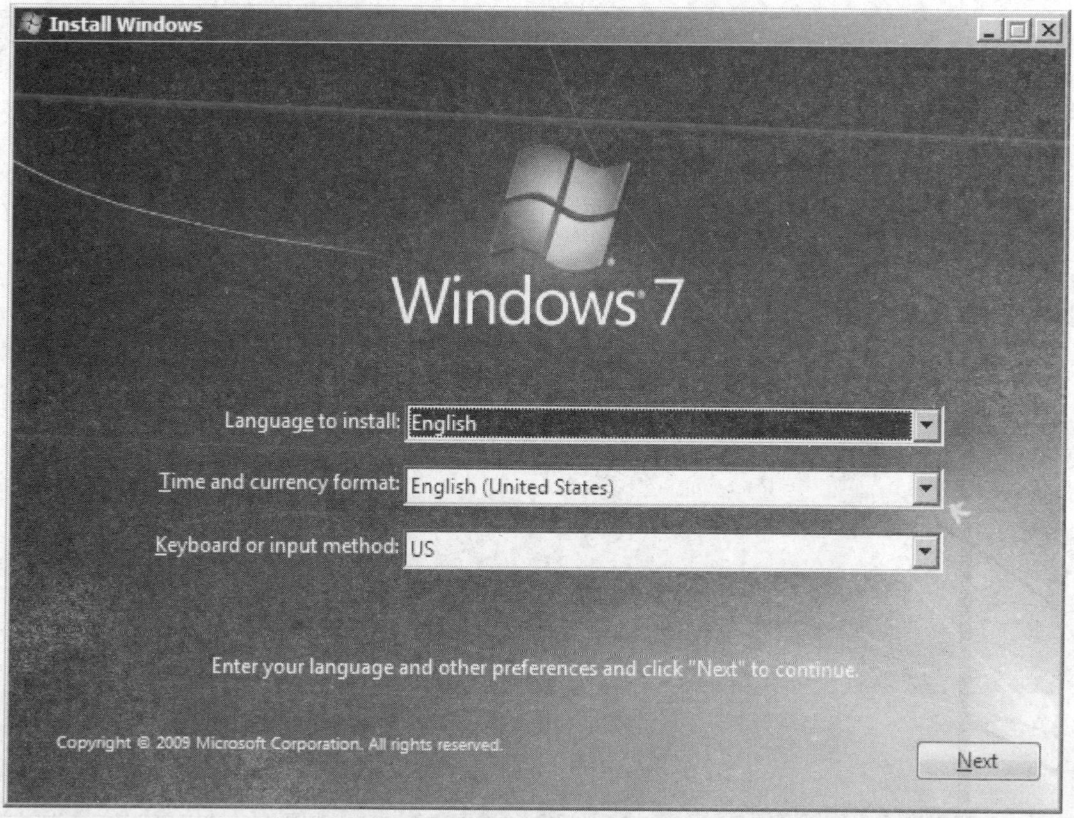


**Figure 5-1** Choosing language and locale settings in Windows 7 setup

After clicking Next, you click Install now and setup continues. You must accept the license terms and then choose the type of installation you want (see Figure 5-2):

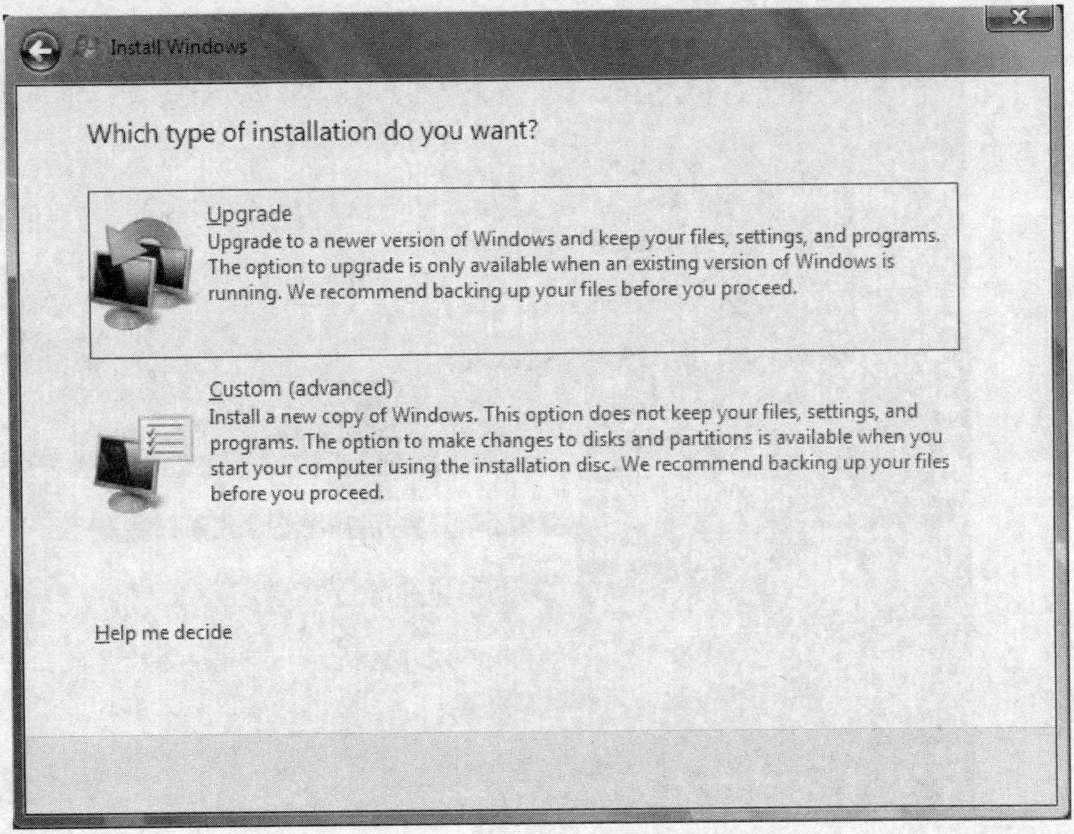


**Figure 5-2** Choosing an Upgrade or Custom installation in Windows 7

Your choices are Upgrade and Custom (advanced). For a clean installation, choose Custom (advanced). An upgrade installation can only be started if you boot the system to an existing OS. Next, you choose where to install Windows. If your disk is empty, as in Figure 5-3, you can accept the default option, and Windows will create a 300 MB System Reserved partition for the boot files and assign the remaining disk space to the C: drive where Windows is installed. Optionally, you can create your own partitions or delete existing partitions by clicking Drive options.

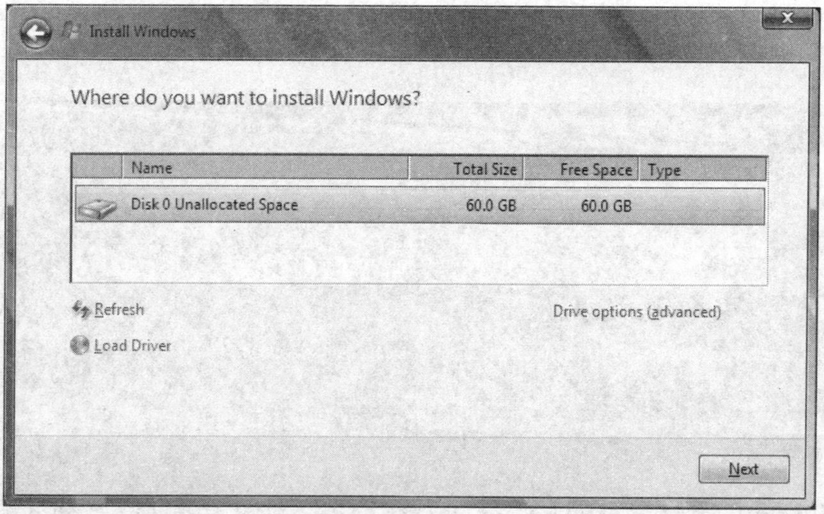


**Figure 5-3** Choosing where to install Windows

Next, Windows copies files needed for installation and the installation continues. Your computer will restart once or twice during installation; when it is complete, you are prompted to create a user and a name for your computer and then create a password. You are then prompted to configure Windows Updates, set the time and time zone, and select your network location (Home, Work, or Public). Windows finalizes settings, the desktop appears, and installation is complete.

Most editions of Windows 7 require you to enter the activation code during installation. An exception is the Enterprise edition, which allows centralized activation for volume license holders.

**Upgrading to Windows 7** There are two approaches to upgrading to Windows 7. One upgrade path is to go from one edition of Windows 7 to a more full-featured edition. You can perform this type of upgrade by purchasing the Windows Anytime Upgrade for Windows 7. Another path is to upgrade from Windows XP or Windows Vista to Windows 7. We'll forego the details of the upgrade paths because at this point in the Windows 7 lifecycle, most updates will be to a more current version of Windows, such as Windows 10.

## Installing and Upgrading Windows 10

The actual installation process for Windows seems to become more streamlined and hands-off with each successive version. The installation process for Windows 10 doesn't differ substantially from that of Windows 7 or Windows 8/8.1 until the initial installation is over and you are asked whether you want to customize settings or use express settings. If you customize settings, you can specify how much information your computer should send to Microsoft for personalizing your experience, whether you want your location and browsing information shared with Windows and apps, whether to send diagnostics to Windows, and whether you should connect automatically to wireless and shared networks. If you choose Customize, you'll see the screen in Figure 5-4.

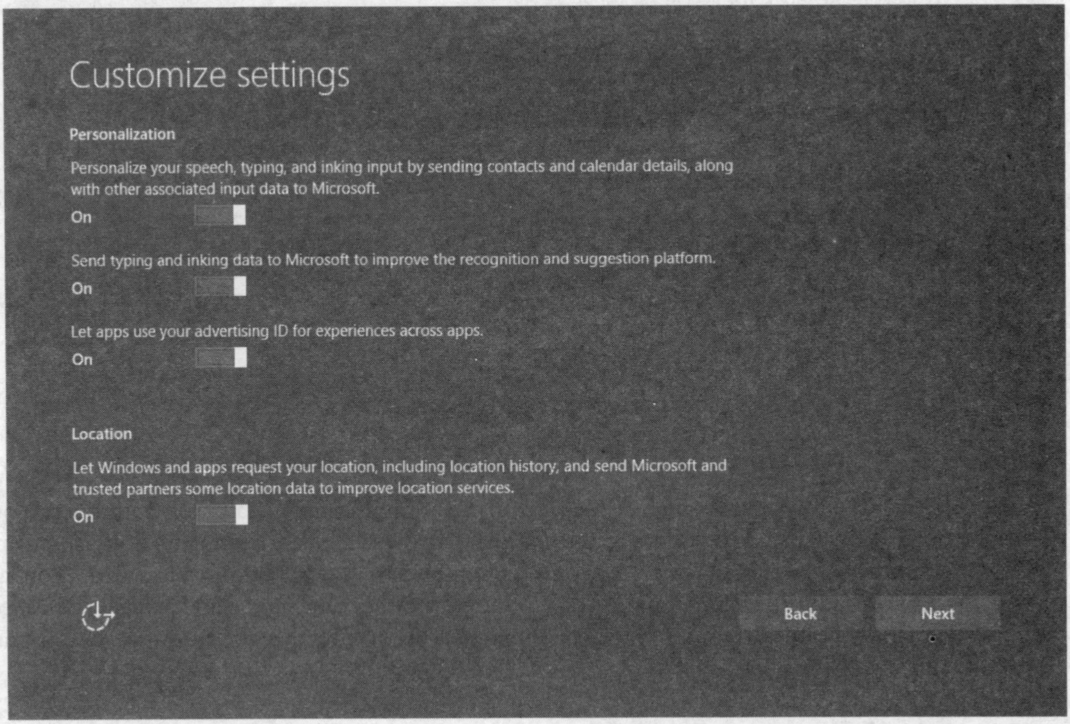


**Figure 5-4** Customizing settings in Windows 10

After you customize settings or accept the express settings, you'll be asked how you want to connect to your organization's network if you're using the Enterprise or Education edition. For all other editions, you'll be asked to sign in to your PC using a Microsoft account. You can create a new Microsoft account or use an existing account by entering your e-mail address. If you want to sign in with a local user account, you are given that option as well. After you log on, Windows finishes installing and configuring your system and displays the Windows desktop. You will have an opportunity to install Windows 10 in a Hands-On Project at the end of the chapter.

All Windows 10 editions except Enterprise require you to enter an activation key during the installation process.

**Upgrading to Windows 10** If you want to upgrade to Windows 10 on a computer with an existing OS installed, you have a number of options. Free in-place upgrades to Windows 10 are supported for Windows 7 and Windows 8/8.1. An **in-place upgrade** essentially overwrites your current OS installation and maintains your applications, settings, and data.

Windows 10 is a free upgrade for qualified editions unless you are running the Enterprise edition of Windows 7 or 8/8.1. If you are running the Enterprise edition, you must upgrade to an Enterprise edition of Windows 10 using your company's volume licensing agreement.

The easiest way to upgrade to Windows 10 is to download the Windows upgrade program. The Windows upgrade program will detect your edition of Windows 7 or 8/8.1 and will install the correct edition of Windows 10. Just open Internet Explorer from the computer you want to upgrade, and go to *www.microsoft.com*. You will be prompted to upgrade to Windows 10, which includes downloading and running the upgrade program. Once started, the upgrade program downloads and then installs the appropriate upgrade version of Windows 10. You can also upgrade by performing a custom installation from the Windows 10 installation DVD. Simply insert the Windows 10 installation media in the DVD drive, navigate to the DVD drive, and double-click Setup. Once the installation is started, there is very little for the user to do except accept the license agreement and let Setup to do the rest. If you do use the installation DVD, you should know which versions of Windows 7 and Windows 8/8.1 can be upgraded to Windows 10, as shown in Table 5-4.

**Table 5-4 Windows 10 upgrade paths**

| Current OS | Edition | Windows 10 edition |
|---|---|---|
| Windows 7 | Starter | Home |
| | Home Basic | Home |
| | Home Premium | Home |
| | Professional | Pro |
| | Ultimate | Pro |
| Windows 8/8.1 | | Home |
| | Pro | Pro |
| | Pro Student | Pro |

If you are running Windows 7 or Windows 8.1, Windows Update will automatically install the Get Windows 10 app, which you can run to verify that your system is compatible with Windows 10.

If you are running a 32-bit version of Windows 7/8/8.1, you must upgrade to the 32-bit version of Windows 10. If you are running a 64-bit version of Windows 7/8/8.1, you must upgrade to the 64-bit version of Windows 10. In addition, upgrading to Windows 10 Enterprise requires a Windows 7/8/8.1 Enterprise edition.

## Installing and Upgrading Windows Server 2008/R2

As with Windows 7, mainstream support for Windows Server 2008 and Windows Server 2008 R2 ended in January 2015 and extended support is scheduled to end in January 2020.

Windows Server 2008/R2 was widely adopted by IT departments. This section will lump together Windows Server 2008 and Windows Server 2008 R2 using the /R2 nomenclature to refer to both versions, while pointing out differences between the two releases as necessary. Most of the new features of Windows Server 2008/R2 were discussed in Chapter 2, but because Windows Server 2008 came five years after Windows Server 2003, there were many significant changes, most of which were carried over to Windows Server 2012. Some of the new features are:

- Centralized server management through the Server Manager tool
- Improved security
- Enhanced Web hosting services
- Hyper-V to create a virtual server environment
- Windows Server Core for running a server strictly through a command-line interface with a smaller network footprint
- Windows PowerShell, which provides a command-line and shell-based environment for creating time-saving computer management scripts

The following list shows some of the enhancements made with Windows Server 2008 R2.

- Active Directory enhancements, such as the Active Directory Administrative Center tool for centralizing tasks related to Active Directory and the Active Directory Recycle Bin that allows administrators to easily restore deleted objects
- File classification and file management tasks to improve file and folder organization
- Hyper-V (virtualization) enhancements, including better processor and networking support, and **live migration**, which allows administrators to move a virtual machine from one server to another with little to no downtime
- Windows AppLocker to better manage how clients access applications and server scripts
- New PowerShell commands to provide better script-based management of Windows servers

The main editions of Windows Server 2008/R2 are:

- *Standard edition*—Designed for basic everyday server needs for small to large businesses, such as file and printer sharing, basic network services including **Domain Name Service (DNS)**, and general management of network access. (DNS is an application protocol that resolves domain and computer names to IP addresses or IP addresses to domain and computer names.)
- *Enterprise edition*—Meets the needs of organizations that deploy networks with applications and Web services requiring high-end servers and a high level of productivity. This edition helps facilitate scaling server services upward as an organization grows, and it provides full clustering services for joining multiple servers in a fail-safe environment.
- *Datacenter edition*—Targeted for organizations that have mission-critical applications that use large databases of information.
- *Web Server edition*—Intended for hosting and deploying Web services and Web applications. This edition is optimized for Microsoft Internet Information Services for Web servers.

- *Itanium edition*—Designed for servers that use the Intel Itanium 64-bit processor but can still run both 32- and 64-bit applications. This OS enables resource-intense applications, such as the accounting system for a large corporation.
- *Windows Server 2008 R2 Foundation edition*—A less full-featured edition intended for small businesses as a file and print server, terminal server, or domain controller (to manage a Windows Server domain). This edition was new to R2.

Microsoft also offers Windows High-Performance Computing (HPC) Server 2008, which is a specialized edition used to cluster high-performance computers to simulate supercomputing capabilities, with support for thousands of CPU cores.

The Standard, Enterprise, and Datacenter editions of the original release of Windows Server 2008 come in 32-bit and 64-bit versions. Starting with Windows Server 2008 R2, only a 64-bit version is available. Also, you can purchase these editions with Microsoft Hyper-V to create a virtual server. A **virtual server** is a computer that can be configured to run multiple virtual machines. A **virtual machine** is a discrete OS running inside virtual server software, such as Hyper-V, on one computer. Multiple virtual machines can run on one virtual server. For example, one virtual server might house three virtual machines, each running its own copy of Windows Server 2008/R2, and two virtual machines, each running a Linux server distribution. In this example, one computer is performing as five servers. Using a virtual server consolidates server management and space and reduces expenses for electricity, resulting in financial savings and increased server manager productivity. As mentioned, virtualization is discussed in more detail in Chapter 8.

**Hardware Requirements** The hardware requirements for Windows Server 2008/R2 are pretty standard for all the primary editions, with the exception of the Itanium edition because it requires a specific CPU. Table 5-5 lists the hardware requirements. Also, be aware that the requirement for the 32-bit version of Windows only applies to the original release, not R2.

**Table 5-5 Windows Server 2008/R2 minimum and recommended system requirements (all editions unless noted)**

| Component | Requirement |
|---|---|
| Processor | Minimum: 1 GHz for x86 CPU or 1.4 GHz for x64 CPU<br>Recommended: 2 GHz or faster<br>(Itanium CPU required for Itanium edition) |
| Memory | Minimum: 512 MB RAM<br>Recommended: 2 GB RAM or more |
| Available disk space | Minimum: 10 GB<br>Recommended: 40 GB or more |
| Additional drives | DVD-ROM |
| Display and peripherals | Super VGA or higher<br>Keyboard and mouse |

In Table 5-5, x86 means 32-bit and x64 means 64-bit.

**Installing Windows Server 2008/R2** There are several ways to install Windows Server 2008. These methods include:

- Traditional DVD clean installation
- Unattended installation that uses specialized files for automating the installation of one or more servers without server administrator intervention
- Installation into a virtual machine, such as in Hyper-V
- Windows Deployment Services, which is a Windows Server 2008 application feature that enables multiple OSs to be installed from a master server over a network

The details of each installation method vary and are too complex to cover in this book. However, the installation steps used for a traditional DVD clean installation are the main steps used for any installation, and are almost identical to a Windows 7 installation.

**Upgrading to Windows Server 2008/R2** Microsoft recommends that you perform a clean installation of Windows Server 2008/R2 rather than perform an upgrade. A server installation affects many more people than a workstation installation. Also, a server is likely to have more critical applications, databases, and other mission-critical information vital to an organization. In an upgrade, there is a greater possibility that compatibility problems or unexpected problems may result with applications and data. It is generally safer to fully back up data, perform a clean installation, reinstall applications, restore data, and spend several weeks testing the new system before releasing it live to users. Because mainstream support for Windows Server 2008/R2 has ended, this book will forego the details of upgrading to Windows Server 2008/R2, as most upgrades should probably be focused on Windows Server 2012 or newer versions.

When testing a new server installation, plan to involve users in the testing so they can help to find problems with the applications and data that are important to them.

Performing an upgrade to Windows Server 2008 is similar to performing a clean installation, but existing applications and data are retained.

## Installing and Upgrading Windows Server 2012/R2

Windows Server 2012 was released to manufacturing in August 2012 with Windows 8, and Windows Server 2012 R2 was released in August 2013 with Windows 8.1. Most of the new features and the various editions were discussed in Chapter 2, but some of the other notable changes from Windows Server 2008/R2 included dropping support for the Itanium processor, dropping Enterprise edition, and the adoption of the Metro-style user interface from Windows

8/8.1. As with Windows 7 and Windows Server 2008/R2, there is very little for the user to do during installation. In fact, all the user really needs to do is select the language and locale settings, enter the activation code, accept the license agreement, and assign a password for the Administrator user. Most of the server configuration comes after the installation. Tasks such as assigning a name to the computer, setting the time zone, configuring the IP address, configuring updates, and installing server roles are all very important, and define how the server will operate in the network. Windows Server 2012/R2 has a convenient configuration panel called Local Server Properties that gives you access to most of these tasks, as shown in Figure 5-5.

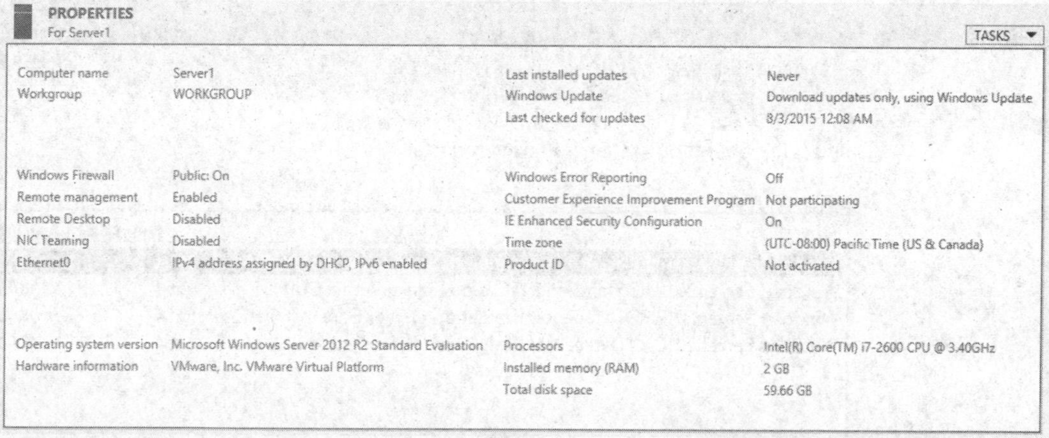


**Figure 5-5** Windows Server 2012 R2 Local Server Properties

**Hardware Requirements** The minimum and recommended hardware requirements for Windows Server 2012/R2 are shown in Table 5-6. The requirements apply to all editions unless noted. (The editions of Windows Server 2012/R2 were discussed in Chapter 2.)

**Table 5-6 Windows Server 2012/R2 minimum and recommended system requirements (all editions unless noted)**

| Component | Requirement |
|---|---|
| Processor | Minimum: 1.4 GHz 64-bit CPU<br>Recommended: 3.1 GHz or faster 64-bit multicore |
| Memory | Minimum: 512 MB RAM (2 GB for Essentials)<br>Recommended: 2 GB RAM or more (8 GB for Essentials) |
| Available disk space | Minimum: 32 GB (90 GB for Essentials)<br>Recommended: 60 GB or more for the system partition |
| Additional drives | DVD drive |
| Network interface card | Gigabit (10/100/1000 BaseT) Ethernet Adapter |
| Display and peripherals | Super VGA or higher<br>Keyboard and mouse<br>Internet access |

The minimum requirements for Essentials are greater than for the other editions because Essentials installs several network services automatically.

**Installing Windows Server 2012/R2** The Windows Server 2012/R2 installation routine is similar to that of Windows Server 2008/R2. You have the same option of installing the OS with a GUI or installing the Server Core version. The only substantial difference is that Microsoft now recommends installing Server Core, so it is the default choice (see Figure 5-6).

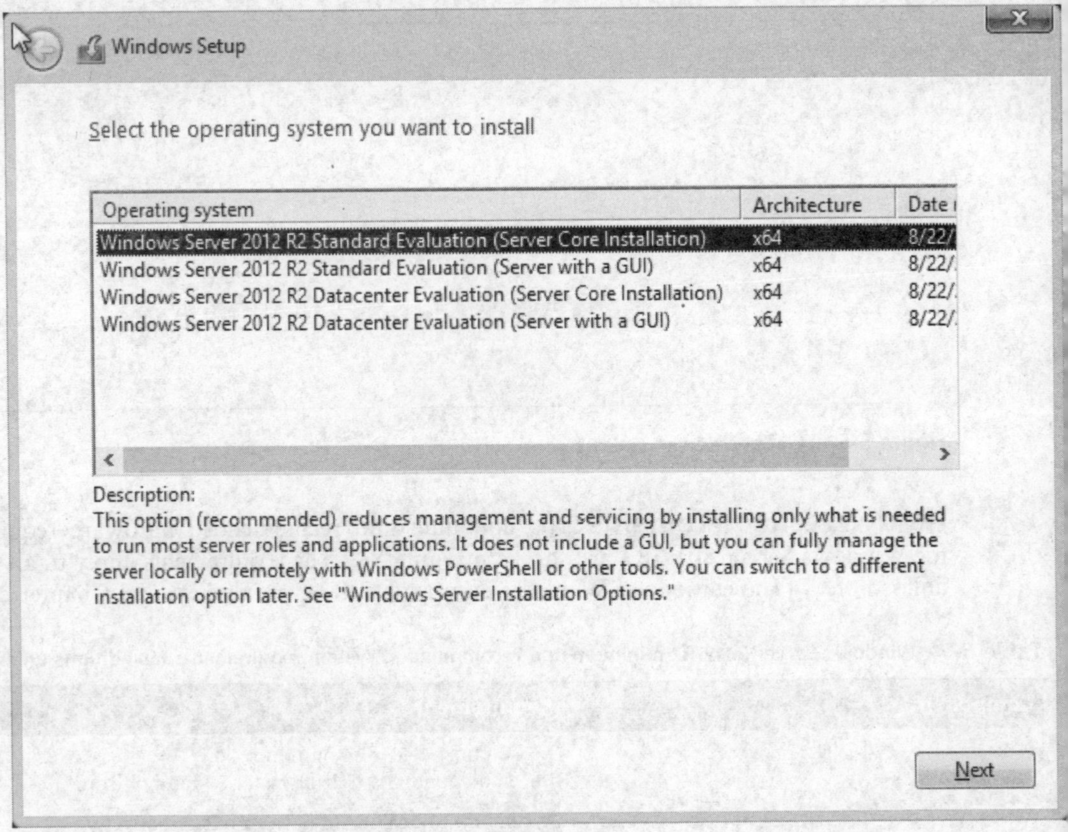


**Figure 5-6** Selecting Server Core or Server with a GUI

**Upgrading Windows Server 2012/R2** When you upgrade to Windows Server 2012/R2, you can use one of two main methods: an in-place upgrade or server role migration. With an in-place upgrade, you boot to the existing OS and run setup.exe from the Windows Server 2012/R2 installation medium. With **server role migration,** you perform a clean installation of Windows Server 2012/R2 and migrate the server roles the old OS version performed. Here's an overview of in-place upgrade considerations, followed by available upgrade paths in Table 5-7:

- The only previous Windows versions supported for upgrade are Windows Server 2008 and Windows Server 2008/R2.
- If you're running Server Core, you can upgrade only to Windows Server 2012/R2 Server Core, but you can install the GUI afterward.
- All Windows Server 2012/R2 versions are 64-bit, and cross-platform upgrades aren't supported, so you can only upgrade the Windows Server 2008 64-bit version to Windows Server 2012/R2. A Windows Server 2008 32-bit version requires a clean installation.
- You can't upgrade to a different language.

**Table 5-7 Windows Server 2012/R2 upgrade paths**

| Current edition | Server 2012/R2 upgrade path |
|---|---|
| Windows Server 2012 Datacenter | Windows Server 2012 R2 Datacenter |
| Windows Server 2012 Standard | Windows Server 2012 R2 Standard or Datacenter |
| Windows Server 2008 Standard or Enterprise | Windows Server 2012/R2 Standard or Datacenter |
| Windows Server 2008 Datacenter | Windows Server 2012/R2 Datacenter |
| Windows Server 2008 R2 Standard or Enterprise | Windows Server 2012/R2 Standard or Datacenter |
| Windows Server 2008 R2 Datacenter | Windows Server 2012/R2 Datacenter |
| Windows Web Server 2008 or Windows Web Server 2008 R2 | Windows Server 2012/R2 Standard |

If you're considering an in-place upgrade, Microsoft recommends removing any third-party software the manufacturer doesn't specifically support for a Windows Server 2012/R2 upgrade before you begin. In addition, make sure your system meets the minimum CPU, RAM, and disk requirements for Windows Server 2012/R2.

An upgrade is similar to a clean installation with a few exceptions. First, you must boot the existing OS and log on. Then you can start the setup.exe program from the installation medium. Next, you're asked whether Windows should go online to get the latest updates for installation. This option is recommended. You aren't prompted for the language, time, currency format, or keyboard layout; they must match the settings for the Windows Server 2012/R2 edition being installed. In addition, you aren't prompted during an upgrade for the location to install Windows. It's installed on the same disk partition as the OS you booted to.

Before an upgrade begins, Windows runs a compatibility check and produces a compatibility report. Any application, hardware, or driver issues discovered during the check are noted; you can't continue the installation until you address issues known to prevent a successful upgrade.

**Migrating from an Earlier Version** As you can see, in-place upgrades are somewhat limiting, and you can run into software incompatibility problems. In addition, upgrading isn't always possible if the specified upgrade path isn't available. For these reasons, Microsoft recommends a clean installation followed by server role migration, when possible.

Windows Server 2012/R2 has a number of tools to help with this process, which avoids most of the upgrade path restrictions. For example, migration allows you to do the following:

- Migrate from a 32-bit Windows server installation to Windows Server 2012/R2.
- Migrate from Windows Server 2003 SP2 and later.
- Migrate from a Windows Server 2008 R2 Server Core installation to a GUI installation and vice versa.

Migrating Windows server roles and features isn't an all-or-nothing proposition. You can migrate roles and features from a server running an earlier version to a Windows Server 2012/R2 server, move a role or feature from one Windows Server 2012/R2 server to another, or move a role or feature from a virtual machine to a physical machine or vice versa. However, language migration isn't supported; both server versions must be running the same language package.

## Installing and Upgrading Linux

In general, installing and upgrading Linux isn't so much different from installing and upgrading Windows. However, there are many distributions of Linux, and details will differ depending on the distribution. This section discusses installing one Linux distribution version—Fedora 23—on the AMD/Intel PC platform. There are numerous other distributions of Linux designed for different hardware platforms. If you understand how Linux installs on the AMD/Intel platform, you should have no problem installing other distributions of Linux.

**Hardware Requirements** As with any OS, the optimal hardware requirements of Linux depend on how the computer will be used. This section only discusses the recommended minimum requirements for Fedora 23, which are shown in Table 5-8.

**Table 5-8 Fedora 23 hardware requirements**

| Hardware | Recommended minimum |
|---|---|
| CPU | 1 GHz or faster processor |
| RAM | 1 GB or more |
| Storage (server) | 10 GB free space |
| Video card | Minimum 800×600 resolution for a GUI installation |
| Removable storage | DVD drive or USB connection for installation or capability to run the OS from external media |

**Installing Linux** Linux is available in free open source and commercial distributions. There is not room in this chapter to cover the installations of all distributions. Fedora 23, the free open source distribution on which the popular commercial Red Hat Enterprise Linux is based, provides a good starting point from which to learn about a Linux installation.

Fedora 23 Live Media can be booted and run from a DVD or Fedora 23 can be loaded as a permanent OS that boots from a computer's hard drive.

In one sense, the Fedora 23 installation from the Live Media DVD is not fully representative because you first start Fedora 23 from the DVD (and load it into memory), boot into the OS's GNOME desktop, and click an icon on the desktop to install Fedora 23 on the hard drive. In many other Linux distributions, including the non-Live Media Fedora 23 distribution, you boot from the DVD and can install Linux without first starting the OS. However, once you get started with the installation using either method, the installation steps are very similar to those of any Linux distribution.

Linux comes with the complete source code for the kernel, all the drivers, and most of the utilities. In particular, it comes with many program development tools, such as compilers for creating executable files that users can run on the computer. Linux distributions also often come with many appealing applications, such as OpenOffice.org, which is a free office suite distribution that is compatible with Microsoft Office.

When you run the live media version of Fedora 23 from the DVD, there are typically fewer applications available than when you install Linux onto the hard drive and simultaneously load a full range of open source applications, such as program language compilers.

Although most Linux distributions can be used as desktop or server OSs, some distributions have a specific version for the desktop and another version for a server. Server versions usually work the same way as desktop versions, but come with software intended for server environments, such as DNS and DHCP server software, Web server software, e-mail server software, account management software, and so on.

**Upgrading Linux** In Linux, the upgrade process works like the installation process. You start the installation in the normal way, and then choose to perform an upgrade. The installer asks for some basic system information, such as which language and keyboard to use. Also, it checks to determine what hard disks to use for the installation. It then gets most of the system information previously stored on the hard disk by the old OS. The appropriate system files are replaced, and the installer asks if you want to customize the package installation. If you select Yes, you can choose specific elements to install or update for each previously installed package. Note that many libraries and programs will be replaced, and if you add software to the computer, you should check carefully to ensure that everything still works as expected after installation.

An important caveat in Linux upgrades is that many configuration files are overwritten during the upgrade. The e-mail system, printing system, window system, and network services may be reconfigured. You should make sure you have backups of these files before you begin an upgrade, and double-check configuration files on these services to make sure they did not change.

## Installing and Upgrading Mac OS X

The installation of Mac OS X uses a graphical interface and a Setup Assistant that functions like the Windows setup wizards. Early versions of Mac OS X up through Mac OS X Leopard can be installed on a computer with a PowerPC processor chip. Mac OS X Leopard can also be installed on a computer that has an Intel processor. Mac OS X Snow Leopard and later versions can only be installed on an Intel-based computer.

Besides the desktop editions of Mac OS X such as Mac OS X El Capitan, there are also server editions of Mac OS X Server. Mac OS X Server was released as a separate product with every desktop version of Mac OS X through Snow Leopard. Starting with Mac OS X Lion, Apple no longer produces a separate server version; rather, users can install an OS X Server add-on package through the Mac App Store for about $20 U.S. The server add-on package includes a number of server applications:

- *File sharing*—Allows more powerful file sharing between Macs, PCs, iPads, and iPhones
- *Caching server*—Speeds downloads and uploads between devices on the network and with cloud-based applications such as App Store, iTunes Store, and iBooks Store
- *Profile manager*—Simplifies the deployment and configuration of Apple devices by centralizing the management of user accounts, mail, calendar, contacts, and so forth
- *Time machine*—Makes any Mac act as a Time Machine backup location for all Macs on the network
- *Xcode server*—Provides team software development tools
- *Wiki server*—Provides a Web server with the capability for users to collaborate on Web pages, including blogs, uploads, and collaboration histories
- *Calendar, contacts, and mail servers*—Allows you to share calendars and contacts, and to manage e-mail with Mac e-mail clients on the Mac, iPad, iPhone, and PCs
- *Xsan 4*—Provides a scalable storage solution for centralized data

**Hardware Requirements for Mac OS X Server Add-On** The Mac OS X Server add-on requirements are shown in Table 5-9. The current version, as of this writing, requires the Mac to run Mac OS X El Capitan.

**Table 5-9** Mac OS X Server hardware requirements and recommendations

| Requirement |
|---|
| Mac computer running Mac OS X El Capitan |
| 2 GB RAM |
| 10 GB available disk space |
| Some features require a valid Apple ID |
| Some features require an Internet connection |

**Installing Mac OS X** Installations of recent versions of Mac OS X are geared toward upgrades because it is assumed that you are already running some version of Mac OS X. You upgrade your current version of Mac OS X by downloading an installer from the App Store and then running the installer app, which installs the most current version of the OS on your system. Upgrading to Mac OS X El Capitan using this method is a safe bet for most Mac models from 2008 onward and for Macs running Snow Leopard or newer versions. In addition, you should make sure your current Mac OS X and the installed apps are up to date before performing the upgrade.

While using the downloadable installer is the easiest way to install the newest Mac OS X on your Mac, you may want to perform a DVD installation—for example, if you must replace your disk. You can create a bootable DVD and perform a clean installation of the OS if you want. To create a bootable DVD, follow these general steps:

- Download the installer for the current version from the Mac App Store.
- Open a terminal window.
- Run the *createinstallmedia* command, which is located in the installer program. The *createinstallmedia* command requires a series of complex options that will be different depending on the Mac you use, so it is not detailed here. To learn more about creating a bootable DVD, do an Internet search for "make a bootable Mac OS X installer disk."
- Boot from the DVD and start the installation, as described next.

A number of third-party DVD creators for Mac OS X will create a bootable DVD you can use to install Mac OS X.

***Performing a Clean Installation from a DVD*** A Macintosh will boot from the DVD drive only if instructed to do so. Simply hold down the option key when you turn on the computer and then select the option to boot from the Mac OS X Installation DVD.

Here are the general steps for installing Mac OS X from scratch:

1. Insert the Mac OS X Installation DVD.
2. Turn on the Macintosh and hold down the option key as it boots.
3. In the OS X Startup Manager, choose the installer drive, and then click the arrow to continue.
4. Click Agree to accept the license agreement.
5. In the Install Mac OS X window, click the drive on which to install the OS.

Before you click Install in the window, notice the Customize button that you can click to customize components that will be installed. Also, you can choose to erase and reformat the drive before you click Install. You might do this, for example, if you suspect the drive has some bad spots or you want to be certain to overwrite any existing data on the drive and start fresh. To do so, click Utilities in the Mac OS X Installer menu bar and then click Disk Utility. Select the drive in the left pane and use the Disk Utility to erase and then format the drive.

6. Click Install. You will be prompted for the administrator password.
7. Wait for the installation process to finish; the computer will restart at least once.
8. In the Welcome window, select the country or region and click Continue.

9. Select the keyboard layout, such as U.S., in the Select Your Keyboard window. Click Continue.
10. In the Do You Already Own a Mac window, select the appropriate option to transfer information to the new Mac, and then click Continue. The options include:
    - From another Mac
    - From another volume on this Mac
    - From a Time Machine backup
    - Do not transfer my information now

    At this point you may need to take appropriate steps for the option you selected. For example, if you have a Time Machine backup on a USB removable hard drive, you need to connect the drive. Time Machine is the software used to back up a Mac.
11. If you see the Select a Wireless Service window, which is likely if you have a modern Mac, select your wireless service from the list. Also, enter the wireless service password if needed, such as that for WPA2 (Wi-Fi Protected Access 2) wireless security. Click Continue.
12. In the Sign in with Your Apple ID window, enter your ID, if applicable, for access to the iTunes store, iCloud, and the Apple Store. If you don't have an Apple ID for these services, leave this information blank. Click Continue.
13. Provide your personal information, including your first and last name, address, and e-mail address, in the Registration Information window. Click Continue.
14. In the A Few More Questions window, enter your answers in the appropriate boxes, including where you will primarily use the computer and what you do for a living. Click Continue.
15. In the Create Your Account window, enter your account name, a short name, the account password, a confirmation of the password, and a password hint. Click Continue.
16. In the Select a Picture For This Account window, select the source for the picture, such as the picture library. Click Continue.
17. In the Thank You window, you see a summary of what the Mac is set up to do, such as organizing your work and e-mail. Click Go to access the Mac.

TIP

Mac OS X comes with Migration Assistant to help you transfer user accounts, files, applications, and computer settings from another Macintosh computer. To run Migration Assistant, make sure Finder is running, click Go in the menu bar, click Utilities, and double-click Migration Assistant.

## Regular Updates for OSs

Every OS vendor has a mechanism to provide bug fixes, security patches for threats such as worms and viruses, and interim upgrades between major releases of their OS. You've already been introduced to the Windows Update feature, which should be used following a Windows installation or upgrade. This section briefly reviews the update features of the OSs covered in this book.

**Windows Updates** Beginning with the Windows 98 release, Microsoft includes Windows Update, a Web-based function that allows you to download and install fixes, updates, and enhancements to your Windows OS.

An easy way to start Windows Update in Windows Vista/7, Windows Server 2008, or Windows Server 2008/R2 is to connect to the Internet, click Start, type Windows Update in the Start Search or "Search programs and files" box, and then click Windows Update. When you click Check (or Scan) for updates, Windows Update will automatically scan your computer to determine your OS and check on the installed updates. It then provides you with a list of updates that you can download and install on your computer.

You should download and install any Critical Updates and Service Packs (SPs) listed for your system. These updates will fix known bugs, security issues, and other problems that should be addressed as soon as possible.

**Linux Updates** Fedora and other Linux systems come with an update module for obtaining the latest updates. In Fedora 23 with the GNOME desktop, you can manually obtain and install updates by clicking Activities, Show Applications, and then Software. Click the Updates tab to list any new updates. You have the option to install the updates or not. To configure automatic updates, open a shell prompt, type *dnf install dnf-automatic*, and press Enter. Next, you must edit the /etc/dnf/automatic.conf file to specify the schedule. Finally, enable and run the update timers using systemctl:

*systemctl enable dnf-automatic.timer && systemctl start dnf-automatic.timer*

**Mac Updates** Mac OS X El Capitan provides updates through the App Store. Check to see if updates are available by clicking the Apple icon in the menu bar and looking for the App Store. If updates are available, you will be informed how many there are (see Figure 5-7). Click the button next to App Store to have Mac OS X download and install the updates. OS X will also display a notification when updates are available; you can choose to install them immediately or wait until later.

**Figure 5-7** Checking for updates in Mac OS X

*Source: Mac OS X El Capitan*

# Chapter Summary

- There are two basic types of installations: a clean installation on a computer with no OS installed or one that completely overwrites an existing installation on a computer, and an upgrade installation on a computer that already has an OS installed and where existing settings, applications, data, and other user files are often retained. The process of installing OSs varies from one OS to another, but all installations can be divided into three general stages: preparation, the installation itself, and any required or optional steps following installation.
- Before installing an OS or upgrading to a new OS, make sure that it is necessary. Also, when you decide to migrate or upgrade, check that your hardware meets the requirements for the new OS, and make sure you have the correct, most up-to-date drivers for the various devices on your system. Gather and document information about your system.
- Before you upgrade, make sure that you have a working backup of the current OS and data. Check your backup after it is made to make sure you can perform a restore from it if the installation or upgrade is unsuccessful, or if you need to retrieve data that was overwritten by the installation.
- Installations and upgrades to Windows, Linux, and Mac OS X are overviewed in the chapter text. Some of these installations are described step by step in the Hands-On Projects.
- After installation, and at regular intervals thereafter, it is a good idea to check for and download OS updates. All of the Windows versions described in this chapter provide the Windows Update tool. Linux provides an update module, and Mac OS X Leopard and Snow Leopard offer the Software Update tool.

# Key Terms

**alpha software** An early development version of software in which there are likely to be bugs, and not all of the anticipated functionality is present. Alpha software is usually tested only by a select few users to identify major problems and the need for new or different features before the software is tested by a broader audience in the beta stage.

**backup** A process of copying files from a computer system to another medium, such as a tape, another hard drive, a removable drive, or a DVD/CD-ROM.

**beta software** During software development, software that has successfully passed the alpha test stage. Beta testing may involve dozens, hundreds, or even thousands of people, and may be conducted in multiple stages: beta 1, beta 2, beta 3, and so on.

**clean installation** An OS installation on a computer that either has no existing OS or an OS that is overwritten by the installation.

**Domain Name Service (DNS)** An application protocol that resolves domain and computer names to IP addresses, or that resolves IP addresses to domain and computer names.

**in-place upgrade** An OS upgrade that overwrites your current OS and maintains your applications, settings, and data.

**live migration** A feature of virtualization that allows a virtual machine to be moved from one server to another with little or no downtime.

**migration** Moving from one OS to another OS, which may or may not involve implementing a new computer as well.

**netbook computers** Small portable or laptop computers that have limited computing capabilities and are designed to be lightweight and portable. Netbook computers are generally used for Web access, e-mail, and basic document creation.

**production computer** Any computer used to perform real work; it should be protected from problems that might cause an interruption in workflow or loss of data.

**release candidate (RC)** The final stage of software testing by vendors before cutting an official release that is sold commercially. A release candidate is usually tested by a very large audience of customers. Some vendors may issue more than one release candidate if problems are discovered in the first RC.

**release to manufacturing (RTM)** A version of a Microsoft OS that is officially released to be sold and has gone through the alpha, beta, and release candidate phases prior to official release.

**server role migration** An alternative to a Windows server OS upgrade in which you perform a clean installation of Windows Server 2012/R2 and migrate the server roles the old OS version performed.

**upgrade installation** An OS installation on a computer that already has an earlier version of the OS; the upgrade replaces the earlier version with a new version, often with the option to retain some or all of the original settings, user accounts, applications, data files, and other existing user files.

**virtual machine** A discrete OS running inside virtual server or virtual desktop software, such as Hyper-V, on one computer. Multiple virtual machines can run on one virtual server. See *virtual server*.

**virtual server** A server computer that can be configured to run multiple virtual machines with multiple server or desktop OSs. See *virtual machine*.

## Review Questions

1. Your manager is very interested in having a new version of an OS, and wants you to install a beta version to use on a server so that your company can be one of the first to take advantage of the new features. What is your advice?
   a. Beta versions are usually very stable and this is a good decision to help stay ahead of the competition.
   b. Beta versions are often sold at a lower cost, which would offer savings to the company.
   c. OS vendors often provide extensive onsite help to users of beta systems in a production environment.
   d. A safer path is to wait for an official release and to avoid using a beta system in a production environment.

2. Under which conditions should you consider a clean installation? (Choose all that apply.)
   a. The installation is performed on a computer that has no OS installed.
   b. You want to replace the current OS but maintain all your settings.
   c. You don't want to have to reinstall applications.
   d. You want to be able to boot to your old OS and the new OS.
3. Which of the following should you do prior to creating a backup in preparation for an OS upgrade? (Choose all that apply.)
   a. Be sure you have the software needed to perform a restore on old and new OSs.
   b. Unmount the disk being backed up.
   c. Close active windows and programs.
   d. Mount all volumes in a volume mount point.
4. You are in a committee meeting in which the members are debating whether the Windows XP Professional computers in a laboratory can be directly upgraded to Windows 10 for free. What is your recommendation?
   a. Check Windows Help on each computer.
   b. Purchase all new computers because Windows 10 can rarely run on computers suited for Windows XP.
   c. Configure the XP computers for the Enterprise edition first.
   d. You will need to perform a clean installation of Windows 10.
5. Which of the following is true about Windows Server 2012?
   a. You can upgrade from Windows Server 2003/R2 SP2.
   b. You can upgrade from Windows Server 2008 x86.
   c. You can upgrade from Server Core to Server with a GUI.
   d. You can't upgrade to a different language.
6. You are running Windows Server 2008 x86 on a 32-bit CPU. You want to upgrade to Windows Server 2012/R2. What can you do?
   a. Run the Windows Server Upgrade program and insert the Windows Server 2012/R2 installation DVD.
   b. First, upgrade to Windows Server 2008/R2, and then upgrade to Windows Server 2012/R2.
   c. Install Windows Server 2012/R2 on a new computer and migrate server roles.
   d. Back up the computer and perform a clean installation of Windows Server 2012/R2, then restore the data and applications.

7. You need to perform a backup in Windows that includes the registry. Which type of backup should you perform?
   a. system state backup
   b. data drive backup
   c. scheduled backup
   d. incremental backup
8. When you install an OS on a computer with a hard drive that has been formatted and does not contain a previous OS, you perform a ________________ installation.
   a. clean
   b. update
   c. upgrade
   d. new
9. Which key should you press to boot a Macintosh computer from an installation DVD?
   a. Esc
   b. Option
   c. Ctrl
   d. Apple
10. Choosing the Customize button during a Mac OS X installation allows you to ________________.
    a. select which OS to install
    b. choose the installation location
    c. choose various OS components you want to install
    d. repartition the hard drive for a different file system
11. Which of the following are possible ways to install Windows Server 2008? (Choose all that apply.)
    a. from a set of floppy disks combined with a CD-ROM
    b. using an unattended installation
    c. into a virtual machine
    d. through Windows Deployment Services
12. You have a Windows Server 2008 server with a 2 GHz, 32-bit processor and 4 GB of memory. You plan to upgrade it to Windows Server 2012/R2. When you attempt the upgrade, the Setup program stops with a message that it cannot continue. Which of the following might be the problem?
    a. There is not enough memory for the upgrade.
    b. You must have a quad-core processor.
    c. You didn't run the setup routine from Windows Server 2008.
    d. Windows Server 2012/R2 requires a 64-bit processor.

13. Mac OS X El Capitan can run on which of the following processors?
    a. PowerPC G3
    b. PowerPC G5
    c. AMD M4
    d. Intel
14. Each OS upgrade is different, but which of the following are general steps you should conduct with every upgrade? (Choose all that apply.)
    a. Test the upgrade on a non-production computer.
    b. Don't upgrade as soon as the new OS is released; wait a few months.
    c. Back up all data and applications before starting the upgrade.
    d. Format the installation disk before starting the upgrade.
15. You have purchased a computer that is loaded with Windows 7 Home Premium. After using the computer for several months, you decide you want to upgrade to Windows 10. Which of the following Windows 10 editions can be upgraded from Windows 7 Home Premium?
    a. Enterprise
    b. Home
    c. Pro
    d. Starter
16. Which of the following is true about the Enterprise edition of Windows 10?
    a. It's only available if it's pre-installed by a computer vendor.
    b. You can upgrade to it from Windows Home Premium.
    c. You don't need to enter an activation key during installation.
    d. It's only available in a 64-bit version.

## Hands-On Projects

### Project 5-1: Change BIOS Settings to Boot to a DVD

Your hardware system BIOS controls many basic functions of your computer. This chapter discusses the need to be able to boot from a DVD. You can find out how your system BIOS handles DVD booting by displaying the BIOS Setup or Configuration screen on your computer.

1. Start your Windows or Linux computer. You must watch carefully for a message that tells you which key to press to enter the BIOS setup. You may also consult the system documentation or ask an instructor. The F1, F2, Esc, and Del keys are commonly used to access BIOS setup. Another way to enter BIOS setup is to hold down a key on the keyboard while booting. The BIOS sometimes generates a keyboard error message and gives you the option to go into setup.

2. Once you are in the BIOS setup, look for settings for boot order or boot sequence. For example, Figure 5-8 displays the PhoenixBIOS Setup Utility with the Boot tab selected. Some BIOS setup routines require you to use the keyboard rather than the mouse to navigate; the navigation keys are often shown on the bottom of the screen, as in Figure 5-8.

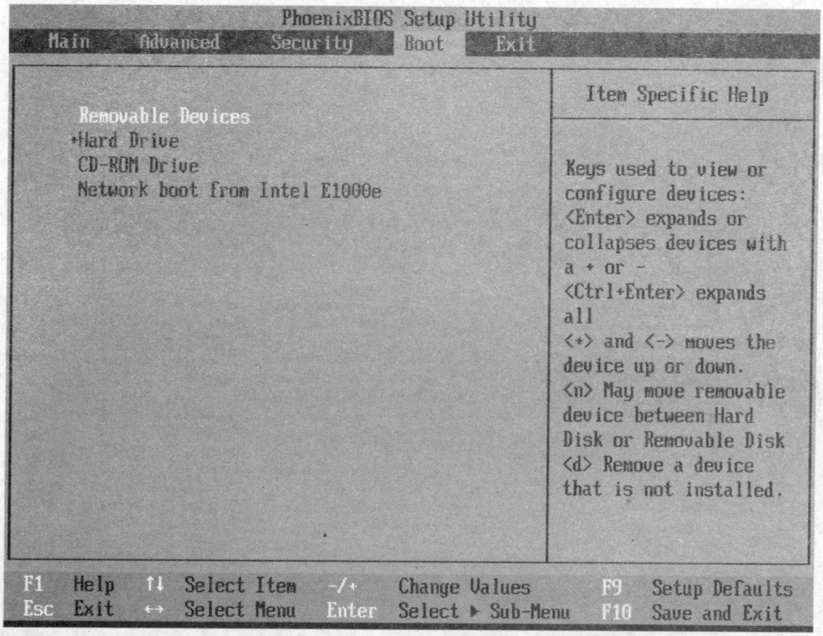


**Figure 5-8** BIOS setup program showing boot options

3. Use the appropriate keys to change the order of boot devices.
4. If available (and with your instructor's permission), choose a DVD or CD-ROM drive, and then save and exit the Setup or Configuration screen.
5. Insert a Windows or Linux OS installation disk and reboot the computer. You may see a message that says, "Press any key to boot to the DVD/CD." Your computer should boot to the installation disk. Do not install the OS now.
6. Restart the computer, change the boot order back to the hard drive, and remove the installation disk. Save the configuration and exit.

Enter
HANDS-ON PROJECTS

## Project 5-2: Document Installed Software in Windows

Before performing a clean installation or upgrading an OS, it is important to know what software is currently installed in the current OS. If you have to do a clean installation or the update doesn't correctly recognize the installed software, you need to have an accurate inventory of all your applications (not those that come with the OS, but those you install after the OS installation) so they can be reinstalled in the new OS, if necessary. This project shows you where to look for installed applications in Windows 10.

1. Start your Windows computer and log on if necessary.
2. Right-click **Start** and click **Control Panel.**
3. In Control Panel, click **Programs** and then click **Programs and Features**. You will see a list of installed programs, as shown in Figure 5-9.

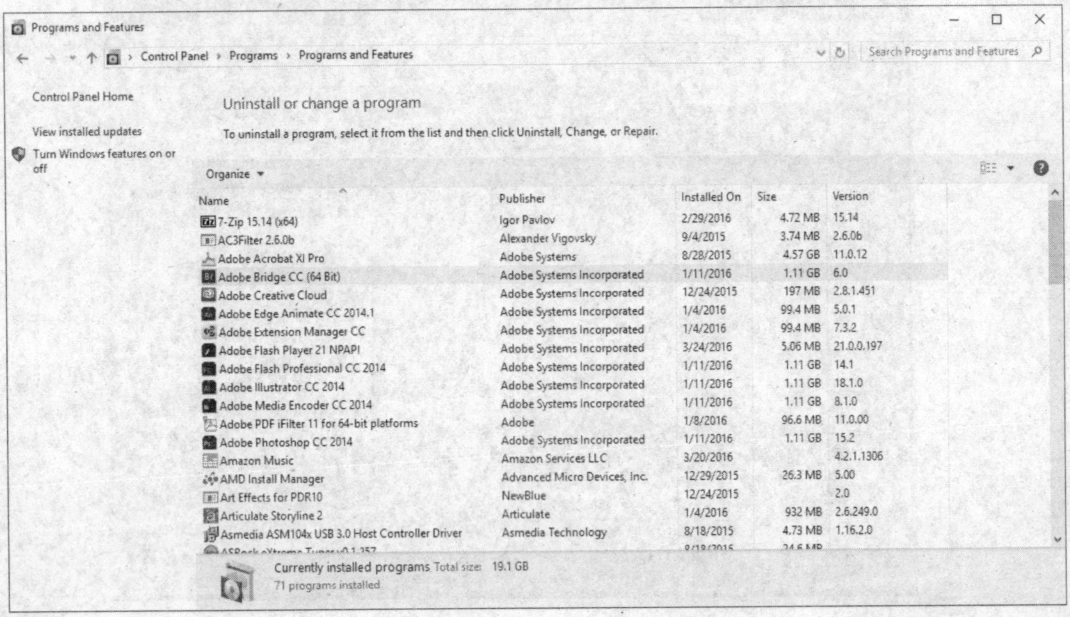


**Figure 5-9** A list of installed programs in Windows

4. Taking a screen shot is probably the easiest way to record the list. In Windows 10, you click in the search box next to Start and type **snip**. In the search results, click **Snipping Tool.**
5. In Snipping Tool, click **New**. Position the mouse in the upper-left corner of the Control Panel window and click and drag until the window is highlighted. When you release the mouse button, the Snipping Tool will open with your screen shot. If you have more programs than will fit on one screen, scroll down and create another screen shot. You can print or save the screen shots.
6. Verify that you have the necessary installation media or setup programs and license codes for all your installed applications before you begin an OS update. If you only have setup files for downloaded applications, be sure to save them on external media before you begin the installation.
7. Close all open windows.
8. Log off or shut down your Windows computer.

## Project 5-3: Document Installed Software in Mac OS X

This project helps you document the installed applications in Mac OS X.

1. Start your Mac OS X computer and log on if necessary. Click **Go** and click **Applications**.
2. The Applications folder displays all installed applications on your Mac, including those that came with the OS and those you installed manually. Scroll through the applications. Take a screen shot of the Applications folder by pressing **Shift+Command+4** and then dragging over the area you want to capture. If you are using a PC keyboard, you can use **Shift+Windows+4**. The screen shot is saved to your Mac desktop.
3. Close the Applications window.
4. If you only want to view the list of applications you installed from the App Store, click the **Apple** icon, and then click **App Store**. Click **Purchased** in the menu bar and sign in with your Apple ID, if necessary. You will see a list of purchased apps.
5. If you only installed apps from the App Store, you probably don't need to document your installed apps. When you install the upgrade, you can connect to the App Store and download any software you previously purchased. Close all open windows and then log off or shut down your Mac.

## Project 5-4: Document Installed Software in Linux

This project helps you document the installed applications in Linux Fedora 23 with GNOME.

1. Start your Linux computer and log on, if necessary. Click **Activities** and **Show Applications**.
2. You will see applications that came installed with Linux and those you installed after Linux was installed. To take a screen shot, press **Shift+PrtScn** on your keyboard. Click and drag the cursor over the area you want to capture. The screen shot is saved to the Pictures folder.
3. You can also use the ScreenShot utility by clicking the search box at the top of the screen and typing **screen**. In the search results, click **Screenshot**. You can take a screen shot of the whole screen, the current window, or a specific area (see Figure 5-10). When you finish, close the Take Screenshot window.

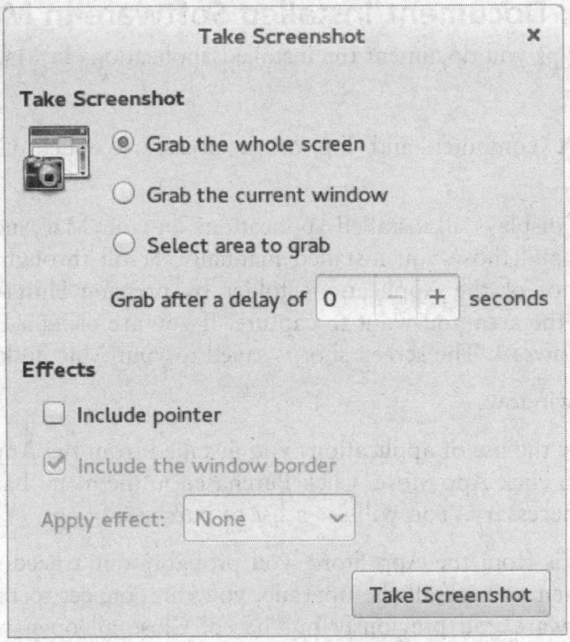


**Figure 5-10** The Linux Screenshot application

*Source: Fedora Linux*

4. To see a list of installed applications using the command line, open a terminal window, type **rpm –qa**, and press **Enter**. You will see a more complete list of applications than you were able to obtain simply by using the Applications menu in the GNOME desktop.

5. You can view each screen of output. Type **rpm –qa | more** and press **Enter**. Press **Space** to scroll through each page of output. Press **q** to quit before viewing all pages.

6. To redirect the output to a file, type **rpm –qa > softwarelist.txt** and press **Enter**. Type **cat softwarelist.txt** and press **Enter** to see the created file. Close the terminal window.

NOTE: The command to view installed software packages is different in various UNIX systems. For example, you enter *pkginfo* in Solaris, *swlist* in HP UNIX, *pkg_info -a* in FreeBSD, and *lslpp -L all* in IBM's AIX.

NOTE: It is highly recommended that you use virtualization software to perform the Hands-On Projects that walk you through the installation of various OSs. If you use virtualization software such as VMware Player, VirtualBox, or Hyper-V, you will not need physical installation media. You can connect the virtual DVD drive to the installation media ISO file, and your virtual machine will boot from the ISO file. If you are using virtualization, do not burn a DVD and insert it into the DVD drive, as instructed in the following projects; connect the virtual DVD drive to the ISO file instead.

## Project 5-5: Install Windows 10

In this project, you install Windows 10 using the DVD installation method. Before you start, you will need the Windows 10 installation DVD. You can get a 90-day evaluation of Windows 10 Enterprise Edition from the Technet Evaluation Center at *www.microsoft.com/en-us/evalcenter/evaluate-windows-10-enterprise*. You will be asked to sign in using your Microsoft account; you can create an account if you don't already have one. After you download the ISO file, burn it to a DVD.

1. Insert the Windows 10 installation DVD in the DVD drive of a computer that meets the minimum requirements for Windows 10.
2. Start your computer if you are sure it will boot to the DVD. (Refer to Hands-On Project 5-1 for details on booting via a DVD.)
3. After the Windows logo is displayed, Windows Setup begins. The screen prompts you to choose your language and location preferences (see Figure 5-1 earlier in this chapter). Click **Next**.
4. On the next screen, you have the option to repair your computer or install the OS. Click **Install now**.
5. If you are using an edition that requires an activation key, enter it on the next screen and click **Next**; otherwise, read the Windows 10 Licensing terms, click **I accept the license terms**, and click **Next**.
6. The next screen asks, "Which type of installation do you want?" (see Figure 5-2 earlier in this chapter). Click **Custom: Install Windows only (advanced)** to perform a clean installation.
7. If you already have an OS installed, your disks will be partitioned like they are in Figure 5-11; otherwise, your screen will look like Figure 5-3 (shown earlier). If you already have an OS installed and you want to keep it on your computer, you will need another partition or disk on which to install Windows 10. To delete the old OS, click each partition and click **Delete**. This project assumes that you have a blank disk on which to install Windows 10. (The name of the disk will include the words "Unallocated Space.").

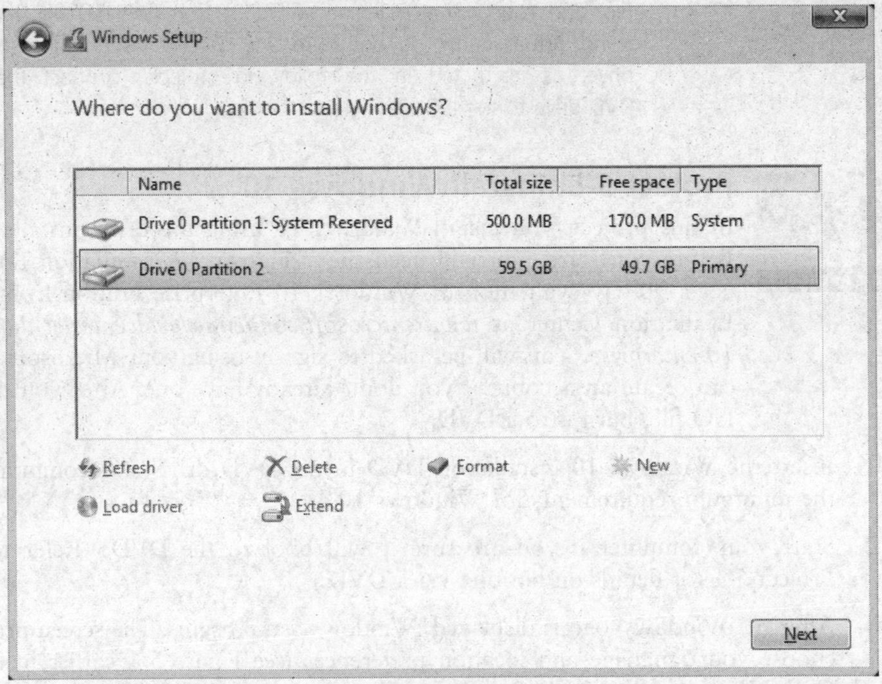


**Figure 5-11** A system with a Windows OS already installed

8. Click the disk on which to install Windows 10, and then click **Next**. The setup program copies files and installs Windows 10. The computer will restart at least once. When the computer restarts, be sure to remove the installation DVD, or the computer might boot to the DVD and start the installation process from the beginning.

9. After the computer restarts, you are prompted to use Express settings or Customize settings. Click **Use Express settings**. The system restarts.

10. If you are using the Enterprise evaluation edition or the Education edition, you are prompted to choose how you'll connect to the network (see Figure 5-12). Click **Join a domain** and then click **Next**.

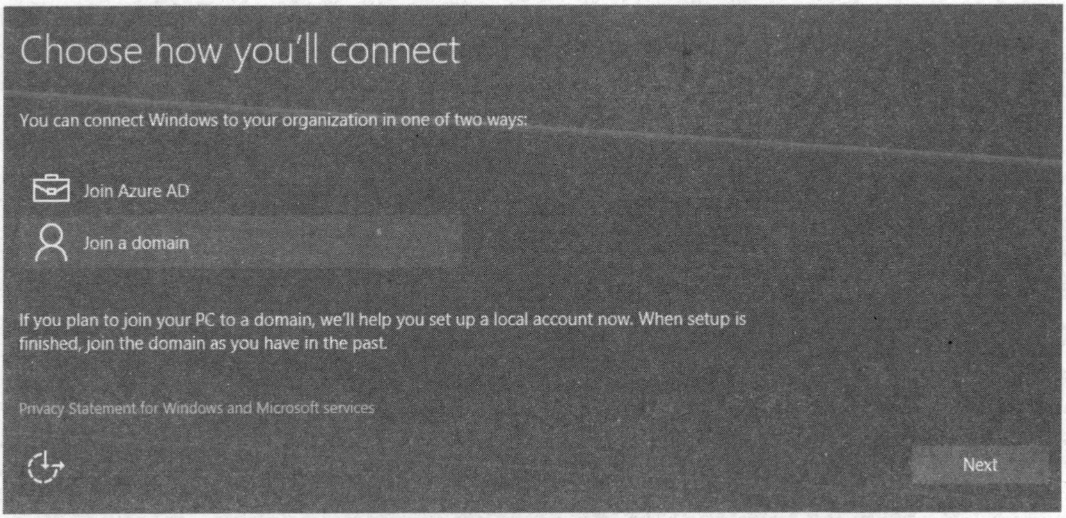


**Figure 5-12** Choose how you'll connect

11. On the "Create an account for this PC" screen (see Figure 5-13), type a user name, a password, and a password hint, and then click **Next.**

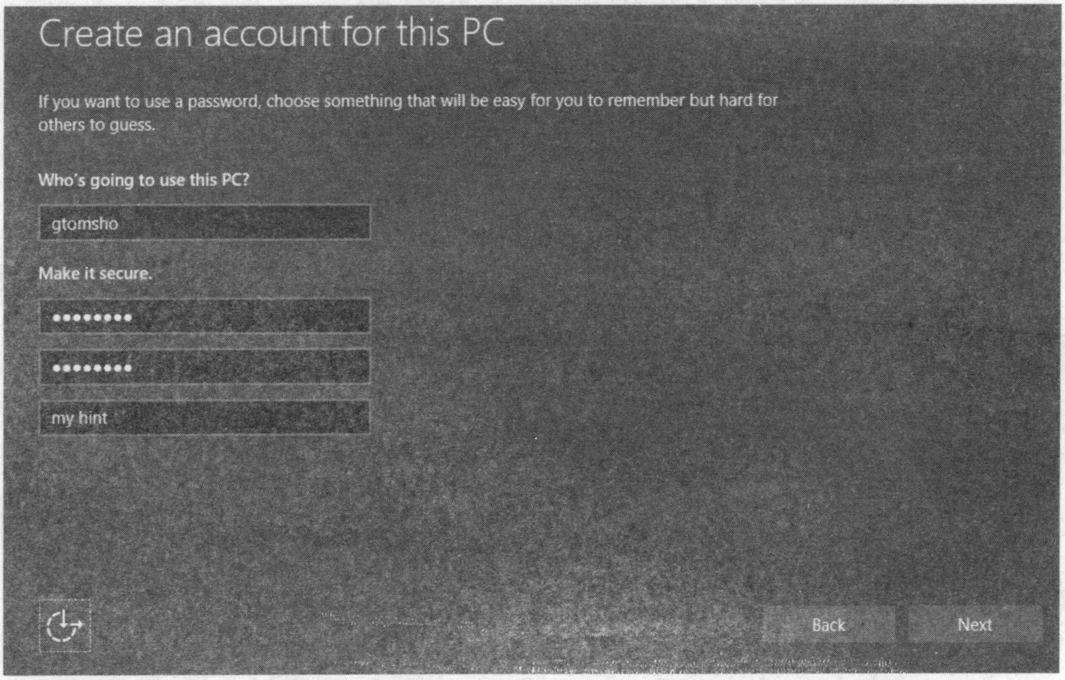


**Figure 5-13** Create an account for this PC

12. Windows 10 completes the setup process and you are logged in.

13. If you are connected to a network, you are asked if you want to allow your PC to be discoverable by other PCs on the network (see Figure 5-14). Click **Yes** unless you are on a public network.

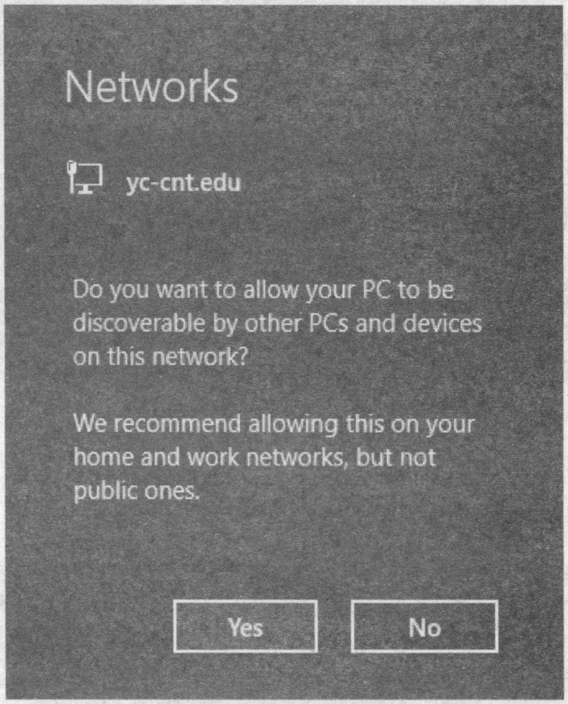


**Figure 5-14** Choosing network behavior

14. Windows will immediately check for updates and install them if you are connected to the Internet. To check on updates, click in the search box next to **Start**, type **update**, and then click **Check for updates** (see Figure 5-15).

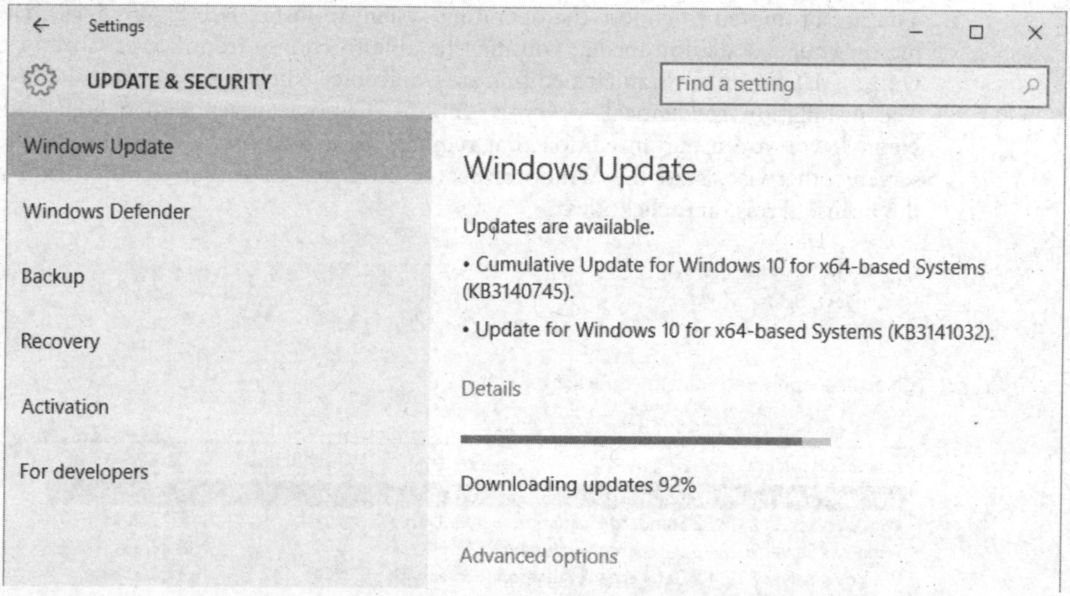


**Figure 5-15** Windows Update

15. Log off or shut down your computer.

## Project 5-6: Install Windows Server 2012 R2

In this project, you install Windows Server 2012 R2. You need the installation DVD for either the Windows Server 2012 R2 Standard or Datacenter edition. You can download a 180-day evaluation of Windows Server 2012 R2 from *www.microsoft.com/en-us/evalcenter/evaluate-windows-server-2012-r2*. You will be asked to sign in using your Microsoft account, which you can create if you don't already have one. After you download the ISO file, burn it to a DVD.

NOTE: The installation procedure for Windows Server 2012 R2 is nearly identical to that of Windows 10 until the system restarts. Only screens that are substantially different are shown in this project. This installation procedure assumes that no other OS is installed on the computer and that the disk is unpartitioned.

1. Insert the Windows Server 2012 R2 installation DVD in the DVD drive of a computer that meets the minimum requirements for Windows Server 2012 R2.
2. Start your computer if you are sure it will boot to the DVD.
3. After the Windows logo is displayed, Windows Setup begins. The screen prompts you to choose your language and location preferences. Click **Next**.
4. On the next screen, you have the option to repair your computer or install the OS. Click **Install now**.

5. You are prompted to choose the operating system to install (see Figure 5-16). Depending on your installation media, you may be able to choose from Server Core or Server with a GUI for either Standard edition or Datacenter edition, as shown in Figure 5-16. The installation is identical for both editions. Choose **Server with a GUI** and click **Next.** If you are using an edition that requires an activation key, enter it on the next screen; otherwise, read the Windows Server 2012 R2 Licensing terms, click **I accept the license terms,** and click **Next.**

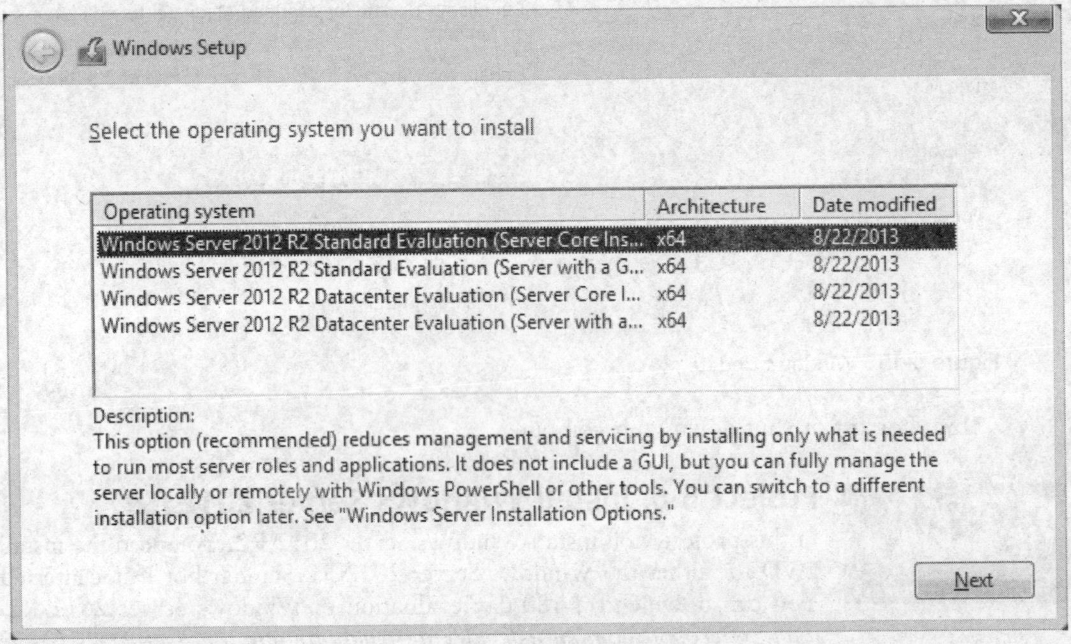


**Figure 5-16** Choosing the edition and interface for Windows Server 2012 R2

6. The next screen asks, "Which type of installation do you want?" Click **Custom** to perform a clean installation.
7. Click the disk on which to install Windows Server 2012 R2, and then click **Next.** The setup program copies files and installs Windows Server 2012 R2. The computer will restart at least once. When the computer restarts, be sure to remove the installation DVD, or the computer might boot to the DVD and start the installation process from the beginning.
8. After the computer restarts, you are prompted to enter a password for the Administrator account. You must use a password that meets minimum requirements. Type **Password01** in the Password and Reenter Password boxes and click **Finish.**
9. To log on to Windows Server 2012 R2, press **Ctrl+Alt+Delete,** enter the password for Administrator, and press Enter.

10. If you are connected to a network, you are asked if you want to allow your PC to be discoverable by other PCs on the network. Click **Yes** unless you are on a public network.
11. Windows Server Manager automatically starts and displays the Windows Server 2012 R2 Server Manager Dashboard (see Figure 5-17).

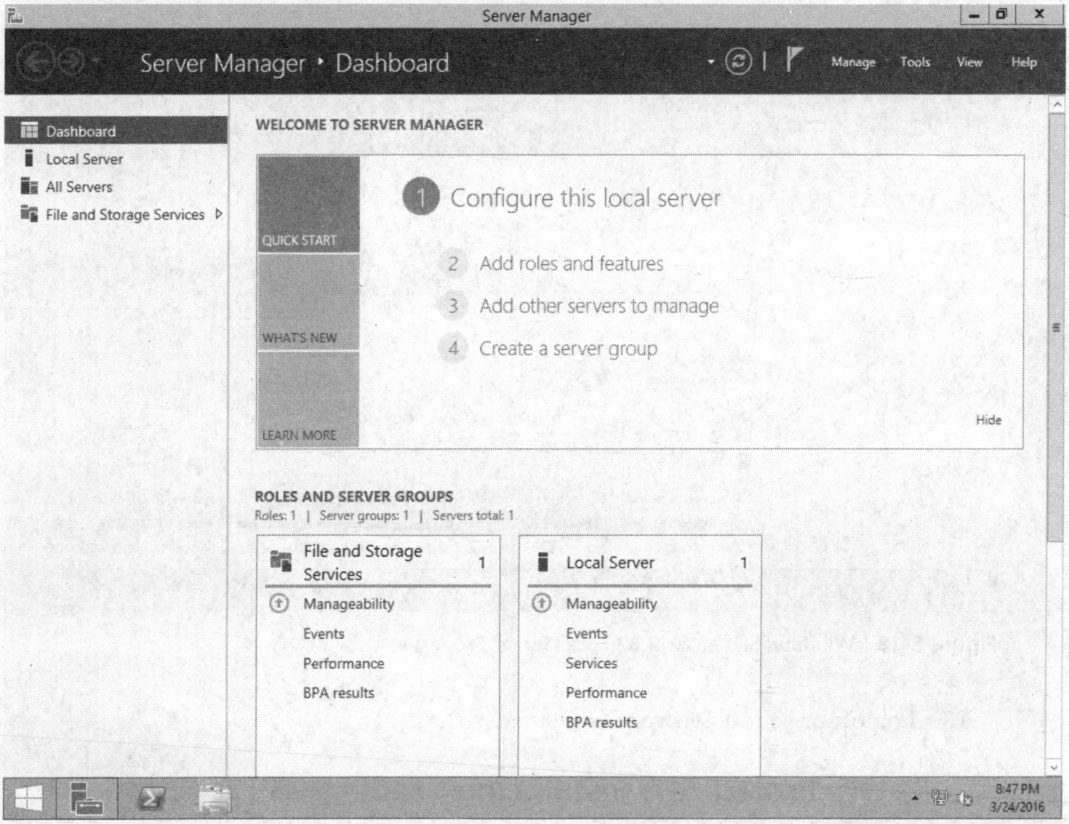


**Figure 5-17** Windows Server 2012 R2 Server Manager Dashboard

12. Click **Local Server** in the left pane to see and change basic settings. On this screen (see Figure 5-18), you can change the computer name, join a workgroup or domain, change IP address settings, configure Windows Update, and so on.

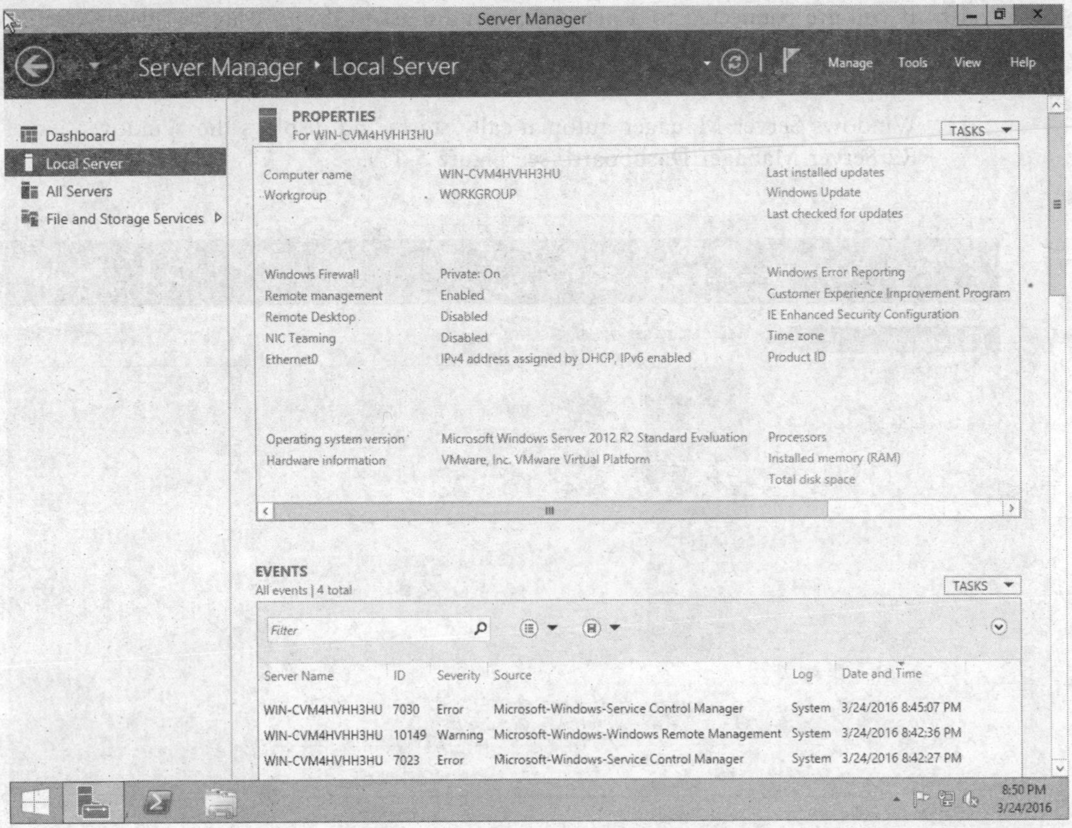


**Figure 5-18** Windows Server 2012 R2 Local Server Properties

13. Log off or shut down your computer.

## Project 5-7: Install Linux Fedora 23 Workstation

In this project, you practice installing Fedora 23 Workstation onto a hard drive. You need the Fedora 23 Workstation installation DVD, which can be downloaded from *https://getfedora.org/en/workstation/download/*. This project assumes you have a blank disk on which to install Fedora 23.

1. Insert the Fedora 23 installation DVD in the DVD drive of a computer that meets the minimum requirements for Fedora 23.
2. Start your computer if you are sure it will boot to the DVD.
3. Fedora Live will start automatically. When Fedora starts, click **Install to Hard Drive** on the Welcome to Fedora screen (see Figure 5-19).
4. On the Welcome to Fedora screen, you are prompted to select the language you want to use. Click the appropriate language and click **Continue**.

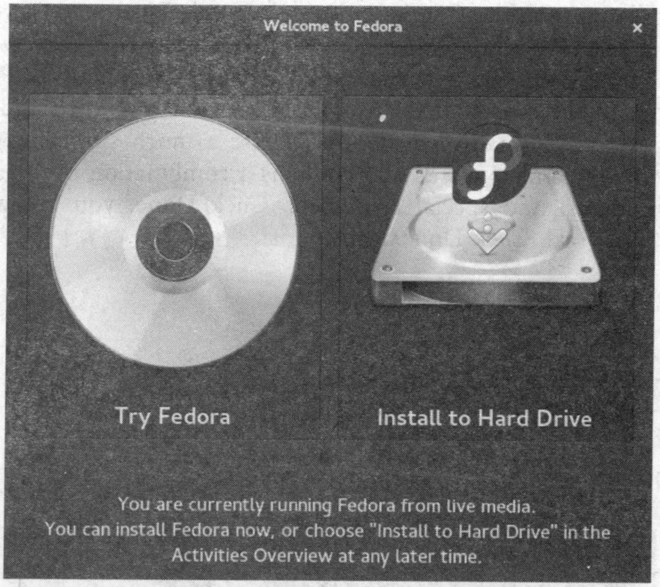


**Figure 5-19** Welcome to Fedora screen

*Source: Fedora Linux*

5. On the Installation Summary screen (see Figure 5-20), review the choices. Click **INSTALLATION DESTINATION** and review the options. Notice that you have the option to encrypt the data on the disk. Click the hard disk you want to use, if necessary, and click **Done.**

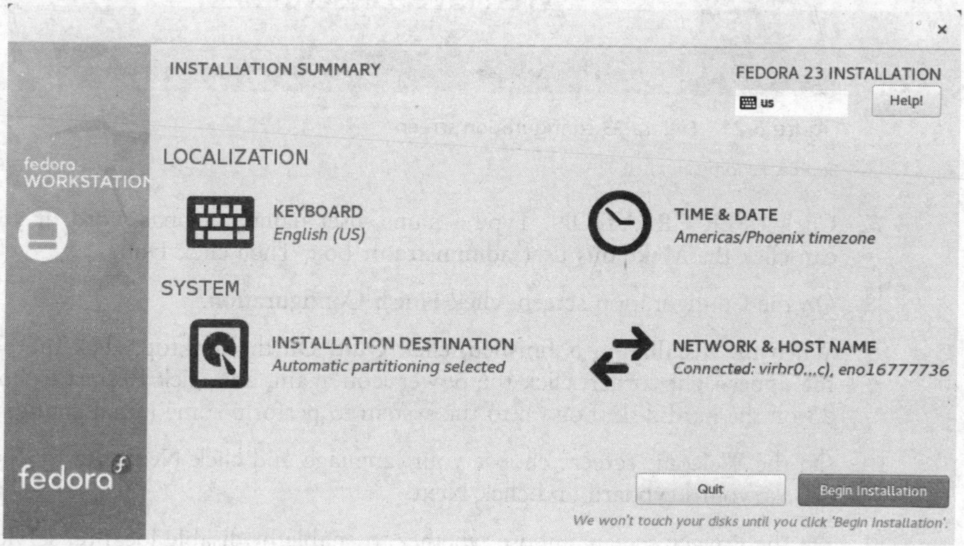


**Figure 5-20** Installation Summary screen in Fedora 23

*Source: Fedora Linux*

6. Click **Begin Installation**. On the Configuration screen (see Figure 5-21), you must perform two tasks before you can continue: create a root password and create a regular user. Click **ROOT PASSWORD** and then type **Password01** in the Root Password box and Confirm box. Linux does a dictionary check on your password and reports that the password is weak. Normally, you would choose a much stronger password that doesn't contain any dictionary words and contains a combination of uppercase letters, lowercase letters, digits, and special characters. Click **Done**; you are warned again about the weak password. Click **Done** again.

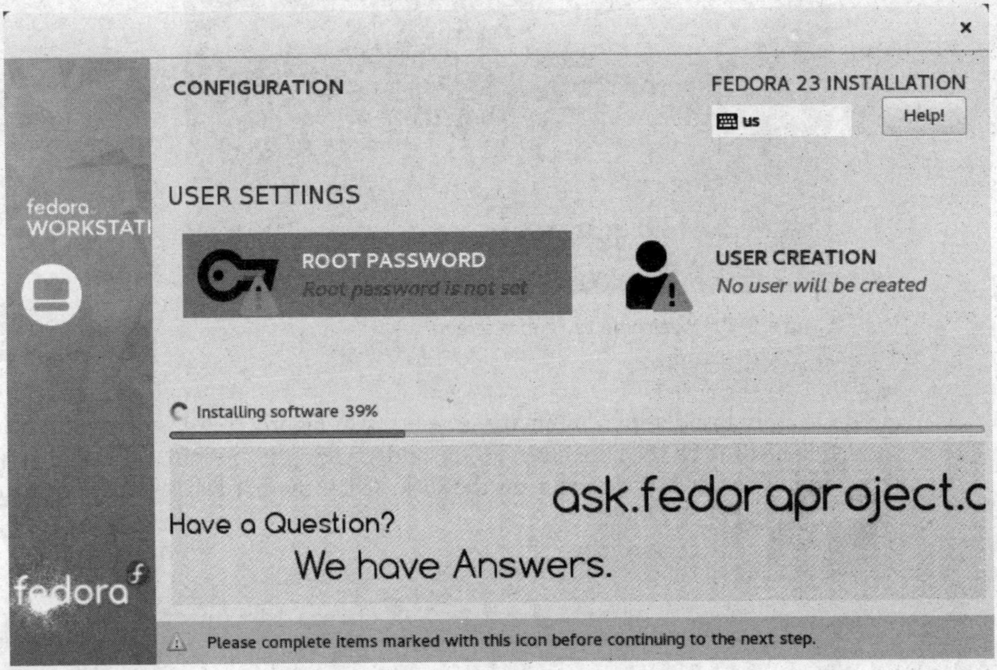


**Figure 5-21** Fedora 23 configuration screen

*Source: Fedora Linux*

7. Click **USER CREATION**. Type a name, user name, and password. If you want, you can click the **Make this user administrator** box. Then click **Done**.
8. On the Configuration screen, click **Finish Configuration**.
9. When the installation is finished, click **Quit**. On the desktop, click the power icon in the upper-right corner, click the power icon again, and click **Restart** to boot to Fedora 23 on the hard disk. Log on to the system to perform some initial configuration tasks.
10. On the Welcome screen, choose your language and click **Next**. On the Typing screen, choose your keyboard and click **Next**.
11. On the Privacy screen, choose whether to enable or disable location services and automatic problem reporting. Click **Next**.
12. On the Online Accounts screen, you can choose any online accounts you want to connect to the Fedora 23 installation. Click **Skip**.

13. On the Ready to Go screen, click **Start using Fedora**. You see a Getting Started (GNOME Help) window that provides tutorials for using GNOME.
14. Log off and shut down the computer.

# Critical Thinking

The following activities give you critical thinking challenges. Challenge Labs give you an opportunity to use the skills you have learned to perform a task without step-by-step instructions. Case projects offer a practical problem for which you supply a written solution. Not all chapters contain Challenge Labs. There is not always a specific right or wrong answer to these critical thinking exercises. They are intended to encourage you to review the chapter material and delve deeper into the topics you have learned.

# Challenge Labs

## Challenge Lab 5-1: Perform a Windows 7/Windows 10 Dual Boot

In this challenge lab, you start from a Windows 7 computer and install Windows 10 while maintaining your Windows 7 installation. Answer the following questions in preparation for this installation:

- What hardware considerations must you take into account before performing the installation? Think about CPU requirements, disk requirements, and memory requirements, plus anything else you can think of.
- What will you need to have on hand before starting the installation?
- What tasks should you perform before beginning the installation?
- What are some of the critical choices you must make during the installation from the time you power on your Windows 7 computer to the time that file copying begins?

# Case Projects

Merlinos Mills is a company that produces flours and grains for grocery stores. It owns mills and distribution centers in the northwestern and midwestern United States. The headquarters in Bend, Oregon employs more than 400 people, most of whom use computers. Also, the headquarters has 28 servers, all running Microsoft Windows Server 2008 Enterprise Edition. The company employees use a full range of OSs, including Windows Vista, Windows 7, Windows 8.1, and Mac OS X Mavericks.

The management of Merlinos Mills wants each department to upgrade to newer OSs. Also, they are very concerned about network security, and they want to install new servers and upgrade their current servers to OS versions that take better advantage of security features. Your role in the process is to work with each department to help ensure that the installations and upgrades go smoothly.

## Case Project 5-1: Determine Preliminary Steps

The master distribution center in Bend, Oregon includes 42 people, including nine Windows Vista users, 22 people using Windows 7 Professional, and 11 people using Windows 8.1. The distribution center is slated to upgrade its computers to Windows 10 Pro. What preliminary steps should be taken before starting the upgrades on these computers? In general, are there any problems involved in upgrading to Windows 10 from each of these OSs?

## Case Project 5-2: Decide to Upgrade or Not

The distribution center's nine Windows Vista users are all certain they need to upgrade to Windows 10 Pro to perform their work. However, the 33 people in the distribution center who are running Windows 8.1 and Windows 7 Professional are currently able to use all software, such as office software, customized distribution software, and inventory software that is integrated with the distribution software. They are resisting the upgrade to Windows 10 Pro, and the distribution manager asks for your opinion about whether to upgrade these computers. Should they upgrade from Windows 8.1 and Windows 7 to Windows 10?

## Case Project 5-3: Install Windows 10 Pro

After considering the issues in Case Project 5-2, management has decided that the distribution center will replace the computers running Windows Vista and Windows 7, and purchase new machines with Windows 10 Pro. The Windows 8.1 users already have computers that can run Windows 10 for a possible upgrade. The user support person for the distribution center has not performed an installation for Windows 10. Tell her generally what to expect when performing this installation.

## Case Project 5-4: Move to Windows Server 2012 R2

The IT Department has already been testing Windows Server 2012 R2, and some time ago purchased licenses to convert all of its Windows Server 2008 Enterprise Edition servers to Windows Server 2012 R2 Enterprise Edition. Two of the servers are running the Server Core installation of Windows Server 2008. Two other servers are running the 32-bit edition of Windows Server 2008. Management wants all servers to run the Server with a GUI installation. Explain the general process the department must follow to convert to Windows Server 2012 R2. Include any caveats or problems they might encounter.

## Case Project 5-5: Upgrade to Mac OS X El Capitan

The Marketing Department strictly uses computers that run Mac OS X Mountain Lion and plans to upgrade to Mac OS X El Capitan. What steps should it follow for the upgrade?

chapter 6

# Configuring Input and Output Devices

**After reading this chapter and completing the exercises, you will be able to:**

- Understand how OSs interface with input and output devices
- Explain the need for device drivers and install devices and drivers
- Describe popular input device technologies
- Discuss the types of printers and install printers
- Explain display adapter technologies
- Install circuit boards for new devices

**Input and output devices enable people to communicate with the computer and** enable the computer to communicate with people. The keyboard is an example of an input device through which you issue commands and enter text. A computer monitor is an output device that enables the computer to communicate back, showing the results of your work in text or rendering eye-catching graphics. A printer lets you output your work on the printed page.

This chapter describes how OSs interface with input and output devices, such as through device drivers. You learn general techniques for installing devices and device drivers for each OS. You also learn about many types of input and output devices, such as keyboards, mice, monitors, scanners, and printers. Further, you learn how to install printers in a variety of OSs.

# OSs and Devices: An Overview

As you learned in Chapter 1, a primary function of any OS is to provide basic input/output (I/O) support for application software—that is, to translate requests from application software into commands that the hardware can understand and carry out. For example, the OS must:

- Handle input from the keyboard, mouse, and other input devices
- Handle output to the screen, printer, and other output devices
- Control information storage and retrieval using various types of disk and optical drives
- Support communications with remote computers through a network

An OS accomplishes these tasks in two ways: through software—device driver code within the OS itself, as well as accessing third-party device driver software—and through hardware controlled by the OS. Specifically, the OS controls chips and circuits inside a computer that communicate with specific input or output devices. Device drivers perform the actual communication between the physical device and the OS. The particular configuration of device drivers and adapters varies, but they function in the same way in each OS.

Likewise, setting up or installing input, output, or storage devices involves three general steps across OSs:

1. Install the device drivers that are required.
2. Connect the input, output, or storage device.
3. Turn on the device, if necessary, and follow any configuration instructions.

Installing and configuring storage devices is covered in Chapter 7.

# Using Device Drivers

A device driver is software that enables the OS and application software to access specific computer hardware, such as a monitor or disk drive. A separate device driver is usually needed for each input or output device used on the computer. The OS provides the basic I/O support for your printer and other hardware, but it doesn't support specific features of individual devices. For that, you need a driver, which may be supplied by the hardware manufacturer or the producer of the OS. (See the discussion of driver software in Chapter 1.)

Computer monitors, flash drives, printers, and disk drives are so much a part of using a computer that it might be surprising that a device driver is necessary for each. However, when you consider that there are thousands of devices and device manufacturers, it makes sense. If all computer OS vendors attempted to incorporate code for all of the possible devices, the OS code would be huge and probably slow. Also, the OS would have to be updated each time a new device or manufacturer came on the market. The advantages of using device drivers are:

- Only essential code is necessary to build into the OS kernel for maximum performance.
- Use of specific devices does not have to be linked to a single OS.
- In a competitive marketplace, the number of I/O devices can expand in virtually unlimited directions to offer computer users a broad range of device selections, functions, and features.
- New devices can come on the market without requiring extensive updates to OSs.

Many hardware manufacturers make drivers for current OSs available as a free download from the Internet or supply a DVD/CD-ROM with the device. While OS vendors supply drivers for many devices as part of the OS installation package, you should generally use the manufacturer's driver, if available, instead of the driver supplied with the OS. Although many OS drivers for specific hardware were developed by the hardware manufacturer in cooperation with the OS producer, they may be generic—designed to support a range of hardware models—or they may be older than the specific hardware you are installing. Using the driver available on the Internet gives you a better chance of having the latest version, and it often provides bug fixes and performance optimizations as well.

TIP

Even if your hardware is brand new, it is good practice to check the manufacturer's Web site for newer driver software. Drivers are usually designated by version number, and sometimes with a date. Drivers with later version numbers and dates may contain fixes for problems identified with earlier releases, and they sometimes enable or improve the performance of some hardware features.

For example, to find drivers for a broad range of Epson hardware products, go to *www.epson.com,* click Support, and then pick your device from the list or search for it by name. Most manufacturers have Web sites that contain support for their products, including troubleshooting tips and downloadable drivers.

Remember that you can usually guess the home page for major companies. Simply type *www.companyname.com* in the address line of your browser, where *companyname* is the name of the manufacturer of your hardware product. If this doesn't work, use a Web search engine to search for information about a particular company or product.

The procedure for installing drivers varies slightly with the source of the driver and the OS you are using. If you download a new driver from a manufacturer's Web site, you'll probably have to uncompress the file before you can use it.

For example, Microsoft has included built-in zip support in its OSs since the late 1990s. PC users can also use the PKZIP or WinZip compression and decompression utilities. Many software producers distribute software that is bundled and compressed with the PKZIP/WinZip format. Compression software not only reduces the size of the supplied files by removing redundant information, it also groups multiple files into a single distribution file. Distribution files may be supplied in self-extraction format, an executable file that decompresses the archive and expands individual files. PC-executable files normally use an .exe file extension. If you download a driver archive that includes this extension, it is a self-extracting file. If the file includes a .zip extension, you can open it directly within the OS; Windows File Explorer supports zip files and can open them just like a normal folder. You can also use a stand-alone program such as PKZIP or WinZip to expand the archive before installing the driver software.

If your OS does not include built-in zip support or you want the PKZIP or WinZip software, you can download it from a variety of Web sites. Other programs perform similar functions. One resource for a wide variety of shareware, freeware, and inexpensive software is *www.tucows.com/downloads.*

Since version 10.3 Tiger, Mac OS X has had built-in zip support. Mac OS X users can use ZIP-format archives, but a more common format is StuffIt, a utility similar to PKZIP, which also bundles multiple files into a single distribution archive. StuffIt products are available for Windows, Linux, and Mac OS X OSs, and for some versions of UNIX. StuffIt files can be self-extracting, or you can use StuffIt Expander or another utility to expand the archive into its individual components. To obtain this utility, visit *my.smithmicro.com*. StuffIt also supports ZIP format, and it lets you retrieve compressed or archived files from Macintosh users. The basic StuffIt Expander is a free download, and you can purchase the full-blown StuffIt Deluxe so you can create archives for Mac and Windows environments. The third-party ZIP utilities available for the Mac don't always produce files that are compatible with Windows systems. The StuffIt Expander software, on the other hand, works both ways quite well.

UNIX/Linux system users may retrieve drivers and other software in a *tar* format. Tar files are also archives that group multiple files into a single distribution file. *Tar* doesn't compress the files; it merely groups files to make it easier to copy and distribute multiple files together. You may find that a *tar* archive is also zipped. UNIX/Linux systems also have a *zip* command that is compatible with the PKZIP software. You can use StuffIt or a UNIX/Linux version of *unzip* to expand the compressed *tar* archive into an uncompressed file, and then you can issue a UNIX/Linux *tar* command to extract individual files from the archive.

Once you locate the driver you want to use, you generally have three choices for installation, depending on the source of the driver: you can use your OS's installation utility, the Plug and Play (PnP) feature, or the installation utility provided by the hardware manufacturer. Procedures are slightly different among OSs, and precise steps differ depending on the equipment (a printer installs differently from a sound card, for example), but the general process is very similar. The following sections discuss manufacturer driver installation and specific steps for installing devices in OSs.

**From the Trenches ...**

An IT professional was called to help a company president's administrative assistant with a printer problem during a board of director's meeting. She tried all types of troubleshooting steps, from turning the printer off and on to testing the network and looking for a paper jam in the printer. After working on the problem for quite some time (and delaying the meeting), the IT professional realized that the printer driver had been removed from the OS used to print the documents. After a quick download and installation from the manufacturer's Web site, the printer was back up and printing correctly.

## Manufacturer Driver Installation

When you use a hardware manufacturer's installation utility, the process is usually fully automatic and well documented. In fact, newer printers, plotters, and other devices frequently come with extensive support material on a DVD or CD-ROM. You might be presented with video or animated training material to teach you how to install or use the device. You shouldn't have to know much about the way your OS installs drivers or interfaces with the device you're installing because the manufacturer's installation routine handles it all for you.

Because each manufacturer has a different procedure with different devices and different OSs, it is difficult to document each system and device type. In general, however, the procedure is to double-click an installation program or insert a DVD/CD-ROM into a drive and either wait for a program to start automatically or run a setup or install utility. Then, simply follow on-screen prompts. If you run into problems, look for a disk-based tutorial or go to the manufacturer's Web site to search for more information. Some software suppliers also include .txt files on installation disks to present new information or tips for the installer. You can use Notepad or any text editor to look for these files and read them.

## Windows Driver Installation

There are several ways to install drivers in Windows. The easiest way to install a driver for a new system is to use the PnP capability to automatically detect the new hardware and install drivers. Another way to install new devices and drivers is to use the Add a device wizard in Windows. You can also use Device Manager to install a new driver, update an existing one, or roll back a driver to a previous version. Each of these methods is explained in the following sections.

**Using PnP to Install a Device and Driver** You can quickly install a new printer, for example, by following these general steps:

1. Install any software drivers that are required.
2. Connect the printer to the computer.
3. Plug the printer into a power outlet and turn it on.
4. Follow any configuration instructions.

When the printer is turned on, the OS recognizes that a new piece of hardware is attached and tries to locate the drivers for it. If Windows already has a built-in driver for this device, the OS finds the driver on the Windows distribution disk or DVD/CD-ROM. Otherwise, you must insert the manufacturer's DVD/CD-ROM into an appropriate drive when the OS asks for it.

**Using a Windows Wizard to Install a Device and Driver** If Windows doesn't recognize newly installed hardware, or if you want to conduct an installation manually or start automatic procedures to detect a hardware device because PnP did not work initially, use the Add a device wizard. In Windows 7 and later versions, open Control Panel and click Add a device under the Hardware and Sound category. Windows will search for the device you are trying to install.

If you have a driver from the device manufacturer, you should probably use it to ensure that the latest driver is installed. When you use the wizard, the drivers may not be the most current ones because Windows uses the drivers from its installation media.

**Using Device Manager to Install or Update a Driver** If you need to install a device driver, update one for a device that is already installed, or roll back a driver to an earlier version, Device Manager (see Figure 6-1) offers a convenient way to accomplish the task. You can also use Device Manager to:

- Determine the location of device driver files
- Check to make sure a device is working properly
- Determine if there is a resource conflict for a device

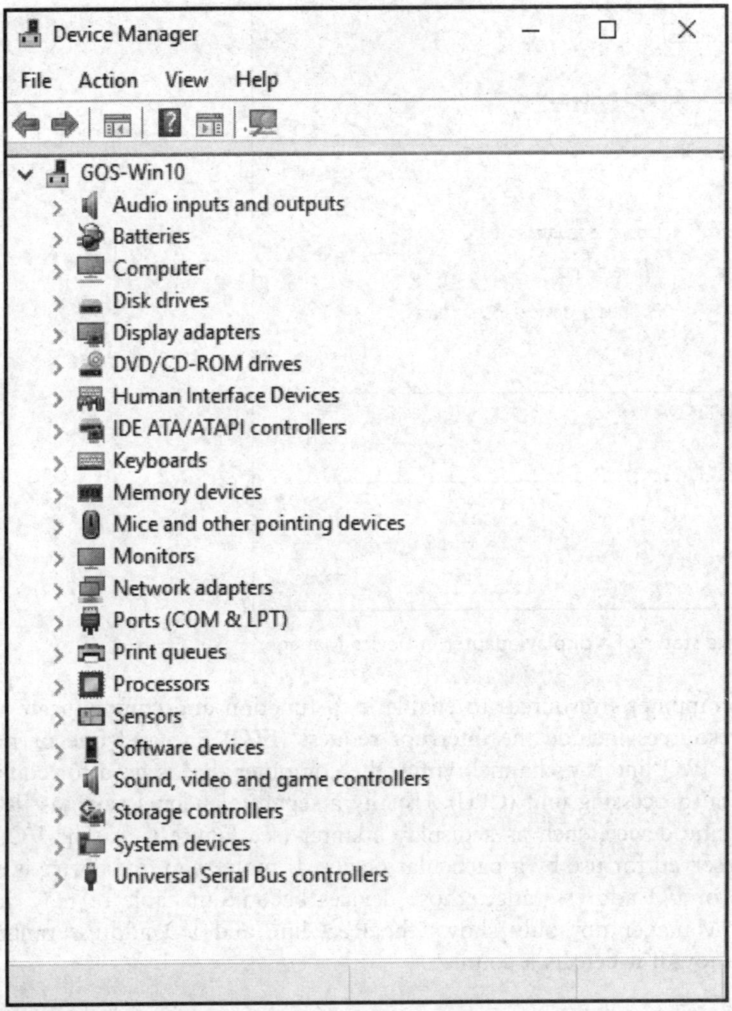


**Figure 6-1** Device Manager in Windows 10

The advantage of determining the location of a device file is that you not only verify that the driver is installed, you can also check the version of the device driver. For example, if you suspect that you have an old driver, check with the manufacturer for the version level or date of the most current driver and then use Device Manager to compare it with the version you have installed.

When you access a device through Device Manager, you can determine if the device is installed in two ways. First, Device Manager places a question mark on the device if there is a problem with the installation or if the driver is not installed. Also, when you use Device Manager to access a device that has a driver set up, the utility checks to verify that the device is working properly. Figure 6-2 shows an example of a display driver in Windows 10 that is working properly.

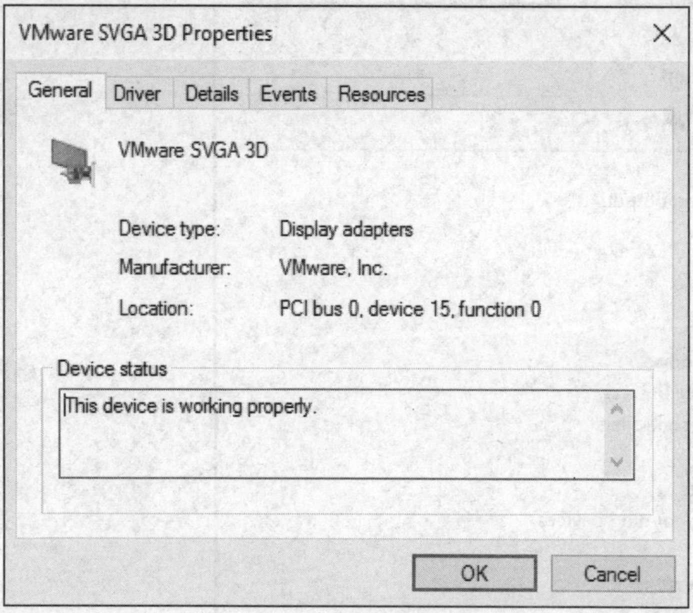


**Figure 6-2** The device status of a display adapter in Device Manager

A device uses the computer's resources to enable it to function and communicate with the computer. These resources include the **interrupt request (IRQ) line** and one or more I/O address ranges. The IRQ line is a channel within the computer that is used for communications with the central processing unit (CPU). Usually a separate channel, such as IRQ 16, is allocated for a specific device, such as a display adapter (see Figure 6-3). The **I/O address range** is memory reserved for use by a particular device. If more than one device is assigned the same IRQ line or I/O address range, those devices become unstable or may not work altogether. Device Manager not only shows the IRQ line and I/O address ranges for a device, it lets you know if it detects a conflict.

You rarely run into resource conflicts on modern PCs. I/O addresses are dynamically configured in cooperation with the BIOS to ensure there are no conflicts. Many devices, such as those that use the PCI Express bus, don't use hardware interrupts (IRQs) at all; instead, a process called *message signaled interrupts* (MSI) uses the data bus to signal a virtual interrupt of sorts.

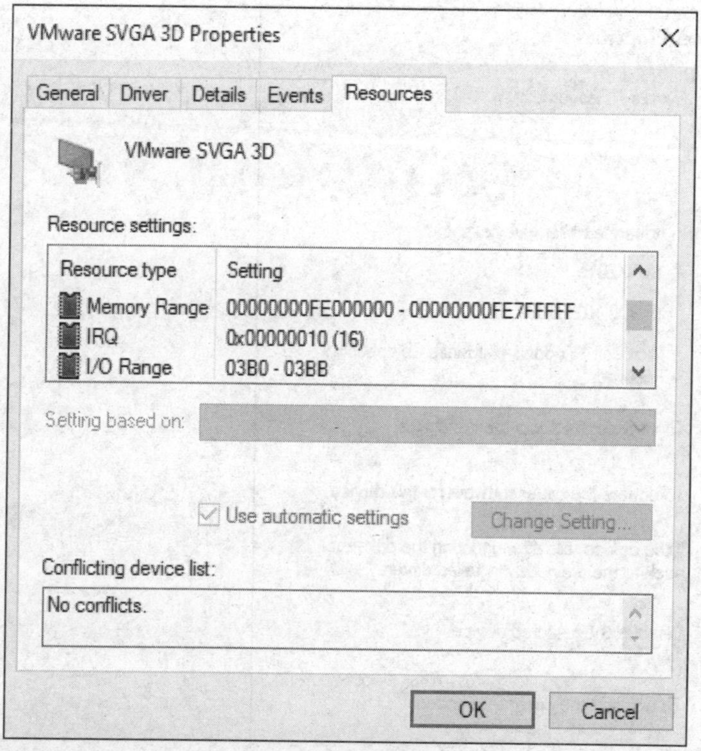


**Figure 6-3** Viewing the resources used by a device

**Updating and Rolling Back Drivers** Aside from checking on the status and resources of a device, Device Manager lets you update a driver or roll it back to an earlier version. You might update a driver if the device is not performing well or is causing system instability. To update a driver from Device Manager, double-click the device and click the Driver tab (see Figure 6-4). When you click the Update Driver button, Windows gives you the option to search your computer and the Internet for an updated driver or to manually browse to the driver file location. If you have recently updated a driver and it is causing system instability or performance problems, you can roll back the driver to an earlier version by clicking the Roll Back Driver button, which is on the same tab as the Update Driver button shown in Figure 6-4. Windows will uninstall the current driver and install the previous version, if available.

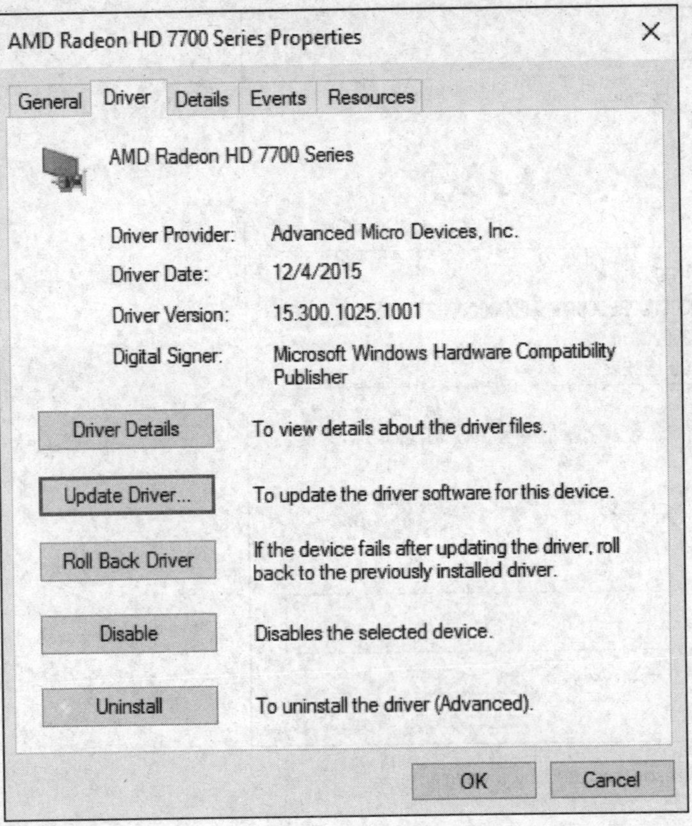


**Figure 6-4** Updating or rolling back a driver

**Configuring Driver Signing** When you install a Windows I/O device, such as a pointing device or a new sound card, Windows makes sure that the device driver has been verified by Microsoft. A unique digital signature is incorporated into the verified driver in a process called **driver signing**. In Windows 10 and newer versions, unsigned drivers are not permitted. Developers of device drivers must use a test signing procedure to test drivers they are developing.

On older Windows versions, you can choose to be warned that a driver is not signed, ignore whether or not a driver is signed, or have the OS prevent you from installing an unsigned driver. The warning level is assigned by default so that you are warned before you install an unsigned driver, but you can still choose to install it. Using driver signing helps to ensure that the driver works properly with the device and in conjunction with other devices. It is also a security feature to ensure that no one has tampered with the driver, such as by incorporating malicious code or a virus.

## UNIX/Linux Driver Installation

The concept of drivers in UNIX/Linux is slightly different from that in other OSs. The central portion of the UNIX/Linux OS, the kernel, is where most of the UNIX/Linux device drivers are loaded. Device drivers are either in the form of kernel modules, which are pieces of code that must be linked into the kernel, or loadable modules, similar pieces of code that are not linked into the kernel but are loaded when the OS is started. Device support in most UNIX/Linux versions is limited when compared to other OSs; manufacturers of devices often provide drivers for special hardware, which are then linked or loaded into the kernel.

UNIX/Linux devices are managed through the use of **device special files**, which contain information about I/O devices that is used by the OS kernel when a device is accessed. In many UNIX/Linux systems, there are three types of device special files:

- **Block special files**, which are used to manage random access devices that handle blocks of data, including DVD/CD-ROM drives, hard disk drives, tape drives, and other storage devices.
- **Character special files**, which handle byte-by-byte streams of data, such as through USB connections. USB is the most common interface for mice, keyboards, external disk drives, and other external hardware such as printers and digital cameras.
- **Named pipes** for handling internal communications, such as redirecting file output to a monitor.

When you install a UNIX/Linux OS, device special files are created for the devices already installed on the system. On many UNIX/Linux distributions, these files are stored in the /dev directory. Table 6-1 provides a sampling of device special files.

**Table 6-1 UNIX/Linux device special files**

| File | Description |
|---|---|
| /dev/console | For the console components, such as the monitor and keyboard attached to the computer (/dev/tty0 is also used at the same time on many systems) |
| /dev/hd*xn* | For Integrated Drive Electronics (IDE) and Enhanced Integrated Drive Electronics (EIDE) hard drives, where *x* is a letter representing the disk and *n* represents the partition number—for example, hda1 for the first disk and partition |
| /dev/modem | Symbolic link to the device special file (typically linked to /dev/ttys1) for a modem |
| /dev/mouse | Symbolic link to the device special file (typically linked to /dev/ttys0) for a mouse or pointing device |
| /dev/sd*xn* | For a hard drive connected to a SCSI or SATA interface, where *x* is a letter representing the disk and *n* represents the partition—for example, sda1 for the first SATA drive and first partition on that drive |
| /dev/st*n* | For a SCSI tape drive, where *n* is the number of the drive—for example, st0 for the first tape drive. The USB devices appear as a SCSI device. |
| /dev/srx | For an IDE CD/DVD drive |

If you need to create a device special file for a new device, use the *mknod* command, as explained in the following general steps:

1. Log in with superuser permissions.
2. Access a terminal window or the command prompt.
3. Type *cd/ dev* and press Enter to switch to the /dev folder.

4. Use the *mknod* command, and then enter the device special file name, such as ttys42. Next, enter the file type, such as character (c) or block (b), and a major and minor node value used by the kernel. (Check with the device manufacturer for these values.) For example, you might type *mknod ttys20 c 8 68*, and press Enter for a new device.

TIP

Some versions of UNIX/Linux also support the *makedev* command for creating a device special file. To determine which commands are supported in your UNIX/Linux version and learn the syntax, use the *man mknod* or *man makedev* command to view the documentation.

To view the I/O device special files that are already on your system, use the *ls* command to see all of the files in the /dev folder. You can view all the PCI (and PCI Express) devices installed on a Fedora Linux system using *lspci*. Another command, *lshw*, provides detailed system information, including installed devices and disks.

## Mac OS X Driver Installation

Mac OS X systems come with device drivers for most hardware that connects to these systems. When you obtain new hardware, make sure that you have an installation DVD/CD-ROM from the hardware manufacturer. The general steps for installing new hardware on a Mac OS X system are:

1. Shut down the OS and turn off the computer.
2. Attach the new hardware.
3. Restart the computer and OS.
4. Insert the DVD/CD-ROM for the hardware.
5. Run the installer program on the DVD/CD-ROM for that hardware.

TIP

If you are having problems with hardware in Mac OS X, it may be necessary to reinstall the OS. In earlier versions of Mac OS X, you can insert the Mac OS X Install Disk 1 DVD/CD-ROM, select the Mac OS X disk as the destination, click Options, and select Archive and Install. In Mac OS X v10.3 and later versions, insert the installation disk and double-click Install Mac OS X; the installation will retain your previous settings and software.

Now that you're familiar with device drivers and the basic process of installing devices and drivers in various OSs, it's time to survey the types of input and output devices and get a more in-depth look into how they relate to OSs.

## Standard Input Devices

There are several standard and universal computer input devices: the keyboard, the mouse, and the touch pad. The keyboard is the most important input device; other important devices include the mouse and touch pad as well as the mouse alternatives, such as a trackball, stylus, and pointing stick. Touch input has become popular; iPads, smartphones, book readers, and tablet touch screens are part of the daily routine for many people.

### Mouse and Keyboard Drivers

Because the I/O routines for the mouse and keyboard are highly standardized across OSs, it is unlikely that you will need to interact with the OS to set up these devices. Although mice and keyboards do use device drivers, unlike printers and other output devices, these drivers are standard and are usually included as part of the OS. The OS provides only general support for output devices like printers; it includes routines to send data out through a USB port, for example, and to receive data sent to the computer from a device connected to this port, but it has no intrinsic routines to support specific printer brands, models, or capabilities. For keyboards and mice, however, most OSs contain intrinsic routines to handle them.

Wireless mice and keyboards are available from computer manufacturers and third-party vendors. You may purchase them as a package or separately. Each device requires batteries to operate, along with a USB receiver for communication between the device and computer. Wireless mice and keyboard packages normally have one USB receiver that both the mouse and keyboard use. Bluetooth mice and keyboards are also available; some come with a USB option and others are Bluetooth only. Almost all mice are now optical. They use either an LED or a laser to illuminate the surface on which they are used, and they contain an optical sensor (a very small camera) that takes thousands of pictures per second. The pictures are compared to calculate the direction and speed of the optical mouse.

Some older mice use a ball on the underside that rotates as you move them across a desk or mouse pad. They are becoming rare as the optical mouse has become the preferred device.

A wired mouse or keyboard uses a USB port, similar to the way a printer uses a USB port. (A wireless mouse uses a receiver.) Like a printer or other output device, a wired keyboard or mouse can also come with drivers and additional software on DVD/CD-ROM. Some OSs include a custom keyboard configuration utility, such as the one from Windows 10, shown in Figure 6-5.

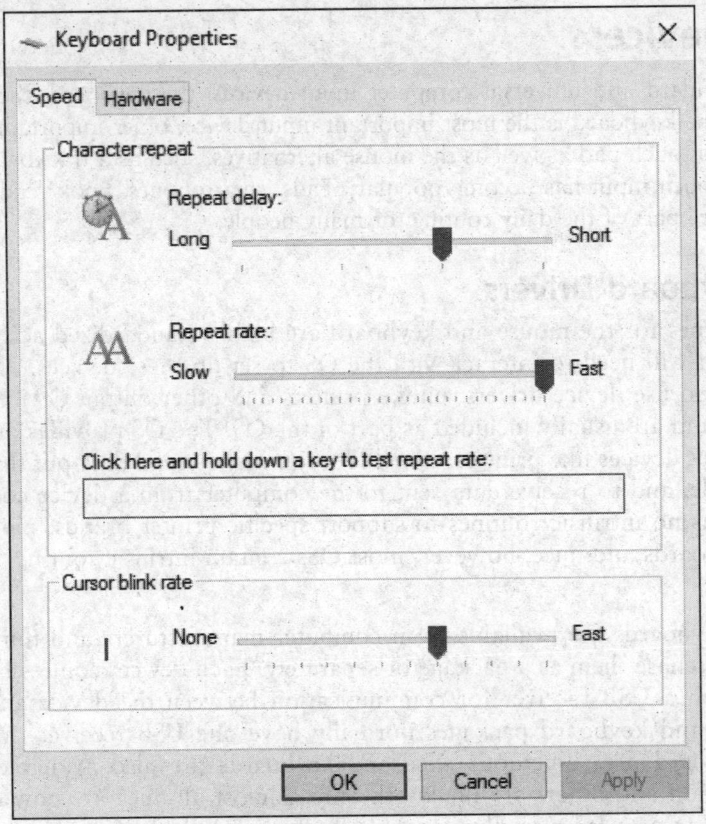


**Figure 6-5** Keyboard settings in Windows 10

As you can see from this figure, the degree of configuration is minimal, which points out the standard nature of the keyboard itself and the drivers that support it. Earlier OSs—particularly non-Windows systems—may have even more limited keyboard configuration options. You plug it in and it either works or not.

As with the keyboard, the intrinsic OS mouse drivers may offer customization options to the user. Mouse preferences in Mac OS X El Capitan are shown in Figure 6-6.

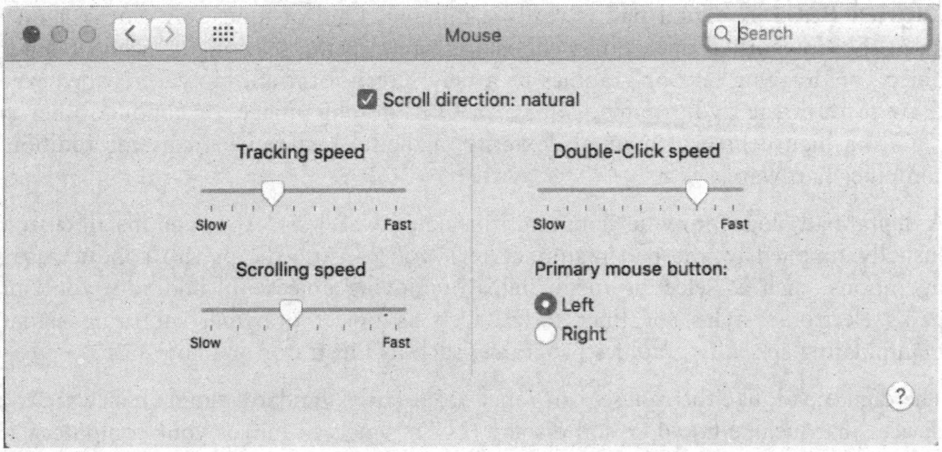


**Figure 6-6** Mac OS X mouse settings

*Source: Mac OS X El Capitan*

Typically, the configuration routines let you set the double-click speed, calibrate mouse movement and direction based on how you hold the mouse as you roll it around the desk, customize the pointer graphic, and a variety of other features. In addition to having special features to enhance the function of the mouse itself, manufacturers' drivers usually provide additional levels of user configuration, such as options to help you quickly find the cursor on the screen or to select a window just by pointing to the title bar.

## Touch Input Drivers

Touch input devices also use device drivers. In most cases, the drivers are included in the OS or preloaded by the computer manufacturer. With a touch screen, you can open files, select items on the screen, and move items with the touch of your finger. Multi-touch technology allows you to use multiple fingers to resize a window, scroll through documents, or page forward or back in your Web browser. To use multi-touch, you need a laptop or monitor equipped with multi-touch technology. Windows 7 and newer versions as well as Linux/Fedora support multi-touch capabilities. Apple has incorporated the touch technology used in the iPad and iPhone into Mac OS X.

A touch pad is another type of touch input. Touch pads are usually found below the keyboard on laptops, but they are also available as a peripheral for desktop computers. A touch pad is a surface that converts finger motion and position to a point on your screen.

## Other Input Devices

The keyboard and mouse are ubiquitous and standard. If your computing needs stop with fairly common business applications such as word processing, spreadsheets, and databases, you probably won't need anything more. On the other hand, if you need your computer for graphics design, Web page development, playing games, making video calls, digital photography, or movie or sound editing, you will use one or more specialty input devices, such as digital pads, scanners, joysticks and gamepads, digital sound input, and digital picture and video input/output. The following sections introduce these devices.

**Digital Pads** A **digital pad** is really a different kind of mouse. A mouse is an excellent input tool for normal operations: choosing from a menu, selecting an icon or other graphic object, or dragging text or graphics to a new screen location. However, when you need to draw pictures, sign your name, color a detailed graphic image, or conduct other tasks that require a high degree of manual dexterity, a digital pad can be a useful addition to your computer hardware.

A digital pad plugs into your computer through a USB port. After you install custom drivers (usually supplied by the pad manufacturer), you can use the pad to conduct usual mouse operations, such as selecting menu items or moving objects. In addition, you can use the pad's electronic stylus for finer tasks, such as object drawing, capturing signatures, or manipulating specialty graphics programs, such as Illustrator or Photoshop.

The digital pad, like the mouse, can range from fairly standard, simple hardware to specialty devices that include liquid crystal display (LCD) panels to mirror your computer's video display. Even the simplest pads require some custom software and a unique installation process.

**Scanners** A **scanner** scans text and images to be manipulated by software on your computer. Once in the computer, the digital image from the scanner can be saved in a variety of graphics image formats, edited, merged with other images or text, transmitted over the Internet or other network connection, and printed.

Scanners may also be used with **optical character recognition (OCR)** software. Instead of scanning text into a digital graphic image, which does not allow for text manipulation, imaging software scans each character on the page as a distinct image. You can then import the scanned results into a word-processing document to work with the text.

If you're using a USB scanner with Windows, installation and configuration should be automatic through PnP. Figure 6-7 shows the Windows Fax and Scan application in Windows 10.

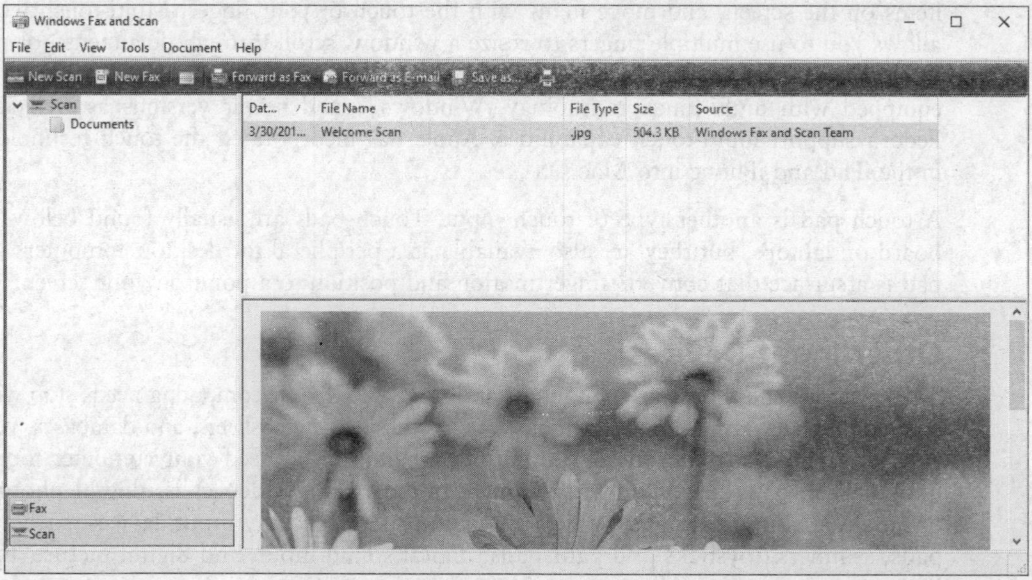


**Figure 6-7** Windows Fax and Scan window

If the built-in Windows Fax and Scan application doesn't suit your needs, you can usually install custom drivers and custom scanning software supplied by the scanner manufacturer. In most cases, the driver software—usually a driver with user interface and scanner control—automatically links with a variety of graphics software. If you're using Photoshop, for example, the scanner may show up as an add-in; if you're using a Microsoft product such as Publisher or Picture Manager, you'll see a scanner icon on your toolbar. When you click the icon, the scanner software will load so you can use the scanner. These drivers and the user interface interact with the OS to control the USB port and capture data supplied by the scanner.

**Joysticks, Gamepads, and Other Controllers** If you run computer simulations, are involved in game development, or enjoy playing games on your computer, you'll most likely have a need for alternative input devices. Some of these may include **joysticks** and **gamepads** along with flight yoke systems and other devices.

A joystick is more like a mouse than a digital pad. Like a mouse, the joystick uses a mechanical or optical device to rotate one or more potentiometers. Changing resistance tells the joystick driver what value to feed to the OS and any associated application software. You use the joystick for three-dimensional movement of an on-screen cursor or other object, such as a car, airplane, or cartoon character. Just as the digital pad makes it easier to input handwriting, picture retouching, and the like, the joystick offers much more control than a mouse when it comes to detailed movements of graphical screen objects. Although games are the primary application for joysticks, Mac users sometimes use them to supplement mouse functionality. Joysticks can be used for virtually any application input task, given the proper driver.

In addition to the three-dimensional movements of the vertical joystick, it usually includes one or more push-button switches that can be associated with gun firings, boxing swings, menu selection, and so on. Like the digital pad, the joystick uses the PC and Mac's USB port. Potentiometer settings or switch closures are sent through the USB port as positive/negative pulses or as variable values on a scale. The OS's basic port I/O routines grab this data, and then it is up to the associated application—a game, for example—to interpret this data in a meaningful way.

Joysticks continue their development to keep up with the games that are being created. There are flight yoke systems, 3D joysticks, attack joysticks, and much more. Logitech and Saitek are just a couple of the vendors that are very active in this arena.

Gamepads come in a wide variety of designs. As the name suggests, they are primarily designed for interaction with games, and include multiple buttons, wheels, or balls to effect movement of a variety of on-screen objects. As with the joystick, the gamepad sends standard signals to the USB port, where the OS I/O routines take the data and pass it off to an application program or custom driver for interpretation. Gamepads from Logitech, Microsoft, and Saitek have become very sophisticated. Some are wireless, some are programmable, and some have LCD displays. There are even vendors that allow your Wii Remote and PS3 controllers to connect to your computer not only to play games, but to control your computer. Apple supports gamepads and sells third-party models on its Web site.

**Digital Sound Input** Every Mac, PC, and workstation computer is supplied with some kind of digital sound card for sound input and output. It may be built into the motherboard or be a separate card. You can connect a microphone to your computer's USB port and record voice mail that you can include with electronic mail, for example, or for narration of slide presentations. Along with your webcam, you can use the microphone to make audio and video calls with Skype and other VoIP (Voice over Internet Protocol) applications. Skype is application software that allows you to make calls with or without video over the Internet. It can also be used for instant messaging and video conferencing (connecting multiple locations via video).

You can download custom sounds or music from Internet sites, such as iTunes, for use within software applications. Voice input to word-processing and other programs is important for people who are unable to use a keyboard or mouse. You can capture digital sound from a digital recorder or digital camera directly into your computer without having to do any conversion in the process. You can also copy digital audio directly from a recorder to your hard drive in much the same way you would copy digital information from one hard drive to another.

There are multiple professional audio I/O standards, but most devices come with a USB port. All you need is a USB cable. Whether you use audio I/O ports or a USB port depends on the external hardware you will interface with your computer. Some high-end digital cameras include more than one digital I/O port, so you can choose which format to use based on personal preference, your need to interface with other users, or which interface you can find. Even high-end digital cameras include a USB port, and most require custom driver software. Also, like scanners, they can usually be controlled and accessed from inside application software, such as digital audio or video editing packages. Once the driver is installed, you can transfer audio information through the USB port from the application you are using to manipulate the audio files.

**Digital Picture and Video Input/Output** Digital picture and video I/O works similarly to digital audio I/O. You need a digital I/O interface and drivers to allow your OS to recognize and use the USB device. As with digital audio, you import digital images into whatever application software you are using for picture or video editing. In some cases, you use a utility supplied by the interface manufacturer to import the digital image, then launch another application, such as Adobe Premier or Photoshop, to conduct the actual editing. On the other hand, some manufacturers include the ability to link their hardware drivers directly into editing software so you can import and export digital files from an external camera and edit the video or still images from the same application.

USB ports are the standard way to connect most devices to a computer. USB 1.0 (version 1.0) had a data transfer rate of 1.5 Mbps. USB 2.0 increased that rate significantly to 480 Mbps and was referred to as Hi-Speed. With SuperSpeed USB 3.0, the data transfer rate has increased to up to 5.0 Gbps, and the newer SuperSpeed+ USB 3.1 standard ups that rate to 10 Gbps.

**1394 Technology** IEEE 1394 (or 1394a) is the original specification for a high-speed digital interface that supports data communication at 100, 200, or 400 megabits per second (Mbps). The newer 1394b specification enables communications at 800 Mbps, 1.6 Gbps, and 3.2 Gbps.

IEEE 1394a and 1394b are technologies currently targeted at multimedia peripherals, which include digital camcorders, music systems, DVDs, digital cameras, and digital TVs. The IEEE 1394b standard also enables data transfer over regular twisted-pair (copper wire) network cable and glass and plastic fiber-optic cable.

FireWire, an IEEE 1394 implementation for bus communications, was developed by Apple Computer and Texas Instruments and is used in computers built by those companies. IEEE 1394 is also known as i.Link (Sony), Lynx (Texas Instruments), and the High Performance Serial Bus (HPSB). The 1394 Trade Association reports that over 2 billion FireWire ports have shipped worldwide. While there is a considerable installed base of 1394 devices, the increases in speed realized by USB 3.0 and USB 3.1 have substantially reduced the popularity and growth of the 1394 standard.

The **Institute of Electrical and Electronics Engineers (IEEE)** is an international organization of scientists, engineers, technicians, and educators that plays a leading role in developing standards for computers, network cabling, and data transmissions, and for other electronics areas, such as consumer electronics and electrical power. Also, visit *www.1394ta.org* for links to information and vendors that support 1394 technologies.

# Printers

A printer is an important part of nearly every computer installation. The following sections outline the most popular types of printers and printer connections. You also learn how to install printers.

## Printer Types

The following types of printers are the most popular today:

- **Inkjet printers** create characters by squirting tiny droplets of ink directly onto the page. Full color—even photographic quality—printing with inkjets is quite common today. Small, quiet, and inexpensive, these printers are popular personal printers in many offices, and dominate the market for schools and homes. Models that deliver color and high resolution are used for proofing by graphics designers and printers, as well as home and office users. With the popularity of digital electronic cameras, high-resolution inkjet printers are used to produce photograph-like output on heavy, slick paper, much like photographic paper stock.
- **Laser printers** use an imaging technology similar to copiers to produce computer output, and are probably the most popular printer for business text and graphics. A typical laser printer contains its own CPU and memory because printed pages are first produced electronically within the printer. Laser printer prices, including those for color printers, have declined sharply over the years so that even small businesses, home offices, and individuals can now afford them.
- **Multifunction printers** combine color inkjet or laser printing, scanning, copying, and faxing into one physical device. Multifunction printers are good for locations that do not

have a lot of desktop space, and can be purchased for as little as $100. The downside to a multifunction printer is that if it breaks, you lose all functions rather than just one.

The cost of printing is more than just the expense of the printer. Ink and laser cartridges add to printing costs. Depending on the cost of the cartridges and the number of pages you can print with each one, many people find that a less expensive printer may cost more in the long run. For example, if you print a high volume of documents, it can be cheaper to use a laser printer than an inkjet printer because one laser cartridge can print tens of thousands of sheets, while one inkjet cartridge may only print hundreds.

In addition to traditional printers, another printer-like device called a **plotter** is popular in engineering, architecture, and other fields where hard copy output (such as blueprints) won't fit on standard paper sizes or can't be produced by standard character or graphics printers. Plotter design is more complex than that of printers, and uses pen and control mechanisms. As with printers, plotters require special drivers to enhance the OS's intrinsic capabilities, but the process of installing plotter hardware and software is similar to that for printers. Likewise, plotters can be installed on a company's network or your computer's USB port in much the same way as printers. (See the next section, "Printer Connections.")

Aside from the three major printer types, other printer designs are used in specialized arenas.

- **3D printers** use an additive process to create one layer of the object at a time. They build the parts from drawings that are cross-sectioned into thousands of layers. There are companies that will create your 3D object from the computer file you send them.
- **Label printers** produce labels and are useful for an eBay seller or shipping business. They only produce labels and do not interfere with other printers attached to your computer.
- **Dot-matrix (impact) printers** produce characters by slamming a group of wires (dots) from a rectangular grid onto a ribbon and then to paper. Although dot-matrix printers have declined in popularity, you'll still find them behind sales counters to support point-of-sale (POS) computers in some businesses. They are also still used when a computer fills out forms or when multiple copies of the same document are needed simultaneously.
- **Line printers** are generally used on older mainframes. These impact printers print an entire line at a time rather than a character at a time. Line printers are fast but extremely noisy because the "line" is usually a metal chain. They use some form of tractor feed or pin feed. Line printers are rare these days; you may see them in government agencies, colleges, universities, or other venues that require large amounts of paper output, particularly output with multiple copies.

Vestiges of the line printer still remain: the main printer port on a PC is designated **LPT1**, which stands for *line print terminal 1*. It is doubtful that many PCs were ever connected to a true line printer, but this big machine terminology stays with us.

- **Thermal-wax transfer printers** exist in two basic designs. One uses rolls of plastic film coated with colored wax, which is melted onto the page one primary color at a time. A second type, known as phase change, melts wax stored in individual colored sticks and sprays the molten, colored wax onto the page. These printers generally produce high-quality color output, but they are also relatively slow. In addition, these printers frequently require special paper, which adds to the cost of the printed output. Thermal-wax transfer and dye sublimation printers are used in many graphics applications when high-quality, color printed output is required.
- **Dye sublimation** (sometimes shortened to *dye sub*) printers have a design that takes the concept of atomizing waxy colors onto paper a step further. Dye sub printers don't just melt pigments and spray them onto the paper, they vaporize them. Colored gas penetrates the surface of the paper to create an image on the page. Dye sub printers produce high-quality output. Moreover, they can mix and blend colors to produce output at near-photographic quality.

High-speed copiers, printers, and most other printing devices found in a printing shop are now connected to a network, which allows the device to receive materials electronically from any computer connected to the network. The operator of these printing devices schedules printing in accordance with the instructions submitted electronically with the materials.

## Printer Connections

Most printers today come standard with a USB port. However, wireless printing provides freedom for computer users and allows printing from handheld devices such as tablets and smartphones. You can print from anywhere in your home, office, or around the world.

Many printers have a direct network connection option that lets you place the printer on a local area network (LAN), where it can be shared by all the computers attached to the LAN. If a particular printer doesn't include a networked option, you can purchase a network printer interface from a third party. These interfaces have one or more network ports plus one or more printer ports. You connect the network on one side and plug in the printer on the other.

It is generally more efficient to use a direct network-attached printer rather than a printer attached to a computer and configured for sharing on the network. Using a printer attached to a computer can be a drain on the computer's resources when others are using the printer, and a network interface is always on, making the printer always available to network users.

## Installing Printers

OSs provide one or more ways to install printers because printing is vital to outputting documents from word processors, spreadsheets, graphics programs, and other software. In the following sections, you learn how to install a printer in the OSs that are the focus of this book.

**Installing Windows Printers** In Windows, many printers can be installed by connecting them to the computer and then letting PnP initiate the installation, as discussed earlier in this chapter. Another option is to connect the printer and use the Add a device wizard, which was also discussed earlier. However, if an installation DVD/CD-ROM comes with the printer, the best approach is to insert the DVD/CD-ROM and follow the instructions. You should not connect the printer until you are instructed to do so. Finally, if you need to perform a manual installation or initiate automatic detection and setup of a new printer, you can use the Add a printer option in Control Panel, as shown in Figure 6-8. Windows will attempt to find a printer connected to your computer or on the network. If no printer is detected, you will be prompted to install one manually.

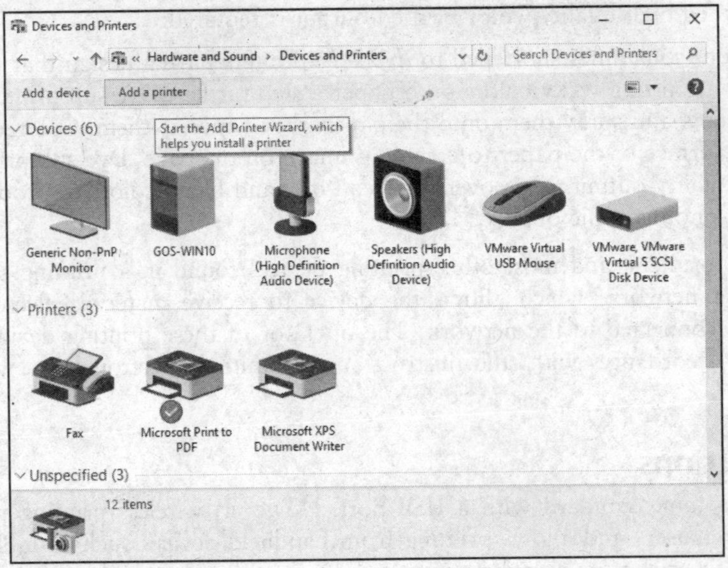


**Figure 6-8** Add a printer option in Windows 10

**Installing UNIX/Linux Printers** When a **print job** is sent from an application, a **print spooler** accepts the job and stores it in a **print queue**, a temporary file used to store jobs until they can be sent to the printer. When the printer is ready, the print spooler sends the job from the queue to the printer. The most common Linux printing system is the Common UNIX Printing System (CUPS). With CUPS, the print spooler is called the *CUPS daemon*, a service that runs on Linux.

Windows also uses a print queue, but users do not have to configure the print queue on a Windows system when installing a new printer.

Older Linux distributions might use the Line Printer Daemon (LPD) printing system. LPD works in a similar manner to CUPS, but CUPS is used in more contemporary distributions and has more features than LPD.

Most of the CUPS configuration files are in /etc/cups. For example, the configuration file for the CUPS daemon is /etc/cups/cupsd.conf, and installed printer configurations are found in /etc/cups/printers.conf. If you have a printer that is directly connected to the computer, the CUPS daemon will usually detect and install it automatically, placing an entry in the printers.conf file. For printers that are not detected, or for network printers, you can edit the printers.conf file directly, but it is better to run the Printers tool in Fedora Linux, as shown in Figure 6-9. The figure shows a network-attached HP LaserJet printer. To access the Printers tool, click Activities, Show Applications, Settings, and then double-click Printers. To add a new printer, click the plus sign on the lower-left side of the Printers tool, or if no printers are currently installed, click the Add New Printer button. Another option is to use the CUPS Web administration tool by opening a Web browser to *http://localhost:631*.

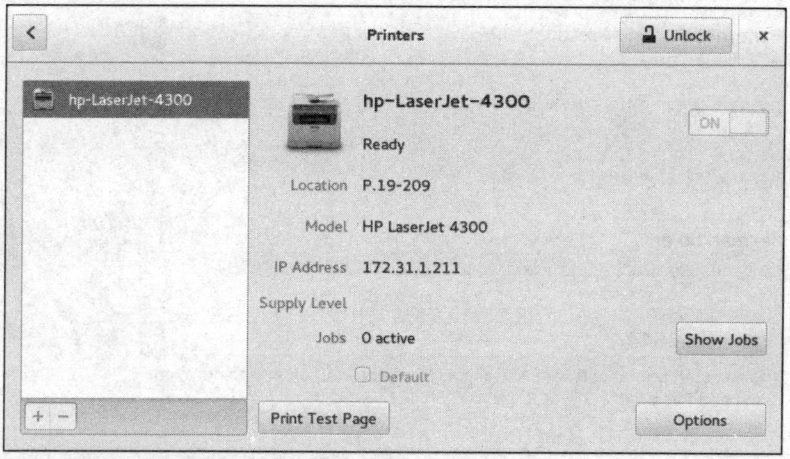


**Figure 6-9** Adding a printer in Linux

*Source: Linux*

A printer connected to one computer can be used to print jobs from another computer. Every computer that wants to use a printer, whether remotely or locally, must first create a print queue for that printer. If one computer has the printer connected and three other Linux computers want to use the printer, a print queue for that printer must be created on all four computers. When a print job is submitted, it is queued in the local print queue. From there, it is submitted to the print queue of the computer to which the printer is connected, and then it spools to the printer.

**Installing Mac OS X Printers** In Mac OS X, most printer drivers are already installed when you install the OS. If not, make sure that the printer you buy has a DVD/CD-ROM to install the new printer driver. To set up a printer, use the Printers & Scanners utility in System Preferences and click the plus sign to add the new printer.

Depending on the setup of your computer, you can add or configure the following types of printers (see Figure 6-10).

- Default
- IP
- Windows

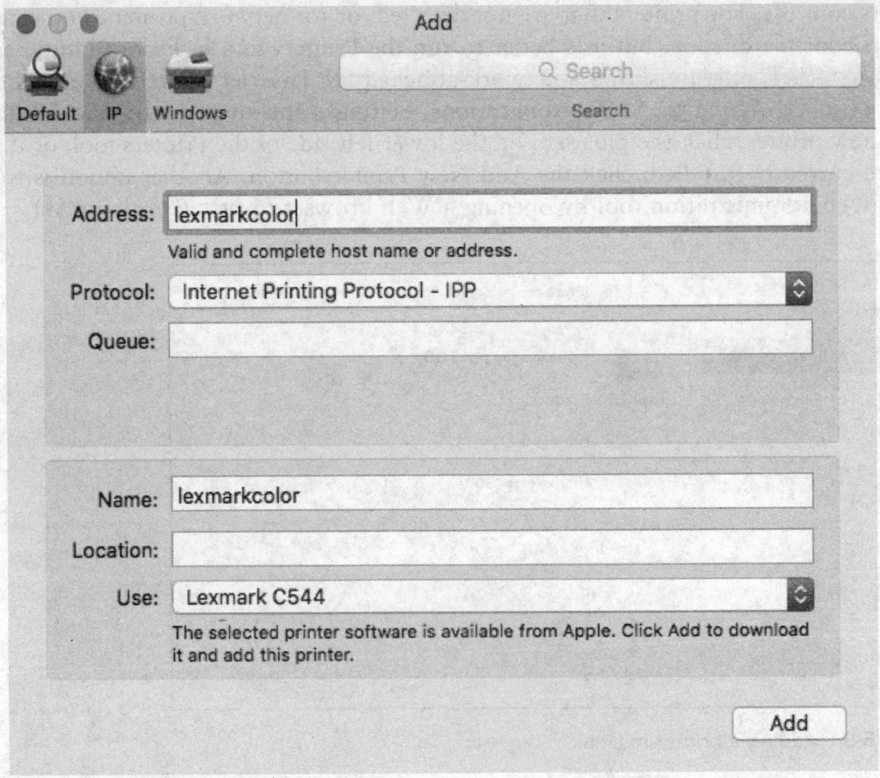


**Figure 6-10** Adding a printer in Mac OS X

*Source: Mac OS X*

Printers listed under Default are those that OS X detects on your local network. Select a listed printer to have OS X install the printer driver. An IP printer is a **network-attached printer** that uses the Internet Printing Protocol (IPP). If OS X doesn't automatically detect a network printer, click IP, and then type the IP address or name of the printer. If Mac OS X finds the printer on the network, click Add to install the necessary driver. The Windows option is for connecting to a shared printer on a Windows computer. If your Mac is on a network that includes Windows computers that are sharing printers, you can use this option to access those printers.

# Display Adapters

Once wildly diverse in design and features, display adapters today have reached a common ground across OSs and hardware platforms. The general industry acceptance of the **Peripheral Component Interconnect** (**PCI**) bus, then the **Accelerated Graphics Port** (**AGP**) bus, and finally the **Peripheral Component Interconnect Express** (**PCIe**) bus standard, has enabled adapter manufacturers to supply one hardware product or a line of hardware products to a variety of hardware platforms. The PCIe bus enables high-performance graphics capabilities and is the current standard for most types of add-on cards, such as display adapters and disk controllers.

## Basic Display Adapter Technology

If you are using a PC with a monitor, you have a display adapter card already installed in your computer. The display adapter is part of a standard computer package. No matter what computer platform you are using, the basic display consists of a number of pixels horizontally and a number of pixels vertically. A **pixel**, remember, is a picture element—actually a small dot of light—that represents one small portion of your overall screen display.

In general, as you display more pixels on the screen, you'll need a larger monitor to comfortably read the displayed data. For a given size of screen, higher-resolution displays can present more data at a time, but this data is presented in a smaller format. Most monitors today offer an optimal resolution setting that you should use. However, most OSs allow you to change the resolution if you want.

Current OSs support devices with the full range of resolution, so the major considerations in choosing an adapter are its resolution capabilities, the amount of memory included with the adapter, the type of video processor, and cost. More memory on the adapter generally means faster performance when rendering screen images; also, when it comes to processors, display adapters may have their own CPU or accelerator to speed things up. As noted previously, you should also consider what kind of monitor you need as you decide on the screen resolution.

Another aspect of screen resolution isn't often discussed: the density of the displayed image, or bit density. A resolution of 1024×768 simply means that images are displayed with 1024 dots of light from left to right and 768 dots of light from top to bottom. However, there is a third consideration to the display, the bit density—the number of dots of light that can be crammed into an inch of display. When you consider graphics programs such as Photoshop or CorelDRAW, or choose a digital camera or other image source, this aspect of resolution becomes important.

These dots are referred to in terms of **dots per inch (dpi)** for printers and **pixels per inch (ppi)** for monitors. These two terms have been used interchangeably, but they are specific to the device you are using.

TIP

When you view graphics on your computer monitor, its bit density will be less than that of your printer. Your printer may be able to reproduce 600, 1200, 1440, or 2880 dpi, or more for some applications. It is important to know this third dimension when you specify printers, plotters, scanners, digital cameras, video editing software, and graphics programs. Print resolution, for example, may be more precise than the resolution of the monitor. The printer may show imperfections that the monitor does not display.

Standard video adapters have color depth capabilities that depend on the OS, software drivers, and video adapter memory. They range from 16 colors at the very low end to 64-bit color. Most computers are set to run at 24-bit or 32-bit color.

Larger monitors are also the norm. For example, a 19-inch display or larger is now common. With a 19-inch monitor, you can routinely set a resolution of 1280×1024 and still see everything you need to see.

**Digital Visual Interface** (DVI) was developed as a high-quality visual standard for flat-panel LCD displays and digital projectors. A resolution of 1920×1200 is the standard for a single cable, and a dual cable can display 3840×2400 at 33 Hz. DVI is mostly compatible with the **High-Definition Multimedia Interface** (HDMI), which is a way to connect digital audio/video devices in televisions, but it is also a popular way to connect devices and computers. **DisplayPort** is a digital interface standard that is projected to replace DVI and HDMI for computers. Both DVI and HDMI signals will run over the DisplayPort interface.

## Installing Display Adapters

There are good reasons for upgrading display hardware. Changes in technology, software, and our personal needs can all require upgrades. Another reason for upgrading or adding a display adapter is to take advantage of multiple monitors. Most OSs support two, three, four, or even more monitors, and you can buy a single display adapter that has up to four outputs to connect multiple monitors. Figure 6-11 shows the Advanced Display Settings control panel in Windows 10 on a system with four monitors.

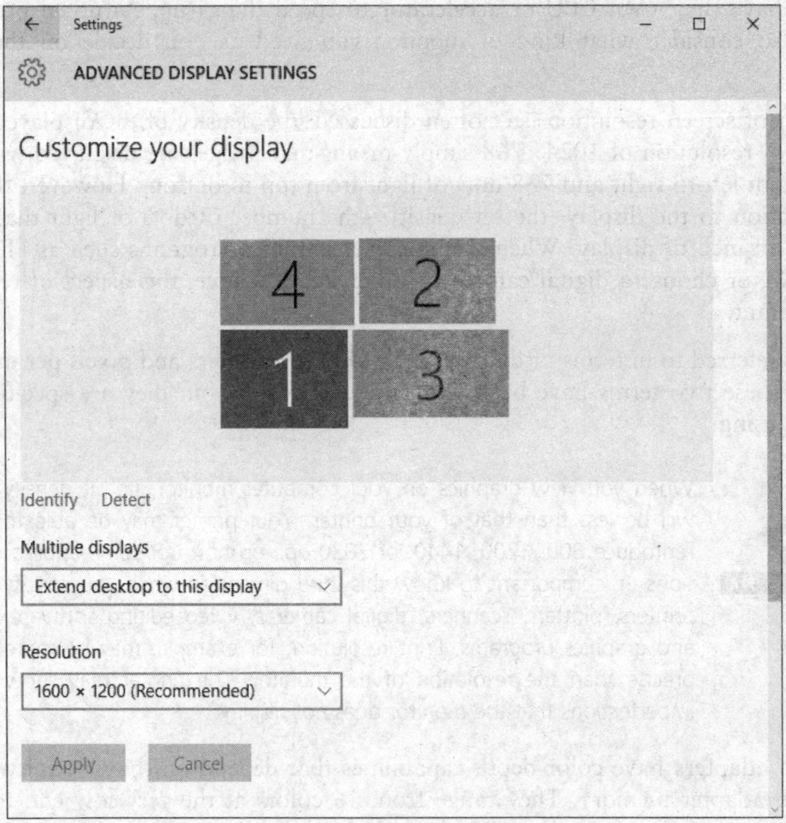


**Figure 6-11** Advanced Display Settings with four monitors

By far, the majority of display adapters are supplied as cards that plug into the PCIe slot on the motherboard. The PCIe bus is the most common expansion bus standard among computer hardware manufacturers, including Intel-based computers, Macintosh computers, and workstations designed for UNIX, Oracle, and other systems. As with printers and other hardware, display adapters are installed in two phases: hardware and software.

Installing any display adapter card is similar to installing circuit boards, as detailed in the last section of this chapter. Thanks to the industry's adoption of the PCIe bus standard and similarities among computer case designs, the installation procedure should be the same across platforms.

### Sound Cards

High-quality sound output and even high-quality recording capabilities have become more important to a broader range of computer users. Businesses use sound as part of documentation or training, sales presentations, and even for music and motion video productions.

The sound card comes preinstalled, and the OS includes integral support for sound input and output on newer computers. However, drivers for individual pieces of sound hardware must be installed, as described earlier in the chapter.

Sound devices are of two general types: hardware integrated with the motherboard and bus cards, which are installed into a bus slot in the same way as a display adapter (see the last section of this chapter). Increasingly you will see sound cards built into the motherboard. This approach provides the easiest installation because the hardware is always there, and all you might need to do is install or configure drivers. The downside to motherboard sound hardware, as with built-in disk controllers, video adapters, and other devices, is that it may be harder to update or change the hardware.

### Other Output Devices

Today's computer marketplace offers so many output options that it would be impossible to cover them all here. Digital video, for example, is a popular consumer and professional feature in computers. Adapter cards are available that let you capture and output digital video to a camera or DVR, and are coupled with capable, low-cost video editing software to help you use them.

Enhanced sound output is also now reasonably priced. Multiport sound cards are available that permit a computer to serve as a fully digital, multichannel recorder for sound studio applications.

As you interact with a variety of computer systems and read specifications for products from a variety of industries, be aware of what hardware and software may be driving the features you are using or reading about. Also, be aware that specialty software is probably required to make everything work properly.

The next section outlines the general steps for installing all types of cards.

## Installing Circuit Boards

Today's computer hardware is pretty rugged. Still, perhaps the biggest enemy of the devices supplied on circuit boards or cards is static electricity—high-voltage, low-current charges that can exist between any two devices, including human bodies. Static discharges are obvious when the voltage is great enough to cause a spark to jump between objects, or from an object to your finger. However, you can damage delicate computer parts with voltages below this sparking level.

To avoid damage to circuit boards during installation, follow these simple guidelines:

- Leave the card inside its protective cover until you are ready to install it.
- Disconnect all power to the computer.
- Prepare the computer by removing the case and any slot covers for the slots you will use.
- Touch a grounded part of the computer to discharge any static. The computer case is a good choice. Then, without removing your hand from the computer, open the bag and remove the card you are about to install. Once you have the card in your hands, you can stop touching the case.

Electrostatic discharge (ESD) straps can be used to prevent damage to your computer and cards. An ESD strap usually consists of a wrist strap with a grounding cord to clip to the computer's metal frame.

- Insert the card carefully into the chosen slot and press it firmly into place. It is helpful to wiggle the card into position, pressing first one end, then the other, until it is firmly seated. You'll quickly get the hang of it as you work with more cards. Just remember that the card itself is quite rugged. Except for static discharge, it isn't likely that you'll hurt a modern computer card during installation.

# Chapter Summary

- An OS handles input and output device communications through device drivers (software) and through hardware such as controller and adapter boards.
- Device drivers are often provided with an OS, but the most up-to-date device drivers come directly from each device manufacturer.
- Manufacturer device and device driver installations are typically performed from a manufacturer's DVD/CD-ROM. Up-to-date drivers can usually be downloaded from the manufacturer's Web site.
- You can install devices and drivers in Windows using PnP, the Add a device wizard, Control Panel options, and Device Manager. Also, plan to configure driver signing to ensure successful and secure device driver installations.
- UNIX/Linux systems use device special files for managing input and output devices.
- For Mac OS X devices, most drivers come with the OS or can be installed from an installation DVD/CD-ROM provided by the device manufacturer.
- Common input devices include mice, keyboards, touch inputs, digital pads, scanners, joysticks, gamepads, digital sound devices, digital picture devices, and a variety of devices that use USB or 1394 technology.

- Printers are common output devices. The most common types are inkjet and laser printers.
- Most OSs include tools for installing printers, such as the Add a device wizard in Windows, Printers in Fedora Linux, and the Printers & Scanners Utility in Mac OS X.
- Besides printers, other examples of common output devices include display adapters and sound cards. Today, many other output devices are available for high-end audio and video processing.

# Key Terms

**3D printer** A printer that uses an additive process to create one layer at a time of a three-dimensional object.

**Accelerated Graphics Port (AGP)** A bus standard that has been replaced by the PCI Express or PCIe standard.

**block special file** In UNIX/Linux, a file used to manage random access devices that handle blocks of data, including DVD/CD-ROM drives, hard disk drives, tape drives, and other storage devices.

**character special file** An I/O management file in UNIX/Linux used to handle byte-by-byte streams of data, such as through a USB connection, including printers and network communications.

**device special file** A file used in UNIX and Linux for managing I/O devices. The file can be one of two types: a *block special file* or a *character special file*.

**digital pad** An alternative input device frequently used by graphic artists and others who need accurate control over drawing and other data input.

**Digital Visual Interface (DVI)** A high-quality visual standard for connecting flat-panel LCD displays and digital projectors.

**DisplayPort** A digital interface standard that is projected to replace DVI and HDMI for computers.

**dot-matrix (impact) printer** An impact character printer that produces characters by arranging a matrix of dots.

**dots per inch (dpi)** Used to measure the resolution of a printer; the number of dots contained in an inch.

**driver signing** A digital signature that Microsoft incorporates into driver and system files as a way to verify the files and to ensure that they are not inappropriately overwritten.

**dye sublimation** A printer technology that produces high-quality color output by creating "sublimated" color mists that penetrate paper to form characters or graphic output.

**gamepad** An input device primarily designed for interaction with games. It includes multiple buttons, wheels, or balls to effect movement of a variety of on-screen objects.

**High-Definition Multimedia Interface (HDMI)** A high-quality visual standard for connecting digital audio and video devices.

**inkjet printer** A printer that forms characters and images by spraying droplets of ink from a nozzle print head onto the paper.

**Institute of Electrical and Electronics Engineers (IEEE)** An international organization of scientists, engineers, technicians, and educators that plays a leading role in developing standards for computers, network cabling, and data transmissions, and for other electronics areas, such as consumer electronics and electrical power.

**interrupt request (IRQ) line** A channel within the computer that is used for communications with the CPU.

**I/O address range** A range of memory addresses used to temporarily store data that is transferred between a computer device or component and the CPU.

**joystick** An input device shaped like a stick that allows for three-dimensional movement of an on-screen cursor or other object, such as a car, airplane, or cartoon character.

**label printers** Special-purpose printers that produce labels only.

**laser printer** A high-quality page printer design that is popular in office and other professional applications.

**line printer** A printer design that prints a full line of character output at a time; it is used for high-speed output requirements.

**LPT1** The primary printer port designation on many desktop computers; also designated as line print terminal 1.

**multifunction printers** Printers that combine printing, scanning, and faxing in one physical device. They can be color inkjet or laser printers.

**named pipe** In UNIX/Linux, a device special file for handling internal communications, such as redirecting file output to a monitor.

**network-attached printer** A printer that has a network interface, is connected to the network, and can be accessed by computers on the network via a host name or IP address.

**optical character recognition (OCR)** Imaging software that scans each character on the page as a distinct image and is able to recognize the character.

**Peripheral Component Interconnect (PCI)** A bus standard that has been replaced by the PCI Express or PCIe standard.

**Peripheral Component Interconnect Express (PCIe)** A bus standard that has enabled adapter manufacturers to supply one hardware product to a variety of hardware platforms.

**pixel** Short for *picture element*; the small dots that make up a computer screen display.

**pixels per inch (ppi)** A unit used to measure the resolution of a display screen; the number of dots (pixels) contained in an inch.

**plotter** Computer hardware that produces high-quality printed output, often in color, by moving ink pens over the surface of paper. Plotters are often used with computer-aided design (CAD) and other graphics applications.

**print job** The data or document sent from an application to a printer and accepted by the print spooler.

**print queue** A temporary file used to store a print job until it can be sent to the printer.

**print spooler** A process that accepts print jobs from applications, stores them in the print queue, and then sends them to the printer when the print device is ready.

**scanner** A digital image created from a hard copy that is then transmitted to the computer.

**tar** A UNIX file archive utility.

**thermal-wax transfer printer** A printer that creates high-quality color printed output by melting colored wax elements and transferring them to the printed page.

## Review Questions

1. The *tar* format for retrieving drivers is used in which of the following?
   a. Windows 10
   b. Windows Server 2012
   c. UNIX/Linux
   d. Windows 7
2. What communicates between the OS and computer devices?
   a. device driver
   b. OS kernel
   c. applications
   d. user interface
3. You need to check a printer parameter for a Linux printer. In what directory should you look for information about the printer configuration?
   a. /dev/printers
   b. /bin/ptr
   c. /usr/printer
   d. /etc/cups
4. When a Linux application prints a document, what accepts the document and stores it in a temporary location before it is sent to the printer?
   a. print device
   b. print spooler
   c. printer service
   d. printer process
5. You support the Windows 10 computers in your organization. A new network interface driver has been issued to plug a security hole. Which tool would you use to quickly install this driver update?
   a. Device Manager
   b. Add Network Interface Wizard
   c. PnP
   d. Registry editor

6. On a Mac OS X computer, what is the name for a 1394 port?
   a. Centronics
   b. FireWire
   c. RS232
   d. USB
7. The Accounting Department needs to purchase a printer that prints receipts for customers. The department also needs three-part carbonless paper. What type of printer would you recommend? (Choose all that apply.)
   a. inkjet printer
   b. laser printer
   c. thermal-wax printer
   d. dot-matrix impact printer
8. Which of the following might be attached to a computer through a USB port? (Choose all that apply.)
   a. mouse
   b. keyboard
   c. printer
   d. video display adapter
9. What type of port is typically used for a scanner?
   a. DVI
   b. AGP
   c. USB
   d. SCSI
10. You installed a new printer in Red Hat Enterprise Linux, but when you print the test page, several characters are not printing correctly. Which of the following should you do first?
    a. Use a different printer cable.
    b. Obtain the latest printer drivers from the printer manufacturer's Web site.
    c. Reconfigure the speed of the printer port.
    d. Return the printer for a refund.
11. Your organization often receives long paper forms to complete and return. Which of the following tools can you use to convert these forms to digital format for faster completion using a word processor? (Choose two.)
    a. SCSI interpreter
    b. scanner
    c. digital picture I/O
    d. OCR software

12. After you install a new sound card and its related device drivers, your monitor frequently pauses or stops working until you reboot. Which of the following is most likely to be the problem?
    a. You need a new monitor.
    b. You need a new display adapter.
    c. There is an I/O address range conflict.
    d. You need to update the driver.
13. You are the computer support person in your small company. One of the employees has installed an off-brand network interface card (NIC) and its drivers on his Windows 10 computer. Now the OS will not run several network-related programs, such as e-mail, a calendar scheduling program, and programs used for remote database access. You suspect a driver problem, so you uninstall the NIC driver and the NIC, and then install a NIC that is known to be Windows 10 compatible. How can you prevent this problem from happening the next time the user installs a device?
    a. Configure driver signing.
    b. Disable Control Panel.
    c. Set up a device block.
    d. Configure a firewall.
14. Which command in Linux enables you to create a device special file?
    a. *tty*
    b. *mknod*
    c. *mkspc*
    d. *devmake*
15. When you create a device special file in Linux, in what folder should it be stored?
    a. /etc
    b. /dev
    c. /sbin
    d. /tmp
16. Where are print jobs stored before being sent to the print device?
    a. spooler
    b. job file
    c. print queue
    d. printer cache
17. What is the most common printing system used in contemporary Linux distributions?
    a. Print Management
    b. IPP
    c. LPD
    d. CUPS

18. A friend was installing a circuit board and damaged it by creating a static discharge at the time of installation. How can this be avoided?
    a. Remove all batteries from circuit boards prior to installation.
    b. Scrape the contacts on the circuit board before you install it.
    c. Turn the computer off, then ground yourself by touching the computer case.
    d. Only purchase self-grounding circuit boards.
19. In UNIX and Linux, which of the following is true about device drivers? (Choose all that apply.)
    a. They must be written in C or Pascal.
    b. They can be loadable modules.
    c. They can be NLMs.
    d. They must never be kernel modules.
20. Which is the most common expansion bus used in personal computers?
    a. PCIe
    b. PCI-X
    c. ISA
    d. AGP

# Hands-On Projects

## Project 6-1: Use the Add a Device Wizard in Windows 10

The Add a device wizard is a valuable tool for installing all types of devices and drivers. In this project, you use the wizard in Windows 10. You need an account that has Administrator privileges; also, your computer should not have newly installed hardware, so that you can manually practice the full range of steps. You do not need to have a connected printer to complete these steps.

1. Start your Windows 10 computer and log on.
2. Right-click **Start**, and click **Control Panel**. Make sure the **Category** View by option is selected. Click **Hardware and Sound**, and then click the **Add a device** link (see Figure 6-12).

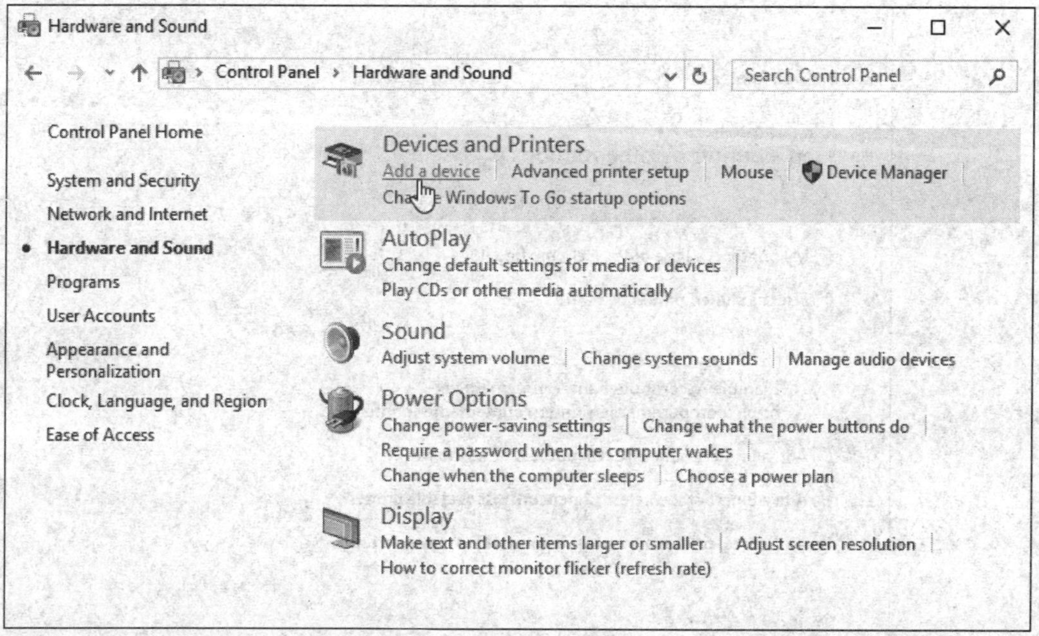


**Figure 6-12** Starting the Add a device wizard

3. Windows looks for a device to add. If Windows can't find one, you must use a different method. For example, to add a printer, click **Advanced printer setup** from the Devices and Printers section of Control Panel. To add other devices, you can try Device Manager. Click **Cancel**.

4. To add a printer, click the **Advanced printer setup** link. Windows looks for a printer to install.

5. When Windows stops looking for the printer, click **The printer that I want isn't listed.**

6. From the Add Printer dialog box (see Figure 6-13), you have several choices, including the option to add a shared, network, or Bluetooth printer.

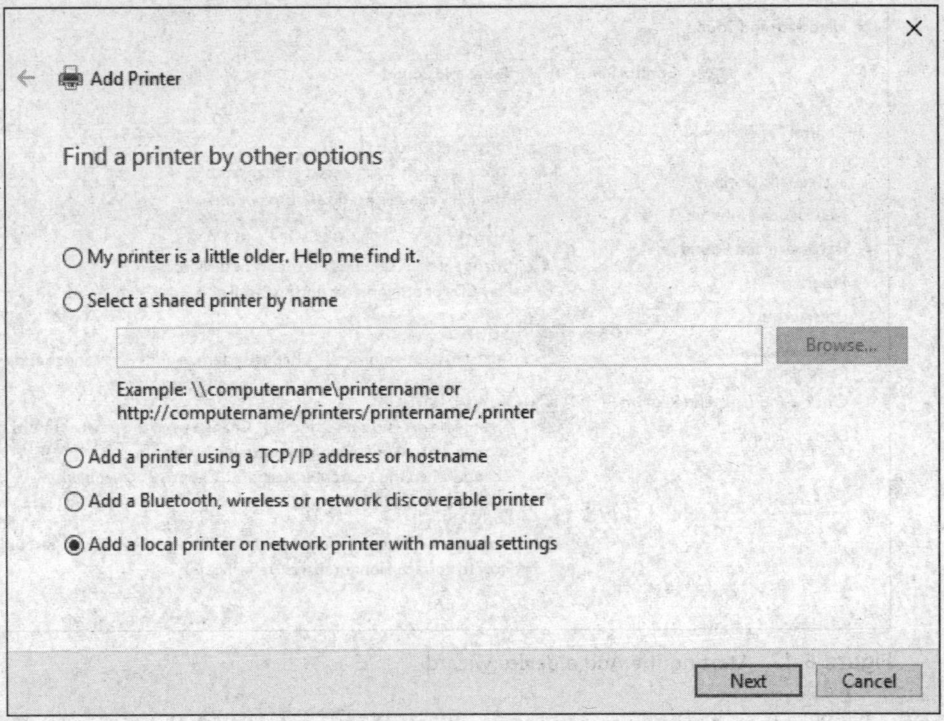


**Figure 6-13** Adding a printer manually

7. Click **Add a local printer or network printer with manual settings.** Click **Next.**
8. Use the default port selection, which is LPT1 (Printer Port), and click **Next.**
9. In the Manufacturer box, click **HP**, and in the Printers box, click **HP Color LaserJet 1600 Class Driver**. On this screen, you also have the option to supply a disk or get the driver via Windows Update. Click **Next.**
10. You can leave the default name for the printer on the next screen. Click **Next.**
11. On the next screen, click **Do not share this printer**, and then click **Next.**
12. Windows installs the printer driver and gives you the option to print a test page. Because you aren't installing an actual printer, click **Finish.**
13. Close all open windows, but stay logged on if you are continuing to the next project.

Enter
HANDS-ON PROJECTS

## Project 6-2: Install a Network Printer in Windows 10

In this project, you install a network-attached printer in Windows 10. Your instructor will have to give you the name or address of the network printer.

1. Log on to your Windows 10 computer, if necessary.
2. Right-click **Start**, and click **Control Panel**. Make sure the **Category** View by option is selected. Click **Hardware and Sound**, and click the **Advanced printer setup** link.

3. Windows looks for a printer. If Windows can't find it, click **The printer that I want isn't listed.**
4. To add a network printer, click **Add a printer using a TCP/IP address or hostname.** Click **Next.**
5. In the next window, type the name or IP address of the printer in the Hostname or IP address text box. Click **Next.**
6. Windows connects to the printer and installs the drivers. In the Printer name text box, type a descriptive name or accept the default name. Click **Next.**
7. In the Printer Sharing window, click **Do not share this printer**, and then click **Next.** (You can share the printer later by accessing the printer properties.)
8. Click **Print a test page** if desired, and click **Finish.**
9. Close all open windows, but stay logged on if you are continuing to the next project.

## Project 6-3: Use Device Manager in Windows 10

In this project, you use Device Manager to view where to install or update a driver in Windows 10. You also use this utility to determine if a device is working properly and to view other information about the device.

1. Log on to your Windows 10 computer, if necessary. Right-click **Start** and click **Device Manager.**
2. Click to expand **Display adapters.**
3. Double-click the specific adapter under Display adapters.
4. Make sure that the **General** tab is displayed. You see the device status, which tells you the device is working properly.
5. Click the **Driver** tab (see Figure 6-14). Notice that you can click the Update Driver button to obtain an updated driver or install a driver if one is not already installed. Also, click the Roll Back Driver button to revert to a previously installed driver if there is a problem with an updated driver. (This button is disabled if you are installing the first driver.) You can click Disable to disable a device without actually installing it, and you can click the Uninstall button to remove a driver.

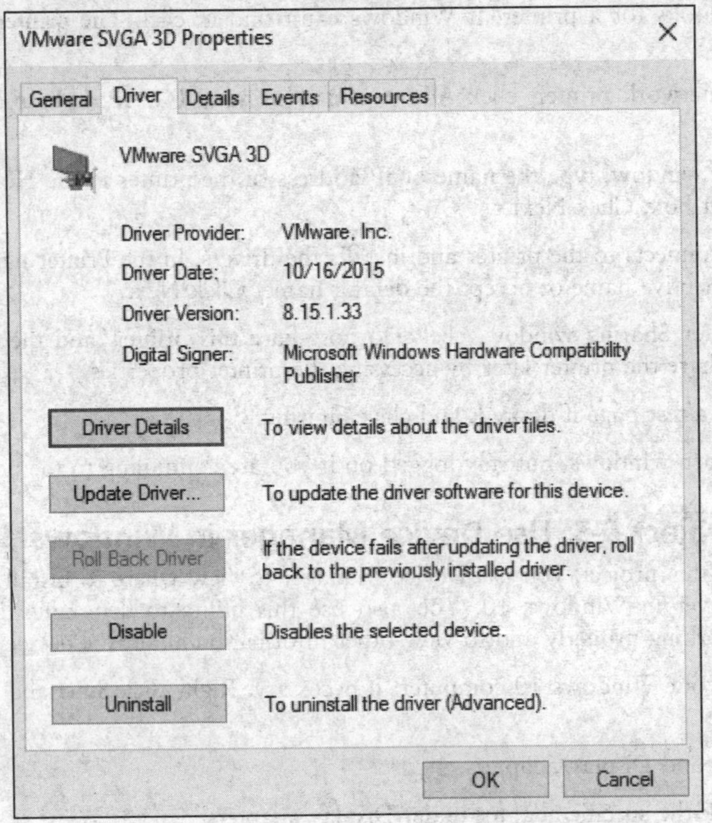


**Figure 6-14** The Driver tab

6. Click the **Driver Details** button.
7. Display drivers usually have a number of associated files. The Driver File Details dialog box lets you view the name and location of the driver files. Click **OK**.
8. Click the **Resources** tab to see the resource settings for the display adapter. Notice there are one or more I/O ranges, one or more memory ranges, and an IRQ setting. A message at the bottom of the dialog box tells you if any conflicts are detected.
9. Click **Cancel** and then close Device Manager.
10. Stay logged on if you are continuing to the next project.

## Project 6-4: Configure Mouse Settings in Windows 10

In this project, you view the settings available for your mouse in Windows 10.

1. Log on to your Windows 10 computer, if necessary.
2. Right-click **Start**, and click **Control Panel**. Click the selection arrow next to **View by** and click **Small icons**.

3. Click **Mouse** to open the Mouse Properties window (see Figure 6-15). Review the options available for changing the behavior of the mouse.

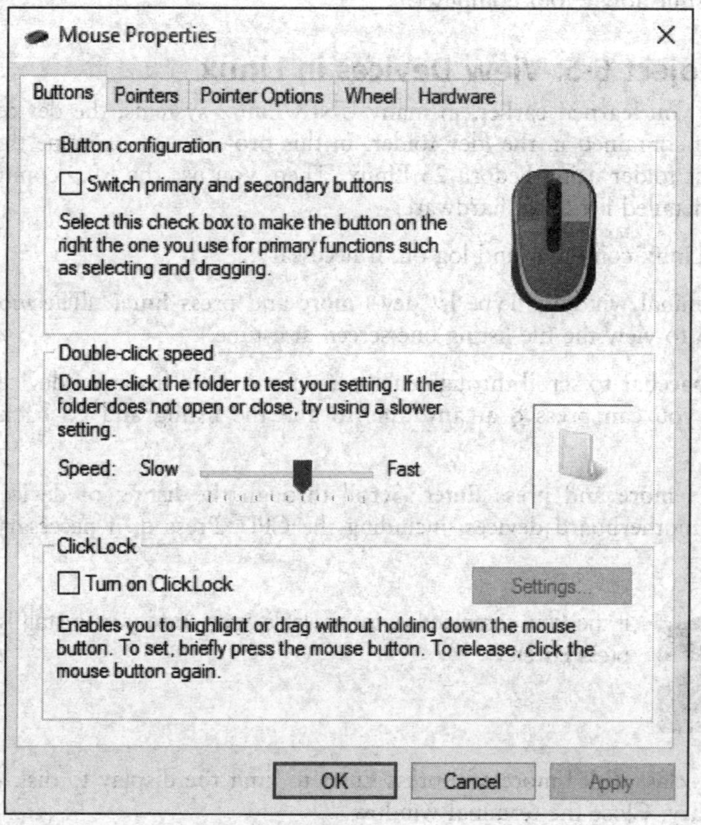


**Figure 6-15** Mouse Properties window

4. Click the **Pointers** tab. Click the selection arrow under Scheme and click **Windows Inverted (extra large) (system scheme)**. Click **OK**.
5. Move your mouse around the screen to see how it changes when you are inside a window. In Control Panel, click **Mouse** again.
6. Click the **Pointers** tab and select **Windows Default (system scheme)** to set the mouse pointer back to its original settings.
7. Click the **Pointer Options** tab, and review the options available. Click the **Show location of pointer when I press the CTRL key** check box. Click **OK**.
8. Press **Ctrl**. Notice the concentric circles displayed around the mouse pointer, which help you locate the mouse pointer easily. The circles are very helpful when you are using multiple monitors.

9. In Control Panel, click **Mouse** again. Click the remaining tabs to see the other mouse configuration options. Click **Cancel** when you are finished.
10. Log off or shut down your computer.

## Project 6-5: View Devices in Linux

As you learned earlier, in many UNIX/Linux systems, the device special files are contained in the /dev folder. In this project, you examine the contents of that folder using Fedora 23 Linux. Then, you use the *lshw* command to view a detailed listing of hardware.

1. Start your Linux computer and log on, if necessary.
2. Open a terminal window. Type **ls/ dev | more** and press **Enter**. (The *more* command enables you to view the file listing one screen at a time.)
3. Press the **Spacebar** to scroll through each screen and see a listing of device special files. (Note that you can press **q** at any time to exit the listing and go back to the shell prompt.)
4. Type **lshw | more** and press **Enter**. Scroll through the listing of devices. You'll see entries for motherboard devices, including the CPU. Press **q**, if necessary, to exit the listing.

NOTE: If the *lshw* command is not available, type **sudo yum install lshw** and press **Enter**.

5. Type **lshw –class disk | more** and press **Enter** to limit the display to disk devices. Press **q**, if necessary. Close the terminal window.
6. Stay logged on if you are continuing to the next project.

## Project 6-6: Use the Settings Menu in Linux

In Fedora 23 Linux with the GNOME desktop, you can configure devices using the Settings menu. This menu enables you to configure Bluetooth devices, desktop effects, the keyboard, monitor, mouse, and other devices and settings. In this project, you use the Settings menu to review settings for one or more monitors connected to the computer, and to review mouse settings.

1. Log on to your Linux computer, if necessary.
2. Click **Activities**, click **Show Applications**, and then click **Settings**. Notice the many devices and settings that can be configured (see Figure 6-16).

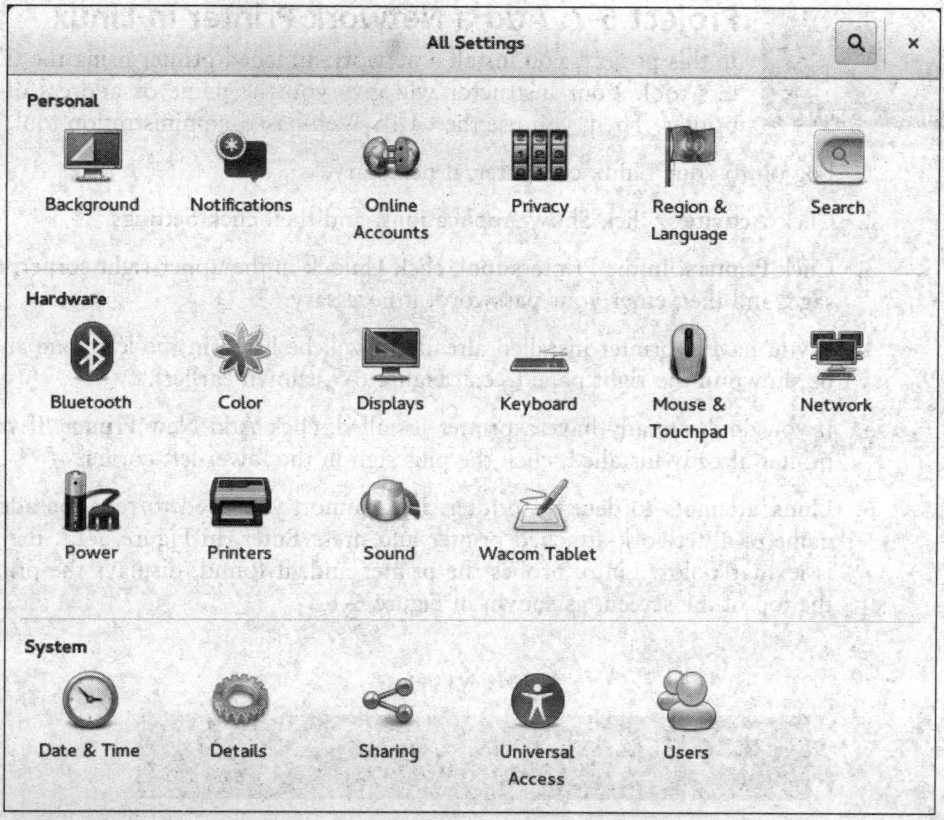


**Figure 6-16** The Linux All Settings window

*Source: Linux*

3. Click **Displays**. Click the monitor icon; it may display a name or it may be labeled Unknown Display. If more than one monitor is attached, you will see a monitor icon for each.

4. You can change the resolution on most monitors, and some allow you to change other settings, such as the refresh rate.

5. Click **Cancel** and then click the arrow in the upper-left corner of the Displays window to return to the All Settings window.

6. Click **Mouse & Touchpad**.

7. Review the available settings and then click the arrow in the upper-left corner of the Mouse & Touchpad window to return to the All Settings window.

8. Click **Sound**. Click each tab to review the available sound options, and then click the arrow in the upper-left corner of the Sound window to return to the All Settings window. Close the All Settings window.

9. Stay logged on if you are continuing to the next project.

## Project 6-7: Add a Network Printer in Linux

In this project, you install a network-attached printer using the GNOME Printers tool. Your instructor will give you the name or address of the network printer. Then, you use the CUPS Web-based administration tool.

1. Log on to your Linux computer, if necessary.
2. Click **Activities**, click **Show Applications**, and then click **Settings**.
3. Click **Printers**. In the Printers tool, click **Unlock** in the upper-right corner, read the message, and then enter your password, if necessary.
4. If you have a printer installed already, it will be listed in the left pane and details will be shown in the right pane (recall Figure 6-9, shown earlier).
5. If you don't already have a printer installed, click **Add New Printer**. If you do have a printer already installed, click the plus sign in the lower-left corner.
6. Linux attempts to detect a printer. If it cannot, you need to type the address or DNS name of a network-attached printer and press **Enter**. In Figure 6-17, the printer name is lexmarkcolor. Linux probes the printer and, if found, displays the printer model at the top of the screen, as shown in Figure 6-17.

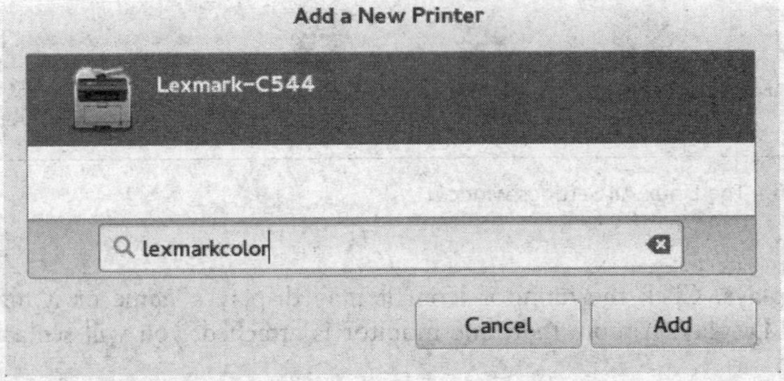


**Figure 6-17** Adding a printer in Linux

*Source: Linux*

7. When the printer is found, click **Add** to install the printer driver. If allowed by the instructor, click **Print Test Page** to verify that the printer is working.
8. Close the Printers window.
9. Open a Web browser. In the address bar, type ***http://localhost:631*** and press **Enter**. The CUPS administration page opens.
10. Click each tab and review the tasks that you can perform. The Administration page is where you add printers and manage printers. Use the Jobs tab to manage print jobs and the Printers tab to view the status of installed printers (see Figure 6-18). Close the Web browser.

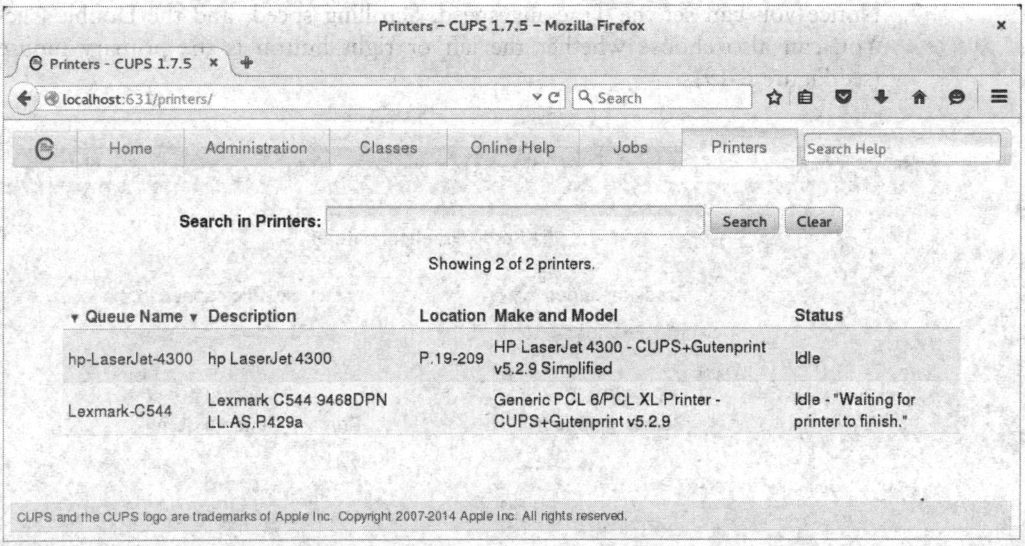


**Figure 6-18** The CUPS Web-based administration page

*Source: Linux*

11. One of the command-line tools for managing CUPS is *lpstat*. Open a terminal window, type **lpstat –p**, and then press **Enter** to see the status of your printers. Type **lpstat –v** and press **Enter** to see the printers and their attached devices. In the case of network printers, you will see the IP address of the printer. Type **man lpstat** and press **Enter** to view the manual pages for *lpstat*. Press **q** after looking at the manual pages.
12. Close the terminal window.
13. Log off or shut down your computer.

## Project 6-8: Use System Preferences in Mac OS X

In this project, you learn how to use the System Preferences tool in Mac OS X and see where to configure the keyboard and mouse. You will need to have a mouse plugged into your computer, and the account you use must have Administrator privileges.

1. Start your Mac computer and log on, if necessary.
2. Click the **Apple** icon and then click **System Preferences**.
3. Click **Keyboard** in the System Preferences window.
4. Ensure that the **Keyboard** tab is selected.
5. Notice that you can set the Key Repeat Rate and Delay Until Repeat parameters.
6. Click the **Back** arrow at the top of the Keyboard window to return to System Preferences. Click **Mouse**.

7. Notice you can set the Tracking speed, Scrolling speed, and the Double-Click speed. You can also choose whether the left or right button is the primary mouse button (see Figure 6-19).

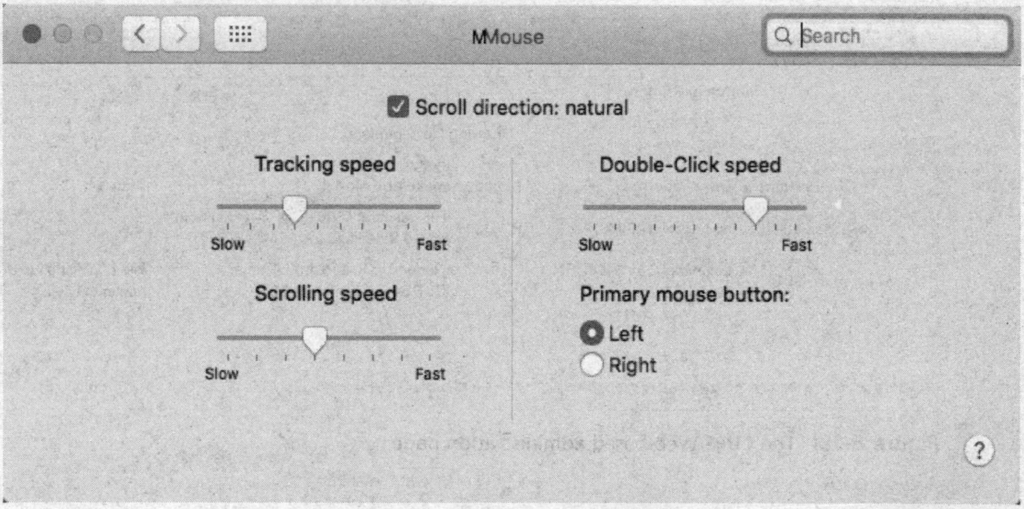


**Figure 6-19** Configuring mouse settings in Mac OS X

*Source: Mac OS X*

8. Click the **Back** arrow at the top of the Mouse window to return to System Preferences.
9. Click **Displays.** Mac OS X will choose the default resolution for the connected monitor. You can configure the resolution by clicking **Scaled** if more than one resolution is available. If you have a compatible AirPlay device, you can select the device for AirPlay Mirroring. AirPlay mirroring allows you to display your Mac screen on an Apple TV device.
10. Click the **Back** arrow at the top of the Display window to return to System Preferences.
11. Leave the System Preferences window open for the next project.

## Project 6-9: Install a Network Printer in Mac OS X

In this project, you install a network-attached printer in Mac OS X. Your instructor will give you the name or address of the network printer.

1. Log on to your Mac and open **System Preferences**, if necessary.
2. Click **Printers & Scanners** in the System Preferences window. The Printers & Scanners dialog box shows currently installed printers (see Figure 6-20).

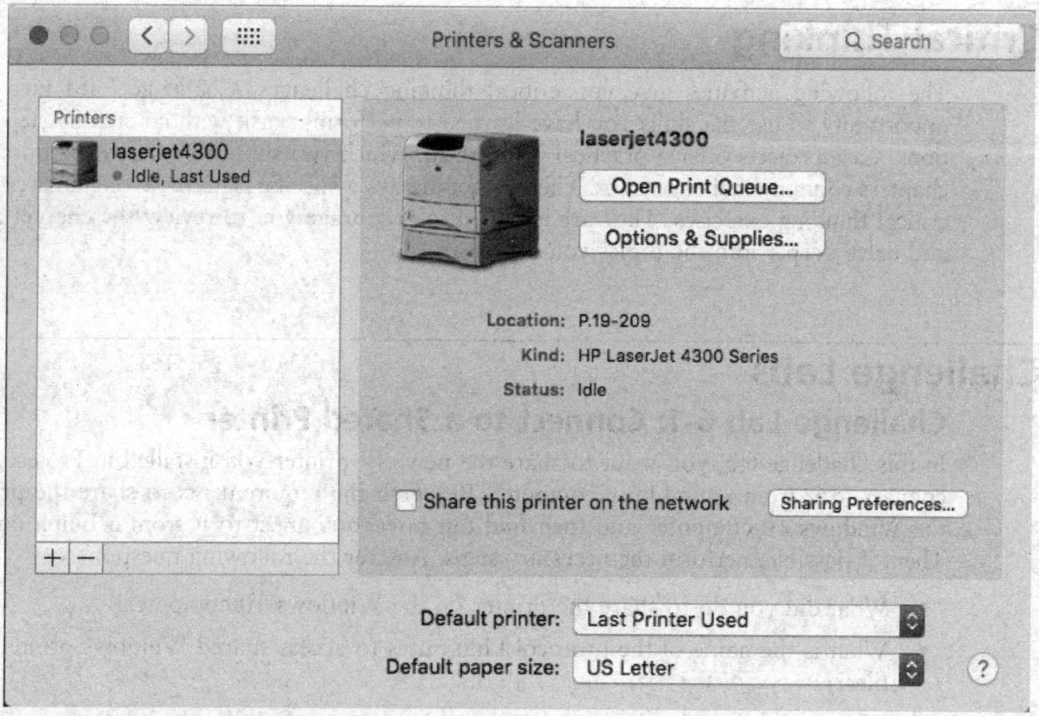


**Figure 6-20** Printers & Scanners dialog box in OS X

*Source: Mac OS X*

3. To add a new printer, click the plus sign (+) in the Printers & Scanners window.
4. You see the Add window. To add a printer already detected by OS X, select it from the list of printers and click the **Add** button. However, for a network printer that is not detected, click **IP**.
5. In the Address text box, type the IP address or name of a printer that is connected to the network (see Figure 6-10 earlier).
6. If OS X finds the printer, click **Add** to install the printer driver.
7. On the Printers & Scanners dialog box, click the printer you just installed and click **Open Print Queue**. The print queue shows any current or pending print jobs. Close the print queue.
8. Close the Printers & Scanners dialog box.
9. Log off or shut down the computer.

# Critical Thinking

The following activities give you critical thinking challenges. Challenge Labs give you an opportunity to use the skills you have learned to perform a task without step-by-step instructions. Case projects offer a practical problem for which you supply a written solution. Not all chapters contain Challenge Labs. There is not always a specific right or wrong answer to these critical thinking exercises. They are intended to encourage you to review the chapter material and delve deeper into the topics you have learned.

# Challenge Labs

## Challenge Lab 6-1: Connect to a Shared Printer

In this challenge lab, you want to share the network printer you installed in Project 6-2 and connect to it from your Linux computer. Research the requirements to share the printer on the Windows 10 computer and then find out how to connect to it from a Linux computer. Then, if possible, perform the necessary steps. Answer the following questions:

- What did you do to share the printer on the Windows 10 computer?
- What is the name of the protocol Linux uses to access shared Windows printers and files?
- What steps were required on the Linux computer to find the shared printer and install the printer driver to access the shared printer?

# Case Projects

Hard Rock makes hard candies that are sold worldwide. One of its specialties is fruit-flavored candies, such as papaya, guava, grapefruit, kiwi, orange, banana, and watermelon. Hard Rock employs 328 people and makes extensive use of computers and networks in the business. Users in the business office have Windows 10. The candy kitchen staff all use Mac OS X, while the shipping unit prefers Fedora Linux. The IT unit uses Fedora Linux for its own desktop computing needs and supports eight Windows Server 2012 R2 servers.

## Case Project 6-1: Install Printers

The business office has just received three new laser printers for installation and wants you to train the printer support coordinator to install printers for the Windows 10 computers. The laser printers have network interfaces and are connected to the network. The printers are named Laser1, Laser2, and Laser3. The business office has three rooms with a network-attached printer in each room. Describe the steps required to install the printers in each room.

## Case Project 6-2: Check the Printer Status for Troubleshooting in Fedora 23 Linux

The shipping unit has a Fedora 23 Linux computer to which it has connected three printers for different uses. One is a color laser printer, one is an inkjet printer, and a third is a dot-matrix printer. The shipping unit is having trouble with the laser printer and wants to check its status. What tools might be useful for this purpose in troubleshooting the problem?

## Case Project 6-3: Solve a Driver Problem in Windows 10

A user downloaded and installed a new driver for her video card on her Windows 10 computer. Now, the user complains that the monitor occasionally flickers and goes black for a few seconds. The system has restarted twice. What should be done to solve this problem?

chapter 7

# Using and Configuring Storage Devices

**After reading this chapter and completing the exercises, you will be able to:**

- Describe computer storage
- Configure local disks
- Work with different types of volumes and virtual disks
- Describe cloud storage
- Describe tape drive technologies
- Work with storage management tools

**Configuring storage is usually one of the first tasks you need to perform on a new** computer; this is particularly true of servers. In the past, computer storage was simply a disk controller and one or two hard drives, but advanced storage solutions are now available to provide fault tolerance and high performance. This chapter covers the basics of computer storage, and then explains how to configure local disks. With virtualization becoming such an important part of computer environments, it's no surprise that more OSs support creating and mounting virtual disks. This chapter describes the basic steps to work with virtual disks. A major enhancement to configuring storage in Windows is Storage Spaces, a new storage model.

# An Overview of Computer Storage

One of the main reasons people use computers is to create, receive, and download files and documents of every type. Everything is stored on digital media now—documents, e-mail, music, photographs, videos—and this trend is continuing. In addition, people want instant access to whatever they store. Just about every large Internet company has its own version of cloud storage, from Dropbox to iCloud to OneDrive. Dozens of cloud storage services are competing to store your files, and although these services are convenient and seemingly work by magic, they all start with a computer and some hard drives. The following sections cover some basics of computer storage: what it is, why you need it, and the common methods for accessing storage.

## What Is Storage?

Generally speaking, storage is any digital medium that data can be written to and later retrieved. Technically, this definition includes random access memory (RAM), but the term *computer storage* generally means long-term storage in which data is maintained without a power source. For example, RAM only holds data when it has electrical power—this is referred to as *volatile storage*. Long-term storage maintains data when the power is turned off, and is referred to as *nonvolatile storage*. Long-term storage includes the following types of media:

- USB memory sticks (flash drives)
- Secure Digital (SD) cards and Compact Flash (CF) cards
- CDs and DVDs
- Magnetic tape
- Solid-state drives
- Hard disk drives

This discussion centers on internal computer storage, which is based on hard disk drives (HDDs), although **solid-state drives (SSDs)** are rapidly closing the price and performance gap with HDDs. SSDs are very popular for applications requiring greater speed, smaller size, and lower power requirements. An SSD uses flash memory and the same type of high-speed interfaces (usually SATA or the newer SATA Express) as traditional hard disks. An SSD has no moving parts, requires less power, and is faster and more resistant to shock than an

HDD, but the cost is higher per gigabyte than an HDD. Also, SSDs don't yet have the capacity of HDDs, so discussions of computer storage are mainly about traditional HDD storage. Nonetheless, most of the discussion of HDD storage applies to SSDs as well, and as technology progresses and prices drop, SSDs will continue to replace HDDs in devices that require high speed and smaller sizes.

## Reasons for Storage

Every computer needs some amount of storage, and servers generally require more than client computers because one of the server's main purposes is to store and serve files when they're requested. The following list isn't exhaustive, but it covers most uses of computer storage:

- *Operating system files*—The OS itself requires substantial storage. The files that make up the OS include boot files, the kernel, device drivers, user interface files, and all the files for additional features you can install. Together, they add up to around 20 GB for a typical Windows 10 and Mac OS X installation, and 8 to 10 GB for Windows Server 2012 and Fedora 23, depending on installed options.
- *User applications*—On client computers, user applications often use the most storage space, especially if users are running entire office suites and multimedia applications like photo editing programs.
- *User documents*—User documents might take up the most space if pictures, videos, and audio files are being stored on the computer. If a server is being used to store the files of dozens or hundreds of users, their documents might be the largest use of disk space on servers. Using disk quotas on servers that store user files is a good idea so that a single user can't monopolize disk space—for example, by storing an entire collection of movies on a network server.
- *Virtual memory*—Most OSs use **virtual memory** to supplement physical RAM. Virtual memory is disk space that is used to store the least recently used pages of memory when more physical RAM is needed but not available. For example, if you have five applications open but you haven't used three for several minutes, and then you open another application, the ones that haven't been used recently may be written to virtual memory if there is not enough free physical RAM. In Windows, virtual memory is stored as a file called **pagefile.sys**, which is usually located at the root of the C: drive. In Linux/UNIX OSs, virtual memory is implemented as a **swap partition**, a separate partition on the disk set aside exclusively for virtual memory. The size of virtual memory varies depending on how much RAM is installed, memory use patterns, and other factors, but it is usually 1 GB or larger on modern systems.
- *Log files*—Most OSs maintain log files to which various system components and applications can write when an event occurs. Log files can be used to track down system or security problems. Log files can slowly eat up disk space unless you keep an eye on their size and delete or archive them periodically.
- *Virtual machines*—If a server is a virtualization server, you need plenty of space to store files for virtual hard disks. Because it is so widely used, virtualization is one of the largest uses of disk space on servers.
- *Database storage*—If a server is running one or more databases, disk storage requirements vary depending on the size of the databases. Because databases can grow

dynamically, it's a good idea to store them on a drive separate from the drive where the OS is installed, preferably on a volume that can have its capacity expanded if needed.

When deciding how much disk space you need for a computer, you should take all the preceding uses into account. Remember that certain storage benefits from being on separate disks from the one where the OS is stored. This advice is particularly true of virtual memory, but ideally, the volume on which the OS is stored should be a separate drive from most other storage uses.

## Storage Access Methods

This discussion of storage access methods revolves around where storage is located in relation to the server. There are four broad categories of storage access methods:

- Local storage
- Direct-attached storage (DAS)
- Network-attached storage (NAS)
- Storage area network (SAN)

**Local Storage** Local storage has been around as long as computers, but the interfaces to storage media have improved as speed and capacity requirements have grown. Local storage is the focus of this chapter; disk interface technologies are discussed later in the "Configuring Local Disks" section.

**Local storage** can be defined as storage media with a direct, exclusive connection to the computer's system board through a disk controller. Local storage is almost always inside the computer's case, and is attached to the disk controller via internal cables and powered by the computer's internal power supply. The term *local storage* usually refers to HDDs or SSDs instead of CD/DVDs or other types of media. Local storage provides rapid and exclusive access to storage media through ever-faster bus technologies. The downside of local storage is that only the system where it's installed has direct access to the storage medium. Data on disks can be shared through network file sharing, but the system with the installed storage must fulfill requests for shared data.

**Direct-Attached Storage** **Direct-attached storage (DAS)** is similar to local storage in that it's connected directly to the server using it. In fact, local storage is a type of DAS because DAS includes hard drives mounted inside the server case. However, DAS can also refer to one or more HDDs in an enclosure with its own power supply. In this case, the DAS device is connected to a server through an external bus interface, such as eSATA, SCSI, USB, FireWire, or Fibre Channel.

A DAS device with its own enclosure and power supply can usually be configured as a disk array, such as a RAID configuration (discussed later in the "Types of Volumes" section). Although most DAS devices provide exclusive use to a single computer, some have multiple interfaces so that more than one computer can access the storage medium simultaneously. Most of the related discussion later in this chapter also applies to DAS devices because the computer usually sees an externally attached DAS device as local storage.

The term *DAS* was created to distinguish it from storage connected to a network, such as NAS and SAN.

**Network-Attached Storage** **Network-attached storage** (NAS), sometimes referred to as a **storage appliance**, has an enclosure, a power supply, slots for multiple HDDs, a network interface, and a built-in OS tailored for managing shared storage. An NAS is designed to make access to shared files easy to set up and easy for users to access. Because an NAS is typically dedicated to file sharing, it can be faster than a traditional server in performing this task because a server often shares its computing and networking resources among several duties. An NAS shares files through standard network protocols, such as Server Message Block (SMB), Network File System (NFS), and File Transfer Protocol (FTP). Some NAS devices can also be used as DAS devices because they often have USB, eSATA, or other interfaces that can be attached directly to a computer.

**Storage Area Network** The most complex type of storage is a **storage area network** (SAN), which uses high-speed networking technologies to give servers fast access to large amounts of shared disk storage. To the server OS, the storage a SAN manages appears to be physically attached to the server. However, it's connected to a high-speed network technology and can be shared by multiple servers. The most common network technologies used in SANs are Fibre Channel and iSCSI. These technologies are designed to connect large arrays of hard drive storage that servers can access and share. Client computers access shared data by contacting servers via the usual method, and the servers retrieve the requested data from the SAN devices and pass it along to the client computer. Figure 7-1 shows a SAN using Fibre Channel, in which disk arrays are connected to a Fibre Channel switch and servers are connected to the Fibre Channel network as well as a traditional network. In this arrangement, all servers have access to the storage medium, which can be shared and allocated as needed.

SANs use the concept of a **logical unit number** (LUN) to identify a unit of storage. A LUN is a logical reference point to a unit of storage that could refer to an entire array of disks, a single disk, or just part of a disk. To the server using the SAN, the LUN is easier to work with because the server doesn't have to know how the storage is provided; it only needs to know how much storage is available.

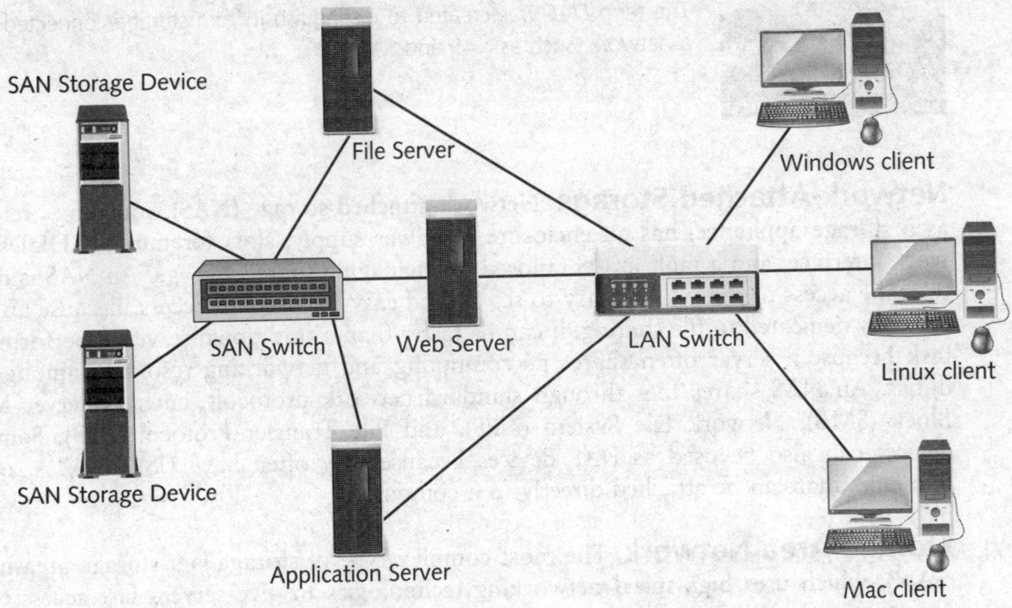


**Figure 7-1** A storage area network

SANs are often used by server clusters so that all cluster members have access to shared storage for the purposes of load balancing and fault tolerance.

# Configuring Local Disks

Configuration of local disks can be divided into two broad categories: physical disk properties and logical properties. Physical disk properties, which must be considered before purchasing disk drives for a server, include disk capacity, physical speed, and the interface for attaching a disk to the system. Logical disk properties include its format and the partitions or volumes created on it. Before you get too far into these properties, however, let's review some disk-storage terms, most of which were introduced in Chapter 4:

- *Disk drive*—A **disk drive** is a physical component with a disk interface connector (such as SATA or SCSI) and a power connector. A mechanical disk drive (usually called an *HDD*) has one or more circular magnetic platters that store the data's actual bits and one or more read/write heads—one for each side of the magnetic platters. The platters spin at high speed, and the read/write heads move from the inside of the platter to the outside to read data on the disk. An SSD has a disk interface and power connector but has flash memory chips instead of magnetic platters, and there are no read/write heads or other moving parts.
- *Volume*—Before an OS can use a disk drive, a volume must be created on the drive. A **volume** is a logical unit of storage that can be formatted with a file system. A disk drive can contain one or more volumes of different sizes. Disk drive space that hasn't been assigned to a volume is said to be unallocated. Volumes can also span two or more

disks in an arrangement called RAID. Volumes, including RAID volumes, are discussed in more detail later in the "Types of Volumes" section.

- *Partition*—This older term means the same thing as *volume*, but is used with basic disks. The term **partition** is still used at times, but in Windows it has largely been replaced by *volume*.
- *Formatting*—Before an OS can use a volume, the volume must be formatted. As you learned in Chapter 4, formatting prepares a disk with a file system that is used to organize and store files. There are different format standards; the format you choose for a disk depends on how the disk will be used. Disk formats were discussed in Chapter 4.

## Disk Capacity and Speed

The disk capacity you need depends entirely on how the disk will be used. Will it be a system disk for storing the OS and related files, a disk for storing documents and other files, a file-sharing disk, a disk storing a database, or maybe one that stores virtual machines? Perhaps you plan to have a combination of uses, but in general, distinct types of data should be kept on separate disks so that you can optimize some of the disk's logical properties for the type of data it will store. Before we talk more about disk capacities, review Table 7-1 for a list of storage capacity units.

**Table 7-1 Storage unit equivalents**

| Storage measurement | Bytes | Base 2 (binary) equivalents |
|---|---|---|
| Kilobyte (KB) | 1,024 | $2^{10}$ |
| Megabyte (MB) | 1,048,576 | $2^{20}$ |
| Gigabyte (GB) | 1,073,741,824 | $2^{30}$ |
| Terabyte (TB) | 1,099,511,627,776 | $2^{40}$ |
| Petabyte (PB) | 1,125,899,906,842,624 | $2^{50}$ |
| Exabyte (EB) | 1,152,921,504,606,846,976 | $2^{60}$ |
| Zettabyte (ZB) | 1,180,591,620,717,411,303,424 | $2^{70}$ |

One byte is 8 bits; bytes are represented by a capital *B*, while bits are represented by a small *b*.

Keep in mind that you might not be basing disk capacity decisions on a single disk because you could be configuring an array of disks in a RAID. HDD capacities are now measured in hundreds of gigabytes, with two, four, and eight terabyte disks being common. (Remember that one terabyte equals 1000 gigabytes.) Disk capacity is fairly inexpensive, and having more than you need is better than having less. Here are some considerations for deciding how much disk capacity to buy and how many disks to use in a server:

- On servers or high-performance workstations, the OS installation should be on a separate disk from the data and applications to get the best performance. An SSD is a good candidate for the OS installation disk.
- Virtual memory should be on its own disk, if possible (pagefile.sys on Windows systems or the swap partition on Linux/UNIX systems). An SSD is also a good candidate for virtual memory. If a separate disk is impractical, at least try to put virtual memory on its own volume.
- Take fault tolerance into account by using a RAID, which combines multiple disks to make a single volume so that data stored on the volume is maintained even if a disk fails. However, overall storage capacity is diminished.

The speed of HDDs is affected by a number of factors. For example, the disk interface technology is an important performance factor, as you will learn in the next section. Other factors include rotation speed and the amount of cache memory installed. The rotation speed of disk platters in HDDs ranges from about 5400 revolutions per minute (rpm) to 15,000 rpm, with speeds of 7200 and 10,000 rpm in between. A server should be outfitted with an HDD that rotates at a minimum of 7200 rpm, but for high-performance applications, look for 10,000 or 15,000 rpm drives.

Even for desktop computers, you should look for HDDs with a rotation speed of 7200 rpm or faster. You can still purchase 5400 rpm HDDs, but they are low-end models that will likely become obsolete in the coming years.

The amount of cache in an HDD allows the drive to buffer read and write data locally, which speeds overall disk access. Cache sizes of 32 and 64 MB are common for server-class drives, but some very fast drives might have as little as 16 MB. The key factor for disk performance is how fast data can be read from and written to the disk—the data rate. When researching disks for performance factors, look for the sustained data rate the manufacturer claims, which tells you how fast the drive can transfer data for an extended period.

## Disk Interface Technologies

The disk interface connects a disk to a computer system, usually with some type of cable. The cable acts as a bus that carries data and commands between the disk and computer. The faster the bus, the faster the system can read from and write to the disk. The most common types of disk interfaces for locally attached disks are SATA, SAS, and SCSI. Each technology has advantages and disadvantages, as you will learn in the following sections.

You might also find a few parallel ATA (PATA) or Integrated Drive Electronics (IDE) drives on the low end and Fibre Channel drives on the high end, but for locally attached drives, the most common by far are SATA, SAS, and SCSI. IDE drives are nearly obsolete, and Fibre Channel drives are most likely to be used in SANs.

**Serial ATA Drives** Serial ATA (SATA) drives have mostly replaced PATA drives and have several advantages over this older technology, including faster transfer times and smaller cable size. Whereas the older PATA interface is limited to about 167 megabytes per second (MB/s), SATA drives boast transfer times of up to 6 gigabits per second (Gb/s; 600 MB/s) and higher. SATA drives are inexpensive, fast, and fairly reliable. They're a good fit both for client computers and lower-end servers. The SATA standard has evolved from SATA 1.0, which supports transfer speeds of 1.5 Gb/s (150 MB/s), to the current SATA 3.2, which supports speeds of up to 16 Gb/s (or 1.6 gigabytes per second, GB/s). However, most readily available devices support SATA 2.0 (3 Gb/s) or SATA 3.0 (6 Gb/s). Even with their high transfer rates, however, SATA drives take a back seat to SCSI and SAS drives in the enterprise server realm.

**SCSI and SAS Drives** **Small computer system interface (SCSI)** drives have been a mainstay in enterprise-class servers for decades, and this drive technology has endured through more than a half-dozen upgrades. The most recent SCSI variation, developed in 2003, is Ultra-640, with up to 640 MB/s transfer rates. SCSI is a parallel technology, like PATA, and has probably reached its performance limits. SCSI, however, has always provided high reliability and enterprise-level command features, such as error recovery and reporting. Its successor is **serial attached SCSI (SAS)**, which maintains the high reliability and advanced commands of SCSI and improves performance, with transfer rates of up to 6 Gb/s and higher speeds under way. SAS enjoys the benefit of having bus compatibility with SATA, so SATA drives can be connected to SAS backplanes. A **backplane** is a connection system that uses a printed circuit board instead of traditional cables to carry signals.

The SAS standard offers higher-end features than SATA drives. SAS drives usually have higher rotation speeds and use higher signaling voltages, which allow their use in server backplanes. Overall, SAS is considered the more enterprise-ready disk interface technology, but enterprise features come with a price—SAS drives are more expensive than SATA drives. As with many other things, disk technologies have a trade-off between performance and reliability versus price.

**Partitioning Methods** Most OSs, including Windows, Mac OS X, and Linux/UNIX, offer two methods for partitioning disks. The most common method, **Master Boot Record (MBR)**, has been around since DOS. MBR partitions support volume sizes of up to 2 TB. MBR-based disks have the advantage of being compatible with most OSs, old and new.

The second and newer method is **GUID Partitioning Table (GPT)**. GPT disks became an option when HDDs larger than 2 TB started becoming common. GPT-partitioned disks support volume sizes of up to 18 exabytes (EB, which is one million terabytes); however, most file systems are only able to support a fraction of that size. For example, Windows file systems currently support volume sizes only up to 256 TB. You can convert an MBR disk to GPT and vice versa, but you must delete existing partitions first, which erases all data, so if you choose to convert, be sure to have a current backup. In addition to larger volume sizes, GPT partitions offer improved reliability in the form of partition table replication (a backup copy of the partition table) and Cyclic Redundancy Check (CRC) protection of the partition table.

GPT partitions contain an area on the disk called the "protective MBR," which is maintained for backward compatibility with disk utilities that work only with MBR disks.

# Types of Volumes

When you create a volume, most OSs have provisions for creating a variety of volume types, from simple single-disk volumes to fault-tolerant multi-disk RAID volumes. **Redundant array of independent disks (RAID)** is a disk configuration that uses space on multiple disks to form a single logical volume. Most RAID configurations offer fault tolerance, and some enhance performance. RAID is commonly configured in one of two ways: by the storage controller in hardware and via the OS storage system in software. Hardware RAID provides better performance by offloading the OS from having to perform the processes involved in RAID, and hardware RAID controllers usually have more options for RAID configurations. Many OSs support at least the three most common configurations: RAID 0, RAID 1, and RAID 5. The following are some of the most common volume types supported by most OSs.

- *Simple volume*—A **simple volume** resides on a single disk. Simple volumes can be extended (made larger) using the OS's disk utilities if unallocated space is available on the disk. A simple volume can also be shrunk. On some OSs, a simple volume can be extended on the same disk or to multiple disks as long as they have unallocated space.
- *Spanned volume*—A **spanned volume** extends across two or more physical disks. For example, a simple volume that has been extended to a second disk is a spanned volume. When the first disk has filled up, subsequent disks are used to store data. Spanned volumes don't offer fault tolerance; if any disk fails, data on all disks is lost. There's also no performance advantage in using a spanned volume compared to a volume that resides on a single disk.
- *RAID 0 volume*—A **RAID 0 volume** extends across two or more disks, but data is written to all disks in the volume equally. For example, if a 10 MB file is written to a RAID 0 volume with two disks, 5 MB is written to each disk. A RAID 0 volume must use at least two disks but can use many more than that; for example, Windows supports RAID 0 volumes with up to 32 disks. RAID 0 volumes don't offer fault tolerance, but they do have a read and write performance advantage over spanned and simple volumes because multiple disks can be accessed simultaneously to read and write files. A RAID 0 volume is also referred to as a *striped volume* because data is said to be striped across each disk. The Windows system and boot volumes can't be on a striped volume. Figure 7-2 shows a RAID 0 volume with two files, F1 and F2. F1 has two parts, F1-a and F1-b, striped across the two disks, and F2 has four parts that are striped across the two disks.

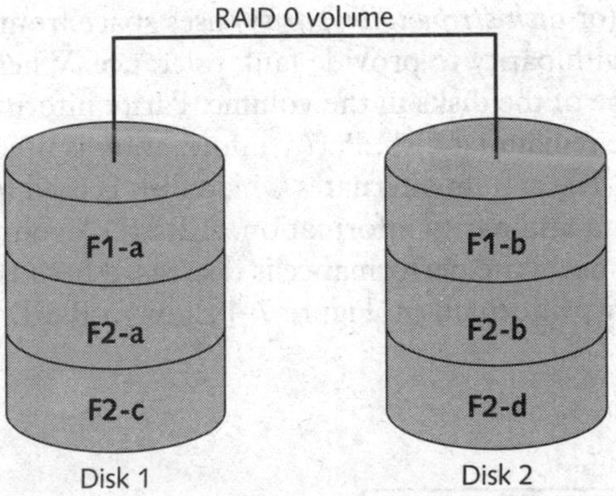


**Figure 7-2** A RAID 0 volume

- *RAID 1 volume*—A **RAID 1 volume** (or *mirrored volume*) uses space from two disks and provides fault tolerance. Data written to one disk is duplicated, or mirrored, to the second disk. If one disk fails, the other disk has a good copy of the data, and the system can continue to operate until the failed disk is replaced. The space used on both disks in a mirrored volume is the same. Mirrored volumes might have a disk read performance advantage, but they don't have a disk write performance advantage. Figure 7-3 shows a RAID 1 volume with the same two files; however, instead of being spread across the disks, they are duplicated so that the contents of disk 1 are also on disk 2.

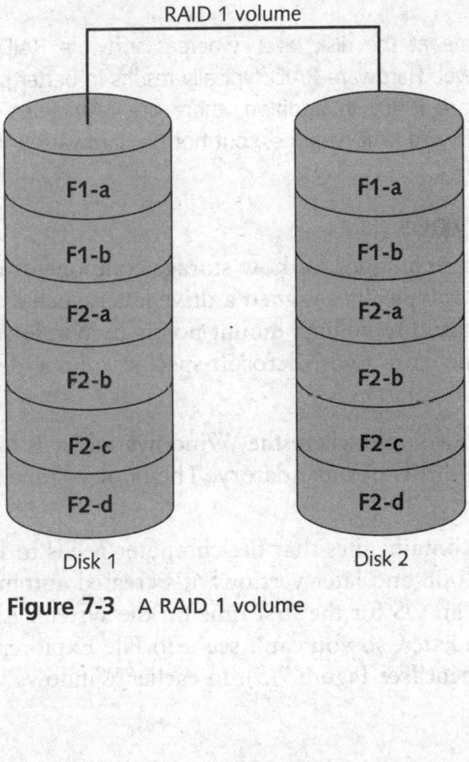


**Figure 7-3** A RAID 1 volume

- *RAID 5 volume*—A **RAID 5 volume** (or *disk stripe with parity*) uses space from three or more disks and uses disk striping with parity to provide fault tolerance. When data is written, it's striped across all but one of the disks in the volume. Parity information derived from the data is written to the remaining disk. Parity information is used to re-create lost data after a disk failure. The system alternates which disk is used for parity information, so each disk has both data and parity information. A RAID 5 volume provides increased read performance, but write performance is decreased because the volume has to calculate and write parity information. Figure 7-4 shows a RAID 5 volume.

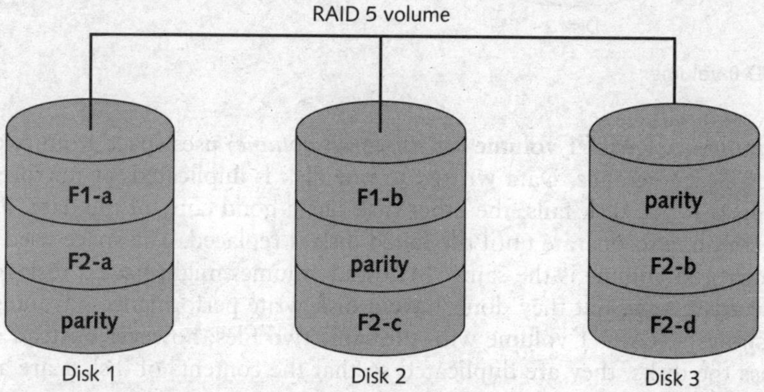


**Figure 7-4** A RAID 5 volume

Hardware RAID is done at the disk level, whereas software RAID is done at the volume level. Hardware RAID typically results in better performance than software RAID. In addition, there are restrictions on placing OS files on software RAID volumes, but not on hardware RAID.

## Windows Volumes and Disk Types

Different OSs use different terminology and techniques for how storage components are identified. On a Windows system, each volume is typically assigned a drive letter, such as C or D, although you learned earlier that you can also use volume mount points in Windows so you can access a volume with a drive letter. There are two Microsoft-specific volume definitions you need to know:

- *Boot volume*—The **boot volume** is the volume where the \Windows folder is located. The usual location is the C drive, but this is not mandatory. The boot volume is also called the *boot partition*.
- *System volume*—The **system volume** contains files that the computer needs to find and load the Windows OS. In Windows 2008 and later versions, it's created automatically during installation if you're installing an OS for the first time on the system. Also, the system volume is not assigned a drive letter, so you can't see it in File Explorer. You can, however, see it in Disk Management (see Figure 7-5). In earlier Windows versions,

the system volume was usually the C drive. In Figure 7-5, it's labeled *Active*, which tells the BIOS to try booting from that volume. The system volume is also called the *system partition*.

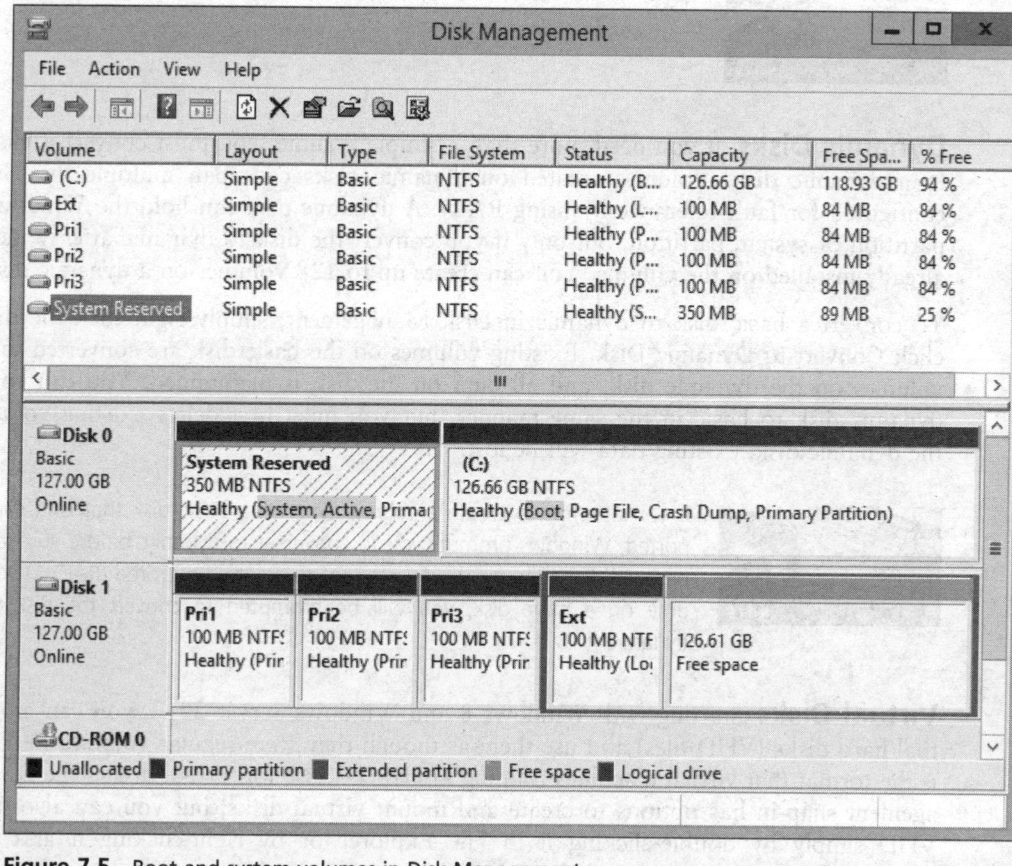


**Figure 7-5** Boot and system volumes in Disk Management

In Windows, the types of volumes you can create on a disk depend on how the disk is categorized. Windows defines two disk categories, which are discussed next: basic and dynamic.

**Basic Disks** As the name implies, a **basic disk** can accommodate only simple volumes. The volumes on a basic disk are also called *partitions*. The Windows Disk Management tool uses both terms in its interface, but the term *partition* is more accurate and distinguishes it from a volume created on a dynamic disk. When Windows detects a new disk drive, it's initialized as a basic disk by default.

As discussed in Chapter 4, you can create a maximum of four partitions on a basic disk. The first three you create with Disk Management are primary partitions. A **primary partition** can be an active partition and can be the Windows system volume. It's usually assigned a drive letter but doesn't have to be, as with the Windows system partition. If you create a fourth partition, it's called an **extended partition**, which can be divided into one or more logical drives, each assigned a drive letter. A logical drive on an extended partition can hold the boot volume, but it can't hold the system volume because it can't be marked as active.

> **NOTE** The Windows boot and system volumes can only be created on basic disks.

**Dynamic Disks** If you need more than a simple volume, you must convert a basic disk to a **dynamic disk**. Volumes created on dynamic disks can span multiple disks and be configured for fault tolerance by using RAID. A dynamic disk can hold the Windows boot partition or system partition, but only if you convert the disk to dynamic after Windows is already installed on the volume. You can create up to 128 volumes on a dynamic disk.

To convert a basic disk to dynamic in Disk Management, simply right-click the disk and click Convert to Dynamic Disk. Existing volumes on the basic disk are converted to simple volumes on the dynamic disk, and all data on the disk is maintained. You can convert a dynamic disk to basic in the same manner, but you must first delete existing volumes on the dynamic disk; existing data will be lost.

> **NOTE** If you attempt to create a volume type on a basic disk that isn't supported, Windows prompts you to convert it to dynamic before you can proceed. For example, if you attempt to create a mirrored (RAID 1) volume on a basic disk, you will be prompted to convert the disk to dynamic first.

**Virtual Disks** Starting with Windows 8 and Windows Server 2012, you can mount virtual hard disks (VHD files) and use them as though they were regular volumes. A **VHD file** is the format that virtual machines running in Hyper-V use for virtual disks. The Disk Management snap-in has options to create and mount virtual disks, but you can also mount a VHD simply by double-clicking it in File Explorer or by right-clicking it and clicking Mount.

You might want to use virtual disks instead of physical volumes to store data. Virtual disks have the advantage of being very portable. Because a virtual disk is just a file on an existing physical volume, you can copy it to any location quickly and easily for the purposes of backing up data on the virtual disk or allowing it to be used by another computer.

> **NOTE** Virtual disks can have a .vhd or .vhdx extension. Windows Server 2012/R2 can mount either file type. The VHDX format, introduced in Windows Server 2012 Hyper-V, has more capacity (up to 64 TB), protection from corruption, and performance improvements than the VHD format.

**Storage Spaces** Storage Spaces, a new feature starting with Windows Server 2012, provides flexible provisioning of virtual storage. It uses the flexibility available with virtual disks to create volumes from storage pools. A **storage pool** is a collection of physical disks from which virtual disks and volumes are created and assigned dynamically. Volumes created from storage pools can be simple volumes, striped volumes, or fault-tolerant RAID volumes.

Unlike traditional physical disks and volumes created in Disk Management, Storage Spaces can allocate storage by using thin provisioning. **Thin provisioning** uses dynamically expanding disks so that you can provision a large volume, even if you have the physical storage for a volume only half the size. Later, you can add physical disks, and Storage Spaces expands into the additional storage as needed. If the disk pool becomes full, Windows takes it offline to alert you that you need to add physical storage to the pool.

Storage Spaces uses the concept of **just a bunch of disks (JBOD)**, in which two or more disks are abstracted to appear as a single disk to the OS but aren't arranged in a specific RAID configuration. JBOD gives you more flexibility because you can simply add a physical disk to a storage pool, and existing volumes can grow into the new space as needed. You can even add external disks to a pool via an external bus architecture, such as SAS or eSATA.

Storage Spaces brings storage flexibility to a Windows server for a fraction of the cost of a traditional SAN, which before Storage Spaces was the best way to achieve similar storage features and performance. Storage Spaces offers the following features that are usually found only in traditional SAN-based storage arrays:

- *Disk pooling*—A collection of physical disks viewed as a single storage space from which volumes can be provisioned for the server's use.
- *Data deduplication*—A new feature in Windows Server 2012 that finds data duplicated on a volume multiple times and reduces it to a single instance, thereby reducing space used on the volume. Data deduplication is a role service that can be installed and then enabled on volumes separately.
- *Flexible storage layouts*—Storage Spaces has three storage options, called **storage layouts**: simple space, which can be a simple volume or RAID 0 volume; mirror space, which is the same as a RAID 1 volume; and parity space, which is the same as a RAID 5 volume.
- *Storage tiering*—A new feature in Windows Server 2012 R2, **storage tiering** combines the speed of SSDs with the low cost and high capacity of HDDs. You can add SSDs to a storage pool with HDDs, and Windows keeps the most frequently accessed data on the faster SSD disks and moves less frequently accessed data to HDDs. This scheme improves performance substantially without the expense of moving all storage to costly SSDs.

Storage Spaces is managed in Windows 10 using the Storage Spaces control panel under System and Security (see Figure 7-6). In Windows Server 2012, open Server Manager, click File and Storage Services, and then click Storage Pools. To use Storage Spaces, you need at least one hard disk that is unallocated—in other words, a disk that has not been partitioned.

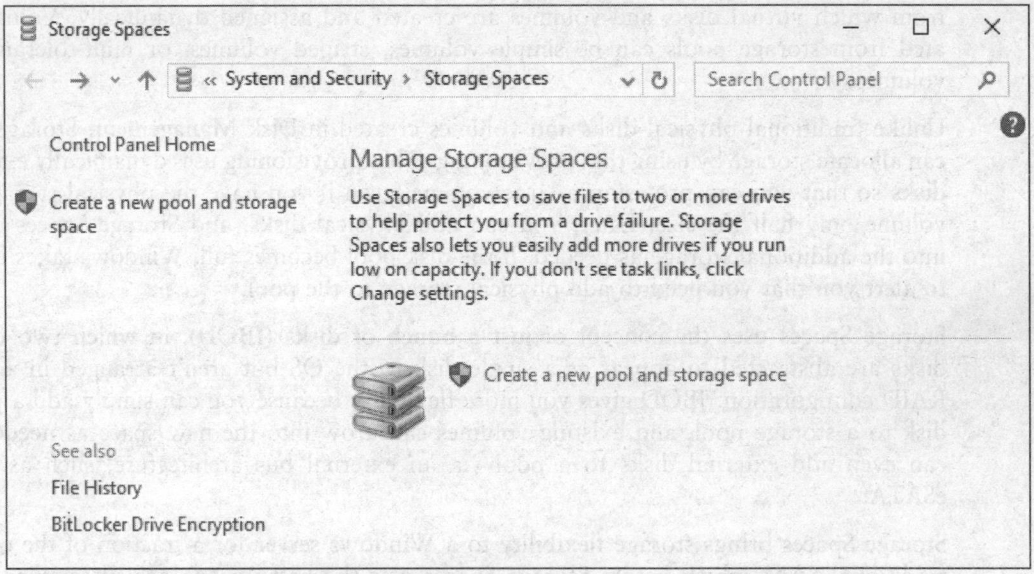


**Figure 7-6** Storage Spaces in Windows 10

**From the Trenches ...**

The network technicians for a small department in a community college operate six Windows Server 2012 R2 servers. Because the department teaches computer and networking technology, the staff feel it is important to build their own servers and maintain their own network. The servers maintain the department domain, and provide DNS, DHCP, Web services, VPN services, virtual machine access, and a host of other services for the faculty and students. A continual problem is maintaining reliable fault tolerance with the disk system. The staff use RAID 1 and RAID 5 disk configurations implemented in hardware, but every time they need to update the OS, they run into problems finding reliable drivers for the RAID controller. Furthermore, when a disk drive fails, they sometimes find it difficult to get a compatible replacement disk because disk models change so often. Enter Storage Spaces on Windows Server 2012. The technicians did away with their hardware RAID controllers and used the RAID 1 and RAID 5 capabilities of Storage Spaces, including tiered storage, to increase the performance of their storage system in a cost-effective manner. Now, they have far fewer worries when a disk drive fails because Storage Spaces doesn't have specific requirements for matching drives, and standard disk controller drivers are less of a problem when OS upgrades occur.

## Volume Types in Linux/UNIX and Mac OS X

Linux/UNIX and Mac OS X share most terminology for managing storage. In fact, if you open a terminal prompt on Mac OS X, you can use most of the same tools that are used in Linux/UNIX. This section will refer to Linux, but most concepts also apply to UNIX and Mac OS X.

Linux volumes can be created using two methods: basic partitions and the **logical volume manager** (LVM). This concept is not so different from using basic disks and dynamic disks in the Windows environment. Using basic partitions, you have the same restriction as with basic disks in Windows: you can have up to four primary partitions or three primary partitions and one extended partition. Using LVM, you can create as many partitions as there is space.

Linux requires only one partition, which is used to hold the root folder (/). However, most Linux systems use separate partitions for various folders such as /home, /usr, and /var, each of which is mounted into the root folder—from a user's point of view, it looks like a single partition.

Basic partitions have substantial limitations; for example, you can't resize them, so if you run out of space, you need to copy all the data on that partition to a new, larger partition, which is inconvenient and inefficient. Using LVM provides more flexibility, and most Linux systems use this method for creating and accessing volumes.

LVM uses physical disk partitions called *volume groups*. From volume groups, logical volumes are created and assigned space. A logical volume can be expanded while the volume is still in use by simply adding more space from the volume group. Volume groups can also be expanded by adding more physical disks or by replacing a smaller disk with a larger disk, all without having to take the volume offline.

In addition, LVMs support RAID configurations like disk mirroring.

**Virtual Disks in Linux** You can work with virtual disks in Linux by creating an image file, installing a file system on it, and mounting it into the file system. Here are the general steps and commands to create and mount a 500 MB virtual disk named mydisk from a Fedora 23 Linux shell prompt:

1. Create a new file using the *fallocate* command: *fallocate -l 500M mydisk.img*
2. Install the ext4 file system: *mkfs -t ext4 mydisk.img*
3. Create a folder to mount the virtual disk: *mkdir /mnt/vdisk*
4. Mount the virtual disk: *mount mydisk.img /mnt/vdisk*

After you have completed the preceding steps, you can use the virtual disk as you would any physical disk that's mounted into the file system. You can also use the Disks utility in GNOME to create a disk image from a hard disk or CD/DVD and attach a disk image. In Mac OS X, you can use the Disk Utility to create an image from an existing device or folder, or you can create a blank disk image, as shown in Figure 7-7. Once the disk image is created, Mac OS X automatically mounts it and places an icon on your desktop. Notice in Figure 7-7 that you have the option to encrypt the disk, which can be useful for storing sensitive documents.

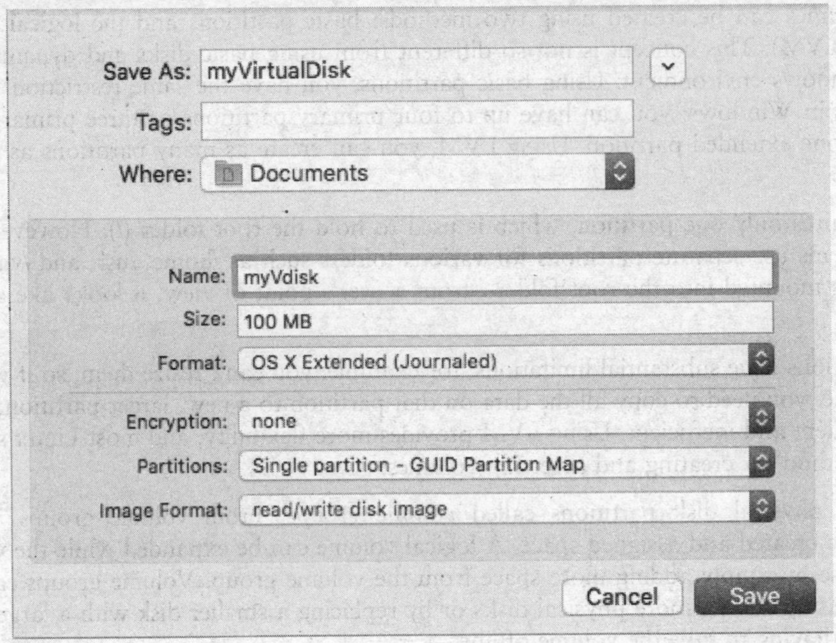


**Figure 7-7** Creating a new disk image in Mac OS X

*Source: Mac OS X*

# Cloud Storage

When a company's storage needs have outgrown its storage capabilities, whether because of physical capacity limits or the lack of personnel to maintain in-house storage, the company can turn to the cloud. With **cloud storage**, some or all of an organization's data is stored on servers located offsite and maintained by a storage hosting company. The customer can manage storage by assigning permissions for user access and allocating storage for network applications without having to physically maintain the servers. If more storage is needed, the customer simply pays the storage hosting company for the additional space. The advantage of this approach is that the details of managing and backing up storage on local servers are offloaded to a third party, which enables a company to focus its monetary and personnel resources on business rather than IT tasks. However, cloud-based storage isn't for everyone. The data a company maintains might be too sensitive to trust to a third party or the data access speed might not be sufficient, for example.

You are probably already familiar with some popular types of public cloud storage. For example, YouTube hosts millions of video files loaded by users. Google Docs enables users to store document files and spreadsheets that can be accessed and manipulated on Google Internet servers. Such files can also be published so that others can access the files through the Internet. Dropbox, Microsoft OneDrive, and Google Drive are popular cloud storage services for individuals and small businesses. For larger applications, there is Google Cloud Storage, Microsoft's OneDrive for Business, Microsoft Azure, and Amazon Web Services, to name just a few of the services in this fast-growing market.

Cloud storage is a comparatively new model in data storage. As you learned in Chapter 1, many services are being offered in the cloud, but the companies that provide cloud storage services use many of the technologies discussed in this chapter.

# Tapes and Tape Drives

Tape backup systems are a relatively inexpensive and traditional choice for backing up large amounts of data. Tapes use magnetic storage and record data in sequential order. The disadvantage of sequential access is that in order to find a file recorded near the end of the tape, the tape drive has to first go through all of the preceding data. This means access to data is typically much slower than that for a removable hard drive, which uses direct access. Tapes, however, are reliable and the technology is well tested because it has been around a long time.

Tapes are most popular for long-term storage, such as backups, or for archiving data that will be stored off-site. With the capacity of disk drives growing into terabytes, a constant need exists to develop tape technologies that can store more and more data on a single tape. The following sections briefly describe several types of tape storage systems. For most tape systems, the actual tape capacity is stated in terms of whether the stored data is compressed. Compressing the data on the tape typically doubles the noncompressed capacity. Table 7-2 lists tape media and their capacities.

**Table 7-2 Tape media capacities**

| Tape medium | Capacity (compressed) |
|---|---|
| Digital audio tape (DAT) | Up to 72 GB |
| Digital linear tape (DLT) | Up to 1.6 TB |
| Super digital linear tape (SDLT) | Up to 2.4 TB |
| Advanced intelligent tape (AIT) and super advanced intelligent tape (S-AIT) | Up to 1.3 TB |
| Linear tape open (LTO) | Up to 1.6 TB |

## DAT Drives

Digital audio tape (DAT) drives use a 4-mm tape. The most common use is the digital data storage (DDS) format. The first DDS (DDS-1) standard has a capacity of 2 GB (4 GB compressed). The current standard is DDS-5, which has a storage capacity of 36 GB (72 GB compressed). The DDS format standard is backward-compatible; for example, you can upgrade to a DDS-5 tape drive and still read DDS-4 tapes. DAT tapes are typically rated to have an archival life of about 10 years. DAT is still used for audio recordings, but its use for data storage has mostly been replaced by other tape technologies.

### DLT and SDLT Drives

**Digital linear tape** (DLT) drives use half-inch-wide magnetic tapes to record data. These tapes record data in tracks that run the whole length of the tape. Each tape contains 128, 168, 208, 240, 352, or 488 tracks, and the data is recorded on the first track from the beginning to the end of the tape. Then, the tape is reversed and the data is written from the end to the beginning. This continues until all the tracks are full. Using this track system with high-speed search capability, a file can often be found in a few seconds, although the search might take a little over a minute, depending on the file's location on the tape. DLT tape drives are used in many automated tape backup systems.

**Super digital linear tape** (SDLT) drives use both magnetic and optical recording methods. This method, along with laser technology, more accurately writes data to the tape and allows for greater density of information—up to 2.4 TB compressed. DLT and SDLT tapes have an archival life of up to 30 years, and some tape manufacturers rate their tapes at up to 500,000 tape passes.

### AIT and S-AIT Drives

**Advanced intelligent tape** (AIT) drives were introduced in 1996 and are used mainly in mid-range servers. The tapes for this drive have an erasable memory chip inside the cartridge that stores the information normally written at the beginning of a tape. This provides the information necessary to fast forward and pinpoint the desired information. AIT drives started with a capacity of 35/90 GB (native/compressed) of recorded data. Today, the **super advanced intelligent tape** (S-AIT) has a capacity of 500 GB/1.3 TB (native/compressed). AIT and S-AIT tapes can sustain up to 30,000 tape passes and have an archival life of around 30 years.

### LTO Drives

The **linear tape open** (LTO) drive is most widely accepted in the high-end server market because of its high-speed performance. LTO is an open standards tape technology, which means that the standards are open to the public and are nonproprietary. The LTO Ultrium format was developed so that LTO tapes could be used in existing DLT tape drives for faster conversion to LTO Ultrium tape technology.

LTO Ultrium tape drives offer fast data transfer speeds of up to 240 MB/s for noncompressed data and 120 MB/s for compressed data. LTO tapes can sustain up to 260 tape passes and have an archival life of 15 to 30 years.

## Storage Management Tools

This section covers some of the operating system tools and commands used to manage storage devices. Also, you will find step-by-step instructions for using some of these tools in the Hands-On Projects at the end of the chapter.

### Windows Storage Management Tools

All modern Windows OSs offer the Windows Disk Management tool for hard drives as well as removable storage. For a hard drive, this tool enables you to create and delete partitions, format partitions for a file system, and generally manage partitions. The tool also recognizes and enables you to manage removable storage, including removable hard drives, DVD/CD-ROM drives, and flash drives. In Windows 10, you can access the Disk Management tool by right-clicking Start or from the Computer Management console. On Windows Server 2012/R2 and newer versions, you can also use the File and Storage Services tool from Server Manager (see Figure 7-8) to manage volumes and Storage Spaces.

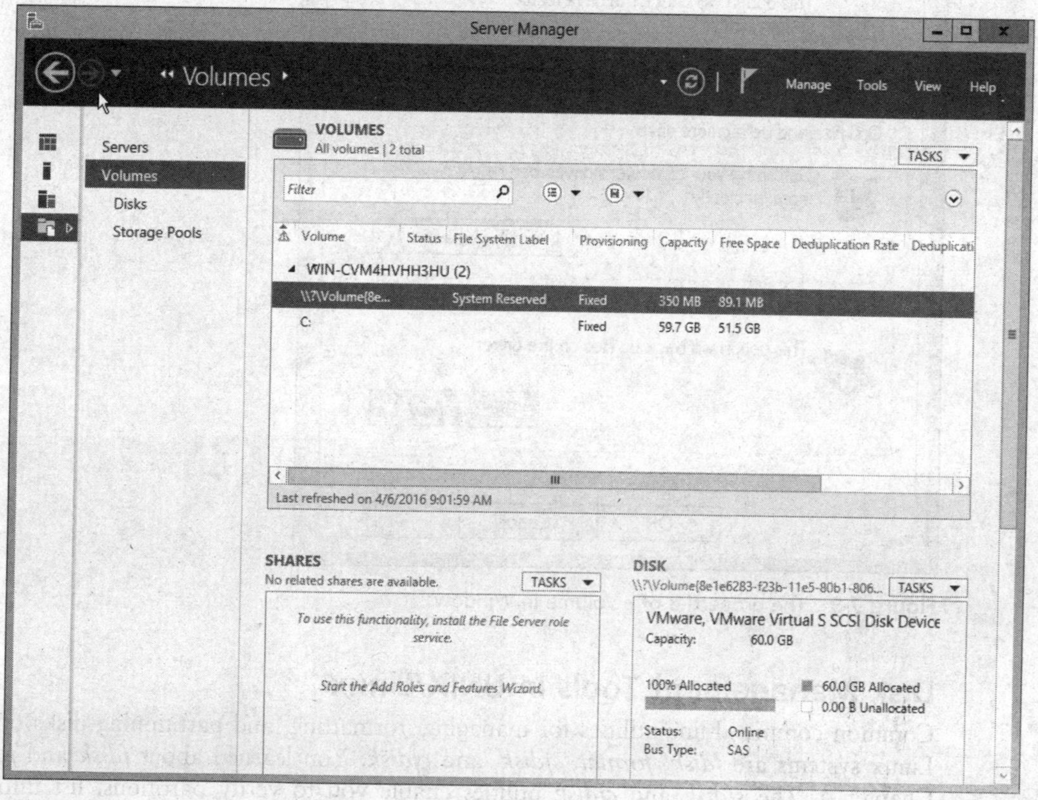


**Figure 7-8** File and Storage Services on Windows Server 2012 R2

One of the easiest ways to manage an existing storage volume is to access its properties. In File Explorer, right-click the volume and click Properties. From the Properties dialog box (see Figure 7-9), you can access several management options, such as viewing free space on the disk, defragmenting or backing up the drive, checking the drive for errors, limiting users' disk space through quotas, and setting permissions.

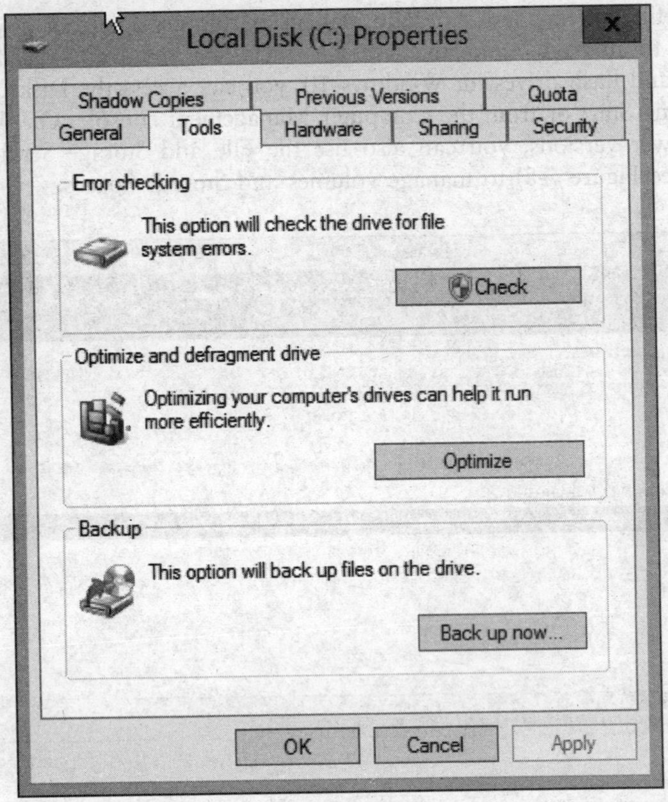


**Figure 7-9** The properties of a volume in Windows

## Disk Management Tools in UNIX/Linux

Common command-line utilities for managing, formatting, and partitioning disks on UNIX/Linux systems are *fdisk*, *format*, *sfdisk*, and *cfdisk*. You learned about *fdisk* and *format* in Chapter 4. The *sfdisk* and *cfdisk* utilities enable you to verify partitions, list information about partitions, such as their size, and repartition a disk. Linux operating systems offer *fdisk*, *sfdisk*, and *cfdisk*, but not *format*, which is used on some UNIX systems.

Further, UNIX/Linux systems offer the *mount* command-line utility, introduced in Chapter 4, to mount a file system so that you can use a disk partition, virtual disk, DVD/CD-ROM drive, or flash drive. Normally, when you boot UNIX/Linux, the main file systems are mounted as part of the boot process—for example, the ext4 file system in Linux. However, you may need to manually mount file systems for DVD/CD-ROM or flash drives (although these are automatically detected and mounted in modern Linux operating systems). For example, to mount a DVD/CD-ROM drive, you would use the following command:

*mount -t iso9660 /dev/cdrom /mnt/cdrom* or *mount -t iso9660 /dev/cdrom /cdrom*

For a DVD formatted for the udf file system, use:

*mount -t udf /dev/cdrom /mnt/cdrom or mount -t udf /dev/cdrom /cdrom*

The *-t iso9660* portion of the first command mounts the iso9660 (CD-ROM) file system. The *-t udf* portion of the second command is for the Universal Disk Format file system, which is a file system that supplants iso9660 for DVDs and other optical media. Further, these commands mount the device, /dev/cdrom, to the mount point, /mnt/cdrom or /cdrom, so that after the DVD or CD-ROM file system is mounted, you can view its files by viewing the contents of /mnt/cdrom or /cdrom.

Use the *umount* command to unmount a file system. For example, you would enter *umount /mnt/cdrom* or *umount /cdrom* to unmount the file system for a DVD/CD-ROM drive. Table 7-3 summarizes UNIX/Linux commands for disk management. These commands typically have many different options, which are documented in the online manual pages. For example, to learn more about the *mount* command, use the command *man mount* to read the documentation.

**Table 7-3 Summary of UNIX/Linux disk management commands**

| Command | Explanation |
|---|---|
| *cfdisk* | Partitions and verifies a hard disk |
| *cpio* | Copies and backs up files to archive them on tape or disk |
| *dump* | Backs up particular files or an entire file system and offers levels to specify the degree to which to back up files; use the *restore* command to restore files backed up by *dump* |
| *fdisk* | Maintains disk partitions, including creating and deleting partitions and flagging the active partition |
| *format* | Partitions and formats a disk in some UNIX distributions, but not in Linux |
| *mount* | Connects or mounts a file system for access in the directory tree |
| *restore* | Restores an entire file system or only specific files backed up by the *dump* command |
| *tar* | Copies files to an archive medium and can restore files; this command is traditionally popular with server administrators |
| *sfdisk* | Provides information about a partition and can be used to create a partition (Caution: This command does not work with PC systems that use a GUID Partitioning Table) |
| *umount* | Disconnects or unmounts a file system partition from access in the directory tree |
| *xfsdump* | Backs up files in the XFS file system; the ext file system is the default option in Linux, but Linux also supports XFS |
| *xfsrestore* | Restores files backed up by *xfsdump* |

If you use Linux with the GNOME desktop, you can use the Disks tool to manage disk storage. For example, to unmount a DVD from the Disks utility, click the CD/DVD drive in the left pane and click the Eject button in the right pane (see Figure 7-10).

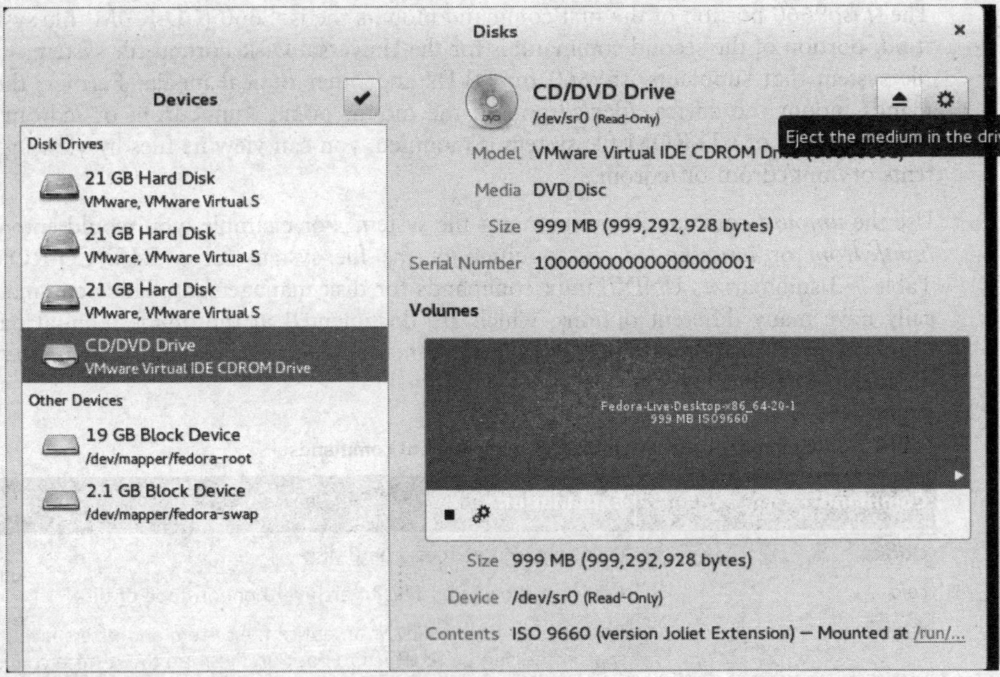


**Figure 7-10** The Disks utility in Linux
*Source: Fedora Linux*

## Mac OS X Disk Utility

The Mac OS X Disk Utility can partition, format, and manage hard drives. It can also manage DVD/CD-ROM drives, removable hard drives, flash drives, and other storage. When you select a storage medium in the left pane, the Disk Utility displays appropriate tabs for the actions you can perform on that storage medium. For example, for a hard disk you can:

- Repair the disk using the First Aid option.
- Erase the contents.
- Partition and format the disk.
- Set up RAID on the disk.
- Restore a disk image or volume.

For removable media, you can use the Disk Utility to mount media, eject media, burn a CD or DVD, and perform other actions. Because Mac OS X is a UNIX-based system, you can also open a terminal window and use the *mount* command to manage storage media. To learn the *mount* command options, type *man mount* and press Enter at the command line.

## Chapter Summary

- Storage is any digital medium that data can be written to and later retrieved. Long-term storage includes USB drives, SD cards, CDs/DVDs, magnetic tape, SSDs, and HDDs.
- All computers require at least some storage, but servers usually require more than client computers. Storage is needed for OS files, page files, log files, virtual machines, database files, and user documents, among others.
- The main methods of storage access are local, DAS, NAS, and SAN. Local and DAS are similar methods, but DAS can also be a separate unit attached through an external interface. NAS is a stand-alone storage device with a network interface. A SAN is the most complex storage device; it uses high-speed networking technologies to provide shared storage.
- Configuration of local disks can be divided into two broad categories: physical disk properties and logical properties. Physical properties include disk capacity, rotation speed, and the disk interface technology. SATA and SAS are the most common disk interfaces.
- Disk types include basic disks, dynamic disks, and virtual disks. Partitioning types include MBR and GPT. Volume types include simple, spanned, RAID 0, RAID 1, and RAID 5.
- Storage Spaces, a new feature starting with Windows 8/8.1 and Windows Server 2012/R2, provides flexible provisioning of virtualized storage by using storage pools. A storage pool is a collection of physical disks from which virtual disks and volumes are created and assigned dynamically.
- Storage Spaces uses the concept of just a bunch of disks (JBOD), in which two or more disks are abstracted to appear as a single disk to the OS but aren't arranged in a specific RAID configuration.
- With cloud storage, some or all of an organization's data is stored on servers located offsite and maintained by a storage hosting company.
- Tape backup systems are a relatively inexpensive and traditional choice for backing up large amounts of data. Tapes use magnetic storage and record data in sequential order. There are several types of tape devices, including DAT, DLT, SDLT, AIT, and LTO.
- Storage management tools in Windows include Disk Management and File and Storage Services. Linux has a number of command-line tools, such as *fdisk*, *format*, and *mount*, plus the Disks GUI tool. Mac OS X includes many of the same Linux command-line tools, plus the Disk Utility tool.

## Key Terms

**advanced intelligent tape (AIT)** A tape drive that has an erasable memory chip and a capacity of up to 1.3 TB.

**backplane** A connection system that uses a printed circuit board instead of traditional cables to carry signals.

**basic disk** A traditional Windows or DOS disk arrangement in which the disk is partitioned into primary and extended partitions. A basic disk can't hold volumes spanning multiple disks or be part of a RAID.

**boot volume** The volume where the \Windows folder is located—usually the C drive, but this location is not mandatory. The boot volume is also referred to as the *boot partition*.

**cloud storage** A storage paradigm in which an individual's or company's storage is hosted by a third party and accessed over the Internet.

**digital audio tape (DAT)** A tape system that uses 4-mm tape and has a capacity of up to 72 GB.

**digital linear tape (DLT)** A tape system that uses half-inch magnetic tapes and has a capacity of up to 1.6 TB.

**direct-attached storage (DAS)** A storage medium directly connected to the server using it. DAS differs from local storage in that it includes externally connected HDDs in an enclosure with a power supply.

**disk drive** A physical component with a disk interface connector (such as SATA or SCSI) and a power connector.

**dynamic disk** A disk arrangement that can hold up to 128 volumes, including spanned volumes, striped volumes, and RAID volumes.

**extended partition** A division of disk space on a basic disk that must be separated into logical drives; it can't be marked active and can't hold the Windows system volume.

**GUID Partitioning Table (GPT)** A disk-partitioning method that supports volume sizes of up to 18 exabytes.

**just a bunch of disks (JBOD)** A disk arrangement in which two or more disks are abstracted to appear as a single disk to the OS but aren't arranged in a specific RAID configuration.

**linear tape open (LTO)** A tape drive used in the high-end server market; it has a storage capacity of up to 1.6 TB.

**local storage** Storage media with a direct and exclusive connection to the computer's system board through a disk controller.

**logical unit number (LUN)** A logical reference point to a unit of storage that could refer to an entire array of disks, a single disk, or just part of a disk.

**logical volume manager (LVM)** A method of creating volumes in Linux that uses physical disk partitions called *volume groups* to create logical volumes.

**Master Boot Record (MBR)** A disk-partitioning method that supports volume sizes of up to 2 TB.

**network-attached storage (NAS)** A storage device that has an enclosure, a power supply, slots for multiple HDDs, a network interface, and a built-in OS tailored for managing shared files and folders.

**pagefile.sys** A system file in Windows used as virtual memory; it is also used to store data produced when the system crashes (dump data), which is used for troubleshooting.

**partition** A logical unit of storage that can be formatted with a file system; it is similar to a volume but used with basic disks.

**primary partition** A division of disk space on a basic disk used to create a volume. It can be assigned a drive letter, be marked as active, and contain the Windows system volume.

**RAID 0 volume** A volume that extends across two or more dynamic disks, but data is written to all disks in the volume equally; it provides no fault tolerance but does provide a performance advantage over simple or spanned volumes.

**RAID 1 volume** A volume that uses space from two dynamic disks and provides fault tolerance. Data written to one disk is duplicated, or mirrored, to the second disk. If one disk fails, the other disk has a good copy of the data, and the system can continue to operate until the failed disk is replaced. This volume is also called a *mirrored volume*.

**RAID 5 volume** A volume that uses space from three or more dynamic disks and uses disk striping with parity to provide fault tolerance. When data is written, it's striped across all but one of the disks in the volume. Parity information derived from the data is written to the remaining disk, which is used to re-create lost data after a disk failure. This volume is also called a *disk stripe with parity*.

**redundant array of independent disks (RAID)** A disk configuration that uses space on multiple disks to form a single logical volume. Most RAID configurations provide fault tolerance, and some enhance performance.

**Serial ATA (SATA)** A common disk interface technology that's inexpensive, fast, and fairly reliable, with transfer speeds up to 6 Gb/s; it is used both in client computers and low-end servers and replaces the older parallel ATA (PATA) technology.

**serial attached SCSI (SAS)** A newer, serial form of SCSI with transfer rates of up to 6 Gb/s and higher; the disk technology of choice for servers and high-end workstations. See also *small computer system interface (SCSI)*.

**simple volume** A volume that usually resides on a single basic or dynamic disk.

**small computer system interface (SCSI)** An older parallel bus disk technology still used on some servers, although it has reached its performance limits at 640 MB/s transfer rates.

**solid-state drive (SSD)** A type of storage medium that uses flash memory, has no moving parts, and requires less power than a traditional HDD. It is faster and more shock resistant than a traditional HDD, but it costs more per gigabyte and doesn't have as much capacity as an HDD.

**spanned volume** A volume that extends across two or more physical disks; for example, a simple volume that has been extended to a second disk is a spanned volume.

**storage appliance** See *network-attached storage (NAS)*.

**storage area network (SAN)** A storage device that uses high-speed networking technologies to give servers fast access to large amounts of shared disk storage. To the server OS, the storage a SAN manages appears to be physically attached to the server.

**storage layout** The method used to create a virtual disk with Storage Spaces; the three methods include simple, mirror, and parity. See also *Storage Spaces*.

**storage pool** A collection of physical disks from which virtual disks and volumes are created and assigned dynamically.

**Storage Spaces** A new feature in Windows 8/8.1 and Windows Server 2012/R2 and later versions that provides flexible provisioning of virtualized storage.

**storage tiering** A feature of Storage Spaces that combines the speed of SSDs with the low cost and high capacity of HDDs to create high-performance volumes.

**super advanced intelligent tape (S-AIT)** A tape system technology that has an erasable memory chip and a capacity of up to 1.3 TB.

**super digital linear tape (SDLT)** A tape system that uses both magnetic and optical recording and has a tape capacity of up to 2.4 TB.

**swap partition** In Linux/UNIX OSs, a separate partition on the disk set aside exclusively for virtual memory.

**system volume** A volume that contains the files a computer needs to find and load the Windows OS. See also *volume*.

**thin provisioning** A method for creating virtual disks in which the virtual disk expands dynamically and uses space from the storage pool as needed until it reaches the specified maximum size.

**VHD file** The format that virtual machines running in Hyper-V use for their virtual disks. VHD files can also be created and mounted with Disk Management and used like physical disks.

**virtual memory** Disk space that stores the least recently used pages of memory when more physical RAM is needed, but not available.

**volume** A logical unit of storage that can be formatted with a file system.

## Review Questions

1. Which of the following is an example of long-term storage? (Choose all that apply.)
   a. magnetic tape
   b. CPU cache
   c. SSD
   d. RAM
2. Which of the following is true about an SSD?
   a. It uses magnetic platters.
   b. It has no moving parts.
   c. It uses a proprietary interface.
   d. It uses EPROM.
3. Which of the following is an example of what a computer stores? (Choose all that apply.)
   a. virtual memory
   b. log files
   c. working memory
   d. documents

4. Which of the following is true about a page file?
   a. It should be stored on a separate disk from the Windows folder.
   b. It's usually stored in fast random access memory.
   c. Windows stores frequently accessed drivers in it.
   d. It is usually smaller than 50 MB.
5. Local storage is rarely direct-attached storage. True or False?
6. You want shared network storage that's easy to set up and geared toward file sharing with several file-sharing protocols, but you don't want the device to be dedicated to file sharing. What should you consider buying?
   a. SAN
   b. DAS
   c. NAS
   d. LAS
7. What type of interface are you likely to find that connects a DAS device to the server that uses it?
   a. SATA
   b. IDE
   c. PATA
   d. eSATA
8. You have four servers that need access to shared storage because you're configuring them in a cluster. Which storage solution should you consider for this application?
   a. NAS
   b. SAN
   c. SCSI
   d. DAS
9. Which of the following is defined as a physical component with a disk interface connector?
   a. format
   b. partition
   c. volume
   d. disk drive
10. You have installed a new disk and created a volume on it. What should you do before you can store files on it?
   a. Format it.
   b. Partition it.
   c. Initialize it.
   d. Erase it.

11. On your Windows server, you're planning to install a new database application that uses an enormous amount of disk space. You need this application to be highly available, so you need a disk system with the capability to auto-correct from disk errors and data corruption. You also want a flexible storage solution that makes it easy to add space and supports deduplication. Which of the following is the best option?
    a. MBR disk with *chkdsk*
    b. NTFS format with EFS
    c. ReFS format and Storage Spaces
    d. GPT disk with shadow copies
12. Which of the following commands can verify a new partition you have configured in Linux? (Choose all that apply.)
    a. *chkdsk*
    b. *vdisk*
    c. *fdisk*
    d. *sfdisk*
13. Which disk interface technology transfers data over a parallel bus?
    a. SATA
    b. USB
    c. SAS
    d. SCSI
14. What is created automatically when you install Windows Server 2012 R2 on a system with a disk drive that has never had an OS installed on it before?
    a. system volume
    b. dynamic disk
    c. GPT
    d. extended partition
15. What type of volumes or partitions can be created on a basic disk? (Choose all that apply.)
    a. spanned volume
    b. striped partition
    c. extended partition
    d. simple volume
16. Which of the following is true about GPT disks?
    a. They support a maximum volume size of 2 TB.
    b. GPT is the default option when initializing a disk in Disk Management.
    c. They use CRC protection for the partition table.
    d. You can't convert a GPT disk to MBR.

17. You have a server with Windows Server 2012 R2 installed on Disk 0, a basic disk. You use the server to store users' documents. You have two more disks that you can install in the server. What should you do if you want to provide fault tolerance for users' documents?
    a. Convert Disk 0 to dynamic. Create a striped volume using Disk 0, Disk 1, and Disk 2.
    b. Create a RAID 1 volume from Disk 1 and Disk 2.
    c. Convert the new disks to GPT. Create a spanned volume using Disk 1 and Disk 2.
    d. Create a RAID 5 volume from Disk 0, Disk 1, and Disk 2.
18. You need a disk system that provides the best performance for a new application that frequently reads and writes data to the disk. You aren't concerned about disk fault tolerance because the data will be backed up each day; performance is the main concern. What type of volume arrangement should you use?
    a. spanned volume
    b. RAID 1 volume
    c. RAID 0 volume
    d. RAID 5 volume
19. You are ordering eight new desktop computers for your small business. Which of the following hard drive technologies is likely to be used in the new computers?
    a. SATA
    b. PATA
    c. SCSI
    d. SAS
20. You come across a file with a .vhd extension on your Windows 10 computer's hard disk. What should you do to see this file's contents?
    a. Right-click the file and click Open.
    b. Open the file in Notepad.
    c. Burn the file to a DVD.
    d. Mount the file.

# Hands-On Projects

## Project 7-1: Use the Windows Disk Management Tool

In this project, you use the Windows Disk Management tool to view existing volumes and create a new volume.

If your Windows 10 computer is configured according to instructions in the "Before You Begin" section of the Introduction, you should have three physical disks. Disk 0 has the Windows OS installed, and Disk 1 and Disk 2 are empty and offline. If you only have two disks in your system, you can still perform this activity. If you only have one disk in your system but have some unallocated space, you can perform this activity with minor changes (see your instructor). If you have no additional disks and no unallocated space, you cannot perform this activity.

1. Start your Windows 10 computer and log on.
2. Right-click **Start** and click **Disk Management.**
3. If you see a message about initializing a disk, click **OK**. There are two panes in Disk Management: The upper pane shows a summary of configured volumes and basic information about each volume. The lower pane shows installed disks and how each disk is being used.
4. Right-click the (C:) volume in the upper pane and note some of the options you have.
5. In the lower pane, find Disk 1. If its status is online and initialized, skip to the next step; otherwise, right-click **Disk 1** and click **Online**. Right-click it again and click **Initialize Disk** to open the dialog box shown in Figure 7-11. Leave the default option **MBR** selected, and click **OK**.

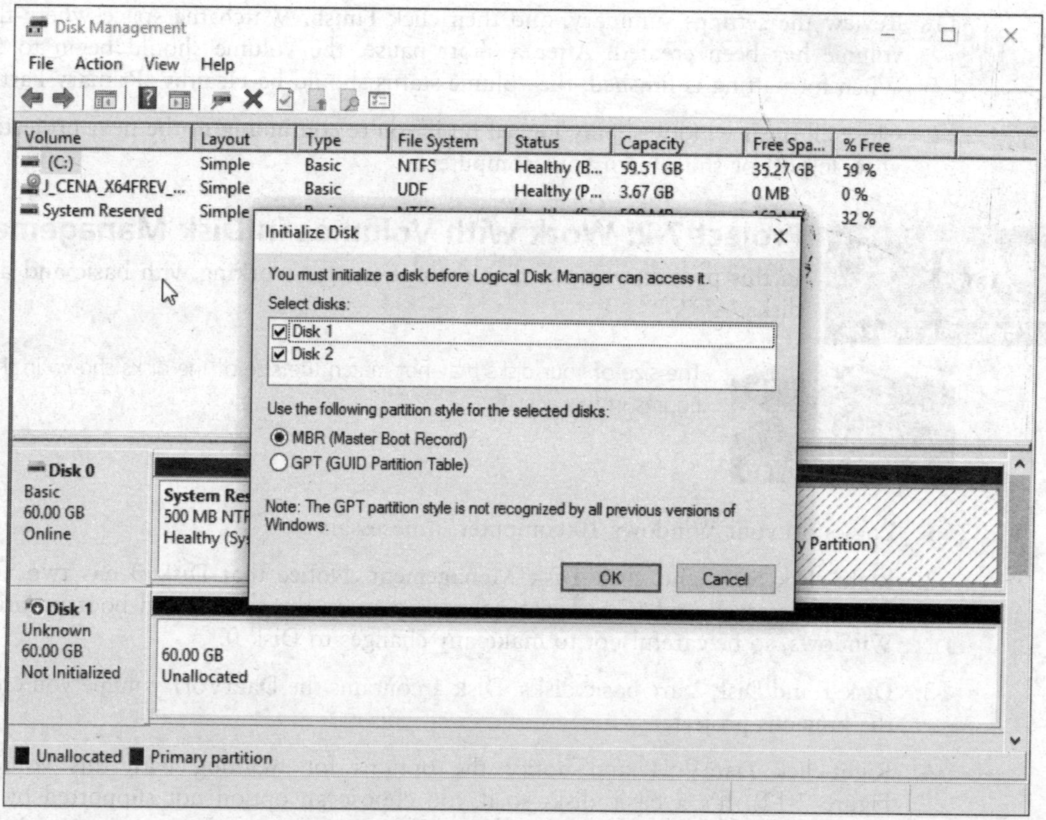


**Figure 7-11** Initializing a disk in Disk Management

6. Right-click the unallocated space of **Disk 1**, and notice the options for making the unallocated space into a new volume. In Windows XP and Windows Server 2003, the term *partition* was used instead of *volume*. In Windows Vista and Windows Server 2008 and newer versions, the term *volume* is often used instead when preparing disks for use.
7. Click **New Simple Volume** to start the New Simple Volume Wizard. In the welcome window, click **Next**.
8. In the Specify Volume Size window, type **500** to make a 500 MB volume, and then click **Next**.
9. In the Assign Drive Letter or Path window, you have the option to assign a drive letter or mount the new volume into a folder on another volume. From the drop-down menu next to "Assign the following drive letter," click drive letter **S**, and then click **Next**. (If the S drive isn't available, ask your instructor which drive letter to select.)
10. In the Format Partition window, click the **File system** list arrow, and note the available options. Click **NTFS** to select it as the file system. In the Volume label text box, type **DataVol1**, and then click **Next**.

11. Review the settings summary, and then click **Finish**. Watch the space where the new volume has been created. After a short pause, the volume should begin to format. When formatting is finished, the volume status should be Healthy (Primary Partition).

12. Close all open windows. Stay logged on if you're continuing to the next project; otherwise, log off or shut down your computer.

## Project 7-2: Work with Volumes in Disk Management

In this project, you examine the options for working with basic and dynamic disks.

The size of your disks may not match the size of the disks shown in the figures in this activity.

1. Log on to your Windows 10 computer, if necessary.

2. Right-click **Start** and click **Disk Management.** Notice that Disk 0 has two volumes: System Reserved and (C:). These volumes contain the system and boot partitions for Windows, so be careful not to make any changes to Disk 0.

3. Disk 1 and Disk 2 are basic disks. Disk 1 contains the DataVol1 volume you created in the previous project.

4. Right-click **DataVol1** and notice the options for working with this volume (see Figure 7-12). It's a basic disk, so if you choose an option not supported by a basic disk, you're prompted to convert the disk to dynamic. If you were working with a FAT/FAT32 volume, you would not have the option to extend, shrink, or add a mirror.

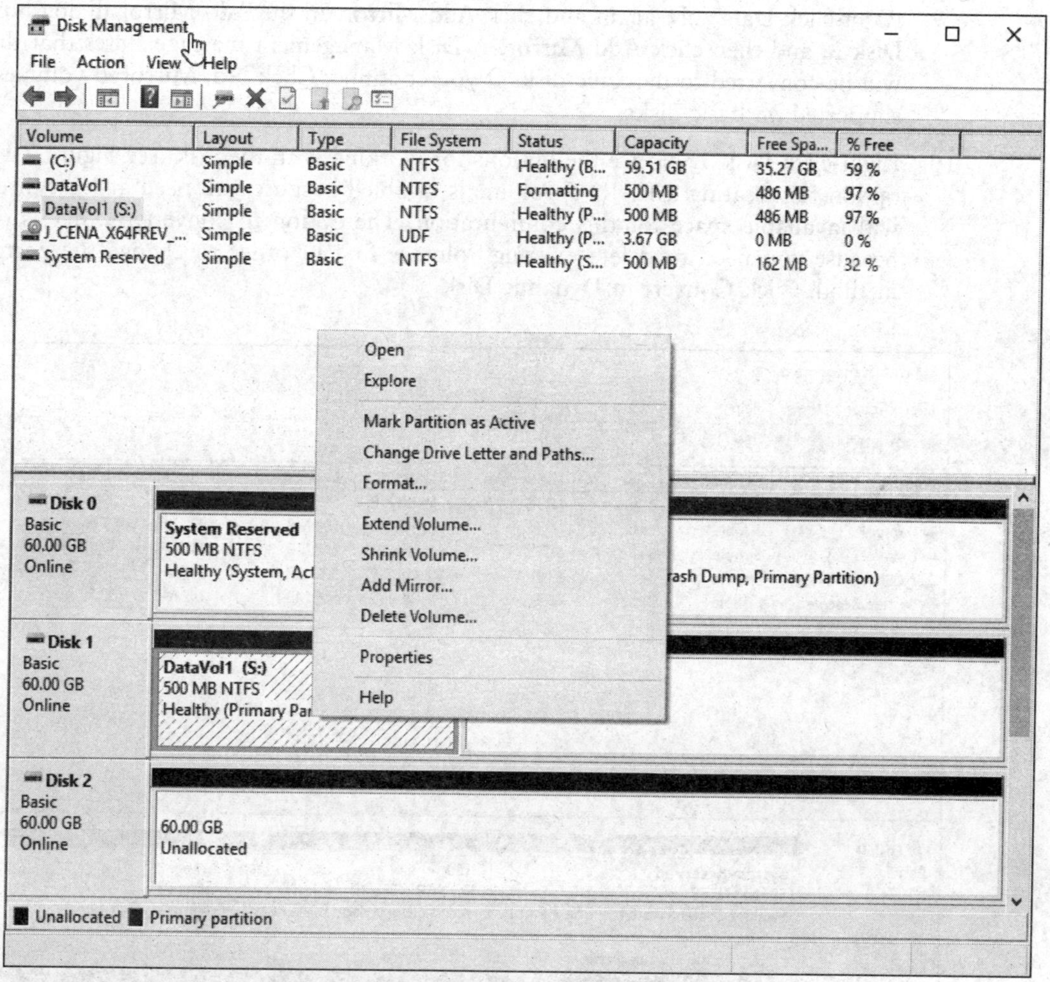


**Figure 7-12** Options for NTFS volumes

5. Right-click **DataVol1** again, if necessary, and click **Extend Volume**. In the Extend Volume Wizard welcome window, click **Next**.

6. In the Select Disks window, you have the option of adding disks to which to extend. If you do so, you're prompted to convert the disk to dynamic because basic disks don't support extending to other disks (disk spanning). In the "Select the amount of space in MB" text box, type **500**, which makes the volume 1 GB. Click **Next**.

7. In the Completing the Extend Volume Wizard window, click **Finish**. The disk is extended to about 1000 MB.

8. In Disk Management, right-click **DataVol1** and then click **Shrink Volume** to open the Shrink S: dialog box. In the "Enter the amount of space to shrink in MB" text box, type **500** and click **Shrink**. The volume is back to 500 MB.

9. Right-click **DataVol1** again and click **Add Mirror**. In the Add Mirror dialog box, click **Disk 2**, and then click **Add Mirror**. A Disk Management message states that the disks will be converted to dynamic disks if you continue. Click **No**. Mirrored volumes aren't supported on basic disks.

10. Right-click **Disk 1**. Notice the options for working with the disk (see Figure 7-13). The option for creating a RAID 5 volume is disabled because you need at least three disks with available space for this configuration. The option to convert to GPT is disabled because you need to delete existing volumes first in order to change the partitioning method. Click **Convert to Dynamic Disk**.

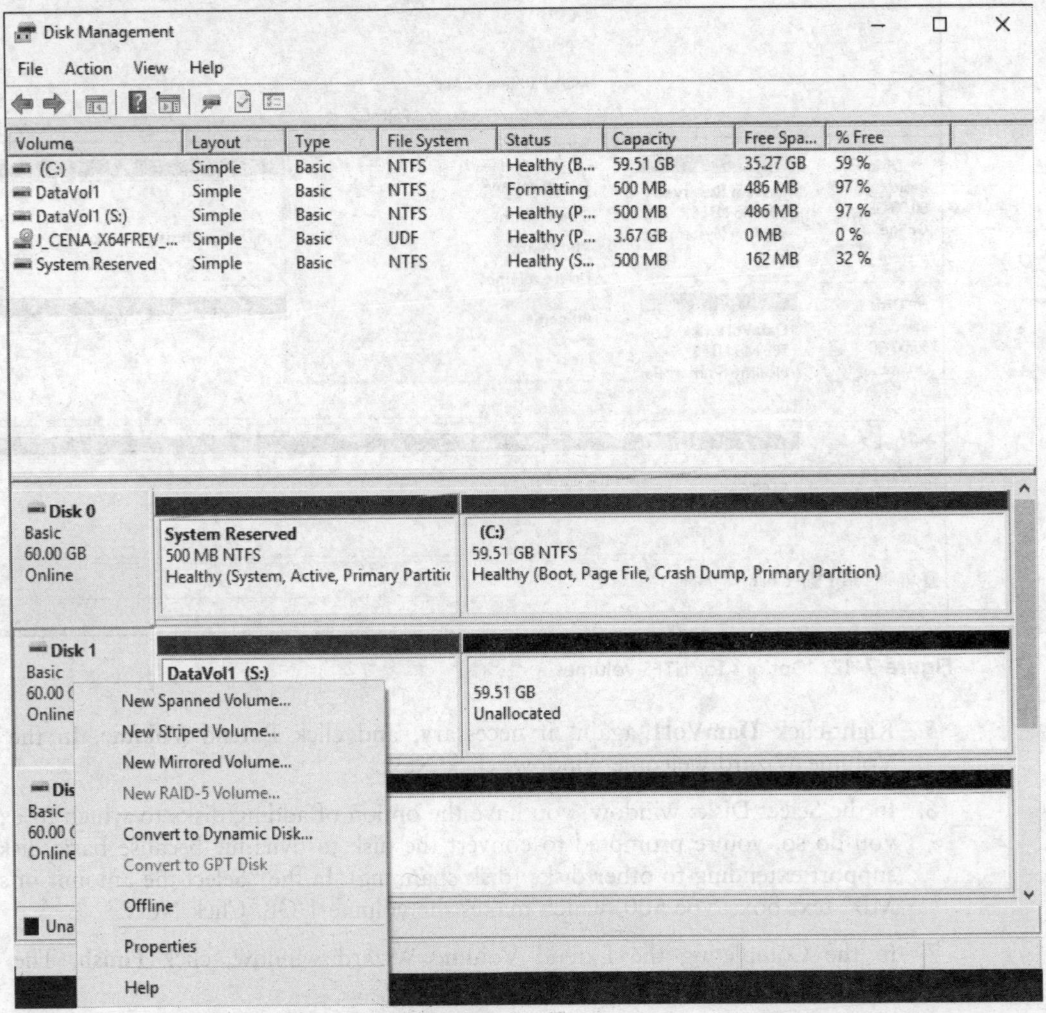


**Figure 7-13** Options for working with Disk 1

11. In the Convert to Dynamic Disk dialog box, you have the option to convert more than one disk to dynamic. Leave the **Disk 1** check box selected and click **OK**. Click **Convert**,

and then click **Yes**. The color of the volume label changes from blue to yellow-green to indicate it's now a simple volume rather than a primary partition.

12. Right-click **DataVol1** and click **Add Mirror**. Click **Disk 2** and then **Add Mirror**. Click **Yes** to confirm that Disk 2 will be converted to a dynamic disk.

13. The volume label changes color to red, indicating a mirrored volume (see Figure 7-14). A status message shows that the volume is resyncing (copying information from the primary disk to the mirrored disk). Disk 2 now has a volume named DataVol1 and assigned the letter S. Close Disk Management.

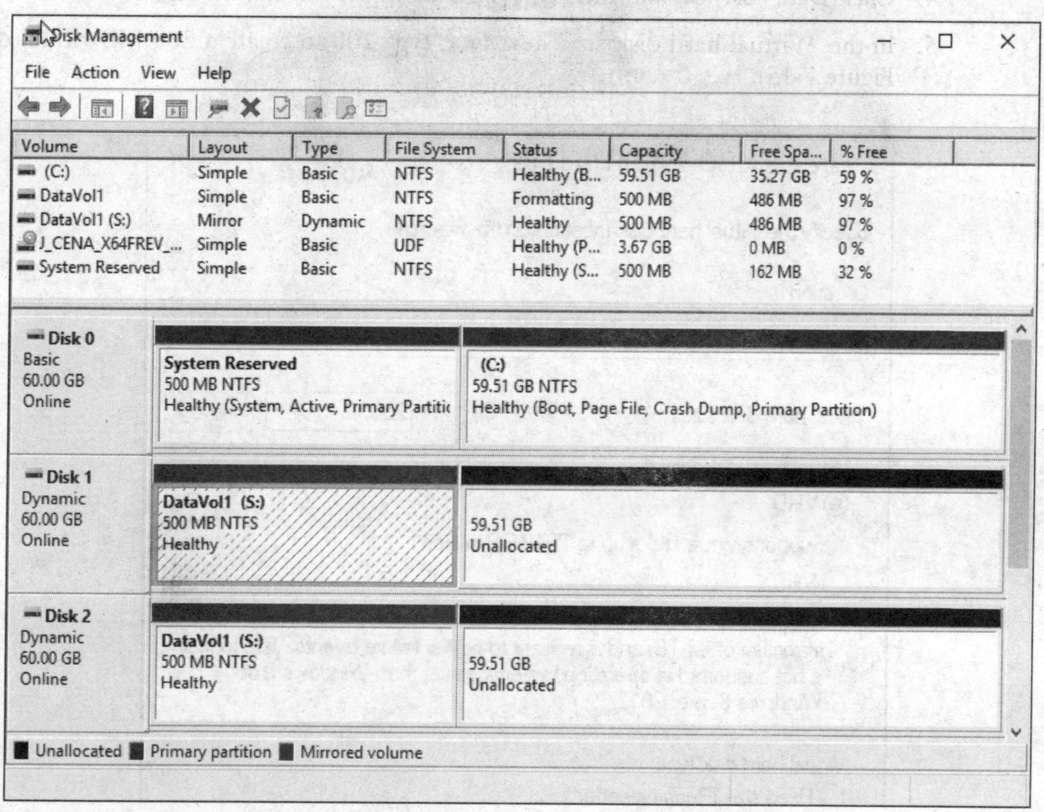


**Figure 7-14** A mirrored volume

14. If you're continuing to the next activity, stay logged on; otherwise, log off or shut down the server.

Disk 1 is an MBR disk and Disk 2 is a GPT disk. You can use disks of different types in RAID configurations.

## Project 7-3: Work with Virtual Disks in Windows

In this project, you create and mount a virtual disk, and then view it in Disk Management and File Explorer.

1. Log on to your Windows 10 computer, if necessary.
2. Open Disk Management. Click the **Action** menu, and then click **Create VHD.**
3. In the Create and Attach Virtual Hard Disk dialog box, click **Browse.**
4. Click **DataVol1 (S:)** and then type **Virtual1** in the File name text box. Click **Save.**
5. In the "Virtual hard disk size" text box, type **200** to create a 200 MB virtual disk (see Figure 7-15).

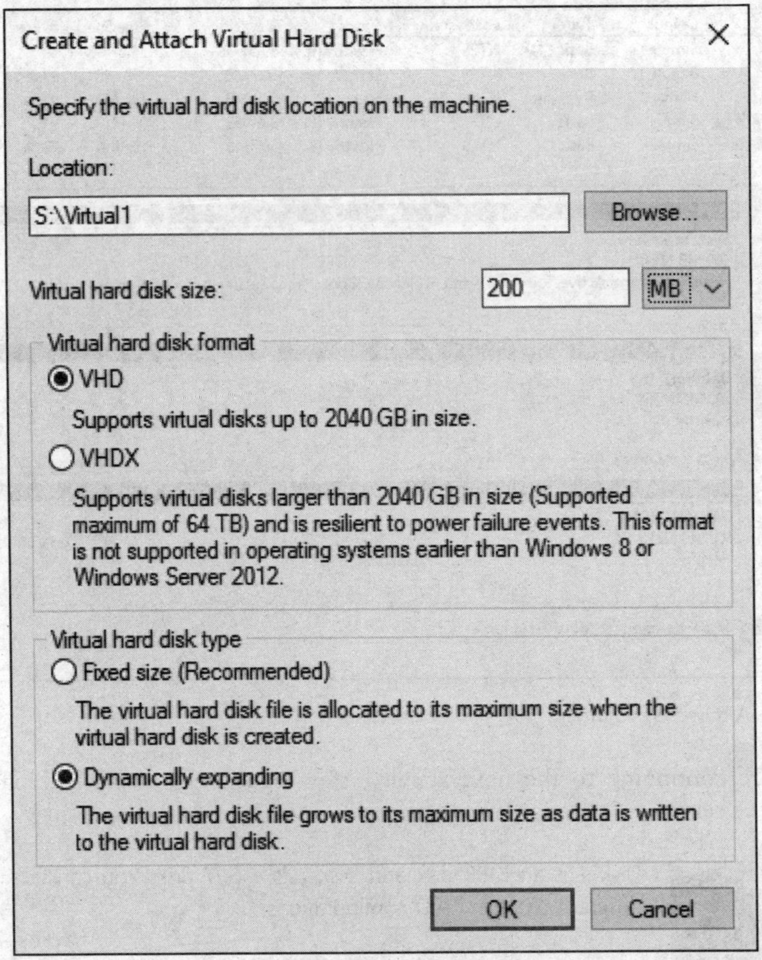


**Figure 7-15** Configuring a virtual hard disk

6. The virtual hard disk format is VHD by default. Because you're creating a small volume, you can accept this default setting. Click the **Dynamically expanding** option button so that the disk's file size is very small at first and then expands as you add data, up to the 200 MB you specified. (Recall that this concept is called *thin provisioning*.) Click **OK**.

7. When you create a VHD file in Disk Management, it's mounted automatically. The disk should be listed as Disk 3, and its status is Not Initialized (see Figure 7-16). Right-click **Disk 3** and notice the Detach VHD option in the menu. Click **Initialize Disk**.

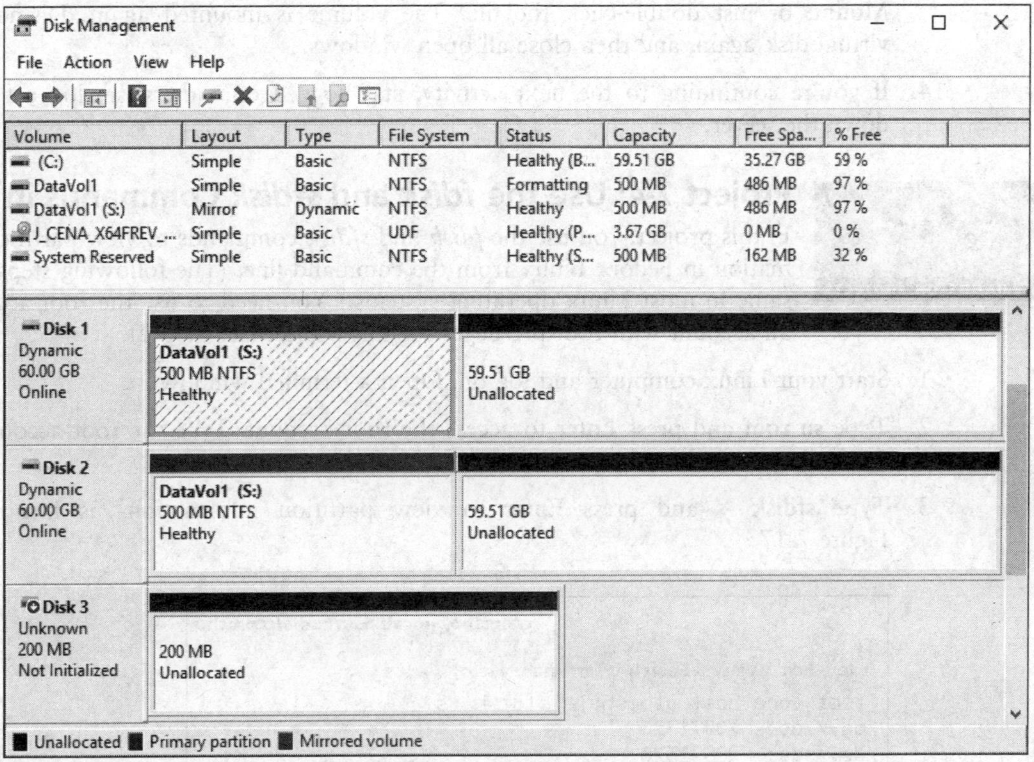


**Figure 7-16** A virtual disk in Disk Management

8. In the Initialize Disk dialog box, click **OK**. Your new virtual disk is initialized and ready to have a volume created on it.

9. Right-click the unallocated space of Disk 3 and click **New Simple Volume**. Follow the New Simple Volume Wizard to select the following settings:

   - Volume size: Use the maximum size.
   - Drive letter: Assign drive letter V:.
   - Format: Use the default settings, but make the volume label **Virtual1**.

10. When the volume has finished formatting, you can access it. The icon color of Disk 3 changes to light blue, indicating a virtual disk. Right-click the volume and click **Explore**.
11. File Explorer treats the virtual disk and volumes in it like any other disk and volume. In File Explorer, click the **S** drive. You should see a file named Virtual1 with an adjacent icon indicating a virtual disk.
12. Right-click **Virtual1 (V:)** in the left pane of File Explorer and then click **Eject**. The disk is no longer shown in File Explorer or Disk Management.
13. In File Explorer, click the **S** drive. Notice that the virtual disk's file size is only about 10 MB. That size expands if you add data to the file. Right-click **Virtual1** and click **Mount**, or just double-click the file. The volume is mounted again. Dismount the virtual disk again, and then close all open windows.
14. If you're continuing to the next activity, stay logged on; otherwise, log off or shut down the server.

## Project 7-4: Use the *fdisk* and *sfdisk* Commands in Linux

In this project, you use the *fdisk* and *sfdisk* commands to view partition information in Fedora Linux from the command line. (The following steps are the same in most Linux operating systems.) You need to use the root account or an account with root privileges for this project (see Step 2).

1. Start your Linux computer and log on. Open a terminal window.
2. Type **su root** and press **Enter** to access the root account. Type the root account password, if requested, and press **Enter**.
3. Type **sfdisk -s** and press **Enter** to view partition information, as illustrated in Figure 7-17.

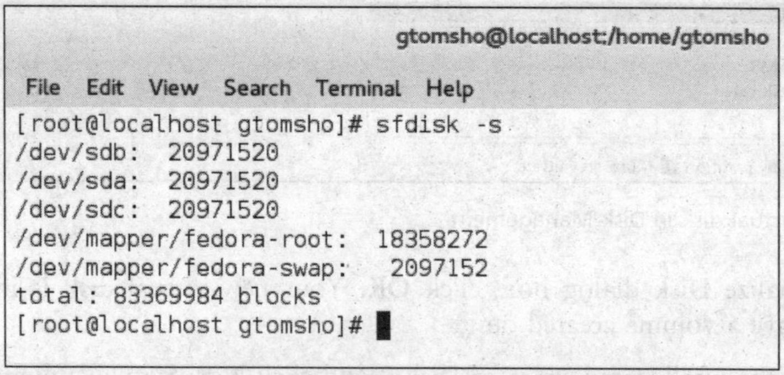


**Figure 7-17** The output from the *sfdisk -s* command

*Source: Fedora Linux*

4. Next, type **fdisk -l** and press **Enter**. Compare the information from the *fdisk* command to the information displayed for the *sfdisk* command.
5. Close the terminal window.

## Project 7-5: Use the Disks Utility in Linux

In this project, you use the Disks utility in Linux to work with a newly installed disk.

> **NOTE:** If your Linux computer is configured according to instructions in the "Before You Begin" section of the Introduction, you should have two physical disks installed. The first disk will have the Linux OS installed and the second disk will be blank. If you don't have more than one disk installed, you can't do this project.

1. Start your Linux computer, and log on.
2. Click **Activities** and click **Show Applications.**
3. Click **Utilities** and then click **Disks** to open the Disks utility (see Figure 7-18). Depending on your system configuration, your Disks utility may look different. In Figure 7-18, there are two hard disks; the Linux system in the figure is running on VMware, so the disks are labeled as VMware disks.

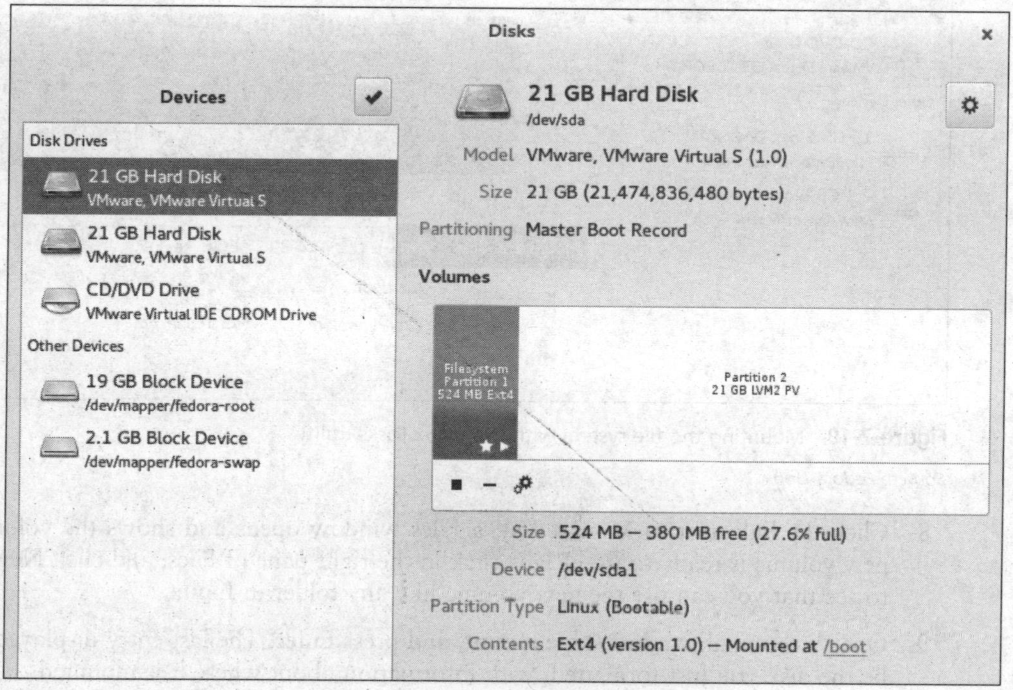


**Figure 7-18** Linux Disks utility

*Source: Fedora Linux*

4. Click the second disk in the left pane. In the right pane, you see that the volume is listed as Unknown.

5. Right-click the **More actions** button under the volume and click **Format**. In the Format Volume dialog box, accept the default Erase and Type options, and type **Vol1** in the Name text box. Click **Format.**

6. The next dialog box asks if you are sure you want to format the volume. Click **Format.** If you are prompted for your password, enter it and click **Authenticate.**

7. Click the **Mount the filesystem** arrow under the volume (see Figure 7-19). If you are prompted for your password, enter it and click **Authenticate.** By default, the volume is mounted in /run/media/*user*/Vol1, where *user* is the logon name of the current user.

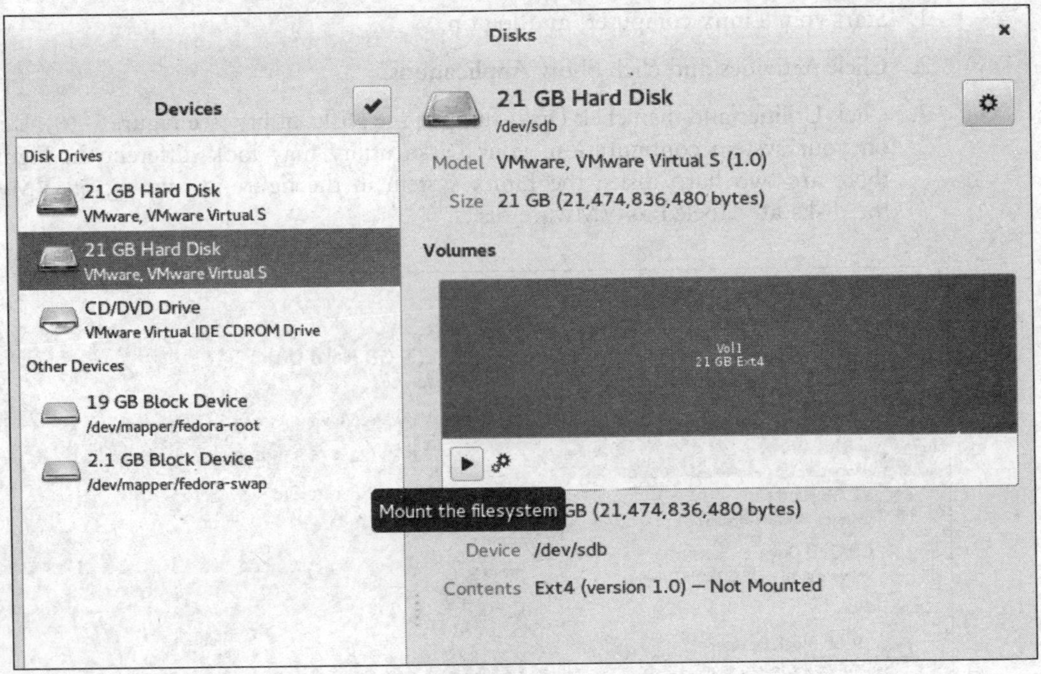


**Figure 7-19** Mounting the file system with the Linux Disks utility

*Source: Fedora Linux*

8. Click the link next to Mounted at; a Files window opens and shows the volume. The new volume is ready to use. Right-click in the right pane of Files, and click **New Folder** to see that you can use the new volume like any folder in Linux.

9. Open a terminal window, type **mount**, and press **Enter**. The last entry displayed should be the disk you just formatted, with information about where it is mounted.

10. To unmount the disk, type **umount /dev/sdb** and press **Enter**. The disk is no longer mounted.

11. Close all windows and log off or shut down your computer.

## Project 7-6: Use the Disk Utility in Mac OS X

Mac OS X provides the Disk Utility for working with storage. In this project, you use the Disk Utility to view information about a disk and see how to partition a disk. You need Administrator privileges to perform this activity.

1. Start your Mac and log on. Make sure that Finder is open (if not, click **Finder** in the Dock). Click the **Go** menu and click **Utilities**.
2. Double-click **Disk Utility**.
3. Click **Macintosh HD** in the left pane.
4. Click the **Info** icon in the menu bar to view information about the disk (see Figure 7-20).

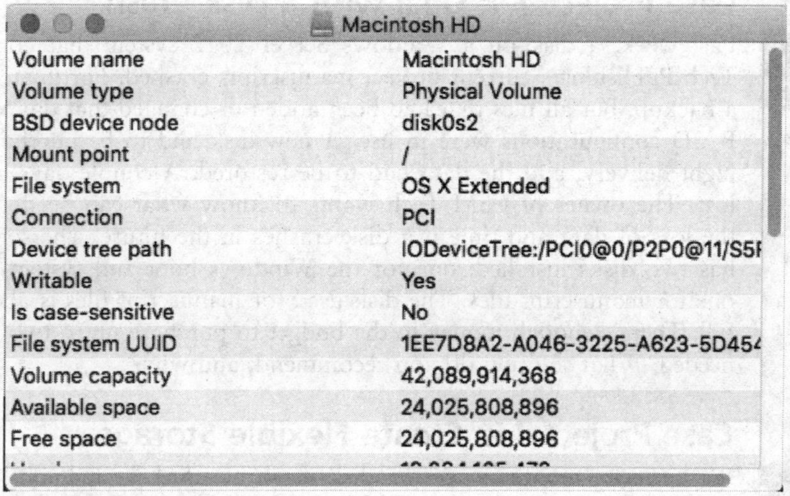


**Figure 7-20** Information about Macintosh HD

*Source: Mac OS X*

5. Close the Information window.
6. In the left pane, click the disk drive above Macintosh HD. Click the **Partition** icon in the menu bar. Read the information displayed about the partition. Notice that the partition scheme is GUID Partition Map, which is the same as GPT, and the format is OS X Extended (Journaled), which is the same as HFS Plus. Click **Cancel**.
7. Close the Disk Utility window and any other open windows.
8. Shut down your computer.

# Critical Thinking

The following activities give you critical thinking challenges. Challenge Labs give you an opportunity to use the skills you have learned to perform a task without step-by-step instructions. Case projects offer a practical problem for which you supply a written solution. Not all chapters contain Challenge Labs. There is not always a specific right or wrong answer to these critical thinking exercises. They are intended to encourage you to review the chapter material and delve deeper into the topics you have learned.

# Case Projects

## Case Project 7-1: Deal with a Disk Crash

Last week, a disk on a Windows Server 2012 system that contained CSM Tech Publishing's current project manuscripts crashed. Fortunately, there was a backup, but all files that had been added or changed that day were lost. No RAID configurations were in use. A new disk had to be purchased for overnight delivery, and the data had to be restored. A couple days of work were lost. The owner of CSM Tech wants to know what can be done to prevent the loss of data and time if a disk crashes in the future. The server currently has two disks installed: one for the Windows boot and system volumes and one for manuscript files. The disk used for manuscript files is about one-third full. There's enough money in the budget to purchase up to two new drives if needed. What solution do you recommend, and why?

## Case Project 7-2: Create Flexible Storage

It's been six months since the disk crash at CSM Tech Publishing, and the owner is breathing a little easier because of the solution you implemented in Case Project 7-1. Business is good, and the current solution is starting to run low on disk space—less than 20 percent of free space remains. In addition, the owner has some other needs that might require more disk space, and he wants to keep the data on separate volumes (what he calls *drives*). He wants a flexible solution in which drives and volumes aren't restricted in their configuration. He also wants to be able to add storage space to existing volumes easily without having to reconfigure existing drives. He has the budget to add a disk storage system that can contain up to 10 HDDs. Which Windows feature can accommodate these needs, and how does it work?

chapter 8

# Virtualization and Cloud Computing Fundamentals

**After reading this chapter and completing the exercises, you will be able to:**

- Describe the components of virtualization
- Use and describe hosted virtualization
- Use and describe bare-metal virtualization
- Describe cloud computing

**OS virtualization has become a mainstream technology in both small and large networks.** Large companies use it to consolidate server hardware and make efficient use of server processing power and network bandwidth. Individuals use virtualization to quickly try a new operating system without having to install the OS to their hard disk. IT professionals use virtualization to perform testing and what-if scenarios. Software developers can test their applications on multiple OSs and multiple versions of an OS without having to configure multiple physical computers. The ability to work at one physical Windows, Mac, or Linux workstation while using one, two, three, or even a dozen other OSs running on virtual machines opens up a world of possibilities. Users and IT professionals can become proficient on multiple OSs while owning just a single physical computer and data center administrators benefit from the ease in which virtual servers can be deployed and managed compared to their physical counterparts.

This chapter introduces you to virtualization, its terminology, and some of the popular virtualization products that can be used on the OSs this book has discussed.

# Virtualization Fundamentals

**Virtualization** is a process that creates a software environment to emulate a computer's hardware and BIOS, allowing multiple OSs to run on the same physical computer at the same time. This environment can be installed on most current OSs, including Windows, Linux, and Mac OS. In this case, a picture is worth a thousand words, so examine Figure 8-1. It shows a Windows 10 client running a Windows Server 2016 (technical preview) virtual machine that uses VMware Workstation virtualization software. Notice the two Start buttons: one on the host desktop and one on the virtual machine.

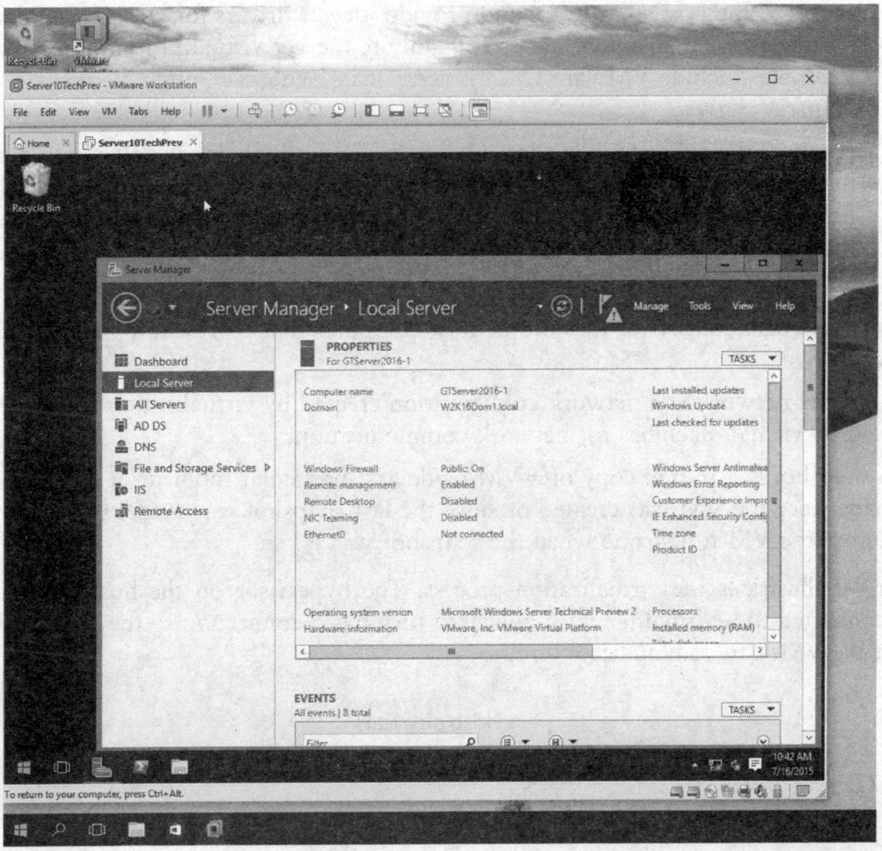


**Figure 8-1** Windows Server 2016 running as a virtual machine in Windows 10

Like all technologies, virtualization comes with a collection of terms that define its operation and components:

- A **virtual machine** (VM) is the virtual environment that emulates a physical computer's hardware and BIOS. A **guest OS** is the operating system installed on a VM.
- A **host computer** is the physical computer on which VM software is installed and VMs run.
- Virtualization software is used for creating and managing VMs and creating the virtual environment in which a guest OS is installed. Examples of this software are VMware Workstation, Oracle VirtualBox, and Microsoft Hyper-V.
- The **hypervisor** is the part of virtualization software that creates and monitors the virtual hardware environment, which allows multiple VMs to share physical hardware resources. On a host computer, the hypervisor acts somewhat like an OS kernel, but instead of scheduling processes for access to the CPU and other devices, it schedules VMs. It's sometimes called the *virtual machine monitor (VMM)*. There are two types of hypervisors:
    - A type 1 hypervisor implements OS virtualization by running directly on the host computer's hardware and controls and monitors guest OSs. It also controls

access to the host's hardware and provides device drivers for guest OSs. Also called **bare-metal virtualization,** it's used mainly for server virtualization in data centers. Examples include VMware ESX Server, Citrix XenServer, and Microsoft Hyper-V Server.

- A type 2 hypervisor implements OS virtualization by being installed in a general-purpose host OS, such as Windows 10 or Linux, and the host OS accesses host hardware on behalf of the guest OS. Also called **hosted virtualization**, it's used mostly for desktop virtualization solutions. Examples include VMware Player and Workstation, Oracle VirtualBox, and OpenVZ for Linux.

- A **virtual disk** consists of files on the host computer that represent a virtual machine's hard drive.
- A **virtual network** is a network configuration created by virtualization software and used by virtual machines for network communication.
- A **snapshot** is a partial copy of a VM made at a particular moment; it contains changes made since the VM was created or since the last snapshot was made. It is used to restore the VM to its state when the snapshot was taken.

Figure 8-2 illustrates the virtualization process. The hypervisor on the host is running two VMs connected to a virtual network, which in turn has a connection to the physical network so that the VMs can communicate on it.

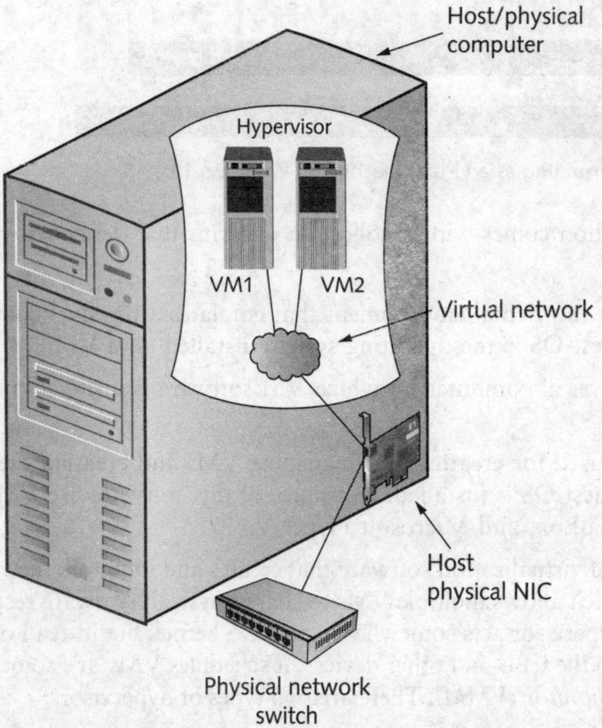


**Figure 8-2** How virtualization works

One of the best ways to understand a technology is to understand why it's used. The reasons to use virtualization are many and varied. They are best discussed by splitting the topic into the two main types of virtualization: hosted and bare-metal.

# Hosted Virtualization

As mentioned, hosted virtualization uses a type 2 hypervisor, which is installed on a standard desktop or server OS. It has the advantage of supporting a wider variety of guest OSs than bare-metal virtualization, mostly because the guest OS uses the host OS to access host hardware, so there are few incompatibility problems between the guest OS and hardware. For example, you can run a distribution of Linux in a virtual machine on a host computer, even if you can't install Linux directly on the physical machine because of driver incompatibilities.

Another advantage of hosted virtualization is that it's easy and straightforward to use. With hosted virtualization, you install the virtualization software on your computer and begin creating virtual machines. There are few hardware requirements, and most products run on Windows versions starting with Windows XP as well as Mac OS X and most Linux distributions. All you need are enough memory to support the host and guest OSs, adequate CPU power, and enough free disk space to store the virtual disk. A system running Windows 10 with 4 GB of RAM, a 2.0 GHz CPU, and a hard drive with 40 GB of free space can run Linux and Windows Server 2016 virtual machines at the same time. Performance might not be stellar, but the virtual machines should work well enough for experimenting or training, which are among the main reasons for using hosted virtualization.

## Hosted Virtualization Applications

Hosted virtualization is flexible and easy to use, so its applications continue to grow as people find different uses for it. Some common applications include the following:

- *OS training*—In the classroom and at home, learning multiple OSs has often been a problem of not having enough computers or a lack of compatibility between the OS and available computers. With virtualization, a computer can have a host OS installed, such as Windows 10, and have virtual machines for numerous Linux distributions, Windows 7, Windows Server 2016, and even Novell NetWare. If you want to learn about past OSs, you can install Windows 3.11, DOS, or OS/2, assuming you can find installation media for them. In addition, you can run multiple VMs at the same time by using a virtual network, which enables you to work with both client and server OSs in situations that would normally take two or more physical computers.
- *Software training*—Students and employees can be trained on new software packages by giving them VMs with preinstalled software.
- *Application isolation*—Not all software plays well together, so if an application conflicts with other installed software, it can be installed in its own VM, effectively isolating it from the host machine's installed software.
- *Network isolation*—Installing certain networking services, such as DHCP, can wreak havoc with an existing network. Virtual networks can be isolated from the rest of the network, however, so you can experiment with these services without causing conflicts.

- *Software development*—Software developers often need to design software that works on multiple OSs and OS versions. Testing on VMs makes this process easier than using a physical computer for each OS to be tested.
- *What-if scenarios*—If you want to try out a software package or see whether a configuration option you read about will actually improve performance, you might not want to risk destabilizing your computer. You can install software and make configuration changes safely on a VM before making the commitment on your production computer.
- *Use of legacy applications*—If you have a favorite application that won't run on a newer OS, you don't have to forego the latest software technology because of one application. You can install the old OS in a VM and run your legacy application on it.
- *Physical-to-virtual conversion*—Your six-year-old machine is getting slow and unreliable, so you bought a new desktop computer. However, you have several applications on your old computer and no longer have the installation media. You can convert your old computer to a virtual machine, and then keep all the software and run it on your new desktop computer as a VM. You'll probably even see a speed boost.

As you can see, virtualization can bring plenty of benefits to your computing experience. You have many choices of products, and the good news is that many are free. The following section describes some products for hosted virtualization.

## Hosted Virtualization Products

Several hosted virtualization products are available. The following are the most well known:

- *VMware Workstation Pro*—VMware, the virtualization pioneer in the PC world, released VMware Workstation in 1999. Of the hosted virtualization products, it offers the most features, including multiple snapshots, extensive guest OS support, and nested virtualization (the capability to run a virtual machine inside another virtual machine).
- *VMware Workstation Player*—This version of VMware Workstation has a streamlined user interface and fewer advanced features than Workstation Pro, but it maintains excellent guest OS support. The current version (Workstation 12 Player) is free for personal, noncommercial use, but it costs about $150 for business or commercial use as of this writing.
- *Microsoft Virtual PC*—This free download from Microsoft enables you to create and run virtual machines. XP mode is a feature available only in Windows 7 Professional or Ultimate that integrates Windows XP virtual machine applications with the Windows 7 desktop. Virtual PC is no longer available in Windows 8 and later versions.
- *VirtualBox*—Originally developed by Innotek, VirtualBox is now developed by Oracle Corporation. Two versions are available: a proprietary version that's free for home users and can be purchased for enterprise use, and a free open-source version with a reduced feature set. VirtualBox runs on Linux, Mac OS X, or Windows hosts. The proprietary version has features similar to VMware Workstation.

TIP

For more information on virtualization products, the platforms they run on, and supported guest OSs, review the article at *http://en.wikipedia.org/wiki/Comparison_of_platform_virtual_machines*.

The preceding products have their strengths and weaknesses; the best approach is to work with different products to see which best serves your needs. The following sections discuss the use of these products.

## Using VMware Workstation

VMware Workstation isn't free, but you can download a free trial version and try it for 30 days. Nonprofit educational institutions can join the VMware Academic program to give students and faculty free downloads of VMware Workstation and other VMware products.

After VMware Workstation is installed, a wizard takes you through the steps of creating a virtual machine. You can choose the size of the virtual disk and set other hardware options or just accept the default settings.

One convenience of installing a guest OS in a VM is being able to boot to the installation program with an ISO file rather than a DVD disk. This way, if you download the ISO file, burning a DVD to install the OS is unnecessary. In addition, the ISO file can be stored on a server and used by multiple users for VM installations.

An advanced feature of VMware Workstation is its flexible networking options. You can configure the network interface card (NIC) on your VM to use one of the five virtual network options or you can create your own custom virtual network. VMware Workstation supports VMs with multiple NICs, and each NIC can be connected to a different virtual network. The five options are as follows (see Figure 8-3):

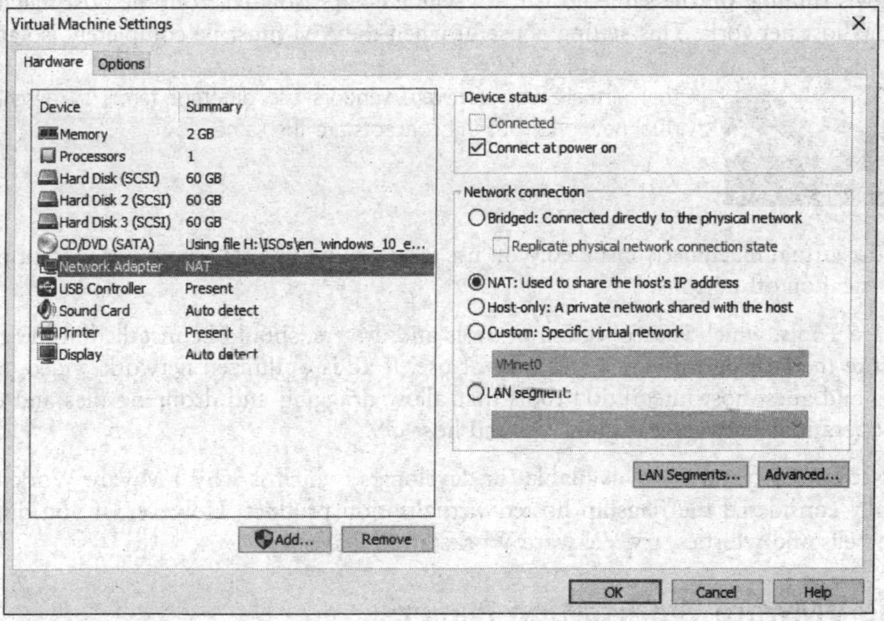


**Figure 8-3** VMware virtual network options

*Source: VMware, Inc., www.vmware.com*

- *Bridged*—This option connects the VM's virtual network to the physical network, and the VM acts like any other computer on the physical network, including having an IP address on the physical network. This option was illustrated in Figure 8-2, which showed that the virtual network has a (virtual) connection to the host's physical NIC.
- *NAT*—Using this default option, the host computer's IP address is shared with the VM by using Network Address Translation (NAT). The main difference between the NAT and Bridged options is that VMs are assigned an IP address from the host computer rather than the physical network, and the host translates the address for incoming and outgoing packets. This option is more secure than the Bridged option because the VM isn't directly accessible on the network. However, it's not a viable option for a VM that provides server functions to the host network.
- *Host-only*—This option isolates the VM from the host network and only allows network communication between VMs running on the host and the host computer. It's the most secure configuration and has the lowest risk that the VM will cause problems with the host network. This configuration works well when you have multiple VMs that must communicate with one another but you don't need to access computers or devices outside the host.
- *Custom*—You can use this option to connect the VM to a virtual network created with the virtual network editor, a tool accessible from the Edit menu in VMware Workstation. With a custom network, you assign a subnet to the network, and you have the option of using DHCP to assign IP addresses to connected VMs. With the virtual network editor, you can make the custom virtual network bridged, NAT, or host-only.
- *LAN segment*—LAN segments are private networks that can be shared with other VMs running on the same host. LAN segments are isolated from the host machine and the host network. This setting is useful when the VM must be completely isolated.

Other virtualization software vendors use different terms to describe virtual networks, but the concepts are the same.

After the virtual machine is installed, you use it as you would any computer, except there are no physical on/off buttons.

VMware Tools, which is a collection of tools and drivers, should be installed in the guest OS to ensure the best performance and ease of use. It adds optimized network, video, and disk drivers and guest-host integration tools that allow dragging and dropping files and cut-and-paste operations between the guest OS and host OS.

Other advanced features are available for developers, which is why VMware Workstation is generally considered the flagship hosted virtualization product. However, if you don't need all the bells and whistles, try VMware Workstation Player.

## Using VMware Workstation Player

VMware Workstation Player is a stripped-down version of VMware Workstation Pro that still offers the basics of desktop virtualization in a streamlined and easy-to-use interface.

You can download a free trial from the VMware Web site, and it's also included with the VMware Workstation package. The opening window of VMware Workstation Player gives you an idea of its clean interface (see Figure 8-4).

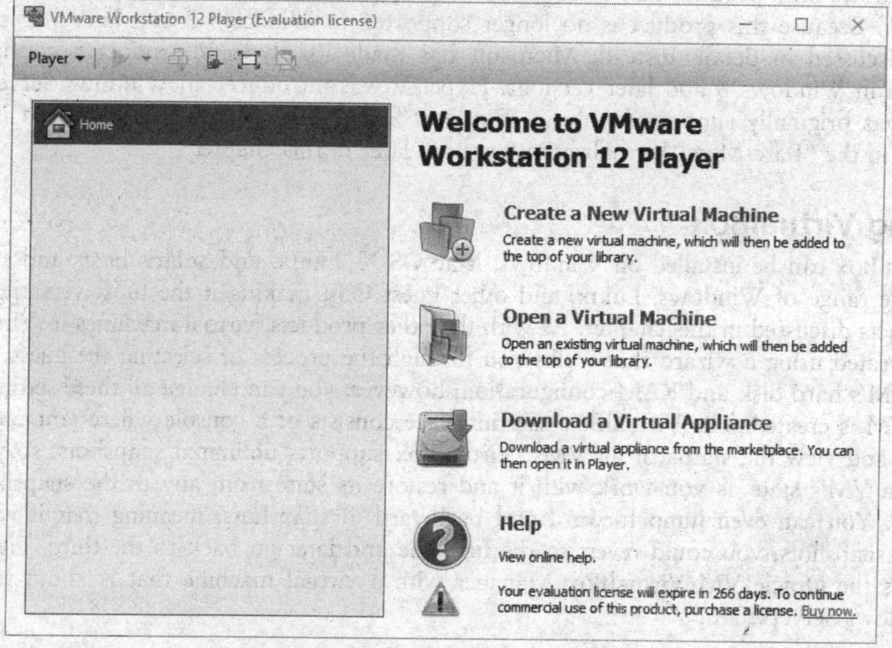


**Figure 8-4** The VMware Workstation Player Welcome window

*Source: VMware, Inc., www.vmware.com*

VMware Workstation 12 Player is now a paid product for business and commercial use. As of this writing, you may still be able to download and install version 7 of the VMware Player, which was the last version that VMware offered as a totally free product. You can download most of VMware's products for a 30-day trial.

To create a VM in VMware Workstation Player, you use a wizard that is nearly identical to the one in VMware Workstation. Notice in Figure 8-4 that you have the option to download a virtual appliance. Virtual appliances are ready-to-use VMs from OS and software vendors that contain a guest OS with preconfigured applications or network services. In some cases, a virtual appliance is just a preinstalled guest OS. A virtual appliance is an easy way to use and evaluate a product or configuration without having to install it yourself. Virtual appliances can be run by VMware Workstation Player or VMware Workstation Pro and sometimes by VMware's bare-metal virtualization products.

VMware Player offers many of the same features as VMware Workstation, with the exception of snapshots, customized virtual networks (although the three preconfigured network options are available), and some advanced network and virtual hardware settings. It's a good choice for new virtualization users and for classroom and training centers where the interface's simplicity is an advantage.

## Using Microsoft Virtual PC

The VMware products just discussed can be installed on both Windows and Linux OSs; another desktop product called VMware Fusion runs in Mac OS X. However, Virtual PC is a Windows-only product that runs in the Windows 7 Professional, Enterprise, or Ultimate edition. Because this product is no longer supported in Windows 8 and later versions, it's not discussed in detail. Instead, Microsoft has made its Hyper-V product a configurable option in Windows 8 and later versions. Hyper-V was introduced in Windows Server 2008 and was originally supported only in Windows Server OSs. Hyper-V is discussed in more detail in the "Bare-Metal Virtualization" section later in this chapter.

## Using VirtualBox

VirtualBox can be installed on Windows, Mac OS X, Linux, and Solaris hosts and supports a wide range of Windows, Linux, and other guest OSs, making it the most versatile of the products discussed in this chapter. As with the other products, virtual machines in VirtualBox are created using a wizard that walks you through the process of selecting the guest OS and the VM's hard disk and RAM configuration; however, you can change all these settings after the VM is created. The VirtualBox user interface consists of a console where you can create VMs and view the status of all VMs. VirtualBox supports unlimited snapshots, so you can save a VM's state as you work with it and restore its state from any of the snapshots you make. You can even jump forward and backward in snapshots, meaning that if you have three snapshots, you could revert to the first one and later go back to the third. Figure 8-5 shows the Oracle VM VirtualBox Manager with a virtual machine that is about to install Windows Server 2016.

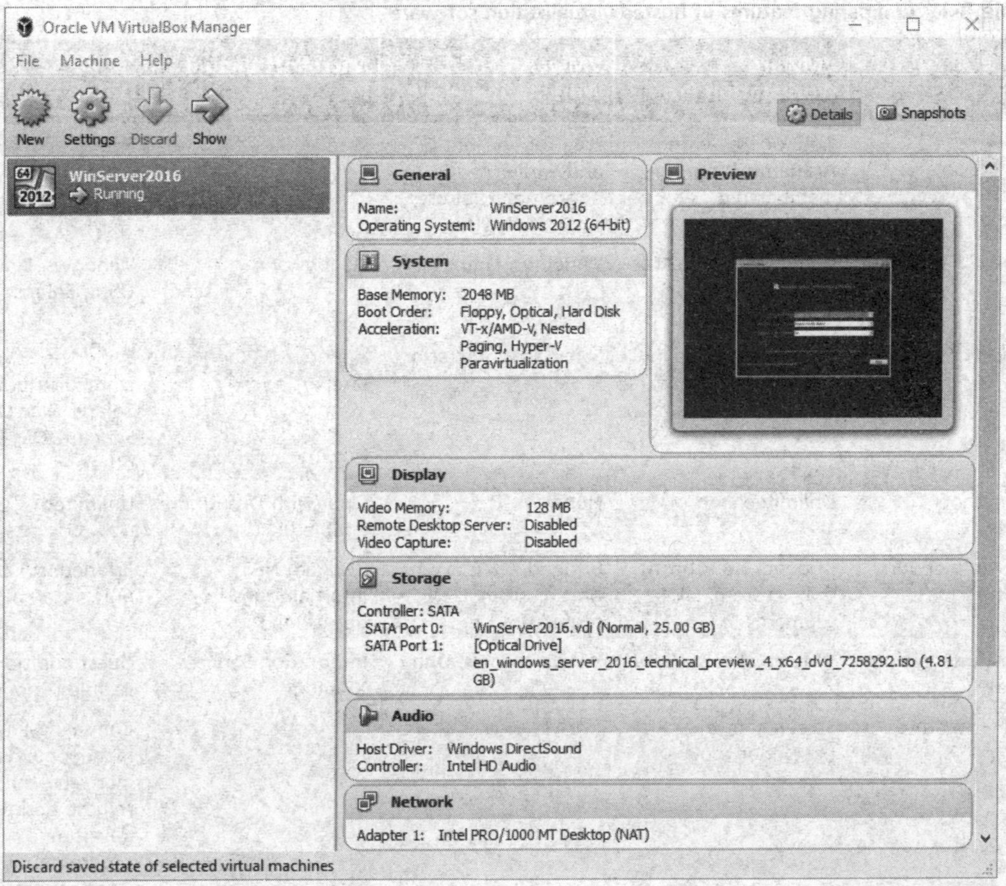


**Figure 8-5** Oracle VM VirtualBox Manager

## Virtualization Software Summary

All the virtualization products discussed so far provide a type 2 hypervisor for hosted virtualization. Table 8-1 summarizes some major features and differences in these products. A benefit is that you can install all of these products and run them at the same time on a single host computer, so you can download and install each one and evaluate it for yourself.

**Table 8-1 Comparing features of hosted virtualization software**

| | VMware Workstation Pro | VMware Workstation Player | Microsoft Virtual PC | Oracle VirtualBox |
|---|---|---|---|---|
| Price | $249 or free with Academic Program membership | Free for versions 7 and earlier or for noncommercial use, $149 otherwise | Free | Free |
| Host OS support | Windows, Linux, Mac OS X (with VMware Fusion) | Windows, Linux | Windows | Windows, Linux, Mac OS X, Solaris |
| Guest OS support | Windows, several Linux distributions, NetWare, Solaris, DOS | Same as Workstation Pro | Windows XP and later | Windows, several Linux distributions, Solaris, Mac OS X Server, DOS, OS/2, others |
| Snapshots | Unlimited | None | One (with Disk Undo enabled) | Unlimited |
| Virtual network options | Bridged, NAT, host-only, custom, LAN segments | Bridged, NAT, host-only, custom, LAN segments | Bridged, NAT, internal (guest-to-guest only) | Bridged, NAT, host-only, internal |
| Host integration tools | VMware Tools, Unity | VMware Tools, Unity | Integration Services, XP mode | Guest additions, seamless mode |
| Other features | Screen capture, developer tools | | | Command-line management interface, built-in remote desktop, developer programming interface, open-source edition |

# Bare-Metal Virtualization

Bare-metal virtualization products (type 1 hypervisors) are targeted mainly for production virtualization in data centers. These products are installed directly on hardware and have more stringent host machine requirements than hosted products. Because they're targeted for IT departments, they have more features for managing VMs and have a performance advantage over hosted virtualization products. Their installation and use tend to require more sophisticated, knowledgeable users. Before learning about specific products, take a look at some applications for bare-metal virtualization products.

## Bare-Metal Virtualization Applications

Bare-metal virtualization products come with a price tag for the virtualization software, the hardware to run it, or both. When considering whether to use virtualization in an IT data center, most IT managers look for a return on their investment in real money or in productivity gains. The following applications show that bare-metal virtualization can deliver both:

- *Consolidate servers*—Server consolidation is probably the original reason for using bare-metal virtualization. It has the following benefits:
  - Retire old or unreliable hardware: Converting physical machines to VMs and running them on the latest hardware means you can get rid of old hardware, thereby gaining a reliability advantage and avoiding the tedious task of reinstalling and reconfiguring a server OS on new hardware. You might also improve performance.
  - Make optimal use of multicore, high-performance servers: Some server roles, such as Active Directory, should be the only major network service running on a server. With multicore server CPUs, you're likely to waste a lot of the server's power if you install a single-role OS. Instead, run two, three, or more VMs on the server, making optimal use of the available performance.
  - Maintain application separation: Some applications and services run best when they're the only major application installed on an OS. You avoid OS resource conflicts and gain stability and reliability.
  - Reclaim rack or floor space: By consolidating a dozen physical servers into three or four host servers, you're no longer tripping over a plethora of towers or wondering whether your rack can handle one more server. You can even clear enough room for an easy chair and a reading lamp so that you can catch up on the latest technical journals in comfort!
  - Reduce cooling and power requirements: By reducing the number of servers (even with higher-performance machines), you usually save money on the costs of cooling and powering a data center, especially when you reduce hundreds of servers down to dozens of virtualization servers.
- *Test installations and upgrades*—Before you install a major software package or upgrade on your server, create a copy of the VM (referred to as *cloning* in some products), and go through a test run to iron out any potential problems or conflicts. If something goes wrong on the production VM, you can revert to a snapshot.
- *Test a preconfigured application*—Are you unsure whether the application the vendor wants to sell you is right for your company? Some vendors offer virtual appliances you can use to evaluate the application without having to install it.
- *Test what-if scenarios*—You can create a virtual network and run clones of your production VMs to test ideas for improving your network's performance, functionality, and reliability. This type of testing on live production systems is never a good idea, but it's ideal on virtual machines.
- *Live migration*—Virtual machines can be migrated to new hardware while they're running for performance or reliability improvements with practically no downtime. Live migration features also ensure VM fault tolerance in clustered server environments.
- *Dynamic provisioning*—Advanced VM management systems can deploy VMs and storage dynamically to meet application requirements. This advanced feature has uses in clustered computing and cloud computing.

VMs that run distributed server applications, such as Active Directory, in which multiple servers synchronize a common database with one another, shouldn't be backed up or moved by copying the virtual hard disk because it might result in database inconsistencies. Use only backup and migration tools approved for the virtualization software.

## Bare-Metal Virtualization Products

VMware dominated the type 1 hypervisor category for years, but now you have a choice of products. The following are the most common bare-metal virtualization products:

- *Microsoft Hyper-V*—Hyper-V was introduced with Windows Server 2008 and can be installed as a server role, in which case the hypervisor is installed as a layer of software between Windows Server and the server hardware. Windows Server acts as a parent or management OS for VMs installed with Hyper-V. Hyper-V is included with Windows Server at no additional cost, or you can download the stand-alone Hyper-V Server free from the Microsoft Web site. (You can install Hyper-V Server directly on the server, with only a command-line interface available for rudimentary management tasks; it's managed remotely by another Windows Server computer.) Hyper-V supports advanced features, such as host server clustering and live migration, and requires a 64-bit CPU with virtualization extensions enabled on the host system. Virtualization extensions offload some virtualization work to the CPU and are present on most current CPUs.

  A big advantage of using Hyper-V is that Microsoft provides virtual instances of the OS with no additional licensing fees. For example, Windows Server 2012 Standard Edition allows you to run two virtual instances (or two VMs) of the OS at no additional cost. Datacenter Edition allows an unlimited number of virtual instances. Hyper-V has guest OS support for Windows Server OSs (Windows 2000 Server and later), SUSE and Red Hat Enterprise Linux distributions, Windows client OSs (Windows XP and later), and more.

  Microsoft has made Hyper-V available with Windows client OSs, too. You can enable Hyper-V in Windows 8 and later versions by opening Programs and Features in Control Panel and clicking "Turn Windows features on or off." After Hyper-V is installed, you need to restart your computer and open Hyper-V Manager (see Figure 8-6) from Administrative Tools in Control Panel.

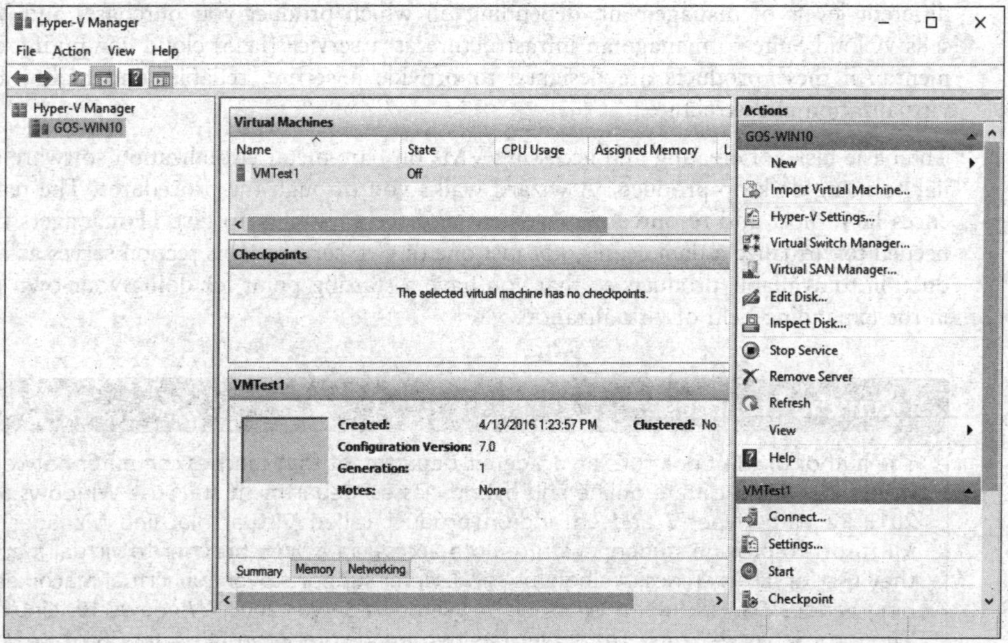


**Figure 8-6** The Hyper-V Manager console

- *Citrix XenServer*—This open-source hypervisor uses Linux as a management OS on the host. It's available free or as a commercial edition that adds enterprise-level features, such as fault tolerance, performance management, and host power management. A number of modified Linux versions and Solaris can run as the management OS, and like Hyper-V, a XenServer host computer requires a 64-bit CPU with virtualization extensions to run Windows guest OSs. Guest OS support includes most Windows OSs, starting with Windows XP, and SUSE, Red Hat, and CentOS Linux distributions. To manage your host and VMs, you download and install XenCenter on a Windows computer or use a command-line interface on the host computer. XenCenter provides virtual machine management, monitoring, and administration from any Windows OS.
- *VMware vSphere*—vSphere includes VMware ESX Server, which is installed directly on the physical server without a management OS. After ESX Server is installed, a basic command-line console based on Linux is available for simple configuration tasks, such as IP address configuration. Most configuration tasks are performed from a remote client OS using vSphere Client, which is downloaded and installed on a Windows or Linux OS. You can also create, manage, and access VMs via a Web browser. ESX Server has the broadest guest OS support of the type 1 hypervisors, including Windows versions back to Windows 3.1, more than a dozen Linux distributions, Novell NetWare, and Solaris.

All these products have extensive management tools for managing up to hundreds of hosts and a wide array of storage resources. These tools are available for a fee from virtualization software vendors. For example, Microsoft offers System Center Virtual Machine Manager (SCVMM) for managing Hyper-V and ESX Server hosts. XenServer offers versions with different levels of management, depending on which product you purchase, and VMware sells vCloud Suite to manage an infrastructure as a service (IaaS) cloud computing environment. All these products are designed to provide a secure, reliable, and highly available virtualization infrastructure.

The basic tasks of creating and accessing VMs on bare-metal virtualization software are similar to using desktop products: A wizard walks you through the procedures. The real differences lie in host and resource management and the capability to give IT managers the tools needed to virtualize a data center, not just one or two servers. This section serves as an introduction to available products so that you have a starting point for doing your own research in the expanding field of virtualization.

**From the Trenches ...**

The author of this book runs an academic department that teaches computer networking technology. To facilitate online and hybrid classes, department staff use Windows Server 2012 R2 with Hyper-V and an add-on product called Virtual Machine Manager from Microsoft to provide students with remote access via a Web browser to virtual machines they use for lab exercises. A single physical server supports over 100 virtual machines running various OSs, including Windows 7, Windows Server 2008, Windows 10, Linux, and Windows Server 2012/R2. The server has two quad-core Xeon CPUs, 64 GB of RAM, two terabytes of disk space, and four 1000BaseT Ethernet ports. To access a virtual machine, students point their Web browser to the server's address and log on. Their logon ID is paired with one or more VMs to which they are assigned. The students can start, log on, and use their VM to complete lab activities. The server can efficiently run about 30 VMs simultaneously, and if students forget to shut down their VM, a PowerShell script runs every 10 minutes automatically and shuts down any VMs that have been running longer than four hours. This is an example of virtualization and private cloud computing.

# Cloud Computing

Many people rely on the Internet's services for communication, research, and entertainment. This trend has continued to the point that many functions once handled in a company's IT center are now handled by servers on the Internet—what's referred to as *cloud computing*. **Cloud computing** is a networking model in which data, applications, and processing power are managed by servers on the Internet; users of these resources pay for what they use rather than for the equipment and software needed to provide resources. It's like paying only for cell phone minutes you use instead of paying for the towers and switching equipment needed to make your phone work.

The word *cloud* is used to obscure the details of equipment and software that actually provide resources. For the most part, customers don't care whether equipment consists of Windows or Linux servers, large tower computers, or rack-mounted computers, as long as it works.

For many companies, cloud computing's allure is based on the following benefits:

- *Reduced physical plant costs*—Having fewer servers means less space is needed to house them, and less electricity and cooling are required to keep servers running.
- *Reduced upfront costs*—Paying only for services and software that are used means a company can avoid the startup costs of purchasing a lot of expensive hardware and software.
- *Reduced personnel costs*—Having fewer servers and applications to support means fewer IT employees are needed to support hardware and applications.

Although cloud computing has seemingly limitless applications, three main categories of cloud computing have taken center stage:

- Software as a service
- Platform as a service
- Infrastructure as a service

The phrase *as a service* simply means that the resource resides on another server or network than the one using the resource, and customers use it as a paid service. You might also hear the term *SPI model*, which is based on the combination of the three aforementioned "as a service" terms (*S*oftware, *P*latform, *I*nfrastructure).

## Software as a Service

Software as a service (SaaS) is also called *hosted applications* or *on-demand applications* because the customer doesn't actually buy any software that's installed on its own equipment. Instead, the customer pays for the use of applications that run on a service provider's network. The most well-known examples are Google Apps and Microsoft Office 365, which a business or a home user can use to run hosted applications, such as e-mail, calendar, word-processing, and spreadsheet programs. More complex applications involve large database systems, such as payroll services from ADP and customer relationship management software offered by companies such as Salesforce.com.

SaaS is usually offered as a subscription based on the number of people using the application. It takes the burden of installation and maintenance off the customer so that companies can focus on maintaining their LANs and Internet access instead of maintaining hundreds of copies of an installed application. In addition, customers can take advantage of new software editions much faster than with the standard deployment times of traditional application upgrades. Some application upgrades require client computer or OS upgrades, but with SaaS, the vendor handles infrastructure upgrades when needed.

In addition, SaaS is available anywhere the customer has a connection to the Internet. Mobile users and telecommuters have access to the same applications they use in the office without having to install the software on their laptops or home computers. Some applications can't even be installed on home computers, but with SaaS, the software runs on remote servers, so local installations aren't necessary.

## Platform as a Service

**Platform as a service (PaaS)**—also called *hosted platform*—is similar to SaaS, but the customer develops applications with the service provider's tools and infrastructure. After applications are developed, they can be delivered to the customer's users from the provider's servers. This setup differs from SaaS, in which the service provider owns the applications delivered to users; with PaaS, the customer develops and owns the application and then delivers it to a third party.

Developers who use PaaS can take advantage of many of the same benefits enjoyed by SaaS users. In addition, after an application is developed with PaaS, the developer can usually deploy the application immediately to customers who access it as a hosted application. The same operating environment used to develop the application is used to run it, which bypasses the sometimes complex and problem-prone process of migrating from a traditional development environment to a production environment.

The most common PaaS products are Salesforce.com's Apex, Azure for Windows, Google's App Engine for Python and Java, WaveMaker for Ajax, and Engine Yard for Ruby on Rails. Others are available, but details on these development platforms are beyond the scope of this book. PaaS is still an evolving model for application development, and platforms will come and go as developers weed out what works and what doesn't. Developing in the cloud is likely here to stay because it offers benefits that aren't usually available in a locally managed environment. In addition, because small businesses and individual developers have access to expensive, full-featured development environments, entrepreneurs can be on an equal footing with the big boys, which increases competition and innovation—and that's always a good thing.

## Infrastructure as a Service

**Infrastructure as a service (IaaS)**, or *hosted infrastructure*, allows companies to use a vendor's storage or even entire virtual servers as needed. Traditionally, if a company needs another 100 GB of storage to house a new database, it has to buy a new hard drive—assuming the server can accommodate a new hard drive. By using IaaS, the company simply pays for another 100 GB of space without worrying about how that space is actually provided. In addition, if a customer needs another server to handle its application workload, it simply pays for the amount of processing and storage the additional server actually requires instead of paying for the physical device. In most cases, IaaS servers run as virtual machines on more powerful physical servers.

IaaS differs from other hosted services because customers mostly rent the resources they're using but are still responsible for application installations and upgrades. Although IT staff can be reduced because the IaaS vendor handles physical device upkeep, customers still need IT staff to configure and manage applications and server OSs.

IaaS isn't just for server infrastructure. Companies can "upgrade" to the latest OSs and desktop applications by using virtualized desktops through their IaaS providers. By accessing desktops remotely, IaaS customers can use thin clients (client computers with minimal hardware resources) or computers with older OSs to make use of the latest desktop OSs and applications. This IaaS feature, virtual desktop infrastructure (VDI), is becoming a popular way for companies to deliver desktop OSs and applications rather than use traditional methods of installing OSs and applications locally.

Examples of IaaS include Amazon Web Services (AWS), Rackspace Cloud, and Microsoft Azure, but many more companies and products are getting into this burgeoning market.

You may hear the term *anything as a service*, which is abbreviated as XaaS. There are also variations on the preceding services, such as storage as a service (SaaS), database as a service (DaaS), and network as a service (NaaS). Other "as a service" functions will undoubtedly be created.

Cloud computing relies heavily on virtualization, which allows a cloud service provider to offer a flexible computing environment to its customers and get the most out of its physical computing devices. With virtualization, a provider can quickly deploy additional computing power for a customer simply by clicking a configuration check box to add more virtual CPUs. Entire virtual servers can be deployed within seconds; using virtual disks, customers can get access to more storage quickly and easily.

Cloud computing isn't for every company or situation, but it offers a flexible array of services that can complement an IT department's existing resources and sometimes replace them. The trend toward cloud computing is growing with no abatement in site.

## Private Cloud Versus Public Cloud

The preceding cloud technologies have been discussed in the context of a third party providing services to customers via the Internet—a **public cloud** solution. In a public cloud, computing resources and their management are the responsibility of the cloud service provider. This arrangement allows a company to focus on its primary business rather than a large IT infrastructure. However, because the cloud resources are in someone else's hands, you must depend on the provider to ensure the reliability and security of the provided service and your data. In addition, you are depending on Internet providers to connect your location with the cloud service provider. If the Internet goes down anywhere in that path, you will be unable to access the cloud service.

Many companies deliver cloud services to their own employees through the use of virtualization technologies, such as VMware and Microsoft Hyper-V—a **private cloud**. VDI, cloud storage, and SaaS are commonly accessed as private cloud services deployed from the company's own data center instead of using a public cloud service. This setup gives a company more control and more security, yet provides its employees many of the benefits of cloud computing. The drawback is the up-front and ongoing costs of maintaining a large IT infrastructure.

# Chapter Summary

- Virtualization is a process that creates a software environment to emulate a computer's hardware and BIOS, allowing multiple OSs to run on the same physical computer at the same time.
- Virtualization can be divided into two categories: hosted virtualization and bare-metal virtualization. Hosted virtualization uses a type 2 hypervisor and bare-metal virtualization uses a type 1 hypervisor.

- Hosted virtualization products are installed on a desktop OS and include VMware Workstation, Virtual PC, and VirtualBox.
- Bare-metal virtualization products are targeted mainly for production virtualization in data centers. These products are installed directly on hardware and have more stringent host machine requirements than hosted products. Bare-metal virtualization software is used in data centers, is installed on servers, and includes products such as Microsoft Hyper-V, VMware vSphere, and Citrix XenServer.
- Cloud computing is a networking model in which data, applications, and processing power are managed by servers on the Internet. Users of these resources pay for what they use rather than for the equipment and software needed to provide resources. Cloud computing models include SaaS, PaaS, and IaaS.

# Key Terms

**bare-metal virtualization** A system in which the hypervisor implements OS virtualization by running directly on the host computer's hardware and controls and monitors guest OSs. See also *virtualization*.

**cloud computing** A networking model in which data, applications, and processing power are managed by servers on the Internet; users of these resources pay for what they use rather than for the equipment and software needed to provide resources.

**guest OS** The operating system installed on a virtual machine.

**host computer** The physical computer on which virtual machine software is installed and virtual machines run.

**hosted virtualization** A system in which the hypervisor implements OS virtualization by being installed in a general-purpose host OS, such as Windows 10 or Linux, and the host OS accesses host hardware on behalf of the guest OS. See also *virtualization*.

**hypervisor** The component of virtualization software that creates and monitors the virtual hardware environment, which allows multiple VMs to share physical hardware resources.

**infrastructure as a service (IaaS)** A category of cloud computing in which a company can use a provider's storage or virtual servers as its needs demand; IaaS is also called *hosted infrastructure*.

**platform as a service (PaaS)** A category of cloud computing in which a customer develops applications with the service provider's development tools and infrastructure. After applications are developed, they can be delivered to the customer's users from the provider's servers. PaaS is also called *hosted platform*.

**private cloud** Cloud services that a company delivers to its own employees.

**public cloud** Cloud services delivered by a third-party provider.

**snapshot** A partial copy of a virtual machine made at a particular moment; it can be used to restore the virtual machine to its state when the snapshot was taken. See also *virtual machine (VM)*.

**software as a service (SaaS)** A category of cloud computing in which a customer pays for the use of applications that run on a service provider's network; SaaS is also called *hosted applications*.

**virtual disk** Files stored on the host computer that represent a virtual machine's hard disk.

**virtual machine (VM)** A software environment that emulates a physical computer's hardware and BIOS.

**virtual network** A network configuration created by virtualization software and used by virtual machines for network communication.

**virtualization** A process that creates a software environment to emulate a computer's hardware and BIOS, allowing multiple OSs to run on the same physical computer at the same time.

## Review Questions

1. Which of the following can best be described as developing applications by using a service provider's development tools and infrastructure?
   a. hosted applications
   b. hosted networking
   c. hosted platforms
   d. hosted infrastructure
2. Which of the following is a partial copy of a VM made at a particular moment that enables you to restore the VM's state?
   a. incremental backup
   b. virtual disk
   c. load balancing
   d. snapshot
3. What can be defined as software that creates and monitors the virtual hardware environment?
   a. host computer
   b. hypervisor
   c. snapshot
   d. guest OS
4. Bare-metal virtualization is best for desktop virtualization. True or False?
5. If you want your virtual machine to have direct access to the physical network, which virtual network option should you configure?
   a. bridged
   b. NAT
   c. host-only
   d. internal

6. Which of the following is the virtual environment that emulates a physical computer's hardware and BIOS?
   a. virtual machine
   b. guest OS
   c. host computer
   d. snapshot
7. Which component of virtualization allows multiple VMs to share physical hardware resources?
   a. virtual machine
   b. snapshot
   c. host computer
   d. hypervisor
8. Which of the following is true about bare-metal virtualization?
   a. It supports a wider variety of guest OSs.
   b. It uses the host OS to access hardware.
   c. It uses a type 1 hypervisor.
   d. VMware Workstation Player is an example.
9. Which virtual network configuration shares an IP address with the host computer?
   a. bridged
   b. NAT
   c. host-only
   d. LAN segment
10. Which virtual network configuration is isolated from the host computer?
    a. bridged
    b. NAT
    c. host-only
    d. LAN segment
11. On which host OS can you run Hyper-V?
    a. Mac OS X
    b. Windows 10
    c. Ubuntu Linux
    d. Solaris

12. Which feature provided by some virtualization products allows you to move a VM to a new host computer while the VM is running?
    a. live migration
    b. snapshots
    c. VM cloning
    d. dynamic provisioning
13. Which of the following are reasons to use bare-metal virtualization?
    a. retiring old hardware
    b. reusing older computers
    c. reducing cooling
    d. reclaiming floor space
14. Which feature of some virtualization products allows you to deploy VMs and storage as needed and has uses in cloud computing?
    a. live migration
    b. snapshots
    c. VM cloning
    d. dynamic provisioning
15. When did Microsoft introduce the Hyper-V product?
    a. with Windows Server 2012
    b. with Windows Server 2008
    c. with Windows Vista
    d. with Windows 7
16. In which cloud computing model does Google Apps best fit?
    a. IaaS
    b. PaaS
    c. SaaS
    d. DaaS

## Hands-On Projects

### Project 8-1: Enable Hyper-V for Windows 10

In this project, you enable Hyper-V on a Windows 10 computer.

1. Start and log on to your Windows 10 computer.
2. Right-click **Start** and click **Control Panel.** In Control Panel, click **Programs.**
3. Under Programs and Features, click **Turn Windows features on or off.**

4. Click **Hyper-V** to select it. Click the plus sign to see the options under Hyper-V. You will enable the management tools and the Hyper-V platform. Click **OK**.
5. When prompted, click **Restart now** to finish the installation.
6. When Windows restarts, log on, click in the search box next to the Start button, and type **admin**. In the search results, click **Administrative Tools**.
7. In Administrative Tools, double-click **Hyper-V Manager**. In the next project, you will create a virtual machine and explore the settings. Leave Hyper-V Manager open if you are continuing to the next project.

## Project 8-2: Create a VM in Hyper-V

You have installed the Hyper-V role on Windows 10 and are ready to create a virtual machine.

1. Log on to your Windows 10 computer and open Hyper-V Manager, if necessary. If your Windows 10 computer is not selected in the left pane, click **Connect to Server** in the Actions pane, click **Local computer**, and then click **OK**.
2. In the Actions pane, click **New**, and then click **Virtual Machine**.
3. Read the information in the Before You Begin window. You can create a default virtual machine simply by clicking Finish in this window, but for this activity, click **Next**.
4. In the Name text box, type **VMTest1**. You can choose a location to store the virtual machine configuration, but for this activity, accept the default location of C:\ProgramData\Microsoft\Windows\Hyper-V by clicking **Next**.
5. In the Specify Generation window, you choose whether to create a generation 1 or generation 2 virtual machine. Leave the default selection, **Generation 1**, and click **Next**.
6. In the Assign Memory window, type **512** in the Startup memory text box, and then click **Next**.
7. In the Configure Networking window, leave the default option, **Not Connected**. Click **Next**.
8. In the Connect Virtual Hard Disk window, you can enter the virtual hard disk's name, size, and location. By default, the size is 127 GB, and Hyper-V assigns the hard disk the same name as the VM, with the extension .vhdx. You can also use an existing virtual disk or attach one later. Write down the location where Hyper-V stores the virtual hard disk by default, in case you want to access the virtual disk later. Click **Next** to accept the default settings.
9. In the Installation Options window, click the **Install an operating system later** option button, if necessary. Click **Next**.
10. The Completing the New Virtual Machine Wizard window displays a summary of your virtual machine configuration. Click **Finish**. After the virtual machine is created,

you return to Hyper-V Manager and see your new VM in the Virtual Machines pane of Hyper-V Manager (see Figure 8-7).

11. Leave Hyper-V Manager open if you're continuing to the next activity.

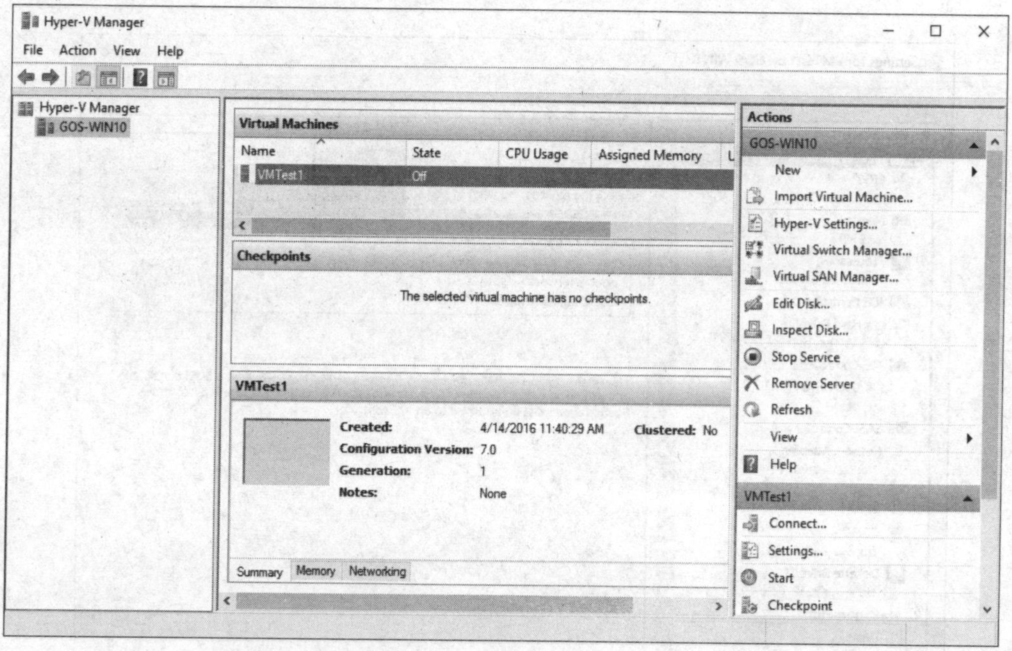


**Figure 8-7** Hyper-V Manager with a VM

## Project 8-3: Install Windows Server 2012 R2 in a VM

You have created a virtual machine and are ready to install Windows Server 2012 R2 as a guest OS using the installation DVD. You need the installation media for Windows Server 2012 R2.

You can download an ISO file for a trial version of Windows Server 2012 R2 from *https://www.microsoft.com/en-us/evalcenter/evaluate-windows-server-2012-r2*. Once downloaded, you can burn a DVD or attach the ISO file to the virtual DVD drive on your virtual machine. These steps assume you have an ISO file that you will attach to the VM's virtual DVD.

You can also use Windows Server 2016, if it's available, for this project. Only the preview was available at the time of this writing, so Windows Server 2012 was used.

1. Log on to your Windows 10 computer and open Hyper-V Manager, if necessary.
2. Click **VMTest1** in the Virtual Machines pane of Hyper-V Manager. In the Actions pane, click **Settings** under VMTest1 to open the Settings for VMTest1 window (see Figure 8-8).

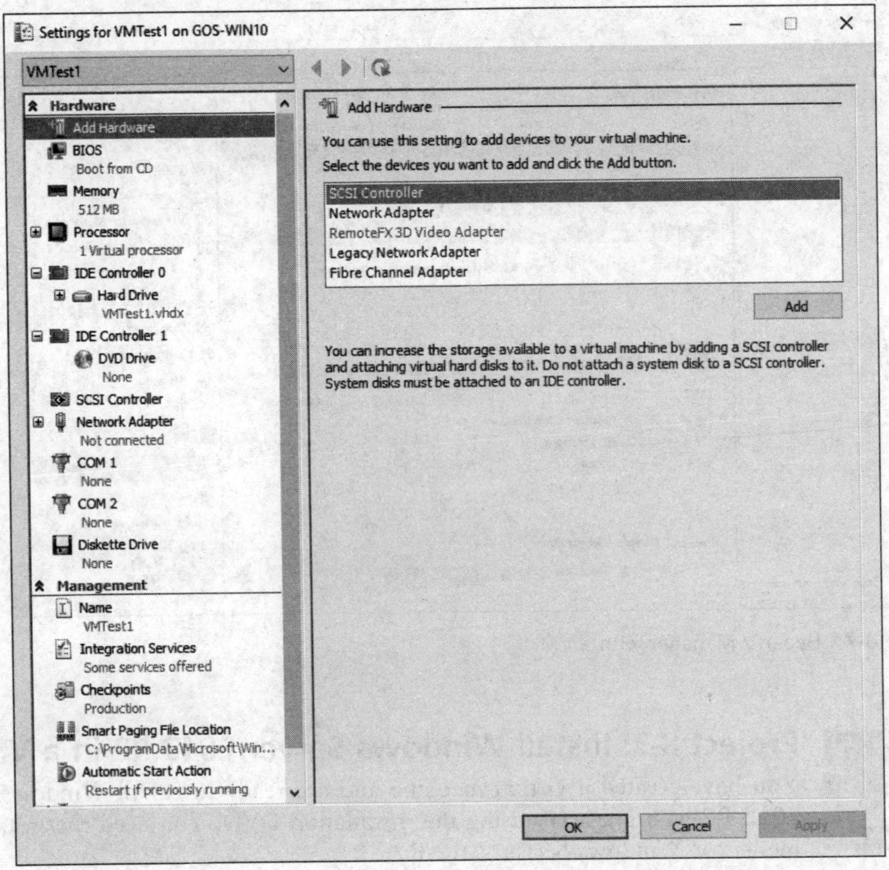


**Figure 8-8** Settings for a Hyper-V VM

3. If you are using a physical DVD, skip to Step 4. Click **DVD Drive** in the left pane. In the right pane, click **Image file** and then click **Browse**. Locate and then click the Windows Server 2012 R2 ISO file. Click **Open**. Click **OK**.
4. Right-click the **VMTest1** virtual machine you created and click **Connect**.
5. Power on VMTest1 by clicking the **Start** toolbar icon or by clicking **Action** and then **Start** from the menu. While the computer is booting, close the Virtual Machine Connection console. Notice that in Hyper-V Manager, the VM's CPU use changes as the Windows installation starts, and the VM screen in the bottom pane changes periodically.

**TIP**

To see a description of any toolbar icon, hover your mouse pointer over it.

6. Double-click the VM screen at the bottom of Hyper-V Manager to open the Virtual Machine Connection console. Begin the installation of Windows Server 2012 R2 by clicking **Next** on the Windows Setup window. From here, the installation steps are the same as installing in a physical computer. As a reminder, review Project 5-6, which walked you through the process of installing Windows Server 2012 R2.
7. After Windows Server 2012 R2 is installed, close the Virtual Machine Connection console and shut down the virtual machine by right-clicking **VMTest1** and clicking **Shut Down**. Click **Shut Down** again to confirm, if necessary.
8. Leave Hyper-V Manager open if you're continuing to the next activity.

## Project 8-4: Work with Virtual Machines in Hyper-V Manager

HANDS-ON PROJECTS

You have installed a test VM that you can use to become familiar with managing virtual machines in Windows Server 2012 R2. In the following steps, you create a checkpoint, make some changes to the OS, and revert to the checkpoint.

1. Log on to your Windows 10 computer and open Hyper-V Manager, if necessary.
2. Right-click **VMTest1** and click **Connect**.
3. Power on VMTest1 by clicking the **Start** toolbar icon.
4. After Windows Server 2012 R2 boots, log on and open Notepad, and then type your name in a new text document. Don't close Notepad or save the file yet. Click the **Save** toolbar icon or click **Action** and then **Save** from the menu of the Virtual Machine Connection console.
5. Close the Virtual Machine Connection console. In Hyper-V Manager, notice that the State column for the VM displays *Saved* or *Saving*. After the state has been saved, open the Virtual Machine Connection console by double-clicking **VMTest1**. Start the VM by clicking the **Start** toolbar icon. You're right where you left off in Notepad.
6. Save the Notepad file to your desktop as **file1.txt**, and then exit Notepad.
7. Click the **Checkpoint** toolbar icon or click **Action** and then **Checkpoint** from the menu. When prompted to enter a name for the checkpoint, type **BeforeDeletingFile1**, and then click **Yes**. In the status bar of the Virtual Machine Connection console, you see a progress bar that reads *Taking checkpoint*.
8. After the checkpoint is finished, minimize the VM, and note that the checkpoint is listed in the Checkpoints section of Hyper-V Manager. Maximize the VM, and delete the Notepad file you created. Empty the Recycle Bin to make sure the file is deleted.
9. Click the **Revert** toolbar icon or click **Action** and then **Revert** from the menu.

10. Click **Revert** when prompted. The VM displays a message that it's reverting. When the desktop is displayed again, you should see the Notepad file back on the desktop. Close the Virtual Machine Connection console.

11. In Hyper-V Manager, right-click **VMTest1** and click **Shut Down**. When prompted, click the **Shut Down** button. The Status column displays *Shutting Down Virtual Machine*.

12. After the VM state changes to Off, delete the checkpoint by right-clicking **BeforeDeletingFile1** in the Checkpoints section and clicking **Delete Checkpoint**. Click **Delete** to confirm.

13. Close Hyper-V Manager, but stay logged on to Windows 10 if you are continuing to the next project.

## Project 8-5: Download and Install VirtualBox

In this project, you download and install VirtualBox.

1. Log on to your Windows 10 computer, if necessary.

2. Start a Web browser, and go to **www.virtualbox.org**. In the left pane, click **Downloads**. Under VirtualBox binaries, click **VirtualBox *version* for Windows hosts, where *version* is the current VirtualBox version.**

3. After downloading the file, start the installation of VirtualBox. Follow the prompts and leave the default options selected.

4. When the installation is finished, VirtualBox should automatically start. If not, double-click the **Oracle VM VirtualBox** shortcut on your desktop to start Oracle VM VirtualBox Manager.

5. You're ready to create a virtual machine. Leave Oracle VM VirtualBox Manager running for the next project.

## Project 8-6: Create a Virtual Machine in VirtualBox

In this project, you create a virtual machine in VirtualBox.

1. If necessary, start Oracle VM VirtualBox Manager.

2. Click **New** to start the Create Virtual Machine wizard.

3. In the "Name and operating system" window, type **VMTest2** in the Name text box.

4. Click the selection arrow next to the Type box, and review the guest OSs that are supported. Click **Microsoft Windows**.

5. Click the selection arrow next to the Version box and click the name of any OS. Click **Next**.

6. In the Memory size window, accept the default setting and click **Next**. In the Hard Disk window, accept the default setting and then click **Create**.

7. In the "Hard disk file type" window, accept the default setting and click **Next**. In the "Storage on physical disk" window, click **Next** to accept the default setting of Dynamically allocated.

8. Click **Create** in the "File location and size" window. The VM is created and you are returned to Oracle VM VirtualBox Manager.

9. Review the information displayed on the details screen (see Figure 8-9).

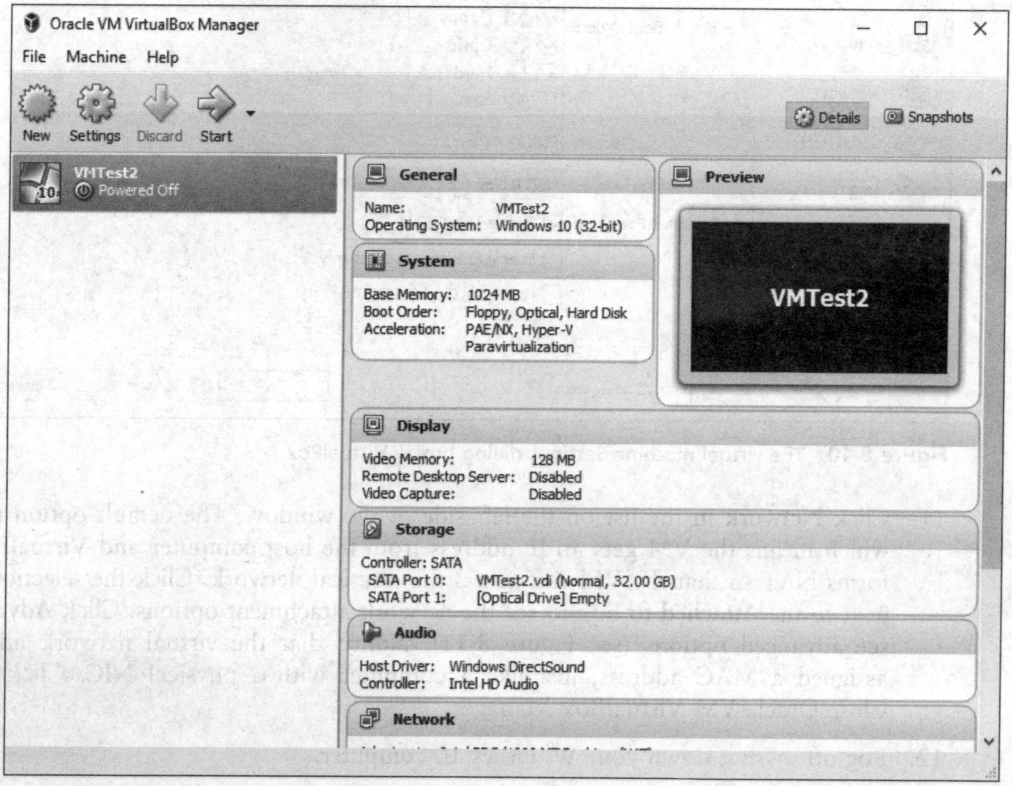


**Figure 8-9** The VirtualBox details screen

10. Installing and working with a VM in VirtualBox is similar to the process in Hyper-V. You can connect the virtual DVD drive to an ISO file or boot from a physical DVD placed in the host. To see and change the VM's settings, right-click **VMTest2** in the left pane and click **Settings**. Select each setting in the left pane to see the configuration options for the VM (see Figure 8-10). In this dialog box, you can change the amount of memory allocated to the VM, change processor options, configure storage, change the virtual network settings, and configure many more settings. You can also add virtual hardware, such as hard disks and network adapters.

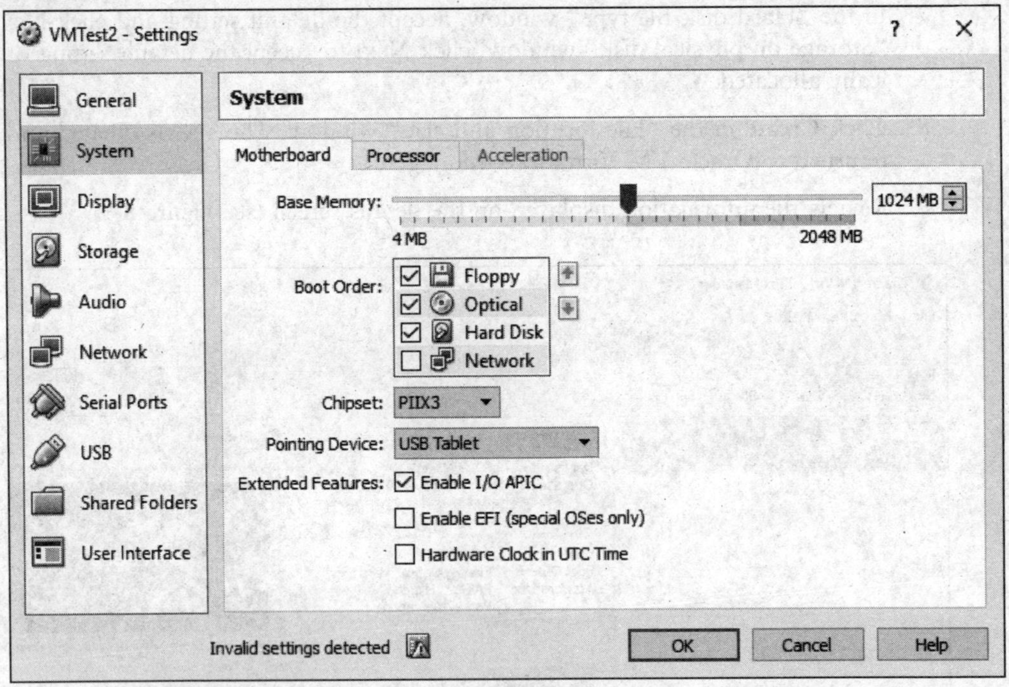


**Figure 8-10** The virtual machine Settings dialog box in VirtualBox

11. Click **Network** in the list on the left side of the window. The default option is NAT, which means the VM gets an IP address from the host computer and VirtualBox performs NAT so that the VM can access the physical network. Click the selection arrow next to the **Attached to** box to see the network attachment options. Click **Advanced** to see advanced options (see Figure 8-11). Notice that the virtual network adapter is assigned a MAC address, just like a computer with a physical NIC. Click **Cancel.** Close Oracle VM VirtualBox Manager.

12. Log off or shut down your Windows 10 computer.

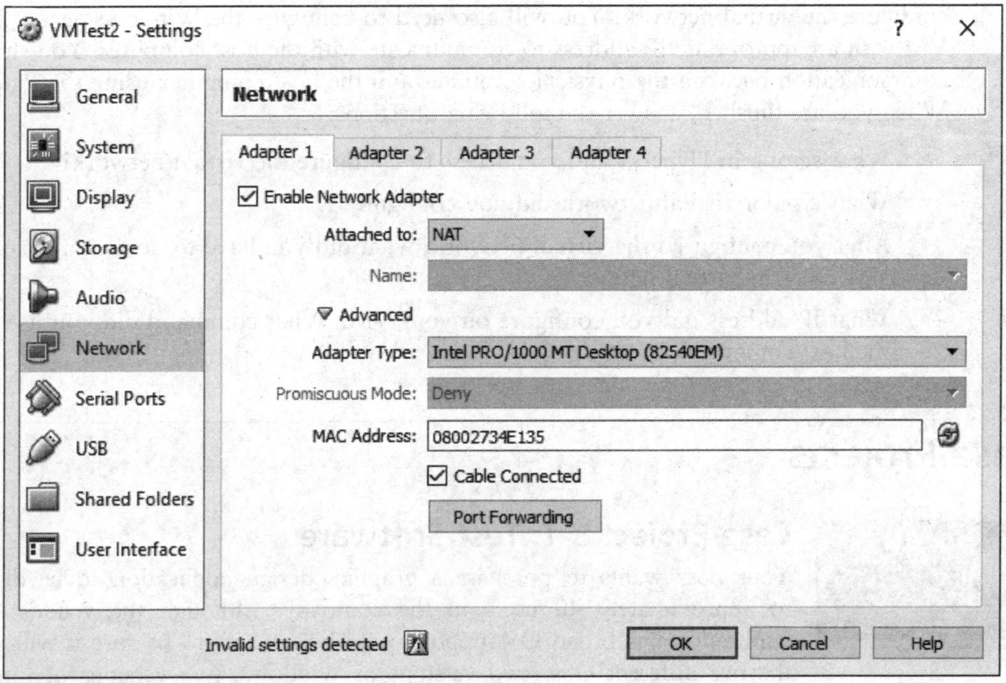


**Figure 8-11** Advanced settings for network adapters in VirtualBox

# Critical Thinking

The following activities give you critical thinking challenges. Challenge Labs give you an opportunity to use the skills you have learned to perform a task without step-by-step instructions. Case projects offer a practical problem for which you supply a written solution. Not all chapters contain Challenge Labs. There is not always a specific right or wrong answer to these critical thinking exercises. They are intended to encourage you to review the chapter material and delve deeper into the topics you have learned.

# Challenge Labs

## Challenge Lab 8-1: Configure Network Settings in Hyper-V

Your Windows Server 2012 R2 server is installed in a VM named VMTest1 that you created in the Hands-On Projects. You are ready to perform postinstallation tasks. One of the things you will need to do is configure the virtual network. Do a little research on configuring the virtual network in Hyper-V. Open Hyper-V Manager and study the configuration tasks you can perform in the Actions pane.

You should configure the virtual network so that VMs you are running in Hyper-V can communicate with each other and with the host computer. You will need to perform two steps to configure the virtual network. You will also need to configure the Windows Server 2012 R2 VM with an appropriate IP address to communicate with the host computer. You should test communication between the physical computer and the host computer using the Ping utility. When you are finished, answer the following questions:

- What setting in Hyper-V did you access to configure the virtual network?
- What type of virtual network did you configure?
- After you configured the virtual network, what did you have to do to make sure your VM used the virtual network?
- What IP address did you configure on your VM? What command did you use to ping the host computer?

## Case Projects

### Case Project 8-1: Test Software

Your boss wants to purchase a graphics design application to be distributed to approximately 40 users in the company. Although the vendor says the application has broad OS support, your boss wants to be sure it will work on the five different OSs (two versions of Windows, two versions of Linux, and the latest Mac OS X) running on the company's user workstations. He wants you to verify compatibility by using evaluation copies of the software without disrupting users or their computers. You have the installation disks for all five OSs your company uses, but you don't have a lot of computers available to install the OSs. What's your plan?

### Case Project 8-2: A Small Business Startup IT Solution

You've been called in to consult with a small startup company that needs advice on how to set up its computer systems and network. The startup company does not have a lot of money to invest in the necessary IT infrastructure, but it will have 30 employees that use computers to run a variety of applications, many of which are server-based. The company wants to run Windows 10 and Mac OS X client stations, and it will need Windows Server and Red Hat Enterprise server. The company already has cabling and switches in place to connect its computers to a LAN, and it has a 50 Mbps Internet connection. What do you advise for this small business to satisfy its IT needs?

chapter 9

# Configuring a Network Connection

**After reading this chapter and completing the exercises, you will be able to:**

- Explain the fundamentals of network communication
- Define common networking terms
- Compare and describe network device types
- Configure and describe network protocols
- Describe the OSI model of networking
- Configure networking in an operating system

**In only a few decades, computer networks have evolved from a complex technology** accessible to only the most tech-savvy users to being part of most people's everyday lives. Computer networks can be found in almost every business, school, and home. Their use is available to anyone with a computer and a network connection, but installation and upkeep of all but the smallest networks still require considerable know-how. This chapter starts you on the path toward acquiring the skills you need to work with network devices and configure an operating system to work in a network. Proper configuration of an operating system in a network is paramount to your overall understanding of operating systems. You cannot properly configure and troubleshoot the operation of a client or server computer in a network unless you have a solid understanding of the technologies and protocols used in building a network and connecting devices to a network.

This chapter begins by discussing the fundamentals of network communication. Many new terms are introduced and defined, and you will learn the fundamentals of the TCP/IP protocol and the OSI model of networking.

# The Fundamentals of Network Communication

A computer **network** consists of two or more computers connected by some kind of transmission medium, such as a cable or airwaves. After they're connected, correctly configured computers can communicate with one another. The primary motivations for networking are to share resources, such as printers and hard drives; to share information, such as word-processing files; and to communicate by using applications such as e-mail. These motivations are important, especially for businesses, but another motivating factor for both businesses and home users is to "get online"—to access the Internet. The Internet, with its wealth of information, disinformation, fun, and games, has had a tremendous impact on how and why networks are used. Indeed, many of the networking technologies described in this book were developed as a result of the Internet explosion.

You might know how to use a network already; in particular, you probably know how to use programs that access the Internet, such as Web browsers and e-mail programs. To understand *how* networks work, however, you need to learn about the underlying technologies and processes used when you open a Web browser or an e-mail program. A good place to start is with the components that help turn a stand-alone computer into a networked computer.

## Network Components

Imagine a computer with no networking hardware or software. It's hard to imagine now, but a computer's main purpose once was to run applications such as word processors and spreadsheets, not Web browsers and e-mail. Such computers had neither the hardware nor software needed to run networked programs, which is why they were called **stand-alone computers**. If you wanted to network a computer, you had to add these required components:

- *Network interface card (NIC)*—A NIC (pronounced *nick*) is an add-on card that's plugged into a motherboard expansion slot and provides a connection between the computer and the network. Most computers have a NIC built into the motherboard, so an additional card is not necessary.

- *Network medium*—This cable plugs into the NIC and makes the connection between a computer and the rest of the network. In networks with just two computers, the other end of the cable can plug into the second computer's NIC. More likely, the other end of the cable plugs into an interconnecting device that accommodates several computer connections. Network media can also be airwaves, as in wireless networks. In this case, the connection is made between the antenna on the NIC and the antenna on another NIC or interconnecting device.
- *Interconnecting device*—Although this component isn't always necessary because two computers can be connected directly with a cable and small wireless networks can be configured without an interconnecting device, most networks include one or several of these components. They allow computers to communicate on a network without being connected directly. Interconnecting devices include switches, hubs, routers, and wireless access points. A small network connected to a switch is shown in Figure 9-1.

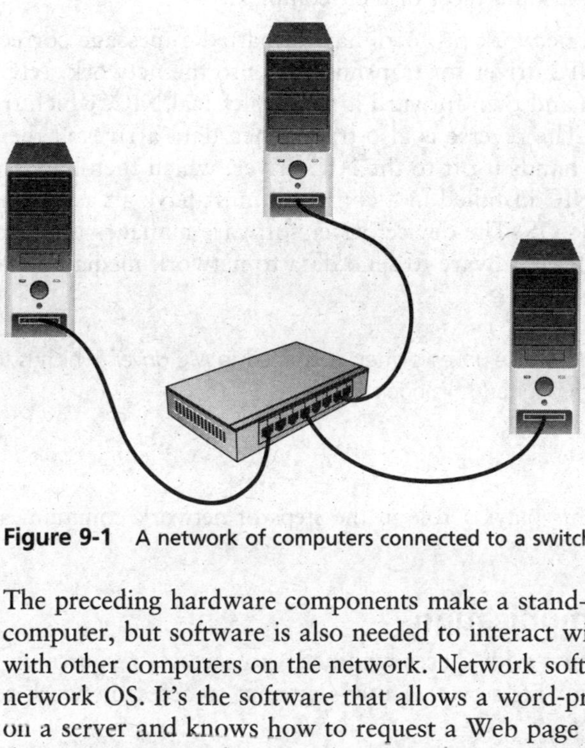

**Figure 9-1** A network of computers connected to a switch

The preceding hardware components make a stand-alone computer into a networked computer, but software is also needed to interact with network hardware and communicate with other computers on the network. Network software transforms a stand-alone OS into a network OS. It's the software that allows a word-processing program to open a document on a server and knows how to request a Web page or send an e-mail. It's also the software that communicates between the OS and network hardware. Network software can be divided into the following categories:

- *Network clients and servers*—**Network client software** requests information that's stored on another network computer or device. **Network server software** allows a computer to share its resources by responding to resource requests generated by network clients. Network client software can be an integral part of well-known applications, such as Web browsers and e-mail programs. A Web browser, for example, sends a request for a Web page to a Web server. Network client software can also run in the background, usually when installed as a networking service. In such cases, it enables programs without built-in client software to access shared network resources on other computers. For example, Client for Microsoft Networks, which is installed automatically in Windows, allows a word-processing program to open a file that's shared on another Windows computer or print to a printer attached to another Windows computer. In this setup, server software called File and Printer Sharing for Microsoft Networks receives the request from the client and provides access to the shared file or printer.

- *Protocols*—When clients and servers need to send information on the network, they must pass it to **network protocols**, which define the rules and formats a computer must use when sending information across the network. A network protocol can be likened to a human language. Just as two people communicate by speaking the same language, two computers communicate by using the same protocol. An example of a network protocol is TCP/IP. Network protocols perform all the behind-the-scenes tasks required to handle networking functions and most of their complexity.
- *NIC device driver*—After a network protocol has formatted a message correctly, it hands the data off to the NIC driver for transmission onto the network. NIC drivers receive data from protocols and then forward it to the physical NIC, which transmits the data onto the medium. The reverse is also true. When data arrives at the NIC from the medium, the NIC hands it off to the NIC driver, which then hands it off to network protocols. Every NIC installed in a computer must have an associated device driver installed in the OS. The device driver software manages the details of communicating with the NIC hardware to send data to network media and receive data from it.

The term *NIC device driver* is often shortened to *NIC driver*, which is the term used throughout this book.

Each of these software components plays a role in the steps of network communication, as described in the next section.

## Steps of Network Communication

Most network communication starts with a user who needs to access a resource on another computer, such as a Web server or file server. A user's attempt to access network resources is summarized in these basic steps:

1. An application tries to access a network resource by attempting to send a message to it.
2. Network client software detects the attempt to access the network. Client software formats the message generated by the application and passes the message on to the network protocol.
3. The protocol packages the message in a format suitable for the network and sends it to the NIC driver.
4. The NIC driver sends the data in the request to the NIC, which converts it into the necessary signals to be transmitted across the network medium.

Remember that there are two sides to a communication session—a client tries to access network resources and a server provides those resources. The steps taken on the server side are essentially the reverse of those on the client side:

1. The NIC on the server receives signals from the network medium and converts them into message data, which is read by the NIC driver.
2. The NIC driver passes the message to the network protocol.
3. The network protocol determines which server software the message is targeting and passes the message to the designated software. Remember that a computer can have many clients and servers running at the same time. For example, a computer running Windows Server 2016 might be acting both as a mail server and as a file server. Each server function requires different server software.
4. The server software receives the message and responds by sending the requested data to the client computer, using the steps outlined previously.

## Layers of the Network Communication Process

Each step a client takes to access network resources is often referred to as a *layer* in the network communication process. Each layer has a specific function, and all the layers work together. Figure 9-2 and Table 9-1 depict this process. Keep in mind that the previous steps simplified the communication process, which is one reason the layered approach is so effective: Complex concepts can be described in simple steps.

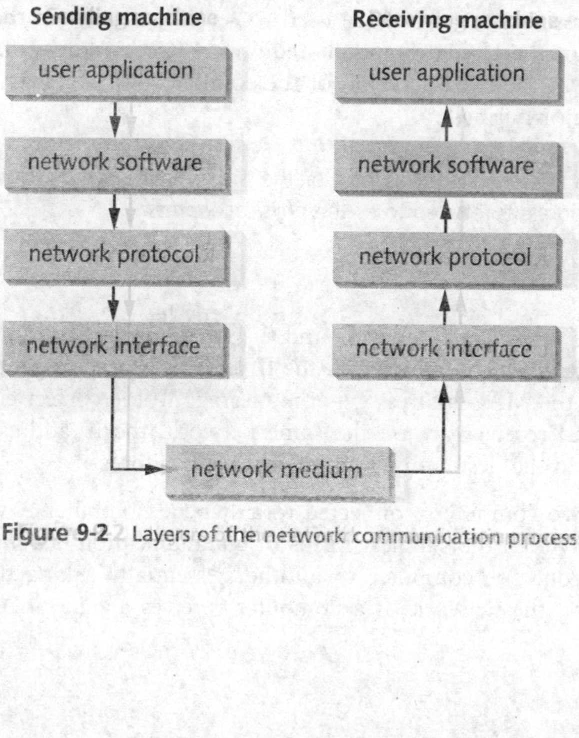


**Figure 9-2** Layers of the network communication process

**Table 9-1 Layers of the network communication process**

| Step | Description | Layer |
|---|---|---|
| 1 | An application tries to access a network resource. | User application |
| 2 | Client software detects the attempt to access the network and passes the message on to the network protocol. | Network client or server software |
| 3 | The protocol packages the message in a format suitable for the network and sends it to the NIC driver. | Network protocol |
| 4 | The NIC driver sends the data in the request to the NIC, which converts it into the necessary signals to be transmitted across the network medium. | Network interface |

The four steps outlined in Table 9-1 give you a basic understanding of the layered approach to networking. A more detailed model for network communication—a universal standard for teaching and designing network communication called the *OSI model*—is discussed later in this chapter.

## How Two Computers Communicate on a LAN

The layers of the network communication process provide an overview of how network communication works. However, there are few details on what each layer accomplishes. This discussion focuses on computer addresses and how they're used during network communication.

In a network that uses a protocol such as TCP/IP (the most common network protocol), computers have two addresses: a logical address and a physical address. The logical address is the IP address, and the physical address is called the Media Access Control (MAC) address. You can look at these two addresses much like those used to send mail through the postal system. When a letter is mailed in the United States, it requires a street address and a zip code. The zip code gets the letter to the correct region of the country, and the street address gets the letter to the correct home or business.

The MAC address is stored as part of the physical NIC, which is why the MAC address is referred to as the *physical address*.

You can liken the zip code to the logical or IP address and the street address to the physical or MAC address. When a message is sent on a network, the IP address is used to get the message to the correct network, and the MAC address gets the message to the correct computer on the network. If the sender and receiver are on the same network, the IP address in the message is used mainly to ascertain the destination computer's MAC address.

For example, Figure 9-3 shows two computers connected to a switch. Computer A wants to communicate with Computer B. One of the simplest forms of communication is a *ping* command, which sends a message from one computer to another, essentially asking the other computer whether it's listening on the network. If a computer receives a ping, it replies so that the sending computer knows the message was received. It's like the cell phone commercial in which the caller asks, "Can you hear me now?" Here are the steps of this communication process:

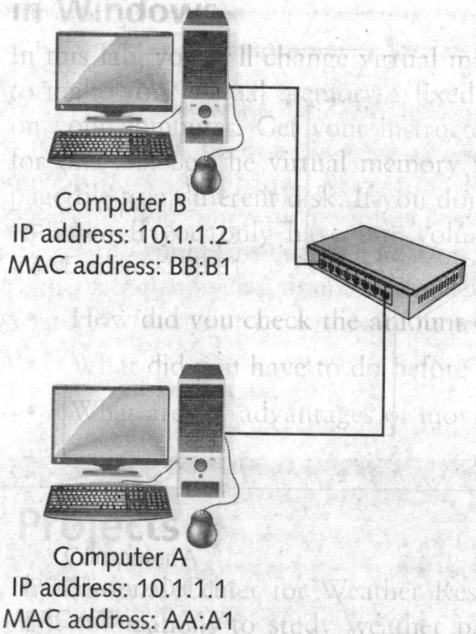


**Figure 9-3** Communication between two computers

1. A user at Computer A types *ping 10.1.1.2* (the IP address of Computer B) at a command prompt.
2. The network software creates a ping message.
3. The network protocol packages the message by adding IP addresses of the sending and destination computers and acquires the destination computer's MAC address.
4. The network interface software adds MAC addresses of the sending and destination computers and sends the message to the network medium as bits.
5. Computer B receives the message, verifies that the addresses are correct, and then sends a reply to Computer A using Steps 2 through 4.

Users don't usually initiate network communication by using a computer's IP address; instead, they use the computer name. However, just as you can't mail a letter with only the recipient's name, you can't communicate over a network with only the computer's name. You certainly know the name of the person you're writing to, but you might have to look up his or her address before you can address the envelope. Similarly, computers use an address book of sorts, called a **name server**, to get a computer's IP address when the name is known. TCP/IP provides name server functions through its Domain Name System (DNS). With this information in mind, the preceding steps can be expanded as follows:

1. A user at Computer A types *ping Computer B* at a command prompt.
2. A name lookup is done to retrieve Computer B's IP address.

3. The network software creates a ping message.
4. The network protocol packages the message by adding IP addresses of the sending and destination computers and acquires the destination computer's MAC address.
5. The network interface software adds MAC addresses of the sending and destination computers and sends the message to the network medium as bits.
6. Computer B receives the message, verifies that the addresses are correct, and then sends a reply to Computer A using Steps 3 through 5.

Next, examine an example of using a network to save a word-processing document to a Windows server and see how the layers of the network communication process are used. Several components are involved in this task, as you will see in Hands-On Project 9-3. In the example shown in Table 9-2, a user at Client A is running a word-processing program, such as Microsoft Word, and wants to save the file to a shared folder on another Windows computer named Server X.

**Table 9-2** **Saving a file with the network communication process**

| Step | Description | Layer |
|---|---|---|
| 1 | The user on Client A clicks Save in the word-processing program and chooses a shared folder on Server X to save the file. | User application |
| 2 | Client for Microsoft Networks detects the attempt to access the network, formats the message, and passes the message to the network protocol. | Network software |
| 3 | The network protocol (in this case, TCP/IPv4) packages the message in a format suitable for the network interface and sends it to the NIC driver. | Network protocol |
| 4 | The NIC driver sends the data in the request to the NIC (in this case, Ethernet0), which converts it into signals to be transmitted across the network medium. | Network interface |
| 5 | Server X's NIC receives the message from the network medium, processes it, and sends the data to TCP/IPv4. | Network interface |
| 6 | TCP/IPv4 on Server X receives the message from the NIC, processes it, and sends the data to the network software (in this case, File and Printer Sharing for Microsoft Networks). | Network protocol |
| 7 | File and Printer Sharing for Microsoft Networks formats the message and requests that the OS save the file to the disk. | Network software |

In Table 9-2, there's no "User application" step on the server. When a server is involved, the last step is typically handled by network software, such as File and Printer Sharing for Microsoft Networks, a Web server, or other server software.

Now that you have an idea of how network communication occurs, you can learn some common terms for describing networks and network components in the next section. Along the way, you see more illustrations of different types of networks.

# Network Terminology

Every profession has its own language with its own terms and acronyms. Learning this language is half the battle of becoming proficient in a profession, and it's no different in computer and networking technology. The following sections explain some common terms used in discussing computer networks. Because some of these terms are associated with network diagrams, a number of figures are included to show different ways of depicting networks.

## LANs, Internetworks, WANs, and MANs

A small network that is limited to a single collection of machines and connected by one or more interconnecting devices in a small geographic area is called a **local area network (LAN)**. LANs also form the building blocks for larger networks called *internetworks*. In Figure 9-4, the computers in a LAN are interconnected by a switch; Figure 9-5 shows a wireless LAN.

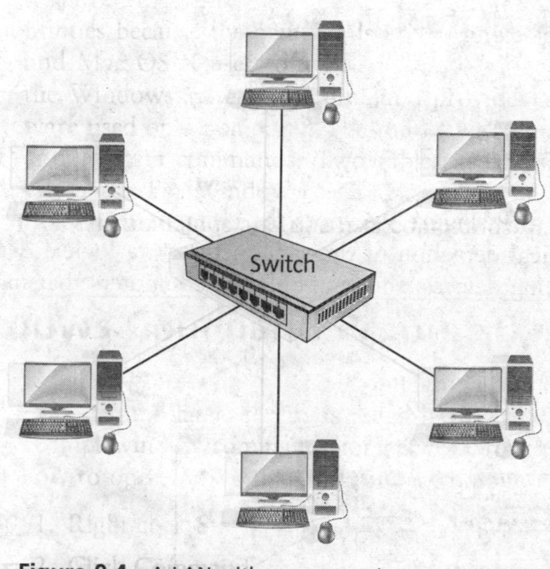


**Figure 9-4** A LAN with computers interconnected by a switch

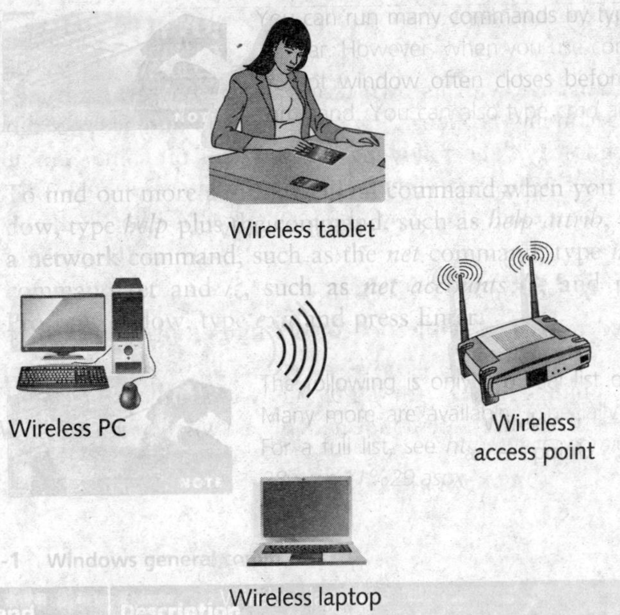


**Figure 9-5** A wireless LAN

LANs are represented in other ways, as in Figure 9-6; note the different symbols for a hub and a switch. Figure 9-7 shows a logical depiction of the same network; a logical depiction leaves out details such as interconnecting devices, showing only the computers that make up the network.

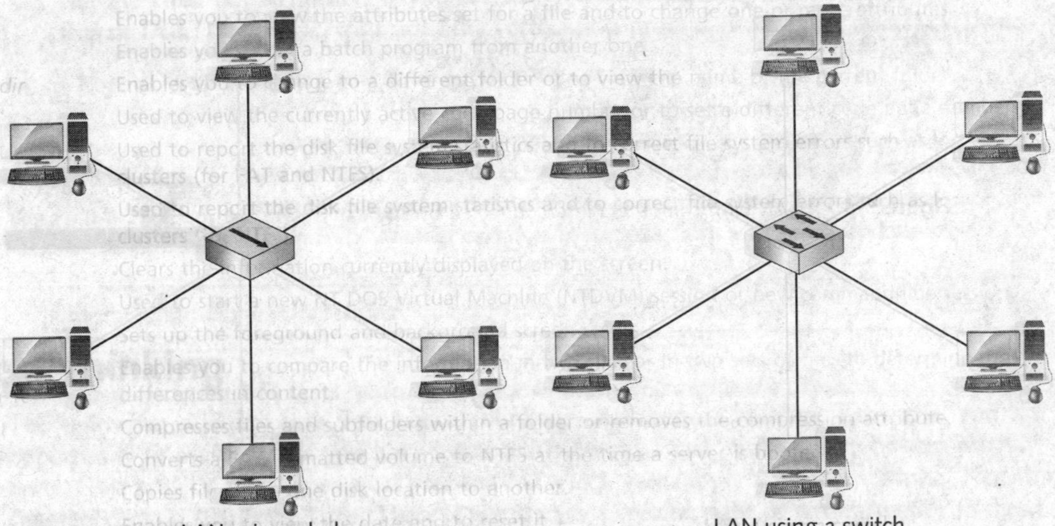


**Figure 9-6** A LAN with a symbolic hub (left) and a symbolic switch (right)

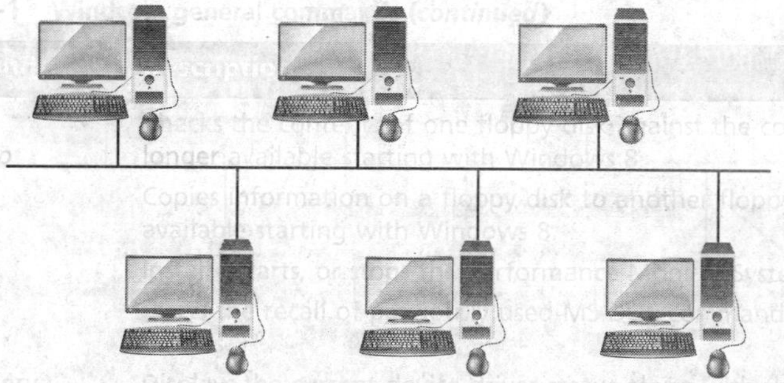

**Figure 9-7** A logical depiction of a LAN

An **internetwork** is a networked collection of LANs tied together by devices such as routers, as discussed later in this chapter. Figure 9-8 shows two LANs interconnected by a router, which is represented by the standard symbol. Internetworks are usually created for the following reasons:

- Two or more groups of users and their computers should be logically separated on the network, yet the groups should be able to communicate. For example, in a school, you might want to logically separate the LAN that contains student computers from the LAN that contains faculty computers. Routers provide this logical separation but still allow communication between groups.
- The number of computers in a single LAN has grown to the point that network communication is no longer efficient. The nature of certain network protocols and devices makes network communication increasingly less efficient as the number of computers on a LAN grows. Routers can be used to separate the computers into two or more smaller LANs, thereby increasing communication efficiency.
- The distance between two groups of computers exceeds the capabilities of most LAN devices, such as switches. This problem can occur, for example, when a company occupies multiple buildings or multiple floors in a building. Routers are often used to communicate between groups of computers that are separated geographically.

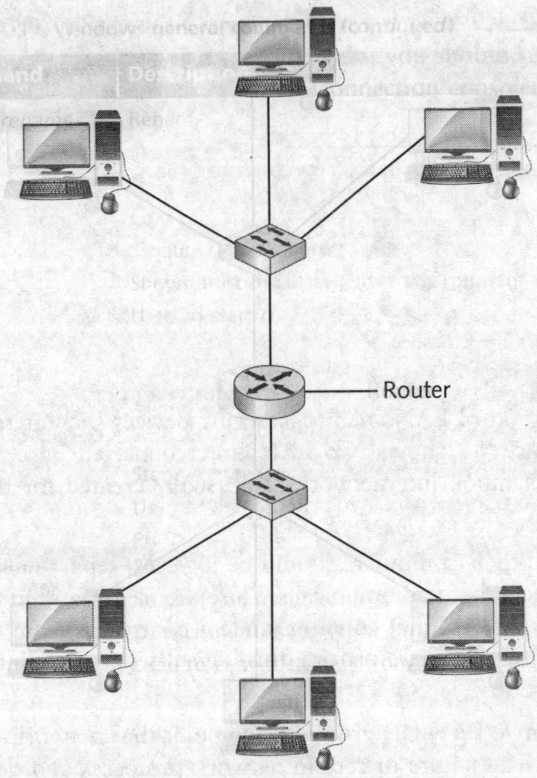


**Figure 9-8** An internetwork with two LANs connected by a router

You might not realize it, but your home computer is probably part of an internetwork. Every time you go online to browse the Web or check your e-mail, your computer or LAN becomes part of the world's largest internetwork: the Internet.

As a network's scope expands to encompass LANs in geographically dispersed locations, internetworks become classified as **wide area networks (WANs)**. A WAN spans distances measured in miles and links separate LANs. WANs use the services of third-party communication providers, such as phone companies, to carry network traffic from one location to another. So, although both internetworks and WANs connect LANs, the difference lies mainly in the LANs' proximity to each other and the technologies used to communicate between LANs. Therefore, the Internet is both an internetwork and, because it spans the globe, a very large WAN.

Occasionally, you might encounter a network type called a **metropolitan area network (MAN)**. MANs use WAN technologies to interconnect LANs in a specific geographic region, such as a county or city. It's not uncommon to find large, complex networks that use all four network types: LANs and internetworks for purely local access, MANs for regional or city-wide access, and WANs for access to remote sites elsewhere in the country or around the world. For example, consider a nationwide bank. The main branch in a large city has a building with multiple floors and hundreds of computers. Each floor constitutes a LAN, and these LANs are connected to form an internetwork. The internetwork at the main branch is connected to other branches throughout the city to form a MAN. In addition, the main branch is connected to other branches in other cities and states to form a WAN.

In network drawings, WANs are often shown with a jagged or thunderbolt-shaped line to represent the connection between two devices, usually routers, and the Internet is usually represented as a cloud. A cloud is used to obscure the details of a large network, as if to say "There's some collection of networks and network devices, but the details aren't important." Figure 9-9 shows a WAN connection between two routers and with a connection to the Internet. A grouping of three computers is often used to represent multiple computers on a LAN when the exact number doesn't matter.

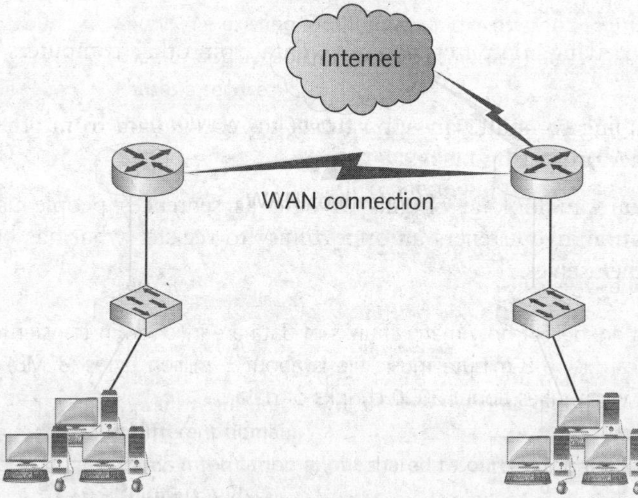


**Figure 9-9** A WAN with a connection to the Internet

## Internet, Intranet, and Extranet

The **Internet** is a worldwide public internetwork that uses standard protocols, such as TCP/IP, DNS, and HTTP, to transfer and view information. It's a public network because devices such as routers and Web servers that make up much of the network are accessible directly through an IP address. An **intranet**, on the other hand, is a private network, such as a school or company network, in which the devices and servers are available only to users connected to the internal network. Many of the same protocols and technologies used on the Internet are used to access information on an intranet. An **extranet** sits somewhere between the Internet and an intranet. It allows limited and controlled access to internal network resources by outside users. It's used when two organizations need to share resources, so controls are put in place to allow the organizations to access resources without making them available to the wider Internet.

## Packets and Frames

When computers transfer information across a network, they do so in short bursts of about 1500 bytes of data. Each burst, or chunk, of data has the same basic structure; specifically, each chunk of data contains the MAC addresses and IP addresses of both the sending (source) and receiving (destination) computers. So, to transfer a small word-processing file, only one burst of data transfer might be needed, but large photo or music files are first divided into several hundred or even thousands of chunks before they're transferred. After each chunk of data is sent, the computer pauses momentarily. Data is transferred in this way for a number of reasons:

- If an error occurs during transmission of a large file, only the chunks of data involved in the error have to be sent again, not the entire file.
- The pause between bursts might be necessary to allow other computers to transfer data during pauses.
- The pause allows the receiving computer to process received data, such as writing it to disk.
- The pause allows the receiving computer to receive data from other computers at the same time.
- The pause gives the sending computer an opportunity to receive data from other computers and perform other processing tasks.

To use another analogy, you can look at chunks of data as sentences people use when speaking. Pauses in conversation give listeners an opportunity to register what has been said and possibly get a word in themselves.

To get an idea of how many chunks of data are involved in transferring a typical file, a 3-minute music file is about 3 million bytes (3 MB) of data, which takes about 2000 chunks of data.

**Packets** The chunks of data sent across the network are usually called *packets* or *frames*. Packet, the more well-known term, is often used generically, but it does have a particular meaning: It's a chunk of data with source and destination IP addresses (as well as other IP protocol information) added to it. Figure 9-10 shows a representation of data to be transferred, and Figure 9-11 shows the packets created after the data has been broken into chunks and IP addresses added.

Lorem ipsum dolor sit amet, consectetuer adipiscing elit. Maecenas porttitor congue massa. Fusce posuere, magna sed pulvinar ultricies, purus lectus malesuada libero, sit amet commodo magna eros quis urna.

Nunc viverra imperdiet enim. Fusce est. Vivamus a tellus.

Pellentesque habitant morbi tristique senectus et netus et malesuada fames ac turpis egestas.

Proin pharetra nonummy pede. Mauris et orci.

Lorem ipsum dolor sit amet, consectetuer adipiscing elit. Maecenas porttitor congue massa. Fusce posuere, magna sed pulvinar ultricies, purus lectus malesuada libero, sit amet commodo magna eros quis urna.

Nunc viverra imperdiet enim. Fusce est. Vivamus a tellus.

Pellentesque habitant morbi tristique senectus et netus et malesuada fames ac turpis egestas.

Proin pharetra nonummy pede. Mauris et orci.

Lorem ipsum dolor sit amet, consectetuer adipiscing elit. Maecenas porttitor congue massa. Fusce posuere, magna sed pulvinar ultricies, purus lectus malesuada libero, sit amet commodo magna eros quis urna.

Nunc viverra imperdiet enim. Fusce est. Vivamus a tellus.

Pellentesque habitant morbi tristique senectus et netus et malesuada fames ac turpis egestas. Proin pharetra nonummy pede. Mauris et orci.

**Figure 9-10** Original data

| | |
|---|---|
| Dest: IP: 172.16.1.2, Source IP: 172.16.1.1 | Lorem ipsum dolor sit amet, consectetuer adipiscing elit. Maecenas porttitor congue massa. Fusce posuere, magna sed pulvinar ultricies. |
| Dest: IP: 172.16.1.2, Source IP: 172.16.1.1 | purus lectus malesuada libero, sit amet commodo magna eros quis urna. Nunc viverra imperdiet enim. Fusce est. Vivamus a tellus. |
| Dest: IP: 172.16.1.2, Source IP: 172.16.1.1 | Pellentesque habitant morbi tristique senectus et netus et malesuada fames ac turpis egestas. Proin pharetra nonummy pede. Mauris et orci |
| Dest: IP: 172.16.1.2, Source IP: 172.16.1.1 | Lorem ipsum dolor sit amet, consectetuer adipiscing elit. Maecenas porttitor congue massa. Fusce posuere, magna sed pulvinar ultricies |
| Dest: IP: 172.16.1.2, Source IP: 172.16.1.1 | Pellentesque habitant tristique senectus et netus et malesuada fames ac turpis egestas. Proin pharetra nonummy pede. Mauris et orci. |

**Figure 9-11** Data divided into several packets

Using the U.S. mail analogy, you can look at a packet as an envelope with the zip code added but not the street address. In relation to the layers of the network communication process, packets are generated and processed by the network protocol.

**Frames** A frame is a packet with the source and destination MAC addresses added to it. In addition, frames have an error-checking code added to the back end of the packet, so the packet is "framed" by MAC addresses (and other network interface information) on one end and an error-checking code on the other. A frame is like a letter that's addressed, stamped, and ready to deliver.

Frames are essentially the final state of data before it's placed on the network medium as bits. The network interface is the layer of the network communication process that works with frames. Figure 9-12 shows what the packets from Figure 9-11 look like after the frame information is added.

| | | | |
|---|---|---|---|
| Dest MAC, Source MAC | Dest IP, Source IP | Lorem ipsum dolor sit amet, consectetuer adipiscing elit. Maecenas porttitor congue massa. Fusce posuere, magna sed pulvinar ultricies, | Error check |
| Dest MAC, Source MAC | Dest IP, Source IP | purus lectus malesuada libero, sit amet commodo magna eros quis urna. Nunc viverra imperdiet enim. Fusce est. Vivamus a tellus. | Error check |
| Dest MAC, Source MAC | Dest IP, Source IP | Pellentesque habitant morbi tristique senectus et netus et malesuada fames ac turpis egestas. Proin pharetra nonummy pede. Mauris et orci | Error check |
| Dest MAC, Source MAC | Dest IP, Source IP | Lorem ipsum dolor sit amet, consectetuer adipiscing elit. Maecenas porttitor congue massa. Fusce posuere, magna sed pulvinar ultricies | Error check |
| Dest MAC, Source MAC | Dest IP, Source IP | Pellentesque habitant tristique senectus et netus et malesuada fames ac turpis egestas. Proin pharetra nonummy pede. Mauris et orci. | Error check |

**Figure 9-12** The packets are now frames and ready for delivery

The error-checking code at the end of a frame is called a *cyclical redundancy check* (CRC).

The process of adding IP addresses and then MAC addresses to chunks of data is called **encapsulation**. Information added at the front of data is called a **header**, and information added at the end of data is called a **trailer**. Data is encapsulated several times as it works its way down from the sending application and makes it to the network interface as a frame. When the destination computer receives the frame, the process is reversed as the network interface de-encapsulates the frame (has the header and trailer removed) so that it becomes a packet again. This process continues until the packet arrives at the receiving application or service as the original data. This process is all part of the layered approach to networking.

## Clients and Servers

You've already learned about the role of client network software and server network software. Unfortunately, the world of networking sometimes uses the same terms to discuss two different things. The following sections clarify what these terms mean and how their meanings can differ depending on how they're used.

**Client** A client, in networking terms, can be a workstation running a client OS, such as Windows 10, or the network software on a computer that requests network resources from a server. In addition, you can refer to a physical computer as a client computer. The meaning of *client*, therefore, depends on the context in which it's used. To clarify, it's typically used in the following three contexts:

- *Client operating system*—The OS installed on a computer is designed mainly to access network resources, even though it might be capable of sharing its own resources. Windows 10 and Mac OS X fit this description, for example, as do certain distributions of Linux. A client OS is also often referred to as a *desktop OS*.
- *Client computer*—This computer's primary role in a network is to run user applications and access network resources. Most computers in a network fit this description.
- *Client software*—This software requests network resources from server software running on another computer. For example, a Web browser, an e-mail client (such as Microsoft Outlook), and Client for Microsoft Networks fit into this category.

**Server** When most people hear the word *server*, they conjure up visions of a large tower computer with lots of hard drives and memory. This image is merely a computer hardware configuration that may or may not be used as a server, however. In short, a computer becomes a **server** when software is installed on it that provides a network service to client computers. In other words, you can install certain software on an inexpensive laptop computer and make it act as a server. By the same token, a huge tower computer with six hard drives and 128 GB of RAM can be used as a workstation for a single user. So, although some hardware configurations are packaged to function as a server, and others are packaged as client or desktop computers, what makes a computer a server is the software installed on it. Just as there are three contexts in which the term *client* is used, so it is with the term *server*:

- *Server operating system*—This term is used when the OS installed on a computer is designed mainly to share network resources and provide other network services. A server OS is tuned to be able to share files efficiently and perform network operations in response to client requests, even though the OS might also be able to run user applications and client software. Windows Server 2012, Mac OS X Server, UNIX, and many Linux distributions fit this description.
- *Server computer*—This term is used when a computer's primary role in the network is to give client computers access to network resources and services. The computers that most often fit this description are usually in the IT room or locked away in a closet.
- *Server software*—This software responds to requests for network resources from client software running on another computer. A Web server (such as Internet Information Services), an e-mail server (such as Microsoft Exchange), and File and Printer Sharing for Microsoft Networks fit into this category.

Microsoft refers to server software components as *services*. Other OSs use other terms; for example, in Linux/UNIX, server software components are referred to as *daemons*.

As you can see, the lines between a client computer and a server computer are often blurred because OSs are designed as network operating systems, and most can take on the roles of both server and client. As you're learning, however, the language of networking is often imprecise, and you must pay attention to the context in which networking terms are used to grasp their meaning. As you get more comfortable with all the terms and better understand how networks work, the nuances of the terminology will fall into place.

## Peer-to-Peer and Client/Server Networks

Network models, which define how and where resources are shared and how access to these resources is regulated, fall into two major types: peer-to-peer and client/server. Client/server networks are the most common in business settings, but understanding both types is essential, especially as they compare with one another.

Peer-to-peer networks running Windows OSs are referred to as *workgroup networks*, and client/server networks running Windows Server are called *domain-based networks*.

In a **peer-to-peer network**, most computers function as clients or servers as circumstances dictate. For example, a computer can act as a server by sharing a printer it's connected to and simultaneously act as a client by accessing a file shared by another computer on the network. In this type of network, there's no centralized control over who has access to network resources; each user maintains control over his or her own shared resources. The computers in peer-to-peer networks usually run desktop or client OSs.

In a peer-to-peer network, every user must act as the administrator of his or her computer's resources. Users can give everyone unlimited access to their resources or grant restricted (or no) access to other users on the network. To grant this access, users must create user accounts and passwords for each user who will access shared resources on their computers. The username and password for accessing a computer are called **credentials**. If you have five computers in a peer-to-peer network, each user might have to remember as many as five different sets of credentials. Because of the lack of centralized authority over resources, controlled chaos is the norm for all but the smallest peer-to-peer networks, and security can be a major concern because not all users might be educated in creating secure passwords.

Another issue that affects peer-to-peer networks is data organization. If every machine can be a server, how can users keep track of what information is stored on which machine? If five users are responsible for a collection of documents, any of those users might have to search through files on all five machines to find a document. The decentralized nature of peer-to-peer networks makes locating resources more difficult as the number of peers increases.

In a **server-based network**, certain computers take on specialized roles and function mainly as servers, and ordinary users' machines tend to function mainly as clients. Windows Server

2012, Red Hat Enterprise Linux, and UNIX are OSs designed primarily for server use. In these networks, servers have centralized authority over who has access to network resources, mainly by providing an environment in which users log on to the network with a single set of credentials maintained by one or more servers running a server OS. Server OSs are designed to handle many simultaneous user logons and requests for shared resources efficiently. In most cases, servers are dedicated to running network services and shouldn't be used to run user applications. You want to reserve servers' CPU power, memory, and network performance for user access to network services.

When you're using Windows server OSs in a server-based network with centralized logons, you're running a Windows domain. A **domain** is a collection of users and computers whose accounts are managed by Windows servers called **domain controllers**. Users and computers in a domain are subject to network access and security policies defined by a network administrator and enforced by domain controllers. The software that manages centralized access and security is a **directory service**. On Windows servers, the directory service software is Active Directory; this software is what makes a Windows server a domain controller.

The Linux OS supports a centralized logon service called Network Information Service (NIS), but more often Linux administrators use a service compatible with Active Directory, called Lightweight Directory Access Protocol (LDAP), if they want to use a directory service. A directory service is one of several network services usually found only on server OSs running in a server-based network. Other services include the following:

- *Naming services*—Translate computer names to their addresses.
- *E-mail services*—Manage incoming and outgoing e-mail from client e-mail programs.
- *Application services*—Grant client computers access to complex applications that run on the server.
- *Communication services*—Give remote users access to an organization's network.
- *Web services*—Provide comprehensive Web-based application services.

Unlike peer-to-peer networks, server-based networks are easier to expand. Peer-to-peer networks should be limited to 10 or fewer users, but server-based networks can handle anywhere from a handful to thousands of users. In addition, multiple servers can be configured to work together, which enables administrators to add more servers to share the load when an application's performance wanes or to provide fault tolerance if a server's hardware malfunctions.

Table 9-3 summarizes the strengths and weaknesses of peer-to-peer/workgroup and server/domain-based networks.

**Table 9-3 Peer-to-peer versus server-based networks**

| Network attribute | Peer-to-peer network | Server-based network |
|---|---|---|
| Resource access | Distributed among many desktop/client computers; makes access to resources more complex | Centralized on one or more servers; streamlines access to resources |
| Security | Users control their own shared resources and might have several sets of credentials to access resources; not ideal when tight security is essential | Security is managed centrally, and users have a single set of credentials for all shared resources; best when a secure environment is necessary |
| Performance | Desktop OS not tuned for resource sharing; access to shared resources can be hindered by users running applications | Server OS tuned for resource sharing; servers are usually dedicated to providing network services |
| Cost | No dedicated hardware or server OS required, making initial costs lower; lost productivity caused by increasing complexity can raise costs in the long run | Higher upfront costs because of dedicated hardware and server OSs; additional ongoing costs for administrative support |

Peer-to-peer networks and server-based networks each have advantages. For this reason, using a combination of the two models isn't uncommon. For example, a user might want to share a printer with a group of users in close proximity or a document folder with a department colleague. With this arrangement, a user is in control of a shared resource, yet can still assign permissions to this resource by using accounts from the central user database on the server. Although sharing the resource is decentralized, the logon credentials to access the resource are still centralized.

# Network Device Fundamentals

LANs, WANs, MANs, and internetworks are built with a variety of network hardware. Your understanding of how the most common network hardware works is crucial to your success in building reliable, high-performance networks. This section begins by discussing the simplest of network devices: the hub, a device that's nearly obsolete but is still found in older installations, or for special purposes. Switches have supplanted hubs in networks large and small and are the main network building block today. Wireless access points are the foundation of wireless networks; you will learn about their operation and basic configuration. Network interface cards have become such an essential component of computers that they're now built into most motherboards. Your understanding of NIC configuration options and properties will help you build a better network. The last topic of this section covers the most complex network devices: routers, the gateway to the Internet that makes it possible for large companies to build vast internetworks and WANs.

## Network Hubs

A hub, also called a *multiport repeater*, is the simplest of the network devices. A hub has the rather straightforward job of receiving bit signals generated by NICs and other devices, strengthening them, and then sending them along (repeating them) to other devices connected to its ports (see Figure 9-13). Think of a hub as a microphone for network signals. When people speak, their voices carry only so far until people in the back of the room can no longer hear what's being said. Network signals, too, carry only so far on their medium before receiving computers can no longer interpret them correctly. A hub enables you to connect computers whose distance from one another would otherwise make communication impossible. Its function is as follows:

- Receives bit signals generated from a connected computer on any one of its ports
- Cleans the signal by filtering out electrical noise
- Regenerates the signal to full strength
- Transmits the regenerated signal to all other ports a computer (or other network device) is connected to

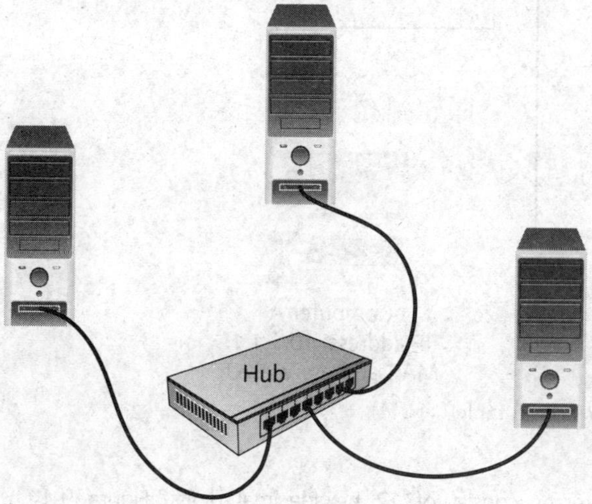


**Figure 9-13** A multiport repeater, or hub

## Network Switches

A network **switch**, like a hub, is used to interconnect multiple computers so that they can communicate with one another. A switch looks just like a hub, with several ports for plugging in network cables. However, instead of simply regenerating incoming bit signals and repeating them to all other ports, a switch actually reads data in the message, determines which port the destination device is connected to, and forwards the message only to that port. So, the first important difference between hubs and switches is that hubs work only with electrical signals and the bits these signals represent, whereas switches work with the actual information these bits compose, to make frames.

By reading the destination MAC address of each frame, the switch can forward the frame to the port the destination computer is on. A switch maintains a **switching table** (see Figure 9-14) of MAC addresses that have been learned and their associated port numbers.

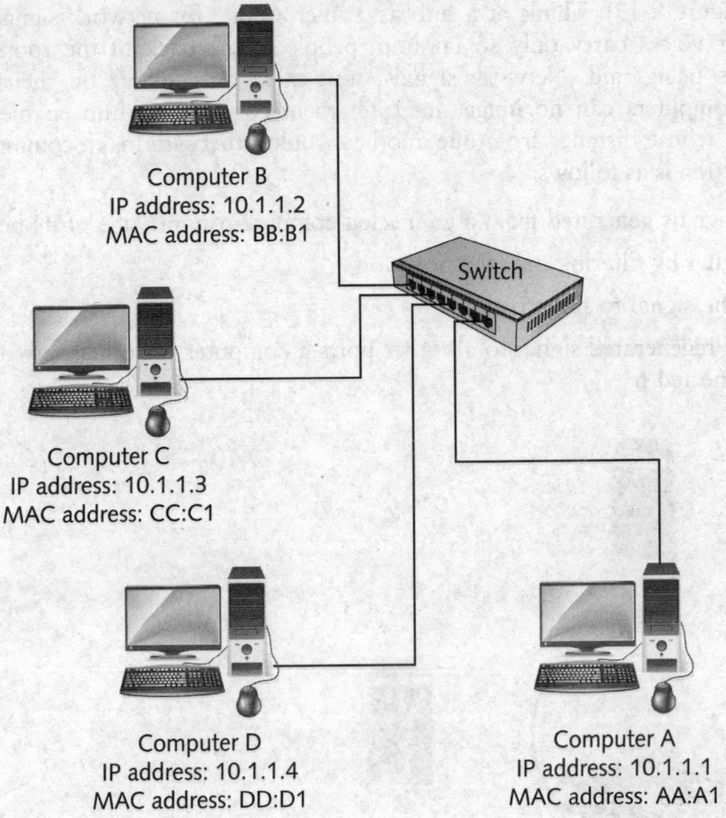


**Figure 9-14** Switches maintain a switching table

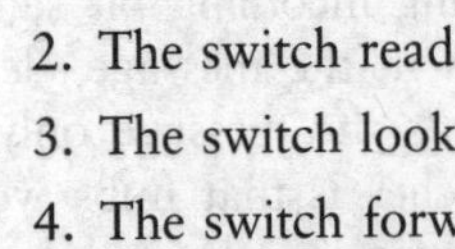


MAC addresses consist of 12 hexadecimal digits. Figure 9-14 uses shorter addresses only as an example.

A switch's operation can be summarized in these steps:

1. The switch receives a frame.
2. The switch reads the source and destination MAC addresses.
3. The switch looks up the destination MAC address in its switching table.
4. The switch forwards the frame to the switch port to which the computer that owns the MAC address is connected.
5. The switching table is updated with the source MAC address and port information.

## Wireless Access Points

Not all networks require a cable to tether the computer to a switch or hub. Wireless networks have become ubiquitous on college and corporate campuses and in many public locations, such as airports and libraries. At the heart of a wireless LAN is the wireless **access point (AP)**. An AP is a lot like a hub, in that all computers send signals through it to communicate with other computers. The obvious difference is that signals don't travel through a physical medium; they travel through the airwaves as radio signals.

Again, an AP is much like a wired hub—all stations hear all network data transmitted by all other wireless devices in the network. All communication goes to the AP, which then retransmits or repeats the transmission to the destination station. However, unlike hubs, communication between two stations requires an extra step. The destination device sends an acknowledgement back to the sending device to indicate that the frame was received. When the sending device receives the acknowledgement, it knows that no error has occurred.

## Network Interface Cards

Attaching a computer to a network requires a NIC to create and mediate the connection between the computer and the networking medium. The networking medium might be copper wire, fiber-optic cable, or the airwaves, but in all cases, data is represented as bit signals that the NIC transmits or receives.

For incoming data, the NIC must be able to interpret the signals used for the network medium, which are electrical for copper wire, light for fiber-optic cable, or radio waves for wireless networks. These signals are then converted to bits and assembled into frames. For outgoing data, the NIC converts frame data into bits and transmits them to the medium in the correct signal format. The following list summarizes the tasks a NIC and its driver perform:

- Provide a connection from the computer to the network medium.
- For incoming messages, receive bit signals and assemble them into frames, verify the frame's destination address, remove the frame header and trailer, and transfer the packet to the network protocol.
- For outgoing messages, receive packets from the network protocol and create frames by adding source and destination MAC addresses and error-checking data.
- Convert the frame data into bit signals in a format suitable for the network medium and transmit the signals.

Figure 9-15 shows a NIC handling incoming data, and Figure 9-16 shows a NIC handling outgoing data.

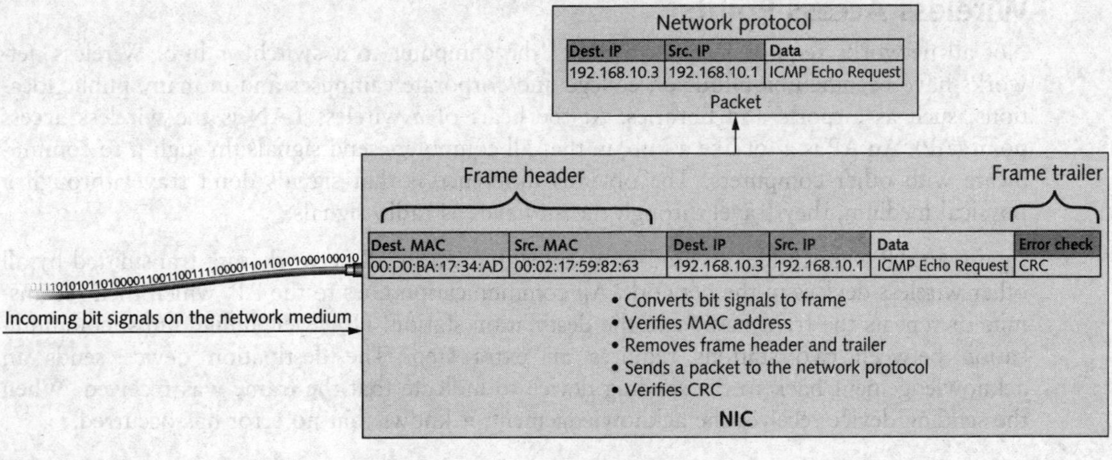


**Figure 9-15** A NIC handles incoming data from the network medium

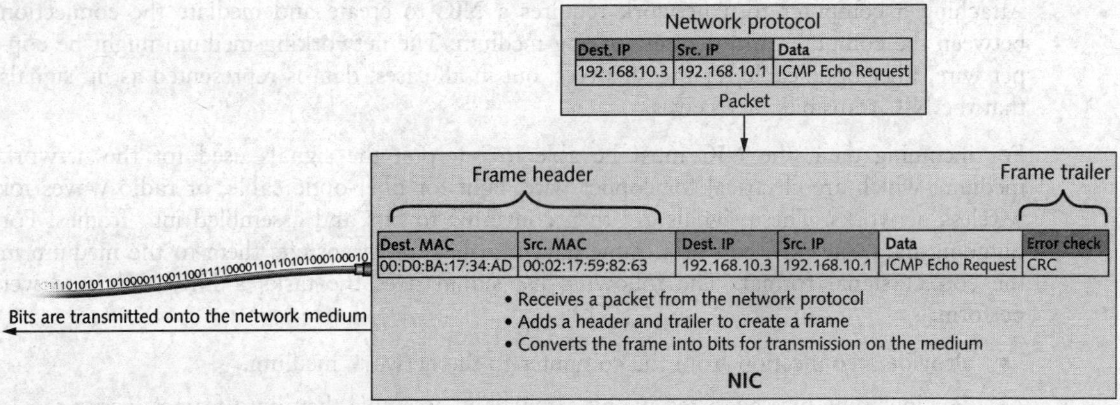


**Figure 9-16** A NIC handles outgoing data to be sent to the network medium

## Routers

Routers are the most complex devices discussed in this chapter. Hubs and switches connect computers to the LAN; routers connect LANs to one another. Routers typically have two or more network ports to which switches are connected to form an internetwork. Figure 9-17 is a diagram of an internetwork, with two LANs connected via a router. Each LAN in this example uses switches to connect workstations and a router port to the LAN. LAN 2 has two switches that are connected.

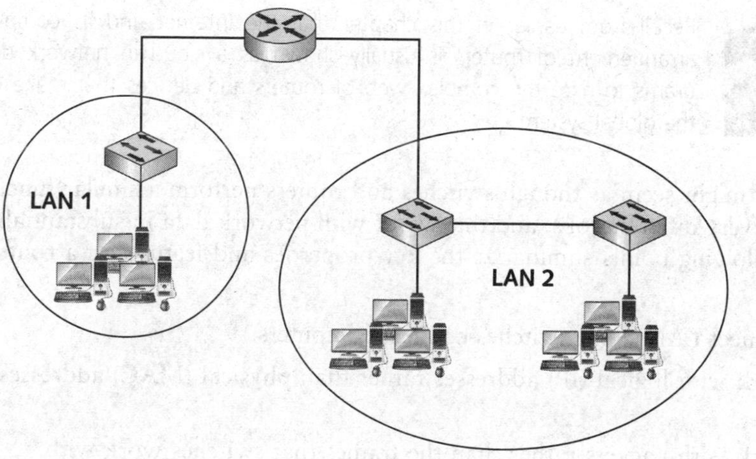


**Figure 9-17** Two LANs connected by a router to make an internetwork

A **router** enables multiple LANs to communicate by forwarding packets from one LAN to another. It also forwards packets from one router to another when LANs are separated by multiple routers. The Internet is built on a vast collection of LANs, all interconnected via routers. Figure 9-18 shows a small business network connected to its Internet service provider (ISP), then to several other Internet routers, and ultimately to a Web server on the Cengage.com network.

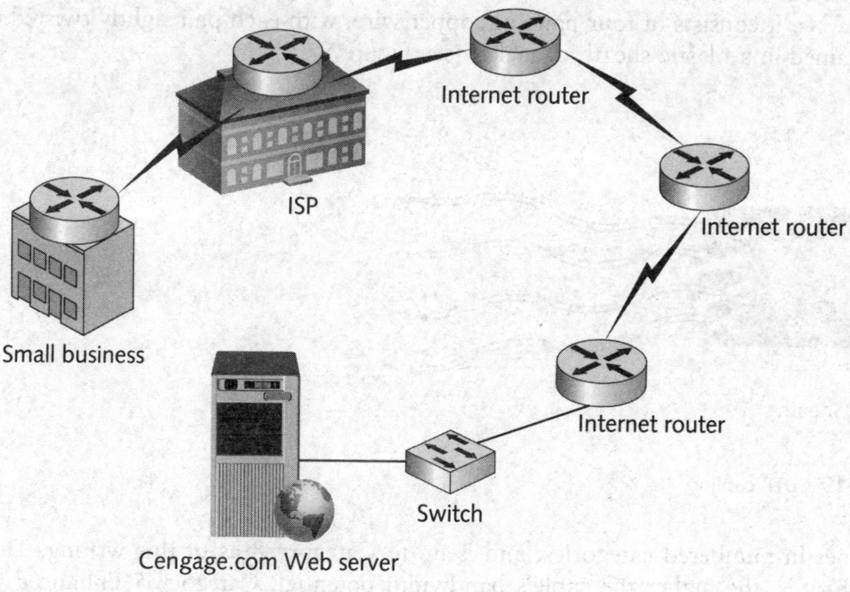


**Figure 9-18** Routers interconnect LANs to form the Internet

Recall from earlier in this chapter that the Internet and its complex arrangement of routers is usually shown as a cloud in network diagrams to hide the complex web of routers and devices that make up the global system.

On the surface, it might seem as though switches and routers perform a similar function, but in reality they do very different jobs, and they work with network data in substantially different ways. The following points summarize the key properties and features of a router versus a switch:

- Routers connect LANs, and switches connect computers.
- Routers work with logical (IP) addresses rather than physical (MAC) addresses, as switches do.
- Routers work with packets rather than the frames that switches work with.
- Routers don't forward broadcast packets, but switches do.
- Routers use routing tables, and switches use switching tables.

## Network Media

Certain network technologies specify the types of media they require to operate. The following sections summarize the most common media types.

**Unshielded Twisted Pair** Unshielded twisted pair (UTP) is the most common media type in LANs. It consists of four pairs of copper wire, with each pair tightly twisted together and contained in a plastic sheath or jacket (see Figure 9-19).

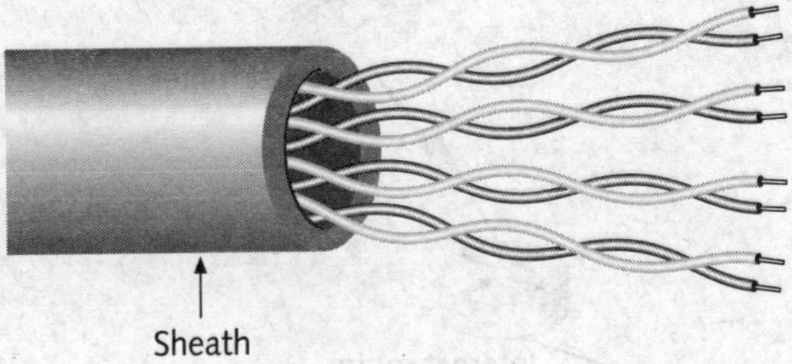


**Figure 9-19** UTP cabling

UTP comes in numbered categories, and is up to Category 8 as of this writing. The higher the category is, the higher the cable's bandwidth potential. Category 5 Enhanced (Cat 5E) and Category 6 (Cat 6) are the most common in wired LANs; they allow speeds of up to 10 Gbps. UTP cabling is used in physical star networks, and the maximum cable length from NIC to switch is 100 meters in LAN applications. UTP cabling is susceptible to electrical interference, which can cause data corruption, so it shouldn't be used in electrically noisy environments.

**Fiber-Optic Cabling** Fiber-optic cabling (see Figure 9-20) uses extremely thin strands of glass to carry pulses of light long distances and at high data rates. It's typically used in large internetworks to connect switches and routers and sometimes to connect high-speed servers to the network. Because of its capability to carry data over long distances (several hundred to several thousand meters), it's also used frequently in WAN applications. Fiber-optic cabling isn't susceptible to electrical interference, so unlike UTP, it can be used in electrically noisy environments. It requires two strands of fiber to make a network connection: one for transmitting and one for receiving.

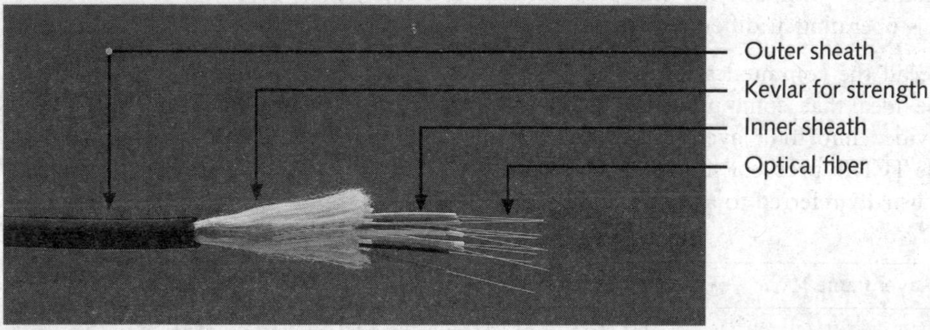


**Figure 9-20** Fiber-optic cabling

**Coaxial Cable** Best known for its use in cable TV, coaxial cable is obsolete as a LAN medium, but it's used as the network medium for Internet access via cable modem. Coaxial cable was the original medium used by Ethernet in physical bus topologies, but its limitation of 10 Mbps half-duplex communication made it obsolete for LAN applications after 100 Mbps Ethernet became the dominant standard.

# Network Protocol Fundamentals

For effective communication across a network, computers must be capable of transmitting data reliably and efficiently. Network protocols are designed to accomplish this goal; some protocols emphasize reliability, others efficiency. Network protocols often work together at different layers of the network communication process to provide both reliability and efficiency. This section discusses network protocols in general but focuses on the most common suite of protocols used in networks: TCP/IP.

The term *protocol* isn't specific to the field of networking. In general, a **protocol** consists of rules and procedures for communication and behavior. Just as two people must share a common set of rules for verbal communication—a language—computers must also "speak" the same language and agree on the rules of communication. You use protocols in other ways as well. Texting, e-mail, and Facebook communication, for example, have their own rules of etiquette and language use.

Until fairly recently, you had a choice of network protocols you could install on your computer, depending on the computing environment. A small network in the 1990s running

Windows 3.1 or Windows 95 probably ran the Windows-specific NetBEUI protocol. A network with Novell NetWare 4.x servers typically ran IPX/SPX. Both these protocols are obsolete now and are found only in networks that haven't been upgraded in more than a decade. Today, you can focus on the TCP/IP protocol suite, the protocol of the Internet and the one all contemporary OSs run.

When a set of protocols works cooperatively, it's called a **protocol suite** (or *protocol stack*). The most common one is **Transmission Control Protocol/Internet Protocol (TCP/IP)**, the Internet protocol suite. Although you can see by its name that TCP/IP consists of at least two protocols—TCP and IP—this protocol suite is actually composed of more than a dozen protocols operating at different layers of the communication process.

Recall the communication process explained earlier. This discussion was an introduction to the idea that communication takes place in layers. The protocols in TCP/IP can also be divided into four layers, with similar names and functions. Figure 9-21 shows the layers of the TCP/IP protocol suite and which protocols operate at each layer. This layered architecture is usually referred to as the *TCP/IP model*.

<table>
<tr><th>Layer name</th><th colspan="4">TCP/IP protocols</th></tr>
<tr><td rowspan="2">Application</td><td>HTTP</td><td>FTP</td><td>DHCP</td><td>TFTP</td></tr>
<tr><td>SMTP</td><td>POP3</td><td>DNS</td><td>SNMP</td></tr>
<tr><td>Transport</td><td colspan="2">TCP</td><td colspan="2">UDP</td></tr>
<tr><td rowspan="2">Internetwork</td><td>ICMP</td><td>ARP</td><td colspan="2">IPsec</td></tr>
<tr><td colspan="4">IPv4 and IPv6</td></tr>
<tr><td>Network access</td><td colspan="4">Ethernet, token ring, FDDI, WAN technologies</td></tr>
</table>

**Figure 9-21** The TCP/IP layered architecture

The Internetwork layer is where computer professionals usually do the most network configuration. It's where the IP protocol operates, and it can be considered the heart of the TCP/IP protocol suite. IP addresses, of course, are defined here, and routing takes place in this layer, too. Without routing, the Internet and World Wide Web wouldn't exist. With all the complexity of configuring routing and managing IP addresses, this layer is also where most errors occur in network configuration. In a large internetwork, a lot of time is typically spent unraveling the intricacies of the Internetwork layer.

The Internetwork layer is responsible for four main tasks, as discussed in the following sections:

- Defines and verifies IP addresses
- Routes packets through an internetwork
- Resolves MAC addresses from IP addresses
- Delivers packets efficiently

## Internet Protocol Version 4

**Internet Protocol version 4 (IPv4)**, or just IP, is an Internetwork layer protocol that provides source and destination addressing and routing for the TCP/IP protocol suite. IPv4 is the most common IP version in networks and the first version that was in widespread use. Earlier versions never really made it out of the lab. One of IP's most important functions is the definition of a logical address, called an **IP address.** IPv4 defines a 32-bit dotted decimal address: 172.31.149.10, for example. Each grouping of numbers separated by a dot (period) is an 8-bit value called an **octet** that can range from 0 to 255. Because an IP address has 32 bits, a total of $2^{32}$ addresses are possible—that's approximately 4 billion addresses, which certainly seems like a lot, but many are wasted, and available addresses to assign to Internet devices are running out.

Part of an IP address specifies the network ID, and the rest of the address specifies a unique host ID in the network. For example, in the address 172.31.149.10, 172.31 is the network ID and 149.10 is the host ID. Determining which part of the IP address is the network ID and which part is the host ID depends on the **subnet mask**, another 32-bit dotted decimal number consisting of a contiguous series of binary 1 digits followed by a contiguous series of binary 0 digits. A contiguous series of eight binary 1s equals the decimal value 255. For example, a typical subnet mask is 255.0.0.0 or 255.255.0.0. In these two examples, for each 255 in the subnet mask, the corresponding octet of the IP address is part of the network ID.

For example, you might configure a computer with the following IP address and subnet mask:

*IP address: 10.1.221.101*

*Subnet mask: 255.0.0.0*

Because the first octet of the subnet mask is 255 (a series of eight binary 1s), the first octet of the IP address is the network ID, which is 10. The network ID is written as 10.0.0.0, and the host ID is 1.221.101. Understand, however, that the network ID and host ID are used together when configuring a computer's IP address, so you will always see them written as 10.1.221.101.

Now take this example:

*IP address: 172.31.100.6*

*Subnet mask: 255.255.0.0*

The first two octets of the subnet mask are 255 (a total of 16 contiguous binary 1s), so the network ID is 172.31, which is written as 172.31.0.0. The host ID is 100.6. When referring to the network ID, you always fill in the host part of the address with 0s.

Continuing with this pattern, say you have the following IP address and subnet mask:

*IP address: 192.168.14.250*

*Subnet mask: 255.255.255.0*

This combination gives you the network ID 192.168.14.0 and the host ID 250. You can't have a subnet mask like 255.0.255.0 because the network ID must be contiguous.

**IPv4 Address Classes** When you enter an IP address in the Internet Protocol Version 4 (TCP/IPv4) Properties dialog box in Windows, as shown in Figure 9-22, Windows fills in a subnet mask automatically. You can change this value if needed. Windows bases the suggested subnet mask on the class of the IP address you enter.

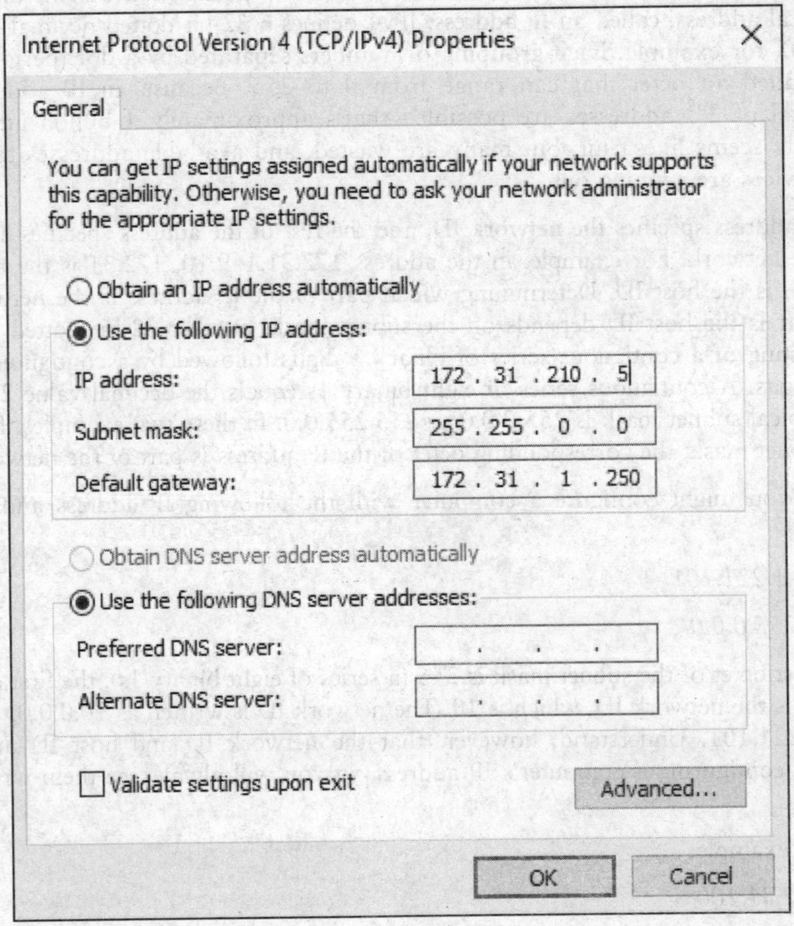


**Figure 9-22** A subnet mask based on the address class

IP addresses are categorized in ranges referred to as Classes A, B, C, D, or E. Only IP addresses in the A, B, and C classes can be assigned to a network device (host). Although the IP address class system has been superseded by a more flexible way to manage IP addresses, called Classless Interdomain Routing (CIDR), the class system is a basis for determining which part of an IP address is the network ID and which part is the host ID. The first octet of an address denotes its class. Review the following facts about IP address classes:

- The value of the first octet for Class A addresses is between 1 and 127. Class A addresses were intended for use by large corporations and governments. An IP address registry assigns the first octet, leaving the last three octets for network administrators to assign to hosts. This allows 24 bits of address space, or 16,777,214 hosts per network address. In a Class A IP address such as 10.159.44.201, for example, the network address is 10.0.0.0. So, the first address in the 10.0.0.0 network is 10.0.0.1, and the last address is 10.255.255.254.

- Class B addresses begin with network IDs between 128 and 191; they were intended for use in medium-sized to large networks. An IP address registry assigns the first two octets, leaving the third and fourth octets available for administrators to assign as host addresses. In the Class B address 172.17.11.4, for example, the network address is 172.17.0.0. Having two octets in the host ID allows 65,534 hosts per network address.
- Class C addresses were intended for small networks. An IP address registry assigns the first three octets, with network IDs ranging from 192 to 223. In the Class C address 203.0.113.254, for example, the network address is 203.0.113.0. These networks are limited to 254 hosts per network.
- Class D addresses are reserved for **multicasting**, in which a packet is addressed so that more than one destination can receive it. Applications using this feature include videoconferencing and streaming media. In a Class D address, the first octet is in the range from 224 to 239. Class D addresses can't be used to assign IP addresses to host computers.
- Class E addresses have a value from 240 to 255 in the first octet. This range of addresses is reserved for experimental use and can't be used for address assignment.

Note a couple of things about the preceding list: First, if you do the math, you can see that a Class C address provides $2^8$ bits of **address space**, which yields 256 addresses, not 254. An address space is the total number of addresses in an IP network number that can be assigned to hosts. The number of addresses specified for Classes A and B are also two fewer than the address space suggests. This discrepancy happens because each network has two reserved addresses: the address in which all host ID bits are binary 0s and the address in which all host ID bits are binary 1s. For example, all the host bits in address 203.0.113.0 are binary 0s; this address represents the network number and can't be assigned to a computer. The host bits in address 203.0.113.255 are binary 1s; this address is the broadcast address for the 203.0.113.0 network and can't be assigned to a computer.

The other note concerns the 127.0.0.0 network. Although technically a Class A address, it's reserved for the **loopback address**, which always refers to the local computer and is used to test the functioning of TCP/IP. A packet with a destination address starting with 127 is sent to the local device and does not reach the network medium. Likewise, the reserved name **localhost** always corresponds to the IP address 127.0.0.1, so that a local machine can always be referenced by this name.

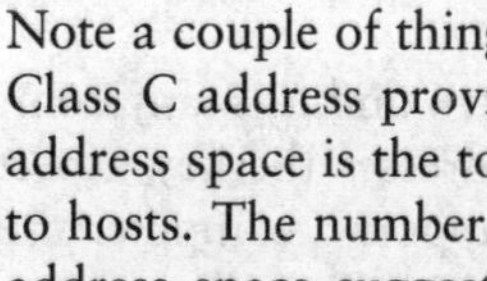


Even though localhost and the loopback address are usually associated with the address 127.0.0.1, any address in the 127.0.0.0 network (except 127.0.0.0 and 127.255.255.255) references the local machine in most OSs.

Table 9-4 summarizes address Classes A, B, and C and the default subnet masks.

**Table 9-4 IPv4 address class summary**

| Class | A | B | C |
|---|---|---|---|
| Value of first octet | 0–127 | 128–191 | 192–223 |
| Default subnet mask | 255.0.0.0 | 255.255.0.0 | 255.255.255.0 |
| Number of network ID bits | 8 | 16 | 24 |
| Maximum number of hosts/network | 16,777,214 | 65,534 | 254 |
| Number of host bits | 24 | 16 | 8 |

## Internet Protocol Version 6

IPv4 has been the driving force on the Internet for decades and continues to be the dominant protocol in use. However, it's showing its age as more and more IPv4 address space is used up and workarounds for security and quality of service must be put in place. IPv4 was developed more than 40 years ago, so it seems natural that as all other aspects of technology slowly get replaced, so will IPv4. This section discusses that replacement: **Internet Protocol version 6 (IPv6)**. IPv6 addresses look very different from IPv4 addresses, and unlike IPv4, IPv6 addresses have a built-in hierarchy and fields with a distinct purpose. Configuring an IPv6 address is clearly different from configuring an IPv4 address. The transition from IPv4 to IPv6 won't happen overnight, so methods have been developed to allow IPv4 and IPv6 networks to coexist and communicate with one another.

This section doesn't attempt to give you a full explanation of IPv6 and its many complexities; there are entire books on this topic. However, this section addresses the key aspects of the IPv6 protocol and what you need to know to configure and support a computer using IPv6. The Internet Engineering Task Force (IETF) started development on IPng (IP next generation) in 1994, and it was later named IPv6. IPv6 was developed to address IPv4's shortcomings. Some of the improvements of IPv6 over IPv4 include the following:

- *Larger address space*—IPv4 addresses are 32 bits, which theoretically provide four billion addresses. IPv6 addresses are 128 bits, meaning there are 340 trillion trillion trillion possible addresses. It's probably safe to say that running out of IPv6 addresses is unlikely.
- *Hierarchical address space*—Unlike IPv4, in which numbers in the address have little meaning other than the address class, network ID, and host ID, IPv6 addresses have a more defined structure. For example, the first part of an address can indicate a particular organization or site.
- *Autoconfiguration*—IPv6 can be self-configuring or autoconfigured from a router or server running IPv6 or through DHCPv6.
- *Built-in Quality of Service (QoS) support*—IPv6 includes built-in fields in packet headers to support QoS strategies without having to install additional protocol components, as IPv4 does. QoS strategies are used to prioritize data packets based on the type or urgency of information they contain.
- *Built-in support for security*—From the ground up, IPv6 is built to support secure protocols, such as Internet Protocol Security (IPsec), whereas IPv4's support for IPsec is an add-on feature.

- *Support for mobility*—With its built-in support for mobility, routing IPv6 packets generated by mobile devices over the Internet is more efficient than with IPv4.
- *Extensibility*—IPv6 uses extension headers instead of IPv4's fixed-size 40-byte header. Extension headers allow adding features to IPv6 simply by adding a new header.

**IPv6 Addresses** An IPv6 address is 128 bits rather than the 32 bits in an IPv4 address. This length increases the number of possible addresses from about 4 billion in IPv4 to $3.4 \times 10^{38}$ addresses (that's 34 followed by 37 zeros!) in IPv6. Unless IP addresses are assigned to every star in the universe, it's safe to say enough IPv6 addresses will be available.

Unlike IPv4 addresses, which are specified in dotted decimal notation in 8-bit sections, IPv6 addresses are specified in hexadecimal format in 16-bit sections separated by a colon, as in this example: 2001:1b20:302:442a:110:2fea:ac4:2b.

If one of the 16-bit numbers doesn't require four hexadecimal digits, the leading 0s are omitted. Furthermore, some IPv6 addresses contain consecutive 0s in two or more 16-bit sections, so a shorthand notation is used to eliminate consecutive 0 values. Two colons replace two or more consecutive 0 values, as the following example shows:

- Longhand notation: 2001:DB8:0:0:0:2ed3:340:ab
- Shorthand notation: 2001:DB8::2ed3:340:ab

The host ID of an IPv6 address is typically 64 bits and uses the interface's MAC address to make up the bulk of the address. Because a MAC address is only 48 bits, the other 16 bits come from the value FF-FE inserted after the first 24 bits of the MAC address. In addition, the first two zeros that compose most MAC addresses are replaced with 02. For example, given the MAC address 00-0C-29-7C-F9-C4, the host ID of an IPv6 address is 02-0C-29-FF-FE-7C-F9-C4.

## Introducing the OSI Model of Networking

The **Open Systems Interconnection (OSI) reference model** for networking explains how networks behave within an orderly, seven-layered model for networked communication. The OSI model isn't specific to a particular network protocol and can be applied to most networking protocols past and present. Many of the networking hardware and software components discussed in this chapter can be identified as working in one or more of the OSI model layers.

Although the OSI model isn't specific to one set of protocols, it's the standard model for discussing, teaching, and learning the field of computer networking. It's unlikely you'll have a course in networking that doesn't at least mention the OSI model, and some courses you take will likely cover it in more detail than this chapter.

Several networking models have sought to create an intellectual framework for clarifying network concepts and activities, but none has been as successful as the OSI model, which was originally proposed by the International Organization for Standardization (ISO). This model is sometimes called the *ISO/OSI reference model*.

NOTE

ISO isn't an acronym; it comes from the Greek prefix *iso*, which means *equal* or *the same*. The ISO, based in Geneva, Switzerland, is a network of national standards institutes from 161 countries. The expanded name differs from language to language. For example, in France the organization is called the Organisation Internationale de Normalisation. The term *ISO* gives the network of institutes a common name.

The OSI reference model has become a key part of networking, in large part because it's a common framework for developers and students of networking to work with and learn from. The attempt to develop a working set of protocols and technologies based on the OSI model and put these efforts into common use never materialized, partly because existing protocols, such as TCP/IP, were already entrenched in the marketplace. However, the OSI reference model has a prominent place in networking as a model and teaching tool. This section briefly covers the model's seven-layer organization, the function of each layer, and the networking devices and components operating at each layer.

NOTE

The set of protocols developed to conform to the OSI model is called *ISO*. You can view the fruits of these labors at *www.protocols.com/pbook/iso*.

## Structure of the OSI Model

The OSI model divides network communication into the seven layers shown in Figure 9-23.

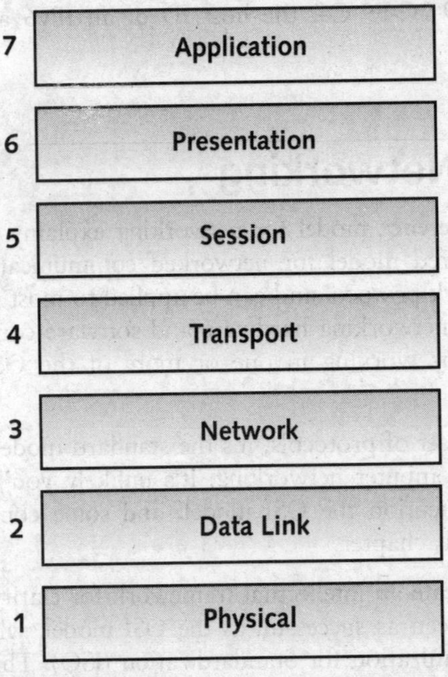


**Figure 9-23** The seven layers of the OSI reference model

TIP

Here are two mnemonics to help you remember the seven layers of the OSI reference model. From the bottom up, starting with the Physical layer, the mnemonic is "People Do Not Throw Sausage Pizza Away." From the top down, starting with the Application layer, try "All People Studying This Need Drastic Psychotherapy" or "All People Seem To Need Data Processing."

At the top, the Application layer provides interfaces that enable user applications—such as File Explorer or Microsoft Word—to access network services. These user applications aren't part of the OSI model, but communicate with its top layer. On the other hand, some user applications, such as Web browsers and e-mail programs, are integrated with functions of the Application layer (as well as the Presentation and Session layers).

At the bottom of the OSI model, the Physical layer is where the network medium and the signals traversing it reside. All the activities needed to handle network communication occur between the top and bottom layers. To comprehend how a network works as a whole, you simply need to understand how each layer functions, what networking components and devices operate at each layer, and how the layers interact with one another.

Each layer in the OSI model has its own well-defined functions, and the functions of each layer communicate and interact with the layers immediately above and below it. For example, the Transport layer works with the Network layer below it and the Session layer above it. The Application layer, although not having a layer above it, interacts with user applications and network services.

TIP

When discussing devices or protocols in relation to the OSI model, the OSI layer number is often used rather than its name. For example, you hear terms such as *Layer 3 switch* or *Layer 7 gateway*.

**Application Layer** The **Application layer** (Layer 7) provides interfaces for applications to access network services, such as file sharing, message handling, and database access. It also handles error recovery for applications, as needed.

Common protocols at the Application layer include HTTP, FTP, SMB/CIFS, TFTP, and SMTP. Computers with network OSs and some security devices operate at Layer 7 because they work with these Application layer protocols.

**Presentation Layer** The **Presentation layer** (Layer 6) handles data formatting and translation. For outgoing messages, it converts data into a format specified by the Application layer, if necessary; for incoming messages, it reverses the conversion if required by the receiving application. In short, Layer 6 "presents" data in a suitable format to the Application layer. The Presentation layer handles protocol conversion, data encryption and decryption, data compression and decompression, data representation incompatibilities between OSs, and graphics commands.

An example of functionality at this level is a Web browser that connects to a secure Web server with encryption protocols that must encrypt data before it's transferred to the server and decrypt data arriving from the Web server.

A software component known as a *redirector* operates at this layer. It intercepts requests for service from the computer; requests that can't be handled locally are redirected across the network to a network resource that can handle the request.

**Session Layer** Layer 5, the **Session layer**, permits two computers to hold ongoing communications—called a *session*—across a network, so applications on either end of the session can exchange data for as long as the session lasts. The Session layer handles communication setup ahead of data transfers when necessary and session teardown when the session ends. Some common network functions this layer handles include name lookup and user logon and logoff.

**Transport Layer** The **Transport layer** (Layer 4) manages data transfer from one application to another across a network. It breaks long data streams into smaller chunks called *segments*. Segmenting the data is important because every network technology has a maximum frame size called the **maximum transmission unit** (MTU). For Ethernet, the MTU is 1518 bytes, which means segments must be small enough to allow for the Network layer and Data Link layer headers and still be no larger than 1518 bytes.

The components working at this layer include TCP and UDP from the TCP/IP protocol suite, although UDP is sometimes called a *pseudo-Transport layer protocol* because it doesn't perform all the functions required of the Transport layer, such as breaking data into segments.

**Network Layer** Layer 3, the **Network layer**, handles logical addressing, translates logical network addresses (IP addresses) into physical addresses (MAC addresses), and performs best path selection and routing in an internetwork. A router performs best path selection when multiple pathways, or routes, are available to reach a destination network; the router attempts to choose the best, or fastest, path.

The software components working at this layer include IP, ARP, ICMP, and several routing protocols from the TCP/IP suite. Routers work at this layer, as do firewalls and certain remote access devices, such as virtual private network (VPN) servers. A switch with routing capabilities, called a *Layer 3 switch*, also works at the Network layer. Essentially, any device that works mainly with packets and their source and destination IP addresses is said to be a Network layer device or Layer 3 device.

**Data Link Layer** Layer 2, the **Data Link layer**, is the intermediary between the Network layer and Physical layer. It defines how computers access the network medium—a process also called *media access control*, which is why the media access control (MAC) address is defined at this layer.

The software component operating at this layer is the NIC driver, and the hardware components include NICs and switches. A NIC operates at this layer because it contains the MAC address and is responsible for media access control. Switches operate at this layer because they do their job by examining MAC addresses and using the information to switch packets from incoming ports to outgoing ports. Networking technologies such as Ethernet and Token Ring operate at this layer.

**Physical Layer** Last but not least, the job of the **Physical layer** (Layer 1) is to convert bits into signals for outgoing messages and signals into bits for incoming messages. The types of signals generated depend on the medium; for example, wire media, such as twisted-pair cable, use electrical pulses, fiber-optic media use pulses of light, and wireless media use radio waves. At this layer, details are specified for creating a physical network connection, such as the type of connectors used to attach the medium to the NIC. The network components working at the Physical layer include all the cables and connectors used on the medium plus repeaters and hubs.

The unit of information at each layer of the OSI model is called a *protocol data unit (PDU)*. For example, at the top three layers, the PDU is simply called *data*. At the Transport layer, the PDU is called a *segment*; at the Network layer, it is called a *packet*; and at the Data Link layer, it is called a *frame*.

**Summary of the OSI Model** The OSI model is a helpful way to categorize and compartmentalize networking activities, and most discussions of protocol suites and networking software use its terminology. Table 9-5 summarizes the actions occurring at each layer. Even though most protocol suites don't adhere strictly to this model (perhaps because so many of them were already implemented in some form before the model's development), they still incorporate its concepts.

**Table 9-5 OSI model summary**

| Layer | PDU | Protocols/ software | Devices | Function |
|---|---|---|---|---|
| 7. Application | Data | HTTP, FTP, SMTP, DHCP | Computers | Provides programs with access to network services |
| 6. Presentation | Data | Redirectors | N/A | Handles data representation to application and data conversions, ensures that data can be read by the receiving system, and handles encryption and decryption |
| 5. Session | Data | DNS, authentication protocols | N/A | Establishes, maintains, and coordinates communication between applications |
| 4. Transport | Segment | TCP, UDP | N/A | Ensures reliable delivery of data, breaks data into segments, handles sequencing and acknowledgements, and provides flow control |
| 3. Network | Packet | IP, ICMP, ARP | Routers, firewalls, Layer 3 switches | Handles packet routing, logical addressing, and access control through packet inspection |
| 2. Data Link | Frame | Ethernet, token ring, FDDI, NIC drivers | Switches, NICs | Provides physical device addressing, device-to-device delivery of frames, media access control, and MAC addresses |
| 1. Physical | Bits | N/A | Network media, hubs/ repeaters, connectors | Manages hardware connections, handles sending and receiving binary signals, and handles encoding of bits |

Although not all networking protocols adhere to the OSI model, a network administrator's clear understanding of the functions at each layer is essential in troubleshooting networks and network equipment and in understanding how network devices operate.

There is a lot more to say about network devices, protocols, network models, and IPv6 and IPv4 addresses, but this book is about operating systems, so we'll turn our attention now to configuring networking in an operating system.

## Configuring Networking in an Operating System

Network configuration in an operating system follows a similar pattern as the steps in the network communication process, the TCP/IP model, and the OSI model. All the functions of the network model must be accounted for, and some but not all might require some level of configuration. We'll start at the bottom, where the physical aspects of the network exist.

### Configuring the Network Interface

The network interface is where the NIC and its driver lives; it comprises the Physical and Data Link layers of the OSI model. In most cases, you don't have to configure the network interface; if a NIC is installed, the OS will usually install the proper driver and the network interface is ready to go. However, it's possible you will need to install a new or different driver if an update becomes available, if the OS is unable to install a driver, or if the OS installs the wrong driver. Installing and updating device drivers was discussed in Chapter 6.

Some network interface drivers provide a number of configuration options. For example, in Figure 9-24, the properties of the Windows network connection have more than 20 configuration options. Some of the options include the speed and duplex mode of the connection, the number of buffers the connection should use, and whether packet prioritization should be enabled. The particular options for a network connection depend on the features of the NIC and its driver.

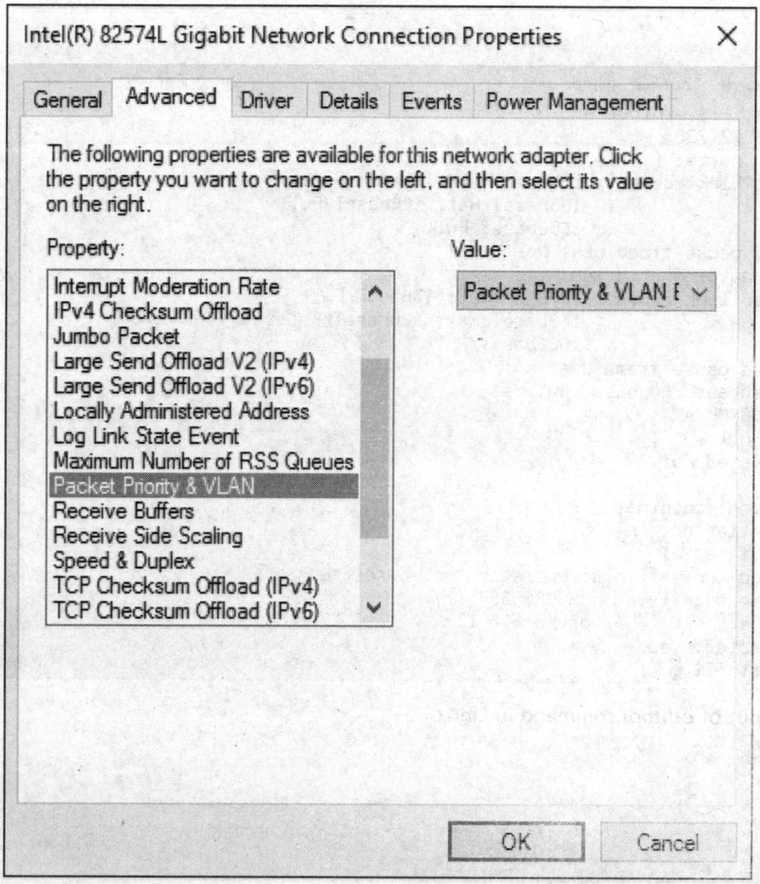


**Figure 9-24** The properties of a network connection in Windows

Linux and Mac OS X also offer configuration settings for the network interface. For example, in Fedora Linux, you can use the command-line tool *ethtool* to display and change network interface settings (see Figure 9-25). In Mac OS X, use the advanced settings in the Network dialog box (see Figure 9-26).

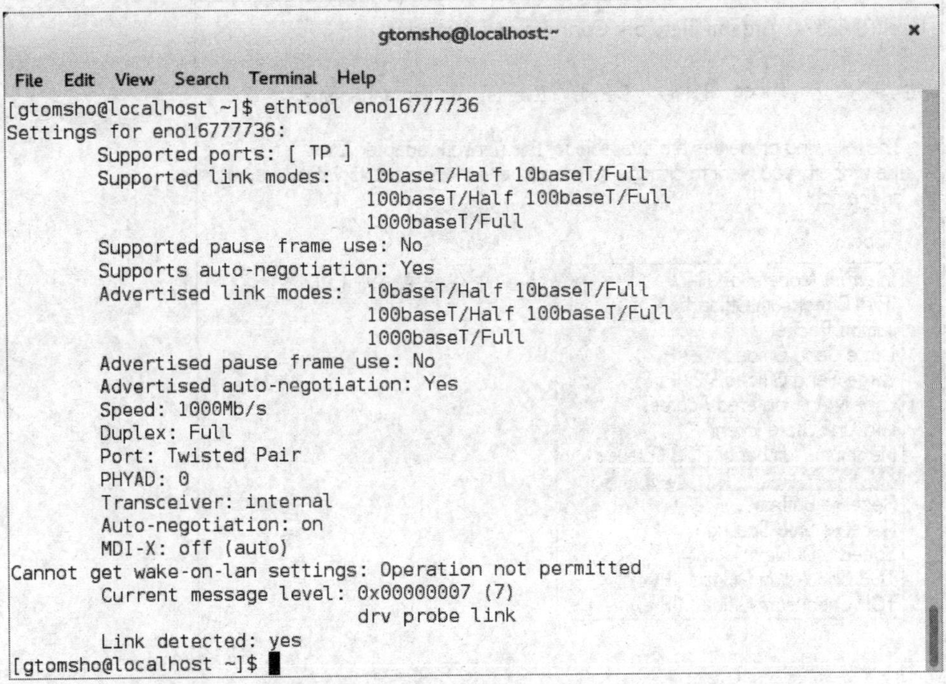


**Figure 9-25** Output of *ethtool* command in Linux

*Source: Fedora Linux*

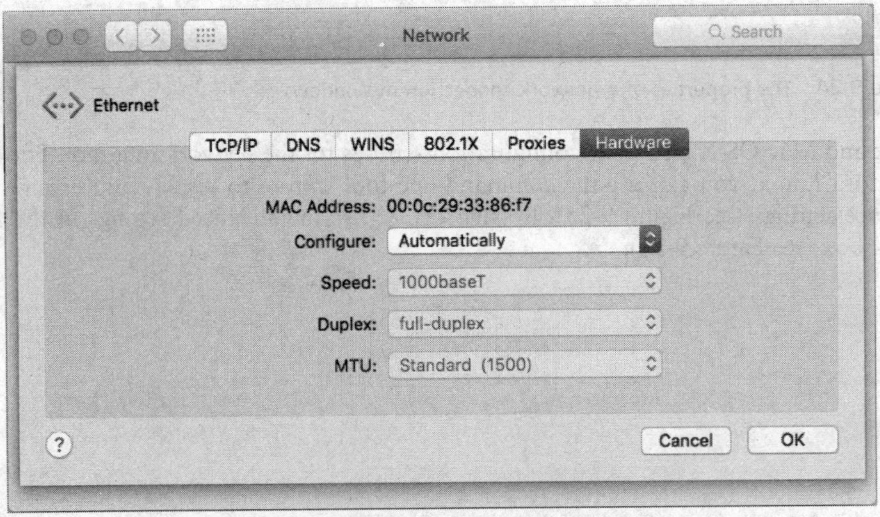


**Figure 9-26** Viewing network interface settings in Mac OS X

*Source: Mac OS X*

## Configuring IPv4 Addresses

The configuration of an IPv4 address consists of the following parts (see Figure 9-27):

- *IP address*—The IP address is required and identifies the computer on the network.
- *Subnet mask*—The subnet mask is required because it determines the network and host IDs.
- *Default gateway*—The default gateway is not required, but is necessary for the computer to access other networks, including the Internet.
- *Preferred DNS server*—The preferred DNS server address is not required but is necessary to translate domain names to addresses. Without a DNS server address, communication with another computer would require you to know the computer's IP address. With a DNS server, your computer can communicate with other computers using their names, such as *server1* and *www.awebserver.com.*
- *Alternate DNS server*—The alternate DNS server address is not required. If the preferred DNS server is not available, the computer will use the alternate DNS server.

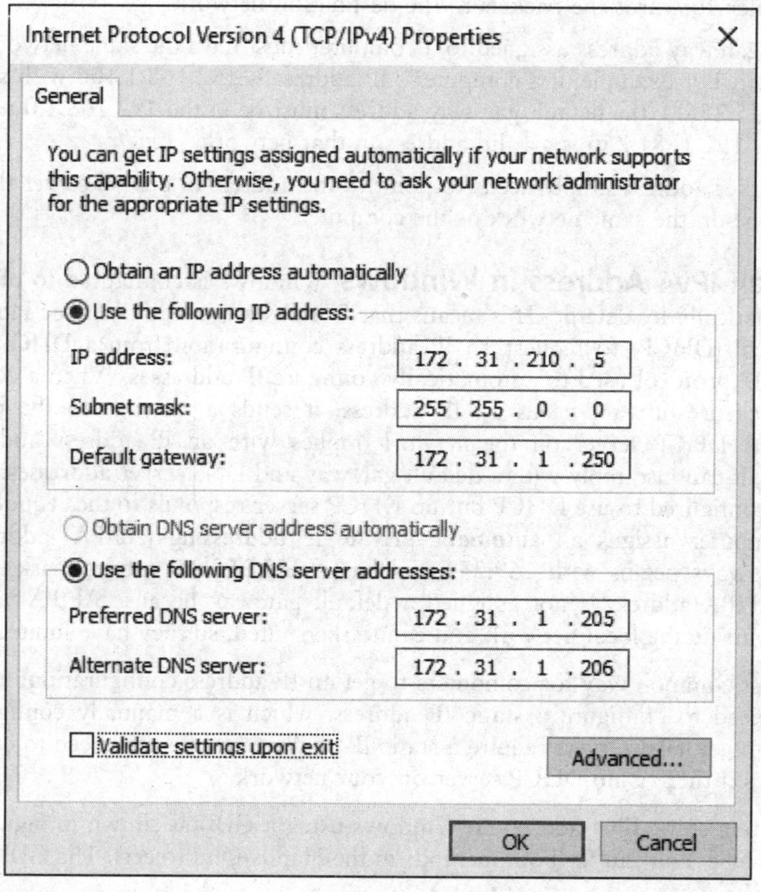


**Figure 9-27** The Internet Protocol Version 4 (TCP/IPv4) Properties dialog box

When you assign a computer an IP address, there are some rules to remember:

- A host can be assigned an IP address only in the range of Class A, Class B, or Class C addresses.
- All hosts on the same network must have the same network ID in their IP addresses. The term *network* in this case means a group of computers connected to one or more switches (or access points), and not separated by a router.
- All host IDs on the same network must be unique.
- You can't assign an IP address in which all the host ID bits are binary 0. This type of IP address is reserved as the network ID. For example, IP address 10.1.0.0 with subnet mask 255.255.0.0 is reserved to identify network 10.1.
- You can't assign an IP address in which all the host ID bits are binary 1. This type of IP address is reserved as the network broadcast address. For example, IP address 10.1.255.255 with subnet mask 255.255.0.0 has all host ID bits set to binary 1 and is reserved as the broadcast address for the 10.1.0.0 network.
- Computers assigned different network IDs can communicate only by sending packets to a router, which forwards the packets to the destination network.
- The default gateway address assigned to a computer must have the same network ID as that computer. For example, if a computer's IP address is 192.168.1.100 with subnet mask 255.255.255.0, the default gateway address must be in the 192.168.1.0 network; for example, 192.1681.250 is a valid address in that network.
- The DNS server address simply needs to point to the address of a DNS server that may or may not be on the same network as the computer.

**Configuring an IPv4 Address in Windows** Windows is configured to obtain an IP address automatically by default. This means that Windows uses the **Dynamic Host Configuration Protocol (DHCP)** to request an IP address configuration from a DHCP server. DHCP is a TCP/IP protocol used to automatically configure IP addresses. When a computer running DHCP client software needs an IP address, it sends a message to the network requesting one. A DHCP server on the network replies with an IP address and subnet mask; optionally, it can also reply with a default gateway and DNS server addresses. If a client computer is configured to use DHCP but no DHCP server responds to the request for an address, the computer assigns an **automatic private IP addressing (APIPA)** address. An APIPA address always begins with 169.254 and has a 255.255.0.0 subnet mask. A computer with an APIPA address is not assigned a default gateway because APIPA addresses cannot be used outside the local network and cannot be routed, so they have limited utility.

DHCP is the most common way for computers to get an IP address configuration; however, sometimes you need to configure a **static IP address**, which is a manually configured IP address. For example, most servers require a static IP address, or you may need to configure static IP addresses if there is no DHCP server on your network.

You can configure a static IPv4 address in Windows using a GUI (as shown in Figure 9-27) or the command line. You can try both methods in the Hands-On Projects. The GUI method is accessed from the properties window of a network connection. To configure an IPv4 address from the command line, use the *netsh* command from a command prompt. You can use the *netsh* command for a wide variety of network configuration tasks. To see a list of *netsh* commands, type *netsh /?* at the command prompt. To configure the IP address of a network interface, you need to know the name of the interface. Windows names its network interfaces Ethernet0, Ethernet1, and so on. You can find the name of your interface from the Network Connections control panel, by typing *netsh interface show interface* from the command prompt, or by typing *ipconfig* from the command prompt. To configure the IP address of an interface named Ethernet0 to 10.1.1.1 with subnet mask 255.255.0.0, use this command:

*netsh interface ipv4 set address "Ethernet0" static 10.1.1.1 255.255.0.0*

You can include the default gateway by adding the address to the end of the command:

*netsh interface ipv4 set address "Ethernet0" static 10.1.1.1 255.255.0.0 10.1.1.250*

To set the primary DNS server for the computer to 10.1.1.100, use the following command:

*netsh interface ipv4 set dns "Ethernet0" static 10.1.1.100 primary*

To view your IP address configuration, use the *ipconfig* command. For extended IP configuration information, use *ipconfig /all*. You'll use *ipconfig* in the Hands-On Projects.

**Configuring an IPv4 Address in Linux and Mac OS X** As with Windows, most Linux distributions use automatically assigned IP addresses using DHCP by default. If you need to configure a static address in Linux, use the *ifconfig* command from a shell prompt. As with the Windows *netsh* command, you need to know the name of your network interface, which you can find out by typing *ifconfig* and pressing Enter to display your current interface configuration. Linux names its interfaces eno*Number*, where *Number* is an 8-digit number. You might also see Linux interface names such as eth0 and eth1. To configure an IP address on an interface named eth0, use the following command from the shell prompt:

*ifconfig eth0 10.1.1.1 netmask 255.255.0.0*

To configure a default gateway in Linux, use the *route* command:

*route add default gw 10.1.1.250*

To configure a DNS server in Linux, you must configure the /etc/resolv.conf file and add an entry that looks like:

*nameserver 10.1.1.100*

Most Linux installations that include a GUI have a GUI tool for configuring the IP address settings. For example, in Fedora 23, you can find the Network utility by clicking Activities, Show Applications, Settings, and then Network. To configure an IP address, click the settings icon and then click IPv4. If you want to use DHCP, leave the setting configured to Automatic (DHCP); otherwise, click Manual to see the dialog box in Figure 9-28.

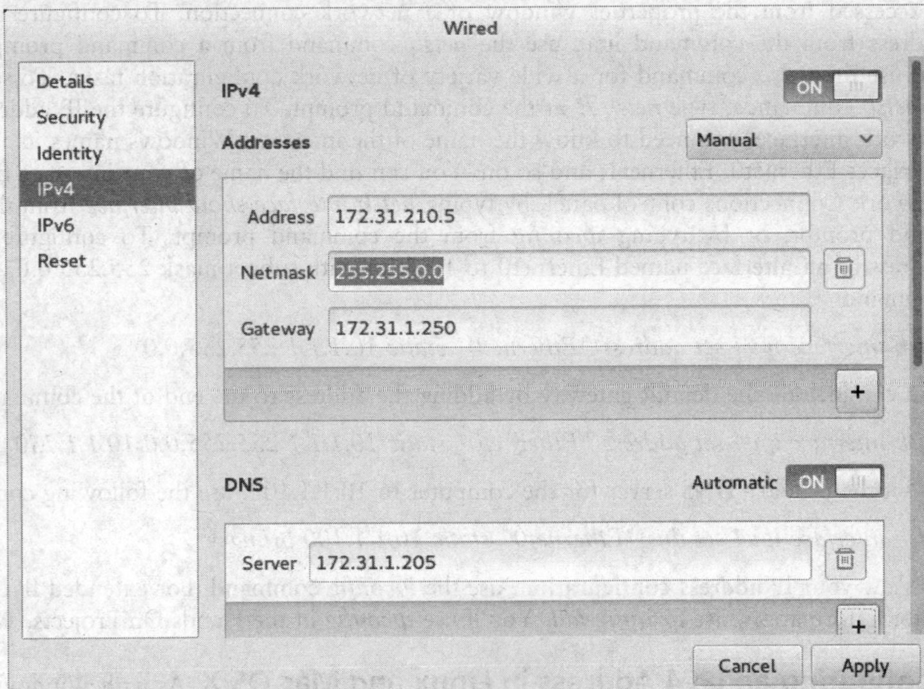


**Figure 9-28** Configuring an IP address in Linux

*Source: Fedora Linux*

As with Linux, you can configure an IP address in Mac OS X using the *ifconfig* command at a shell prompt. To use a GUI in Mac OS X, click the Apple icon, click System Preferences, and then click Network to see the window shown in Figure 9-29.

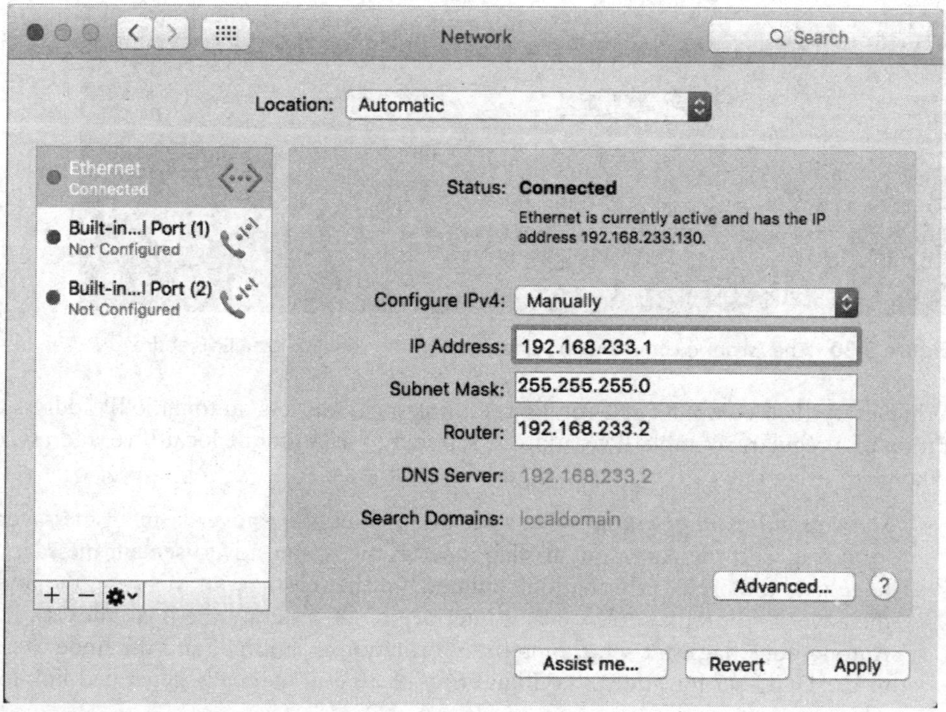


**Figure 9-29** Configuring an IP address in Mac OS X

*Source: Mac OS X*

## Configuring IPv6 Addresses

Like IPv4, IPv6 can configure itself automatically, which is the preferred method of IPv6 configuration. Static configuration is also an option, when necessary. A computer with IPv6 enabled is always automatically assigned a **link-local IPv6 address**. A link-local address always begins with *fe80* and is self-configuring, using the MAC address or a random value for the host ID. Link-local addresses can't be routed and are somewhat equivalent to APIPA addresses in IPv4. These addresses can be used for computer-to-computer communication in small networks where no routers are needed. When you display your IP configuration in Windows, Linux, or Mac OS X, you will see your link-local IPv6 address, as shown in the output of the *ipconfig* command in Figure 9-30.

```
C:\WINDOWS\system32>ipconfig

Windows IP Configuration


Ethernet adapter Ethernet 3:

   Connection-specific DNS Suffix  . :
   Link-local IPv6 Address . . . . . : fe80::2421:5ac1:6a44:b979%3
   IPv4 Address. . . . . . . . . . . : 172.31.210.1
   Subnet Mask . . . . . . . . . . . : 255.255.0.0
   Default Gateway . . . . . . . . . : 172.31.1.250
```

**Figure 9-30** The *ipconfig* command in Windows showing the link-local IPv6 address

While every IPv6 computer self-configures a link-local address, automatic IP address configuration of a regular, routable IPv6 address, referred to as a **unique local IPv6 address**, can also take place using one of two autoconfiguration methods:

- *Stateless autoconfiguration*—The node listens for router advertisement messages from a local router. If the Autonomous flag is set in the router advertisement message, the node uses the prefix information contained in the message. In this case, the node uses the advertised prefix and its 64-bit interface ID to generate the IPv6 address. If the Autonomous flag isn't set, the prefix information is ignored, and the node can attempt to use DHCPv6 for address configuration or an automatically generated link-local address.
- *Stateful autoconfiguration*—The node uses an autoconfiguration protocol, such as DHCPv6, to get its IPv6 address and other configuration information. A node attempts to use DHCPv6 to get IPv6 address configuration information if no routers on the network provide router advertisements or if the Autonomous flag isn't set in router advertisements.

Static assignment of IPv6 addresses is always an option. For Windows, you can use the properties dialog box for Internet Protocol Version 6 (TCP/IPv6) or the *netsh* command. For Linux and Mac OS X, you use the *ifconfig* command or the GUI utilities described earlier in the "Configuring IPv4 Addresses" section. You will configure IP addresses in all three OSs in the Hands-On Projects.

## Chapter Summary

- The components needed to make a stand-alone computer into a networked computer include a NIC, a network medium, and usually an interconnecting device. In addition, network client and server software, protocols, and the NIC driver are needed to enable a computer to communicate on a network.
- The layers of the network communication process can be summarized as user application, network software, network protocol, and network interface.
- The terms for describing networks of different scopes are *LAN*, *internetwork*, *WAN*, and *MAN*. A LAN is a single collection of devices operating in a small geographic

area. An internetwork is a collection of LANs tied together by routers, and a WAN and MAN are geographically dispersed internetworks.

- Packets and frames are the units of data handled by different network components. Packets, which are processed by the network protocol, are units of data with the source and destination IP addresses added. Frames, which are processed by the network interface, have MAC addresses and an error-checking code added to the packet.
- A client is the computer or network software that requests network data, and a server is the computer or network software that makes network data available to requesting clients.
- A peer-to-peer network model has no centralized authority over resources; a server-based network typically uses a directory service for centralized logon, security settings, and resource management.
- LANs, WANs, MANs, and internetworks are built with a variety of network hardware. Network hubs take incoming bit signals and repeat them at their original strength out of all connected ports. Network switches read the destination MAC address in the frame to determine which port the destination device is connected to and forward the frame only to that port. Access points are a central device in a wireless network and perform a function similar to hubs. Network interface cards create and mediate the connection between the computer and network medium. Routers connect LANs to one another and forward packets from one LAN to another, according to the destination IP address specified in the packet. Routers use routing tables to determine where to forward packets.
- TCP/IP is the main protocol suite used in networks. Like most facets of networking, TCP/IP takes a layered approach and is organized into four layers: Application, Transport, Internetwork, and Network access.
- The Open Systems Interconnection (OSI) reference model for networking explains how networks behave within an orderly, seven-layered model for networked communication. The OSI model isn't specific to a particular network protocol and can be applied to most networking protocols past and present.
- Network configuration in an operating system follows a similar pattern as the steps in the network communication process, the TCP/IP model, and the OSI model. All the functions of the network model must be accounted for, and some but not all might require some level of configuration.

## Key Terms

**access point (AP)** A wireless device that serves as the central connection point of a wireless LAN and mediates communication between wireless computers.

**Active Directory** The directory service used by Windows servers.

**address space** The number of addresses available in an IP network number that can be assigned to hosts.

**Application layer** Layer 7 in the OSI model, which provides interfaces that enable applications to request and receive network services. See also *Open Systems Interconnection (OSI) reference model.*

**automatic private IP addressing (APIPA)** A private range of IP addresses assigned to an APIPA-enabled computer automatically when an IP address is requested via DHCP but no DHCP server responds to the request. See also *Dynamic Host Configuration Protocol (DHCP).*

**client** The term used to describe an OS designed mainly to access network resources, a computer's primary role in a network (running user applications and accessing network resources), and software that requests network resources from servers.

**credentials** A username and password or another form of identity used to access a computer.

**Data Link layer** Layer 2 in the OSI model, which is responsible for managing access to the network medium and delivery of data frames from sender to receiver or from sender to an intermediate device, such as a router. See also *Open Systems Interconnection (OSI) reference model.*

**directory service** The software that manages centralized access and security in a server-based network.

**domain** A collection of users and computers in a server-based network whose accounts are managed by Windows servers called *domain controllers*. See also *domain controller*.

**domain controller** A computer running Windows Server with Active Directory installed; it maintains a database of user and computer accounts as well as network access policies in a Windows domain. See also *directory service.*

**Dynamic Host Configuration Protocol (DHCP)** An Application layer protocol used to configure a host's IP address settings dynamically.

**encapsulation** The process of adding header and trailer information to chunks of data.

**extranet** A private network that allows limited and controlled access to internal network resources by outside users, usually in a business-to-business situation.

**frame** A packet with source and destination MAC addresses added and an error-checking code added to the back end. Frames are generated and processed by the network interface. See also *packet.*

**header** Information added to the front end of a chunk of data so it can be correctly interpreted and processed by network protocols.

**Internet** A worldwide public internetwork that uses standard protocols, such as TCP/IP, DNS, and HTTP, to transfer and view information.

**Internet Protocol version 4 (IPv4)** A connectionless Internetwork layer protocol that provides source and destination addressing and routing for the TCP/IP protocol suite; IPv4 uses 32-bit dotted decimal addresses.

**Internet Protocol version 6 (IPv6)** A connectionless Internetwork layer protocol that provides source and destination addressing and routing for the TCP/IP protocol suite. IPv6 uses 128-bit hexadecimal addresses and has built-in security and QoS features.

**internetwork** A networked collection of LANs tied together by devices such as routers. See also *local area network (LAN)*.

**intranet** A private network in which devices and servers are available only to users connected to the internal network.

**IP address** A 32-bit dotted decimal address used by IP to determine the network a host resides on and to identify hosts on the network at the Internetwork layer.

**link-local IPv6 address** Similar in function to IPv4 APIPA addresses, link-local IPv6 addresses begin with *fe80*, are self-configuring, and can't be routed. See also *Automatic private IP addressing (APIPA)*.

**local area network (LAN)** A small network limited to a single collection of machines and linked by interconnecting devices in a small geographic area.

**localhost** A reserved name that corresponds to the loopback address in an IP network. See also *loopback address*.

**loopback address** An address that always refers to the local computer; in IPv4, it's 127.0.0.1, and in IPv6, it's ::1. This address is used to test TCP/IP functionality on the local computer.

**maximum transmission unit (MTU)** The maximum frame size allowed to be transmitted across a network medium.

**metropolitan area network (MAN)** An internetwork confined to a geographic region, such as a city or county; a MAN uses third-party communication providers to supply connectivity between locations. See also *internetwork*.

**multicasting** A network communication in which a packet is addressed so that more than one destination can receive it.

**name server** A computer that provides the service of name-to-address resolution; for example, it resolves a host and domain name to an IP address.

**network** Two or more computers connected by a transmission medium that allows them to communicate.

**network client software** An application or OS service that can request information stored on another computer.

**network interface card (NIC)** A device that creates and mediates the connection between a computer and the network medium.

**Network layer** Layer 3 of the OSI model, which handles logical addressing and routing of PDUs across internetworks. See also *Open Systems Interconnection (OSI) reference model*.

**network protocols** The software that defines the rules and formats a computer must use when sending information across the network.

**network server software** The software that allows a computer to share its resources by fielding requests generated by network clients.

**octet** An 8-bit value; a number from 0 to 255 that's one of the four numbers in a dotted decimal IP address.

**Open Systems Interconnection (OSI) reference model** ISO Standard 7498 defines a frame of reference for understanding networks by dividing the process of network communication into seven layers. Each layer is defined in terms of the services and data it handles on behalf of the layer above it and the services and data it needs from the layer below it.

**packet** A chunk of data with source and destination IP addresses (as well as other IP information) added to it. Packets are generated and processed by network protocols.

**peer-to-peer network** A network model in which all computers can function as clients or servers as needed, and there's no centralized control over network resources.

**Physical layer** Layer 1, the bottom layer of the OSI model, transmits and receives signals and specifies the physical details of cables, NICs, connectors, and hardware behavior. See also *Open Systems Interconnection (OSI) reference model.*

**Presentation layer** At Layer 6 of the OSI model, data can be encrypted and/or compressed to facilitate delivery. Platform-specific application formats are translated into generic data formats for transmission or from generic data formats into platform-specific application formats for delivery to the Application layer. See also *Open Systems Interconnection (OSI) reference model.*

**protocol** Rules and procedures for communication and behavior. Computers must use a common protocol and agree on the rules of communication.

**protocol suite** A set of protocols working cooperatively to provide network communication. Protocols are "stacked" in layers, and each layer performs a unique function required for successful communication. Also called a *protocol stack*.

**router** A device that enables LANs to communicate by forwarding packets from one LAN to another. Routers also forward packets from one router to another when LANs are separated by multiple routers.

**server** The term used to describe an OS designed mainly to share network resources, a computer with the main role of giving client computers access to network resources, and the software that responds to requests for network resources from client computers.

**server-based network** A network model in which servers take on specialized roles to provide client computers with network services and to maintain centralized control over network resources.

**Session layer** Layer 5 of the OSI model, which is responsible for setting up, maintaining, and ending communication sequences (called *sessions*) across a network. See also *Open Systems Interconnection (OSI) reference model.*

**stand-alone computer** A computer that doesn't have the necessary hardware or software to communicate on a network.

**static IP address** A manually configured IP address.

**subnet mask** A 32-bit dotted decimal number consisting of a contiguous series of binary 1 digits followed by a contiguous series of binary 0 digits. The subnet mask determines which part of an IP address is the network ID and which part is the host ID.

**switch** A network device that reads the destination MAC addresses of incoming frames to determine which ports should forward the frames.

**switching table** A table of MAC address and port pairs that a switch uses to determine which port to forward frames it receives.

**trailer** Information added to the back end of a chunk of data so it can be correctly interpreted and processed by network protocols.

**Transmission Control Protocol/Internet Protocol (TCP/IP)** The most common protocol suite, the default protocol in contemporary OSs, and the protocol of the Internet.

**Transport layer** Layer 4 of the OSI model, which is responsible for reliable delivery of data streams across a network. Layer 4 protocols break large streams of data into smaller chunks and use sequence numbers and acknowledgements to provide communication and flow control. See also *Open Systems Interconnection (OSI) reference model.*

**unique local IPv6 address** An address for devices on a private network that can't be routed on the Internet.

**wide area networks (WANs)** Internetworks that are geographically dispersed and use third-party communication providers to supply connectivity between locations. See also *internetwork.*

## Review Questions

1. An IPv6 address is made up of how many bits?
   a. 32
   b. 48
   c. 64
   d. 128
   e. 256
2. The subnet mask of an IP address does which of the following?
   a. provides encryption in a TCP/IP network
   b. defines network and host portions of an IP address
   c. allows automated IP address configuration
   d. allows users to use a computer's name rather than its address
3. What's the term for each grouping of 8 bits in an IP address?
   a. quartet
   b. quintet
   c. hexadecimal
   d. octet
4. Which of the following IPv6 features is an enhancement to IPv4? (Choose all that apply.)
   a. larger address space
   b. works at the Internetwork and Transport layers
   c. built-in security
   d. connectionless communication

5. Which protocol can configure a computer's IP address and subnet mask automatically?
   a. TCP
   b. IP
   c. ARP
   d. DNS
   e. DHCP
6. When a Windows computer is configured to use DHCP but no DHCP server is available, what type of address is configured automatically for it?
   a. PAT
   b. APIPA
   c. NAT
   d. static
7. Which OSI layer determines the route a packet takes from sender to receiver?
   a. 7
   b. 1
   c. 3
   d. 4
8. Which of the following best describes a MAC address?
   a. a 24-bit number expressed as 12 decimal digits
   b. an address with 12 hexadecimal digits
   c. a 48-bit number composed of 12 octal digits
   d. a dotted decimal number burned into the NIC
9. Which OSI model layer takes a large chunk of data from the Application layer and breaks it into smaller segments?
   a. Network access
   b. Internetwork
   c. Transport
   d. Application
10. You have just installed a new NIC in your PC to replace the old one that had started malfunctioning. What additional software must be installed to allow the OS to communicate with the new NIC?
    a. network application
    b. device driver
    c. BIOS
    d. protocol

11. Which of the following requests information stored on another computer?
    a. NIC
    b. network client
    c. network server
    d. network protocol
    e. device driver
12. Choose the correct order for the process of a user attempting to access network resources:
    1. network protocol
    2. application
    3. network client
    4. NIC driver
        a. 4, 2, 1, 3
        b. 3, 2, 1, 4
        c. 1, 4, 2, 3
        d. 2, 3, 1, 4
        e. 3, 1, 2, 4
13. TCP/IP is an example of which of the following?
    a. NIC
    b. network client
    c. network server
    d. network protocol
    e. device driver
14. In network communication, what address is used to deliver a frame to the correct computer on the network? (Choose all that apply.)
    a. MAC
    b. logical
    c. IP
    d. physical
15. What type of message is used to determine whether a computer is listening on the network?
    a. MAC
    b. ping
    c. IP
    d. TCP

16. What does TCP/IP use to look up a computer's IP address when its name is known?
    a. DNS
    b. ping
    c. MAC
    d. TCP
17. What is the unit of information that contains MAC addresses and an error-checking code that's processed by the network interface layer?
    a. packet
    b. ping
    c. frame
    d. chunk
18. Data is processed from the time an application creates it to the time it reaches the network medium. This process includes adding information such as addresses and is called ____________________.
    a. packetization
    b. encapsulation
    c. de-encapsulation
    d. layering
19. You're the network administrator for a company that has just expanded from one floor to two floors of a large building, and the number of workstations you need has doubled from 50 to 100. You're concerned that network performance will suffer if you add computers to the existing LAN. In addition, new users will be working in a separate business unit, and there are reasons to logically separate the two groups of computers. What type of network should you configure?
    a. WAN
    b. MAN
    c. internetwork
    d. extended LAN
20. Which of the following best describes a client?
    a. A computer's primary role in the network is to give other computers access to network resources and services.
    b. A computer's primary role in the network is to run user applications and access network resources.
    c. It's the software that responds to requests for network resources.
    d. The OS installed on a computer is designed mainly to share network resources.

21. You work for a small company with four users who need to share information on their computers. The budget is tight, so the network must be as inexpensive as possible. What type of network should you install?
    a. server-based network
    b. peer-to-peer network
    c. wide area network
    d. storage area network
22. Which of the following characteristics is associated with a peer-to-peer network? (Choose all that apply.)
    a. decentralized data storage
    b. inexpensive
    c. user-managed resources
    d. centralized control
    e. uses a directory service
23. A device interconnects five computers and a printer in a single office so users can share the printer. This configuration is an example of which of the following?
    a. LAN
    b. MAN
    c. WAN
    d. internetwork
24. A company has just made an agreement with another organization to share their two networks' resources by using TCP/IP protocols. What best describes this arrangement?
    a. MAN
    b. LAN
    c. intranet
    d. extranet
25. You have installed Windows Server 2012 on a new server and want to centralize user logons and security policies. What type of software should you install and configure on this server?
    a. naming services
    b. application services
    c. communication services
    d. directory services

# Hands-On Projects

## Project 9-1: Upgrade a Stand-Alone Computer to a Networked Computer

In this project, you install a NIC and connect it to an interconnecting device with a cable. This project can be done in groups or as an instructor demonstration. It's intended only to familiarize you with the hardware components needed to make a stand-alone computer into a networked computer. You will need a computer, a network interface card (NIC), a patch cable, and a switch. A USB NIC is a good option if you don't want to open the computer case. Even though most computers have a built-in NIC, you may need to add a stand-alone NIC if the built-in interface fails or you want a computer with two or more NICs, a common feature on servers.

1. Install the NIC, following the steps your instructor provides. This process might involve opening the computer case or simply plugging a USB NIC into a USB slot.

2. Turn on the computer. If necessary, insert a disk that contains the NIC driver and follow the instructions for installing it.

3. Using the supplied cable, plug one end into the NIC and the other end into the interconnecting device, which should be a hub or a switch.

4. Examine the indicator lights on the NIC and the hub or switch. There might be one or two lights on each port of the device, depending on its features. At least one indicator on the NIC and on each port of the hub or switch is usually referred to as a *link light*. The link light glows when a data connection has been made between the NIC and the hub or switch. Your instructor can supply more details about the indicator lights available on your hub or switch.

5. When the computer is finished booting, view your IP address settings by opening a command prompt and typing *ipconfig* (for a Windows computer) or *ifconfig* (for a Linux or Mac OS X computer).

6. If your classmates are plugged into the same switch, exchange IP addresses with them and then type **ping *IPaddress*** and press **Enter**, replacing *IPaddress* with the IP address of one of your classmates. You'll work more with *ping* in other Hands-On Projects in this chapter.

7. Shut down the computer, and then unplug and put away the cables.

## Project 9-2: Examine NIC Properties in Windows 10

In some of the following Hands-On Projects, you will work with network settings. Note that the name of the interface referenced in these projects (for example, Ethernet0) may be different from the actual interface name on your computer. Substitute the correct interface name, if necessary.

When you describe a NIC as a component of networking, you're referring to both the hardware NIC and its driver. NIC drivers are configured in the OS in which they're installed and control certain operational aspects of the network interface as a whole. In this project, you examine the properties of your installed NIC. You also use the NIC's MAC address to look up the vendor. Not all NICs or NIC drivers have equivalent features, so your NIC might have more or fewer features than are described here.

1. Start your Windows computer and log on.
2. Right-click **Start**, and click **Network Connections.** (You can get to Network Connections in Windows 7 and earlier versions by going to Control Panel, opening Network and Sharing Center, and clicking Change adapter settings). Right-click **Ethernet0** and click **Status.** The Ethernet0 Status window shows a summary of information about your network connection. To see more information, click **Details** to open the Network Connection Details window (see Figure 9-31).

The *ipconfig /all* command shows much of the same information shown in the Network Connection Details window.

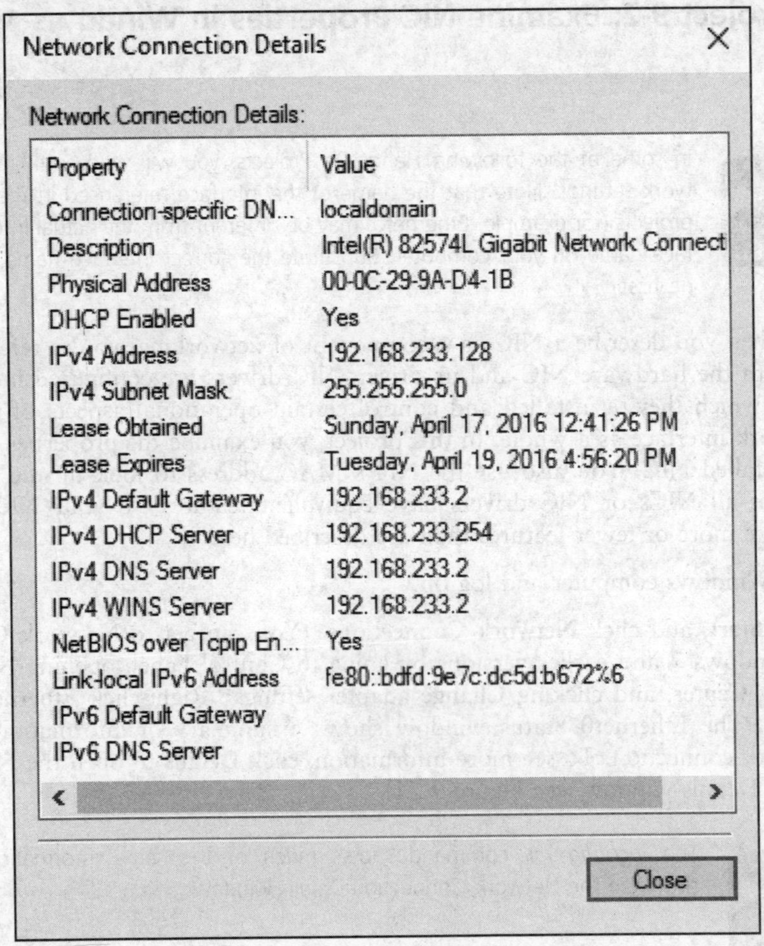


**Figure 9-31** The Network Connection Details window

3. The Network Connection Details window shows information about your connection, including the NIC model, the physical (MAC) address, and your IP address configuration. Write down your MAC address, which you will use later to look up the NIC vendor. Review the remaining information, and then click **Close**.

   MAC address: ______________________

4. In the Ethernet0 Status window, click **Properties**. In the Ethernet0 Properties dialog box, click the **Configure** button under the "Connect using" text box. In the Network Connection Properties dialog box, click the **Advanced** tab (see Figure 9-32). Your NIC might have fewer, more, or different options.

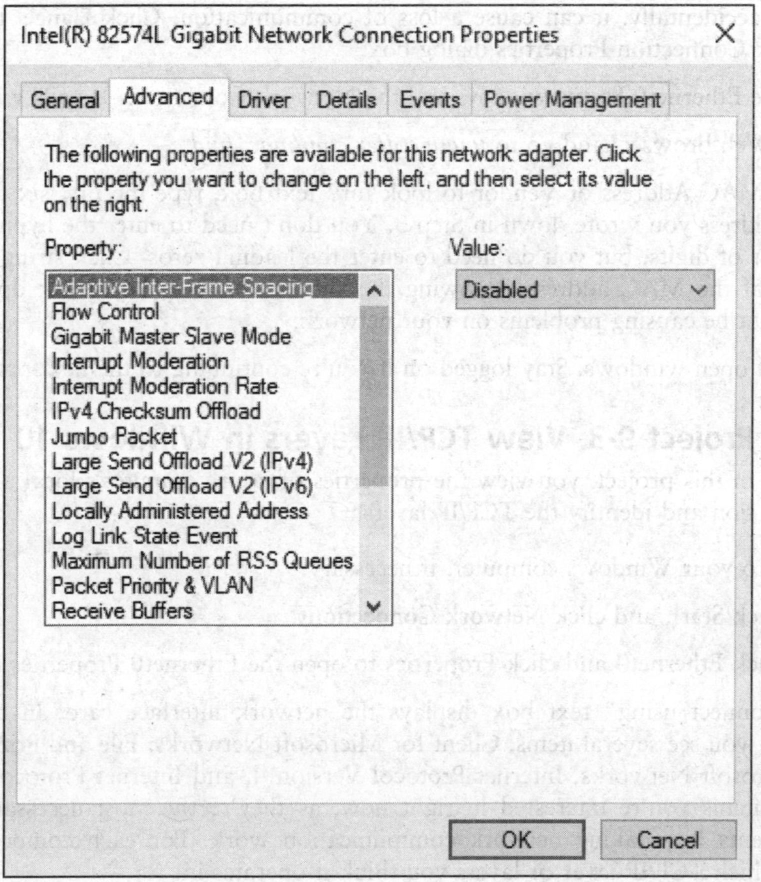


**Figure 9-32** Viewing advanced settings in the Network Connection Properties dialog box

5. Review the available properties for your NIC. When you select a property, you can see its possible values in the Value drop-down list.
6. Click **Speed & Duplex** (or Link Speed and Duplex), and then click the **Value** list arrow to see the possible values. On most NICs, the default value is Auto Negotiation, which means the NIC and switch exchange signals to determine the optimum operational mode. Other modes usually include combinations of 10, 100, and 1000 Mbps, full-duplex, and half-duplex. Normally, you don't need to change these values unless auto-negotiation fails to work. If this happens, you'll probably see the link status light change from on to off repeatedly or never turn on at all.
7. Click the **Locally Administered Address** property. (It might also be listed as Network Address, Physical Address, or MAC Address.) In most cases, this property's value is set to Not Present. You can use this property to override the NIC's burned-in MAC address by entering a new address in the Value text box. Normally, however, you shouldn't override the burned-in MAC address because if you duplicate an existing

address accidentally, it can cause a loss of communication. Click **Cancel** to close the Network Connection Properties dialog box.

8. Close the Ethernet0 Status window and the Network Connection Details window.
9. Start a Web browser, and go to *www.coffer.com/mac_find*.
10. In the "MAC Address or Vendor to look for" text box, type the first six digits of the MAC address you wrote down in Step 3. You don't need to enter the hyphen between each pair of digits, but you do need to enter the leading zeros. Click **string** to find the vendor of the MAC address. Knowing the vendor can help you track down devices that might be causing problems on your network.
11. Close all open windows. Stay logged on if you're continuing to the next project.

## Project 9-3: View TCP/IP Layers in Windows 10

In this project, you view the properties of your computer's local area connection and identify the TCP/IP layers.

1. Log on to your Windows computer, if necessary.
2. Right-click **Start**, and click **Network Connections**.
3. Right-click **Ethernet0** and click **Properties** to open the Ethernet0 Properties dialog box.
4. The "Connect using" text box displays the network interface card. In the list box under it, you see several items. Client for Microsoft Networks, File and Printer Sharing for Microsoft Networks, Internet Protocol Version 4, and Internet Protocol Version 6 are the items you're interested in right now, as they're the most necessary software components for making network communication work. For each component, write down which TCP/IP layer or layers you think it operates in:
    - NIC displayed in the "Connect using" text box: ______________________
    - Client for Microsoft Networks: ______________________
    - File and Printer Sharing for Microsoft Networks: ______________________
    - Internet Protocol Version 4: ______________________
    - Internet Protocol Version 6: ______________________
5. Close all open windows, but leave your computer running for the next project.

## Project 9-4: Use *ipconfig*, *ping*, and *arp* in Windows 10

In this project, you use command-line tools to view your network configuration and test your computer's capability to communicate with other computers. The *ipconfig* command displays the IP address configuration of network interfaces. The *ping* command sends a message to a computer to verify the capability to communicate with it, and the *arp* command displays the MAC (physical) addresses your computer has discovered. You will work with one or more partners in this project.

1. Log on to your Windows computer, if necessary.
2. Right-click **Start** and click **Command Prompt** to open a command prompt window. At the command prompt, type **ipconfig** and press **Enter.** You should see a screen similar to that shown earlier in Figure 9-30, although the numbers will vary. The *ipconfig* command lists the IP address configuration for network interfaces as well as other network settings.
3. To see more details about your network configuration, type **ipconfig /all** and press **Enter.** You can scroll up the command prompt window to see all the output. Under the heading "Ethernet adapter Ethernet0," find the row labeled Physical Address (see Figure 9-33). The number in this row is the MAC address. Also, find the IP address in the IPv4 Address row. Write down these two addresses:

   ______________________________________________

   ______________________________________________

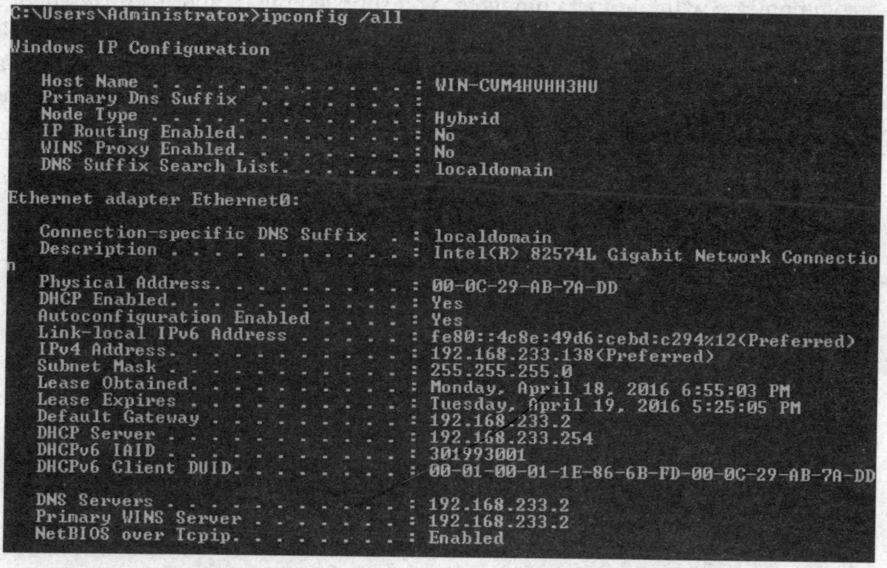


**Figure 9-33** Using *ipconfig /all* to list physical (MAC) and IP addresses

4. Tell your partner your IP address and make a note of your partner's IP address. At the command prompt, type **ping *IPaddress*** and press **Enter** (replacing *IPaddress* with your partner's IP address). You should see output similar to that in Figure 9-34.

```
C:\Users\NetAdmin>ping 172.31.1.250

Pinging 172.31.1.250 with 32 bytes of data:
Reply from 172.31.1.250: bytes=32 time<1ms TTL=128
Reply from 172.31.1.250: bytes=32 time<1ms TTL=128
Reply from 172.31.1.250: bytes=32 time<1ms TTL=128
Reply from 172.31.1.250: bytes=32 time<1ms TTL=128

Ping statistics for 172.31.1.250:
    Packets: Sent = 4, Received = 4, Lost = 0 (0% loss),
Approximate round trip times in milli-seconds:
    Minimum = 0ms, Maximum = 0ms, Average = 0ms

C:\Users\NetAdmin>_
```

**Figure 9-34** Results of the *ping* command

5. Remember that your computer needs both the destination IP address and MAC address to communicate with another computer. You supplied the IP address by typing it at the command prompt. Your computer discovered the MAC address of your partner's computer by using Address Resolution Protocol (ARP). To see this address, type **arp -a** and press **Enter**. The output should be similar to that in Figure 9-35. You might see more lines of output, depending on what other devices your computer has been communicating with.

```
C:\Users\Administrator>arp -a

Interface: 192.168.233.138 --- 0xc
  Internet Address      Physical Address      Type
  192.168.233.2         00-50-56-e3-8d-08     dynamic
  192.168.233.254       00-50-56-e9-23-93     dynamic
  192.168.233.255       ff-ff-ff-ff-ff-ff     static
  224.0.0.22            01-00-5e-00-00-16     static
  224.0.0.252           01-00-5e-00-00-fc     static
  255.255.255.255       ff-ff-ff-ff-ff-ff     static
```

**Figure 9-35** The *arp -a* command displays MAC addresses

6. Use the **ping** command to communicate with other computers and devices on your network.
7. Close all open windows, but leave your computer running for the next project.

## Project 9-5: Configure the IP Address in Windows 10

In this project, you configure your IP address in Windows 10.

1. Log on to your Windows computer, if necessary.
2. Right-click **Start** and click **Network Connections.**
3. Right-click **Ethernet0** and click **Properties** to open the Ethernet0 Properties dialog box. Click **Internet Protocol Version 4 (TCP/IPv4)** and then click **Properties.**

4. If your IP settings have the "Obtain an IP address automatically" option enabled, click **Use the following IP address.** You use this option to set a static IP address. If your address is already static, make a note of it, and skip entering the information in Step 5.
5. For the following IP address settings, enter the information shown unless your instructor tells you to use different values. Click **OK** when you're finished:
   - IP address: **192.168.100.*XX*** (replacing *XX* with a number provided by your instructor)
   - Subnet mask: **255.255.255.0**
   - Default gateway: provided by your instructor
   - Preferred DNS server: provided by your instructor
6. Click **Close.** If you're prompted to set a network location, click **Work network**, and then click **Close.**
7. Test the configuration using the *ping* command to communicate with another student's computer or with your default gateway (if provided).
8. To configure an address using the *netsh* command, open a command prompt with administrator privileges (right-click **Start** and click **Command Prompt (Admin)**). To display your current configuration using *netsh*, type **netsh interface ipv4 show addresses** and press **Enter.**
9. To configure your Ethernet0 interface with the same IP address and subnet mask shown in Step 5, type **netsh interface ipv4 set address "Ethernet0" static 192.168.100.*XX* 255.255.255.0** and press **Enter**. Be sure to replace *XX* with an appropriate number.
10. If your interface was using DHCP before you started this project, type **netsh interface ipv4 set address "Ethernet0" dhcp** and then press **Enter.** This command changes the settings back to using DHCP.
11. To configure a static IPv6 address, type **netsh interface ipv6 set address "Ethernet0" 2001:db8::*XX*** and press **Enter**, replacing *XX* with a value assigned by your instructor. The value *db8* in the address is not required, but it designates the address as one used for testing.
12. To test the configuration, type **ping -6 2001:db8::*XX*** and press **Enter**, replacing *XX* with the address of another student's computer. The -6 in the *ping* command tells *ping* to use IPv6 addresses.
13. Close all open windows and shut down your Windows 10 computer.

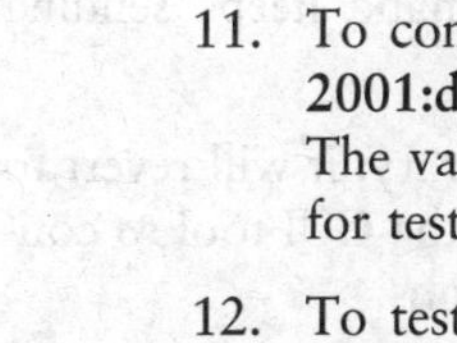


## Project 9-6: Configure the IP Address in Linux

In this project, you configure the IP address in Linux using the *ifconfig* command. You can use *ifconfig* in Mac OS X as well.

1. Start and log on to your Linux computer.
2. Open a terminal window.

3. Type **ifconfig** and press **Enter** to view your current interface settings (see Figure 9-36). Make a note of the interface that is listed on the first line of the output. In Figure 9-36, the interface name is eno16777736. You see your IPv4 address (the number after *inet* in the output) and your IPv6 address (the number after *inet6* in the output).

```
[gtomsho@localhost ~]$ ifconfig
eno16777736: flags=4163<UP,BROADCAST,RUNNING,MULTICAST>  mtu 1500
        inet 192.168.233.131  netmask 255.255.255.0  broadcast 192.168.233.255
        inet6 fe80::20c:29ff:fe95:9b92  prefixlen 64  scopeid 0x20<link>
        ether 00:0c:29:95:9b:92  txqueuelen 1000  (Ethernet)
        RX packets 39030  bytes 4186034 (3.9 MiB)
        RX errors 0  dropped 0  overruns 0  frame 0
        TX packets 21588  bytes 1440243 (1.3 MiB)
        TX errors 0  dropped 0 overruns 0  carrier 0  collisions 0

lo: flags=73<UP,LOOPBACK,RUNNING>  mtu 65536
        inet 127.0.0.1  netmask 255.0.0.0
        inet6 ::1  prefixlen 128  scopeid 0x10<host>
        loop  txqueuelen 0  (Local Loopback)
        RX packets 20  bytes 1940 (1.8 KiB)
        RX errors 0  dropped 0  overruns 0  frame 0
        TX packets 20  bytes 1940 (1.8 KiB)
        TX errors 0  dropped 0 overruns 0  carrier 0  collisions 0
```

**Figure 9-36** Output from the *ifconfig* command
*Source: Linux*

4. To configure your interface with an IPv4 address of 192.168.100.XX and a subnet mask of 255.255.255.0, type **ifconfig *InterfaceName* 192.168.100.*XX* netmask 255.255.255.0** and press **Enter**, being sure to replace *InterfaceName* with the name of the interface in the output and *XX* with a number provided by your instructor. If you get an "Operation not permitted" error, you need root permissions, so type **sudo** followed by the command above and then enter your password when prompted.

5. To test the configuration, type **ping *IPAddress*** and press **Enter**, replacing *IPAddress* with the address of another computer. In Linux, the *ping* command keeps sending packets until you stop it. Press **Ctrl+C** to stop the *ping* command.

6. When you use *ifconfig* to configure the IP address, it is only temporary; it will revert to permanent settings (such as using DHCP) at the next boot. To use the GUI tool to configure an IP address, click **Activities** and then click **Show Applications**.

7. Click **Settings** and then click **Network**. Click the settings button in the lower-right corner and then click **IPv4**. To change how Linux receives its IP address, click the list box next to Addresses, then click Automatic (DHCP) to use DHCP or the Manual option to enter an address manually. Click **Cancel**. Close all open windows and shut down your Linux computer.

## Project 9-7: Configure the IP Address in Mac OS X

In this project, you configure the IP address in Mac OS X using the Network preferences utility. You can also use the *ifconfig* command in Mac OS X.

1. Start and log on to your Mac OS X computer.
2. Click the **Apple** icon and then click **System Preferences**. Click **Network**.

3. Be sure that Ethernet is selected in the left pane and click the selection arrow next to **Configure IPv4** in the right pane (see Figure 9-37). Make a note of your current settings.

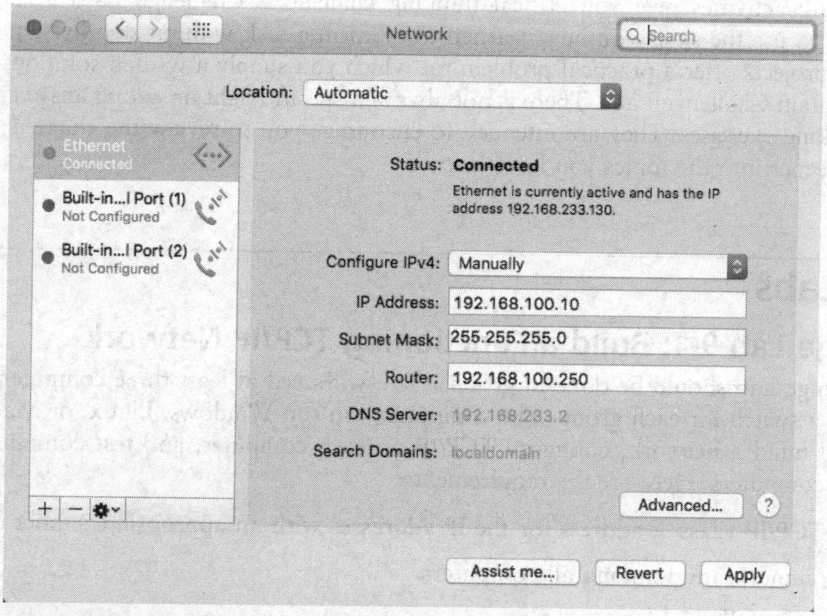


**Figure 9-37** Configuring IPv4 in Mac OS X

*Source: Mac OS X*

4. Click **Manually**, if necessary. Then type the following values:
   - IP Address: **192.168.100.*XX*** (replacing *XX* with a number provided by your instructor)
   - Subnet Mask: **255.255.255.0**
   - Router: provided by your instructor
5. Click **Apply**.
6. To test the configuration, open a terminal window by clicking **Finder** in the Dock. Next, click **Go**, click **Utilities**, and then double-click **Terminal**. Type **ping *IPAddress*** and press **Enter**, replacing *IPAddress* with the address of another computer. As in Linux, the *ping* command keeps sending packets until you press Ctrl+C. Press **Ctrl+C**, close the terminal window, and then close the Utilities window.
7. In the Network window, click **Advanced**. Click each tab to see the options for configuring the network settings. Click the **Hardware** tab. You can use this tab to configure certain properties of the network interface, such as the speed and duplex mode.
8. Click the **TCP/IP** tab. Configure the IP address settings as they were originally set; for example, click the selection arrow next to **Configure IPv4** and click **Using DHCP** if that was the original setting. Click **OK** and click **Apply**.
9. Close all windows and log off or shut down your computer.

# Critical Thinking

The following activities give you critical thinking challenges. Challenge Labs give you an opportunity to use the skills you have learned to perform a task without step-by-step instructions. Case projects offer a practical problem for which you supply a written solution. Not all chapters contain Challenge Labs. There is not always a specific right or wrong answer to these critical thinking exercises. They are intended to encourage you to review the chapter material and delve deeper into the topics you have learned.

# Challenge Labs

## Challenge Lab 9-1: Build a Functioning TCP/IP Network

This Challenge Lab should be done in groups. You will need at least three computers, patch cables, and a switch for each group. The computers can run Windows, Linux, or Mac OS X. You should build a network, configure TCP/IP on each computer, and test communication among the computers. Here are the requirements:

1. Use a TCP/IP Class A address for the IP addresses with an appropriate subnet mask.
2. Test communication among all computers.
3. Answer the following questions.
    - What IP network address did you use?
    - What subnet mask did you use?
    - What command did you use to test communication?
    - What would you need to add to the network to gain access to other networks, including the Internet? How would your TCP/IP configuration change?

# Case Projects

## Case Project 9-1: Peer-to-Peer or Server-Based Network?

Networking Gadgets, Inc. currently employs eight people but plans to hire 10 more in the next four months. Users will work on multiple projects, and only users assigned to a project should have access to the project files. You're instructed to set up the network to make it easy to manage and back up, yet still provide centralized storage for project files. Would you choose a peer-to-peer network, a server-based network, or a combination? Why?

## Case Project 9-2: Peer-to-Peer or Server-Based Network?

CNT Books hired you as a productivity consultant. Currently, it employs six people who will be moving into a new office space. You are to configure a network that allows them to share files and printers. Employees must also be able to control resources on their own machines. The company wants the least expensive solution and only minimal training for employees. Would you choose a peer-to-peer network or a server-based network? Write a list of supplies you might need to purchase to perform this task. What computer configuration tasks might you need to perform?

## Case Project 9-3: What Type of Network?

CNT Books has expanded considerably since you got the network up and running three years ago. The company now occupies an entire floor in the building, and its LAN has grown to include several servers and more than 60 workstations. CNT Books has recently purchased another book company and needs more space and computers. Expansion plans include leasing another floor four stories above the current offices in the same building and adding 35 workstations and at least one more server immediately, with additional equipment purchases expected. What type of network is called for—LAN, WAN, MAN, or internetwork? What additional devices might be needed to ensure efficient network communication?

## Case Project 9-4: Troubleshoot an IP Configuration

You work at a help desk and have just received a call from an employee who says she can't access network resources. You want the employee to view her IP address configuration. Write an e-mail to the employee explaining what command-line program to use and how she can use it to find the information you need. After following your instructions, the employee tells you that her IP address is 169.254.14.11 with the subnet mask 255.255.0.0. What conclusion can you make from this information?

chapter 10

# Sharing Resources and Working with Accounts

**After reading this chapter and completing the exercises, you will be able to:**

- Configure file and printer sharing
- Manage user and group accounts

**One of the primary reasons networks were built was to facilitate the sharing of** information. In this chapter, you learn about sharing files and printers in Windows, Linux, and Mac OS X. In order to secure access to shared files, you need to configure user and group accounts, then assign permissions to these accounts to determine who can access the shared resources and what type of access they have (read or write, for example). You will learn about different types of user accounts and groups, how to create them, and how to assign permissions to shared resources.

# File and Printer Sharing

File and printer sharing is one reason businesses began to outfit computers with network interfaces and network software. Sharing files and printers with other computers on the network requires a file sharing client and a file sharing protocol. The dominant file sharing protocol is **Server Message Block (SMB)**, the native protocol used by Windows; it is also supported by Linux and Mac OS X. **Network File System (NFS)** is the native Linux/UNIX file sharing protocol, and it is supported by Windows and Mac OS X. The protocol you use depends on which client OS is most prevalent on your network—for most networks, it is Windows, so the SMB protocol is the focus of this chapter.

NFS support for Windows is available in Windows Server 2008 and in Windows Vista and later versions.

Printer sharing also uses the SMB protocol in Windows, Linux, and Mac OS X. The native Linux printer sharing protocols are line printer daemon/line printer remote (LPD/LPR) and Common UNIX Printing System (CUPS). CUPS has become the more popular protocol because it is based on the Internet Printing Protocol (IPP).

## Sharing Files in Windows

File sharing in Windows is based on Client for Microsoft Networks on the client side and File and Printer Sharing for Microsoft Networks on the server side. To see these client/server components, view the properties of your network connection, as shown in Figure 10-1. Neither Client for Microsoft Networks nor File and Printer Sharing for Microsoft Networks has any configuration options other than the ability to disable them on a particular network connection.

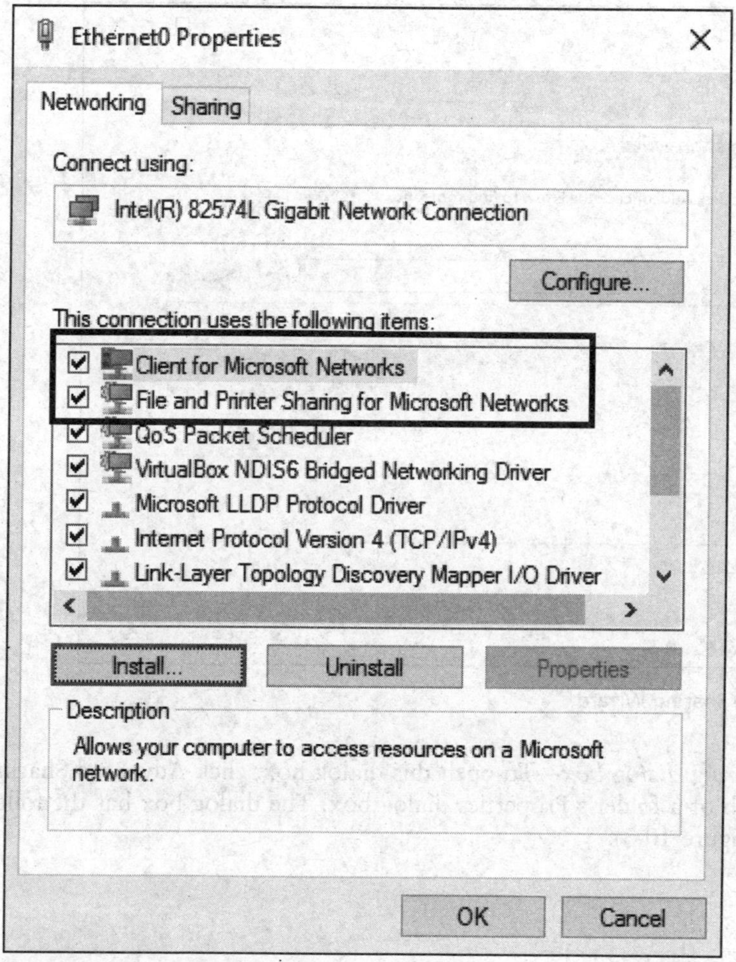


**Figure 10-1** File sharing components in Windows

To share files in Windows, you share the folder in which the files are located. You can use the following methods to configure folder sharing in Windows. The procedures are similar in Windows client OSs:

- *File Sharing Wizard*—To start this wizard, right-click a folder, point to Share with, and then click Specific people. The File Sharing Wizard (see Figure 10-2) simplifies sharing for novices by simplifying the permissions settings.

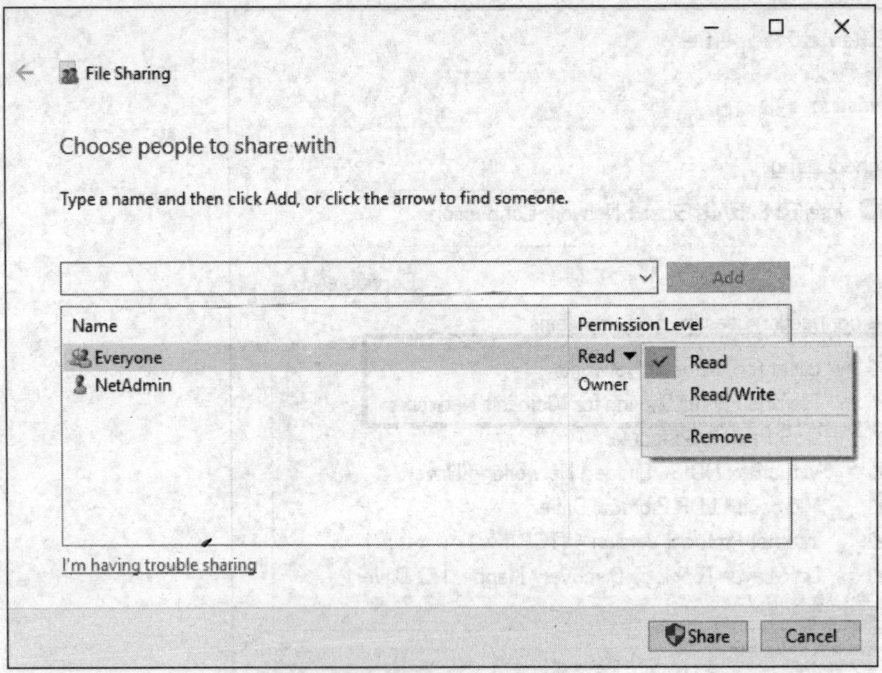


**Figure 10-2** The File Sharing Wizard

- *Advanced Sharing dialog box*—To open this dialog box, click Advanced Sharing in the Sharing tab of a folder's Properties dialog box. The dialog box has the following options (see Figure 10-3):

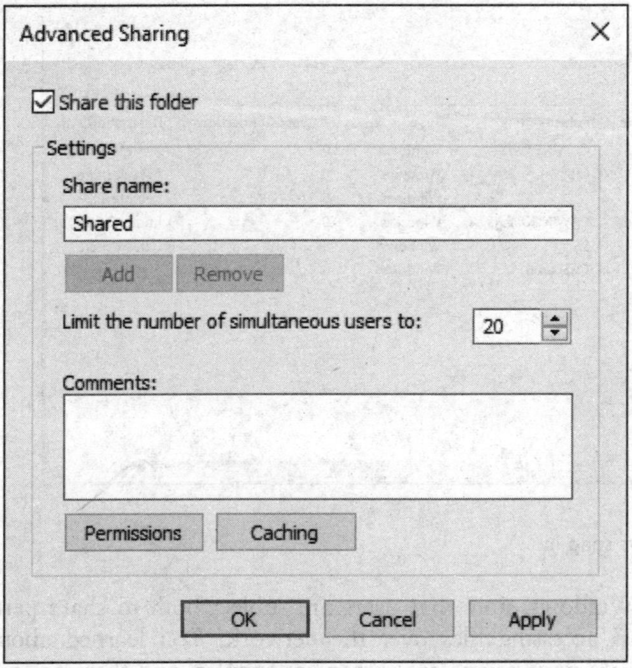


**Figure 10-3** The Advanced Sharing dialog box

- *Share this folder:* To enable folder sharing, click this check box.
- *Share name:* Users see the folder share name in the Network folder of File Explorer or when using the net share command. In other words, it's the name you use to access the folder with the UNC path (\\server\share name). You can add or remove share names. A single folder can have multiple share names and different permissions, a different number of simultaneous users, and caching settings for each share name.
- *Limit the number of simultaneous users to:* In Windows Server, the default limit is 16,777,216, which is practically unlimited. In Windows client OSs, up to 20 users can access a share simultaneously.
- *Comments:* You can enter a description of the share's contents and settings in this text box.
- *Permissions:* Click this button to open the Permissions dialog box.
- *Caching:* This option controls how offline files are configured. Offline files enable users to disconnect from the network and still have access to the shared files they were using.

- *Shared Folders snap-in*—Use this component of the Computer Management console (see Figure 10-4) to monitor, change, and create shares on the local computer or a remote computer. To create a share, right-click the Shares node under the Shared Folders snap-in and click New Share. The Create A Shared Folder Wizard walks you through the processes of selecting a folder to share or creating a new folder to share, naming the share, configuring offline files, and setting permissions.

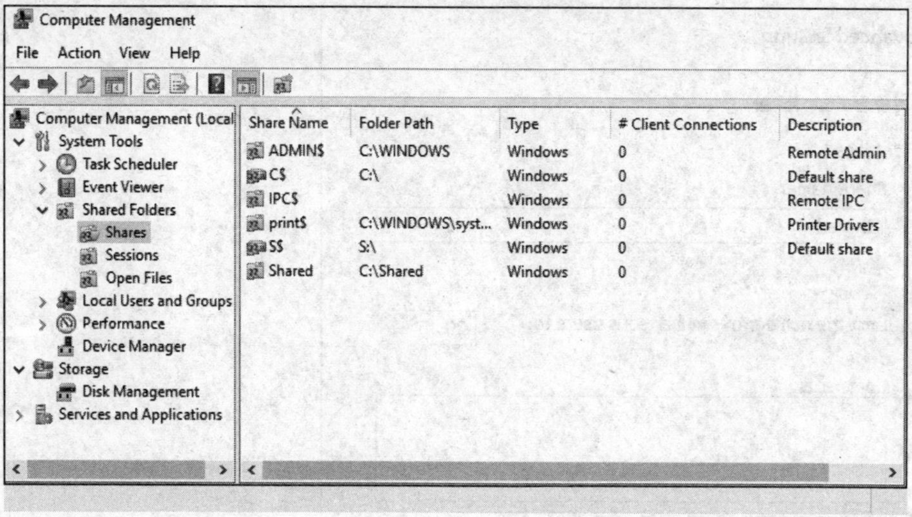


**Figure 10-4** The Shared Folders snap-in

When using file sharing in Windows, note that users are subject both to share permissions and NTFS permissions when accessing files over the network. You learned about NTFS permissions in Chapter 4. Share permissions are somewhat simpler, and there are only three (see Figure 10-5):

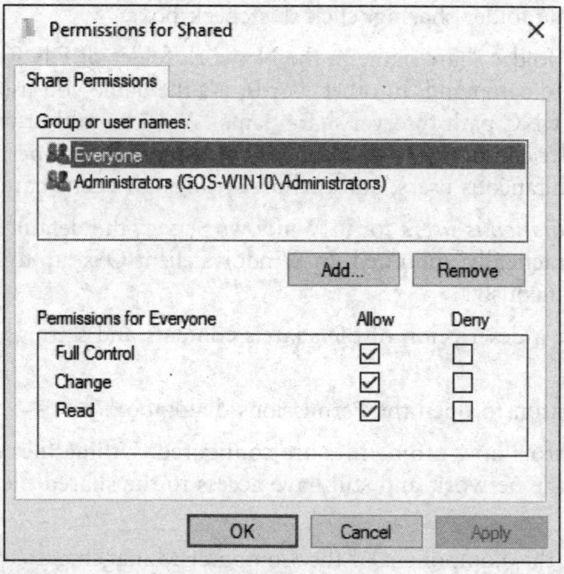


**Figure 10-5** Viewing share permissions

- *Read*—Users can view contents of files, copy files, run applications and script files, open folders and subfolders, and view file attributes.

- *Change*—Users have all the permissions granted by Read, as well as the ability to create files and folders, change their contents and attributes, and delete files and folders.
- *Full Control*—Users have all the permissions granted by Change; they can also change file and folder permissions as well as take ownership of files and folders.

Windows assigns default permissions depending on how a folder is shared. Generally, the default share permission is Read for the Everyone group. On FAT/FAT32 volumes, share permissions are the only way to secure files accessed through the network because these file systems don't support local file permissions.

Sharing files on the network isn't difficult in a Windows environment. Nonetheless, you should be familiar with some techniques and options before setting up a file sharing server.

**Accessing Shared Files in Windows** A file sharing client requests access to shared files and printers on a network server. When a user or an application requests a resource—such as a printer or a data file—a **redirector** intercepts the request and then examines it to determine whether the resource is local (on the computer) or remote (on the network). If the resource is local, the redirector sends the request to the local software component for processing. If the resource is remote, the redirector sends the request over the network to the server hosting the resource.

With redirectors, network resources can be accessed as though they were local. For example, a user or user application doesn't distinguish between a printer connected to a local USB port and one connected to the network. In addition, with drive mapping, shared network folders are accessed just like a drive that's physically attached to the system—at least from the user's point of view. In Windows, the redirector component is part of Client for Microsoft Networks. The two most common ways to access a shared resource in Windows are by using the UNC path and mapping a drive.

The UNC path is used to access a shared folder, and has the syntax *server-name**sharename*. The *server-name* is the name of the computer where the shared resource resides. You can also use the server's IP address in place of its name. The *sharename* is the name given to the folder or printer when it was shared. You can directly access a subfolder or file in the share by continuing the UNC path, as in *server-name**sharename**subfolder**file.extension*.

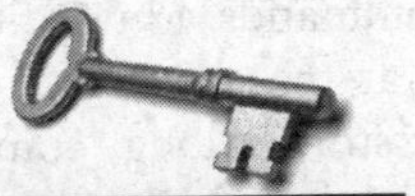
TIP

Linux and Mac OS X systems also use the UNC path to access shared resources, but forward slashes are used in place of backslashes.

You can use the UNC path to access shared folders and printers, but you must type the path every time you need it or create a shortcut with the UNC path as the target. In Windows, one common method of simplifying access to shared files (particularly those that are used often) is drive mapping, which associates a drive letter with the UNC path to a shared folder. Drives are usually mapped by using File Explorer or the *net* command. To use File Explorer, simply type the server portion of the UNC path in the Search text box on the taskbar to see a list of shared folders and printers the server is hosting. Right-click a shared folder and click Map network drive, as shown in Figure 10-6. You can then pick a drive letter that's not already in use and choose to have Windows reconnect to the share with the same drive letter every time you log on.

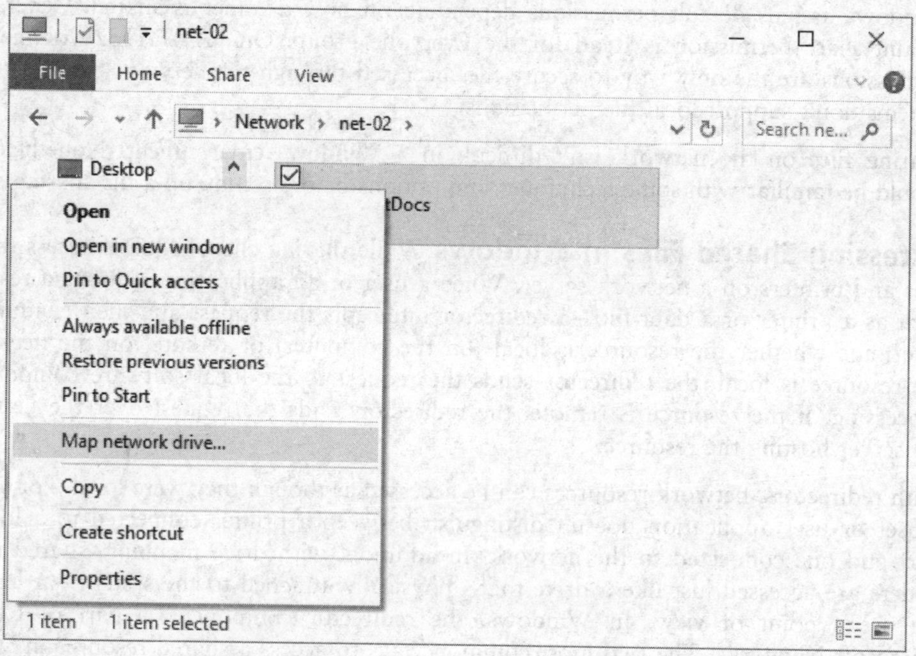


**Figure 10-6** Mapping a drive in File Explorer

Another method of mapping a drive is to use the *net* command. This method is often used by administrators in a logon script, which consists of commands that run when a user logs on to a Windows domain. The command syntax to map a drive with the *net* command is *net use drive-letter: \\server-name\sharename*.

The *drive-letter* is an unused drive letter, and it must be followed by a colon (:). The command can be entered at the command prompt or placed in a batch file. A **batch file** is a text file with a .bat or .cmd extension that contains a list of commands you ordinarily type at the command prompt. To run a batch file, enter its name at the command prompt or double-click the file in File Explorer. Batch files are useful for storing long, complex commands that are used often or a series of commands that are always used together.

As you've learned, Linux and Mac OS X don't use drive letters at all. Instead, their file systems are based on the concept of a file system root designator, which is simply the / character. All local and network drives and folders are accessed from the root as folders. A drive or network share is mounted into an empty directory so that it becomes part of the file system hierarchy. To access a shared folder in Linux or Mac OS X, you create a new directory at the root of the file system or in a subdirectory, and then mount the shared folder in the new directory.

**Sharing Printers in Windows** To understand how to work with and share printers in a Windows environment, first you need to know the terminology for defining the components of a shared printer:

- *Print device*—The physical printer to which print jobs are sent. There are two basic types of print devices:
  - *Local print device:* A printer connected to a port on a computer with a parallel or USB cable or through a TCP/IP port, which is used to access a printer attached directly to the network through the printer's NIC
  - *Network print device:* A printer attached to and shared by another computer
- *Printer*—The icon in the Printers folder that represents print devices. Windows programs use a printer driver to format the print job and send it to the print device or print server. A printer can be a local printer, which prints directly to a local or network print device, or a network printer, which prints to a print server.
- *Print server*—A Windows computer that shares a printer. It accepts print jobs from computers on the network and sends jobs to the printer.
- *Print queue*—A storage location for pending print jobs. In Windows, the print queue is implemented as a folder (by default, C:\Windows\System32\Spool\Printers) where files are stored until they're sent to the print device or print server.

A configured print server can perform a host of functions that aren't possible when users' computers print directly to a print device:

- *Access control*—Using permissions, administrators can control who may print to a printer and manage print jobs and printers.
- *Printer pooling*—A single printer represents two or more print devices. The print server sends the job to the print device that's least busy.
- *Printer priority*—Two or more printers can represent a single print device. In this case, printers can be assigned different priorities so that jobs sent to the higher-priority printer are printed first.
- *Print job management*—Administrators can pause, cancel, restart, reorder, and change preferences on print jobs waiting in the print queue.
- *Availability control*—Administrators can configure print servers so that print jobs are accepted only during certain hours of the day.

To configure a print server, you just need to share a printer. After a printer is installed, right-click its icon, click Printer properties, and then click the Sharing tab. The Sharing tab of a print server's Properties dialog box contains the following options:

- *Share this printer*—When this check box is selected, the print server is shared. By default, everyone is assigned print permissions to shared printers.
- *Share name*—By default, it's the name of the print server in the Printers folder. You can enter a shorter share name or one that's easier to remember.
- *Render print jobs on client computers*—When this check box is selected (the default setting), client computers process the print job and send it to the print server in a

format that's ready to go directly to the print device. If this option isn't selected, more processing occurs on the print server.

- *List in the directory*—This option is shown if the computer on which the printer is being shared is a member of a Windows Active Directory domain. When this check box is selected, the print server is displayed in Active Directory and can be found by Active Directory searches. By default, this option isn't selected.
- *Additional drivers*—When a client connects to a shared printer, the printer driver is downloaded to the client from the server automatically when possible. You can click this button to install different printer drivers on the server to support different Windows versions.

## Sharing Files and Printers in Linux

Linux supports Windows file sharing by using SMB in a software package called *Samba*. Depending on the Linux distribution, you might have to install this component. On a Linux system with Samba installed, you can share a folder using the Samba Server Configuration GUI tool (see Figure 10-7) or by editing the /etc/samba/smb.conf file. When you use the GUI tool to configure Samba, changes to the smb.conf file are made automatically. Figure 10-8 shows part of the smb.conf file after the folder named Folder1 has been shared using the GUI tool.

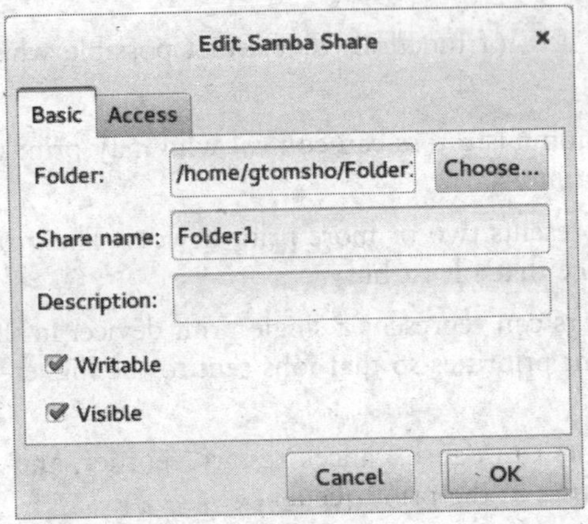


**Figure 10-7** Sharing a folder in Linux

*Source: Linux*

```
[Folder1]
        path = /home/gtomsho/Folder1
        read only = no
        browseable = yes
;       guest ok = yes
```

**Figure 10-8** The smb.conf file

*Source: Linux*

Once a folder is shared in Linux, it can be accessed by another computer using the UNC path; for example, to access the shared folder named Folder1 on a Linux server named LinuxSrv from Windows, you would type the UNC path \\LinuxSrv\Folder1 into a File Explorer or Run box.

Printer sharing in Linux is straightforward after Samba has been installed. When you create a printer in Linux, it's shared automatically. To configure additional printer sharing options, you must edit the /etc/samba/smb.conf file and look for the line that starts with "[printers]."

**Accessing Shared Files in Linux** To access shared files on another computer from a Linux client, you can use the Files tool and browse the network. If you see the computer that contains the shared files, click the computer's icon and enter your credentials, if necessary. Otherwise, click Connect to Server in the left pane and enter the path to the server. You must preface the path with *smb:* so Linux knows you are trying to connect to an SMB share (see Figure 10-9).

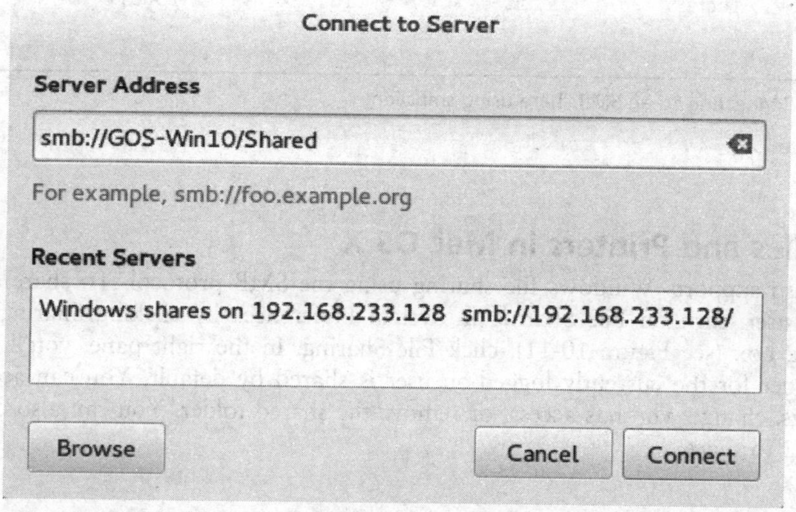


**Figure 10-9** Connecting to an SMB share in Linux

*Source: Linux*

Linux also comes with a command-line program called *smbclient* for accessing SMB shares. To use smbclient, type *smbclient //servername/share* and press Enter. You will see a prompt for *smb*, from which you can enter commands to upload and download files. To see a list of these commands, type *?* and press Enter at the smb: \> prompt (see Figure 10-10).

```
[gtomsho@localhost ~]$ smbclient //gregs-mac.local/folder1
Enter gtomsho's password:
Domain=[GREGS-MAC] OS=[Darwin] Server=[@(#)PROGRAM:smbd  PROJECT:smbx-347
smb: \> ?
?              allinfo        altname        archive        backup
blocksize      cancel         case_sensitive cd             chmod
chown          close          del            dir            du
echo           exit           get            getfacl        geteas
hardlink       help           history        iosize         lcd
link           lock           lowercase      ls             l
mask           md             mget           mkdir          more
mput           newer          notify         open           posix
posix_encrypt  posix_open     posix_mkdir    posix_rmdir    posix_unlink
print          prompt         put            pwd            q
queue          quit           readlink       rd             recurse
reget          rename         reput          rm             rmdir
showacls       setea          setmode        stat           symlink
tar            tarmode        timeout        translate      unlock
volume         vuid           wdel           logon          listconnect
showconnect    tcon           tdis           tid            logoff
..             !
smb: \>
```

**Figure 10-10** Connecting to an SMB share using smbclient

*Source: Linux*

## Sharing Files and Printers in Mac OS X

Mac OS X also supports Windows file sharing using the SMB protocol. To share a folder with another user, turn on File Sharing in System Preferences by clicking Sharing. In the Sharing dialog box (see Figure 10-11), click File Sharing. In the right pane, you'll see that the Public folder for the currently logged-on user is shared by default. You can accept the default settings, change who has access, or remove the shared folder. You can also choose a different folder to share.

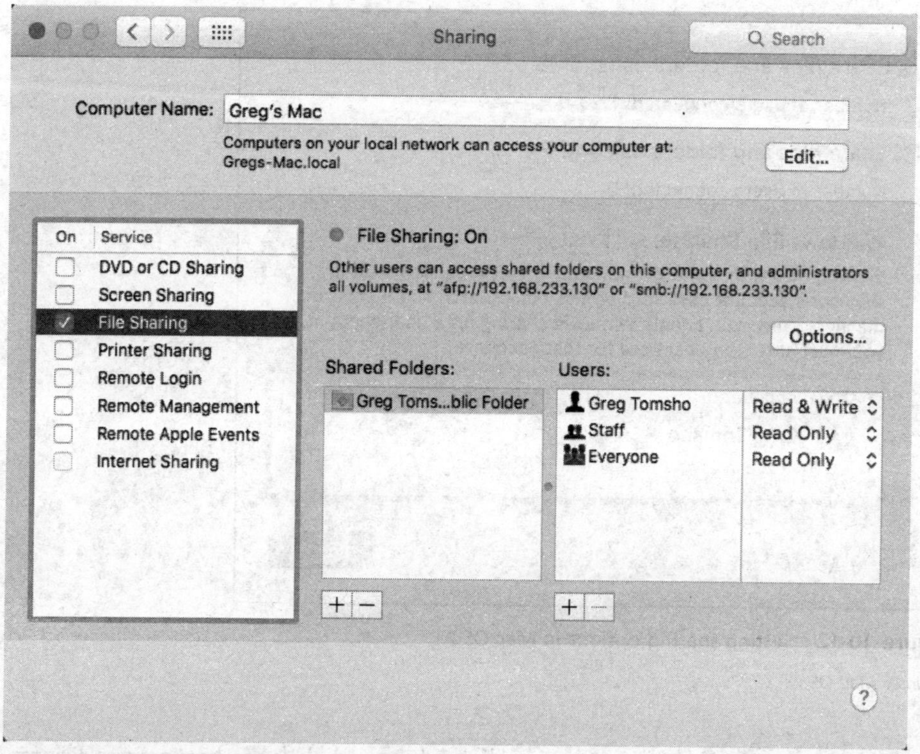


**Figure 10-11** Sharing a folder in Mac OS X

*Source: Mac OS X*

After you have chosen the folder you want to share and set the permissions, click Options to turn on sharing for SMB if you want to share your files with Windows or Linux users. For Windows file sharing, you must enable sharing for each user (see Figure 10-12).

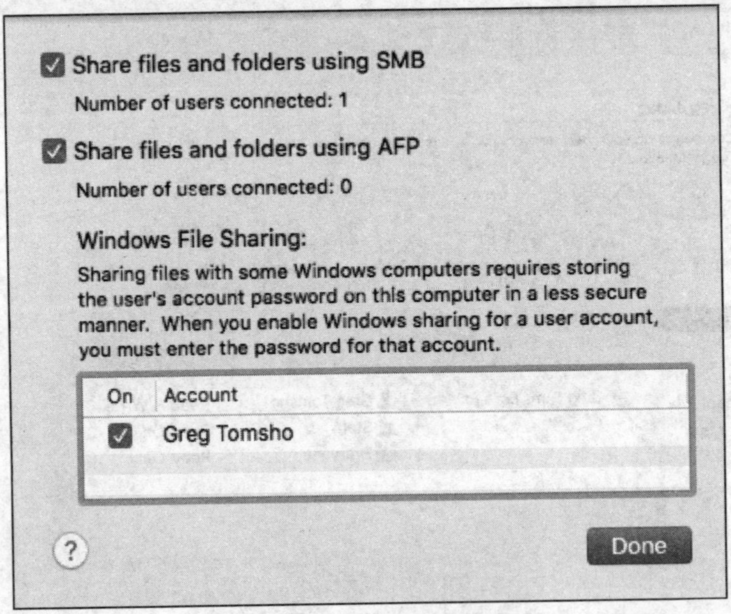


**Figure 10-12** Setting sharing options in Mac OS X

*Source: Mac OS X*

To share printers, use the same Sharing dialog box and click the box next to Printer Sharing. In the right pane, you are presented with a list of printers you can share. Select the printers you want to share and the users with whom you want to share them.

**Accessing Shared Files in Mac OS X** To access shared files on another computer from a Mac OS X client, click Go and then click Network to browse the network. If you see the computer that contains the shared files, click its icon and enter your credentials, if necessary. Otherwise, click Go, click Connect to Server, and enter the path to the server. You must preface the path with *smb:*, as with Linux. Once connected, you will see the computer in the Network browse window, so you won't need to connect to it each time you want to access shared files on the server.

# Managing User and Group Accounts

If you share files and printers, you'll usually want to control access to those shared resources through user accounts, group accounts, and permissions. Working with user accounts is one of an administrator's key tasks. User accounts are the link between people and network resources, so user account management requires both technical expertise and people skills. When users can't log on to the network or access the resources they need, IT staff members get the phone calls. Your understanding of how user accounts work and how to configure them can reduce the frequency of these calls. User accounts have two main functions in a network:

- *Provide a method for users to authenticate themselves to the network*—Using a username and password is the most common way for users to log on to a network and gain access to network resources. This process is called **authentication.** User accounts can also contain restrictions about when and where a user can log on. Administrators use user accounts to assign permissions to network resources and define the types of actions a user can perform on the system, such as installing software, configuring hardware, or accessing files. This process is called **authorization.** Many tasks require elevated access, such as administrator access in Windows or root access in Linux.
- *Provide detailed information about a user*—User accounts can hold information such as a user's phone number, office location, and department. This information can be used in a company directory or by the IT department to identify users for support purposes.

Group accounts are used to organize users so that resource permissions and rights can be managed more easily than working with dozens or hundreds of user accounts. For example, an administrator can make a group account for each department in the company and add the users in each department as members of the corresponding group. Then, when a department creates a shared folder and documents for its users, the administrator just needs to assign permission to the group, which gives all its members the necessary permission. If a user changes departments, the administrator moves the account from one group to another, thereby changing the resources to which the user has permissions.

## Account and Password Conventions

In a small network with only a few users and network resources, establishing a naming convention for accounts might be more trouble than it's worth. When you're working with dozens of servers and hundreds or thousands of users, however, a scheme for naming user and group accounts as well as network devices is crucial. For user accounts, considerations for a naming convention include the following:

- Should user account names have a minimum and maximum number of characters?
- Should the username be based on the user's real name? If security is of utmost importance, should usernames be more cryptic and difficult to guess?
- Some OSs distinguish between uppercase and lowercase letters. Should usernames contain both as well as special characters, such as periods and underscores?

There's no right or wrong answer to these questions, but after you devise a policy, you should stick to it so that when it's time to create a new user account, your naming conventions make the process straightforward.

Passwords are also part of creating user accounts. The considerations for password naming conventions include the following:

- *Minimum length—In* environments where a user account is based on a user's real name, all that's needed to access the account is to correctly guess the password. Longer passwords are harder to guess and therefore more secure.

- *Complexity requirements*—Using uppercase and lowercase letters along with numbers and special symbols (such as @, $, and %) makes passwords considerably more difficult to guess, even with password-guessing software.
- *User or administrator created*—In most cases, users create their own passwords after an administrator gives them an initial password. However, to ensure that passwords are complex enough, administrators can use dictionary attacks and other brute-force methods to attempt to crack them.
- *Password change frequency*—Many networks require frequent password changes to enhance security. However, if changes are required too frequently, users are more apt to write down their passwords, which is a major security risk.

There are other considerations for working with passwords, some of which are particular to the OS on which the user account is created. You learn more about password-handling options in the next section.

Group account names also warrant careful planning. The group name should reflect the group membership or the resource to which the group is assigned permissions or rights. For example, the group name might simply be a department name, or it might reflect a resource permission assignment, such as *NAS_4thFloor*, which indicates that group members have access to the NAS server on the 4th floor. In some cases, a group name might reflect the role that group members have in the company, such as supervisors, administrators, or executives. The most important aspect of naming conventions is establishing and sticking to them; only users who are well versed in these conventions should be allowed to create accounts.

## Working with Accounts in Windows

This section discusses user and group accounts in Windows Server 2016 with Active Directory; you will also work with accounts in a Windows 10 client OS in the Hands-On Projects at the end of this chapter. A key point to remember when working with accounts in Active Directory is that they're used to log on to the Windows domain and can access resources on all computers that are domain members. By contrast, an account created in a Windows client OS is used only to log on to a particular computer and access resources only on that computer.

When Windows is installed, two users are created: Administrator and Guest. On a Windows Server 2016 domain controller, the Guest account is disabled, and in Windows 10, both Administrator and Guest are disabled. In Windows 10, you create a user with administrator privileges during installation. The Guest account is rarely used and poses a security risk, which is why it's disabled. You can enable the account if you like, but best practices dictate creating new accounts for guest users of your network. The Administrator account has full access to a computer, and in a Windows domain, the domain Administrator account's access is extended to all computers that are domain members. You must carefully consider who can log on as Administrator and who is a member of the Administrators group.

**Creating User Accounts in Windows Domains** Windows domain users are created in Active Directory Users and Computers (shown in Figure 10-13), in Active Directory Administrative Center (ADAC), or with command-line tools. As you can see, several folders are available for organizing users, groups, and other domain elements. You can also create your own folders, called *organizational units (OUs)*, to match your company's organizational scheme. For example, you can create a folder for each department or create folders that represent office locations. In Figure 10-13, the open folder named Users contains the Administrator and Guest accounts and many of the default groups created when Active Directory is installed. You can create additional users in this folder, but it's better to add OUs and then create users and groups in the OU structure you specify.

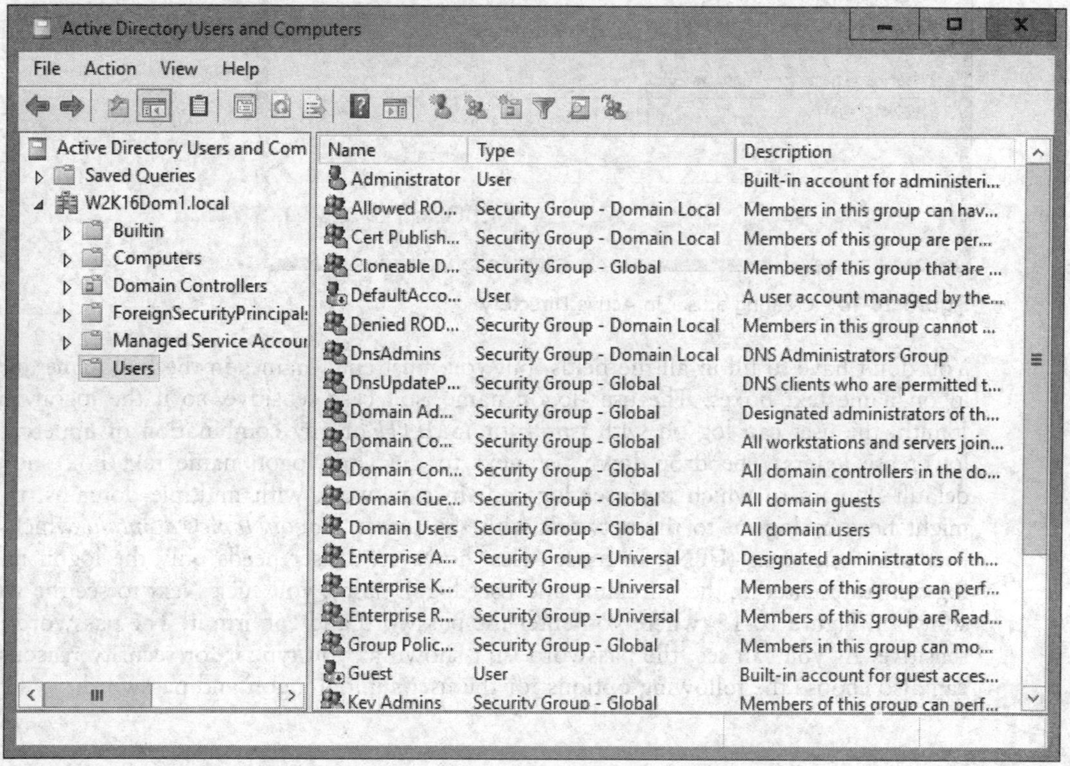


**Figure 10-13** The Active Directory Users and Computers management console

To create a user account, select the folder where you want to create it. Right-click the folder, point to New, and then click User, or click the user icon on the Active Directory Users and Computers toolbar. The New Object - User dialog box opens (see Figure 10-14). Everything you create in Active Directory is considered an object.

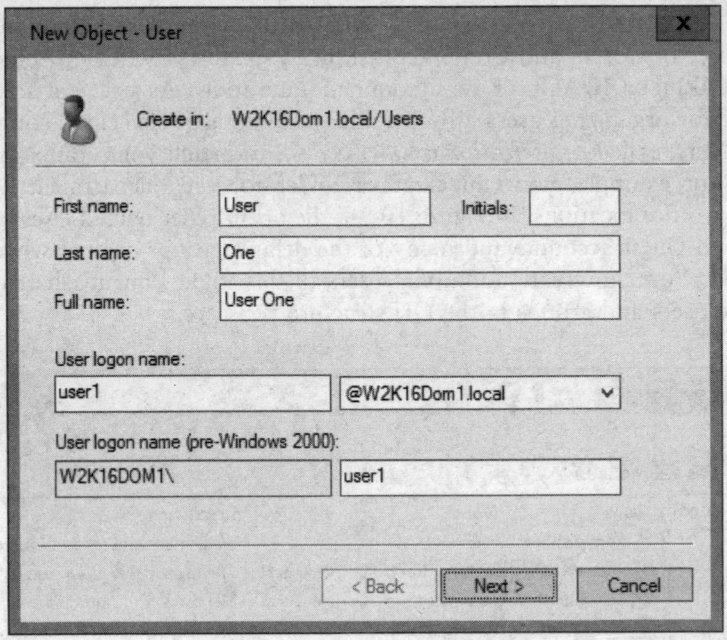


**Figure 10-14** Creating a user in Active Directory

You don't have to fill in all the fields, but you must enter names in the Full name and User logon name text boxes. The user logon name isn't case sensitive, so if the logon name is JSmith, the user can log on with *jsmith* or *JSMITH* or any combination of uppercase and lowercase letters. The drop-down list next to the User logon name text box shows the default domain to which the user logs on. In a network with multiple domains, the user might need to log on to the network with the syntax *LogonName@domain*, which is the user principal name (UPN). In most cases, however, a user needs only the logon name to log on. After entering the full name and user logon name, you click Next to see the window shown in Figure 10-15, where you enter the password and confirm it. The password is case sensitive. As you can see, the password isn't shown as you type it for security reasons. You can also choose the following options for the user's initial logon and password:

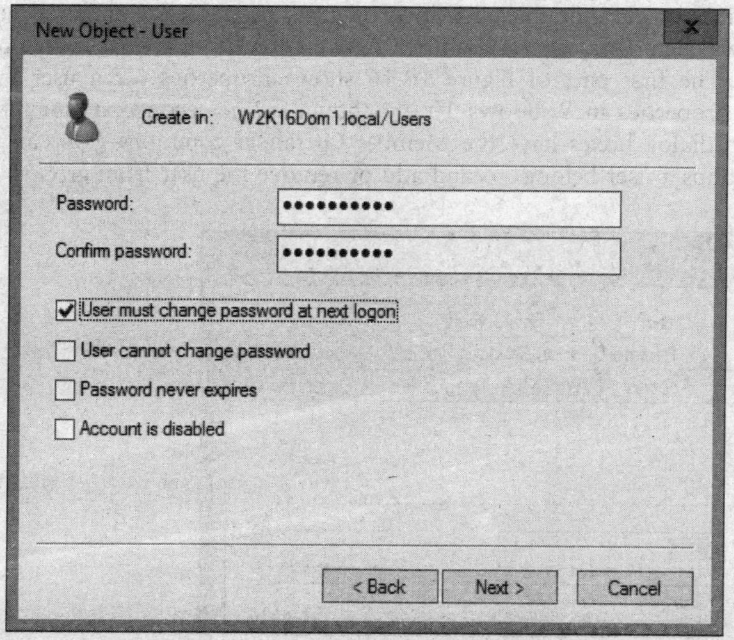


**Figure 10-15** Setting the password and additional account options

- *User must change password at next logon*—The user is prompted to change the password at the next logon. Administrators sometimes create accounts with a default password based on the user's name or phone number that must be changed at the next logon. This option can also be set when users forget their passwords and the support staff changes passwords for them.
- *User cannot change password*—When the administrator wants to maintain control of passwords, this option can be set to prevent users from changing their own. It's also used when multiple users have a common generic account for logging on (such as "salesperson").
- *Password never expires*—Users can be required to change their passwords periodically. If this option is set, users aren't subject to the password change requirement.
- *Account is disabled*—If a user account is created several days before it will be used, the account can be disabled at first and then enabled when the user joins the company. In addition, if a user leaves the company or will be gone for an extended period, the account can be disabled. When a user leaves the company, the account is often disabled rather than deleted so that the replacement can use the same account after it is renamed and the password is changed. In this way, the new user has all the same permissions and rights as the previous user.

After a user account is created, double-click it to open its properties. Compared with user accounts in Windows client OSs, user accounts in Active Directory have far more properties you can configure. The first part of Figure 10-16 shows properties for a user in Active Directory; account properties in Windows 10 are shown in the second part of the figure. Notice that the two dialog boxes have the Member Of tab in common—you can use this tab to see which groups a user belongs to and add or remove the user from groups.

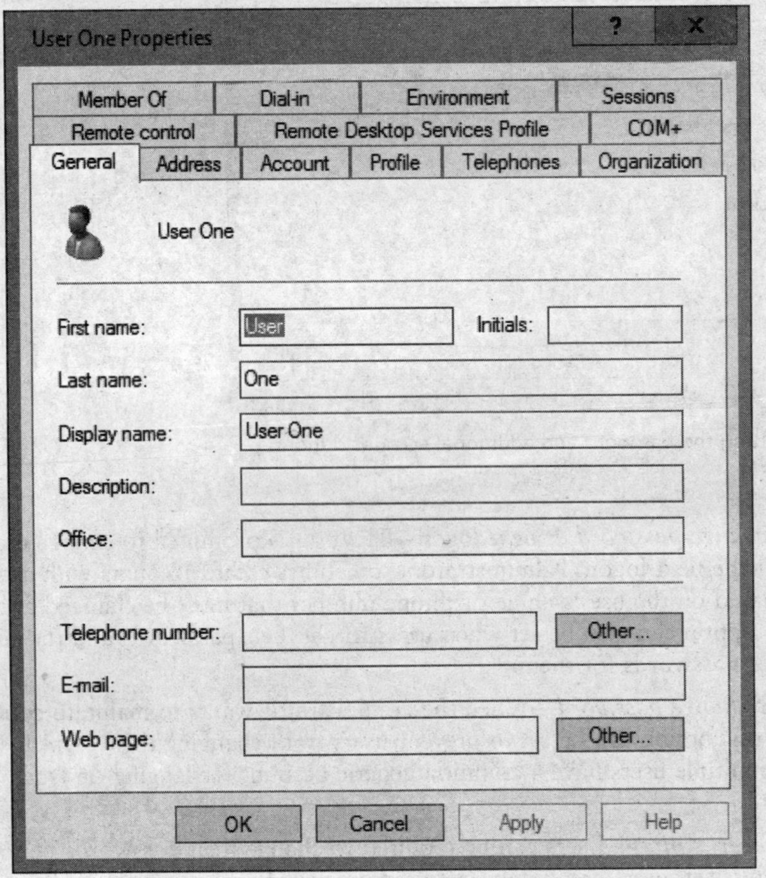


**Figure 10-16** User properties in Active Directory and in Windows 10

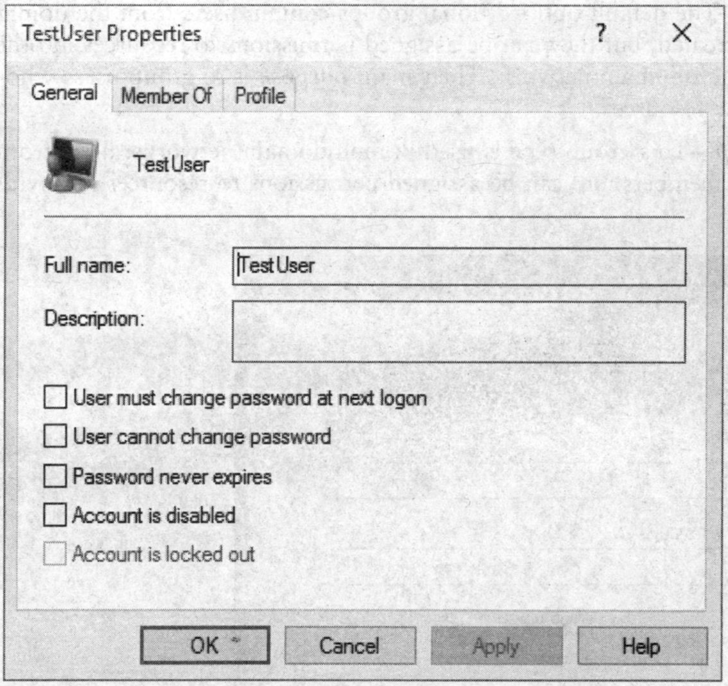


**Figure 10-16** User properties in Active Directory and in Windows 10 *(continued)*

When a user is added to a group or removed from it, the setting takes effect the next time the user logs on; if a user is already logged on, he or she must log off and log on again.

**Creating Group Accounts in Windows Domains** Group accounts are easy to create. All they require is a name; after they're created, you can begin adding users as members. The process is similar to creating a user account. In Active Directory, the New Object - Group dialog box looks like Figure 10-17. The "Group name (pre-Windows 2000)" text box is used for backward compatibility with older Windows OSs. The other options, group scope and group type, are used only in Windows domains. The **group scope** lets you create one of three different group types:

- *Domain local group*—This group type can be used to assign permissions to resources only in the domain in which the group is created. Although domain local groups can contain users from any domain, they're used mainly to hold global groups and assign permissions to global group members.

- *Global group*—The default option, global groups contain users from the domain in which they're created, but they can be assigned permissions to resources in other domains in a multidomain network. Their main purpose is to group users who require access to similar resources.
- *Universal group*—This group type is used in multidomain networks; users from any domain can be members and can be assigned permissions to resources in any domain.

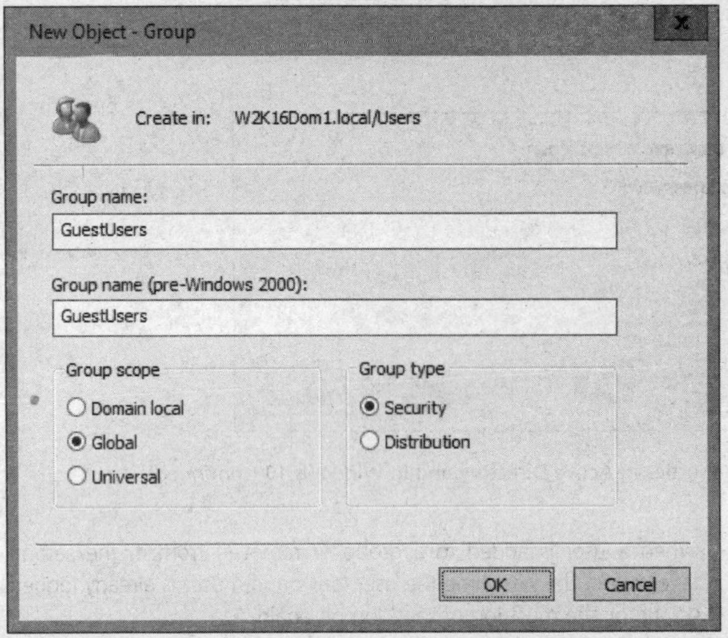


**Figure 10-17** Creating a group in Active Directory

A detailed discussion of group scope is beyond the scope of this book. For a complete discussion, see *MCSA Guide to Installing and Configuring Microsoft Windows Server 2012/R2* (Cengage Learning, 2015, ISBN 9781285868653).

The Group type option is set to Security by default. Distribution groups are used only for tasks like sending all group members an e-mail when you run an Active Directory-integrated e-mail program, such as Microsoft Exchange.

**Windows Default Groups** Aside from groups you create to organize users and assign permissions, Windows defines some **default groups,** which have preassigned rights that apply to all group members. Table 10-1 shows the most important default domain local groups in Windows Server running Active Directory. The table also shows the rights assigned to these groups.

**Table 10-1 Some Windows Server default domain local groups**

| Group | Rights |
|---|---|
| Administrators | Has complete control over the computer and domain |
| Account Operators | Can administer user and group accounts for the local domain |
| Backup Operators | Can back up and restore files that users can't normally access |
| Guests | Is allowed guest access to domain resources; same access as the Users group |
| Print Operators | Can add, delete, and manage domain printers |
| Server Operators | Can administer domain servers |
| Users | Has the same default access rights that ordinary user accounts have |

In addition, Windows Server has numerous default global groups, including Domain Admins, Domain Users, and Domain Guests. These groups apply to entire domains rather than a single machine, and are essentially the same as domain local groups with similar names.

**Special Identity Groups** **Special identity groups**, as described in Table 10-2, don't appear as objects in Active Directory Users and Computers or in Local Users and Groups, but they can be assigned permissions and rights. Membership in these groups is controlled dynamically by Windows, can't be viewed or changed manually, and depends on how an account accesses the OS. For example, membership in the Authenticated Users group is assigned to a user account automatically when the user logs on to a computer or domain.

**Table 10-2 Some Windows special identity groups**

| Special identity group | Description |
|---|---|
| Authenticated Users | Members belong to any user account (except Guest) that can be used to log on to a computer or domain with a valid username and password. |
| Creator Owner | A user becomes a member automatically for a resource he or she created, such as a folder. |
| Everyone | Refers to all users who access the system; similar to the Authenticated Users group but includes the Guest user. |
| Interactive | Members are users who are logged on to a computer locally or through Remote Desktop Services. |
| Network | Members are users who are logged on to a computer through a network connection. |
| System | Refers to the Windows OS. |
| Self | Refers to the object on which permissions are being set. |

**From the Trenches ...**

The author manages a small departmental network and hires students to help with classroom lab maintenance. Sometimes, the tasks performed by students require administrative access to the client workstations. In Windows, a domain administrator has full permissions and rights to all client and server computers in the domain. However, it is not good security practice to give all users domain administrator access. The goal is to give students temporary administrator access to client workstations when they need it but not to provide them with the administrator account username and password. The solution is to use groups wisely. A Global group called clientAdmins is created in the domain; then, using a feature of Group Policy, this group is made a member of the Administrators local group on the client workstations. When students need to perform a task that requires local administrator access, their user accounts are added as members of the clientAdmins Global group. When they log on to client workstations, they have local administrator access. When they finish the task, their accounts are removed from the clientAdmins group and their privileges revert to regular user privileges.

## Working with Accounts in Linux

User and group accounts in Linux have the same purposes as in Windows: user authentication and authorization. Linux OSs also have a default user named root who has full control over all aspects of the system. As in Windows, the root user account is used only when you're performing tasks that require root privileges, such as creating additional system users. In fact, some Linux distributions require creating a user during installation because logging on as root isn't allowed; you can access root privileges only by entering a special command.

Most Linux administration takes place at the command line. In its simplest form, user creation is a matter of using the *useradd newuser* command; you replace *newuser* with the logon name for the user account you're creating. Then you create a password for the user with the *passwd newuser* command. Both the logon name and password are case sensitive in Linux.

On most Linux systems, you can't run *useradd* and similar commands unless you're logged on as the root user or you preface the command with *sudo*, as in *sudo useradd newuser*. The *sudo* command, which stands for "superuser do," executes the command with root privileges. If you know you will use many commands that require root privileges, you can change to the root user temporarily with the *su* command (which means "switch user"). This command attempts to switch to the root user when no user is specified, and you must enter the root user's password when prompted.

When some commands are entered with a username, as in *passwd testuser*, the command is executed only for the specified user account. If the commands are entered without a username, they're executed only for the current user. For example, users or administrators can change a user's password with the *passwd* command. You can change user information with the *usermod* command and delete users with the *deluser* command.

The *useradd* command has many options. For example, you can specify a different home directory and assign group memberships. You practice using this command in a Hands-On Project at the end of this chapter.

TIP

As with most commands, you can see extensive help for the commands used to create and modify users and groups in Linux by prefacing the command with *man*, as in *man useradd*.

All users must belong to at least one group in Linux. When a user is created, a group with the same name as the user is also created, and the new user is made a member of this group. However, you can create groups and add users to them, just as you can in Windows.

Groups are created with the aptly named *groupadd* command. To add users as members of a group, you can specify this option when you create the user account. You can also use the *useradd username groupname* command or the *usermod* command.

To view the list of users, display the /etc/passwd file's contents with the *cat /etc/passwd* command; to view the list of groups, display the /etc/group file's contents with the *cat /etc/group* command. The *cat* command lists a text file's contents onscreen.

For those who prefer a GUI to manage users and groups, most Linux distributions have convenient graphical interfaces for doing so. In Fedora Linux, the Users tool is available to manage users (see Figure 10-18).

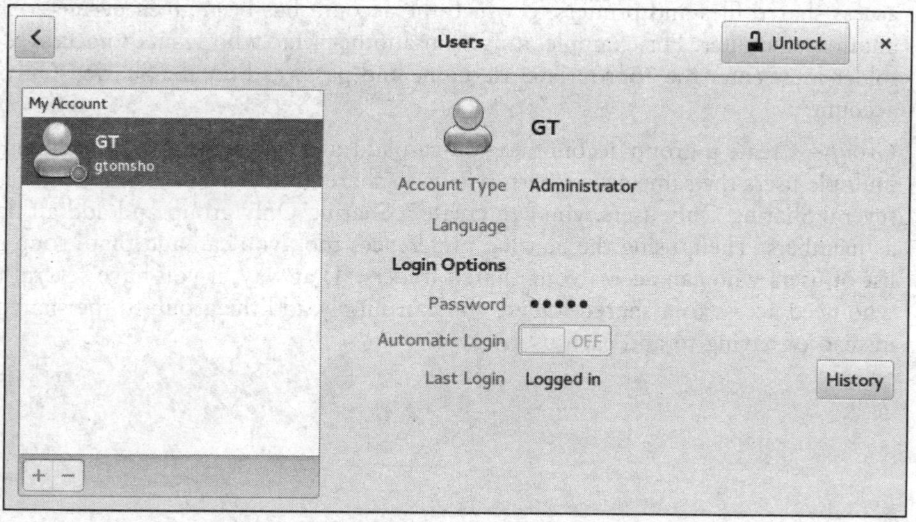


**Figure 10-18** The Users control panel in Fedora Linux

*Source: Fedora Linux*

Many administrators prefer the command-line method for creating users because they can import user information from a text file and add many users at one time by using the *newusers* command.

## Working with Accounts in Mac OS X

In Mac OS X, you create users and groups using the Users & Groups tool in System Preferences. To create a user, click the plus sign in the left pane of Users & Groups, click the selection arrow next to New Account (see Figure 10-19) to choose the type of account you want to create, and then enter the user's full name, account name, and password. If the user already has an iCloud account, you can use the existing iCloud password or enter a new password. You can also include a password hint.

You can choose one of the following account types:

- *Administrator*—The user has full access to the Mac OS X computer, can create and manage user and group accounts, and can change any of the Mac OS X settings.
- *Standard*—Users can run applications and create files in their home folder but cannot perform administrative actions such as installing devices, formatting drives, and changing network settings. Standard users can install apps and change settings for their own use.
- *Managed with parental controls*—Parental controls can be enforced for users, including which apps they can run, which Web sites they can visit, and how long they can use the computer during a session.
- *Sharing Only*—This type of user cannot log on to the local Mac computer, but can access shared files and printers to which the account has been given permission from another computer. For example, a user on another Mac who wants to access a shared folder must enter the appropriate username and password for the Sharing Only user account.
- *Group*—Create a group account so you can add user accounts as members and assign multiple users the same access permissions to shared folders. For example, if you create several Sharing Only users, you can create a Sharing Only group and add all the users as members. Then, using the Sharing preferences tool, you can add that group to the list of users who can access your shared folders. That way, if you have several users who need access to a shared folder, you can simply add the group to the shared folder instead of having to add each user.

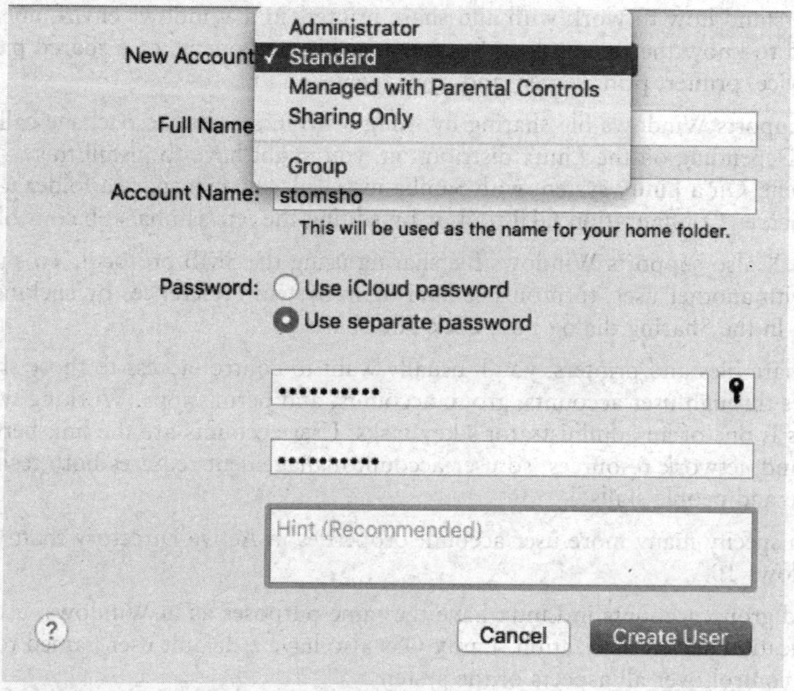


**Figure 10-19** Creating a new account in Mac OS X

*Source: Mac OS X*

This chapter provided basic details for sharing resources in an operating system. A more comprehensive treatment is beyond the scope of this book, but you now have a starting point from which to explore this topic further on the three OS platforms.

## Chapter Summary

- File and printer sharing is one reason businesses began to outfit computers with network interfaces and network software. Sharing files and printers with other computers on the network requires a file sharing client and a file sharing protocol. The dominant file sharing protocol is Server Message Block (SMB), the native protocol used by Windows; it is also supported by Linux and Mac OS X.
- File sharing in Windows is based on Client for Microsoft Networks on the client side and File and Printer Sharing for Microsoft Networks on the server side. To share files in Windows, you share the folder in which the files are located. Windows assigns default permissions depending on how a folder is shared. Generally, the default share permission is Read for the Everyone group.
- When a user or an application requests a resource—such as a printer or a data file—a redirector intercepts the request and then examines it to determine whether the resource is local (on the computer) or remote (on the network).

- To understand how to work with and share printers in a Windows environment, first you need to know the terminology for defining the components of a shared printer: print device, printer, print server, and print queue.
- Linux supports Windows file sharing by using SMB in a software package called Samba. Depending on the Linux distribution, you might have to install this component. On a Linux system with Samba installed, you can share a folder using the Samba Server Configuration GUI tool or by editing the /etc/samba/smb.conf file.
- Mac OS X also supports Windows file sharing using the SMB protocol. To share a folder with another user, turn on File Sharing in System Preferences by clicking Sharing. In the Sharing dialog box, click File Sharing.
- If you share files and printers, you'll usually want to control access to those shared resources through user accounts, group accounts, and permissions. Working with user accounts is one of an administrator's key tasks. User accounts are the link between people and network resources, so user account management requires both technical expertise and people skills.
- You can specify many more user account properties in Active Directory than you can in Windows 10.
- User and group accounts in Linux have the same purposes as in Windows: user authentication and authorization. Linux OSs also have a default user named root who has full control over all aspects of the system.
- In Mac OS X, you create users and groups using the Users & Groups tool in System Preferences. To create a user, click the plus sign in the left pane of Users & Groups, click the selection arrow next to New Account to choose the type of account you want to create, and then enter the user's full name, account name, and password.

# Key Terms

**authentication** The process of identifying who has access to the network. The most common form of authentication is a logon with a username and password.

**authorization** The process of granting or denying an authenticated user's access to network resources.

**batch file** A text file that contains a list of commands you ordinarily type at the command prompt.

**default groups** Special groups with rights already assigned; these groups are created during installation in a Windows environment.

**domain local group** A group scope recommended for assigning rights and permissions to domain resources.

**global group** A group scope used mainly to group users from the same domain who have similar access and rights requirements. A global group's members can be user accounts and other global groups from the same domain. See also *group scope*.

**group scope** A property of a group that determines the reach of a group's application in a domain—for example, which users can be group members and to which resources a group can be assigned rights or permissions.

**Network File System (NFS)** The native Linux/UNIX file sharing protocol.

**redirector** An OS client component that intercepts resource requests and determines whether the resource is local or remote.

**Server Message Block (SMB)** The Windows file sharing protocol; SMB is also supported by Linux and Mac OS X as Samba.

**special identity group** A type of group in Windows in which membership is controlled dynamically by Windows, can't be viewed or changed manually, and depends on how an account accesses the OS. For example, membership in the Authenticated Users group is assigned to a user account automatically when the user logs on to a computer or domain.

**universal group** A group scope that can contain users from any domain and be assigned permissions to resources in any domain. See also *group scope*.

## Review Questions

1. Which of the following is the correct syntax for mapping drive letter W to a shared folder named Accounting on the Finance server?
   a. net use W: \\Finance\Accounting
   b. net share W: \\Accounting\Finance
   c. net use W: \\Accounting\Finance
   d. net share W: \\Finance\Accounting
2. A text file that contains a list of commands is called which of the following?
   a. logon process file
   b. service file
   c. task file
   d. batch file
3. Which of the following is the default protocol Windows uses to share folders?
   a. NFS
   b. SMB
   c. WPA
   d. FTP
4. Which of the following is the native Linux/UNIX file sharing protocol?
   a. NFS
   b. SMB
   c. WPA
   d. FTP

5. Which of the following is a native printer sharing protocol used on Linux? (Choose all that apply.)
   a. CUPS
   b. PPP
   c. NFS
   d. LPD
6. Which of the following group scopes can only contain users from the domain in which the group is created?
   a. global
   b. domain local
   c. universal
   d. distribution
7. Which of the following is *not* a Windows share permission?
   a. Read
   b. Write
   c. Change
   d. Full Control
8. Which component of a file sharing client determines whether the resource is local or remote?
   a. redirector
   b. SMB
   c. active directory
   d. UNC path
9. Which of the following correctly specifies a file named salaries.xls in a shared folder named Budget on a server named Accounting when accessing the file remotely from a Windows computer?
   a. \\Accounting.budget.salaries.xls
   b. /Accounting/Budget/salaries.xls
   c. \\Budget.Accounting\salaries.xls
   d. \\Accounting\Budget\salaries.xls
10. What is a storage location for pending print jobs?
    a. print queue
    b. print server
    c. print directory
    d. print path

11. What file can you edit on a Linux system to configure shared folders using Samba?
    a. /samba/smb.cnf
    b. /etc/smb/samba.conf
    c. /etc/samba/smb.conf
    d. /smb/samba.cnf
12. Which of the following is a Linux command to access shared files using Samba?
    a. *netsh*
    b. *samba*
    c. *smbclient*
    d. *nfsclient*
13. Which of the following defines the types of actions a user can perform on a system?
    a. authentication
    b. authorization
    c. logon
    d. permission
14. A user has called you to complain that he does not have access to a file. While on the phone, you add the user to the appropriate group that has permission to access the file. You ask the user to try to access the file again, but he still cannot. What should you do?
    a. Tell the user to log off and log on again.
    b. Delete the user account and re-create it.
    c. Add the user to the permission list for the file.
    d. Shut down the server and restart it.
15. Which group scope can be used to assign permissions to resources only in the domain in which the group is created?
    a. global
    b. universal
    c. domain local
    d. local

# Hands-On Projects

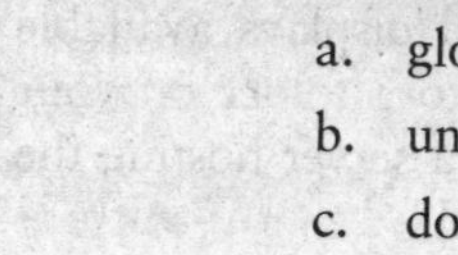


## Project 10-1: Map a Drive Letter in Windows

In this project, you create a shared folder and then map a drive letter to it. You wouldn't normally map a drive letter to a share on your own computer, but this project shows you how to perform the process without using a second computer.

1. Start your Windows computer and log on.
2. Click **Start**, and then click **File Explorer**. Click **This PC** in the left pane, and then click **Local Disk (C:)**.
3. Create a folder named **MyShare**. Right-click **MyShare**, point to **Share with**, and click **Specific people**. You see that the currently logged-on user has the permission level Owner. You can add users who may access the share in this dialog box, but because only you will access it, click **Share**. You're notified that the folder is now shared, and you see the path listed as *ComputerName*\MyShare, where *ComputerName* is the name of your computer (see Figure 10-20). Click **Done**.

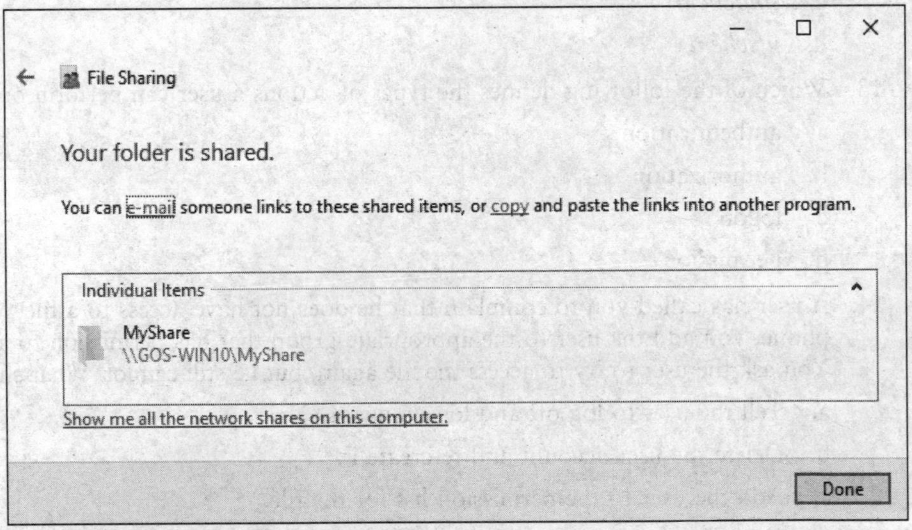


**Figure 10-20** Sharing a folder in Windows

4. Click in the Search text box on the taskbar, type **\\localhost**, and press **Enter**. The *localhost* refers to your own computer, so a window opens and displays available shares, including MyShare. Normally, you wouldn't map a drive to a folder on your own computer, and you would replace *localhost* with the name of a server hosting the share. You're using localhost just for practice. Click the search result.
5. In File Explorer, right-click **MyShare** and click **Map network drive**. You can choose a drive letter to map to this share. Click the **Drive** list arrow and click **X:**. Click to clear the **Reconnect at sign-in** check box. If you leave this option selected, the drive is mapped to the share each time you log on. Notice that you can also choose to connect to the share with different credentials (username and password). Click **Finish**.
6. A File Explorer window opens and displays the share's contents (it's currently empty). Close all windows. Click **Start** and then click **File Explorer**. You see the drive letter and share name listed under This PC. Right-click **MyShare (\\localhost) (X:)** and click **Disconnect** to delete the drive mapping. (You might need to press F5 to refresh the File Explorer window and see that the drive mapping has been deleted.)

7. Open a command prompt window. To map a drive letter from the command line, type **net use x: \\localhost\MyShare** and press **Enter**. You should see the message "The command completed successfully." To display current connections to shared resources, type **net use** and press **Enter**.
8. Click in the File Explorer window. The X drive letter is listed under This PC again.
9. At the command prompt, type **net use /?** and press **Enter** to see a list of options for the *net use* command. You can use the */persistent* option to make a drive mapping reconnect each time you log on. You can also connect with a different set of credentials. Type **net use x: /delete** and press **Enter** to delete the drive mapping, and then close the command prompt window. In File Explorer, verify that the drive mapping has been deleted.
10. To create a batch file for mapping a drive, open Notepad and type the following two lines:

```
net use x: /delete
net use x: \\localhost\MyShare
```

11. The first command deletes any existing drive mappings for the X drive. Click **File** and then **Save As** from the menu. In the left pane of the Save As dialog box, click **Desktop**. Click the **Save as type** list arrow, and then click **All Files**. In the File name text box, type **mapX.bat** and click **Save**. Close Notepad. Batch files can come in handy if you need to connect to another computer periodically but don't want a permanent drive mapping. Batch files are especially useful if you need to enter long commands because you don't have to remember and re-enter them each time you need them.
12. On your desktop, double-click **mapX**. In File Explorer, verify that the X drive mapping has been created. Right-click **MyShare (\\localhost) (X:)** and click **Disconnect**.
13. To review what you've learned, write the command to map drive letter G to a share named Accounting on a server named Finance:

_______________________________________________

14. Close all open windows, and leave Windows running for the next project.

TIP

To learn more about creating and using batch files in Windows, read the TechNet article at *https://technet.microsoft.com/en-us/library/bb490869.aspx*.

HANDS-ON PROJECTS

## Project 10-2: Create and Connect to a Shared Printer in Windows

This project walks you through the process of creating a printer, sharing it, and then connecting to the shared printer. Note that you won't actually connect to a physical printer.

1. If necessary, log on to your Windows computer.
2. Click in the Search text box on the taskbar, type **Devices and Printers**, and press **Enter**. Click **Add a printer** in the Devices and Printers window. Windows searches for devices. Click **The printer that I want isn't listed**.
3. Click **Add a local printer or network printer with manual settings**, and then click **Next**. In the "Choose a printer port" window, leave the default option **Use an existing port** selected, and then click **Next**. In the "Install the printer driver" window, you would normally select the printer's manufacturer and model, but because there's no physical printer, just accept the default selection and then click **Next**.
4. In the "Type a printer name" window, click **Next**. In the Printer Sharing window, make sure **Share this printer so that others on your network can find and use it** is selected. For the share name, type **MyPrinter**, and then click **Next**. Click to clear the **Set as the default printer** check box (note that you might not see this check box). If you were actually installing a printer, you would click "Print a test page," but for this project, just click **Finish**.
5. To connect to a shared printer, ask your instructor whether a printer share is set up or you can use another student's shared printer. In Windows, you can't connect to your own printer, as you did with the shared folder. Click in the Search text box on the taskbar, type ***computer*, where** computer **is the name of the computer sharing the printer, and press Enter.**
6. When the window opens, right-click the shared printer and click **Connect**. In the Devices and Printers window, verify that the printer was created. It's listed as "*Printer make and model* on *computer*," where *Printer make and model* is the make and model of the printer and *computer* is the name of the computer on which the printer is shared.
7. Close all open windows but stay logged on if you're continuing to the next project.

## Project 10-3: Create Users in a Windows Client OS

In this project, you create a user in the Computer Management console.

1. Log on to your Windows computer, if necessary. There are two tools for creating user accounts in a Windows client OS. One is User Accounts in Control Panel, which is used mostly for home users. The other tool is Local Users and Groups in the Computer Management console. Local Users and Groups gives administrators more control over user properties and has more in common with Active Directory Users and Computers, so it's used in this project.

2. Right-click **Start** and click **Computer Management.** In the left pane, click to expand **Local Users and Groups,** which has two folders under it: Users and Groups. Click **Users** to display a list of users in the right pane (see Figure 10-21). Notice that the Administrator, DefaultAccount, and Guest users in the figure are shown with a black arrow in a white circle to indicate that the accounts are disabled.

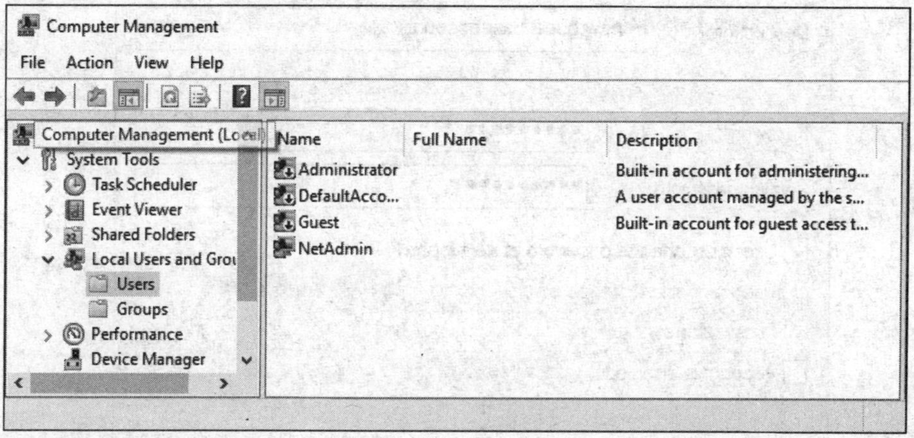


**Figure 10-21** Viewing Users in Computer Management

3. Right-click an empty space in the right pane and click **New User.** In the New User dialog box, type **NewGuest1** as the User name. In the Full name text box, type **New Guest User 1**, and in the Description text box, type **A new guest user account.**

4. Type **guestpass** in the Password text box and again in the Confirm password text box.

5. Leave the **User must change password at next logon** check box selected (see Figure 10-22), and click **Create.** The New User dialog box clears so you can create another user. Click **Close.**

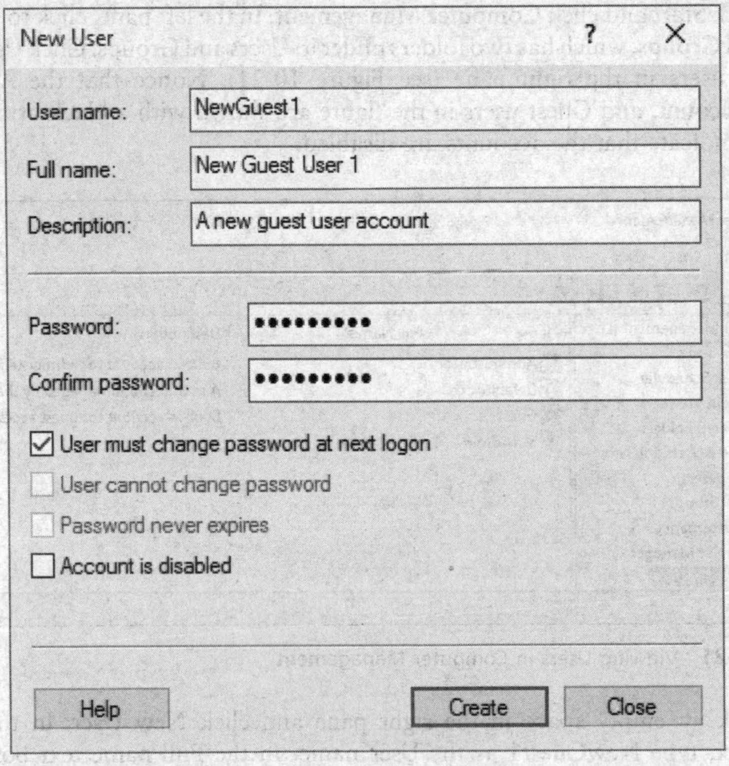


**Figure 10-22** Creating a user in Windows 10

6. In Local Users and Groups, double-click **NewGuest1** to view its properties. Click the **Member Of** tab. By default, all new users are put in a group called Users; this is also the case when a user is created in Active Directory. Click **Cancel**.
7. Click the **Groups** folder in the left pane to see a list of default groups that Windows creates. Double-click the **Users** group. You'll see a list of users who are members of the Users group, including NewGuest1. You'll probably also see some special groups named Authenticated Users and INTERACTIVE, which are internal groups used by Windows. Click **Cancel**.
8. Log off Windows. When the logon window opens, New Guest User 1 is shown as a user. Click **New Guest User 1**. Type **guestpass** in the Password text box and press **Enter**, or click the arrow to log on. When prompted to change your password, click **OK**, and then type **Password01** in the New password and Confirm password text boxes. Press **Enter** or click the arrow.
9. In the message box stating that the password has been changed, click **OK**. Do not sign in, but leave Windows running for the next project.

## Project 10-4: Work with Groups in a Windows Client OS

In this project, you create a group in the Computer Management console and then add a user to the group.

1. Log on to your Windows computer as an administrator.
2. Right-click **Start** and click **Computer Management**. Click to expand **Local Users and Groups**, and then click **Groups**.
3. Right-click an empty space in the right pane, and then click **New Group**. In the New Group dialog box, type **GuestUsers** as the Group name. In the Description text box, type **A group for guest users of this computer.**
4. Click **Add**. Examine the Select Users dialog box shown in Figure 10-23. It's similar to what you see when adding a user to a group in Active Directory.

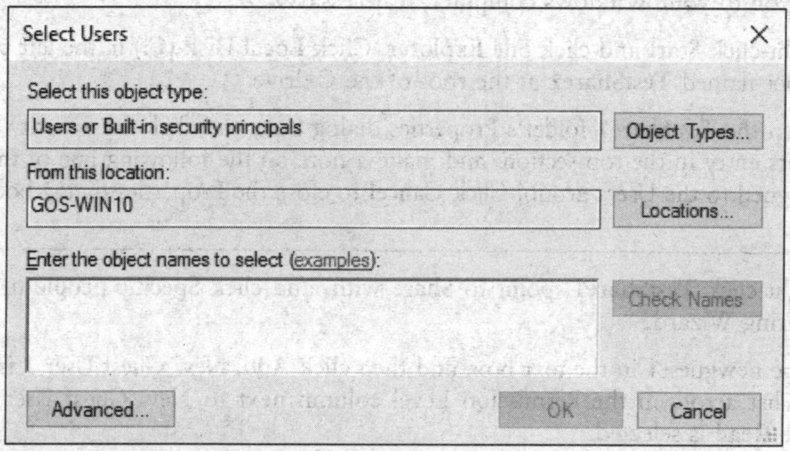


**Figure 10-23** Selecting users to add to a group

5. You can use the Object Types button to limit the types of objects Windows displays if you click the Advanced button to search for objects to add to a group. Click **Locations**. You have only one option unless your computer is a member of a domain. If so, you can select objects from the domain; otherwise, you can only choose objects created on your computer. Click **Cancel**.
6. You can type the group members' names in the text box, but to select them from a list, click **Advanced**. Click **Find Now** to list available users and groups you can add as group members. Click **NewGuest1** and then click **OK**. Notice in the Select Users dialog box that the user is specified as *ComputerName\NewGuest1*. *ComputerName* is the name of the computer or domain where the user was created; in this case, it's the computer. Click **OK**.

7. NewGuest1 is listed as a member of the group. Click **Create** to finish creating the group, and then click **Close**.

8. NewGuest1 is now a member of both the GuestUsers and Users groups. Remember that the result of changing group membership takes effect the next time the user logs on. If you wanted to remove NewGuest1 from the default Users group, you would double-click the Users group, right-click NewGuest1, and click Remove. However, doing so removes NewGuest1 from the list of users in the Windows 10 logon window. For now, leave this account as a member of both groups. Log off Windows for the next project.

## Project 10-5: Share a Folder and View Permissions

In this project, you use the File Sharing Wizard to see how it sets permissions automatically.

1. Log on to your Windows computer, if necessary.
2. Right-click **Start** and click **File Explorer**. Click **Local Disk (C:)** in the left pane. Create a folder named **TestShare1** at the root of the C drive.
3. Open the TestShare1 folder's Properties dialog box, and click the **Security** tab. Click the **Users** entry in the top section, and make a note on the following line of the permissions assigned to the Users group. Click **Cancel** to close the Properties dialog box.

4. Right-click **TestShare1**, point to **Share with**, and click **Specific people** to start the File Sharing Wizard.
5. Type **newguest1** in the text box, and then click **Add**. New Guest User 1 is added. Click the list arrow in the Permission Level column next to New Guest User 1, and make sure **Read** is selected.
6. Click **Share**. The UNC path for the share is displayed. Click **Done**.
7. Right-click **TestShare1** and click **Properties**. Click the **Sharing** tab, and then click **Advanced Sharing**.
8. Click **Permissions**. The Administrators and Everyone groups have Full Control permission to the share. As you will see in the next step, the NTFS permissions restrict New Guest User 1's permissions to Read & execute, List folder contents, and Read, which effectively allows the user to open and view the file. Click **Cancel** twice.
9. In the TestShare1 folder's Properties dialog box, click the **Security** tab. Click **New Guest User 1**, and notice that the account's NTFS permissions are Read & execute, List folder contents, and Read.
10. Close all open windows and then log off or shut down your Windows computer.

## Project 10-6: Work with Users and Groups in Linux

In this project, you create users with the *useradd* command and groups with the *groupadd* command. Next, you add users as members of these groups with the *useradd* and *usermod* commands.

1. Log on to your Linux computer and open a terminal window.
2. At the shell prompt, type **man useradd** and press **Enter** to get an overview of the man pages for the *useradd* command. Press the **Page Up** and **Page Down** keys to scroll through the man pages. Type **q** when you're finished.
3. To view current users on the Linux system, type **cat /etc/passwd** and press **Enter**. Another way to view a text file is with the *less* option. Type **less /etc/passwd** and press **Enter**. Use the arrow keys or Page Up and Page Down keys to scroll through the file. Many of the user accounts you see in this file are system accounts that are not used to log on to the OS. Type **q** to quit.
4. Display the list of groups by typing **less /etc/group** and pressing **Enter**. When you're finished, type **q**.
5. To create a user, type **useradd testuser1** and press **Enter**. If you aren't logged on as root, you see a message stating that permission is denied. Type **su** and press **Enter** to switch to the root user, if necessary; type your password when prompted. The last character in the prompt changes from a *$* to a # to indicate that you're now operating as the root user.
6. Type **useradd testuser1** and press **Enter**. To create a password for the user, type **passwd testuser1** and press **Enter**. Type **Password01** and press **Enter**. (Notice that your keystrokes aren't displayed.) You see a message that the password is bad and fails a dictionary check. However, the password is still accepted, and you're prompted to retype it. Type **Password01** and press **Enter** again. You should see a message stating "passwd: all authentication tokens updated successfully."

If you don't enter the same password when asked to retype it, you get a message stating that the passwords don't match, and you're prompted to try again.

7. Create another user with the logon name **testuser2**.
8. Type **less /etc/passwd**, press **Enter**, and page to the bottom of the file, where you see the users you created. Type **q** and then display the group file to see that groups named testuser1 and testuser2 were also created. (*Hint*: Remember that you can use the arrow keys to scroll through recently used commands.)
9. Type **groupadd testgroup1** and press **Enter**. To add testuser1 to testgroup1, type **usermod -a -G testgroup1 testuser1** and press **Enter**. Repeat the command for **testuser2**. Type **cat /etc/group** and press **Enter** to list all groups. You should see the new group at the end of the file along with a list of its members.

10. You can view a user's group memberships with the *groups* command. Type **groups testuser1** and press **Enter**. Testuser1 is listed as a member of the testuser1 and testgroup1 groups.
11. Close the terminal window and shut down the Linux computer.

## Project 10-7: Create a User in Mac OS X

In this project, you create users and groups in Mac OS X.

1. Log on to your Mac OS X computer.
2. Click the **Apple** icon and then click **System Preferences.**
3. In System Preferences, click **Users & Groups.** At the bottom of the window, click the **lock** icon so you can make changes. Type your password when prompted and click **Unlock.**
4. At the bottom of the left pane, click the plus (+) sign, as shown in Figure 10-24.

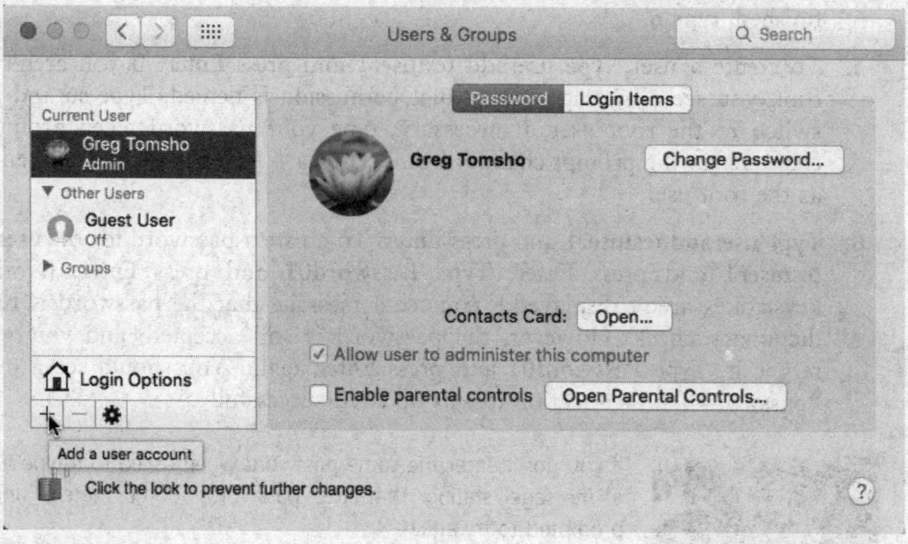


**Figure 10-24** Creating a new user in Mac OS X

*Source: Mac OS X*

5. In the next dialog box, click the list arrow next to New Account to review the account types you can create. In the Full Name text box, type **John Doe**; in the Account Name text box, type **jdoe**. Type **Password01** in the Password and Verify text boxes. Optionally, you can add a password hint.
6. Click **Create User.**
7. Click the plus (+) sign again. In the New Account list box, click **Group**. In the Full Name text box, click **MyGroup** and then click **Create Group.**

8. In the left pane, make sure MyGroup is selected. In the right pane, click the check box next to John Doe to add the account to the group.
9. Close all open windows, but stay logged on if you're continuing to the next project.

## Project 10-8: Share a Folder and Assign Permissions in Mac OS X

In this project, you share a folder and assign permissions in Mac OS X.

1. Log on to your Mac OS X computer, if necessary.
2. On the desktop, double-click **Macintosh HD**. Right-click in **Macintosh HD** and click **New Folder**. Type your password if prompted and click **OK**. Click the folder name and rename it **SharedFolder**.
3. Click the **Apple** icon and then click **System Preferences**. In System Preferences, click **Sharing**. In the Sharing dialog box, click the **File Sharing** check box to enable file sharing.
4. Click the plus (+) sign under Shared Folders. Click **Macintosh HD** in the left pane and click **Shared Folder** in the right pane. Click **Add**.
5. In the Sharing dialog box, click the plus (+) sign under **Users**. Click **MyGroup** and then click **Select** (see Figure 10-25).

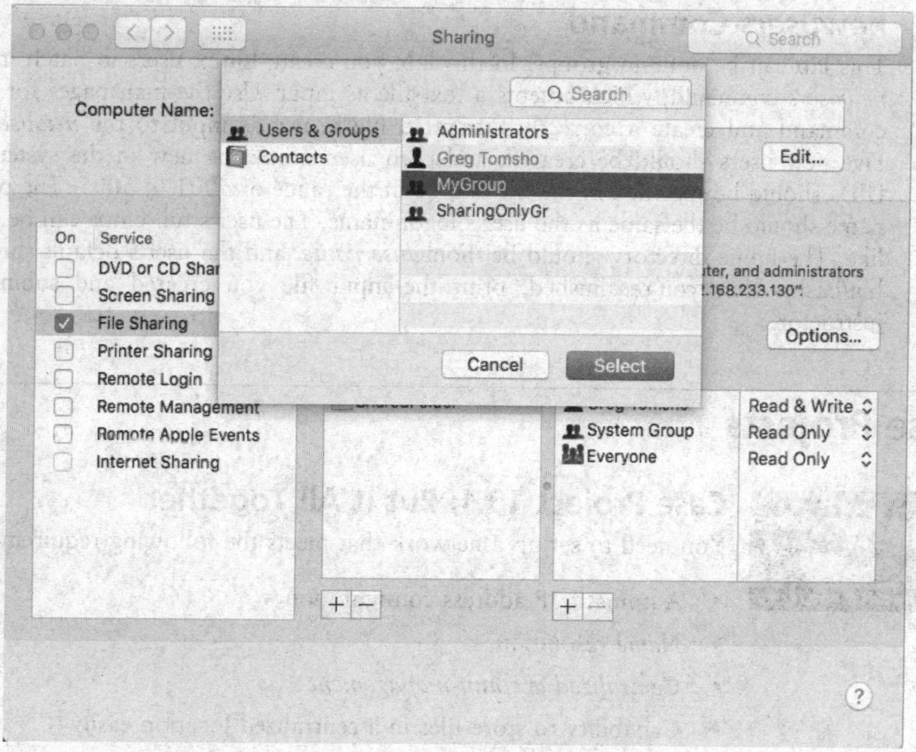


**Figure 10-25** Sharing a folder and assigning permissions

*Source: Mac OS X*

6. Notice that the default permission is Read Only for MyGroup. Click the arrow next to **Read Only** in the MyGroup row to see the possible permission settings. Click **Read & Write**. To remove a user or group from the permission list, click the user or group and click the minus (–) sign. Close the Sharing dialog box.
7. Shut down your Mac OS X computer.

# Critical Thinking

The following activities give you critical thinking challenges. Challenge Labs give you an opportunity to use the skills you have learned to perform a task without step-by-step instructions. Case projects offer a practical problem for which you supply a written solution. Not all chapters contain Challenge Labs. There is not always a specific right or wrong answer to these critical thinking exercises. They are intended to encourage you to review the chapter material and delve deeper into the topics you have learned.

# Challenge Labs

## Challenge Lab 10-1: Create Users in Linux with the *newusers* Command

This lab can be done in groups. In this lab, you create Linux users in batch mode with the *newusers* command, which accepts a text file as input. Use the man pages for the *newusers* command and create a correctly formatted file to use as input to the *newusers* command. Five new users should be created, and each user should be new in the system. The users' UIDs should be specified in the file and be in the range of 5001 to 5005. The primary group name should be the same as the user's logon name. The user's full name can be whatever you like. The home directory should be /home/*username*, and the user's default shell should be /bin/bash. After you're finished, print the input file you created and submit it to your instructor.

# Case Projects

## Case Project 10-1: Put It All Together

You need to set up a network that meets the following requirements:

- Automatic IP address configuration
- *Name resolution*
- *Centralized account management*
- Capability to store files in a centralized location easily

Write a memo explaining what services must be installed on the network to satisfy each requirement.

CASE PROJECTS

## Case Project 10-2: Share Files with Multiple OSs

You have been called in to consult for a company that is running 15 Windows 10 computers, two Linux computers, and three Mac OS X computers. Your boss wants all of these computers to be able to share files. What file sharing protocol do you recommend and why? Should you configure this network as a peer-to-peer network or as a client/server network? Explain your answer.

chapter 11

# Operating Systems Management and Maintenance

**After reading this chapter and completing the exercises, you will be able to:**

- Explain file system maintenance techniques for different operating systems
- Perform regular file system maintenance by finding and deleting unused files and folders
- Perform disk maintenance that includes defragmenting, relocating files and folders, running disk and file repair utilities, and selecting RAID options
- Explain the types of backups and develop a backup plan
- Explain how to install software for best performance
- Tune operating systems for optimal performance

**Computer operating systems are similar to cars in that they need regular maintenance** to achieve the best performance. A new car, like a new computer, delivers fast response, and every component usually functions perfectly. To keep the car at its best, you must perform regular maintenance, such as changing the oil and performing tune-ups. If you neglect this maintenance, the car's performance suffers and the wear shows quickly. Maintenance is just as important for computers because it does not take long for an operating system, software, and hardware to degrade in performance. Operating system maintenance consists of deleting unnecessary files, tuning memory, regularly backing up files, defragmenting disks, and repairing damaged files. Maintenance is particularly important for networked computer systems because a poorly responding computer has an impact on network operations.

In this chapter, you learn a variety of techniques for maintaining and tuning workstations and servers. One of the most important steps in disk and file maintenance is to start with a well-designed folder structure, which makes finding unused files and folders a straightforward process. Two other important tasks are performing regular backups and running disk maintenance utilities. How and where software is installed is also vital to how a computer performs. Finally, there are tuning options that can immediately enhance performance, such as adjusting virtual memory.

# File System Maintenance

Successful file system maintenance is closely linked to a computer's folder structure. On desktop and server operating systems, a well-planned folder structure makes it easy to locate files, update files, share folders and files, back up and archive files, and delete unwanted files. In addition, on server operating systems, well-designed folder structures help network performance and security. The importance of a well-designed folder structure and the default folder structures for Windows, Linux/UNIX, and Mac OS X were described in Chapter 4. As a reminder, here are some basic rules for creating and maintaining a folder structure:

- Keep a manageable number of folders in the root folder.
- Keep operating system files in the default folders recommended by the vendor.
- Keep different versions of software in their own folders.
- Keep data files in folders on the basis of their functions.
- Design home folders to match the functions of users in an organization.
- Group files with similar security needs within the same folders.

Operating system folders are typically placed in the root folder and have appropriate subfolders under a main folder. It's important that you know the locations of system files so you know where to look if you need to troubleshoot a problem with system files. Table 11-1 illustrates typical locations for system files in various operating systems.

**Table 11-1 Essential operating system folders**

| Operating system | Essential system folders at the root level for 32-bit systems | Essential system folders at the root level for 64-bit systems |
|---|---|---|
| Mac OS X | bin, dev, etc, Library, Network, sbin, System, var, and Volumes | bin, dev, etc, Library, Network, sbin, System, var, and Volumes |
| UNIX/Linux | bin, dev, etc, lib, mnt, proc, sbin, and var | bin, dev, etc, lib, mnt, proc, sbin, and var |
| Modern Windows desktop and server versions | Windows, including the Boot, System, and System32 subfolders | Windows, including the Boot, System, System32, and sysWOW64 subfolders |

There are several advantages to leaving operating system files in the folders created by the OS instead of using other folder locations. For example, it is easier for others to help with computer problems as they arise. Also, in organizations that have help desks or support centers, it is easier for support professionals to solve problems with drivers and network access when system files are easy to find. Finally, many software installations expect operating system files to be in their default locations, and these installations work best when it is easy to find specific subfolders and key files related to the operating system.

When you install server operating systems, you may be tempted to hide or rename default system folders as a way to protect them from intruders. However, most intruders will not be deterred by these efforts. A better approach is to understand and implement the security features available in the operating system. One security precaution is to periodically back up OS files in all operating systems, including the system state data in Windows operating systems.

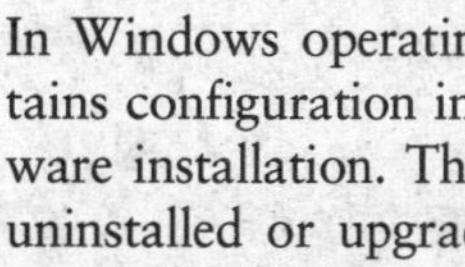


In modern Windows operating systems, such as Windows 10, you can configure system protection to return to a previous system configuration in case one or more system files are deleted or if the installation of a new device causes operating system problems. To configure system protection in Windows 10, right-click Start, click System, and click System protection in the left pane. On the System Protection tab, configure the System Restore settings.

In Windows operating systems, installed software is also tracked in the registry, which contains configuration information as well as information about individual components of a software installation. Thus, it is easier for the operating system to assist when software must be uninstalled or upgraded because the OS can quickly identify and find the relevant components. In Windows desktop and server operating systems, these vital files are kept in the OS's folder and subfolders. For example, these files might be located in the \Windows, \Windows \System, or \Windows\System32 folders. Table 11-2 lists some typical Windows application software components and their associated file extensions. Table 11-3 lists the same types of components for UNIX/Linux and Mac OS X. Application software and operating system enhancements are easier to install when these components are in known locations.

**Table 11-2 Examples of Windows-based application software components**

| File type | File extension | File type | File extension |
|---|---|---|---|
| Application | .exe | Initialization | .ini |
| ActiveX control | .ocx | Installation | .inf |
| Backup | .bak | Microsoft Common Console document | .mcs |
| Bitmap image | .bmp | Microsoft Office settings file | .pip |
| Compiled HTML help file | .chm | OLE common control (.ocx is now part of the ActiveX control set) | .ocx |
| Control Panel extension | .cpl | Precompiled setup information | .pnf |
| Configuration | .cfg | Screen saver | .scr |
| Data | .dat | Security catalog | .cat |
| Device driver | .drv | Temporary file | .tmp |
| Dynamic link library | .dll | Text | .txt |
| Help | .hlp | TrueType font | .ttf |
| Help context | .cnt | Virtual device driver | .vxd |

**Table 11-3 Examples of UNIX/Linux and Mac OS X application software components**

| File type | File extension | File type | File extension |
|---|---|---|---|
| awk script (for running reports) | .awk | Program header for a C or C++ program | .h |
| Backup | .bak | Hypertext Markup Language | .html |
| C program file containing source code | .c | Log file | .log |
| C++ program file containing source code | .C or .cc | Matlab script | .mat |
| CGI script for a Web page | .cgi | Object code file | .o |
| Configuration | .cfg | Perl script/program | .pl |
| Data | .dat | Python program | .py |
| Document | .doc | Shell archive | .shar |
| Emacs Lisp source code file | .el | Scheme source code | .ss |
| Emacs Lisp compiled file | .elc | Text | .txt |
| Source code in Fortran | .for or .f | Tape archive (made from the *tar* command) | .tar |
| Source code in Fortran 77 | .f77 | Uuencoded | .uue |

> **NOTE**
>
> The Windows registry is an extensive database of information about the operating system, including customized settings and software installations. The registry contains data about all hardware components and software. It contains information about Windows services that are started automatically, manually, or are disabled. Desktop configuration data is stored in the registry, as is information about user accounts, group policies, networking, and system boot data. The registry is an essential component of the system state data.

Sometimes, particularly on network servers, several versions of a software application must be available for different uses. For example, an organization may have some users who still use earlier versions of Microsoft Word or even WordPerfect, so these versions must be maintained in case a specific version needs to be reinstalled on a client's computer over the network. In an organization that develops software applications, it may be necessary to keep different versions of compilers or development tools available. Some users may have operating systems that only support 32-bit applications, whereas other users may have operating systems that support 32-bit and 64-bit applications. In these situations, one way to handle having more than one version of the same software is to put different versions in different subfolders under a main applications folder. For example, in Windows Server, you can support different versions of Microsoft Word by having a Program Files folder and subfolders called Word2013 and Word2016. In this case, one version is installed to run locally and the other version is available to clients for network installations. Also, Microsoft 64-bit operating systems offer the Program Files and Program Files (x86) folders to separate 64-bit and 32-bit applications.

## Finding and Deleting Files

Having a solid computer file structure makes it easier to find and delete unneeded files on a regular schedule. Files can quickly accumulate and occupy a large amount of disk space—an example is the temporary files created when you install new software and run many types of applications. Most installations create a temporary folder and a set of temporary files that are stored under the root folder or an account's home folder. Some software applications do not completely delete temporary files when the installation is finished. Also, some software applications create temporary files that are not deleted when the application is closed or improperly terminated, either because of a power failure or other malfunction. For example, many word-processing programs create temporary files that are used for backup purposes or to save the most immediate changes.

Web browsers also write an impressive number of temporary Internet files that are not deleted unless you set an expiration date or delete them using an OS utility or browser utility. In most cases, the files can be deleted regularly; however, some **cookies** may be kept because they contain specialized information for accessing particular Web sites. Many cookies are deleted because they only take up space and contain no information the user needs. Some users regularly delete all cookies because new ones are created anyway when users re-access Web sites. Cookies are text files that have the preface *cookie*:—for example, in many Windows operating systems, a cookie created after you access the Microsoft Web site from your account is *cookie:accountname@microsoft.com*. Temporary Internet files often have extensions such as .html, .htm, .jpg, and .gif.

It is a good practice to implement a regular schedule for finding and deleting unneeded files. The following sections explain these methods in different operating systems.

Deleting files is vital for making the best use of disk storage resources, and it can help extend the life of hard disks. One rule of thumb is that hard disk drives should be kept less than 80 percent full. Otherwise, the drive is subject to excessive wear, and is more likely to have problems or fail.

## Deleting Temporary Files in Windows

Temporary files accumulate in Windows operating systems and can be deleted using several approaches. In Windows, temporary files are typically located in the \Temp and \Windows \Temp folders, or in users' home folders. Temporary Internet files from Internet Explorer are stored in the Users*accountname*\AppData\Local\Microsoft\Windows\Temporary Internet Files folder.

Temporary Internet files can also be stored in other locations, depending on the operating system, Web browser in use, and individual settings specified by the user.

A convenient way to delete unneeded files in Windows operating systems is to use the Disk Cleanup tool. You can start this tool by typing Disk Cleanup in the search text box on the taskbar and then clicking Disk Cleanup.

When you start Disk Cleanup (see Figure 11-1), it scans your disk to determine the amount of space that can be restored after removing specific types of files. In Windows 8 and later versions, the Disk Cleanup tool is scheduled to automatically run on the system drive where Windows is installed whenever the computer is idle for an extended period.

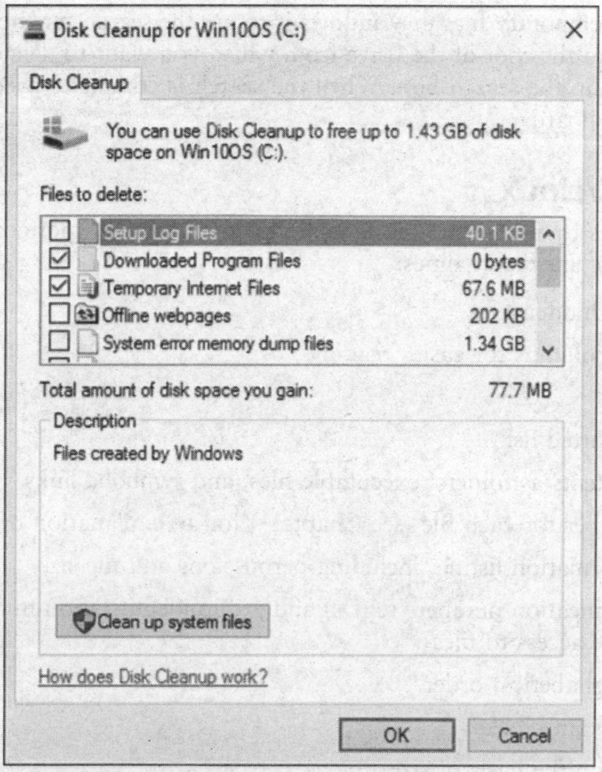


**Figure 11-1** The Disk Cleanup tool in Windows

TIP

To quickly delete all temporary files without using Disk Cleanup in Windows operating systems, you can open the Command Prompt window and enter the command *dir *.tmp /s* to list all temporary files that have the .tmp extension. The * works as a wildcard to search for all .tmp files. The */s* switch lists files in subfolders. If you determine that you want to delete all of the listed files, enter the *del *.tmp /s* command. Files that are currently in use will not be deleted.

Windows comes with a Recycle Bin, which contains files that have been deleted. You should regularly open the Recycle Bin and delete its files, which purges them from the system permanently. You can delete files in the Recycle Bin by using the Disk Cleanup tool, but the fastest way to delete these files is to keep the Recycle Bin icon on the desktop, right-click the icon, and then click Empty Recycle Bin on the shortcut menu.

NOTE

By default, the Recycle Bin can grow to occupy 10 percent of available hard disk storage. Computers that are configured for two or more volumes have a Recycle Bin on each volume. You can resize the maximum allocation for the Recycle Bin by right-clicking its desktop icon, selecting Properties, and configuring the maximum size. When the Recycle Bin is full and you continue to delete files to send to the Recycle Bin, the oldest files in the Recycle Bin are purged first.

Another approach to deleting temporary files in Windows is to use the search function in File Explorer. In File Explorer, go to the root of the drive from which you want to delete temporary files, and then type *.tmp in the search box. When the search is complete, select all the files and press Del on your keyboard.

## Deleting Files in UNIX/Linux

You can view UNIX/Linux files by using the *ls* command along with one or more of the following options for listing particular file qualities:

- *-a* lists all files, including hidden files
- *-C* formats the listing in columns for easier reading
- *-d* lists folders
- *-f* displays files in an unsorted list
- *-F* identifies the list's contents as folders, executable files, and symbolic links
- *-i* displays the inode number for each file (see Chapter 4 for an explanation of inodes)
- *-l* presents a detailed information listing, including permissions and file size
- *-n* displays the user identification numbers (UIDs) and group identification numbers (GIDs) of those who have access to files
- *-r* sorts files in reverse alphabetical order
- *-s* displays the size of files (in blocks)
- *-S* sorts files and folders on the basis of size
- *-t* sorts files and folders based on when they were last modified

For example, to list all files, including hidden files, use the command *ls -a*. If you are only looking for large files, use the command *ls -sa* to show file and folder sizes for all listings, including hidden files. You can use the command *ls -la* to show more detailed information, including file and folder sizes and the permissions associated with each file and folder. Notice that you can combine options, such as using the *-la* option to show detailed information for all files, including hidden files.

Files and folders are deleted in UNIX/Linux using the remove (*rm*) command. Two options commonly added to this command are *-i* and *-r*. The *-i* or interactive option results in a prompt that asks if you really want to delete the file or folder; the *-r* or recursive command is used to delete an entire folder's contents, including all its subfolders and files.

Use the *rm -r* command carefully; it deletes all files and subfolders within a folder. When you delete a folder, you should add the *-i* option, such as in *rm -ir foldername*, so that the operating system asks you to verify the deletion first.

For example, let's say you want to list all files in the /home/mjackson/docs folder that end with .txt so you can determine whether to delete them. You would enter:

*ls -a /home/mjackson/docs/*.txt*

In the preceding command, the * is a wildcard that lists all files ending in .txt. To delete the files, you would enter:

*rm /home/mjackson/docs/*.txt*

As another example, assume that you want to delete your /work folder, but first you want to view its contents, including hidden files. As a safety precaution, you also want the command to include a prompt that queries whether you really want to delete the folder and its contents. You would enter the following commands:

*ls -a /work*

*rm -ri /work*

**TIP**

If the /work folder is in your home folder, you can use the ~ symbol to represent your home folder path, no matter what folder you are currently in. In the preceding example, you could enter *ls -a ~/work* and then enter *rm -ri ~/work*.

In the Linux GNOME Files tool, you can delete a file by browsing to the folder that contains it, clicking the appropriate file in the display of the folder's contents, and pressing the Del key on your keyboard.

To find a file, use the *find* command. You can use this command and its various options to find files based on their filenames, file size, and the last time they were accessed or modified. You can also use wildcard characters. For example, to find and print a list of all temporary files modified in the last 30 days, you could enter *find -name temp* -mtime -30 -print*. (Hands-On Project 11-5 shows you how to delete temporary files in UNIX/Linux.)

The *find* command has options that let you search for files using several criteria:

- *-atime* for last accessed time
- *-ctime* for last changed time of file attributes
- *-mtime* for last modification time of file data
- *-name* for the filename (wildcards can be used)
- *-print* to print the results of the search
- *-size* for file size (in blocks or bytes; bytes are specified by a *c* after the size value)
- *-user* to find files by ownership

For example, assume that you are looking for a file called *file1* to delete from your home folder. To find the file, you would use the following command:

*find ~ -name file1*

As another example, consider a server administrator who wants to find all files in the /usr folder that are owned by the user lpadron. To find the files, he would use the following command:

*find /usr -user lpadron*

To search all folders under the root and find all files owned by user lpadron, enter the following command:

*find / -user lpadron*

To find all files owned by user lpadron and then delete them, you can use the | symbol with the *rm* command:

*find / -user lpadron | rm*

Like the Recycle Bin in Windows, the Linux GNOME Files tool offers a trash can for deleting files permanently. The trash can appears in the left pane of the Files tool and is aptly named Trash. Periodically view the contents of Trash and then purge the files by clicking Trash in Files and clicking Empty.

UNIX/Linux provides commands to help you assess the allocation of disk space in a file system. One command is *df*, which provides statistics on the total number of blocks in a file system, the number used, the number available, and the percent of capacity used. While the *df* command provides information for the file system as a whole, the *du* command displays similar statistics for a given folder and its subfolders or for a particular subfolder.

Table 11-4 lists a summary of the UNIX/Linux commands discussed in this section.

**Table 11-4 UNIX/Linux commands for finding and removing files**

| Command | Explanation |
|---|---|
| *df* | Reports how disk space is employed, including free and used space on a mounted file system |
| *du* | Displays file statistics for a folder and its subfolders |
| *find* | Finds specific files and includes these options:<br>• *-atime* for last accessed time<br>• *-ctime* for last changed time<br>• *-mtime* for last modification time<br>• *-name* for the filename (wildcards can be used)<br>• *-print* to print the results of the search<br>• *-size* for file size (in blocks or bytes; bytes are specified by a c after the size value)<br>• *-user* to find files by ownership |
| *ls* | Lists files and includes these options:<br>• *-a* lists all files, including hidden files<br>• *-C* formats the listing in columns for easier reading<br>• *-d* lists folders<br>• *-f* displays files in an unsorted list<br>• *-F* identifies the list's contents as folders, executable files, and symbolic links<br>• *-i* displays the inode number for each file<br>• *-l* presents a detailed information listing, including permissions and file size<br>• *-n* displays the user identification numbers (UIDs) and group identification numbers (GIDs) of those who have access to files |

**Table 11-4** **UNIX/Linux commands for finding and removing files (*continued*)**

| Command | Explanation |
|---|---|
| | • *-r* sorts files in reverse alphabetical order<br>• *-s* displays the size of files (in blocks)<br>• *-S* sorts files and folders by their size<br>• *-t* sorts files and folders based on when they were last modified |
| *rm* | Removes files and folders and includes the following options:<br>• *-i* is used to avoid unintentional deletions by prompting the user to verify the deletion<br>• *-r* is used to delete a folder and all of its contents |

## Deleting Files in Mac OS X

Mac OS X is generally effective in automatically cleaning out many temporary, log, and other files on a regular basis. However, it is still important to find and delete unneeded files periodically to make sure you do not run out of disk space. Mac OS X windows often have a list option that shows files and their sizes. Click the List view button in the window to see file sizes (see Figure 11-2).

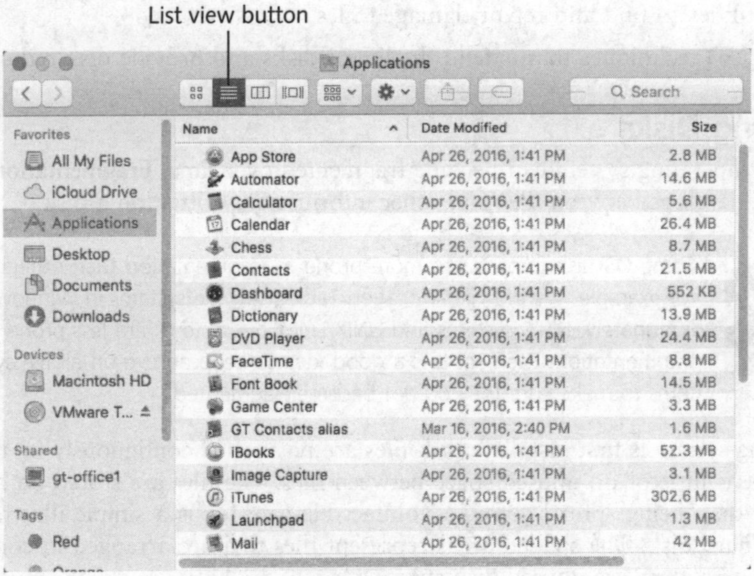


**Figure 11-2** Viewing file sizes in Mac OS X

*Source: Mac OS X*

TIP

Mac OS X has a Find utility that you can use to find files that are no longer needed. To use the Find utility, click File in the menu bar, click Find, and enter the object of your search in the box with the magnifying glass. Alternatively, you can click the Spotlight icon in the menu bar and enter the search request in Spotlight. When you find an unneeded file, drag it into the Trash. If necessary, you can retrieve the deleted item from the Trash by opening it and moving the item back to a folder or the desktop. Files are not truly deleted until you purge them by emptying the Trash; perform this task on a regular schedule to free up disk space. (You will learn how to empty the trash in Mac OS X in Hands-On Project 11-8.)

# Maintaining Disks

In addition to finding and deleting unneeded files, other disk maintenance tasks and techniques are valuable in terms of maintaining the integrity of files and ensuring disk performance:

- Defragmenting disks
- Moving files to spread the load between multiple disks
- Using disk utilities to find and repair damaged files
- Deploying RAID techniques that extend the life of disks and provide disk redundancy

## Defragmenting Disks

Hard disks in any operating system can become fragmented over time. **Fragmentation** means that unused space develops between files and other information written on a disk.

NOTE

Some OS disk formats are more prone to fragmentation than others—for example, the old File Allocation Table (FAT) file systems in Windows. Fortunately, NTFS systems and UNIX/Linux file systems are less prone to fragmentation. Even so, it is a good idea to keep an eye on all file systems to make sure they do not become fragmented.

When an operating system is first installed, disk files are positioned contiguously on the disk, which means there is little or no unused space between files. The files are stored on consecutive blocks rather than being spread across a volume. Figure 11-3 is a simple illustration of an unfragmented hard disk. The shaded areas represent files that are arranged in contiguous fashion, and the white areas are unused disk space.

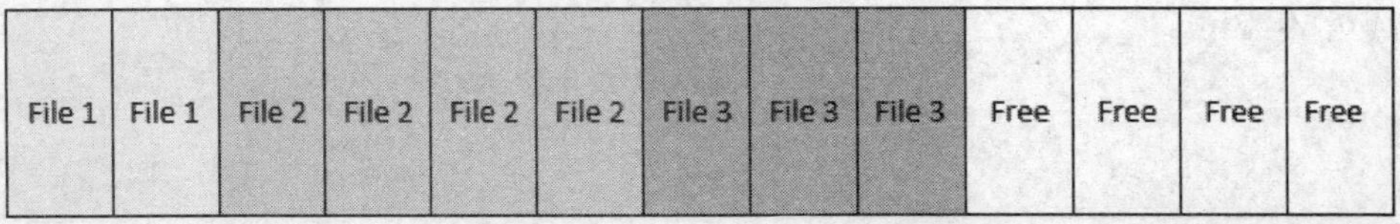


**Figure 11-3** An unfragmented disk

As the operating system deletes, creates, and modifies files, the unused space between them grows and becomes scattered throughout the disk, and the files themselves become scattered throughout the disk (see Figure 11-4). The greater the fragmentation, the more space is wasted. Equally important, the disk read/write head must work harder to find individual files and data in files, which leads to two problems: First, disk performance suffers because it takes the read/write head longer to find information, and it takes longer to find an appropriate unused location on which to write information. The second problem is that the read/write head works harder when there is more disk fragmentation, which increases the chances of hardware failure.

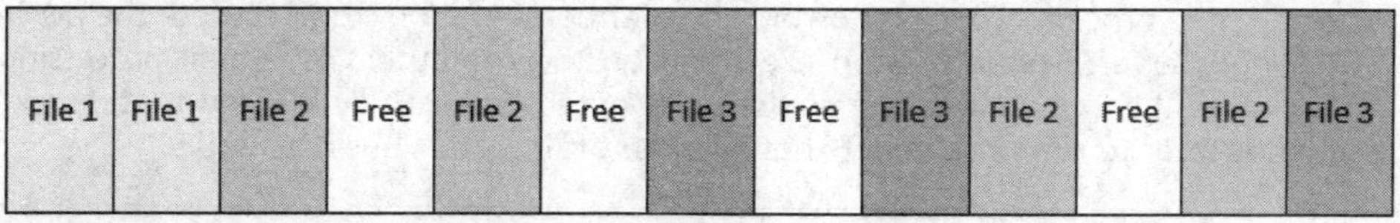


**Figure 11-4** A fragmented disk

**Defragmentation** is the process of removing the empty pockets between files and other information on a hard disk drive. An older defragmentation method is to take a complete backup of a disk's contents and perform a full restore. Some administrators also run a **surface analysis** of a disk before performing the full restore as a means of finding damaged disk sectors and tracks. Some surface analysis tools are destructive to data and attempt to reformat the damaged area to determine if it can be recovered. Other tools are not destructive to data because they relocate information from a damaged disk area to an undamaged location, and then mark the damaged area as off limits so no files can be written there.

As a precaution, back up a hard disk before running a disk surface analysis or defragmenting it. Also, consult the documentation to determine whether a disk analysis tool is destructive to data before you run it. For example, some computer manufacturers provide disk analysis tools on a system troubleshooting disk; these tools perform a format along with the disk surface analysis.

A second option, which is usually easier than backing up and restoring a hard disk, is to run a disk defragmentation tool. Some operating systems come with a built-in tool to defragment disks. For example, Windows operating systems come with a disk defragmenter tool called Optimize Drives in Windows 8 and newer versions. Some defragmentation tools can run in the background as you continue to use the operating system. Many also provide a quick analysis of the hard disk and advise whether it is necessary to defragment it. For example, if disk fragmentation is 20 percent or less, the disk does not usually need to be defragmented immediately. Because server operating systems often experience more rapid fragmentation than client operating systems, server administrators should develop a regular schedule to defragment hard disks. Some administrators defragment between once a week and once a month, always during times when no one is on the server other than the administrator. In some situations where a server is under constant and heavy use, such as one used for a client/server or cloud-based application, it can be necessary to defragment disks every few days.

In Windows 8, Windows Server 2012, and later versions of both, the disk defragmentation tool defrag.exe is scheduled to run automatically on all volumes when the system is idle, so manual defragmentation is rarely needed.

**From the Trenches ...**

A new server administrator checked the server at her company and found that the hard drive was severely fragmented. She felt it should be defragmented right away and started the process. To her horror, the defragmentation tool caused the Microsoft Exchange Server process to stop executing on the computer. All e-mail processing was down until the Exchange Server could be rebooted. She quickly learned that defragmentation is safer to run on a server that is taken offline after business hours.

If a disk contains an error, the Optimize Drives tool in Windows detects the error and requires that it be repaired prior to defragmenting the disk. Errors can be repaired using the *chkdsk* utility, which is discussed later in this chapter.

In UNIX/Linux and Mac OS X, file systems are designed to reduce the need for defragmenting a disk. These file systems first write to a hidden journal, which is loaded into memory; the contents are then written to disk in a linear fashion, not sequentially. Writing in linear fashion means that the data is temporarily stored and written all at one time in contiguous spaces. Writing in sequential fashion means the data is not stored, but is written as soon as it is created to whatever disk areas are immediately open. Using a hidden journal and writing data in linear fashion means that these file systems use methods that minimize fragmentation, which is why defragmentation tools are usually not included with them.

As with any system, an alternative to defragmenting disks on UNIX/Linux and Mac OS X systems is to perform a full backup and restore.

## Moving Disk Files to Spread the Load

Another technique that can help extend the life of disk drives is to spread files evenly across them when there are multiple disks. This technique is used mainly on computers with multiple-user access, such as servers, and on computers with frequent disk activity. Before files are moved, the server administrator examines disk and file activity to determine how to spread files across the disk drives to achieve even loading. Also, files must be moved based on their functions so files that contain related information are on the same drive.

Disk activity is monitored in Windows operating systems using Task Manager, Resource Monitor, and Performance Monitor. Performance Monitor provides the most in-depth information and can be configured to log information to a file so activity can be examined over a longer period of time. For a quick look at current disk utilization, use Resource Monitor (see Figure 11-5).

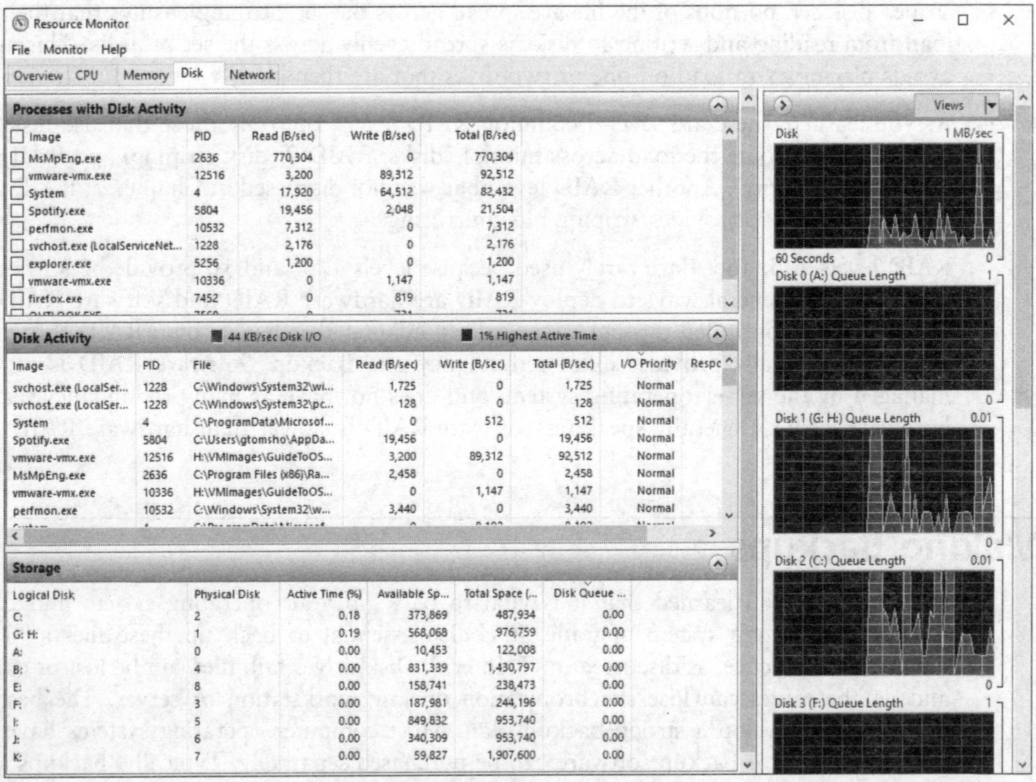

**Figure 11-5** Using Resource Monitor to view disk usage

## Using Disk Utilities to Repair Damaged Files

Some operating systems have utilities that enable you to repair damaged files and file links. Four examples of these utilities are listed here and were discussed in Chapter 4.

- Disk First Aid in the Mac OS X Disk Utility
- *fsck* and *p_fsck* in UNIX/Linux
- *chkdsk* in Windows

## Deploying RAID Techniques

As you learned in Chapter 7, deploying RAID is a technique used by server operating systems and some client OSs for three purposes:

- Increased reliability by providing data recovery when a disk drive fails and extending the useful life of disks
- Increased storage capacity
- Increased speed

This section focuses on how RAID extends the life of a set of disks using **disk striping**, a technique for spreading data over multiple disk volumes. For example, when a file is written to a striped disk set, portions of the file are spread across the set. Striping ensures that the resulting load from reading and writing to disks is spread evenly across the set of disks. This approach avoids placing extra load on one or two disks that are then likely to wear out sooner.

As you learned, there are several common RAID levels, but only those that use disk striping techniques distribute the load across multiple disks: RAID 0 (disk striping) and RAID 5 (disk striping with parity). Another RAID level that was not discussed in Chapter 7, RAID 10 (also called RAID 1+0), provides striping plus mirroring.

RAID levels 2, 3, and 4 are rarely used because levels 1, 5, and 10 provide better fault tolerance. The two general ways to deploy RAID are hardware RAID and software RAID. Hardware RAID is controlled through a specialized adapter that has its own RAID software on a chip, which usually provides extra redundancy and backup. Software RAID is set up and managed by the server operating system, and does not have as many redundancy features as hardware RAID. Generally speaking, software RAID is slower than hardware RAID.

## Making Backups

In Chapter 5, you learned that it is vital to back up your operating system and data files before an operating system upgrade. It is also essential to back up these files as a regular maintenance practice, as discussed in Chapter 7. Disk drives fail, files can be lost or corrupted, and database files can lose synchronization on any workstation or server. The best line of defense is to develop a strong backup plan. Most computer operating systems have built-in backup utilities, or backup software can be purchased separately. Typically, backups are written to tape or to a removable hard drive, but other backup options include flash drives, CDs, and DVDs, depending on the space required, the type of backup, and the required reliability of the media. Chapter 7 covers these different media and includes information about their projected life spans.

There are several types of backups. One type is called a **binary backup** because it backs up the disk contents in binary format to create an exact image of the disk contents. The advantages of this type of backup are its simplicity of operation and its inclusion of everything on the disk. The disadvantages are that in many versions, you cannot restore individual files or folders, and that when you perform a restore, the target disk drive must be the same size or larger than the disk drive from which the backup was made.

Another backup type is called a **full file-by-file backup**, in which all of the disk contents are backed up, but as individual folders and files. This type of backup is commonly used on workstations because it enables you to restore a single folder or a set of files without restoring the entire disk's contents. Full file-by-file backups are also performed on servers, depending on the backup scheme that is in place. Some backup schemes call for a full file-by-file backup to be performed at the end of each workday, as long as the total amount of information on the disks is not prohibitive. If the disks hold a great amount of information, it is common to perform a full file-by-file backup once a week and partial backups on the other days of the week.

There are typically two kinds of partial backups—differential and incremental. A **differential backup** only backs up files that have changed since the last full backup. An **incremental backup** backs up any files that have changed since the last full or incremental backup.

The differences between using differential or incremental backups as opposed to full backups depend on the amount of media required for these backups, such as tapes or DVDs, and the number of days of work that must be restored when a complete restore is necessary.

A basic backup scheme for a business might be to perform a full file-by-file backup to tape each Saturday evening and to perform differential backups to tape Monday through Friday. The business might also have four sets of tapes that are rotated each week. The first tape set would be used in week 1, the second tape set in week 2, and so on. In this way, if one tape set goes bad, one of the other tape sets from a previous week can be used to restore a server. In this scenario, if a catastrophic disk failure occurs on Thursday, the business can recover after the disk drive or drives are replaced by restoring the full file-by-file backup from the previous Saturday and then restoring the differential backup from Wednesday night. If the business had been performing incremental backups, it would restore the full file-by-file backup from Saturday and then restore the incremental backups from Monday, Tuesday, and Wednesday.

For small server and individual workstation backups, a simple solution is to use the ability of the native backup software to periodically back up new files and file modifications on the same day they are made. Mac OS X Time Machine, for example, enables you to leave a removable hard drive connected to the computer so it can back up any file changes shortly after they occur. This backup technique can be performed to supplement a full backup. Another option is to always have an internal disk or removable disk connected so that the native backup software automatically performs an image or full file-by-file backup at a scheduled time each day or one day during the week. Windows operating systems enable this type of regular backup.

TIP

Some removable disks provide software to perform backups, including software that regularly backs up recent changes to files.

Whether you are a home user, have a client computer in a business, or manage a server, it is important to develop a solid backup strategy. Consider the following elements as you develop your approach:

- *Determine what information needs to be backed up and how often*—Some files, such as the operating system files, need only infrequent backups—for example, after you change the settings on your computer or install new software. More frequent backups are required for other information, such as new word-processing files, spreadsheets, and other documents that you create daily. Develop a plan that enables you to back up the operating system as needed and to back up specific files as often as they are modified or are created.
- *Use scheduling software*—Windows native backup software, Mac OS X Time Machine, open source backup software for UNIX/Linux, and other third-party software can help you schedule backups. Set up the scheduling software to make sure backups are regularly performed so you don't inadvertently miss a backup.
- *Choose the right backup media*—Many kinds of backup media exist, including dedicated internal hard drives for backups, removable hard drives or flash drives, DVDs, and tapes. Choose the media that match your backup needs. For example, if you are a

home user who does not plan to store backups for years and years, a removable hard drive might match your needs. For personal information that needs to be stored for years, such as tax returns and precious family photos, use long-lasting DVDs for backup. If you are a server administrator who needs to back up and store large amounts of data for years or decades, consider using reliable, high-quality tapes and a tape subsystem.

- *Rotate backup media*—Even the longest-lasting backup medium can be damaged or broken accidentally. To protect against failures, rotate the media every week, every two weeks, or once a month, depending on the value of your data. Rotating media means having one or more full sets of media. If you are a home user, you might rotate the media once a month; a server administrator might rotate every week. For example, if it takes four tapes to back up the data files on your server, purchase an extra set of four tapes. Use one set one week and use the other set the second week, and then rotate the two sets every other week. For even better backup assurance, such as for a server in a credit union, purchase three or four sets of tapes so that each set is used only one week per month.
- *Store a set of backups in an off-site location*—Supplement your rotation strategy by storing one full set of backups in an off-site location, such as a bank vault. You might rotate one set to the off-site location once a month. If your home or place of business is damaged by a fire or flood, at least your data will be protected.
- *Regularly use file repair tools and a virus checker*—Regularly run file repair software, such as *chkdsk* or *fsck*, to make sure the data you back up is usable. Also, regularly scan with a virus checker so you do not back up viruses or malware.
- *Investigate third-party backup software*—After you develop your backup plan, you may discover that the backup software that comes with your operating system does not fully match your needs. For example, a server administrator may want to use backup software that helps track all media in a tape rotation or stored off site. In this case, investigate commercial and open source backup software to find a match for your needs.

# Optimizing Software Installation

The following list provides some general guidelines for optimizing software installation and uninstallation:

- One aspect of software installation already discussed in this chapter is to plan and set up a well-organized folder structure. The folder structure influences ease of installation, provides the ability to keep different versions in separate places, and enables you to smoothly uninstall software. The following is a checklist of additional guidelines for software installation:
  - Make sure that the software is compatible with your operating system.
  - Check the central processing unit (CPU), RAM, disk storage, audio, video, and other requirements to make sure your computer is a match for the software.

- Find out if there are different installation options, such as one with or without tutoring applications to help you learn the software.
- Use the utilities provided by the operating system for installing or uninstalling applications. In particular, Windows operating systems usually have a Windows-compatible setup program that comes with the software. Also, use the Programs and Features tool in the Windows Control Panel to uninstall applications (see Figure 11-6).

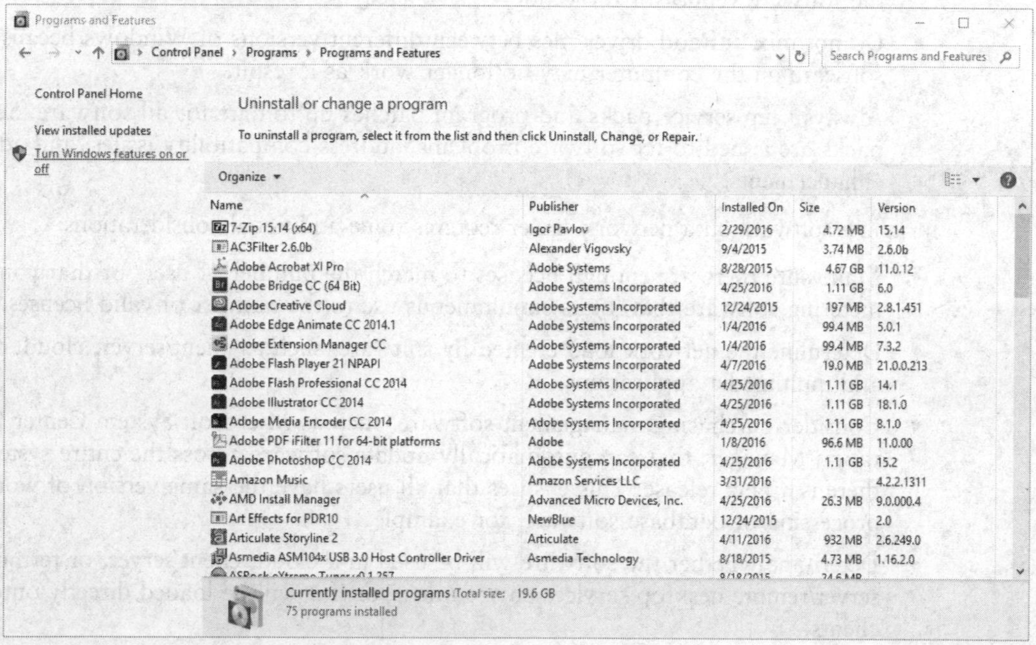


**Figure 11-6** Programs and Features in Control Panel

When you need to remove an application in Windows, always use the uninstall capability in Control Panel. This practice helps to ensure that all components are removed, such as .dll and configuration files, so that the system folders do not become cluttered with files that are no longer needed. If you don't use the uninstall tools and instead simply delete the program's subfolder, such as the one in the Program Files folder, you might see delays in the operating system and other unexpected consequences.

- Check the vendor's "bug" list for the software to make sure the bugs will not affect the way you use it. Bug lists are often posted on the vendor's Web site in the software support area.
- Make sure that the software is well documented and supported by the vendor and that the vendor can provide the required drivers, if applicable.
- Determine in advance how to back up important files associated with the software, and find the locations and purposes of all program and data files, including hidden files.

- Determine whether running the program requires adjustments to page or swap files used by the operating system. (Page files and swap files are discussed in the next section.)
- Find out what temporary files are created by the program and where they are created.
- For Windows-based software, always install the latest versions of components, including .dll, .ocx, .ini, .inf, and .drv files. These files are generally available directly from the software vendor or the vendor's Web site.
- Do not mix .inf and driver files between different versions of Windows because other software on the computer may no longer work as a result.
- Always keep service packs and program patches up to date for all software. **Service packs** are issued to fix software problems, address compatibility issues, and add enhancements.

Installing software on a network server requires some additional considerations:

- Make sure there are enough licenses to match the number of users or that you have metering software that limits simultaneous use to the number of valid licenses.
- Determine the network load created by software, such as client/server, cloud, database, and multimedia applications.
- Consider purchasing management software, such as Microsoft System Center Configuration Manager, that can automatically update software across the entire system when there is a new release. This ensures that all users have the same version of word-processing or database software, for example.
- Determine whether the software will be used in a cloud, client/server, or terminal server/remote desktop services environment, or if it will be loaded directly onto server clients.
- Determine whether the server or client workstations must be tuned for the software in a particular way, such as by modifying page files or registry entries.
- For operating systems that support two or more file systems, make sure the software is compatible with the file system used by the operating system.

## Tuning the Operating System

After an operating system is installed, you may notice that it doesn't perform as well as you expected or that performance seems to suffer with time. Just as a car needs periodic tuning, so do desktop and server operating systems. One critical reason for tuning operating systems is that slow workstations and servers have a cumulative impact on a network. Sometimes, poor network performance is not the result of network problems or too little bandwidth; instead, a preponderance of workstations and servers cannot keep up with the network. This is an often overlooked area that can result in significant savings for an organization if addressed. It is much less expensive to tune servers and workstations (often at no cost) than to invest in faster, very expensive network devices such as routers and switches. There are many ways to tune operating systems to achieve better performance, including tuning virtual memory, installing operating system updates and patches, and tuning for optimal network communications.

## Tuning Virtual Memory

Most operating systems supplement RAM by employing virtual memory techniques. **Virtual memory** is disk storage used when there is not enough RAM for a particular operation or for all processes currently in use. The operating system can swap to disk (virtual memory) the processes and data in RAM that temporarily have a low priority or are not currently in use. When the operating system needs to access certain information on a disk, it swaps other information to disk and reads the information it needs back into RAM using a process called *paging*. The information that is swapped back and forth from RAM to disk and vice versa is stored in a specially allocated disk area called the **page file**, *paging file*, or **swap file**. (In UNIX/Linux, this area is called the *swap file system*.)

Some operating systems that use virtual memory and paging enable you to tune the page file by adjusting its size. Tuning the page file can result in better operating system performance.

Virtual memory in Windows operating systems is adjusted to set an initial size and a maximum size to which it can grow. Generally, the rule for sizing the page file is to set the initial size to 1.5 times the amount of RAM. The maximum page file size should allow for adequate growth to handle the most active times. In Windows 8, Windows Server 2012, and later versions, the paging file size is configured by default to be automatically managed by Windows (see Figure 11-7). You can change this configuration and specify a size and location for the paging file; however, if you are using a solid state disk (SSD) for the Windows system disk, you should let Windows manage the paging file size. In addition, because the paging file is extensively used, you should locate it on a separate physical disk from the Windows system disk (where the \Windows folder is located). By doing so, you reduce disk contention because the system disk is also heavily used. This advice extends to Linux/UNIX systems—the swap partition should be located on a separate disk from the Linux/UNIX system files. Also, on a Windows system, you can free up considerable space on the system disk by moving the page file to another volume or disk. You learn where to configure the paging file in Hands-On Project 11-3 and in Challenge Lab 11-1.

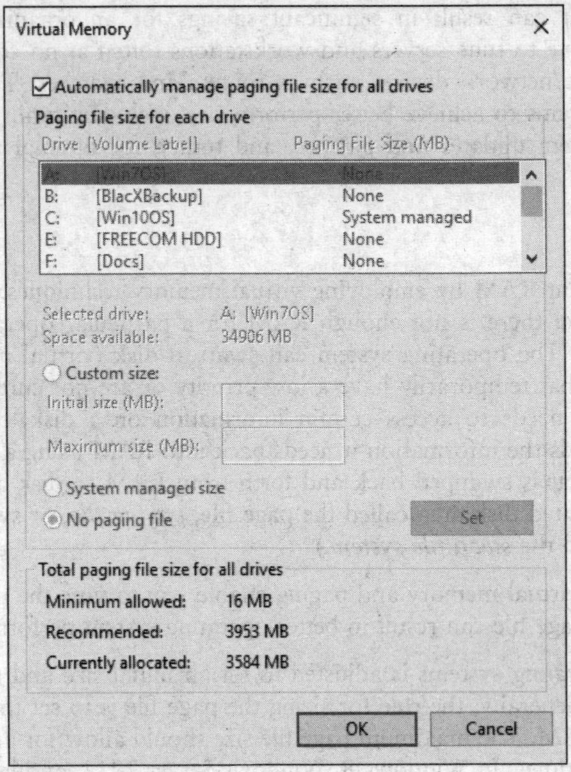


**Figure 11-7** Configuring the paging file in Windows

**TIP**

Windows operating systems also offer Performance Monitor for monitoring paging and many other activities, but a discussion of Performance Monitor is beyond the scope of this chapter. To access Performance Monitor, right-click Start, click Computer Management, click to expand Performance in the left pane, and then click Monitoring Tools.

In UNIX/Linux, you can use the *vmstat* command-line utility to monitor paging. Paging in UNIX/Linux is accomplished with a swap file system, which is automatically created when you install most UNIX/Linux distributions. If a swap file system is not already created, you can use the *mkfs* command in Linux to create it. The swap file system is mounted like any other file system. If it is consistently more than 80 percent full, increase its size. Also, if there is a regularly high rate of swapping, consider spreading the swap space over multiple disks on different controllers.

In Mac OS X, there is no option for turning on or configuring virtual memory because it is always enabled. The use of virtual memory is built into the operating system and is not subject to user intervention.

## Installing Operating System Updates and Patches

One of the most important ways to keep your operating system tuned is by installing system updates issued by the vendor. Problems with an operating system are often not fully discovered until it has been released and used by thousands, or even millions, of users. Once enough problems are discovered and reported, vendors create updates. For example, you can obtain updates by using the Windows Update utility in all Windows operating systems (see Chapter 5). Windows Update requires an Internet connection and downloads updates from Microsoft's Web site. By default, Windows 10 is configured to automatically download and install updates. Restarts are scheduled during the maintenance window, which is usually around 3 a.m. You can configure Windows Update to notify you when a restart is required rather than restarting automatically (see Figure 11-8). An automatic restart may be okay with a client OS, but you should only restart a server when no client applications are using it.

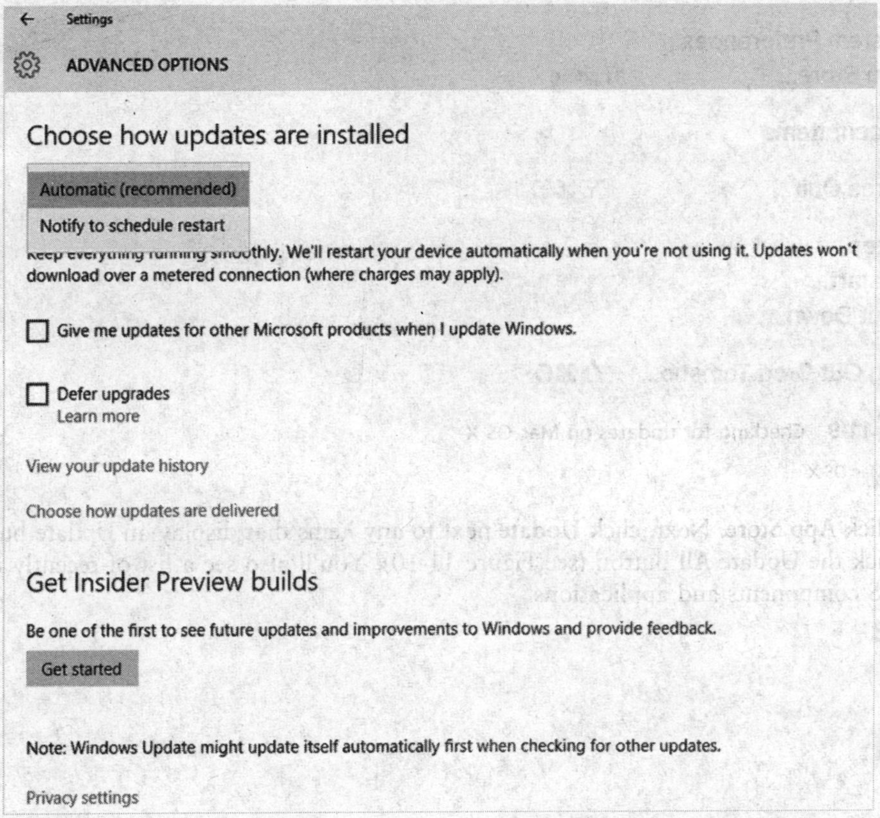


**Figure 11-8** Windows Update

Many Linux distributions with the GNOME desktop have a software update tool that enables you to automatically obtain operating system updates through the Internet. The general steps to start the tool in Fedora Linux with the GNOME desktop are:

1. Click **Activities.**
2. Click **Show Applications.**

3. Click **Software.**
4. Click the **Updates** tab to see if any installed applications or OS files need to be updated.

Mac OS X uses the App Store to deliver updates. As long as the Mac has an Internet connection, the App Store is periodically contacted to look for updates to the OS and installed applications. You can check for updates using the following steps:

1. Click the Apple icon.
2. If any updates are detected, you will see a notification next to App Store (see Figure 11-9).

**Figure 11-9** Checking for updates on Mac OS X

*Source: Mac OS X*

3. Click **App Store.** Next, click **Update** next to any items that display an Update button, or click the **Update All** button (see Figure 11-10). You'll also see a list of recently updated OS components and applications.

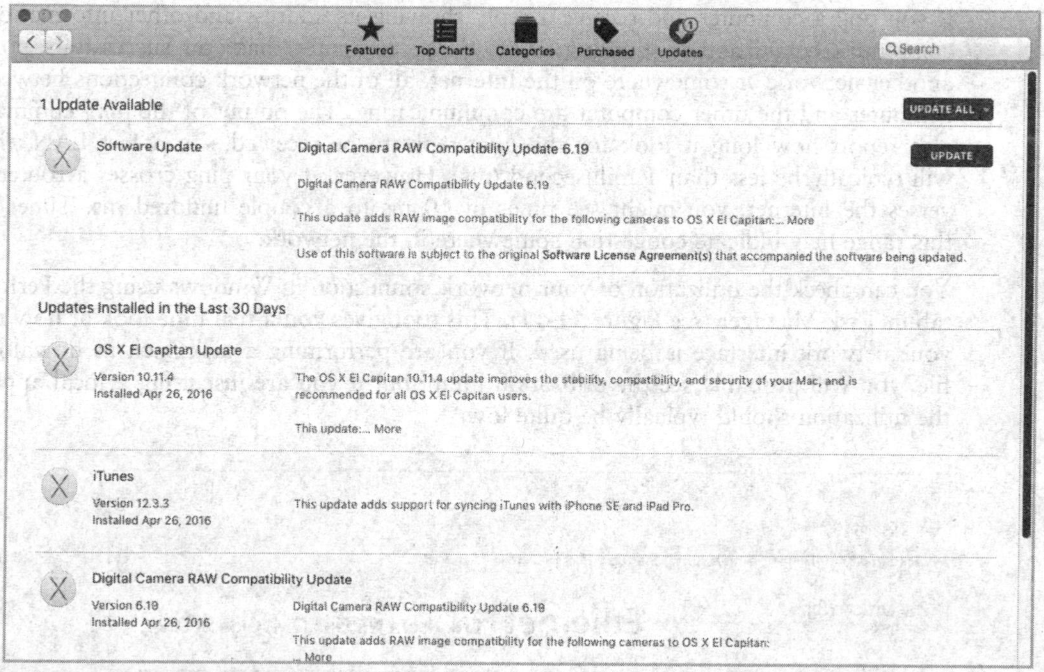


**Figure 11-10** Updating Mac OS X

*Source: Mac OS X*

TIP

Sometimes it is helpful to contact the operating system vendor or an independent support organization for help with a system problem. The representative will ask what service releases, upgrades, or patches you have installed, and may request that you install them as the first step in solving the problem.

## Tuning for Network Communications

Any computer connected to a network should be checked periodically to make sure that its connectivity is optimized. When a network interface card (NIC) is purchased, it should be of high quality and designed for use in the computer's fastest expansion slot, usually a PCIe slot.

Just as operating systems need periodic patches, so do NIC drivers. Check the NIC vendor's Web site occasionally for updated drivers that you can download and use immediately. Another problem with NICs is that they sometimes have problems that cause them to saturate the network with repeated packet broadcasts, called a *broadcast storm*. Network administrators can regularly monitor the network and individual nodes to make sure they are not creating excessive traffic.

## Testing Network Connectivity

Questions often arise about whether the network is working or a particular workstation's network connection is working. Anyone can poll another network device using the *ping* utility, as you learned in Chapter 9. All of the operating systems covered in this book support *ping* as a command-line utility.

If you poll a computer and receive a reply showing its address and other information, your computer's connection is working. Also, if the computer that you successfully poll is on another network or somewhere on the Internet, all of the network connections between your computer and the other computer are communicating. The output of the *ping* command will also report how long it took for the *ping* reply to be received. On a fast LAN, this time will typically be less than 1 millisecond (ms). However, if your ping crosses a router or traverses the Internet, you might see times of 10 ms to a couple hundred ms. Times beyond this range may indicate congestion somewhere in the network.

You can check the utilization of your network connection in Windows using the Performance tab in Task Manager (see Figure 11-11). This tool gives you a real-time look at how much of your network interface is being used. If you are performing a task such as downloading a file, you will probably see the utilization jump, but if you are just using a local application, the utilization should typically be quite low.

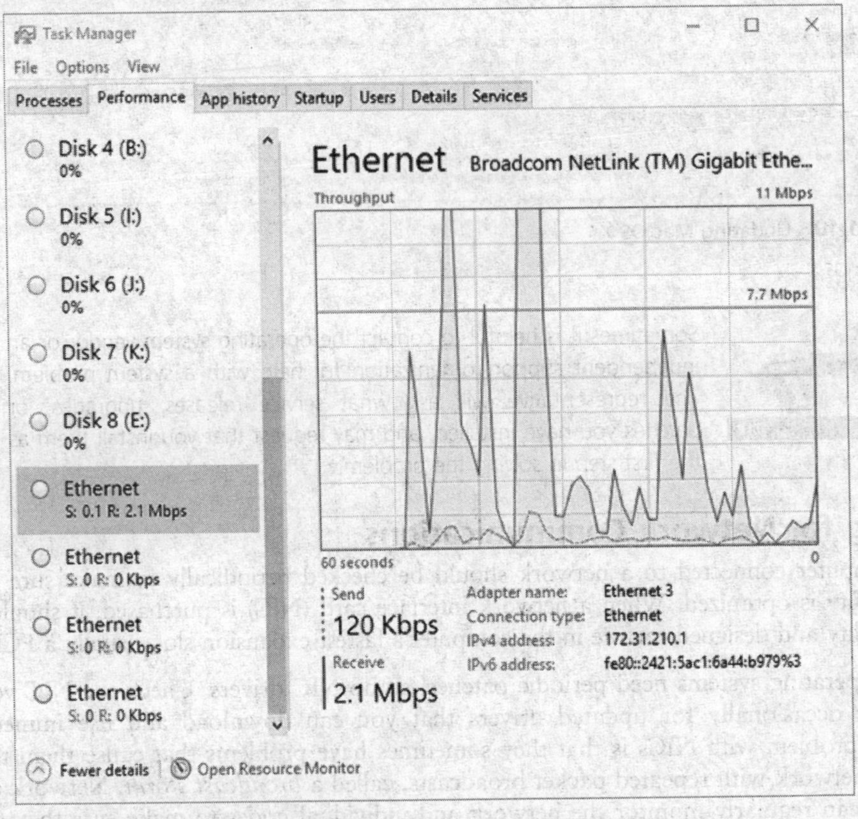


**Figure 11-11** Checking network interface utilization in Windows

To check the utilization of your interface in Linux, you may need to download and install a utility such as *netdiag* or *netwatch*, but you can use a simple command-line utility called *ifstat* that is available in most Linux distributions and provides basic statistics for your network interface. On Mac OS X, you can run Activity Monitor and check the Network tab to see which processes are using network bandwidth and to see basic statistics for the number of packets received and sent.

## Chapter Summary

- Successful file system maintenance is closely linked to a computer's folder structure. On desktop and server operating systems, a well-planned folder structure makes it easy to locate files, update files, share folders and files, back up and archive files, and delete unwanted files.
- The file structure established on a computer should be easy to maintain over the long term. Keeping files in a logical structure means it is easier to identify files that don't belong, that are out of date, or may be causing problems.
- One important practice for maintaining an operating system is to regularly find and delete unused files. Disk space is often at a premium, and there is no reason to leave unused files on a system because they are easy to delete. To find and delete unused files, use the Disk Cleanup tool in Windows, the *find*, *ls*, and *rm* commands in Linux, and the Find utility in Mac OS X.
- Other ways to maintain disks include defragmenting them, moving files to relatively unused disks, finding and repairing disk problems, and setting up RAID. Some operating systems have built-in utilities that can determine if disks are fragmented and then defragment them. Regularly defragmenting disks is an inexpensive method of extending disk life and improving performance. Disk scan and repair tools are another inexpensive way to address disk problems and prevent them from growing more serious. Equalizing the disk load by periodically moving files is an effective way to extend the life of disks. RAID techniques are also frequently used to extend disk life and to protect data when a disk fails.
- An important part of maintaining a system is to make regular backups. Backups can be vital when a hard disk fails or after you delete files you wish you had retained. Backups can also be used to restore drivers or other operating system files that were damaged or overwritten.
- An important consideration for optimizing software installations is to make sure the software is compatible with the computer hardware and operating system. When uninstalling software, use the uninstall options built into the operating system.
- All operating systems should be tuned periodically. Adjusting paging is one way to tune for better performance. Another way is to keep current with operating system patches and updates. Networked systems should be tuned so that NIC drivers are kept current and checked to ensure that no NIC is causing excessive network traffic. TCP/IP-based network systems include the *ping* utility for testing a network connection.

## Key Terms

**binary backup** A technique that backs up the entire contents of one or more disk drives in a binary or image format.

**cookie** A text-based file used by Web sites to obtain information about a user, such as the user's name, the user's password to access the site, and information about how to customize the Web page display.

**defragmentation** The process of removing empty pockets between files and other information on a hard disk drive.

**differential backup** A method that only backs up files that have changed since the last full backup.

**disk striping** A disk storage technique that divides portions of each file over all volumes in a set as a way to minimize wear on individual disks.

**fragmentation** The accumulation of empty pockets of space between files on a disk due to frequent writing, deleting, and modifying of the files and their contents.

**full file-by-file backup** A technique that backs up the entire contents of one or more disk drives, including all folders, subfolders, and files, so that any of these contents can be restored.

**incremental backup** A method that only backs up files that have changed since the last full or incremental backup.

**page file** Also called the *paging file* or *swap file*, an allocated portion of disk storage reserved to supplement RAM when the available RAM is exceeded. See *swap file*.

**service packs** Software "fixes" issued by a vendor to repair software problems, address compatibility issues, and add enhancements.

**surface analysis** A disk diagnostic technique that locates and marks damaged disk areas. Some surface analysis tools are destructive to data because they also format the disk. Other tools can run without altering data, except to move it from a damaged location to one that is not.

**swap file** Also called the *page file*, *paging file*, or *swap file system*, an allocated portion of disk storage reserved to supplement RAM when the available RAM is exceeded. See *page file*.

**virtual memory** Disk storage used when there is not enough RAM for a particular operation or for all processes currently in use.

# Review Questions

1. After you start your Windows 10 computer, you attempt to access your organization's network to open an inventory program, but you can't make a network connection. Which of the following commands tests your computer's ability to connect to the network?
   a. *find net*
   b. *net test*
   c. *ping*
   d. *listen*

2. When examining the contents of the Windows folder in Windows 10, which of the following subfolders would you expect to find? (Choose all that apply.)
   a. sbin
   b. System
   c. etc
   d. System32
3. Your organization's Windows Server 2012 server has 8 GB of RAM but has been running a little slow, so you decide to check the virtual memory configuration. You find that the paging file is located on the C: drive, where Windows is installed. The paging file is about 12 GB. Is there anything you can do to configure the paging file for optimal performance?
   a. Decrease the paging file size to 4 GB.
   b. Move it to another disk.
   c. Increase the paging file size to 24 GB.
   d. No, it is configured optimally.
4. How can you purge a file in Mac OS X?
   a. Send the file to the Trash and then delete it from the Trash.
   b. Right-click the file and click Purge.
   c. Copy the file to another hard drive and then delete it.
   d. Mac OS X files are always purged as soon as they are deleted.
5. You want to check on the size of virtual memory on your Linux computer. Where should you look?
   a. the /vmem folder
   b. the swap file system
   c. the /etc/swapconfig.cnf file
   d. the pagefile.sys file
6. Your Linux workstation runs slowly when you use certain applications. You decide to determine how much virtual memory is used when you run these applications. Which of the following commands enables you to determine virtual memory usage?
   a. *sfiles*
   b. *vmstat*
   c. *netstat*
   d. *vfiles -s*

7. Which of the following utilities in Windows 10 can find and delete temporary files created by programs?
   a. Disk Tracker
   b. Recovery Console
   c. File Manager
   d. Disk Cleanup
8. How do you check for software updates in Mac OS X?
   a. Click the Apple icon and then click App Store.
   b. Click Go and then click System Update.
   c. Click Go, click Utilities, and then click Updates.
   d. Click the Apple icon, click System Preferences, and then click Updates.
9. Which Windows tool lets you monitor paging activity?
   a. Device Manager
   b. Performance Monitor
   c. Disk Management
   d. Storage Spaces
10. In Linux, you are preparing to delete the tprice user account because this user has just left the company. However, before you delete the account, you want to list all files owned by tprice so you can decide which files to keep. What command enables you to view all files owned by the tprice account?
    a. *ls -owner tprice*
    b. *lsuser tprice*
    c. *find / -user tprice*
    d. *scan -owner tprice*
11. Temporary Internet files often have which of the following extensions? (Choose all that apply.)
    a. .html
    b. .cooky
    c. .gif
    d. .htm
12. Which of the following RAID levels involve disk striping? (Choose all that apply.)
    a. level 0
    b. level 1
    c. level 5
    d. level 10

13. How are files stored on the disk when an OS is first installed?
    a. randomly
    b. alphabetically
    c. contiguously
    d. fragmented
14. In Windows operating systems, which of the following methods backs up any files that have changed since the last full or incremental backup?
    a. copy
    b. incremental
    c. daily
    d. differential
15. Which backup scheme requires the fewest tapes to perform a full restore?
    a. full backup plus differential
    b. full backup plus daily
    c. daily backup plus incremental
    d. full backup plus incremental
16. What is the default Windows Update configuration in Windows 10?
    a. manually download, automatic install
    b. automatically download, prompt to install
    c. disabled
    d. automatically download and install
17. When you attempt to access an application in Mac OS X, you see a message that the disk is corrupted. Which of the following tools enables you to examine the disk, find the problem, and attempt to fix it?
    a. Inode Checker
    b. *chkdsk*
    c. Disk First Aid in the Disk Utility
    d. File Checker in the Preferences window
18. Your Windows 10 workstation hard drive seems to be laboring to find files, possibly because you added and deleted hundreds of files without performing any special disk maintenance. What is the most likely problem?
    a. The *defrag* program is not scheduled to run.
    b. The *chkdsk* program is not working properly.
    c. The page file is too small.
    d. Automatic disk cleanup is not working.

19. You use the Internet frequently. What simple step should you perform on a regular basis to maintain your computer?
    a. Tune your Internet browser to automatically shrink all cookies.
    b. Reset the protocol binding order in the Web browser to give priority to HTTP communications because accessing multiple sites can change the binding order.
    c. Check to make sure that your browser's speed is always maintained between 1 Mbps and 20 Mbps.
    d. Use your browser or an operating system utility to regularly delete temporary Internet files.

20. This morning you modified five large data files in your home folder in Linux, and now you want to find and delete the files because you no longer need them. Which of the following commands can you use to list and sort files based on the time they were modified?
    a. *locate -d*
    b. *ls -t*
    c. *rm -m*
    d. *df -d*

# Hands-On Projects

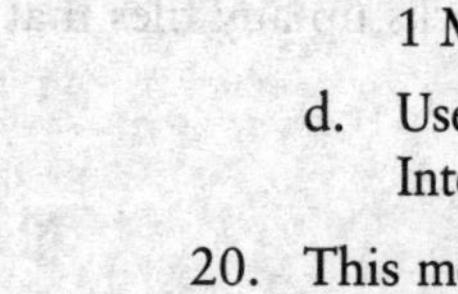


## Project 11-1: Use Disk Cleanup in Windows

In this project, you use the Disk Cleanup tool in Windows to delete temporary Internet files and temporary files created by applications. You need Administrator privileges for this project.

1. Start and log on to your Windows computer.
2. In the search box on the taskbar, type **Disk Cleanup** and then click **Disk Cleanup** in the search results.
3. In the Disk Cleanup: Drive Selection dialog box, be sure that the drive where Windows is installed is selected, and click **OK**.
4. In the Disk Cleanup for (C:) dialog box (see Figure 11-12), click to select the boxes for **Temporary Internet Files** and **Temporary files**. Remove checks from any other boxes. Click **OK**.

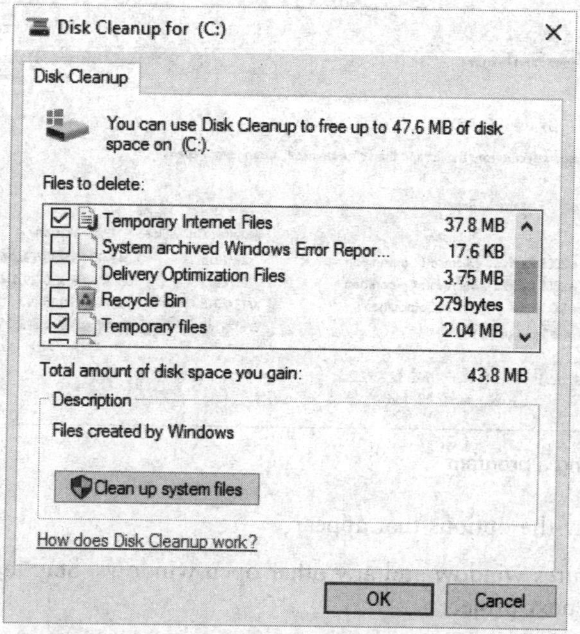


**Figure 11-12** Cleaning up files with Disk Cleanup

5. Click **Delete Files** to verify that you want to delete the files. The Disk Cleanup utility begins. Depending on how many files you're deleting, the process could take a few seconds or several minutes.
6. Stay logged on if you are continuing to the next project.

## Project 11-2: Use Programs and Features in Windows

In this project, you use the Programs and Features tool in Windows to see options for changing or uninstalling a program.

1. Log on to your Windows computer, if necessary. Right-click **Start** and click **Control Panel.**
2. If Control Panel is in Category view, click the **Uninstall a program** link under Programs. If Control Panel is in icon view, click **Programs and Features.**
3. Click a program in the list (see Figure 11-13). Notice that the option bar just above the list of programs displays the options available for the program. Possible options include Uninstall, Change, and Repair.

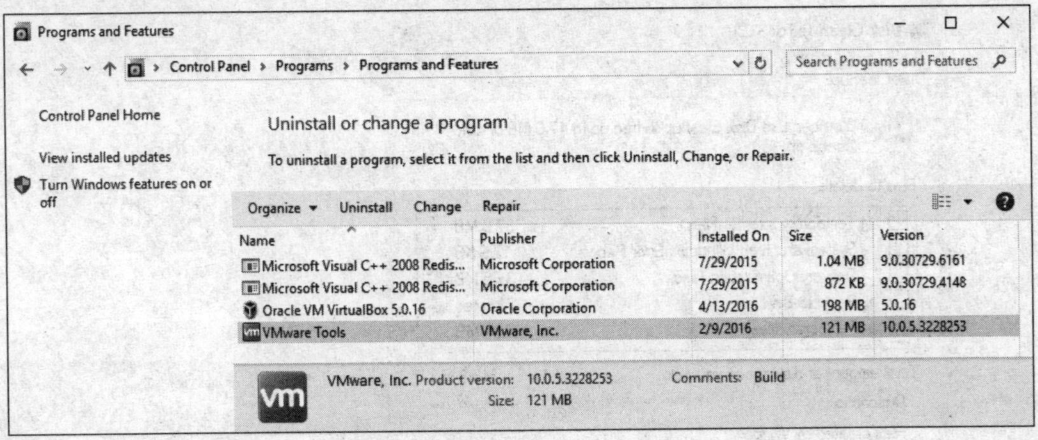


**Figure 11-13** Uninstalling or changing a program

4. Click other programs to view the options that appear.
5. Close the Program and Features window and any other open windows. Stay logged on if you are continuing to the next project.

## Project 11-3: View Virtual Memory Configuration in Windows

In this project, you view the virtual memory configuration in Windows.

1. Log on to your Windows computer, if necessary. Right-click **Start** and click **System.**
2. Click **Advanced system settings** in the left pane.
3. In the System Properties dialog box, click the **Advanced** tab.
4. On the Advanced tab, click **Settings** under the Performance section.
5. Click the **Advanced** tab in the Performance Options dialog box.
6. Under Virtual memory, you can see the total amount of virtual memory that has been allocated. Click the **Change** button.
7. At the bottom of the Virtual Memory dialog box, notice the minimum, recommended, and currently allocated sizes set for virtual memory.
8. Notice the check box (**Automatically manage paging file size for all drives**) at the top of the dialog box. If you cleared this check box, you could make changes to virtual memory, if needed. For example, you could put the page file on a different physical disk to optimize performance. For now, leave the check box selected. Click **Cancel** to close the Virtual Memory dialog box.
9. Click **Cancel** in the Performance Options dialog box and then click **Cancel** in the System Properties dialog box.
10. Close all open windows but stay logged on if you are continuing to the next activity.

HANDS-ON PROJECTS

## Project 11-4: Check Network Utilization in Windows

In this project, you check network utilization in Windows using Task Manager.

1. Log on to Windows, if necessary. Right-click the taskbar and click **Task Manager.**
2. Click **More details,** if necessary, to see more information in the Performance tab. Click the **Performance** tab.
3. In the left pane, click **Ethernet.** In the right pane, you see a graph of network utilization on the Ethernet interface. Create some network activity by opening a Web browser and browsing to some Web sites. You should see activity in the graph. Keep the Web browser window open.
4. To see more details of network usage, click **Open Resource Monitor** at the bottom of the Task Manager window. Click the **Network** tab.
5. The top pane displays processes that are using the network. Your browser should be displayed in the list. Browse to some other Web sites, such as Microsoft.com or Espn.com, to create some network traffic. The graphs in the right pane should show plenty of activity (see Figure 11-14).

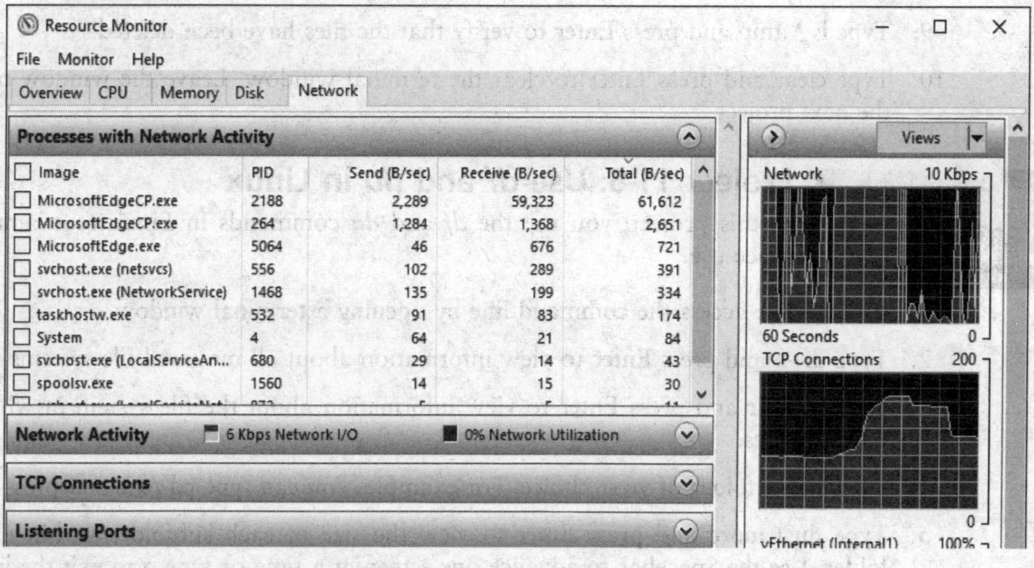

**Figure 11-14** Monitoring network activity with Resource Monitor

6. Close Resource Monitor and Task Manager.
7. Close all open windows and shut down Windows.

## Project 11-5: Delete Files in Linux

In this project, you create a couple of test files and then practice deleting them in Linux. Log on to your account for this project rather than the root account.

1. Start and log on to your Linux computer. Open a terminal window.
2. Create two files that you can practice deleting. First, type **touch practice1.tmp** and press **Enter**. Next, type **touch practice2.tmp** and press **Enter**.
3. Type **ls *.tmp** and press **Enter**. You can see the files you just created.
4. Type **rm *.tmp** and press **Enter**. If prompted, type **Y** and press **Enter** to confirm the files' removal.
5. Type **ls *.tmp** and press **Enter**. No files are found.
6. Create the two files again by entering the commands from Step 2.
7. Type **find / -type f –name "*.tmp"** and press **Enter**. This command finds all files with the .tmp extension in the entire file system. You may see some "access denied" errors as the *find* command attempts to look in folders for which you don't have permission.
8. To delete all files with the .tmp extension, type **find / -type f –name "*.tmp" -delete** and press **Enter**.
9. Type **ls *.tmp** and press **Enter** to verify that the files have been deleted.
10. Type **clear** and press **Enter** to clear the terminal window. Leave the window open for the next project.

## Project 11-6: Use *df* and *du* in Linux

In this project, you use the *df* and *du* commands in Linux to examine disk space use.

1. If necessary, access the command line by opening a terminal window.
2. Type **df -a** and press **Enter** to view information about all mounted file systems.
3. Type **df /var** and press **Enter** to view information about the file system in which that folder resides.
4. Switch to a folder of your choice. For example, you can type **cd /usr** and press **Enter**.
5. Type **du | more** and press **Enter** to view the size of each subfolder within the main folder. Use the Spacebar to advance one screen at a time or type **q** to exit the listing of information.
6. Stay logged on if you are continuing to the next project.

## Project 11-7: Use the *fsck* Command in Linux

In this project, you learn more about the *fsck* command in Linux by reviewing its online documentation.

1. Log on to your Linux computer and open a terminal window, if necessary.
2. Type **man fsck** and press **Enter**.
3. Use the **Spacebar** to scroll forward one page at a time or use the **up** and **down** arrows to scroll up or down one line at a time.
4. Unfortunately, you can't run *fsck* while the file system is mounted, but if you use Linux, you should be familiar with this command in case you need to perform file system maintenance. Press **q** to exit the documentation when you are finished.
5. Close the terminal window and shut down Linux.

## Project 11-8: Perform Disk Maintenance in Mac OS X

In this project, you empty the trash and use Disk First Aid in Mac OS X.

1. Start and log on to your Mac OS X computer. Click the **Trash** icon on the Dock to view its contents.
2. Make sure there are no files you want to salvage from the trash. If you want to salvage files, drag them out of the trash and into the appropriate folder or folders.
3. Click **Finder** on the menu bar.
4. Click **Empty Trash.**
5. Click **Empty Trash** again to confirm that you want to permanently delete the files.

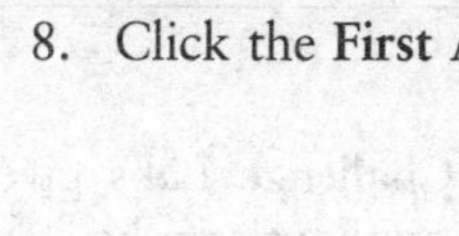


In Mac OS X, the Trash icon appears either as an empty wire basket on the Dock or as a can with papers inside.

6. Click **Go** in the menu bar, click **Utilities,** and double-click **Disk Utility.**
7. Click **Macintosh HD** in the left pane.
8. Click the **First Aid** button at the top of the Disk Utility window (see Figure 11-15).

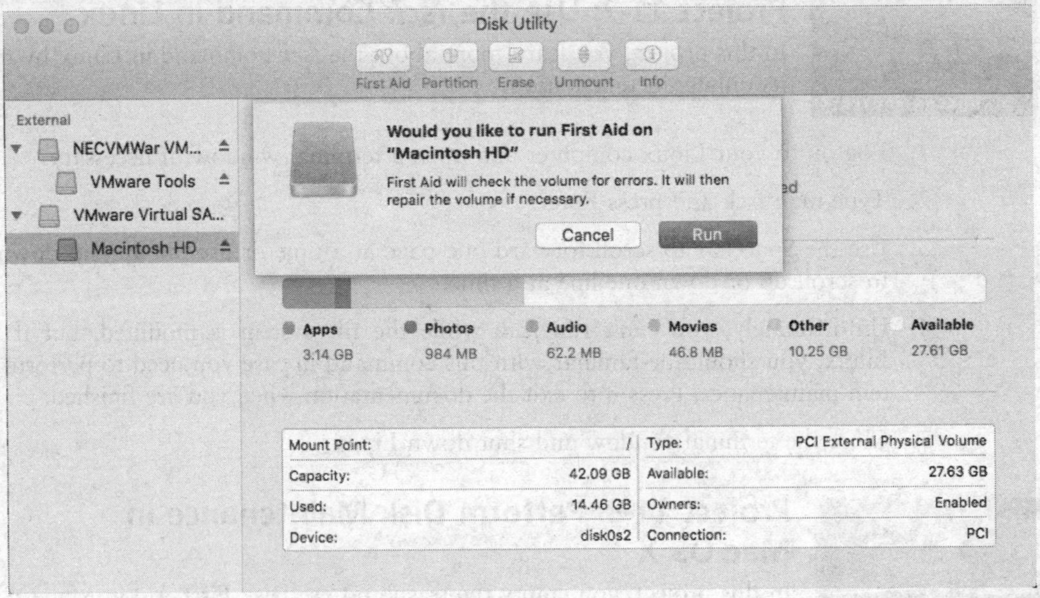


**Figure 11-15** The Disk Utility in Mac OS X running First Aid

*Source: Mac OS X*

9. Click **Run.**
10. Click **Show Details** to see the progress and status.
11. If the disk needs to be repaired, you'll see messages in red and the recommendation to run the Disk Repair utility. If you see this recommendation, click **OK** and then click **Repair Disk.** Otherwise, wait until the verification process is complete and click **Done.**
12. Close all open windows and shut down your computer.

In some cases when disk repair is necessary, the Repair Disk option will not start. In such cases, try starting the disk repair by first booting from the installation DVD and then using Disk Utility from the installation DVD. Another option is to run *fsck* from a terminal window.

# Critical Thinking

The following activities give you critical thinking challenges. Challenge Labs give you an opportunity to use the skills you have learned to perform a task without step-by-step instructions. Case projects offer a practical problem for which you supply a written solution. Not all chapters contain Challenge Labs. There is not always a specific right or wrong answer to these critical thinking exercises. They are intended to encourage you to review the chapter material and delve deeper into the topics you have learned.

# Challenge Labs

## Challenge Lab 11-1: Change Virtual Memory Settings in Windows

In this lab, you will change virtual memory settings on a Windows 10 computer. You want to make your virtual memory a fixed size and, if possible, move it to another physical disk on your computer. Get your instructor's approval if you plan to use classroom computers for this lab. Set the virtual memory to 1.5 times the size of physical RAM and move the page file to a different disk. If you don't have a second disk, move the page file to a different volume. (If you only have one volume, don't move the page file.) Answer the following questions:

- How did you check the amount of RAM installed on your computer?
- What did you have to do before you could change the virtual memory settings?
- What are the advantages of moving the page file to a different disk?

# Case Projects

The National Center for Weather Research (NCWR) is funded by 22 state universities and eight foundations to study weather patterns, forecasting, cloud seeding, and other weather phenomena. NCWR's building has a network consisting of 295 workstations, including systems that run Linux, Mac OS X, and Windows 10. There are also Windows Server 2012/R2 servers on the network. All users have access to the Internet.

## Case Project 11-1: Discuss Options for Additional Storage

More than 50 users who run Windows 10 are certain they need to purchase additional disks because they are nearly out of space. However, the budget is tight and it is important to eliminate unnecessary purchases. What options can you explain to them before their department heads order new disks?

## Case Project 11-2: Repair Disk and File Problems

Your boss hired a new computer professional who formerly worked as a database support specialist in the business office, but who is relatively inexperienced in operating systems. The boss assigned you to train your new colleague. Today you will teach him how to find and repair disk and file problems. Explain the tools available for the following operating systems:

- Linux
- Mac OS X
- Windows 10

## Case Project 11-3: Outline Maintenance Tasks on Mac OS X

The director of publications uses Mac OS X and has been working on so many projects for the past six months that she hasn't had time to perform maintenance tasks. She wants to spend some time tomorrow morning on these tasks. What maintenance tasks do you recommend?

Appendix A

# Operating System Command-Line Commands

**You can accomplish many tasks by using command-line commands in an operating** system, including creating a user account or configuring a network interface card (NIC). Many UNIX/Linux users prefer using commands instead of graphical user interface (GUI) utilities because the commands are so universal and are often quicker to execute. Windows and Mac OS X users often find commands to be powerful, step-saving tools. For example, the Windows *systeminfo* command provides an instant snapshot of the hardware and software used on a computer. The following sections provide tables for quick reference to operating system commands. Two tables are presented for each operating system discussed in this book. For Windows, Fedora/Red Hat Enterprise Linux, and Mac OS X, one table lists general commands and one lists commands that relate to network functions.

## Windows Command Prompt Commands

Table A-1 presents general Command Prompt window commands for Windows versions from XP and later, except as noted in the Description column. Table A-2 presents Command Prompt window commands for network functions in Windows. The following steps explain how to open the Command Prompt window in Windows 8.1 and later versions:

1. Right-click **Start**.
2. Click **Command Prompt** or **Command Prompt (Admin)** if the commands require administrator access.

Starting with Windows Vista, Microsoft introduced a powerful new command-line scripting environment called *PowerShell*. PowerShell allows administrators to manage almost every aspect of the OS environment using the command line and PowerShell scripts. PowerShell is a subject for an entire book and is not covered here, but you can learn more about it at *https://msdn.microsoft.com/en-us/library/ms714469%28v=vs.85%29.aspx*.

You can run many commands by typing them in the search box on the taskbar. However, when you use commands in this way, the Command Prompt window often closes before you can view the results of the command. You can also type *cmd* and press Enter in the search box.

To find out more about a general command when you are using the Command Prompt window, type *help* plus the command, such as *help attrib*, and press Enter. To learn more about a network command, such as the *net* command, type *net /?* and press Enter, or type the full command set and */?*, such as *net accounts /?*, and press Enter. To leave the Command Prompt window, type *exit* and press Enter.

The following is only a partial list of commands available in Windows. Many more are available, especially on a Windows Domain Controller. For a full list, see *https://technet.microsoft.com/en-us/library/cc754340%28v=ws.11%29.aspx*.

**Table A-1 Windows general commands**

| Command | Description |
|---|---|
| *assoc* | Used to view and change file associations in Windows. |
| *at* | Enables you to schedule one or more programs to run at a designated date and time. This command has been replaced by *schtasks* in Windows 8 and later versions. |
| *attrib* | Enables you to view the attributes set for a file and to change one or more attributes. |
| *bcdedit* | Manages the boot configuration data (BCD) store. |
| *break* | Causes the system to check for a break key only during standard operations, such as while making input or output (*break off*) or during all program execution options (*break on*). |
| *cacls* | Enables you to view the attributes set for a file and to change one or more attributes. |
| *call* | Enables you to call a batch program from another one. |
| *cd* or *chdir* | Enables you to change to a different folder or to view the name of the current folder. |
| *chcp* | Used to view the currently active code page number or to set a different code page number. |
| *chkdsk* | Used to report the disk file system statistics and to correct file system errors such as lost clusters (for FAT and NTFS). |
| *chkntfs* | Used to report the disk file system statistics and to correct file system errors such as lost clusters (for NTFS). |
| *cls* | Clears the information currently displayed on the screen. |
| *cmd* | Used to start a new NT DOS Virtual Machine (NTDVM) session or new command-line session. |
| *color* | Sets up the foreground and background screen colors. |
| *comp* or *fc* | Enables you to compare the information in two files or in two sets of files to determine the differences in content. |
| *compact* | Compresses files and subfolders within a folder or removes the compression attribute. |
| *convert* | Converts a FAT-formatted volume to NTFS at the time a server is booted. |
| *copy* | Copies files from one disk location to another. |
| *date* | Enables you to view the date and to reset it. |
| *del* or *erase* | Deletes specified files on a volume. |
| *dir* | Lists files and subfolders within a folder. |

**Table A-1 Windows general commands (*continued*)**

| Command | Description |
|---|---|
| *diskcomp* | Checks the contents of one floppy disk against the contents of another. This command is no longer available starting with Windows 8. |
| *diskcopy* | Copies information on a floppy disk to another floppy disk. This command is no longer available starting with Windows 8. |
| *diskperf* | Installs, starts, or stops the Performance Monitor/System Monitor disk counters. |
| *doskey* | Starts the recall of previously used MS-DOS commands and is used to create command macros. |
| *driverquery* | Displays the current device driver status along with the properties. |
| *echo* | Shows an associated message or turns screen messages on or off. |
| *exit* | Used to close the Command Prompt session. |
| *find* | Used to find a designated set of characters contained in one or more files. |
| *findstr* | Used to find one or more sets of characters within a set of files. |
| *format* | Formats a disk. |
| *fsutil* | Configures and displays the file system properties. |
| *ftype* | Provides detailed information about file associations and is used to change associations so as to link them with a designated program. |
| *goto* | Moves to a labeled line in the batch program. |
| *gpresult* | Displays group policy information. |
| *graftabl* | Displays characters and code-page switching for a color display monitor. This command is no longer available starting with Windows 8. |
| *help* | Provides a list of the Windows command-line commands and is used to display help about a particular command. |
| *icacls* | Allows you to display, modify, back up, and restore ACLs (Access Control Lists). |
| *if* | Performs conditional processing in a batch routine. |
| *keyb* | Enables you to set the keyboard language or layout (only available in Windows XP/Windows Server2003). |
| *label* | Modifies the label on a disk volume. |
| *md* or *mkdir* | Used to set up a new folder. |
| *mklink* | Sets up symbolic and hard links (not available in Windows XP). |
| *mode* | Sets up parameters for a device or a communications port. |
| *more* | Used to limit the display to one screen at a time so information does not rush by faster than it can be read. |
| *move* | Enables you to move files from one disk location to another on the same volume. |
| *openfiles* | Displays, queries, and disconnects open files. |
| *path* | Used to establish the path or list of folders to search in order to run a program or command. |
| *pause* | Suspends processing of a batch file. |
| *popd* | Deletes a specified drive letter that was temporarily created by *pushd*. |
| *print* | Prints a designated file. |
| *prompt* | Modifies the format of the command prompt shown in the Command Prompt window. |
| *pushd* | Creates a temporary drive letter to a network resource. |
| *rd* or *rmdir* | Deletes a folder or subfolder. |
| *recover* | Enables you to try recovering files and data from a damaged or unreadable disk. |
| *reg, regedit,* or *regedt32* | Starts the GUI-based Registry editor. |

(*continues*)

**Table A-1 Windows general commands (*continued*)**

| Command | Description |
|---|---|
| *ren* or *rename* | Renames a file or a group of files. |
| *replace* | Compares files in two disks or folders and synchronizes the files in one to those on another. |
| *robocopy* | Utility to copy files and trees (available for Windows XP in the Windows Resource Kit). |
| *sc* | Configures and displays services. |
| *schtasks* | Schedules commands to run. |
| *set* | Shows a list of currently set environment variables and is used to modify those variables. |
| *setlocal* | Used to start command process extensions via a batch file, such as for detecting error-level information. |
| *shift* | Shifts the position of replaceable parameters in batch files. |
| *shutdown* | Allows for shutdown of the computer. |
| *sort* | Sorts lines input into a file that is written to the screen or sent to a printer from a file. |
| *start* | Starts a new Command Prompt window in which to run a program or a command. |
| *subst* | Used to link a path or volume with a designated drive letter. |
| *systeminfo* | Provides a wealth of information about hardware and software (not available in Windows 2000). |
| *taskkill* | Stops a task from running. |
| *tasklist* | Displays all running tasks. |
| *time* | Used to view the time of day and to reset it. |
| *title* | Modifies the title in the title bar of the Command Prompt window. |
| *tree* | Used to show a graphic of the folder and subfolder tree structure. |
| *type* | Shows a file's contents on the screen or sends the contents to a file. |
| *ver* | Shows the current version of the operating system. |
| *verify* | Instructs the operating system to verify that each file is accurately written to disk at the time it is created, copied, moved, or updated. |
| *vol* | Used to view the volume label, if there is one, and the volume serial number. |
| *wmic* | Displays WMI (Windows Management Instrumentation) information in an interactive command shell. |
| *xcopy* | Designed as a fast copy program for files, folders, and subfolders. |

TIP

A very useful command called *msconfig* starts the graphical System Configuration utility, which enables you to configure files that automatically run when the operating system boots, specify which programs to run at startup, and enable or disable services. You can start *msconfig* from the command line or a Run dialog box.

**Table A-2 Windows network commands**

| Command | Description |
|---|---|
| *ipconfig* | Displays information about the TCP/IP setup. |
| *nbtstat* | Shows the server and domain names registered to the network (used only on server versions). |
| *net accounts* | Used to change account policy settings and to synchronize BDCs (Backup Domain Controllers). |
| *net computer* | Adds or removes a computer in a domain. |

**Table A-2 Windows network commands (*continued*)**

| Command | Description |
|---|---|
| *net config* | Shows the started services that can be configured from this command, such as the Server and Workstation services. |
| *net continue* | Resumes a service that has been paused. |
| *net file* | Shows the currently open shared files and file locks and is used to close designated files or to remove file locks. |
| *net group* | Shows the existing global groups and is used to modify those groups. |
| *net help* | Displays help information for the *net* command. |
| *net helpmsg* | Used to determine the meaning of a numeric network error message. |
| *net localgroup* | Shows the existing local groups and is used to modify those groups. |
| *net name* | Used to display, add, or remove computer names that can participate in the Messenger service. |
| *net pause* | Pauses a service. |
| *net print* | Used to view and manage queued print jobs by computer, share name, and job number. |
| *net send* | Sends a message to designated users or to all users currently connected to the server. |
| *net session* | Shows the users currently connected to the server and is used to disconnect designated user sessions or all user sessions. |
| *net share* | Used to create, delete, or show information about a shared resource. |
| *net start* | Shows the started services or is used to start a designated service. |
| *net statistics* | Shows the accumulated statistics about the server or workstation service. |
| *net stop* | Stops a network service on a server. |
| *net time* | Used to synchronize the server's clock with that of another computer in the same domain or in a different domain, or to view the time set on another computer in the same domain or in a different domain. |
| *net use* | Shows information about shared resources or is used to configure, connect, and disconnect shared resources. |
| *net user* | Used to view, add, or modify a user account set up on the server or in a domain. |
| *net view* | Presents a list of domains, the computers and servers in a domain, and all resources shared by a computer in a domain. |
| *netsh* | Allows you to display and modify the network configuration. |
| *netstat* | Used to display information about the Transmission Control Protocol/Internet Protocol (TCP/IP) session at the server. |
| *nslookup* | Queries information on Domain Name System (DNS) servers. |
| *ping* | Used to poll another TCP/IP node to verify that you can communicate with it. |
| *tracert* | Used to view the number of hops and other routing information on the path to the specified server or host. |

# Linux Commands

The commands presented in Table A-3 are general Linux commands, and the commands in Table A-4 are network-related commands. If you are using the GNOME interface in Fedora or Red Hat Enterprise Linux, open a terminal window using the following steps:

1. Click **Activities.**
2. Click **Show Applications.**
3. Click **Utilities** and then click **Terminal.**

To close the window, type *exit* and then press Enter. To access documentation for any of these commands, type *man* and the command, such as *man at*, and press Enter. Press Enter to advance through lines in the documentation or press the Spacebar to view pages. Type *q* in the text window to leave it and return to the normal command prompt. Another way to find information about a command is to type *info* plus the command, such as *info at*, and press Enter. Press Enter or the Spacebar to read the information and then press *q* to exit.

Not all commands are available in all installations of Linux. For example, *lpr* and related commands are only available if the *lpr* package is installed. In addition, other commands will be available depending on the packages installed on the system.

**Table A-3 Linux commands**

| Command | Description |
|---|---|
| *at* | Runs a command or script at a given time. |
| *atq* | Shows the jobs that are scheduled to run. |
| *atrm* | Removes a job that is scheduled to run. |
| *awk* | Finds and replaces text in a file. |
| *batch* | Runs a command or script and is really a subset of the *at* command that takes you to the *at>* prompt if you type only *batch* (in Red Hat Enterprise Linux and Fedora, you should run this command when the system load is at an acceptable level). |
| *cat* | Displays the contents of a file to the screen. |
| *cd* | Changes to another directory. |
| *cfdisk* | Partitions and verifies a hard disk. |
| *chgrp* | Changes group ownership of a file. |
| *chmod* | Controls file security. |
| *chown* | Changes file ownership. |
| *chsh* | Sets your login shell. |
| *clear* | Clears the screen. |
| *cmp* | Used to compare two files. |
| *cp* | Copies a file to another directory; you can rename the file at the same time. |
| *cpio* | Copies and backs up files to archive them on tape or disk. |
| *crontab* | Schedules a command to run at a specific time. |
| *date* | Displays the date and time. |
| *df* | Shows a report of how the disk space is used. |
| *du* | Displays file statistics for a directory and its subdirectories. |
| *dump* | Backs up files. |
| *echo* | Displays a message on the screen. |
| *fdisk* | Formats and partitions a disk. |
| *file* | Displays the file type. |
| *find* | Finds specific files. |
| *fsck* | Performs a verification of the file system. |
| *grep* | Searches for a particular string of characters in a file. |
| *groupadd* | Creates a new group. |
| *groupdel* | Deletes an existing group. |

**Table A-3 Linux commands (*continued*)**

| Command | Description |
|---|---|
| *groupmod* | Modifies an existing group. |
| *groups* | Prints the names of groups for a user. |
| *info* | Displays information and documentation about a command or a utility. |
| *kill* | Stops a process. |
| *less* | Shows the contents of a file, and offers the ability to go back or move ahead in the file. |
| *ln* | Creates symbolic file links. |
| *locate* | Finds a file. |
| *lpd* | Configures a printer. |
| *lpq* | Checks a print queue. |
| *lpr* | Prints a file. |
| *lprm* | Removes print jobs from the queue. |
| *ls* | Lists the contents of a directory. |
| *man* | Displays documentation in Linux. |
| *mkdir* | Creates a directory. |
| *mkfs* | Creates a file system (but requires more parameters than *newfs*). |
| *more* | Displays text in a file one screen at a time. |
| *mount* | Lists the disks currently mounted; also mounts file systems and devices (such as a CD-ROM). |
| *mv* | Moves a file to a different directory. |
| *newfs* | Creates a new file system. |
| *passwd* | Used to change a password. |
| *paste* | Merges lines of a file. |
| *pr* | Formats a file into pages or columns for printing. |
| *printenv* | Prints environment variables that are already set up. |
| *ps* | Shows currently running processes. |
| *pwck* | Checks the /etc/passwd and /etc/shadow files to make sure password authentication entries are valid. |
| *pwd* | Shows the directory you are in. |
| *restore* | Restores files (from a dump). |
| *rm* | Removes a file or directory. |
| *rmdir* | Deletes a directory that is empty. |
| *sfdkisk* | Provides information about a partition and can be used to create a partition. |
| *shutdown* | Shuts down Linux. |
| *sort* | Sorts the contents of a text file. |
| *swapon/swapoff* | Turns page file devices on or off. |
| *sync* | Forces information in memory to be written to disk. |
| *tar* | Archives files. |
| *top* | Shows a report of the main, current processes engaging the central processing unit (CPU). |
| *touch* | Creates an empty file. |
| *umount* | Dismounts a file system. |
| *uname* | Shows information about the operating system. |
| *useradd* | Configures a new user account. |
| *userdel* | Removes an existing user account. |

(*continues*)

**Table A-3** Linux commands (*continued*)

| Command | Description |
|---|---|
| *usermod* | Modifies an existing user account. |
| *users* | Lists currently logged-in users. |
| *vmstat* | Displays a report about virtual memory use. |
| *whereis* | Locates information about a specific file, such as a program. |
| *who* | Shows who is logged on. |

**Table A-4** Linux network commands

| Command | Description |
|---|---|
| *finger* | Provides information about a user. |
| *ftp* | Enables file transfers. |
| *ifconfig* | Sets up a network interface. |
| *ipchains* | Manages a firewall. This command has largely been replaced by *system-config-firewall* on most modern Linux systems. |
| *netstat* | Shows network connection information. |
| *nfsstat* | Shows statistics for Network File System (NFS) file upload and download activity. |
| *nslookup* | Queries information on Domain Name System (DNS) servers. |
| *ping* | Polls another TCP/IP node to verify that you can communicate with it. |
| *rcp* | Copies files between two computers. |
| *route* | Displays routing table information and can be used to configure routing. |
| *showmount* | Shows clients that have mounted volumes on an NFS server. |
| *traceroute* | Traces the route to the host. |
| *who* | Shows who is logged on. |
| *wvdial* | Controls a Point-to-Point Protocol (PPP)-based modem dialer. |

# Mac OS X Commands

The Mac OS X kernel (also called Darwin, the open source core of OS X) is based on Berkeley Software Distribution (BSD) UNIX, which means that you can access a terminal window and execute UNIX commands. To open the Mac OS X terminal window:

1. Make sure Finder is open or click the Finder icon in the Dock.
2. Click **Go** in the menu bar.
3. Click **Utilities**.
4. Double-click **Terminal**.

Tables A-5 and A-6 list commands that you can use in the Mac OS X terminal window. Notice that these commands are nearly identical to those available in Linux, including the use of *man* to read manual pages and *info* to learn more about a command.

**Table A-5 Mac OS X commands**

| Command | Description |
|---|---|
| *awk* | Finds and replaces text within a file. |
| *cat* | Displays the contents of a file to the screen. |
| *cd* | Changes to another directory. |
| *chgrp* | Changes group ownership of a file. |
| *chmod* | Controls file security. |
| *chown* | Changes file ownership. |
| *chsh* | Sets your login shell. |
| *clear* | Clears the screen. |
| *cmp* | Compares two files. |
| *cp* | Copies a file to another directory; you can rename the file at the same time. |
| *date* | Displays the date and time. |
| *df* | Shows a report of how the disk space is used. |
| *dump* | Backs up files. |
| *edquota* | Edits disk quotas associated with user accounts. |
| *fdisk* | Formats and partitions a disk. |
| *file* | Displays the file type. |
| *find* | Finds specific files. |
| *fsck* | Performs a verification of the file system. |
| *grep* | Looks for a string of characters in a file. |
| *groups* | Displays groups to which a user belongs. |
| *kill* | Stops a process. |
| *less* | Shows the contents of a file and offers the ability to go back or move ahead in the file. |
| *ln* | Creates symbolic file links. |
| *locate* | Finds a file. |
| *lpq* | Checks a print queue. |
| *lpr* | Prints a file. |
| *lprm* | Removes print jobs from the queue. |
| *ls* | Lists the contents of a directory. |
| *man* | Displays documentation. |
| *mkdir* | Creates a directory. |
| *more* | Displays text in a file one screen at a time. |
| *mount* | Lists the disks currently mounted; also mounts file systems and devices (such as a CD-ROM). |
| *mv* | Moves a file to a different directory. |
| *newfs* | Creates a new file system. |
| *open* | Opens a file or folder. |
| *passwd* | Changes a password. |
| *pr* | Formats a file into pages or columns for printing. |
| *printenv* | Prints environment variables that are already set up. |
| *ps* | Shows currently running processes. |
| *pwd* | Displays the directory you are in. |
| *quota* | Displays the disk quota for users. |
| *quotacheck* | Verifies the disk quota files, including reporting disk usage. |

**Table A-5 Mac OS X commands (*continued*)**

| Command | Description |
|---|---|
| *quotaon/quotaoff* | Enables or disables disk quotas. |
| *rcp* | Performs a remote copy. |
| *repquota* | Makes a report of disk quotas. |
| *restore* | Restores files (from a dump). |
| *rm* | Removes a file or directory. |
| *rmdir* | Deletes a directory that is empty. |
| *scp* | Uses a secure version of ftp or rcp (remote copy procedure). |
| *screencapture* | Captures the screen image. |
| *sort* | Sorts the contents of a text file. |
| *ssh* | Uses a secure version of ftp. |
| *sync* | Forces information in memory to be written to disk. |
| *tar* | Archives files. |
| *telnet* | Remotely connects to another computer. |
| *top* | Shows a report of the main, current processes engaging the CPU. |
| *touch* | Creates an empty file. |
| *umount* | Dismounts a file system. |
| *uname* | Shows information about the operating system. |
| *uptime* | Displays how long the system has been running. |
| *vm_stat* | Displays a report about virtual memory use. |
| *whereis* | Locates a specific file. |
| *who* | Shows who is logged on. |

**Table A-6 Mac OS X network commands**

| Command | Description |
|---|---|
| *curl* | Transfers data from one server to another. |
| *finger* | Provides information about a user. |
| *ftp* | Enables file transfers. |
| *ifconfig* | Used to set up a network interface. |
| *netstat* | Shows network connection information. |
| *networksetup* | Sets up and modifies network and system preferences. |
| *nfsstat* | Shows statistics for NFS file upload and download activity. |
| *nslookup* | Queries information on DNS servers. |
| *ping* | Polls another TCP/IP node to verify that you can communicate with it. |
| *route* | Displays routing table information and can be used to configure routing. |
| *showmount* | Shows clients that have mounted volumes on an NFS server. |
| *traceroute* | Traces the route to the host. |
| *who* | Shows who is logged on. |

# Glossary

**3D printer** A printer that uses an additive process to create one layer at a time of a three-dimensional object.

**8.3 filenames** An older filename format in which the name of the file can be up to eight characters long, followed by a period and an extension of three characters. See also *extension.*

**Accelerated Graphics Port (AGP)** A bus standard that has been replaced by the PCI Express or PCIe standard.

**access point (AP)** A wireless device that serves as the central connection point of a wireless LAN and mediates communication between wireless computers.

**activate** To register your copy of a Windows operating system, starting with the Windows XP version. Without this activation, you can only run your operating system for a very brief time.

**Active Directory** The directory service used by Windows servers; a Windows Server installable service that consists of a database of computers, users, shared printers, shared folders, and other network resources and resource groupings used to manage a network and enable users to quickly find a particular resource.

**active partition** The logical portion of a hard disk drive that is currently being used to store data. In a PC system, the partition that contains the bootable operating system.

**ActiveX** An internal programming standard that allows various software running under the Windows operating system to communicate with Windows and other programs.

**address bus** An internal communications pathway inside a computer that specifies the source and target address for memory reads and writes.

**address space** The number of addresses available in an IP network number that can be assigned to hosts.

**advanced intelligent tape (AIT)** A tape drive that has an erasable memory chip and a capacity of up to 1.3 TB.

**alias** In the Macintosh file system, a feature that presents an icon representing an executable file. Equivalent to the UNIX/Linux link and the Windows shortcut.

**allocation block** In the Macintosh file system, a division of hard disk data, equivalent to the Windows disk cluster. Each Macintosh volume is divided into $2^{16}$ (65,535) individual units.

**alpha software** An early development version of software in which there are likely to be bugs, and not all of the anticipated functionality is present. Alpha software is usually tested only by a select few users to identify major problems and the need for new or different features before the software is tested by a broader audience in the beta stage.

**Application layer** Layer 7 in the OSI model, which provides interfaces that enable applications to request and receive network services. See also *Open Systems Interconnection (OSI) reference model.*

**application programming interface (API)** Functions or programming features in an operating system that programmers can use for network links, links to messaging services, or interfaces to other systems.

**application software** A word processor, spreadsheet, database, computer game, or other type of application that a user runs on a computer. Application software consists of computer code that is formatted so the computer or its operating system can translate the code into a specific task, such as writing a document.

**arithmetic logic unit (ALU)** A component of a CPU that executes instructions.

**authentication** The process of identifying who has access to the network. The most common form of authentication is a logon with a username and password.

**authorization** The process of granting or denying an authenticated user's access to network resources.

**automatic private IP addressing (APIPA)** A private range of IP addresses assigned to an APIPA-enabled computer automatically when an IP address is requested via DHCP but no DHCP server responds to the request. See also *Dynamic Host Configuration Protocol (DHCP).*

**backplane** A connection system that uses a printed circuit board instead of traditional cables to carry signals.

**backup** A process of copying files from a computer system to another medium, such as a tape, another hard drive, a removable drive, or a DVD/CD-ROM.

**backward compatibility** The ability of features from an older chip to function on a newer chip.

**bad clusters** On a hard disk drive, areas of the surface that cannot be used to safely store data. Bad clusters are usually identified by the *format* command or one of the hard drive utilities, such as *chkdsk* or *fsck.*

**bare-metal virtualization** A system in which the hypervisor implements OS virtualization by running directly on the host computer's hardware and controls and monitors guest OSs. See also *virtualization.*

**basic disk** A traditional Windows or DOS disk arrangement in which the disk is partitioned into primary and extended partitions. A basic disk can't hold volumes spanning multiple disks or be part of a RAID.

**basic input/output system (BIOS)** Low-level program code that conducts basic hardware and software communications inside the computer. A computer's BIOS basically resides between computer hardware and the higher-level operating system, such as UNIX or Windows.

**batch file** A text file that contains a list of commands you ordinarily type at the command prompt.

**batch processing** A computing style frequently employed by large systems. A request for a series of processes is submitted to the computer; information is displayed or printed when the batch is complete. Batches might include the processing for all of the checks submitted to a bank for a day, or for all of the purchases in a wholesale inventory system, for example. Compare to *sequential processing*.

**Beginner's All-purpose Symbolic Instruction Code (BASIC)** An English-like computer programming language originally designed as a teaching tool, but which evolved into a useful and relatively powerful development language.

**Berkeley Software Distribution (BSD)** A variant of the UNIX operating system upon which a large proportion of today's UNIX software is based.

**beta software** During software development, software that has successfully passed the alpha test stage. Beta testing may involve dozens, hundreds, or even thousands of people, and may be conducted in multiple stages: beta 1, beta 2, beta 3, and so on.

**binary backup** A technique that backs up the entire contents of one or more disk drives in a binary or image format.

**blade enclosure** A large box with slots for blade servers; the box also provides cooling fans, electrical power, connection to a shared monitor and pointing device, and even network connectivity. The actual design depends on the manufacturer.

**blade server** A server unit that looks like a card that fits into a blade enclosure. Blade servers are intended to save space. See *blade enclosure*.

**block allocation** A hard disk configuration scheme in which the disk is divided into logical blocks, which in turn are mapped to sectors, heads, and tracks.

**block device** In the UNIX/Linux file system, a device that is divided or configured into logical blocks. See also *raw device*.

**block special file** In UNIX/Linux, a file used to manage random access devices that handle blocks of data, including DVD/CD-ROM drives, hard disk drives, tape drives, and other storage devices.

**boot block** The UNIX/Linux and Mac OS X equivalent of the Windows Master Boot Record (MBR), the area of the hard disk that stores partition information for the disk. For example, on a Mac-formatted disk, the first two sectors are boot blocks that identify the filing system, the names of important system files, and other important information. See also *volume information block*.

**boot volume** The volume where the \Windows folder is located—usually the C drive, but this location is not mandatory. The boot volume is also referred to as the *boot partition*.

**bus** A path or channel between a computer's CPU and the devices it manages, such as memory and I/O devices.

**cache controller** Internal computer hardware that manages the data going into and loaded from the computer's cache memory.

**cache memory** Special computer memory that temporarily stores data used by the CPU. Cache memory is physically close to the CPU and is faster than standard system memory, enabling faster retrieval and processing time.

**catalog b-tree** In the Macintosh file system, a list of all files on a given volume. Similar to a folder in the Windows file system.

**CD-ROM File System (CDFS)** A 32-bit file system used on CD-ROMs and DVDs.

**character special file** An I/O management file in UNIX/Linux used to handle byte-by-byte streams of data, such as through a USB connection, including printers and network communications.

**clean installation** An OS installation on a computer that either has no existing OS or an OS that is overwritten by the installation.

**client** The term used to describe an OS designed mainly to access network resources, a computer's primary role in a network (running user applications and accessing network resources), and software that requests network resources from servers.

**client/server systems** A computer hardware and software design in which different portions of an application execute on different computers, or on different components of a single computer. Typically, client software supports user I/O and server software conducts database searches, manages printer output, and the like.

**cloud computing** A networking model in which data, applications, and processing power are managed by servers on the Internet; users of these resources pay for what they use rather than for the equipment and software needed to provide resources.

**cloud storage** A storage paradigm in which an individual's or company's storage is hosted by a third party and accessed over the Internet.

**cluster** In Windows-based file systems, a logical block of information on a disk containing one or more sectors. Also called an *allocation unit*.

**clustering** The ability to share computing load and resources by linking two or more discrete computer systems (servers) to function as though they are one.

**command-line interface** An interface that enables the user to display a command line from which to enter commands. These interfaces include the Command Prompt window in Windows operating systems and the terminal window in Linux and Mac OS X.

**compiler** A computer program that takes a high-level language like C# or Java and turns it into assembly code that is executed by the CPU.

**complementary metal oxide semiconductor (CMOS)** A type of memory that stores a computer's BIOS configuration. A CMOS chip uses a low-power memory technology that is powered by a small battery.

**Complex Instruction Set Computing (CISC)** A computer CPU architecture in which processor components are reconfigured to conduct different operations as required. Such computer designs require many instructions and more complex instructions than other designs. Compare to *Reduced Instruction Set Computing (RISC)*.

**Component Object Model (COM)** Standards that enable a software object, such as a graphic, to be linked from one software component to another one.

**computer program** A series of instructions executed by the computer's CPU.

**control bus** An internal communications pathway that keeps the CPU informed of the status of particular computer resources and devices, such as memory and disk drives.

**control unit (CU)** A component of a CPU that provides timing and coordination between the other parts of the CPU, such as the arithmetic logic unit, registers, and system bus.

**cookie** A text-based file used by Web sites to obtain information about a user, such as the user's name, the user's password to access the site, and information about how to customize the Web page display.

**cooperative multitasking** A computer hardware and software design in which the operating system temporarily hands off control to an application and waits for the application to return control to the operating system. Compare to *preemptive multitasking*.

**core** The part of a processor used to read and execute instructions.

**creator codes** Hidden file characteristics in the Macintosh file system that indicate the program (software application) that created the file. See *type code*.

**credentials** A username and password or another form of identity used to access a computer.

**data bus** An internal communications pathway that carries data between the CPU and memory locations.

**data fork** The portion of a file in the Macintosh file system that stores the variable data associated with the file. Data fork information might include word-processing data, spreadsheet information, and so on.

**Data Link layer** Layer 2 in the OSI model, which is responsible for managing access to the network medium and delivery of data frames from sender to receiver or from sender to an intermediate device, such as a router. See also *Open Systems Interconnection (OSI) reference model*.

**default groups** Special groups with rights already assigned; these groups are created during installation in a Windows environment.

**defragmentation** The process of removing empty pockets between files and other information on a hard disk drive.

**defragmenter** A tool that rearranges data on a disk in a continuous fashion, ridding the disk of scattered open clusters.

**desktop operating system** A computer operating system that is typically installed on a PC, usually used by one person at a time, and may or may not be connected to a network. Also called a *client operating system*.

**device driver** Computer software designed to provide the operating system and application software access to specific computer hardware.

**device special file** A file used in UNIX and Linux for managing I/O devices. The file can be one of two types: a *block special file* or a *character special file*.

**differential backup** A method that only backs up files that have changed since the last full backup.

**digital audio tape (DAT)** A tape system that uses 4-mm tape and has a capacity of up to 72 GB.

**digital linear tape (DLT)** A tape system that uses half-inch magnetic tapes and has a capacity of up to 1.6 TB.

**digital pad** An alternative input device frequently used by graphic artists and others who need accurate control over drawing and other data input.

**Digital Visual Interface (DVI)** A high-quality visual standard for connecting flat-panel LCD displays and digital projectors.

**direct-attached storage (DAS)** A storage medium directly connected to the server using it. DAS differs from local storage in that it includes externally connected HDDs in an enclosure with a power supply.

**directory** An organizational structure that contains files and may additionally contain subdirectories under it. A directory contains information about files, such as filenames, file sizes, date of creation, and file type. More commonly referred to as a *folder* in modern OSs.

**directory service** The software that manages centralized access and security in a server-based network.

**disk drive** A physical component with a disk interface connector (such as SATA or SCSI) and a power connector.

**disk label** The UNIX/Linux equivalent of a partition table in MS-DOS or Windows systems. The disk label is a table containing information about each partition on a disk, such as the type of partition, size, and location.

**disk quota** Allocation of a specific amount of disk space to a user or application with the ability to ensure that the user or application cannot use more disk space than is specified in the allocation.

**disk striping** A disk storage technique that divides portions of each file over all volumes in a set as a way to minimize wear on individual disks.

**DisplayPort** A digital interface standard that is projected to replace DVI and HDMI for computers.

**Distributed File System (DFS)** A set of client and server services to organize distributed shared files into a logical file system.

**Distributed Link Tracking** A technique introduced in NTFS 5 so that shortcuts, such as those on the desktop, are not lost when files are moved to another volume.

**distribution** An issuance of UNIX or Linux that is based on a standard kernel, but that also has customizations added by a particular private or commercial development group.

**domain** A collection of users and computers in a server-based network whose accounts are managed by Windows servers called *domain controllers*. See also *domain controller*.

**domain controller** A computer running Windows Server with Active Directory installed; it maintains a database of user and computer accounts as well as network access policies in a Windows domain. See also *directory service*.

**domain local group** A group scope recommended for assigning rights and permissions to domain resources.

**Domain Name Service (DNS)** An application protocol that resolves domain and computer names to IP addresses, or that resolves IP addresses to domain and computer names.

**dot-matrix (impact) printer** An impact character printer that produces characters by arranging a matrix of dots.

**dots per inch (dpi)** Used to measure the resolution of a printer; the number of dots contained in an inch.

**driver signing** A digital signature that Microsoft incorporates into driver and system files as a way to verify the files and to ensure that they are not inappropriately overwritten.

**dye sublimation** A printer technology that produces high-quality color output by creating "sublimated" color mists that penetrate paper to form characters or graphic output.

**dynamic disk** A disk arrangement that can hold up to 128 volumes, including spanned volumes, striped volumes, and RAID volumes.

**Dynamic Host Configuration Protocol (DHCP)** An Application layer protocol used to configure a host's IP address settings dynamically.

**embedded system** A computer that has a dedicated function within a larger system, such as a piece of machinery.

**encapsulation** The process of adding header and trailer information to chunks of data.

**Extended (HFS+)** A file system released in 1998 with Mac OS 8.1 and the file system used in Mac OS X.

**extended file system (ext or ext fs)** The file system designed for Linux that is installed by default in Linux operating systems.

**extended partition** A division of disk space on a basic disk that must be separated into logical drives; it can't be marked active and can't hold the Windows system volume.

**extension** In MS-DOS and Windows-based systems, the part of a filename that typically identifies the type of file associated with the name. File extensions are typically three characters long and include standard notations such as .sys, .exe, .bat, and so on.

**extents b-tree** A file system component that keeps track of the location of file fragments, or extents, in the Mac OS HFS file system.

**external clock speed** The speed at which the processor communicates with the memory and other devices in the computer; usually one-fourth to one-half the internal clock speed.

**external commands** Operating system commands that are stored in separate program files on disk. When these commands are required, they must be loaded from disk storage into memory before they are executed.

**extranet** A private network that allows limited and controlled access to internal network resources by outside users, usually in a business-to-business situation.

**failover clustering** A group of two or more servers configured so that if one server fails, another server can resume the services the first one was providing.

**file** A set of data that is grouped in some logical manner, assigned a name, and stored on the disk.

**file allocation table (FAT)** A file management system that defines the way data is stored on a disk drive. The FAT stores information about a file's size and physical location on the disk.

**file attributes** File characteristics stored with the filename in the disk folder; attributes specify certain storage and operational parameters associated with the file, such as hidden, read-only, archive, and so on.

**File Classification Infrastructure (FCI)** A system that allows files to be located on servers in an organization based on predetermined naming conventions.

**file system** A design for storing and managing files on a disk drive; the method by which an OS stores and organizes files and manages access to files on a storage device.

**floating point unit (FPU)** A component of a CPU that executes floating point mathematical operations.

**folder** See *directory*.

**formatting** The process of installing a file system on a disk partition.

**fragmentation** The accumulation of empty pockets of space between files on a disk due to frequent writing, deleting, and modifying of the files and their contents.

**frame** A packet with source and destination MAC addresses added and an error-checking code added to the back end. Frames are generated and processed by the network interface. See also *packet*.

**full file-by-file backup** A technique that backs up the entire contents of one or more disk drives, including all folders, subfolders, and files, so that any of these contents can be restored.

**gadgets** Small applications for readily accessing information and tools.

**gamepad** An input device primarily designed for interaction with games. It includes multiple buttons, wheels, or balls to effect movement of a variety of on-screen objects.

**global group** A group scope used mainly to group users from the same domain who have similar access and rights requirements. A global group's members can be user accounts and other global groups from the same domain. See also *group scope*.

**graphical user interface (GUI)** An interface between the user and an operating system that presents information in an intuitive graphical format, including multiple colors, figures, icons, windows, toolbars, and other features. A GUI is usually deployed with a pointing device, such as a mouse, to make the user more productive.

**group scope** A property of a group that determines the reach of a group's application in a domain—for example, which users can be group members and to which resources a group can be assigned rights or permissions.

**guest OS** The operating system installed on a virtual machine.

**GUID Partitioning Table (GPT)** A disk-partitioning method that supports volume sizes of up to 18 exabytes.

**hard link** In Windows versions starting with Windows 2000 and UNIX/Linux, a file management technique that permits multiple folder entries to point to the same file.

**hardware** The physical devices in a computer, including the CPU, circuit boards (cards), disk drives, monitor, and modem.

**header** Information added to the front end of a chunk of data so it can be correctly interpreted and processed by network protocols.

**Hierarchical Filing System (HFS)** An early Apple Macintosh file system storage method that uses a hierarchical folder structure.

**High-Definition Multimedia Interface (HDMI)** A high-quality visual standard for connecting digital audio and video devices.

**high-level formatting** A process that prepares a disk partition (or removable media) for a specific file system.

**host computer** The physical computer on which virtual machine software is installed and virtual machines run.

**hosted virtualization** A system in which the hypervisor implements OS virtualization by being installed in a general-purpose host OS, such as Windows 10 or Linux, and the host OS accesses host hardware on behalf of the guest OS. See also *virtualization*.

**hot fix** A procedure used by a file system that can detect a damaged disk area and then automatically copy information from that area to another disk area that is not damaged.

**Hyper-Threading (HT)** A feature of some Intel CPUs that allows two threads to run on each CPU core simultaneously.

**Hyper-V** A Windows feature that allows a server to run multiple independent operating systems at the same time and to run multiple virtual servers on one physical server.

**hypervisor** The component of virtualization software that creates and monitors the virtual hardware environment, which allows multiple VMs to share physical hardware resources.

**I/O address range** A range of memory addresses used to temporarily store data that is transferred between a computer device or component and the CPU.

**in-place upgrade** An OS upgrade that overwrites your current OS and maintains your applications, settings, and data.

**incremental backup** A method that only backs up files that have changed since the last full or incremental backup.

**Infrared Data Association (IrDA)** A group of peripheral manufacturers that developed a set of standards for transmitting data using infrared light. Printers were some of the first devices to support the IrDA specifications.

**infrastructure as a service (IaaS)** A category of cloud computing in which a company can use a provider's storage or virtual servers as its needs demand; IaaS is also called *hosted infrastructure*.

**inkjet printer** A printer that forms characters and images by spraying droplets of ink from a nozzle print head onto the paper.

**inode** Short for *information node*. In UNIX/Linux, a system for storing key information about files.

**input/output (I/O)** Input is information taken in by a computer device to handle or process; an example is characters typed at a keyboard. Output is information sent out by a computer device after the information is handled or processed; an example is the display of typed characters on the monitor.

**Institute of Electrical and Electronics Engineers (IEEE)** An international organization of scientists, engineers, technicians, and educators that plays a leading role in developing standards for computers, network cabling, and data transmissions, and for other electronics areas, such as consumer electronics and electrical power.

**instruction set** In a computer CPU, the group of commands (instructions) the processor recognizes. These instructions are used to conduct the operations required of the CPU by the operating system and application software.

**internal clock speed** The speed at which the CPU executes internal commands, measured in megahertz (millions of clock ticks per second) or gigahertz (billions of clock ticks per second). Internal clock speeds can be as low as 1 MHz or more than 4 GHz.

**Internet** A worldwide public internetwork that uses standard protocols, such as TCP/IP, DNS, and HTTP, to transfer and view information.

**Internet Protocol version 4 (IPv4)** A connectionless Internetwork layer protocol that provides source and destination addressing and routing for the TCP/IP protocol suite; IPv4 uses 32-bit dotted decimal addresses.

**Internet Protocol version 6 (IPv6)** A connectionless Internetwork layer protocol that provides source and destination addressing and routing for the TCP/IP protocol suite. IPv6 uses 128-bit hexadecimal addresses and has built-in security and QoS features.

**internetwork** A networked collection of LANs tied together by devices such as routers. See also *local area network (LAN)*.

**interrupt request (IRQ)** A request to the processor so that a currently operating process, such as a read from a disk drive, can be interrupted by another process, such as a write into memory.

**interrupt request (IRQ) line** A channel within the computer that is used for communications with the CPU.

**intranet** A private network in which devices and servers are available only to users connected to the internal network.

**IP address** A 32-bit dotted decimal address used by IP to determine the network a host resides on and to identify hosts on the network at the Internetwork layer.

**IP Security (IPsec)** A way to secure Internet Protocol (IP) traffic by encrypting and authenticating each packet.

**journaling** The ability of a file system or software (such as database software) to track file changes so that if a system crashes unexpectedly, it is possible to reconstruct files or to roll back changes with minimal or no damage.

**joystick** An input device shaped like a stick that allows for three-dimensional movement of an on-screen cursor or other object, such as a car, airplane, or cartoon character.

**just a bunch of disks (JBOD)** A disk arrangement in which two or more disks are abstracted to appear as a single disk to the OS but aren't arranged in a specific RAID configuration.

**Kerberos** A security system and authentication protocol that authenticates users and grants or denies access to network resources based on a user's log-on name and password. Kerberos creates a unique encryption key for each communication session.

**kernel** An essential set of programs and computer code built into a computer operating system to control processor, disk, memory, and other functions central to a computer's basic operation. The kernel communicates with the BIOS, device drivers, and the API to perform these functions. It also interfaces with the resource managers.

**label printers** Special-purpose printers that produce labels only.

**laser printer** A high-quality page printer design that is popular in office and other professional applications.

**level 1 (L1) cache** Cache memory that is part of the CPU hardware. See *cache memory*.

**level 2 (L2) cache** Cache memory that is somewhat slower than L1 cache but is much larger. See *cache memory*.

**level 3 (L3) cache** Cache memory that is slower than L1 or L2 cache but is much larger. L3 cache is located on the CPU chip on most modern CPUs, and is shared among multiple cores. See *cache memory*.

**level 4 (L4) cache** Cache memory that is found on some advanced modern CPUs. See *cache memory*.

**library** A combination of folders that can be in any location on the local computer or the network.

**line editor** An editor that is used to create text one line at a time.

**line printer** A printer design that prints a full line of character output at a time; it is used for high-speed output requirements.

**linear tape open (LTO)** A tape drive used in the high-end server market; it has a storage capacity of up to 1.6 TB.

**link-local IPv6 address** Similar in function to IPv4 APIPA addresses, link-local IPv6 addresses begin with *fe80*, are self-configuring, and can't be routed. See also *Automatic private IP addressing (APIPA)*.

**linked list** Used in FAT file systems so that when a file is written to disk, each cluster containing that file's data has a pointer to the location of the next cluster of data.

**live migration** A feature of virtualization that allows a virtual machine to be moved from one server to another with little or no downtime.

**local area network (LAN)** A small network limited to a single collection of machines and linked by interconnecting devices in a small geographic area.

**local storage** Storage media with a direct and exclusive connection to the computer's system board through a disk controller.

**localhost** A reserved name that corresponds to the loopback address in an IP network. See also *loopback address*.

**logical drive** A software definition that divides a physical hard drive into multiple drives for file storage.

**logical unit number (LUN)** A logical reference point to a unit of storage that could refer to an entire array of disks, a single disk, or just part of a disk.

**logical volume manager (LVM)** A method of creating volumes in Linux that uses physical disk partitions called *volume groups* to create logical volumes.

**long filename (LFN)** A name for a file, folder, or folder in a file system in which the name can be up to 255 characters in length. Long filenames in Windows, UNIX/Linux, and Mac OS systems are also POSIX compliant in that they honor uppercase and lowercase characters.

**loopback address** An address that always refers to the local computer; in IPv4, it's 127.0.0.1, and in IPv6, it's ::1. This address is used to test TCP/IP functionality on the local computer.

**low-level format** A software process that marks tracks and sectors on a disk. A low-level format is necessary before a disk can be partitioned and formatted.

**LPT1** The primary printer port designation on many desktop computers; also designated as line print terminal 1.

**Macintosh Filing System (MFS)** The original Macintosh filing system, introduced in 1984. MFS was limited to keeping track of 128 documents, applications, or folders.

**Master Boot Record (MBR)** A disk-partitioning method that supports volume sizes of up to 2 TB; an area of a hard disk in MS-DOS and Windows that stores partition information about the disk. MBRs are not found on disks that do not support multiple partitions.

**Master File Table (MFT)** A storage organization system used with the NTFS file system. The MFT is located at the beginning of the partition.

**maximum transmission unit (MTU)** The maximum frame size allowed to be transmitted across a network medium.

**metadata** Information that describes data but is not the actual data.

**metropolitan area network (MAN)** An internetwork confined to a geographic region, such as a city or county; a MAN uses third-party communication providers to supply connectivity between locations. See also *internetwork*.

**microarchitecture** The description of the internal circuitry of a CPU that defines characteristics such as the technology used to create the chip, the supported instruction set, and the bit size.

**microcode** A small program inside a CISC CPU that must interpret and execute each instruction.

**Microsoft Disk Operating System (MS-DOS)** The first widely distributed operating system for microcomputers, created by Tim Paterson and a team at Microsoft that included Bill Gates. This generic computer code was used to control many basic computer hardware and software functions. MS-DOS is sometimes referred to as DOS.

**Microsoft Management Console (MMC)** A flexible system that allows server administrators to configure the servers and monitor their function in one place.

**migration** Moving from one OS to another OS, which may or may not involve implementing a new computer as well.

**mount** A process that makes a disk partition or volume available for use by the operating system.

**multicasting** A network communication in which a packet is addressed so that more than one destination can receive it.

**multifunction printers** Printers that combine printing, scanning, and faxing in one physical device. They can be color inkjet or laser printers.

**multiprocessor computer** A computer that uses more than one CPU.

**multitasking** A technique that allows a computer to run two or more programs at the same time.

**multithreading** Running several program processes or parts (threads) at the same time.

**multiuser system** A computer hardware and software system designed to service multiple users who access the computer's hardware and software applications simultaneously.

**name server** A computer that provides the service of name-to-address resolution; for example, it resolves a host and domain name to an IP address.

**named pipe** In UNIX/Linux, a device special file for handling internal communications, such as redirecting file output to a monitor.

**.NET Framework** A large library, available to all programming languages supported by .NET, that allows multiple programming languages to use code from other languages.

**netbook computers** Small portable or laptop computers that have limited computing capabilities and are designed to be lightweight and portable. Netbook computers are generally used for Web access, e-mail, and basic document creation.

**network** Two or more computers connected by a transmission medium that allows them to communicate.

**network client software** An application or OS service that can request information stored on another computer.

**Network File System (NFS)** The native Linux/UNIX file sharing protocol.

**network interface card (NIC)** A device that creates and mediates the connection between a computer and the network medium.

**Network layer** Layer 3 of the OSI model, which handles logical addressing and routing of PDUs across internetworks. See also *Open Systems Interconnection (OSI) reference model.*

**network protocols** The software that defines the rules and formats a computer must use when sending information across the network.

**network server software** The software that allows a computer to share its resources by fielding requests generated by network clients.

**network-attached printer** A printer that has a network interface, is connected to the network, and can be accessed by computers on the network via a host name or IP address.

**network-attached storage (NAS)** A storage device that has an enclosure, a power supply, slots for multiple HDDs, a network interface, and a built-in OS tailored for managing shared files and folders.

**New Technology File System (NTFS)** The file storage system that is the native system in Windows versions starting with Windows NT.

**octet** An 8-bit value; a number from 0 to 255 that's one of the four numbers in a dotted decimal IP address.

**Open Systems Interconnection (OSI) reference model** ISO Standard 7498 defines a frame of reference for understanding networks by dividing the process of network communication into seven layers. Each layer is defined in terms of the services and data it handles on behalf of the layer above it and the services and data it needs from the layer below it.

**operating system (OS)** A specialized computer program that provides a user interface, file system, services, and a kernel to a computer. An OS runs on computer hardware and facilitates application execution.

**optical character recognition (OCR)** Imaging software that scans each character on the page as a distinct image and is able to recognize the character.

**packet** A chunk of data with source and destination IP addresses (as well as other IP information) added to it. Packets are generated and processed by network protocols.

**page file** Also called the *paging file* or *swap file*, an allocated portion of disk storage reserved to supplement RAM when the available RAM is exceeded. See *swap file.*

**pagefile.sys** A system file in Windows used as virtual memory; it is also used to store data produced when the system crashes (dump data), which is used for troubleshooting.

**partition** A logical unit of storage that can be formatted with a file system; it is similar to a volume but used with basic disks.

**partition table** A table containing information about each partition on a disk, such as the type of partition, size, and location. Also, the partition table provides information to the computer about how to access the disk.

**partitioning** Blocking a group of tracks and sectors to be used by a particular file system, such as FAT or NTFS. Partitioning is a hard disk management technique that permits the installation of multiple file systems on a single disk or the configuration of multiple logical hard drives that use the same file system on a single physical hard drive.

**peer-to-peer network** A network model in which all computers can function as clients or servers as needed, and there's no centralized control over network resources.

**Peripheral Component Interconnect (PCI)** A bus standard that has been replaced by the PCI Express or PCIe standard.

**Peripheral Component Interconnect Express (PCIe)** A bus standard that has enabled adapter manufacturers to supply one hardware product to a variety of hardware platforms.

**physical drive** A hard drive in a computer that you can physically touch and that can be divided into one or more logical drives.

**Physical layer** Layer 1, the bottom layer of the OSI model, transmits and receives signals and specifies the physical details of cables, NICs, connectors, and hardware behavior. See also *Open Systems Interconnection (OSI) reference model.*

**pipelining** A CPU design that permits the processor to operate on one instruction at the same time it is fetching one or more subsequent instructions from the operating system or application.

**pixel** Short for *picture element*; the small dots that make up a computer screen display.

**pixels per inch (ppi)** A unit used to measure the resolution of a display screen; the number of dots (pixels) contained in an inch.

**platform as a service (PaaS)** A category of cloud computing in which a customer develops applications with the service provider's development tools and infrastructure. After applications are developed, they can be delivered to the customer's users from the provider's servers. PaaS is also called *hosted platform.*

**plotter** Computer hardware that produces high-quality printed output, often in color, by moving ink pens over the surface of paper. Plotters are often used with computer-aided design (CAD) and other graphics applications.

**Plug and Play (PnP)** Software utilities that operate with compatible hardware to facilitate automatic hardware configuration. Windows versions starting with 95 recognize PnP hardware when it is installed, and in many cases can configure the hardware and install required software without significant user intervention.

**Portable Operating System Interface for UNIX (POSIX)** A UNIX standard designed to ensure portability of applications among various versions of UNIX.

**power-on self test (POST)** Tests, such as memory and hardware component tests, that are run by the BIOS when a computer starts and that must complete before the operating system is loaded. See *basic input/output system (BIOS).*

**preemptive multitasking** A computer hardware and software design for multitasking of applications in which the operating system retains control of the computer at all times. See *cooperative multitasking* for comparison.

**Presentation layer** At Layer 6 of the OSI model, data can be encrypted and/or compressed to facilitate delivery. Platform-specific application formats are translated into generic data formats for transmission or from generic data formats into platform-specific application formats for delivery to the Application layer. See also *Open Systems Interconnection (OSI) reference model.*

**primary partition** A division of disk space on a basic disk used to create a volume. It can be assigned a drive letter, be marked as active, and contain the Windows system volume.

**print job** The data or document sent from an application to a printer and accepted by the print spooler.

**Print Management Console** A console that allows a system administrator to manage printers and printing throughout the network.

**print queue** A temporary file used to store a print job until it can be sent to the printer.

**print spooler** A process that accepts print jobs from applications, stores them in the print queue, and then sends them to the printer when the print device is ready.

**private cloud** Cloud services that a company delivers to its own employees.

**privileged mode** A feature of the operating system kernel introduced in Windows NT that protected it from problems created by a malfunctioning program or process.

**process** A program that is loaded into memory and run by the CPU. It can be an application a user interacts with, such as a word-processing program or a Web browser, or a program with no user interface that communicates with other processes and provides services to them.

**production computer** Any computer used to perform real work; it should be protected from problems that might cause an interruption in workflow or loss of data.

**protocol** Rules and procedures for communication and behavior. Computers must use a common protocol and agree on the rules of communication.

**protocol suite** A set of protocols working cooperatively to provide network communication. Protocols are "stacked" in layers, and each layer performs a unique function required for successful communication. Also called a *protocol stack.*

**public cloud** Cloud services delivered by a third-party provider.

**rack-mounted server** CPU boxes mounted in racks that can hold multiple servers, each with its own power cord and network connection—and that often share one monitor and pointing device.

**RAID 0 volume** A volume that extends across two or more dynamic disks, but data is written to all disks in the volume equally; it provides no fault tolerance but does provide a performance advantage over simple or spanned volumes.

**RAID 1 volume** A volume that uses space from two dynamic disks and provides fault tolerance. Data written to one disk is duplicated, or mirrored, to the second disk. If one disk fails, the other disk has a good copy of the data, and the system can continue to operate until the failed disk is replaced. This volume is also called a *mirrored volume.*

**RAID 5 volume** A volume that uses space from three or more dynamic disks and uses disk striping with parity to provide fault tolerance. When data is written, it's striped across all but one of the disks in the volume. Parity information derived from the data is written to the remaining disk, which is used to re-create lost data after a disk failure. This volume is also called a *disk stripe with parity.*

**raw device** In the UNIX/Linux file system, a device that has not been divided into logical blocks. See also *block device.*

**read-only memory (ROM)** Memory that contains information that is not erased when the power is removed from the memory hardware.

**real-time operating system (RTOS)** An operating system that receives and processes inputs and produces the required outputs in a specified amount of time.

**redirector** An OS client component that intercepts resource requests and determines whether the resource is local or remote.

**Reduced Instruction Set Computing (RISC)** A computer CPU design that dedicates processor hardware components to certain functions. This design reduces the number and complexity of required instructions and often results in faster performance than CISC CPUs. Compare to *Complex Instruction Set Computing (CISC)*.

**redundant array of independent disks (RAID)** A disk configuration that uses space on multiple disks to form a single logical volume. Most RAID configurations provide fault tolerance, and some enhance performance.

**register** A temporary holding location in a CPU where data must be placed before the CPU can use it.

**registry** A Windows database that stores information about a computer's hardware and software configuration.

**release candidate (RC)** The final stage of software testing by vendors before cutting an official release that is sold commercially. A release candidate is usually tested by a very large audience of customers. Some vendors may issue more than one release candidate if problems are discovered in the first RC.

**release to manufacturing (RTM)** A version of a Microsoft OS that is officially released to be sold and has gone through the alpha, beta, and release candidate phases prior to official release.

**Resilient File System (ReFS)** A file system in Windows Server 2012 and later that is used in large file-sharing applications and that can correct some types of data corruption automatically.

**resource fork** In the Macintosh file system, the portion of a file that contains fixed information, such as a program's icons, menu resources, and splash screens.

**resource managers** Programs that manage computer memory and CPU use.

**root folder** The highest-level folder in the structure of files and folders in a file system.

**router** A device that enables LANs to communicate by forwarding packets from one LAN to another. Routers also forward packets from one router to another when LANs are separated by multiple routers.

**scanner** A digital image created from a hard copy that is then transmitted to the computer.

**sectors** Equally sized portions of a disk track. See *tracks*.

**sequential processing** A computer processing style in which each operation is submitted, acted upon, and the results displayed before the next process is started. Compare to *batch processing*.

**Serial ATA (SATA)** A common disk interface technology that's inexpensive, fast, and fairly reliable, with transfer speeds up to 6 Gb/s; it is used both in client computers and low-end servers and replaces the older parallel ATA (PATA) technology.

**serial attached SCSI (SAS)** A newer, serial form of SCSI with transfer rates of up to 6 Gb/s and higher; the disk technology of choice for servers and high-end workstations. See also *small computer system interface (SCSI)*.

**server** The term used to describe an OS designed mainly to share network resources, a computer with the main role of giving client computers access to network resources, and the software that responds to requests for network resources from client computers.

**server-based network** A network model in which servers take on specialized roles to provide client computers with network services and to maintain centralized control over network resources.

**Server Core** A scaled-back version of Windows Server 2008 in which all configurations and maintenance are done via the command-line interface.

**Server Message Block (SMB)** The Windows file sharing protocol; SMB is also supported by Linux and Mac OS X as Samba.

**server operating system** A computer operating system usually found on more powerful PC-based computers than those used for desktop operating systems. A server OS is connected to a network and can act in many roles to enable multiple users to access information via e-mail, files, software, and other means.

**server role migration** An alternative to a Windows server OS upgrade in which you perform a clean installation of Windows Server 2012/R2 and migrate the server roles the old OS version performed.

**service** A process that runs in the background because there is no user interface. See *process*.

**service packs** Software "fixes" issued by a vendor to repair software problems, address compatibility issues, and add enhancements.

**Session layer** Layer 5 of the OSI model, which is responsible for setting up, maintaining, and ending communication sequences (called *sessions*) across a network. See also *Open Systems Interconnection (OSI) reference model.*

**shell** An interface that enables users to interact with an operating system kernel. The shell enables the user to execute commands. See *kernel.*

**simple volume** A volume that usually resides on a single basic or dynamic disk.

**single-processor computer** A computer capable of supporting only a single CPU.

**single-tasking** A computer hardware and software design that can manage only a single task at a time.

**single-user system** A computer hardware and software system that enables only one user to access its resources at a particular time.

**small computer system interface (SCSI)** An older parallel bus disk technology still used on some servers, although it has reached its performance limits at 640 MB/s transfer rates.

**snapshot** A partial copy of a virtual machine made at a particular moment; it can be used to restore the virtual machine to its state when the snapshot was taken. See also *virtual machine (VM).*

**software as a service (SaaS)** A category of cloud computing in which a customer pays for the use of applications that run on a service provider's network; SaaS is also called *hosted applications.*

**solid-state drive (SSD)** A type of storage medium that uses flash memory, has no moving parts, and requires less power than a traditional HDD. It is faster and more shock resistant than a traditional HDD, but it costs more per gigabyte and doesn't have as much capacity as an HDD.

**spanned volume** A volume that extends across two or more physical disks; for example, a simple volume that has been extended to a second disk is a spanned volume.

**special identity group** A type of group in Windows in which membership is controlled dynamically by Windows, can't be viewed or changed manually, and depends on how an account accesses the OS. For example, membership in the Authenticated Users group is assigned to a user account automatically when the user logs on to a computer or domain.

**Spotlight** The new way to search in Mac OS X, starting with version 10.4 Tiger. Spotlight stores a virtual index of everything on the system.

**stand-alone computer** A computer that doesn't have the necessary hardware or software to communicate on a network.

**static IP address** A manually configured IP address.

**status bits** Bits used as part of a folder entry to identify the type of file contained in each entry. The status bits in use are Volume, Folder, System, Hidden, Read-only, and Archive.

**storage appliance** See *network-attached storage (NAS).*

**storage area network (SAN)** A storage device that uses high-speed networking technologies to give servers fast access to large amounts of shared disk storage. To the server OS, the storage a SAN manages appears to be physically attached to the server.

**storage layout** The method used to create a virtual disk with Storage Spaces; the three methods include simple, mirror, and parity. See also *Storage Spaces.*

**storage pool** A collection of physical disks from which virtual disks and volumes are created and assigned dynamically.

**Storage Spaces** A new feature in Windows 8/8.1 and Windows Server 2012/R2 and later versions that provides flexible provisioning of virtualized storage.

**storage tiering** A feature of Storage Spaces that combines the speed of SSDs with the low cost and high capacity of HDDs to create high-performance volumes.

**subnet mask** A 32-bit dotted decimal number consisting of a contiguous series of binary 1 digits followed by a contiguous series of binary 0 digits. The subnet mask determines which part of an IP address is the network ID and which part is the host ID.

**super advanced intelligent tape (S-AIT)** A tape system technology that has an erasable memory chip and a capacity of up to 1.3 TB.

**super digital linear tape (SDLT)** A tape system that uses both magnetic and optical recording and has a tape capacity of up to 2.4 TB.

**superblock** In the UNIX/Linux file system, a special data block that contains information about the layout of blocks, sectors, and cylinder groups on the file system. This information is the key to finding anything on the file system, and it should never change.

**supercomputer** A computer that has extreme processing power and speed to handle complex computations that are beyond the reach of other computers.

**surface analysis** A disk diagnostic technique that locates and marks damaged disk areas. Some surface analysis tools are destructive to data because they also format the disk. Other tools can run without altering data, except to move it from a damaged location to one that is not.

**swap file** Also called the *page file*, *paging file*, or *swap file system*, an allocated portion of disk storage reserved to supplement RAM when the available RAM is exceeded. See *page file.*

**swap partition** In Linux/UNIX OSs, a separate partition on the disk set aside exclusively for virtual memory.

**switch** A network device that reads the destination MAC addresses of incoming frames to determine which ports should forward the frames. Also, an operating system command option that changes the way certain commands function. Command options, or switches, are usually entered as one or more letters, separated from the main command by a forward slash (/) in Windows and by a dash (-) in UNIX/Linux.

**switching table** A table of MAC address and port pairs that a switch uses to determine which port to forward frames it receives.

**symbolic link** A special file in the UNIX/Linux file system that permits a folder link to a file that is on a different partition.

**system architecture** The computer hardware design that includes the processor (CPU) and communication routes between the CPU and the hardware it manages, such as memory and disk storage.

**System V Release 4 (SVR4)** A variation of the UNIX operating system. It is very popular today along with the Berkeley Software Distribution (BSD).

**system volume** A volume that contains the files a computer needs to find and load the Windows OS. See also *volume*.

**tar** A UNIX file archive utility.

**task supervisor** A process in the operating system that keeps track of applications running on the computer and the resources they use.

**task switching** A hybrid between single-tasking and multitasking that permits the user or application software to switch among multiple single-tasking operations.

**thermal-wax transfer printer** A printer that creates high-quality color printed output by melting colored wax elements and transferring them to the printed page.

**thin provisioning** A method for creating virtual disks in which the virtual disk expands dynamically and uses space from the storage pool as needed until it reaches the specified maximum size.

**thread** The smallest piece of computer code that can be independently scheduled for execution.

**time-sharing system** A central computer system, such as a mainframe, that is used by multiple users and applications simultaneously.

**total cost of ownership (TCO)** The cost of installing and maintaining computers and equipment on a network. TCO includes hardware, software, maintenance, and support costs.

**tracks** Concentric rings that cover an entire disk like grooves on a phonograph record. Each ring is divided into sectors in which to store data.

**trailer** Information added to the back end of a chunk of data so it can be correctly interpreted and processed by network protocols.

**Transmission Control Protocol/Internet Protocol (TCP/IP)** The most common protocol suite, the default protocol in contemporary OSs, and the protocol of the Internet.

**Transport layer** Layer 4 of the OSI model, which is responsible for reliable delivery of data streams across a network. Layer 4 protocols break large streams of data into smaller chunks and use sequence numbers and acknowledgements to provide communication and flow control. See also *Open Systems Interconnection (OSI) reference model.*

**type code** In the Macintosh file system, embedded file information that denotes which applications were used to create the files. Mac OS type codes are used in much the same way as Windows file extensions that identify file types with .txt, .doc, and other extensions. See *creator codes.*

**Unicode** A 16-bit character code that allows for the definition of up to 65,536 characters.

**unique local IPv6 address** An address for devices on a private network that can't be routed on the Internet.

**Universal Disk Format (UDF)** A removable disk formatting standard used for large-capacity CD-ROMs and DVD-ROMs.

**universal group** A group scope that can contain users from any domain and be assigned permissions to resources in any domain. See also *group scope.*

**Universal Plug and Play (UPnP)** An initiative of more than 80 companies to develop products that can be quickly added to a computer or network. These products include intelligent appliances for the home. For more information, go to *http://openconnectivity.org/upnp*.

**Universal Serial Bus (USB)** A serial bus designed to support up to 127 discrete devices with data transfer speeds up to 5 Gbits/s (gigabits per second).

**UNIX file system (ufs)** A file system supported in most versions of UNIX/Linux; ufs is a hierarchical (tree structure) file system that is expandable, supports large storage, provides excellent security, and is reliable. Ufs employs information nodes (inodes).

**upgrade installation** An OS installation on a computer that already has an earlier version of the OS; the upgrade replaces the earlier version with a new version, often with the option to retain some or all of the original settings, user accounts, applications, data files, and other existing user files.

**User Account Protection (UAP)** A feature of some Microsoft operating systems that allows for better protection of user accounts by controlling permissions and limiting the software applications that can be run from an account.

**user interface** A component of an operating system that provides a method for users to interact with the computer, usually with a keyboard and mouse or touch screen.

**VHD file** The format that virtual machines running in Hyper-V use for their virtual disks. VHD files can also be created and mounted with Disk Management and used like physical disks.

**virtual disk** Files stored on the host computer that represent a virtual machine's hard disk.

**virtual machine (VM)** A software environment that emulates a physical computer's hardware and BIOS.

**virtual memory** Disk space that stores the least recently used pages of memory when more physical RAM is needed, but not available.

**virtual network** A network configuration created by virtualization software and used by virtual machines for network communication.

**virtual private network (VPN)** A private network that is like an encrypted tunnel through a larger network—such as the Internet, an enterprise network, or both—and is restricted to designated member clients.

**virtual server** A server computer that can be configured to run multiple virtual machines with multiple server or desktop OSs. See *virtual machine*.

**virtualization** A process that creates a software environment to emulate a computer's hardware and BIOS, allowing multiple OSs to run on the same physical computer at the same time.

**volume** A logical unit of storage that can be formatted with a file system.

**volume information block** On a Mac-formatted disk, the sector after the boot blocks. See also *boot block*. The volume information block points to other important areas of information, such as the location of the system files and the catalog and extents trees.

**volume label** A series of characters, commonly used as a nickname, that identify a volume.

**volume mount point** An empty folder into which a volume is mounted. See *mount*.

**wide area networks (WANs)** Internetworks that are geographically dispersed and use third-party communication providers to supply connectivity between locations. See also *internetwork*.

**Windows Hardware Error Architecture (WHEA)** An architecture that supports memory and cache error recovery without the operating system being aware of the process.

**X Window** A windowed user interface for UNIX and other operating systems.

# Index

## E



## F

## J



## K

## L



## M

## T

## X